The Leader's Companion

THE
LEADER'S
COMPANION

Insights on Leadership Through the Ages

Edited by

J. THOMAS WREN

THE FREE PRESS

New York

The Free Press
A Division of Simon & Schuster Inc.
1230 Avenue of the Americas, New York, N.Y. 10020

Printed in the United States of America

printing number

8 9 10

Text design by Carla Bolte

Library of Congress Cataloging-in-Publication Data

The leader's companion : insights on leadership through the ages /
edited by J. Thomas Wren.
    p.   cm.
  ISBN 0-02-874005-X (cloth).—ISBN 0-02-874091-2 (pbk)
  1. Leadership—History.   I. Wren, J. Thomas
HM141.L375   1995
303.3'4'09—dc20   95-2850
                                                  CIP

CONTENTS

PREFACE

Leadership has become one of the hot topics in the popular consciousness. Bookstores are filled with "how to" books on leadership, and colleges and corporations have discovered that the study of leadership is both popular and potentially quite useful. Unfortunately, leadership remains an ambiguous, amorphous, and frequently misunderstood concept, and is often portrayed in a negative light. Indeed, the well-respected commentator James MacGregor Burns once called leadership "one of the most observed and least understood phenomena on earth."[1]

There is a widespread perception of a lack of leadership in our society, in the face of increasingly challenging problems and needs. Governments at all levels confront increasing demands for services, even as resources to satisfy those demands contract. Political leaders appear to have no plan of action or, worse, waffle as competing constituencies successively claim the leaders' attention. The very complexity of issues such as health care, crime, and the problems of the poor give pause to anyone seeking an effective resolution. Similarly on the international scene perplexing and often dangerous questions constantly arise, while leaders and their constituents flounder in response. In the private sector, corporations seek skilled leaders to guide them in their struggle to adapt to rapidly changing conditions. Unfortunately, in such organizations, "leadership" is often confused with "management," to the detriment of both. Even families seek the reassurance of effective leadership, yet family members do not understand how to realize this objective while maintaining healthy interrelationships.

This desire for effective leadership is hindered by a lack of understanding about the phenomenon of leadership. When one seeks advice on leadership in the "how to" books of the popular literature, one often finds a distressingly shallow treatment of complex human and organizational interactions. On the other hand, while many evince a lack of understanding about leadership or decry its absence, others are put off by an excessive focus on leadership. They fear a leader's manipulation of others for selfish or evil ends (and they can produce an impressive list of examples from the recent past to buttress their position).

This volume seeks to counter the lack of understanding concerning leadership and misperceptions about its nature through the insights of a number of thoughtful commentators, scholars, and practitioners. Its contents spring from several premises which should be made clear at the outset. The first premise is that leadership is central to the human condition. Leadership is not a "fad," but a concept that is both current and timeless. If leadership is viewed as a process by which groups, organizations, and societies attempt to achieve common goals, it encompasses one of the fundamental currents of the human experience. In one form or another, then, the leadership process has been central to human interaction since the dawn of society. At the same time, the particularly intractable problems facing today's society have generated a seemingly universal call for leadership which gives the topic special currency today.

A corollary to the premise that leadership is a fundamental aspect of the human condition is that its study should be as all-embracing as the human experience itself. Such a broad view of leadership permits our investigation to rise above the current popular literature and seek insights in some of the great thought and literature of the past. Although such writers and philosophers rarely used the term "leadership," it is the leadership process which often engaged their attention. Moreover, alongside the popular literature (albeit less visible), there has grown up in recent decades a substantial body of solid scholarship on leadership which yields real insights. In sum, because the issues relating to leadership cut across all types of human activity and thought, true understanding of such a complex phenomenon requires a broadly conceived approach, which this book seeks to represent.

The second premise of *The Leader's Companion* is that leadership is the province of all, not just a privileged few. This collection of readings does not treat leadership as an elitist undertaking; rather, it is portrayed as a process ubiquitous in its presence and broad in its scope. Leadership in its full compass is neither a position or title nor the actions of an identifiable "leader." It is instead an interactive process in which leaders and followers engage in mutual interaction in a complex environment to achieve mutual goals. Viewed in this light, leadership occurs at all levels of society and engages all humans. A proper approach to leadership must acknowledge all elements of the process, not just the actions of the leader.

The third and most important premise of this book is that it is important to understand leadership. Knowing more about leadership and how the process operates permits one to realize the real end of leadership: the achievement of mutual goals which are intended to enhance one's group, organization, or society. This book assumes that the more that is known and understood about the process of leadership by all who participate in it, the more likely it is that the fruits of the combined efforts of leaders and followers will yield satisfactory results.

The Leader's Companion seeks to fulfill the promise of an approach to leadership which is broadly conceived. It draws from a wide range of sources: observations on leadership by classical writers, seminal articles from major leadership scholars, insights from recent observers which expand the frontiers of our understanding of leadership, and the wisdom of leaders. Moreover, these eclectic readings have been organized into thirteen parts in a purposeful fashion to guide the reader through the complex phenomenon we call leadership. Part I is an introduction designed to orient the reader to some of the issues of leadership and to suggest some profitable ways of thinking about the topic. Part II explores the concept of leadership itself: what the term means, and how one might go about learning more about it. Part III pulls together insights on leadership from classical philosophers, literary greats and practitioners, while Part IV turns to the understanding provided by modern scholars. Parts V through VIII contain some of the best current writing on the essential elements of the leadership process—i.e., the leader, followers, and leadership environment, and how they interact. This part of the book, as others, considers how issues of gender, diversity, and multiculturalism influence leadership. Parts IX and X look at the process itself: how leaders and followers work together to achieve mutual goals. With the understanding gleaned in the previous sections as backdrop, Part XI turns to a consideration of the competencies needed to be effective in the practice of leadership. Part XII adds the insights of several leadership practitioners. Finally, Part XIII seeks to reinforce the desired ends of leadership by focusing on the application of this understanding of leadership to moral means and ends.

Taken together, these selections should enhance the reader's understanding and practice of an enormously important process which lies at the heart of all of our efforts to improve our surroundings, our lives, and our world.

This is not to say that the selections assembled here are the only ones—or even the best choices—to achieve this goal. One of the beauties of exploring leadership is the remarkable richness and diversity of relevant source materials. Nevertheless, this collection is intended as a starting point for those who want to know more about the art and science of leadership.

ACKNOWLEDGMENTS

This book, even more than most, is the product of many hands. It had its genesis as a collection of readings for the introductory course on leadership at the Jepson School of Leadership Studies at the University of Richmond. If there is such a thing as a truly collaborative work, this collection of readings embodies it. Every member of the faculty of the Jepson School has played a major role in shaping its organization and content. The founding faculty of the school—Howard Prince, Stephanie Micas, Richard Couto, Joanne Ciulla, and Karin Klenke—devoted an entire semester to little else than the development of these materials. William Howe joined the faculty in time to teach the first version of the course, and he then fashioned a significant revision of the materials prior to the second iteration of the course. Gill Hickman and the current editor came on board at that point, and had the opportunity to shape the third version of the readings. The present volume represents yet another revision, and this time the editor had the sage counsel and unfailing good humor contributed by two new additions to the Jepson faculty, Marc Swatez and Fred Jablin. To all I am heavily indebted.

In order to fashion a collection of readings on leadership which would serve the needs of a broad constituency of potential readers—leadership practitioners; students of business, management, and organizations; as well as those in the liberal arts—I called upon the expertise of numerous colleagues in related fields. I am deeply appreciative of the extensive feedback on the present volume provided by participants of the Leadership Education Conference held in Richmond in July, 1994. I also had the benefit of extensive comments and suggestions from a number of reviewers: Charles Beitz, Jr., Chair of

Department of Business and Economics, Mount Saint Mary's College; Roger Casey, Department of English, Birmingham Southern College; Donald Davis, Psychology Department, Old Dominion University; Karen Ristau, Graduate School of Education, Professional Psychology, and Social Work, University of St. Thomas; Lonnie D. Timmerman, Director, The Center for Leadership Studies, Drake University; and Kevin N. Wright, School of Education and Human Development, Binghamton University.

The production of this volume has been facilitated by the skills of Judy Mable and Charlotte Chandler of the Jepson School, and Carol Mayhew at The Free Press. I owe an enormous debt of gratitude to my editor at The Free Press, Beth Anderson, who provided counsel and support, and always found a gentle way to tell me that 50 percent of my prose was superfluous. I deeply appreciate her continued faith in the worthiness of this project.

As is usually the case, the most important acknowledgment is saved for last. Without the love and support of Suzanne, I could not have finished this book, nor would I have wanted to. And I thank Jack, who did everything in his power to keep his Daddy from finishing this work, and thereby kept first things first.

PART I

THE CRISIS OF LEADERSHIP

Many groups of people—citizens, workers, students, politicians and business exec-utives—are troubled by a lack of strong leadership. Is this a valid concern? Part I addresses this issue. In the first two selections, two giants in the field of leadership studies, John Gardner and James MacGregor Burns, suggest that there is indeed a "crisis of leadership" in today's society, and that it is incumbent upon all responsible individuals to redress the problem. In the third reading, Richard Couto takes issue with the premise that there is a dearth of good leadership in our society. Couto ar-gues that individuals who make such statements are simply looking in the wrong places for effective leadership; it exists in the form of great numbers of "citizen lead-ers." This debate is moderated by Robert Greenleaf in the final reading of this initial section, who articulates a middle way between the jeremiads of Gardner and Burns and the optimism of Couto. Greenleaf is well aware of the challenges to leadership in today's world, and presents a solution to the "crisis of leadership" which parallels the "citizen leader" of Couto. Greenleaf argues that what is really needed in our at-tempt to address society's woes are "servant leaders"—in our neighborhoods, in pol-itics, and in private industry.

1

1

The Cry for Leadership

John W. Gardner

John Gardner has served six presidents of the United States in various leadership capacities. He was Secretary of Health, Education and Welfare, founding chairman of Common Cause, co-founder of the Independent Sector, chairman of the National Coalition, and president of the Carnegie Corporation and Foundation. He is currently the Miriam and Peter Haas Centennial Professor at Stanford Business School.

Why do we not have better leadership? The question is asked over and over. We complain, express our disappointment, often our outrage; but no answer emerges.

When we ask a question countless times and arrive at no answer, it is possible that we are asking the wrong question—or that we have misconceived the terms of the query. Another possibility is that it is not a question at all but simply convenient shorthand to express deep and complex anxieties. It would strike most of our contemporaries as old-fashioned to cry out, "What shall we do to be saved?" And it would be time-consuming to express fully

Reprinted with the permission of The Free Press, a Division of Simon & Schuster, from *On Leadership* by John W. Gardner. Copyright © 1990 by John W. Gardner. Reprinted by permission of Sterling Lord Literistic, Inc. Copyright © 1990 by John W. Gardner.

our concerns about the social disintegration, the moral disorientation, and the spinning compass needle of our time. So we cry out for leadership.

To some extent the conventional views of leadership are shallow, and set us up for endless disappointment. There is an element of wanting to be rescued, of wanting a parental figure who will set all things right. Such fantasies for grown-up children should not lead us to dismiss the need for leaders nor the insistent popular expression of that need. A great many people who are not given to juvenile fantasies want leaders—leaders who are exemplary, who inspire, who stand for something, who help us set and achieve goals.

Unfortunately, in popular thinking on the subject, the mature need and the childlike fantasies interweave. One of [my] tasks . . . is to untangle them, and to sketch what is realistically possible.

Leadership is such a gripping subject that once it is given center stage it draws attention away from everything else. But attention to leadership alone is sterile—and inappropriate. The larger topic of which leadership is a subtopic is *the accomplishment of group purpose*, which is furthered not only by effective leaders but also by innovators, entrepreneurs and thinkers; by the availability of resources; by questions of morale and social cohesion; and by much else that I discuss. . . . It is not my purpose to deal with either leadership or its related subjects comprehensively. I hope to illuminate aspects of the subject that may be of use in facing our present dilemmas—as a society and as a species.

The Issues Behind the Issues

We are faced with immensely threatening problems—terrorism, AIDS, drugs, depletion of the ozone layer, the threat of nuclear conflict, toxic waste, the real possibility of economic disaster. Even moderately informed citizens could extend the list. Yet on none of the items listed does our response acknowledge the manifest urgency of the problem. We give every appearance of sleepwalking through a dangerous passage of history. We see the life-threatening problems, but we do not react. We are anxious but immobilized.

I do not find the problems themselves as frightening as the questions they raise concerning our capacity to gather our forces and act. No doubt many of the grave problems that beset us have discoverable, though difficult, solutions. But to mobilize the required resources and to bear what sacrifices are necessary calls for a capacity to focus our energies, a capacity for sustained commitment. Suppose that we can no longer summon our forces to such effort. Suppose that we have lost the capacity to motivate ourselves for arduous exertions in behalf of the group. A discussion of leadership cannot avoid such questions.

Could it be that we suppress our awareness of problems—however ominous—because we have lost all conviction that we can do anything about them? Effective leaders heighten both motivation and confidence, but when these qualities have been gravely diminished, leaders have a hard time leading.

Suppose that fragmentation and divisiveness have proceeded so far in American life that we can no longer lend ourselves to any worthy common purpose. Suppose that our shared values have disintegrated to the point that we believe in nothing strongly enough to work for it as a group. Shared values are the bedrock on which leaders build the edifice of group achievement. No examination of leadership would be complete without attention to the decay and possible regeneration of the value framework.

Suppose that our institutions have become so lacking in adaptiveness that they can no longer meet new challenges. All human institutions must renew themselves continuously; therefore, we must explore this process as it bears on leadership.

I think of such matters—motivation, values, social cohesion, renewal—as the "issues behind the issues," and I shall return to them often in the pages that follow.

Our Dispersed Leadership

In this society, leadership is dispersed throughout all segments of the society—government, business, organized labor, the professions, the minority communities, the universities, social agencies, and so on. Leadership is also dispersed down through the many levels of social functioning, from the loftiest levels of our national life down to the school principal, the local union leader, the shop supervisor.

We have always associated both kinds of dispersion with our notions of democracy and pluralism. But as our understanding of the principles of organization has developed, we have come to see that there is really no alternative to such dispersal of leadership if large-scale systems are to retain their vitality. The point is relevant not only for our society as a whole but also for all the organized subsystems (corporations, unions, government agencies, and so forth) that compose it.

Most leadership today is an attempt to accomplish purposes through (or in spite of) large, intricately organized systems. There is no possibility that centralized authority can call all the shots in such systems, whether the system is a corporation or a nation. Individuals in all segments and at all levels must be prepared to exercise leaderlike initiative and responsibility, using their local knowledge to solve problems at their level. *Vitality at middle and lower levels of leadership can produce greater vitality in the higher levels of leadership.*

In addition to all people down the line who may properly be called leaders at their level, there are in any vital organization or society a great many individuals who *share leadership tasks* unofficially, by behaving responsibly with respect to the purposes of the group. Such individuals, who have been virtually ignored in the leadership literature, are immensely important to the leader and to the group. (And as I point out later, even the responsible dissenter may be sharing the leadership task.)

Understanding Leadership

I have seen a good many leaders in action. My first chore for a president was for Eisenhower, whom I had known earlier when he headed Columbia University. Of the seven presidents since then, I have worked with all but two. But I have learned powerful lessons from less lofty leaders—from a top sergeant in the Marine Corps, from university presidents, corporate chief executive officers, community leaders, bankers, scientists, union leaders, school superintendents, and others. I have led, and have worked in harness with other leaders.

The development of more and better leaders is an important objective that receives a good deal of attention in these pages. But this is not a how-to-do-it manual. The first step is not action; the first step is understanding. The first question is how to think about leadership. I have in mind not just political buffs who want more and better leaders on the political scene, nor just CEOs who wonder why there are not more leaders scattered through their huge organizations. I have in mind citizens who do not want to be victimized by their leaders, neighborhood organizations that want to train their future leaders, the young people who dream of leadership, and all kinds of people who just want to comprehend the world around them.

Citizens must understand the possibilities and limitations of leadership. We must know how we can strengthen and support good leaders; and we must be able to see through the leaders who are exploiting us, playing on our hatred and prejudice, or taking us down dangerous paths.

Understanding these things, we come to see that much of the responsibility for leaders and how they perform is in our own hands. If we are lazy, self-indulgent, and wanting to be deceived; if we willingly follow corrupt leaders; if we allow our heritage of freedom to decay; if we fail to be faithful monitors of the public process—then we shall get and deserve the worst. . . .

Leadership Development

How many dispersed leaders do we need? When one considers all the towns and city councils, corporations, government agencies, unions, schools and colleges, churches, professions and so on, the number must be high. In order to have a target to think about, and setting precision aside, let us say that it is 1 percent of the population—2.4 million men and women who are prepared to take leaderlike action at their levels. How can we ever find that many leaders?

Fortunately, the development of leaders is possible on a scale far beyond anything we have ever attempted. As one surveys the subject of leadership, there are depressing aspects but leadership development is not one of them. Although our record to date is unimpressive, the prospects for improvement are excellent.

Many dismiss the subject with the confident assertion that "leaders are born not made." Nonsense! Most of what leaders have that enables them to lead is learned. Leadership is not a mysterious activity. It is possible to describe the tasks that leaders perform. And the capacity to perform those tasks is widely distributed in the population. Today, unfortunately, specialization and patterns of professional functioning draw most of our young potential leaders into prestigious and lucrative nonleadership roles.

We have barely scratched the surface in our efforts toward leadership development. In the mid-twenty-first century, people will look back on our present practices as primitive.

Most men and women go through their lives using no more than a fraction—usually a rather small fraction—of the potentialities within them. The reservoir of unused human talent and energy is vast, and learning to tap that reservoir more effectively is one of the exciting tasks ahead for humankind.

Among the untapped capabilities are leadership gifts. For every effectively functioning leader in our society, I would guess that there are five or ten others with the same potential for leadership who have never led or perhaps even considered leading. Why? Perhaps they were drawn off into the byways of specialization . . . or have never sensed the potentialities within them . . . or have never understood how much the society needs what they have to give.

We can do better. Much, much better.

2

The Crisis of Leadership

James MacGregor Burns

James MacGregor Burns won a Pulitzer Prize and a National Book Award for his study of Franklin D. Roosevelt. His book *Leadership* is considered to be a seminal work in leadership studies. Burns has been Woodrow Wilson Professor of Government at Williams College, and he has served as president of the American Political Science Association.

One of the most universal cravings of our time is a hunger for compelling and creative leadership. Many of us spent our early years in the eras of the titans—Freud and Einstein, Shaw and Stravinsky, Mao and Gandhi, Churchill and Roosevelt, Stalin and Hitler and Mussolini. Most of these colossi died in the middle years of this century; some lingered on, while a few others—de Gaulle, Nehru, perhaps Kennedy and King—joined the pantheon of leadership. These giants strode across our cultural and intellectual and political horizons. We—followers everywhere—loved or loathed them. We marched for them and fought against them. We died for them and we killed some of them. We could not ignore them.

In the final quarter of our century that life-and-death engagement with leadership has given way to the cult of personality, to a "gee whiz" approach to celebrities. We peer into the private lives of leaders, as though their sleeping habits, eating preferences, sexual practices, dogs, and hobbies carry messages of profound significance. Entire magazines are devoted to trivia about "people" and serious newspapers start off their news stories with a personality anecdote or slant before coming to the essence of the matter. Huge throngs parade in Red Square and in the T'ien An Men Square with giant portraits of men who are not giants. The personality cult—a cult of devils as well as heroes—thrives in both East and West.

The crisis of leadership today is the mediocrity or irresponsibility of so many of the men and women in power, but leadership rarely rises to the full need for it. The fundamental crisis underlying mediocrity is intellectual. If we know all too much about our leaders, we know far too little about *leadership*. We fail to grasp the essence of leadership that is relevant to the modern age and hence we cannot agree even on the standards by which to measure, recruit, and reject it. Is leadership simply innovation—cultural or political? Is it essentially inspiration? Mobilization of followers? Goal setting? Goal fulfillment? Is a leader the definer of values? Satisfier of needs? If leaders require followers, who leads whom from where to where, and why? How do leaders lead followers without being wholly led *by* followers? Leadership is one of the most observed and least understood phenomena on earth.

It was not always so. For two millennia at least, leaders of thought did grapple with the vexing problems of the rulers vs. the ruled. Long before modern sociology Plato analyzed not only philosopher-kings but the influences on rulers of upbringing, social and economic institutions, and responses of followers. Long before today's calls for moral leadership and "profiles in courage," Confucian thinkers were examining the concept of leadership in moral teaching and by example. Long before Gandhi, Christian thinkers were preaching nonviolence. Long before modern biography, Plutarch was writing brilliantly about the lives of a host of Roman and Greek rulers and orators, arguing that philosophers "ought to converse especially with 'men in power,'" and examining questions such as whether "an old man should engage in public affairs." From this biographer Shakespeare borrowed for his *Antony and Cleopatra*.

A rich literature on rulership flourished in the classical and middle ages. Later—for reasons we must examine—the study of rulership and leadership ran into serious intellectual difficulties. Leadership as a concept has dissolved into small and discrete meanings. A recent study turned up 130 definitions of the word. A superabundance of facts about leaders far outruns theories of leadership. The world-famous New York Public Library has tens of thousands of biographies, monographs, and newspaper clippings on individual political leaders, but only one catalogue entry to "political leadership" (referring to an obscure politician of forty years ago).

There is, in short, no school of leadership, intellectual or practical. Does it matter that we lack standards for assessing past, present, and potential leaders? Without a powerful modern philosophical tradition, without theoretical and empirical cumulation, without guiding concepts, and without considered practical experiences, we lack the very foundations for knowledge of a phenomenon—leadership in the arts, the academy, science, politics, the professions, war—that touches and shapes our lives. Without such standards and knowledge we cannot make vital distinctions between types of leaders; we cannot distinguish leaders from rulers, from power wielders, and from despots. Hitler called himself—and was called—the Leader; his grotesque *führerprinzip* is solemnly examined as a doctrine of leadership. But Hitler, once he gained power and crushed all opposition, was no leader—he was a tyrant. A leader and a tyrant are polar opposites.

Although we have no school of leadership, we do have in rich abundance and variety the *makings* of such a school. An immense reservoir of data and analysis and theories has been developed. No central concept of leadership has yet emerged, in part because scholars have worked in separate disciplines and subdisciplines in pursuit of different and often unrelated questions and problems. I believe, however, that the richness of the research and analysis and thoughtful experience, accumulated especially in the past decade or so, enables us now to achieve an intellectual breakthrough.

3

Defining a Citizen Leader

Richard A. Couto

Richard Couto currently serves as professor in the Jepson School of Leadership Studies at the University of Richmond. He has worked with community organizations and leaders in the Appalachian region and has published reports and articles related to that work. His recent, award-winning work, *Lifting the Veil*, examines the history of civil rights efforts in one county in Tennessee since Reconstruction.

There I was trying to impress members of the search committee during lunch and sitting across the table from James MacGregor Burns, Pulitzer Prize-winning patriarch of leadership studies. It was difficult to eat and talk without embarrassment, so I did little eating. I talked a lot. I heard myself counter points made by one search committee member about a recent coal miners' strike in Virginia—an impolitic step. Late in our luncheon conversation, Burns lamented the dearth of leadership in contemporary America. I took issue with his point as well, suggesting that the amount and quality of leadership varied depending on where you looked. Leadership at the local community level, I asserted, is abundant and of extraordinarily high quality. Suddenly, I realized that I felt more about leadership than I thought about it.

Reprinted from *Public Leadership Education: The Role of the Citizen Leader* (Dayton: The Kettering Foundation, 1992). By permission of the author.

I had lived it more than I had studied it. I had worked 20 years with an array of leaders in low-income communities of the rural South, Appalachia, and several urban areas. Like them, I had spent far less time thinking about the "why's" and "how's" of leadership than on the "what's to be done" questions of leadership. I had what Michael Polanyi calls "personal knowledge" rather than scholarship. This realization gave me pause, but only momentarily. Undeterred, I forged on.

Burns and I eventually agreed on the disappointing dearth of political and national leadership and ascribed it, in large measure, to the fragmentation of America's political structures. We also agreed that possibly we have more and better leadership at the local level of American life than we give ourselves credit for. Fortunately, I got the job. Burns and I became colleagues and eventually traveled through parts of Appalachia to meet some of the community leaders I had had in mind when I spoke.

This trip, my new job, and that luncheon conversation challenged me to examine what I had taken for granted: What is citizen leadership? And why is it important? As I learned more about leadership, I recognized that I was dealing with only one form of citizen leadership. Legislators, labor union officers, social service agency heads, directors of nonprofit organizations, civic and business leaders, elected and appointed political officials are all citizens and they are also leaders to one degree or another. I was tempted to stretch a definition from that luncheon conversation to cover all these people. Such a definition, however, would risk becoming a Fourth of July celebrative elaboration of the virtues of American life, and certainly would obscure the distinguishing characteristics of the citizen leaders with whom I have worked. What sets these largely ignored leaders apart?

The citizen leaders I have in mind facilitate organized action to improve conditions of people in low-income communities and to address other basic needs of society at the local level. Their goal is to raise the floor beneath all members of society, rather than to enable a few to touch its vaulted ceiling. Sometimes citizen leaders work for change, protesting proposed toxic waste dumping near their homes, for example. In all cases, they exhibit the leadership which occurs when people take sustained action to bring about change that will permit them continued or increased well-being. They recognize the existence of community, a set of relationships among people forged by some special bond. Sometimes that bond includes residence in a particular place. It *always* includes the common human condition with all of its aspirations and potentials.

There are obvious similarities between this form of citizen leadership and broader concepts of leadership. It entails follower-leader relationships and collaboration, exchanges, and interchanges. The citizen leaders about whom I write are transforming leaders who engage others in efforts to reach higher levels of human awareness and relationships. With time, citizen leaders also become transactional leaders and some of them acquire the administrative competencies needed to manage an organization. Burns has referred to "cobblestone leadership" and the "second and third tier" of leadership. These citizen leaders embody those concepts as well.

On the other hand, as I learned more about leadership, I understood the differences between the citizen leadership I knew and other concepts of leadership. For example, in my first class on leadership studies, I asked my students to draw pictures of leadership. In response, students drew an array of images of money, power, prestige, and superiority—leaders were in front of or above others. Few scholars would define leadership in such terms, yet my students probably reflected accurately the lessons they had acquired from popular culture.

Citizen leaders contrast markedly with such popular conceptions of power and, to a lesser extent, with academic conceptions as well. For one thing, citizen leaders usually do not choose leadership. They do not even seek it. They leave their private lives reluctantly for these public roles. Often they intend to take some public action, to achieve their purpose quickly, and then to return to private matters. Customarily, their first action is to approach the people in charge to get something done about a specific problem. It is only when they are rebuffed or rebuked that citizen leaders go farther, eventually entering into a chain of events and actions that leads to the achievement of their original purpose. Somewhere in that chain, the people I have in mind acquire the truly distinguishing characteristic of leadership: the gift of trust bestowed by others with whom they work. Their groups may establish a formal organization—"Concerned citizens of . . ." is a frequently used name—and citizen leaders will be elected or delegated to act on behalf of the group. Whatever their titles, citizen leaders have a deeper sense of responsibility and higher sense of authority that comes from the trust others have bestowed informally upon them to act on behalf of the group.

Citizen leadership brings new responsibilities, new contacts, media exposure, and other trappings of leadership that, more often than not, citizen leaders would prefer to shed. They would like to return to their "normal" lives. Ten years ago, Larry Wilson and his wife, Sheila, backed into leadership positions in the controversy over pollution of Yellow Creek near their eastern Kentucky home. Today, they direct a regional environmental program of the

Highlander Research and Education Center. He attended the United Nations Earth Summit in Brazil in the summer of 1992. At the same time, she visited other citizen leaders in Northern Ireland who had traveled to Appalachia earlier to observe her work. Larry Wilson calls local environmental citizen leaders "reluctant warriors," who pay for their leadership:

> These people have to raise families in the contaminated areas, punch a time clock within an organization that is frequently opposed to their environmental activities, be sensitive to rocking the political boat, [and] maintain social ties in a community divided by the issue they are working on.

The Wilsons' full-time work creates an alter ego that separates them from other local citizen leaders to whom they feel kindred. As Larry Wilson put it, "I wake up in a different world every morning." His expanded role of citizen leader requires him to accept that new world, but to adjust it to a world he does not want to leave behind.

The loss of what is familiar prompts citizen leader William Saunders to maintain adamantly that he did not and would not choose the role. His work on the Sea Islands of South Carolina, and his direction of the 100-day hospital workers' strike in Charleston in 1969, earned him a place in the film, *You Got to Move*, which dramatizes citizen leadership. Saunders now runs a radio station in Charleston, South Carolina, and continues to be an important part of the civil rights movement and antipoverty programs in the area. Like Martin Luther King, Jr., Saunders understands citizen leadership as a burden, a cross that few would take up willingly. After all, he points out, the transforming aspect of citizen leadership transforms the personal lives of leaders as well as the conditions they intend to change:

> It's not the kind of life you choose. You get caught up in it. But you wouldn't choose to be misunderstood. A preacher near here gave a sermon, "Being Picked Out to be Picked On." That's a heavy subject. To see things clearly ahead of your time carries a heavy price. You're friendless. There's no one you can talk with straight across the board, not even your family. Ten years later, they may see what you are saying, but by that time, you've gone on.

Citizen leadership is leadership with far fewer perks and far less glamour than that which marks those in the threadbare political and national leadership we lament. At the same time, citizen leadership comes with the same or greater personal costs as other forms of leadership.

Despite their reluctance, citizen leaders act from fairly simple motives. One does not hear long, complicated analyses of Abraham Maslow's hierarchy of needs. Instead, citizen leaders speak in simple terms about the basic dignity of every human being. They act from the conviction that we, as a society, are responsible for redressing the conditions that undermine and understate the human dignity of any of its members. While others may accept the needs and deprivation of some groups without a sense of moral responsibility, citizen leaders cannot. They are compelled to pass on to the next generation a society less tolerant of human and environmental degradation. For citizen leaders, with bonds to specific low-income communities, success has a single, clear measure: Will our children have a reasonable choice to live with dignity in their community as adults? Eventually, their assertion of social responsibility for the human condition becomes exceedingly troublesome. It means entering the value of "community" into economic calculations in which community has no monetary value. It means giving voice and stature to groups of people without political influence. Citizen leadership means making a political, economic, and social system accountable for whom it serves and fails to serve.

Citizen leaders express the simplicity of their motives in anger mixed with humor and determination to persuade those who impede them to recognize the human dignity of individuals and the worth of community. Eula Hall helped establish a health center in Mud Creek in eastern Kentucky. She still works at the center to assure residents of the area access to medical care providers and to the rights and benefits to which they are entitled. She exemplifies the sophisticated competencies citizen leaders acquire to conduct their work. She has an outstanding record of victories in black lung hearings, for example. Press her for her reasons for a 30-year career in full-time citizen leadership and she echoes Fannie Lou Hamer: "You just get sick and tired of seeing people get pushed around."

Citizen leaders are not showered with traditional forms of recognition. Colleges and universities, for example, often ignore them or delay recognizing their achievements. Citizen leaders are likely to be pressing the medical school's hospital on its policy for indigent care. They are likely to be protesting conditions in the rental property of a university's landlord, or protesting the inadequacy of pollution controls at the plant of a major university contributor. It serves the interest of many institutions to ignore the reality citizen leaders work to make us aware of. Colleges interested in instructing students about the workings of the American economy are more likely to encourage them to speak to people in corporate offices than in picket lines.

Recognition does come to citizen leaders. First, and fewest, are the awards that recognize them for addressing an issue of injustice or inequality. In general, these awards come from organizations and institutions, including some foundations, that understand themselves as part of a process of basic social change. Larry Wilson was designated an environmental hero by *Mother Jones*. Second, and most frequent, are the awards that recognize citizen leaders for individual courage within a context of need but separate from the political and social issues that underlie that need. These awards make citizen leaders into heroes and heroines by emphasizing their personal traits. *People* magazine, for example, depicted Eula Hall as a crusader when it included her among 25 "Amazing Americans!"

Eventually, some citizen leaders are recognized by institutions that previously shunned them. This form of award measures the acceptance of positions that citizen leaders took and the transformation of society and some of its institutions. Bill Saunders, for example, served as chairman of the Democratic Party of Charleston County. The leadership path that led him to this position began with a protest against racial barriers that prevented him and others from voting and joining a political party. Often this recognition comes long after the controversy has subsided, after the citizen leader has passed on the mantle of leadership to others, or even after he or she has died.

As I thought about why citizen leadership is important, I came back to our luncheon consensus about the dearth of national and political leadership. Citizen leadership protests and mitigates the shortcomings of our national and political leadership. In the absence of strong formal political leadership, leadership slips over into the hands of those with economic and social power. We not only recognize this dispersion of political power, we praise it. We teach pluralism as a political system which provides a high probability that an active and legitimate group can make itself heard effectively in the process of decision making. Our first inclination is to include citizen leadership in that pantheon, but that would miss the importance of the form of citizen leadership with which I am concerned.

Citizen leadership demands that the political system expand its notion of "legitimate" groups beyond economic and social elites. It constantly presses the static boundaries of our political system to broaden, to incorporate new issues, and to involve new groups. For citizen leaders, politics is the public expression of society's sense of community and of the common interests of its members. Invariably, citizen leaders are criticized early on in their efforts precisely because of their efforts to wake sleeping dogs and to expand the public agenda. Any political system throws up barriers to resist change. If there is one thing that citizen leaders are about, it is taking down those barriers. The greater the change, the more likely the resistance. Citizen leaders soon understand that their form of leadership is intolerable for some. All the people mentioned in this essay have stories of being shot at and threatened with physical harm and arson.

Eventually, most citizen leaders learn to work within "the system," but it is a system changed by their presence. Eula Hall invited the representative of her congressional district to the ground-breaking ceremony for the new clinic in Mud Creek. Twenty years before, that would have been inconceivable. But, in the intervening time, Hall's aspirations and leadership had acquired legitimacy. Likewise, any listing of the political elite of Charleston and, perhaps, South Carolina today will include Bill Saunders. Larry Wilson and the Concerned Citizens of Yellow Creek initiated forums to discuss issues with candidates for local political positions.

In a sense, citizen leadership is a parallel government, a shadow government, or a government in exile depending on the degree of change entailed in its demands. As a "parallel government," citizen leaders carry out changes before political leaders are prepared to do the same. Addressing the needs of the homeless is the most recent case in point. In cases where needed changes exceed the capacity of citizen leaders, they may become a "shadow government," the loyal opposition of those with political power, to demand public action for public problems heretofore ignored or considered "illegitimate." The demand for public responses to the AIDS crisis illustrates the point on a national scale. When the demand for change exceeds the capacity of public officials to act, citizen leaders also become a "government in exile" waiting for the day that issues, long denied, become crises demanding action.

Through protest, demands for fairer portions of public resources for some groups, and a vision of a transformed state of society in which the bonds of community are more apparent, citizen leaders pursue and establish change. In some measure, the dearth of political leadership that we lament reflects the inability or unwillingness of elected and appointed leaders to express the degree of compassion, concern, and community that animates citizen leadership. In part, this failure is structural and needs to be fixed. In another sense, however, it represents a valuable gap worth preserving. As long as our citizen leaders exceed the quality of our elected and appointed leaders, the latter have someone to follow—what could be more central to a vital democracy?

4

Servant Leadership

Robert K. Greenleaf

Robert Greenleaf developed his theory of servant leadership while an executive at AT&T, and subsequently lectured at Harvard Business School, Dartmouth College, and the University of Virginia. He founded The Center for Applied Ethics, now known as the Robert K. Greenleaf Center.

Servant and leader—can these two roles be fused in one real person, in all levels of status or calling? If so, can that person live and be productive in the real world of the present? My sense of the present leads me to say yes to both questions. This chapter is an attempt to explain why and to suggest how.

The idea of *The Servant as Leader* came out of reading Hermann Hesse's *Journey to the East.* In this story we see a band of men on a mythical journey, probably also Hesse's own journey. The central figure of the story is Leo who accompanies the party as the *servant* who does their menial chores, but who also sustains them with his spirit and his song. He is a person of extraordinary presence. All goes well until Leo disappears. Then the group falls into disarray and the journey is abandoned. They cannot make it without the servant Leo. The narrator, one of the party, after some years of wandering finds Leo and is taken into the Order that had sponsored the journey. There he discovers that Leo, whom he had known first as *servant,* was in fact the titular head of the Order, its guiding spirit, a great and noble *leader.*

One can muse on what Hesse was trying to say when he wrote this story. We know that most of his fiction was autobiographical, that he led a tortured life, and that *Journey to the East* suggests a turn toward the serenity he achieved in his old age. There has been much speculation by critics on Hesse's life and work, some of it centering on this story which they find the most puzzling. But to me, this story clearly says that *the great leader is seen as servant first,* and that simple fact is the key to his greatness. Leo was actually the leader all of the time, but he was servant first because that was what he was, *deep down inside.* Leadership was bestowed upon a man who was by nature a servant. It was something given, or assumed, that could be taken away. His servant nature was the real man, not bestowed, not assumed, and not to be taken away. He was servant first.

I mention Hesse and *Journey to the East* for two reasons. First, I want to acknowledge the source of the idea of *The Servant as Leader.* Then I want to use this reference as an introduction to a brief discussion of prophecy.

Fifteen years ago when I first read about Leo, if I had been listening to contemporary prophecy as intently as I do now, the first draft of this piece might have been written then. As it was, the idea lay dormant for eleven years until, four years ago, I concluded that we in this country were in a leadership crisis and that I should do what I could about it. I became painfully aware of how dull my sense of contemporary prophecy had been. And I have reflected much on why we do not hear and heed the prophetic voices in our midst (not a new question in our times, nor more critical than heretofore).

I now embrace the theory of prophecy which holds that prophetic voices of great clarity, and with a quality of insight equal to that of any age, are speaking cogently all of the time. Men and women of a stature equal to the greatest of the past are with us now addressing the problems of the day and pointing to a better way and to a personeity better able to live fully and serenely in these times.

The variable that marks some periods as barren and some as rich in prophetic vision is in the interest, the level of seeking, the responsiveness of the hearers. The variable is not in the presence or absence or the relative quality and force of the prophetic voices. Prophets grow in stature as people respond to their message. If their early attempts are ignored or spurned, their talent may wither away.

It is *seekers,* then, who make prophets, and the initiative of any one of us in searching for and responding to the voice of contemporary prophets may mark the turning point in their growth and service. But since we are the product of our own history, we see current prophecy within the context of past wisdom. We listen to as wide a range of contemporary thought as we can attend to. Then we *choose* those we elect to heed as prophets—*both old and new*—and meld their advice with our own leadings. This we test in real-life experiences to establish our own position. . . .

One does not, of course, ignore the great voices of the past. One does not awaken each morning with the compulsion to reinvent the wheel. But if one is *servant*, either leader or follower, one is always searching, listening, expecting that a better wheel for these times is in the making. It may emerge any day. Any one of us may find it out from personal experience. I am hopeful.

I am hopeful for these times, despite the tension and conflict, because more natural servants are trying to see clearly the world as it is and are listening carefully to prophetic voices that are speaking *now*. They are challenging the pervasive injustice with greater force and they are taking sharper issue with the wide disparity between the quality of society they know is reasonable and possible with available resources, and, on the other hand, the actual performance of the whole range of institutions that exist to serve society.

A fresh critical look is being taken at the issues of power and authority, and people are beginning to learn, however haltingly, to relate to one another in less coercive and more creatively supporting ways. A new moral principle is emerging which holds that the only authority deserving one's allegiance is that which is freely and knowingly granted by the led to the leader in response to, and in proportion to, the clearly evident servant stature of the leader. Those who choose to follow this principle will not casually accept the authority of existing institutions. *Rather, they will freely respond only to individuals who are chosen as leaders because they are proven and trusted as servants.* To the extent that this principle prevails in the future, the only truly viable institutions will be those that are predominantly servant-led.

I am mindful of the long road ahead before these trends, which I see so clearly, become a major society-shaping force. We are not there yet. But I see encouraging movement on the horizon.

What direction will the movement take? Much depends on whether those who stir the ferment will come to grips with the age-old problem of how to live in a human society. I say this because so many, having made their awesome decision for autonomy and independence from tradition, and having taken their firm stand against injustice and hypocrisy, find it hard to convert themselves into *affirmative builders* of a better society. How many of them will seek their personal fulfillment by making the hard choices, and by undertaking the rigorous preparation that building a better society requires? It all depends on what kind of leaders emerge and how they—we—respond to them.

My thesis, that more servants should emerge as leaders, or should follow only servant-leaders, is not a popular one. It is much more comfortable to go with a less demanding point of view about what is expected of one now. There are several undemanding, plausibly-argued alternatives to choose. One, since society seems corrupt, is to seek to avoid the center of it by retreating to an idyllic existence that minimizes involvement with the "system" (with the "system" that makes such withdrawal possible). Then there is the assumption that since the effort to reform existing institutions has not brought instant perfection, the remedy is to destroy them completely so that fresh new perfect ones can grow. Not much thought seems to be given to the problem of where the new seed will come from or who the gardener to tend them will be. The concept of the servant-leader stands in sharp contrast to this kind of thinking.

Yet it is understandable that the easier alternatives would be chosen, especially by young people. By extending education for so many so far into the adult years, the normal participation in society is effectively denied when young people are ready for it. With education that is preponderantly abstract and analytical it is no wonder that there is a preoccupation with criticism and that not much thought is given to "What can *I* do about it?"

Criticism has its place, but as a total preoccupation it is sterile. In a time of crisis, like the leadership crisis we are now in, if too many potential builders are taken in by a complete absorption with dissecting the wrong and by a zeal for instant perfection, then the movement so many of us want to see will be set back. The danger, perhaps, is to hear the analyst too much and the artist too little.

Albert Camus stands apart from other great artists of his time, in my view, and deserves the title of *prophet*, because of his unrelenting demand that each of us confront the exacting terms of our own existence, and, like Sisyphus, *accept our rock and find our happiness in dealing with it*. Camus sums up the relevance of his position to our concern for the servant as leader in the last paragraph of his last published lecture, entitled *Create Dangerously*:

One may long, as I do, for a gentler flame, a respite, a pause for musing. But perhaps there is no other peace for the artist than what he finds in the heat of combat. "Every wall is a door," Emerson correctly said. Let us not look for the door, and the way out, anywhere but in the wall against which we are living.

Instead, let us seek the respite where it is—in the very thick of battle. For in my opinion, and this is where I shall close, it *is* there. Great ideas, it has been said, come into the world as gently as doves. Perhaps, then, if we listen attentively, we shall hear, amid the uproar of empires and nations, a faint flutter of wings, the gentle stirring of life and hope. Some will say that this hope lies in a nation, others, in a man. I believe rather that it is awakened, revived, nourished by millions of solitary individuals whose deeds and works every day negate frontiers and the crudest implications of history. As a result, there shines forth fleetingly the ever-threatened truth that each and every man, on the foundations of his own sufferings and joys, builds for them all. . . .

Who Is the Servant-Leader?

The servant-leader *is* servant first—as Leo was portrayed. It begins with the natural feeling that one wants to serve, to serve *first*. Then conscious choice brings one to aspire to lead. That person is sharply different from one who is *leader* first, perhaps because of the need to assuage an unusual power drive or to acquire material possessions. For such it will be a later choice to serve—after leadership is established. The leader-first and the servant-first are two extreme types. Between them there are shadings and blends that are part of the infinite variety of human nature.

The difference manifests itself in the care taken by the servant first to make sure that other people's highest priority needs are being served. The best test, and difficult to administer, is: Do those served grow as persons? Do they, *while being served*, become healthier, wiser, freer, more autonomous, more likely themselves to become servants? *And*, what is the effect on the least privileged in society; will they benefit, or, at least, not be further deprived? . . .

All of this rests on the assumption that the only way to change a society (or just make it go) is to produce people, enough people, who will change it (or make it go). The urgent problems of our day—the disposition to venture into immoral and senseless wars, destruction of the environment, poverty, alienation, discrimination, overpopulation—are here because of human failures, individual failures, one person at a time, one action at a time failures.

If we make it out of all of this (and this is written in the belief that we will make it), the "system" will be whatever works best. The builders will find the useful pieces wherever they are, and invent new ones when needed, all without reference to ideological coloration. "How do we get the right things done?" will be the watchword of the day, every day. And the context of those who bring it off will be: all men and women who are touched by the effort grow taller, and become healthier, stronger, more autonomous, *and* more disposed to serve.

Leo the *servant*, and the exemplar of the *servant-leader*, has one further portent for us. If we may assume that Hermann Hesse is the narrator in *Journey to the East* (not a difficult assumption to make), at the end of the story he establishes his identity. His final confrontation at the close of his initiation into the Order is with a small transparent sculpture: two figures joined together. One is Leo, the other is the narrator. The narrator notes that a movement of substance is taking place within the transparent sculpture.

> I perceived that my image was in the process of adding to and flowing into Leo's, nourishing and strengthening it. It seemed that, in time . . . only one would remain: Leo. He must grow, I must disappear.
>
> As I stood there and looked and tried to understand what I saw, I recalled a short conversation that I had once had with Leo during the festive days at Bremgarten. We had talked about the creations of poetry being more vivid and real than the poets themselves.

What Hesse may be telling us here is that Leo is the symbolic personification of Hesse's aspiration to serve through his literary creations, creations that are greater than Hesse himself; and that his work, for which he was but the channel, will carry on and serve and lead in a way that he, a twisted and tormented man, could not—except as he created.

Does not Hesse dramatize, in extreme form, the dilemma of us all? Except as we venture to create, we cannot project ourselves beyond ourselves to serve and lead.

To which Camus would add: *Create dangerously!*

PART II

WHAT IS LEADERSHIP?

Here we turn to one of the solutions to the crisis of leadership outlined by Gardner and Burns. Both of those authors imply that the real answer to the perceived "cry for leadership" is a greater understanding of leadership itself. Thomas Cronin picks up on this and ponders the question of whether leadership is indeed something which can be learned. Irving Spitzberg, Jr., poses a series of specific questions which must be addressed if one is to gain any real understanding of leadership. According to Spitzberg, "the first task . . . is to develop a tentative definition of leadership. . . ." While Spitzberg's insight is logical enough, the task of defining "leadership" is not at all a simple one. Indeed, it is an issue over which there has been much disagreement, and, as Bernard Bass states, "there are almost as many definitions of leadership as there are persons who have attempted to define the concept." Nevertheless, it is possible to come up with a definition which is serviceable, as Hughes, Ginnett and Curphy (selection 8) demonstrate.

5

Thinking and Learning about Leadership

Thomas E. Cronin

Thomas Cronin is a former White House Fellow and White House aide. In 1986, he won the American Political Science Association's Charles E. Merriam Award for significant contributions to the art of government. He is widely published, and currently serves as President of Whitman College.

Leadership is one of the most widely talked about subjects and at the same time one of the most elusive and puzzling. Americans often yearn for great, transcending leadership for their communities, companies, the military, unions, universities, sports teams, and for the nation. However, we have an almost love-hate ambivalence about power wielders. And we especially dislike anyone who tries to boss us around. Yes, we admire the Washingtons and Churchills, but Hitler and Al Capone were leaders too—and that points up a fundamental problem. Leadership can be exercised in the service of noble, liberating, enriching ends, but it can also serve to manipulate, mislead and repress.

"One of the most universal cravings of our time," writes James MacGregor Burns, "is a hunger for compelling and creative leadership." But exactly what

Reprinted from *Presidential Studies Quarterly* 14 (Winter, 1984), pp. 22–24, 33–34. Permission granted by the Center for the Study of the Presidency, publisher of *Presidential Studies Quarterly*.

is creative leadership? A *Wall Street Journal* cartoon had two men talking about leadership. Finally, one turned to the other in exasperation and said: "Yes, we need leadership, but we also need someone to tell us what to do." That is to say, leadership for most people most of the time is a rather hazy, distant and even confusing abstraction. Hence, thinking about or defining leadership is a kind of intellectual leadership challenge in itself.

What follows are some thoughts about leadership and education for leadership. These thoughts and ideas are highly personal and hardly scientific. As I shall suggest below, almost anything that can be said about leadership can be contradicted with counter examples. Moreover, the whole subject is riddled with paradoxes. My ideas here are the product of my studies of political leadership and my own participation in politics from the town meeting level to the White House staff. Some of my ideas come from helping to advise universities and foundations and the Houston-based American Leadership Forum on how best to go about encouraging leadership development. Finally, my thoughts have also been influenced in a variety of ways by numerous conversations with five especially insightful writers on leadership—Warren Bennis, James MacGregor Burns, David Campbell, Harlan Cleveland and John W. Gardner.

Teaching Leadership

Can we teach people to become leaders? Can we teach leadership? People are divided on these questions. It was once widely held that "leaders are born and not made," but that view is less widely held today. We also used to hear about "natural leaders" but nowadays most leaders have learned their leadership ability rather than inherited it. Still there is much mystery to the whole matter. In any event, many people think colleges and universities should steer clear of the whole subject. What follows is a set of reasons why our institutions of higher learning generally are "bashful about teaching leadership." These reasons may overstate the case, but they are the objections that serious people often raise.

First, many people still believe that leaders are born and not made. Or that leadership is somehow almost accidental or at least that most leaders emerge from circumstances and normally do not create them. In any event, it is usually added, most people, most of the time, are not now and never will be leaders.

Second, American cultural values hold that leadership is an elitist and thus anti-American phenomenon. Plato and Machiavelli and other grand theorists might urge upon their contemporaries the need for selecting out and training a select few for top leadership roles. But this runs against the American grain. We like to think that anyone can become a top leader here. Hence, no special training should be given to some special select few.

Third is the complaint that leadership training would more than likely be preoccupied with skills, techniques, and the *means* of getting things done. But leadership for what? A focus on *means* divorced from *ends* makes people—especially intellectuals—ill at ease. They hardly want to be in the business of training future Joe McCarthys or Hitlers or Idi Amins.

Fourth, leadership study strikes many as an explicitly vocational topic. It's a practical and applied matter—better learned in summer jobs, in internships or on the playing fields. You learn it on the job. You learn it from gaining experience, from making mistakes and learning from these. And you should learn it from mentors.

Fifth, leadership often involves an element of manipulation or deviousness, if not outright ruthlessness. Some consider it as virtually the same as learning about jungle-fighting or acquiring "the killer instinct." It's just not "clean" enough a subject matter for many people to embrace. Plus, "leaders" like Stalin and Hitler gave "leadership" a bad name. If they were leaders, then spare us of their clones or imitators.

Sixth, leadership in the most robust sense of the term is such an ecumenical and intellectually all-encompassing subject that it frightens not only the timid but even the most well educated of persons. To teach leadership is an act of arrogance. That is, it is to suggest one understands far more than even a well educated person can understand—history, ethics, philosophy, classics, politics, biography, psychology, management, sociology, law, etc. . . . and [is] steeped deeply as well in the "real world."

Seventh, colleges and universities are increasingly organized in highly specialized divisions and departments all geared to train specialists. While the mission of the college may be to educate "the educated person" and society's future leaders, in fact the incentive system is geared to training specialists. Society today rewards the expert or the super specialist—the data processors, the pilots, the financial whiz, the heart surgeon, the special team punt returners, and so on. Leaders, however, have to learn to become generalists and usually have to do so well after they have left our colleges, graduate schools and professional schools.

Eighth, leadership strikes many people (and with some justification) as an elusive, hazy and almost mysterious commodity. Now you see it, now you don't. So much of leadership is intangible, you can't possibly define all the parts. A person may be an outstanding leader here, but fail there. Trait theory has been thoroughly debunked. In fact, leadership is highly situational and contextual. A special chemistry develops between leaders and followers and it is usually context specific. Followers often do more to determine the leadership they will get than can any teacher. Hence, why not teach people to be substantively bright and well-read and let things just take their natural course.

Ninth, virtually anything that can be said about leadership can be denied or disproven. Leadership studies, to the extent they exist, are unscientific. Countless paradoxes and contradictions litter every manuscript on leadership. Thus, we yearn for leadership, but yearn equally to be free and left alone. We admire risk-taking, entrepreneurial leadership, but we roundly criticize excessive risk-taking as bullheadedness or plain stupid. We want leaders who are highly self-confident and who are perhaps incurably optimistic—yet we also dislike hubris and often yearn for at least a little self-doubt (e.g., Creon in *Antigone*). Leaders have to be almost singleminded in their drive and commitment but too much of that makes a person rigid, driven and unacceptable. We want leaders to be good listeners and represent their constituents, yet in the words of Walter Lippmann, effective leadership often consists of giving the people not what they want but what they will learn to want. How in the world, then, can you be rigorous and precise in teaching leadership?

Tenth, leadership at its best comes close to creativity. And how do you teach creativity? We are increasingly made aware of the fact that much of creative thinking calls upon unconscious thinking, dreaming and even fantasy. Some fascinating work is being done on intuition and the nonrational—but it is hardly a topic with which traditional disciplines in traditional colleges are comfortable. . . .

Learning About Leadership

Permit me to return again to the question of whether leadership can be learned, and possibly taught. My own belief is that students cannot usually be taught to be leaders. But students, and anyone else for that matter, can profitably be exposed to leadership, discussions of leadership skills and styles, and leadership strategies and theories. Individuals can learn in their own minds the strengths as well as limitations of leadership. People can learn about the paradoxes and contradictions and ironies of leadership, which, however puzzling, are central to appreciating the diversity and the dilemmas of problem-solving and getting organizations and nations to function.

Learning about leadership means recognizing bad leadership as well as good. Learning about leadership means understanding the critical linkage of ends and means. Learning about leadership also involves the study of the special chemistry that develops between leaders and followers, not only the chemistry that existed between Americans and Lincoln, but also between Mao and the Chinese peasants, Lenin and the Bolsheviks, between Martin Luther King, Jr., and civil rights activists, between Jean Monnet and those who dreamed of a European Economic Community.

Students can learn to discern and define situations and contexts within which leadership has flourished. Students can learn about the fallibility of the trait theory. Students can learn about the contextual problems of leadership, of why and when leadership is sometimes transferable, and sometimes not. Students can learn about the crucial role that advisors and supporters play in the leadership equation. Students can also learn about countless problem-solving strategies and theories, and participate in role playing exercises that sharpen their own skills in such undertakings.

Students of leadership can learn widely from reading biographies about both the best and the worst leaders. Plutarch's *Lives* would be a good place to start. Much can be learned from mentors and from intern-participant observing. Much can also be learned about leadership by getting away from one's own culture and examining how leaders in other circumstances go about the task of motivating and mobilizing others. Countless learning opportunities exist that can sharpen a student's skills as a speaker, debater, negotiator, problem clarifier and planner. Such skills should not be minimized. Nor should anyone underestimate the importance of history, economics, logic, and a series of related substantive fields that help provide the breadth and the perspective indispensible to societal leadership.

Above all, students of leadership can make an appointment with themselves and begin to appreciate their own strengths and deficiencies. Personal mastery is important. So too the ability to use one's intuition, and to enrich one's creative impulses. John Gardner suggests, "It's what you learn after you know it all that really counts." Would-be leaders learn to manage their time more wisely. Would-be leaders learn that self-pity and resentment are like toxic substances. Would-be leaders learn the old truth that most people are not for or against you but rather preoccupied with themselves. Would-be leaders learn to break out of their comfortable imprisonments; they learn to cast aside dull routines and habits that enslave most of us. Would-be leaders learn how to become truly sharing and caring people—in their families, their professions and in their communities. And would-be leaders constantly learn too that they have more to give than they have ever given, no matter how much they have given.

Let me conclude by paraphrasing from John Adams:

We must study politics [and leadership] and war [and peace] that our sons [and daughters] have the liberty to study mathematics and philosophy, geography, natural history and naval architecture, navigation, commerce, and agriculture, in order to give their children a right to study painting, poetry, music, architecture, statuary, tapestry, and porcelain.

6

Paths of Inquiry into Leadership

Irving J. Spitzberg, Jr.

Irving Spitzberg, Jr., has degrees from Columbia, Yale and Oxford. He has been a college professor, college administrator, and practicing attorney. Spitzberg served as executive director of the Council on Liberal Learning of the Association of American Colleges and Universities. He is president of The Knowledge Company, and serves of counsel to the Spirer Law Group, Washington, D.C.

Between 500 and 600 campuses are paying attention to developing their students as leaders, either in the classroom or in extracurricular activities and programs. The extracurricular activities often originate either in a student development office or in direct student initiative. The academic courses may be loosely divided into two categories: those that draw mainly on social psychological and management studies literatures, the traditional homes of leadership studies; and liberal arts academic courses that place the study of leadership in the context of both the humanities and social sciences—a multidisciplinary approach, in essence.

Each of these kinds of courses raises a number of issues, and the issues, in

Reprinted with permission from *Liberal Education*, Vol. 73 #2, March/April 1987, Copyright, 1987, by the Association of American Colleges and Universities (AAC & U), 1818 R Street, NW, Washington, DC 20009.

turn, raise questions. In two years of working with the general topic of leadership, I have developed what I like to refer to as a "laundry list" of these questions. It is a "laundry list" because I have no grand theoretical construct for generating and organizing these questions.

It is essential that I state my skepticism about supposedly interdisciplinary inquiries. I think true interdisciplinary is rare. Indeed, with the exception of some sciences such as biochemistry and biophysics, which evolved from interdisciplinary research into disciplines themselves, I have yet to see an interdisciplinary inquiry. But there are many fields that require knowledge from many disciplines to be understood: education, cognitive science, and intercultural studies, for example. Leadership, like these multidisciplinary fields, requires fancy footwork in modes of inquiry and standards of evidence and argument. To admit this limitation at the start is to encourage prudence and caution, not to dismiss or belittle the value of the enterprise.

The first task in a class, a course, or a program is to develop a tentative definition of leadership and criteria about what constitutes a leader. The various literatures are full of definitions that focus upon the ability to change group behavior, the exercise of power, the validation of authority, and the existence of followers. There is little consideration of how we use the concept in different institutional and organizational settings. And there is almost no debate about the various definitions used. In fact, most discussion assumes that we will know leadership when we see it, and that leaders are simply known.

In order to impart some rigor to considering the concept, I would pose these permutations of the question, "What is leadership?": Do leaders require followers? Does the concept of leadership have different meanings in different institutional, national, or historical settings? Does the role of leader assume authority? Does this authority require consent? How do power and authority relate in the concept of leadership? How do leaders actually lead? How do we assess how well they lead?

I have not listed a number of traditional questions—is leadership a trait, for example—because I find this sort of question to be less than interesting and probably unanswerable. While the particular question about environment versus character is now passé, however, the significance of understanding the environmental features that interact with personality and character in the recruitment and success of leadership should never be underestimated.

Conceptual questions seldom arise from leaders who are leading, but answers to them will influence how we answer more practical questions, which are the stuff of the exercise of leadership and interest those engaged in self-conscious leadership development.

Questions Arising from Practice

How are leaders recruited and selected? When we look at governance systems, issues of election and selection play a significant role. Their answers require an ethical framework and the careful collection of empirical data.

- Where do leaders come from demographically?
- What is the connection between recruitment and selection (or election)?
- Are leaders selected or self-selected?
- What is the impact of institutions that are self-consciously committed to a culture of leadership (for example, the military academies and Ivy League schools) on the recruitment and selection of leaders throughout society?

How do leaders lead? These sorts of questions inform the approach of a number of scholars of leadership, particularly in the applied social sciences. How does one learn to be a leader? Once one is anointed, what skills are necessary and what is the nature of the activity of leadership?

Students in leadership courses are reading some of the thousands of biographies of leaders. While each biography describes how heroes go about the leadership business, there is a paucity of comparisons of different leaders with attention to similarities and differences of techniques of leadership. Students should be considering:

- Do leaders use incentives or sanctions or both?
- Do leaders at different times use different techniques?
- Does institutional setting affect leadership style and techniques?
- Are there techniques of leadership, such as time management, which account for its constructive exercise? How do leaders communicate?
- Are there important gender or ethnic differences in leadership style? What are they?
- Is the exercise of leadership an incremental (transactional) or discontinuous (transformational) process or both?
- How do standards of leadership vary according to context?

What is the nature of the relationship between leader and followers? To understand leaders is to understand followers. Whether one is a leader or follower depends upon the situation and the institutional context. Lincoln was a political leader but a religious follower; he set ethical standards in the political system but was not a theological pacesetter. The leader/follower nexus can pose a series of interesting questions that can best be pursued by careful analysis of crises and decision making.

- What is the connection among individual characteristics, organizational features, and historical moment that casts the same individual in different roles in different settings at different moments?
- How does the communication system between leaders and followers work?
- What are the rights and duties of leaders in relation to followers and vice versa?

How ought we evaluate the quality of leadership? Much of the literature, while seeming to focus on the nature of leadership, in fact evaluates particular qualities of specific leaders. We need to develop detailed strategies for evaluating leadership according to standards that are set in the context of a particular organization and a society at a specific historical moment. Even with these qualifications, students of leadership can generate criteria and standards. This requires both analytical and political acumen: Understanding the quality of leadership requires an analytical framework; evaluating for purposes of improving or changing leadership requires political agreement in regard to all of these questions.

- What is the culture of the particular organization and/or society?
- How does the leader understand and respond to that culture?
- What substantive changes occurred while a particular leader stood watch?
- What values are appropriate to evaluate a particular leadership record?
- How might one evaluate a particular group of leaders who operate in similar settings and whose activity affects each other?
- What are the systems for holding leaders accountable? How ought they vary? . . .

In framing my questions, I have viewed myself as trying to understand leadership, not explicitly trying to develop leaders. Those who wish to develop leaders must understand much more than the current state of knowledge about leadership if they are to do more than engage in the documentation of trivia. Leadership development is an important personal and social goal. But it is a goal dependent upon better understanding the nature of leadership.

7

The Meaning of Leadership

Bernard M. Bass

Bass & Stogdill's Handbook of Leadership has been the leading reference work for serious students of leadership for two decades. Bernard Bass has been a prolific leadership writer. His 1985 book *Leadership and Performance Beyond Expectations* is also a classic. Bass has served as president of the Division of Organizational Psychology of the International Association of Applied Psychology, and is distinguished professor of management and director of the Center for Leadership Studies at the State University of New York, Binghamton. He is a founding editor of *The Leadership Quarterly*.

The word leadership is a sophisticated, modern concept. In earlier times, words meaning "head of state," "military commander," "princeps," "proconsul," "chief," or "king" were common in most societies; these words differentiated the ruler from other members of society. A preoccupation with leadership, as opposed to headship based on inheritance, usurpation, or appointment, occurred predominantly in countries with an Anglo-Saxon heritage. Although the *Oxford English Dictionary* (1933) noted the appearance of the word "leader" in the English language as early as the year 1300, the word "leadership" did not appear until the first half of the nineteenth century in writings about the political influence and control of British Parliament. And the word did not appear in the most other modern languages until recent times.

Defining Leadership

There are almost as many different definitions of leadership as there are persons who have attempted to define the concept.[1] Moreover, as Pfeffer noted,[2] many of the definitions are ambiguous. Furthermore, the distinction between leadership and other social-influence processes is often blurred.[3,4] The many dimensions into which leadership has been cast and their overlapping meanings have added to the confusion. Therefore, the meaning of leadership may depend on the kind of institution in which it is found.[5] Nevertheless, there is sufficient similarity among definitions to permit a rough scheme of classification. Leadership has been conceived as the focus of group processes, as a matter of personality, as a matter of inducing compliance, as the exercise of influence, as particular behaviors, as a form of persuasion, as a power relation, as an instrument to achieve goals, as an effect of interaction, as a differentiated role, as initiation of structure, and as many combinations of these definitions.

8

What Is Leadership?

Richard L. Hughes, Robert C. Ginnett,
and Gordon R. Curphy

Richard L. Hughes has a Ph.D. in clinical psychology and heads the Department of Behavioral Sciences and Leadership at the United States Air Force Academy. Robert C. Ginnett has a Ph.D. in organizational behavior from Yale University and is currently deputy department head for leadership programs and counseling at the United States Air Force Academy. Gordon Curphy's graduate work was in industrial/organizational psychology. He was an associate professor at the Air Force Academy, and is now a senior consultant at Personnel Decisions, Inc.

In the spring of 1972, an airplane flew across the Andes mountains carrying its crew and 40 passengers. Most of the passengers were members of an amateur Uruguayan rugby team en route to a game in Chile. The plane never arrived. It crashed in snow-covered mountains, breaking into several pieces on impact. The main part of the fuselage slid like a toboggan down a steep valley, finally coming to rest in waist-deep snow. Although a number of people died immediately or within a day of the impact, the picture for the 28 survivors was not much better. The fuselage initially offered little protection from the extreme cold, food supplies were scant, and a number of passengers had serious injuries from the crash. Over the next few days, several of the passengers became psychotic and several others died from their injuries. Those passengers who were relatively uninjured set out to do what they could to improve their chances of survival.

Several worked on "weatherproofing" the wreckage, others found ways to get water, and those with medical training took care of the injured. Although shaken from the crash, the survivors initially were confident they would be found. These feelings gradually gave way to despair, as search and rescue teams failed to find the wreckage. With the passing of several weeks and no sign of rescue in sight, the remaining passengers decided to mount several expeditions to determine the best way to escape. The most physically fit were chosen to go on the expeditions, as the thin mountain air and the deep snow made the trips extremely taxing. The results of the trips were both frustrating and demoralizing; the expeditionaries determined they were in the middle of the Andes mountains, and walking out to find help was believed to be impossible. Just when the survivors thought nothing worse could possibly happen, an avalanche hit the wreckage and killed several more of them.

The remaining survivors concluded they would not be rescued and their only hope was for someone to leave the wreckage and find help. Three of the fittest passengers were chosen for the final expedition, and everyone else's work was directed toward improving the expedition's chances of success. The three expeditionaries were given more food and were exempted from routine survival activities; the rest spent most of their energies securing supplies for the trip. Two months after the plane crash, the expeditionaries set out on their final attempt to find help. After hiking for 10 days through some of the most rugged terrain in the world, the expeditionaries stumbled across a group of Chilean peasants tending cattle. One of the expeditionaries stated, "I come from a plane that fell in the mountains. I am Uruguayan. . . ." Eventually, 14 other survivors were rescued.

When the full account of their survival became known, it was not without controversy. It had required extreme and unsettling measures; the survivors had lived only by eating the flesh of their deceased comrades. Nonetheless, their story is one of the most moving survival dramas of all time, magnificently told by Piers Paul Read in *Alive* (1974).[1] It is a story of tragedy and courage, and it is a story of leadership.

Perhaps a story of survival in the Andes is so far removed from everyday experience that it does not seem to hold any relevant lessons about leadership for you personally. But consider for a moment some of the basic issues the Andes survivors faced; for example, tension between individual and group goals, dealing with the different needs and personalities of group members, and keeping hope alive in the face of adversity. These issues are not so very different from those facing many groups we're a part of. We can also look at the Andes experience for examples of the emergence of informal leaders in groups. Before the flight, a boy named Parrado was awkward and shy, a "second-stringer" both athletically and socially. Nonetheless, this unlikely hero became the best loved and most respected among the survivors for his courage, optimism, fairness, and emotional support. Persuasiveness in group decision making also was an important part of leadership among the Andes survivors. During the difficult discussions preceding the agonizing decision to survive on the flesh of their deceased comrades, one of the rugby players made his reasoning clear: "I know that if my dead body could help you stay alive, then I would want you to use it. In fact, if I do die and you don't eat me, then I'll come back from wherever I am and give you a good kick in the ass."[1]

This story . . . provides vivid examples of many of the phenomena examined by leadership researchers. However, you may find it surprising that leadership researchers disagree considerably over what does and does not constitute leadership. Most of this disagreement stems from the fact that leadership is a complex phenomenon involving the leader, the followers, and the situation. Some leadership researchers have focused on the personality, physical traits, or behaviors of the leader; others have studied the relationships between leaders and followers; still others have studied how aspects of the situation affect the ways leaders act. Some have extended the latter viewpoint so far as to suggest there is no such thing as leadership; they argue that organizational successes and failures often get falsely attributed to the leader, but the situation often has a much greater impact on how the organization functions than does any individual, including the leader.[2]

Perhaps the best way for you to begin to understand the complexities of leadership is to see some of the ways leadership has been defined. Leadership researchers have defined leadership as follows:

- The creative and directive force of morale (Munson, 1921).[3]
- The process by which an agent induces a subordinate to behave in a desired manner (Bennis, 1959).[4]
- The presence of a particular influence relationship between two or more persons (Hollander & Julian, 1969).[5]
- Directing and coordinating the work of group members (Fiedler, 1967).[6]

- An interpersonal relation in which others comply because they want to, not because they have to (Merton, 1969).[7]
- Transforming followers, creating visions of the goals that may be attained, and articulating for the followers the ways to attain those goals. (Bass, 1985; Tichy & Devanna, 1986).[8,9]
- The process of influencing an organized group toward accomplishing its goals (Roach & Behling, 1984).[10]
- Actions that focus resources to create desirable opportunities. (Campbell, 1991).[11]

As you can see, these definitions differ in many ways and have resulted in different researchers exploring very different aspects of leadership. For example, if we were to apply these definitions to the survival scenario described earlier, researchers adopting Munson's definition would focus on the behaviors Parrado used to keep up the morale of the survivors; researchers adopting Fiedler's definition would focus on the behaviors Parrado used to direct the survivors' activities in support of the final expedition; and researchers using Roach and Behling's definition would examine how Parrado managed to convince the group to stage and support the final expedition. Each group of researchers would focus on a different aspect of leadership, and each would tell a different story regarding the leader, the followers, and the situation.

Although such a large number of leadership definitions may seem confusing, it is important to understand that there is no single "correct" definition. The various definitions can help us appreciate the multitude of factors that affect leadership, as well as different perspectives from which to view it. For example, in Bennis's definition, the word *subordinate* seems to confine leadership to downward influence in hierarchical relationships; it seems to exclude informal leadership. Fiedler's definition emphasizes the directing and controlling aspects of leadership, and thereby may deemphasize emotional aspects of leadership. The emphasis Merton placed on subordinates "wanting to" comply with a leader's wishes seems to exclude coercion of any kind as a leadership tool. Further, it becomes problematic to identify ways in which a leader's actions are "really" leadership if subordinates voluntarily comply when a leader with considerable potential coercive power merely asks others to do something without explicitly threatening them. Similarly, Campbell used the phrase *desirable opportunities* precisely to distinguish between leadership and tyranny.

All considered, we believe the definition provided by Roach and Behling[10] to be a fairly comprehensive and helpful one. Therefore, . . . [we] also define leadership as "the process of influencing an organized group toward accomplishing its goals." One aspect of this definition is particularly worth noting: Leadership is a social influence process shared among *all* members of a group. Leadership is not restricted to the influence exerted by someone in a particular position or role; followers are part of the leadership process, too.

PART III

HISTORICAL VIEWS OF LEADERSHIP

*P*art III turns to the insights of leaders and thinkers throughout the centuries. Several of the earlier selections in this anthology have noted that modern attempts to understand leadership often ignore the considerable insights provided by great figures of the past. In the first selection, Bernard M. Bass demonstrates that leadership was a recognized phenomenon from the emergence of civilization. With that as introduction, we turn to the commentators themselves. Carlyle, Tolstoy, Plato, Aristotle, Machiavelli, Lao-tzu, Gandhi, and Du Bois represent a sampling of thinking about leadership from differing perspectives as well as from various time periods and cultures. Moreover, their writings highlight the timeless nature of the key issues identified by Spitzberg: the importance of the leader, the recruitment of leaders, the process of leadership, and the relationship between leaders and followers.

Carlyle and Tolstoy provide a stark contrast in their views of the importance of the leader in any social system. Carlyle's essay championing the leader as "Great Man" to whom all subordinate themselves has become a classic of its type. Tolstoy suggests the opposite. While both Carlyle and Tolstoy discuss (among others) Napoleon, their conclusions about his rise to power and his freedom of action could hardly be more different. Tolstoy's perception of leaders as "history's slaves" contrasts sharply with the powerful leader depicted by Carlyle.

Similarly, Plato and Aristotle address (and disagree on) such key leadership issues as the recruitment of leaders, the role of the leader, and the relationship between leaders and followers. In the initial portion of his selection Plato voices his view of democracy. His deep suspicion of it (ironic in a work entitled The Republic) grew out of his own unfortunate experiences with the anarchy of Greece in the late-fifth-century/early-fourth-century B.C. The second portion of the reading provides his antidote—Plato's famous "philosopher-kings." In perusing this selection, one should note not only the characteristics of such leaders but also Plato's insistence that the cadre of leaders remain distinct from those of lesser attainments—the followers. The reader should note that Plato's views are conveyed in the form of fictional conversations (dialogues) between Plato (who refers to himself as "Socrates" but who will be labeled "P" in the dialogue) and another person (here, "Glaucon," labeled "G").

Aristotle disagreed with his mentor Plato on many matters, including the notion of a higher order of philosopher-kings. Aristotle's notion of the recruitment of leaders and the relationship of leaders and followers likewise differed. While it can only be speculation, Aristotle's retreat from his mentor's position might be due in part to the fact that Aristotle composed this in a later period when the evils of overbearing power were as evident as was the anarchy which stemmed from an excess of democracy in Plato's time. Despite their differences, it should be noted that Aristotle's articulation of the purpose of leadership (the "perfect life" of peace and leisure) was similar to that envisioned by Plato.

Another example of how contrasting viewpoints can highlight important leadership issues can be seen in the writings of Machiavelli and Lao-tzu. Machiavelli's infamous The Prince is another example of a leadership commentary closely tied to its own place and time, yet articulating timeless issues which resonate to the present day. In the selection reprinted here, Machiavelli discusses the need for a leader to deceive followers in order to retain his position. In stark contrast to Machiavelli and much Western thought, Lao-tzu, a sixth-century B.C. Chinese philosopher, advocates selflessness and non-directive leadership, themes typical of Eastern philosophy. It is interesting to note that many current leadership commentators are now advocating an approach to leadership which is remarkably similar to what Lao-tzu articulated 2,500 years ago.

It is appropriate to conclude our sampling of historical views of leadership by comparing the views of two leaders of important twentieth-century social movements. In his efforts to reform India, Gandhi advocated an approach to leadership reminiscent of Lao-tzu. The selection of his writings has been entitled "satyagraha," which can be roughly translated to mean "truth-force" or, more specifically, non-violent resistance. Gandhi never claimed that he was a leader and, despite the fact that millions followed his lead, he disclaimed followers. A close reading of the selection, however, will reveal keen insights into leadership—the phenomenon we have defined as "the process of influencing a . . . group toward accomplishing its goals" (see *selection 8*). *A contemporary of Gandhi, W. E. B. Du Bois took a different tack in his efforts to help the American black community "pull itself up by its own bootstraps" and assume its rightful place in the American social fabric. In Du Bois' emphasis on an educated leadership cadre, you might detect echoes of Plato more than the wisdom of Gandhi.*

These philosophers, men of letters, and leaders differed greatly in their perceptions of leadership; nevertheless the rich variety of approaches suggests the insights which may be obtained by the careful reading of the commentators of the past.

9

Concepts of Leadership:
The Beginnings

Bernard M. Bass

Bass & Stogdill's Handbook of Leadership has been the leading reference work for serious students of leadership for two decades. Bernard Bass has been a prolific leadership writer. His 1985 book *Leadership and Performance Beyond Expectations* is also a classic. Bass has served as president of the Division of Organizational Psychology of the International Association of Applied Psychology, and is distinguished professor of management and director of the Center for Leadership Studies at the State University of New York, Binghamton. He is a founding editor of *The Leadership Quarterly*.

Leadership is one of the world's oldest preoccupations. The understanding of leadership has figured strongly in the quest for knowledge. Purposeful stories have been told through the generations about leaders' competencies, ambitions, and shortcomings; leaders' rights and privileges; and the leaders' duties and obligations.

The Beginnings

Leaders as prophets, priests, chiefs, and kings served as symbols, representatives, and models for their people in the Old and New Testaments, in the Upanishads, in the Greek and Latin classics, and in the Icelandic sagas. In the *Iliad*, higher, transcendental goals are emphasized: "He serves me most, who serves his country best" (Book X, line 201). The *Odyssey* advises leaders to maintain their social distance: "The leader, mingling with the vulgar host, is in the common mass of matter lost" (Book III, line 297). The subject of leadership was not limited to the classics of Western literature. It was of as much interest to Asoka and Confucius as to Plato and Aristotle.

Myths and legends about great leaders were important in the development of civilized societies. Stories about the exploits of individual heroes (and occasionally heroines) are central to the Babylonian *Gilgamesh, Beowolf*, the *Chanson de Roland*, the Icelandic sagas, and the Ramayana (now they would be called cases). All societies have created myths to provide plausible and acceptable explanations for the dominance of their leaders and the submission of their subordinates.[1] The greater the socioeconomic injustice in the society, the more distorted the realities of leadership—its powers, morality and effectiveness—in the mythology.

The study of leadership rivals in age the emergence of civilization, which shaped its leaders as much as it was shaped by them. From its infancy, the study of history has been the study of leaders—what they did and why they did it. Over the centuries, the effort to formulate principles of leadership spread from the study of history and the philosophy associated with it to all the developing social sciences. In modern psychohistory, there is still a search for generalizations about leadership, built on the in-depth analysis of the development, motivation, and competencies of world leaders, living and dead.

Written philosophical principles emerged early. As can be seen in Figure 1, the Egyptian hieroglyphics for leadership (*seshemet*), leader (*seshemu*) and the follower (*shemsu*) were being written 5,000 years ago.

In 2300 B.C. in the Instruction of Ptahhotep, three qualities were attributed to the Pharoah. "Authoritative utterness is in thy mouth, perception is in thy heart, and thy tongue is the shrine of justice."[2] The Chinese classics, written as early as the sixth century B.C., are filled with hortatory advice to the country's leaders about their responsibilities to the people. Confucius urged leaders to set a moral example and to manipulate rewards and punishments for teaching what was right and good. Taoism emphasized the need for the leader to work himself out of his job by making the people believe that successes were due to their efforts.

Greek concepts of leadership were exemplified by the heroes in Homer's *Iliad*. Ajax symbolized inspirational leadership and law and order. Other qualities that the Greeks admired and thought were needed (and sometimes

FIGURE 1
Egyptian Hieroglyphics
for Leadership, Leader,
and Follower

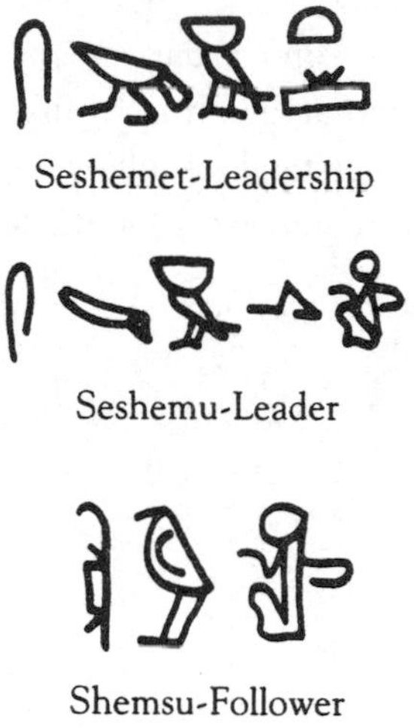

Seshemet-Leadership

Seshemu-Leader

Shemsu-Follower

wanting) in heroic leaders were (1) justice and judgment (Agamemnon), (2) wisdom and counsel (Nestor), (3) shrewdness and cunning (Odysseus), and (4) valor and activism (Achilles).[3] (Shrewdness and cunning are not regarded as highly in contemporary society as they once were.) Later, Greek philosophers, such as Plato in the *Republic*, looked at the requirements for the ideal leader of the ideal state (the philosopher king). The leader was to be the most important element of good government, educated to rule with order and reason. In *Politics*, Aristotle was disturbed by the lack of virtue among those who wanted to be leaders. He pointed to the need to educate youths for such leadership. Plutarch, although he was involved with prosocial ideals about leadership, compared the traits and behavior of actual Greek and Roman leaders to support his point of view in *The Parallel Lives*.[4]

A scholarly highlight of the Renaissance was Machiavelli's (1513) *The Prince*.[5] Machiavelli's thesis that "there is nothing more difficult to take in hand, more perilous to conduct, or more uncertain in its success, than to take the lead in the introduction of a new order of things" is still a germane description of the risks of leadership and the resistance to it. Machiavelli was the ultimate pragmatist. He believed that leaders needed steadiness, firmness, and concern for the maintenance of authority, power, and order in government. It was best if these objectives could be accomplished by gaining the esteem of the populace, but if they could not, then craft, deceit, threat, treachery, and violence were required.[4] Machiavelli is still widely quoted as a guide to an effective leadership of sorts, which was the basis for a modern line of investigation with the Mach scale.[6] A 1987 survey of 117 college presidents reported that they still found *The Prince* highly relevant.

In the same way, a fundamental principle at West Point today can be traced back to Hegel's (1830) *Philosophy of Mind*[7] which argued that by first serving as a follower, a leader subsequently can best understand his followers. Hegel thought that this understanding is a paramount requirement for effective leadership.

10

The Hero As King

Thomas Carlyle

Thomas Carlyle (1795–1881) was a Scottish historian and essayist. His most famous works were *French Revolution* and *On Heroes, Hero Worship, and the Heroic in History*.

We come now to the last form of Heroism; that which we call Kingship. The Commander over Men; he to whose will our wills are to be subordinated, and loyally surrender themselves, and find their welfare in doing so, may be reckoned the most important of Great Men. He is practically the summary for us of *all* the various figures of Heroism; Priest, Teacher, whatsoever of earthly or of spiritual dignity we can fancy to reside in a man, embodies itself here, to *command* over us, to furnish us with constant practical teaching, to tell us for the day and hour what we are to *do*. He is called *Rex*, Regulator, *Roi*: our own name is still better; King, *Könning*, which means *Can*-ning, Able-man.

Numerous considerations, pointing towards deep, questionable, and indeed unfathomable regions, present themselves here: on the most of which we must resolutely for the present forbear to speak at all. As Burke said that perhaps fair *Trial by Jury* was the soul of Government, and that all legislation,

Thomas Carlyle, *On Heroes, Hero Worship, and the Heroic in History* (New York: Ginn & Co., 1902), pp. 225–226.

administration, parliamentary debating, and the rest of it, went on, in order 'to bring twelve impartial men into a jury-box;'—so, by much stronger reason, may I say here, that the finding of your *Ableman* and getting him invested with the *symbols of ability*, with dignity, worship (*worth*-ship), royalty, kinghood, or whatever we call it, so that *he* may actually have room to guide according to his faculty of doing it,—is the business, well or ill accomplished, of all social procedure whatsoever in this world! Hustings-speeches, Parliamentary motions, Reform Bills, French Revolutions, all mean at heart this; or else nothing. Find in any country the Ablest Man that exists there; raise *him* to the supreme place, and loyally reverence him: you have a perfect government for that country; no ballot-box, parliamentary eloquence, voting, constitution-building, or other machinery whatsoever can improve it a whit. It is in the perfect state; an ideal country. The Ablest Man; he means also the truest-hearted, justest, the Noblest Man: what he *tells us to do* must be precisely the wisest, fittest, that we could anywhere or anyhow learn;—the thing which it will in all ways behove us, with right loyal thankfulness, and nothing doubting, to do! Our *doing* and life were then, so far as government could regulate it, well regulated; that were the ideal of constitutions.

11

Rulers and Generals Are "History's Slaves"

Leo Tolstoy

Leo Tolstoy (1828–1910) was a Russian novelist. His greatest works were *War and Peace* and *Anna Karenina*.

From the close of the year 1811 an intensified arming and concentrating of the forces of Western Europe began, and in 1812 these forces—millions of men, reckoning those transporting and feeding the army—moved from the west eastwards to the Russian frontier, toward which since 1811 Russian forces had been similarly drawn. On the twelfth of June, 1812, the forces of Western Europe crossed the Russian frontier and war began, that is, an event took place opposed to human reason and to human nature. Millions of men perpetrated against one another such innumerable crimes, frauds, treacheries, thefts, forgeries, issues of false money, burglaries, incendiarisms, and murders as in whole centuries are not recorded in the annals of all the law courts of the world, but which those who committed them did not at the time regard as being crimes.

What produced this extraordinary occurrence: What were its causes? The historians tell us with naïve assurance that its causes were the wrongs inflict-

Reprinted from Leo Tolstoy, *War and Peace*, translation by Louise and Aylmer Maude (New York: Oxford University Press, 1933).

ed on the Duke of Oldenburg, the nonobservance of the Continental System,[1] the ambition of Napoleon, the firmness of Alexander, the mistakes of the diplomatists, and so on.

Consequently, it would only have been necessary for Metternich, Rumyánstev, or Talleyrand, between a levee and an evening party, to have taken proper pains and written a more adroit note, or for Napoleon to have written to Alexander: "My respected Brother, I consent to restore the duchy to the Duke of Oldenburg"—and there would have been no war.

We can understand that the matter seemed like that to contemporaries. It naturally seemed to Napoleon that the war was caused by England's intrigues (as in fact he said on the island of St. Helena). It naturally seemed to members of the English Parliament that the cause of the war was Napoleon's ambition; to the Duke of Oldenburg, that the cause of the war was the violence done to him; to businessmen that the cause of the war was the Continental System which was ruining Europe; to the generals and old soldiers that the chief reason for the war was the necessity of giving them employment; to the legitimists of that day that it was the need of re-establishing *les bons principes*, and to the diplomatists of that time that it all resulted from the fact that the alliance between Russia and Austria in 1809 had not been sufficiently well concealed from Napoleon, and from the awkward wording of Memorandum No. 178. It is natural that these and a countless and infinite quantity of other reasons, the number depending on the endless diversity of points of view, presented themselves to the men of that day; but to us, to posterity who view the thing that happened in all its magnitude and perceive its plain and terrible meaning, these causes seem insufficient. To us it is incomprehensible that millions of Christian men killed and tortured each other either because Napoleon was ambitious or Alexander was firm, or because England's policy was astute or the Duke of Oldenburg wronged. We cannot grasp what connection such circumstances have with the actual fact of slaughter and violence: why because the Duke was wronged, thousands of men from the other side of Europe killed and ruined the people of Smolensk and Moscow and were killed by them.

To us, their descendants, who are not historians and are not carried away by the process of research and can therefore regard the event with unclouded common sense, an incalculable number of causes present themselves. The deeper we delve in search of these causes the more of them we find; and each separate cause or whole series of causes appears to us equally valid in itself and equally false by its insignificance compared to the magnitude of the events, and by its impotence—apart from the cooperation of all the other coincident causes—to occasion the event. To us, the wish or objection of this or that French corporal to serve a second term appears as much a cause as Napoleon's refusal to withdraw his troops beyond the Vistula[2] and to restore the duchy of Oldenburg; for had he not wished to serve, and had a second, a third, and a thousandth corporal and private also refused, there would have been so many less men in Napoleon's army, and the war could not have occurred.

Had Napoleon not taken offense at the demand that he should withdraw beyond the Vistula, and not ordered his troops to advance, there would have been no war; but had all his sergeants objected to serving a second term then also there could have been no war. Nor could there have been a war had there been no English intrigues and no Duke of Oldenburg, and had Alexander not felt insulted, and had there not been an autocratic government in Russia, or a Revolution in France and a subsequent dictatorship and Empire, or all the things that produced the French Revolution, and so on. Without each of these causes nothing could have happened. So all these causes—myriads of causes—coincided to bring it about. And so there was no one cause for that occurrence, but it had to occur because it had to. Millions of men, renouncing their human feelings and reason, had to go from west to east to slay their fellows, just as some centuries previously hordes of men had come from the east to the west, slaying their fellows.

The actions of Napoleon and Alexander, on whose words the event seemed to hang, were as little voluntary as the actions of any soldier who was drawn into the campaign by lot or by conscription. This could not be otherwise, for in order that the will of Napoleon and Alexander (on whom the event seemed to depend) should be carried out, the concurrence of innumerable circumstances was needed without any one of which the event could not have taken place. It was necessary that millions of men in whose hands lay the real power—the soldiers who fired, or transported provisions and guns—should consent to carry out the will of these weak individuals, and should have been induced to do so by an infinite number of diverse and complex causes.

We are forced to fall back on fatalism as an explanation of irrational events (that is to say, events the reasonableness of which we do not understand). The more we try to explain such events in history reasonably, the more unreasonable and incomprehensible do they become to us.

Each man lives for himself, using his freedom to attain his personal aims, and feels with his whole being that he can now do or abstain from doing this or that action; but as soon as he has done it, that action performed at a certain moment in time becomes irrevocable and belongs to history, in which it has not a free but a predestined significance.

There are two sides to the life of every man, his individual life, which is the more free the more abstract its interests, and his elemental hive life in which he inevitably obeys laws laid down for him.

Man lives consciously for himself, but is an unconscious instrument in the attainment of the historic, universal, aims of humanity. A deed done is irrevocable, and its result coinciding in time with the actions of millions of other men assumes an historic significance. The higher a man stands on the social ladder, the more people he is connected with and the more power he has over others, the more evident is the predestination and inevitability of his every action.

"The king's heart is in the hands of the Lord."

A king is history's slave.

History, that is, the unconscious, general, hive life of mankind, uses every moment of the life of kings as a tool for its own purposes.

Though Napoleon at that time, in 1812, was more convinced than ever that it depended upon him, *verser (ou ne pas verser) le sang de ses peuples* [to shed (or not to shed) the blood of his peoples]—as Alexander expressed it in the last letter he wrote him—he had never been so much in the grip of inevitable laws, which compelled him, while thinking that he was acting on his own volition, to perform for the hive life—that is to say, for history—whatever had to be performed.

The people of the west moved eastwards to slay their fellow men, and by the law of coincidence thousands of minute causes fitted in and coordinated to produce that movement and war: reproaches for the nonobservance of the Continental System, the Duke of Oldenburg's wrongs, the movement of troops into Prussia [undertaken, as it seemed to Napoleon, only for the purpose of securing an armed peace], the French Emperor's love and habit of war coinciding with his people's inclinations, allurement by the grandeur of the preparations, and the expenditure on those preparations and the need of obtaining advantages to compensate for that expenditure, the intoxicating honors he received in Dresden,[3] the diplomatic negotiations which, in the opinion of contemporaries, were carried on with a sincere desire to attain peace, but which only wounded the self love of both sides, and millions and millions of other causes that adapted themselves to the event that was happening or coincided with it.

When an apple has ripened and falls, why does it fall? Because of its attraction to the earth, because its stalk withers, because it is dried by the sun, because it grows heavier, because the wind shakes it, or because the boy standing below wants to eat it?

Nothing is the cause. All this is only the coincidence of conditions in which all vital organic and elemental events occur. And the botanist who finds that the apple falls because the cellular tissue decays and so forth is equally right with the child who stands under the tree and says the apple fell because he wanted to eat it and prayed for it. Equally right or wrong is he who says that Napoleon went to Moscow because he wanted to, and perished because Alexander desired his destruction, and he who says that an undermined hill weighing a million tons fell because the last navvy struck it for the last time with his mattock. In historic events, the so-called great men are labels giving names to events, and like labels they have but the smallest connection with the event itself.

Every act of theirs, which appears to them an act of their own will, is in an historical sense involuntary and is related to the whole course of history and predestined from eternity.

12

The Republic

Plato

Plato (428–347 B.C.) grew up in Athens and was a student of Socrates. In 387 B.C. he founded the Academy, the first permanent institution in Western civilization devoted to education and research. His dialogues, in which he explores the nature of good and the construction of an ideal society, have become among the most famous works in all literature.

P. Democracy comes into being after the poor have conquered their opponents, slaughtering some and banishing some, while to the remainder they give an equal share of freedom and power; and this is the form of government in which the magistrates are commonly elected by lot. . . .

This, then, seems likely to be the fairest of States, being like an embroidered robe which is spangled with every sort of flower. And just as women and children think a variety of colors to be of all things most charming, so there are many men to whom this State, which is spangled with the manners and characters of mankind, will appear to be the fairest of States.

G. Yes. . . .

P. Say then, my friend, in what manner does tyranny arise?—that it has a democratic origin is evident. . . . democracy has her own good, of which the insatiable desire brings her to dissolution.

Excerpted from *The Republic of Plato: An Ideal Commonwealth* (translated by Benjamin Jowett) rev. ed. (New York: Colonial Press, 1901).

G. What good?

P. Freedom . . . ; which, as they tell you in a democracy, is the glory of the State—and that therefore in a democracy alone will the freeman of nature deign to dwell.

G. Yes; the saying is in everybody's mouth.

P. I was going to observe, that the insatiable desire of this and the neglect of other things introduce the change in democracy, which occasions a demand for tyranny.

G. How so? . . .

P. [Such a State] would have subjects who are like rulers, and rulers who are like subjects: these are men after her own heart, whom she praises and honors both in private and public. Now, in such a State, can liberty have any limit?

G. Certainly not.

P. By degrees the anarchy finds a way into private houses, and ends by getting among the animals and infecting them.

G. How do you mean?

P. I mean that the father grows accustomed to descend to the level of his sons and to fear them, and the son is on a level with his father, he having no respect or reverence for either of his parents; and this is his freedom; and the metic is equal with the citizen, and the citizen with the metic, and the stranger is quite as good as either.

G. Yes, . . . that is the way.

P. And these are not the only evils . . .—there are several lesser ones: In such a state of society the master fears and flatters his scholars, and the scholars despise their masters and tutors; young and old are all alike; and the young man is on a level with the old, and is ready to compete with him in word or deed; and old men condescend to the young and are full of pleasantry and gayety; they are loth to be thought morose and authoritative, and therefore they adopt the manners of the young.

G. Quite true. . . .

P. The last extreme of popular liberty is when the slave bought with money, whether male or female, is just as free as his or her purchaser; nor must I forget to tell of the liberty and equality of the two sexes in relation to each other. . . . And above all, . . . and as the result of all, see how sensitive the citizens become; they chafe impatiently at the least touch of authority, and at length, as you know, they cease to care even for the laws, written or unwritten; they will have no one over them.

G. Yes, . . . I know it too well.

P. Such, my friend, . . . is the fair and glorious beginning out of which springs tyranny.

G. Glorious indeed. . . . But what is the next step?

P. The ruin of oligarchy is the ruin of democracy; the same disease magnified and intensified by liberty overmasters democracy—the truth being that the excessive increase of anything often causes a reaction in the opposite direction; and this is the case not only in the seasons and in vegetable and animal life, but above all in forms of government.

G. True.

P. The excess of liberty, whether in States or individuals, seems only to pass into excess of slavery. . . .

G. How so? . . .

P. The people have always some champion whom they set over them and nurse into greatness.

G. Yes, that is their way.

P. This, and no other, is the root from which a tyrant springs; when he first appears above ground he is a protector.

G. Yes, that is quite clear.

P. How, then, does a protector begin to change into a tyrant? . . .

At first, in the early days of his power, he is full of smiles, and he salutes everyone whom he meets; he to be called a tyrant, who is making promises in public and also in private! liberating debtors, and distributing land to the people and his followers, and wanting to be so kind and good to everyone!

G. Of course. . . .

P. But when he has disposed of foreign enemies by conquest or treaty, and there is nothing to fear from them, then he is always stirring up some war or other, in order that the people may require a leader.

G. To be sure.

P. Has he not also another object, which is that they may be impoverished by payment of taxes, and thus compelled to devote themselves to their daily wants and therefore less likely to conspire against him?

G. Clearly.

P. And if any of them are suspected by him of having notions of freedom, and of resistance to his authority, he will have a good pretext for destroying them by placing them at the mercy of the enemy; and for all these reasons the tyrant must be always getting up a war.

G. He must.

P. Now he begins to grow unpopular.

G. A necessary result. . . .

P. Then some of those who joined in setting him up, and who are in power, speak their minds to him and to one another, and the more courageous of them cast in his teeth what is being done.

G. Yes, that may be expected.

P. And the tyrant, if he means to rule, must get rid of them; he cannot stop while he has a friend or an enemy who is good for anything.

G. He cannot.

P. Thus liberty, getting out of all order and reason, passes into the harshest and bitterest form of slavery.

G. True. . . .

P. Very well; and may we not rightly say that we have sufficiently discussed the nature of tyranny, and the manner of the transition from democracy to tyranny?

G. Yes, quite enough. . . .

P. I think . . . that there might be a reform of the State if only one change were made, which is not a slight or easy though still a possible one.

G. What is it? . . .

P. . . . Until philosophers are kings, or the kings and princes of this world have the spirit and power of philosophy, and political greatness and wisdom meet in one, and those commoner natures who pursue either to the exclusion of the other are compelled to stand aside, cities will never have rest from their evils—no, nor the human race, as I believe—and then only will this our State have a possibility of life and behold the light of day." Such was the thought, my dear Glaucon, which I would fain have uttered if it had not seemed too extravagant; for to be convinced that in no other State can there be happiness private or public is indeed a hard thing.

G. Socrates, what do you mean? . . .

P. . . . we must explain. . . . whom we mean when we say that philosophers are to rule in the State . . . There will be discovered to be some natures who ought to study philosophy and to be leaders in the State; and others who are not born to be philosophers, and are meant to be followers rather than leaders.

G. Then now for a definition. . . .

P. Follow me, . . . and I hope that I may in some way or other be able to give you a satisfactory explanation. . . . In the first place, as we began by observing, the nature of the philosopher has to be ascertained. We must come to an understanding about him, and, when we have done so, then, if I am not mistaken, we shall also acknowledge that such a union of qualities is possible, and that those in whom they are united, and those only, should be rulers in the State.

G. What do you mean?

P. Let us suppose that philosophical minds always love knowledge of a sort which shows them the eternal nature not varying from generation and corruption.

G. Agreed.

P. And further, . . . let us agree that they are lovers of all true being; there is no part whether greater or less, or more or less honorable, which they are willing to renounce; as we said before of the lover and the man of ambition. . . . Then, besides other qualities, we must try to find a naturally well-proportioned and gracious mind, which will move spontaneously toward the true being of everything. . . . Well, and do not all these qualities, which we have been enumerating, go together, and are they not, in a manner, necessary to a soul, which is to have a full and perfect participation of being?

G. They are absolutely necessary. . . .

P. And must not that be a blameless study which he only can pursue who has the gift of a good memory, and is quick to learn—noble, gracious, the friend of truth, justice, courage, temperance, who are his kindred?

G. The god of jealousy himself . . . could find no fault with such a study.

P. And to men like him, . . . when perfected by years and education, and to these only you will intrust the State. . . . Observe, Glaucon, that there will be no injustice in compelling our philosophers to have a care and providence of others; we shall explain to them that . . . we have brought you into the world to be rulers of the hive, kings of yourselves and of the other citizens, and have educated you far better and more perfectly than they have been educated, and you are better able to share in the double duty.

13

Politics

Aristotle

Aristotle (384–322 B.C.) was Plato's most gifted pupil and critic. He tutored Alexander the Great and founded and taught at the Lyceum. Aristotle is known for his teaching and writing on a broad range of topics, including logic, metaphysics, rhetoric, poetry, ethics, and politics.

Since every political society is composed of rulers and subjects let us consider whether the relations of one to the other should interchange or be permanent. For the education of the citizens will necessarily vary with the answer given to this question. Now, if some men excelled others in the same degree in which gods and heroes are supposed to excel mankind in general (having in the first place a great advantage even in their bodies, and secondly in their minds), so that the superiority of the governors was undisputed and patent to their subjects, it would clearly be better that once for all the one class should rule and the other serve. But since this is unattainable, and kings have no marked superiority over their subjects, such as Scylax affirms to be found among the Indians, it is obviously necessary on many grounds that all the citizens alike should take their turn of governing and being governed. Equality consists in the same treatment of similar persons, and no government can

Excerpted from Aristotle, A *Treatise on Government* (Trans. William Ellis, ed. Ernest Rhys) (London: J. M. Dent & Sons, 1900), pp. 226–227.

stand which is not founded upon justice. For if the government be unjust every one in the country unites with the governed in the desire to have a revolution, and it is an impossibility that the members of the government can be so numerous as to be stronger than all their enemies put together. Yet that governors should excel their subjects is undeniable. How all this is to be effected, and in what way they will respectively share in the government, the legislator has to consider. The subject has been already mentioned. Nature herself has provided the distinction when she made a difference between old and young within the same species, of whom she fitted the one to govern and the other to be governed. No one takes offence at being governed when he is young, nor does he think himself better than his governors, especially if he will enjoy the same privilege when he reaches the required age.

We conclude that from one point of view governors and governed are identical, and from another different. And therefore their education must be the same and also different. For he who would learn to command well must, as men say, first of all learn to obey. As I observed in the first part of this treatise, there is one rule which is for the sake of the rulers and another rule which is for the sake of the ruled; the former is a despotic, the latter a free government. Some commands differ not in the thing commanded, but in the intention with which they are imposed. Wherefore, many apparently menial offices are an honour to the free youth by whom they are performed; for actions do not differ as honourable or dishonourable in themselves so much as in the end and intention of them. But since we say that the virtue of the citizen and ruler is the same as that of the good man, and that the same person must first be a subject and then a ruler, the legislator has to see that they become good men, and by what means this may be accomplished, and what is the end of the perfect life. . . .

The whole of life is further divided into two parts, business and leisure, war and peace, and of actions some aim at what is necessary and useful, and some at what is honourable. And the preference given to one or the other class of actions must necessarily be like the preference given to one or other part of the soul and its actions over the other; there must be war for the sake of peace, business for the sake of leisure, things useful and necessary for the sake of things honourable. All these points the statesman should keep in view when he frames his laws; he should consider the parts of the soul and their functions, and above all the better and the end; he should also remember the diversities of human lives and actions. For men must be able to engage in business and go to war, but leisure and peace are better; they must do what is necessary and indeed what is useful, but what is honourable is better.

14

How Princes Should Keep Faith

Niccolo Machiavelli

Niccolo Machiavelli (1469–1527) was trained as a humanist and served as an active diplomat for Florence. He was exiled, and there wrote his most famous work, *The Prince*, a classic on the pragmatic use of power. While *The Prince* addresses winning and maintaining individual power by any means necessary, his other famous work, the *Discourses*, describes the advantages of a republic.

Every one understands how praiseworthy it is in a Prince to keep faith, and to live uprightly and not craftily. Nevertheless, we see from what has taken place in our own days that Princes who have set little store by their word, but have known how to overreach men by their cunning, have accomplished great things, and in the end got the better of those who trusted to honest dealing.

Be it known, then, that there are two ways of contending, one in accordance with the laws, the other by force; the first of which is proper to men, the second to beasts. But since the first method is often ineffectual, it becomes necessary to resort to the second. A Prince should, therefore, understand how to use well both the man and the beast. . . .

Excerpted from Niccolo Machiavelli, *The Prince* (1513) trans. Ninian Hill Thompson (1813) (New York: Limited Editions Club, 1954).

. . . a prudent Prince neither can nor ought to keep his word when to keep it is hurtful to him and the causes which led him to pledge it are removed. If all men were good, this would not be good advice, but since they are dishonest and do not keep faith with you, you, in return, need not keep faith with them; and no prince was ever at a loss for plausible reasons to cloak a breach of faith. . . .

It is necessary, indeed, to put a good colour on this nature, and to be skilful in simulating and dissembling. But men are so simple, and governed so absolutely by their present needs, that he who wishes to deceive will never fail in finding willing dupes. . . .

A Prince should therefore be very careful that nothing ever escapes his lips which is not . . . the embodiment of mercy, good faith, integrity, humanity, and religion. . . .

It is not essential, then, that a Prince should have all the good qualities which I have enumerated above, but it is most essential that he should seem to have them; I will even venture to affirm that if he has and invariably practises them all, they are hurtful, whereas the appearance of having them is useful. Thus, it is well to seem merciful, faithful, humane, religious, and upright, and also to be so; but the mind should remain so balanced that were it needful not to be so, you should be able and know how to change to the contrary.

And you are to understand that a Prince, and most of all a new Prince, cannot observe all those rules of conduct in respect whereof men are accounted good, being often forced, in order to preserve his Princedom, to act in opposition to good faith, charity, humanity, and religion. He must therefore keep his mind ready to shift as the winds and tides of Fortune turn, and, as I have already said, he ought not to quit good courses if he can help it, but should know how to follow evil courses if he must. . . .

Moreover, in the actions of all men, and most of all of Princes, where there is no tribunal to which we can appeal, we look to results. Wherefore if a Prince succeeds in establishing and maintaining his authority, the means will always be judged honourable and be approved by every one. For the vulgar are always taken by appearances and by results, and the world is made up of the vulgar, the few only finding room when the many have no longer ground to stand on.

A certain Prince of our own days, whose name it is as well not to mention, is always preaching peace and good faith, although the mortal enemy of both; and both, had he practised them as he preaches them, would, oftener than once, have lost him his kingdom and authority.

15

Tao Te Ching

Lao-tzu

Lao-tzu was an ancient Chinese sage of the sixth century B.C. He compiled a lifetime of meditation and careful observation into his book *Tao Te Ching*, or How Things Work. The volume was intended for the political leaders of his day; it has become a classic of world literature.

7. Selflessness

True self-interest teaches selflessness.

Heaven and earth endure because they are not simply selfish but exist in behalf of all creation.

The wise leader, knowing this, keeps egocentricity in check and by doing so becomes even more effective.

Enlightened leadership is service, not selfishness. The leader grows more and lasts longer by placing the well-being of all above the well-being of self alone.

Paradox: By being selfless, the leader enhances self.

Reprinted with permission from *The Tao of Leadership* by John Heider, Copyright 1985 by Humanics Limited, Atlanta, Georgia, USA.

8. Water

The wise leader is like water.

Consider water: water cleanses and refreshes all creatures without distinction and without judgment; water freely and fearlessly goes deep beneath the surface of things; water is fluid and responsive; water follows the law freely.

Consider the leader: the leader works in any setting without complaint, with any person or issue that comes on the floor; the leader acts so that all will benefit and serves well regardless of the rate of pay; the leader speaks simply and honestly and intervenes in order to shed light and create harmony.

From watching the movements of water, the leader has learned that in action, timing is everything.

Like water, the leader is yielding. Because the leader does not push, the group does not resent or resist.

10. Unbiased Leadership

Can you mediate emotional issues without taking sides or picking favorites?

Can you breathe freely and remain relaxed even in the presence of passionate fears and desires?

Are your own conflicts clarified? Is your own house clean?

Can you be gentle with all factions and lead the group without dominating?

Can you remain open and receptive, no matter what issues arise?

Can you know what is emerging, yet keep your peace while others discover for themselves?

Learn to lead in a nourishing manner.
Learn to lead without being possessive.
Learn to be helpful without taking the credit.
Learn to lead without coercion.

You can do this if you remain unbiased, clear, and down-to-earth.

17. Being a Midwife

The wise leader does not intervene unnecessarily. The leader's presence is felt, but often the group runs itself.

Lesser leaders do a lot, say a lot, have followers, and form cults.

Even worse ones use fear to energize the group and force to overcome resistance.

Only the most dreadful leaders have bad reputations.

Remember that you are facilitating another person's process. It is not your process. Do not intrude. Do not control. Do not force your own needs and insights into the foreground.

If you do not trust a person's process, that person will not trust you.

Imagine that you are a midwife; you are assisting at someone else's birth. Do good without show or fuss. Facilitate what is happening rather than what you think ought to be happening. If you must take the lead, lead so that the mother is helped, yet still free and in charge.

When the baby is born, the mother will rightly say: "We did it ourselves!"

16

Satyagraha

Mohandas Gandhi

Mohandas Gandhi (1869–1948) was educated in law but dedicated his career, first in South Africa and then in his native India, to the achievement of a better life for the downtrodden. His causes included gaining independence for India from Great Britain, Hindu–Muslim unity, and the end of "untouchability"—the discrimination against the lower orders. But it was not his issues so much as his method which has earned him fame (and the honorific title "Mahatma"— Great Soul). Gandhi preached—and practiced—non-violence, and inspired millions to emulate his example.

Moral Requirements for Satyagraha

Reader: I deduce that passive resistance[1] is a splendid weapon of the weak, but that when they are strong they may take up arms.

Editor: This is gross ignorance. Passive resistance, that is, soul-force, is matchless. It is superior to the force of arms. How, then, can it be considered only a weapon of the weak? Physical-force men are strangers to the courage that is requisite in a passive resister. Do you believe that a coward can ever

These selections are published by permission of the Navajivan Trust, Ahmedabad, India.

disobey a law that he dislikes? Extremists are considered to be advocates of brute force. Why do they, then, talk about obeying laws? I do not blame them. They can say nothing else. When they succeed in driving out the English and they themselves become governors, they will want you and me to obey their laws. And that is a fitting thing for their constitution. But a passive resister will say he will not obey a law that is against his conscience, even though he may be blown to pieces at the mouth of a cannon.

What do you think? Wherein is courage required—in blowing others to pieces from behind a cannon, or with a smiling face to approach a cannon and be blown to pieces? Who is the true warrior—he who keeps death always as a bosom-friend, or he who controls the death of others? Believe me that a man devoid of courage and manhood can never be a passive resister.

This, however, I will admit: that even a man weak in body is capable of offering this resistance. One man can offer it just as well as millions. Both men and women can indulge in it. It does not require the training of an army; it needs no jiu-jitsu. Control over the mind is alone necessary and when that is attained, man is free like the king of the forest and his very glance withers the enemy.

Passive resistance is an all-sided sword, it can be used anyhow; it blesses him who uses it and him against whom it is used. Without drawing a drop of blood it produces far-reaching results. It never rusts and cannot be stolen. Competition between passive resisters does not exhaust. The sword of passive resistance does not require a scabbard. It is strange indeed that you should consider such a weapon to be a weapon merely of the weak.

Reader: You have said that passive resistance is a speciality of India. Have cannons never been used in India?

Editor: Evidently, in your opinion, India means its few princes. To me it means its teeming millions on whom depends the existence of its princes and our own.

Kings will always use their kingly weapons. To use force is bred in them. They want to command, but those who have to obey commands do not want guns: and these are in a majority throughout the world. They have to learn either body-force or soul-force. Where they learn the former, both the rulers and the ruled become like so many mad men; but where they learn soul-force, the commands of the rulers do not go beyond the point of their swords, for true men disregard unjust commands. Peasants have never been subdued by the sword, and never will be. They do not know the use of the sword, and they are not frightened by the use of it by others. That nation is great which rests its head upon death as its pillow. Those who defy death are free from all fear. For those who are labouring under the delusive charms of brute-force, this picture is not overdrawn. The fact is that, in India, the nation at large has generally used passive resistance in all departments of life. We cease to co-operate with our rulers when they displease us. This is passive resistance.

Hind Swaraj or Indian Home Rule, chap. XVII

Conditions for Successful Satyagraha

There can be no Satyagraha in an unjust cause. Satyagraha in a just cause is vain, if the men espousing it are not determined and capable of fighting and suffering to the end; and the slightest use of violence often defeats a just cause. Satyagraha excludes the use of violence in any shape or form, whether in thought, speech, or deed. Given a just cause, capacity for endless suffering and avoidance of violence, victory is a certainty.

Young India, 27-4-'21

Qualifications for Satyagraha

Satyagraha presupposes self-discipline, self-control, self-purification, and a recognized social status in the person offering it. A Satyagrahi must never forget the distinction between evil and the evil-doer. He must not harbour ill-will or bitterness against the latter. He may not even employ needlessly offensive language against the evil person, however unrelieved his evil might be. For it should be an article of faith with every Satyagrahi that there is none so fallen in this world but can be converted by love. A Satyagrahi will always try to overcome evil by good, anger by love, untruth by truth, *himsa* by *ahimsa*. There is no other way of purging the world of evil. Therefore a person who claims to be a Satyagrahi always tries by close and prayerful self-introspection and self-analysis to find out whether he is himself completely free from the taint of anger, ill-will and such other human infirmities, whether he is not himself capable of those very evils against which he is out to lead a crusade. In self-purification and penance lies half the victory of a Satyagrahi. A Satyagrahi has faith that the silent and undemonstrative action of truth and love produces far more permanent and abiding results than speeches or such other showy performances.

But although Satyagraha can operate silently, it requires a certain amount of action on the part of a Satyagrahi. A Satyagrahi, for instance, must first mobilize public opinion against the evil which he is out to eradicate, by means of a wide and intensive agitation. When public opinion is sufficiently roused against a social abuse even the tallest will not dare to practise or openly to lend support to it. An awakened and intelligent public opinion is the most potent weapon of a Satyagrahi.

Young India, 8-8-'29

For "Followers"

A friend sends me the following:

> "It will be very helpful if you will kindly guide your followers about their conduct when they have to engage in a political controversy. Your guidance on the following points is particularly needed: (a) Vilification so as to lower the opponent in public estimation; (b) Kind of criticism of the opponent permissible; (c) Limit to which hostility should be carried; (d) Whether effort should be made to gain office and power."

I have said before in these pages that I claim no followers. It is enough for me to be my own follower. It is by itself a sufficiently taxing performance. But I know that many claim to be my followers. I must therefore answer the questions for their sakes. If they will follow what I endeavour to stand for rather than me they will see that the following answers are derived from truth and *ahimsa*.

(a) Vilification of an opponent there can never be. But this does not exclude a truthful characterization of his acts. An opponent is not always a bad man because he opposes. He may be as honourable as we may claim to be and yet there may be vital differences between him and us.

(b) Our criticism will therefore be if we *believe* him to be guilty of untruth to meet it with truth, of discourtesy with courtesy, of bullying with calm courage, of violence with suffering, of arrogance with humility, of evil with good. "My follower" would seek not to condemn but to convert.

(c) There is no question of any limit to which hostility may be carried. For there should be no hostility to persons. Hostility there must be to acts when they are subversive of morals or the good of society.

(d) Office and power must be avoided. Either may be accepted when it is clearly for greater service.

Young India, 7-5-'31

The Future

A friend writing from America propounds the following two questions:

1. Granted that Satyagraha is capable of winning India's independence, what are the chances of its being accepted as a principle of State policy in a free India? In other words, would a strong and independent India rely on Satyagraha as a method of self-preservation, or would it lapse back to seeking refuge in the age-old institution of war, however defensive its character? To restate the question on the basis of a purely theoretic problem: Is Satyagraha likely to be accepted only in an up-hill battle, when the phenomenon of martyrdom is fully effective, or is it also to be the instrument of a sovereign authority which has neither the need nor the scope of behaving on the principle of martyrdom?

2. Suppose a free India adopts Satyagraha as an instrument of State policy how would she defend herself against probable aggression by another sovereign State? To restate the question on the basis of a purely theoretic problem: What would be the Satyagrahic action-patterns to meet the invading army at the frontier? What kind of resistance can be offered the opponent before a common area of action, such as the one now existing in India between the Indian nationalists and the British Government, is established? Or should the Satyagrahis withhold their action until after the opponent has taken over the country?

The questions are admittedly theoretical. They are also premature for the reason that I have not mastered the whole technique of non-violence. The experiment is still in the making. It is not even in its advanced stage. The nature of the experiment requires one to be satisfied with one step at a time. The distant scene is not for him to see. Therefore, my answers can only be speculative.

In truth, as I have said before, now we are not having unadulterated non-violence even in our struggle to win independence.

As to the first question, I fear that the chances of non-violence being accepted as a principle of State policy are very slight, so far as I can see at present. If India does not accept non-violence as her policy after winning independence, the second question becomes superfluous.

But I may state my own individual view of the potency of non-violence. I believe that a State can be administered on a non-violent basis if the vast majority of the people are non-violent. So far as I know, India is the only country which has a possibility of being such a State. I am conducting my experiment in that faith. Supposing, therefore, that India attained independence through pure non-violence, India could retain it too by the same means. A non-violent man or society does not anticipate or provide for attacks from without. On the contrary, such a person or society firmly believes that nobody is going to disturb them. If the worst happens, there are two ways open to non-violence. To yield possession but non-co-operate with the aggressor. Thus, supposing that a modern edition of Nero descended upon India, the representatives of the State will let him in but tell him that he will get no assistance from the people. They will prefer death to submission. The second way would be non-violent resistance by the people who have been trained in the non-violent way. They would offer themselves unarmed as fodder for the aggressor's cannon. The underlying belief in either case is that even a Nero is not devoid of a heart. The unexpected spectacle of endless rows upon rows of men and women simply dying rather than surrender to the will of an aggressor must ultimately melt him and his soldiery. Practically speaking there will be probably no greater loss in men than if forcible resistance was offered; there will be no expenditure in armaments and fortifications. The non-violent training received by the people will add inconceivably to their moral height. Such men and women will have shown personal bravery of a type far superior to that shown in armed warfare. In each case the bravery consists in dying, not in killing. Lastly, there is no such thing as defeat in non-violent resistance. That such a thing has not happened before is no answer to my speculation. I have drawn no impossible picture. History is replete with instances of individual non-violence of the type I have mentioned. There is no warrant for saying or thinking that a group of men and women cannot by sufficient training act non-violently as a group or nation. Indeed the sum total of the experience of mankind is that men somehow or other live on. From which fact I infer that it is the law of love that rules mankind. Had violence, i.e. hate, ruled us, we should have become extinct long ago. And yet the tragedy of it is that the so-called civilized men and nations conduct themselves as if the basis of society was violence. It gives me ineffable joy to make experiments proving that love is the supreme and only law of life. Much evidence to the contrary cannot shake my faith. Even the mixed non-violence of India has supported it. But if it is not enough to convince an unbeliever, it is enough to incline a friendly critic to view it with favour.

Harijan, 13-4-'40

17

The Talented Tenth

W. E. B. Du Bois

W. E. B. Du Bois (1868–1963) was the first black to receive a Ph.D. from Harvard. He is considered one of the fathers of modern black militancy (he became involved in the black movement, at least partially, in reaction to the conciliatory tactics of Booker T. Washington). Du Bois was a founder of the Niagara Movement and the National Association for the Advancement of Colored People. He wrote extensively, but is perhaps best known for his *The Souls of Black Folk*. Later in life he became disillusioned with the prospects of complete freedom for black people in the United States. He spent the last years of his life in Ghana.

The Negro race, like all races, is going to be saved by its exceptional men. The problem of education, then, among Negroes must first of all deal with the Talented Tenth; it is the problem of developing the Best of this race that they may guide the Mass away from the contamination and death of the Worst, in their own and other races. . . .

If this be true—and who can deny it—three tasks lay before me; first to show from the past that the Talented Tenth as they have risen among American Negroes have been worthy of leadership; secondly, to show how these

Excerpted from W. E. Burghardt Du Bois, "The Talented Tenth," in *The Negro Problem* (New York: James Pott & Company, 1903).

men may be educated and developed; and thirdly, to show their relation to the Negro problem.

You misjudge us because you do not know us. From the very first it has been the educated and intelligent of the Negro people that have led and elevated the mass, and the sole obstacles that nullified and retarded their efforts were slavery and race prejudice. . . .

And so we come to the present—a day of cowardice and vacillation, of strident wide-voiced wrong and faint hearted compromise; of double-faced dallying with Truth and Right. Who are to-day guiding the work of the Negro people? The "exceptions" of course. And yet so sure as this Talented Tenth is pointed out, the blind worshippers of the Average cry out in alarm: "These are exceptions, look here at death, disease and crime—these are the happy rule." Of course they are the rule, because a silly nation made them the rule: Because for three long centuries this people lynched Negroes who dared to be brave, raped black women who dared to be virtuous, crushed dark-hued youth who dared to be ambitious, and encouraged and made to flourish servility and lewdness and apathy. But not even this was able to crush all manhood and chastity and aspiration from black folk. A saving remnant continually survives and persists, continually aspires, continually shows itself in thrift and ability and character. . . .

Can the masses of the Negro people be in any possible way more quickly raised than by the effort and example of this aristocracy of talent and character? Was there ever a nation on God's fair earth civilized from the bottom upward? Never; it is, ever was and ever will be from the top downward that culture filters. The Talented Tenth rises and pulls all that are worth the saving up to their vantage ground. This is the history of human progress; and the two historic mistakes which have hindered that progress were the thinking first that no more could ever rise save the few already risen; or second, that it would better the unrisen to pull the risen down.

How then shall the leaders of a struggling people be trained and the hands of the risen few strengthened? There can be but one answer: The best and most capable of their youth must be schooled in the colleges and universities of the land.

But I have already said that human education is not simply a matter of schools; it is much more a matter of family and group life—the training of one's home, of one's daily companions, of one's social class. Now the black boy of the South moves in a black world—a world with its own leaders, its own thoughts, its own ideals. In this world he gets by far the larger part of his life training, and through the eyes of this dark world he peers into the veiled world beyond. Who guides and determines the education which he receives in his world? His teachers here are the group-leaders of the Negro people—the physicians and clergymen, the trained fathers and mothers, the influential and forceful men about him of all kinds; here it is, if at all, that the culture of the surrounding world trickles through and is handed on by the graduates of the higher schools. Can such culture training of group leaders be neglected? Can we afford to ignore it? Do you think that if the leaders of thought among Negroes are not trained and educated thinkers, that they will have no leaders? On the contrary a hundred half-trained demagogues will still hold the places they so largely occupy now, and hundreds of vociferous busy-bodies will multiply. You have no choice; either you must help furnish this race from within its own ranks with thoughtful men of trained leadership, or you must suffer the evil consequences of a headless misguided rabble. . . .

Men of America, the problem is plain before you. Here is a race transplanted through the criminal foolishness of your fathers. Whether you like it or not the millions are here, and here they will remain. If you do not lift them up, they will pull you down. Education and work are the levers to uplift a people. Work alone will not do it unless inspired by the right ideals and guided by intelligence. Education must not simply teach work—it must teach Life. The Talented Tenth of the Negro race must be made leaders of thought and missionaries of culture among their people. No others can do this work and Negro colleges must train men for it. The Negro race, like all other races, is going to be saved by its exceptional men.

PART IV

MODERN VIEWS OF LEADERSHIP

With the past as prologue, our attention next shifts to the wealth of knowledge about leadership provided by modern thinkers. Martin Chemers, a prominent leadership scholar, provides a cogent summary of leadership research in the twentieth century. Attention then turns to a more thorough consideration of a few key current approaches to leadership.

In selection 19, James MacGregor Burns identifies two forms of leadership: "transactional" and "transforming." While both have been influential, it is Burns' "transforming" leadership which has become a driving force in leadership thought and practice. Burns' focus on the interaction of leader and follower as each seeks to transform the other to higher levels of conduct has fundamentally influenced our perception of leadership. In the next selection, Richard A. Couto traces the evolution of transforming leadership as it has been applied in organizations, focusing specifically upon Bernard Bass's influential "transformational" leadership. A related yet distinct area of investigation has focused on "charismatic" leadership. Selection 21 is an article by David A. Nadler and Michael L. Tushman which explores the role of charismatic leadership.

Our overview of modern conceptions of leadership ends with the consideration of an issue that has caused for many a certain amount of conceptual difficulty—the distinction between leadership and management. John Kotter notes that management deals with complexity, while leadership deals with change. Given the reality that in today's world all organizations face both complexity and change, both managers and leaders are equally valuable and necessary.

18

Contemporary Leadership Theory

Martin M. Chemers

Martin M. Chemers is Professor of Psychology at Claremont McKenna College. He received his Ph.D. in psychology from the University of Illinois, and is the author of several books and articles, including *Leadership and Effective Management* and *Improving Leadership Effectiveness: The Leader Match Concept*.

A Brief History

The scientific study of leadership can be roughly divided into three periods: the trait period, from around 1910 to World War II, the behavior period, from the onset of World War II to the late 1960s, and the contingency period, from the late 1960s to the present.

Traits

The early research on leadership emergence and leadership effectiveness proceeded from the premise that, somehow, those who became leaders were different from those who remained followers. The objective of the research was

Martin M. Chemers, "The Social, Organizational, and Cultural Context of Effective Leadership", in Kellerman, Barbara, ed. *Leadership: Multidisciplinary Perspectives*, pp. 93–108, ® 1984, Reprinted by permission of Prentice-Hall Inc., Englewood Cliffs, NJ.

to identify specifically what unique feature of the individual was associated with leadership. The success of the mental testing movement in the early part of the century encouraged researchers to employ the recently developed "personality tests" in their search for the leadership trait. A large number of studies were done in which leaders and followers were compared on various measures hypothesized to be related to leadership status or effectiveness. Measures of dominance, social sensitivity, moodiness, masculinity, physical appearance, and many others were used. The typical research design involved the administration of one or more individual difference measures to members of an organization that had leaders and followers (for example, a military unit, industrial organization, or university student bodies). The scores of leaders and followers on the measures were compared for significant differences.

In 1948, Ralph Stogdill[1] reviewed over 120 such trait studies in an attempt to discern a reliable and coherent pattern. His conclusion was that no such pattern existed. The mass of inconsistent and contradictory results of the trait studies led Stogdill to conclude that traits alone do not identify leadership. He pointed out that leadership situations vary dramatically in the demands which they place upon the leader. For example, compare the desirable traits and abilities for a combat military officer with those for a senior scientist on a research team. Stogdill predicted that leadership theorizing would be inadequate until personal and situational characteristics were integrated.

Behaviors

The failure of the trait approach and the growing emphasis on behaviorism in psychology moved leadership researchers in the direction of the study of leadership behavior. A classic study of leadership styles was conducted by Kurt Lewin and his associates.[2] These researchers trained graduate research assistants in behaviors indicative of three leadership styles: autocratic, democratic, and laissez-faire. The autocratic style was characterized by the tight control of group activities and decisions made by the leader. The democratic style emphasized group participation and majority rule, while the laissez-faire leadership pattern involved very low levels of any kind of activity by the leader. Groups of preadolescent boys were exposed to each leadership style and the effects measured. Results indicated that the democratic style had somewhat more beneficial results on group process than the other styles. The importance of this study is not so much in its results but in its definition of leadership in terms of behavioral style. Also the emphasis on autocratic, directive styles versus democratic and participative styles had a profound impact on later research and theory.

In the 1950s, the research focus turned even more basic and behavioral. A number of independent researchers using rating scales,[3] interviews,[4] and observations[5] attempted to identify the specific, concrete behaviors in which leaders engaged. Here the emphasis was to move away from the focus on the internal state of leaders (that is, their values or personalities, as well as any preconceived leadership styles) to the more basic question of what it is that leaders actually do.

The most comprehensive study of leader behavior employed a rating scale labeled the Leader Behavior Description Questionnaire (LBDQ).[6] After extensive observation and rating of large numbers of military and industrial leaders, it was found that most of the variation in leader behavior could be described by two major clusters or factors of behavior. One factor which included items relating to interpersonal warmth, concern for the feelings of subordinates, and the use of participative two-way communication was labeled *Consideration* behavior. A second factor whose items stressed directiveness, goal facilitation, and task-related feedback was labeled *Initiation of Structure*. A number of other research projects confirmed the existence of these two general behavioral configurations, although they might be labeled *employee oriented* versus *production oriented*[7] or *task* versus *socioemotional*.[8]

The identification of two reliable dimensions of leader behavior was a major step forward for the field of leadership. Optimism was high that research had finally cracked open the complexity of leadership effects. Unfortunately, attempts to relate the behavioral factors to group and organizational outcomes proved quite difficult. Although the leader's consideration behavior was generally associated with subordinate satisfaction, this was not always the case. Furthermore, the relationship between leader-structuring behavior and group productivity revealed very few consistent patterns.[9]

During both the trait and behavior eras, researchers were seeking to identify the "best" style of leadership. They had not yet recognized that no single style of leadership is universally best across all situations and environments. For this reason, leadership theorists were quite disappointed when the behavior patterns which they had identified were not consistently related to important organizational outcomes such as group productivity and follower satisfaction.

Current Theory

Contingency Approaches

The reliable prediction of the effects of leadership style on organizational outcomes awaited the development of the modern contingency theories. The first of these was developed by Fred Fiedler.[10,11] Fiedler's approach centered on a personality measure called the "esteem for the least-preferred co-worker" or LPC scale which he found to be related to group performance. The person who fills out the scale is asked to rate an individual with whom the rater had difficulty accomplishing an assigned task. The most widely accepted interpretation of the meaning of this measure is that a person who gives a *very negative* rating to a poor co-worker is the kind of person for whom task success is very important. Such a person might be labeled "task motivated." A leader who gives a least-preferred co-worker a relatively positive rating would appear to be more concerned with the interpersonal than the task aspects of the situation, and is called "relationship motivated."[12–15]

A considerable body of research[16] indicates that the task-motivated leader is more attentive to task-related aspects of the leadership situation, more concerned with task success, and under most circumstances, more inclined to behave in a structuring, directive, and somewhat autocratic style. The relationship-motivated leader, on the other hand, is more attentive and responsive to interpersonal dynamics, more concerned with avoiding conflict and maintaining high morale, and more likely to behave in a participative and considerate leadership style.

After a very extensive series of studies covering some fifteen years, Fiedler[16] determined that leadership style alone was not sufficient to explain leader effectiveness. He set about to develop a model which integrated situational parameters into the leadership equation. He saw the most important dimension of the situation to be the degree of certainty, predictability, and control which the leader possessed. Fiedler developed a scale of *situational control* based on three features of the situation. These were: 1) leader-member relations, that is, the degree of trust and support which followers give the leader; 2) task structure, that is, the degree to which the goals and procedures for accomplishing the group's task are clearly specified; and 3) position power, that is, the degree to which the leader has formal authority to reward and punish followers. The research results indicate that neither style is effective in all situations. In *high control* situations, where predictability is assured by a clear task and a cooperative group, the task-motivated leader is calm and relaxed but maintains a strong emphasis on successful task accomplishment, which is very effective. However, under conditions of *moderate control*, caused by an ambiguous task or an uncooperative group, the task-motivated leader becomes anxious, overconcerned with a quick solution, and sometimes overly critical and punitive. The more open, considerate, and participative style of the relationship-motivated leader can address the problems of low morale or can create an environment conducive to successful problem solving and decision making, making the relationship-motivated leader more effective under these conditions. The crisis nature of the *low control* situation calls for a firm and directive leadership style which is supplied by the task-motivated leader. Such a situation is too far gone to be quickly solved via a participative or considerate style, although such styles may be effective in the long run.

The Contingency Model, as Fiedler's theory is called, has been the subject of considerable controversy.[17-19] Arguments have raged over the meaning of the LPC scale, the appropriateness of situational variables, and the general predictive validity of the theory. However, a recent extensive review[20] indicated that the predictions of the theory are strongly supported by data from both laboratory and organizational studies.

Research on the Contingency Model has been quite extensive and broad. The person/situation perspective has provided insights into leadership phenomena which were obscured by "one best way" approaches. One example is in the area of leadership training. Reviews of research on leadership training[21] had concluded that such training had few consistent effects on group performance or subordinate satisfaction. However, Contingency Model research on the effects of leadership training[22,23] has shown that training has its most powerful effects on the leader's situational control. Training provides the leader with knowledge, procedures, and techniques which increase his or her sense of control over the group's task activities. Since the relationship of leadership style to group performance varies across different levels of situational control, the increased control provided by training can either improve or lower a particular leader's performance. For example, if a situation was of moderate control for untrained leaders, the relationship-motivated leaders would perform most effectively. Leadership training which clarified and structured the task would change the situation into one of high control. Under these conditions, the task-motivated leaders would perform better than the relationship-motivated leaders. With the task-motivated leaders getting better and the relationship-motivated leaders getting worse, the net effect of training would appear to be null. However, when both leadership style and situational control are analyzed, the effects of training become clear. These findings helped to explain why leadership training has not been found to be a consistent positive factor in leadership effectiveness. More importantly, the utility of the situational-control dimension as a mediator of leadership effectiveness gained further support, suggesting that aspects of certainty, predictability, and control could well be the most critical factors in the leadership equation.

A number of other contingency-oriented leadership theories have also addressed the relationship of leadership decision-making style to group performance and morale. The best known of these approaches is the Normative Decision Theory presented by Vroom and Yetton.[24] These authors have identified a range of decision-making styles. These include *autocratic* styles, in which the leader makes a decision alone without consulting subordinates; *consultative* styles, in which the leader makes the decision, but after consulting with subordinates; and a *group* style, in which the leader allows subordinates to share in the decision-making responsibility. The dimension which underlies the range of decision styles is the degree to which the leader allows the followers to participate in the process of decision making. As the word *normative* in the name of the theory implies, the model specifies which of the styles is most likely to yield effective decisions under varying situations. Like Fiedler's Contingency Model, and other contingency theories, it is assumed that there is no one best way to make decisions, and that the most effective style will depend on the characteristics of the situation.

The situational characteristics which are considered most important in this model are 1) the expected support, acceptance, and commitment to the decision by subordinates and 2) the amount of structured, clear, decision-relevant information available to the leader. Three general rules determine which styles or sets of styles will be most effective. The first rule is that, other things being equal, autocratic decisions are less time-consuming and, therefore, more efficient. However, the second rule specifies that if the leader does not have sufficient structure and information to make a high-quality decision, he or she must consult with subordinates to gain the necessary information and enlist their aid and advice. The third general rule specifies that if the leader does not have sufficient support from subordinates to be assured that they will accept the decision, the leader must gain subordinate acceptance and commitment through participation in decision making.

Research support for the Normative Decision Theory is somewhat sparse.[25,26] Managers who are asked to recall and describe the characteristics of good and poor decisions that they have made in the past have been shown to usually describe situations and styles that would be predicted by the theory. Such recollective analyses are clearly open to distortion and bias. However, a comparison of Normative Decision Theory with the Contingency Model, described earlier, helps to strengthen and clarify both theories.

The two most important features of Fiedler's situational-control dimension are leader-member relations and task structure, which are extremely similar to Vroom and Yetton's characteristics of follower acceptance and structured information availability. Thus, the various situations presented in Vroom and Yetton's analysis would fit closely into Fiedler and situational-control dimension. Further, Fiedler's task-motivated and relationship-motivated leaders are typically described as using decision styles which fall toward the two poles of Vroom and Yetton's dimension of style. Task-motivated leaders are more likely to tend toward autocratic or minimally consultative styles while relationship-motivated leaders more often use group-oriented and participative styles.[27–29] The two theories make very similar predictions. Autocratic decisions are likely to be efficient and effective when the leader has a clear task and the support of followers. Relatively more participative decisions will fare better when either support or clarity is absent.

Despite the similarity of the two theories, they diverge sharply on the question of the ability of people to modify and change their decision styles. The normative model assumes that leaders can quickly and easily change their behavior to fit the demands of the situation, while Fiedler sees leadership style arising out of stable, enduring, well-learned personality attributes which are quite difficult to change. Some research by Bass and his associates[30] on decision styles is relevant to this question. Bass and others identified five decision styles which are quite close to those already discussed. These are called directive, negotiative, consultative, participative, and delegative. In a large survey conducted in several organizations, Bass asked managers to rate a number of features of the leadership situation which affect or are affected by these decision styles. The results do indicate that the effects of decision style on group performance and subordinate satisfaction depend on the situation, although the pattern of results in these studies is not yet clear and consistent. However, of great interest was Bass's finding that the various leadership styles were not independent of one another. The directive and negotiative styles seem to form one related set, while consultative, participative, and delegative form another. This suggests that some leaders across many situations tend to use more directive, task-oriented, autocratic styles while another type of leader is more likely to employ the participative, open, relationship-oriented styles. The possibility, then, that leadership decision and behavioral style are stable and enduring aspects of the individual leaders seems reasonable.

Another prominent contingency theory of leadership is the Path Goal Theory.[31,32] This is a more restricted theory which deals primarily with the effects of specific leader behavior on subordinate motivation and satisfaction, rather than the more general issues of decision making and performance. The Path-Goal research has studied the effects of the Leader Behavior Description Questionnaire categories of considerate and structuring behavior. The theory predicts that leader-structuring behavior will have the most positive effects on subordinate psychological states when the subordinate's task is unclear and/or difficult, that is, unstructured. The structure provided by the leader helps to clarify the *path* to the *goal* for the subordinates. On the other hand, consideration behavior will have its most positive effects when subordinates have a boring or distasteful job to perform. Subordinates then appreciate the "strokes" provided by their boss, more than they would if their job were intrinsically satisfying.

It is difficult to integrate Path Goal Theory with the more general theories of leadership discussed earlier. It is not concerned with participative decision styles. In fact, it is not concerned with decisions at all, and might more properly be thought of as a theory of supervision under conditions where the supervisor has high clarity and follower support. However, even with this model, the dimension of clarity, predictability, and certainty of the situation is a variable of critical importance. Research support for the Path-Goal Theory is variable. The most clear and consistent results show up on studies of follower satisfaction rather than group performance. However, a most interesting recent finding by Griffin[33] indicates that in addition to job characteristics, the needs, attitudes, and expectations of the follower have an important effect on the follower's reaction to leader behavior. Griffin found that managers who scored high on a measure of the need for personal growth preferred not to receive structuring supervision, even under conditions of ambiguity. These subordinates would rather work the problem out for themselves. Conversely, subordinates low in growth need were not upset by a boring, routine job. The supervisor's considerate behavior had little effect since the subordinates were not really suffering. This result is especially important because the theoretical orientations of the three theories described so far tend to largely ignore the characteristics of subordinates.

Transactional Approaches

The theories discussed above might all be regarded as "leader oriented" approaches. They tend to focus most of their attention on the leader's actions and attitudes. Although followers make their appearance in features related to leader-subordinate relationships, the leader is clearly the central figure and prime actor. However, some transactional or exchange theories of leadership addressing the relationship between leader and followers have had considerable impact.

One of the most important bodies of research in leadership are the studies of leader legitimation by Hollander.[34,35] Hollander developed the notion of "idiosyncrasy credit" to refer to the freedom which valued group members are given to deviate somewhat from group norms, that is, to act idiosyncratically. Idiosyncrasy credits are earned through the demonstration of competence and shared values which serve to make the group member more indispensable to the group. The individual's achieved value, which is the same as status, allows him or her to introduce new ideas and new ways of doing things into the group or society, thus creating adaptability and change. Hollander's work shows us that the legitimation of leadership is a process of social exchange. Members of groups exchange their competence and loyalty for group-mediated rewards which range from physical rewards such as income or protection to the less tangible rewards of honor, status, and influence.

The work of George Graen and his associates[36-38] has shown that the nature of exchange processes between leaders and subordinates can have far-reaching effects on group performance and morale. Research with the Vertical Dyad Linkage model has shown that a leader or manager develops a specific and unique exchange with each of his or her subordinates. These exchanges might range from a true partnership in which the subordinate is given considerable freedom and autonomy in defining and developing a work-related role to exchanges in which the subordinate is restrained, controlled, and little more than a "hired hand." As might be expected, the more positive exchanges are associated with higher subordinate satisfaction, reduced turnover, and greater identification with the organization.[39]

On the one hand, these findings are not surprising. Good interpersonal relationships in dyads make people feel better about each other, themselves, and their work. The importance of this research is that it redirects our attention to the relationship between leader, follower, and situation, and encourages a broader and more dynamic approach to the study of the leadership phenomenon. However, the Vertical Dyad Linkage Model does not elucidate the causes of good and poor exchanges.

Over the years, a number of studies have examined follower effects on the leadership process. Although not organized into a comprehensive theory, the research makes some interesting and important points. For example, a number of studies[40-42] have shown that leader activity, specifically the leader's willingness to engage in attempts to move the group toward its goals, is dramatically affected by followers' responses to the influence attempts. Leaders lead more with follower acceptance.

Individual differences in follower attitude or personality traits have long been associated with leadership effects. Early studies by Haythorn[43] and Sanford[44] showed that differences in authoritarian versus egalitarian attitudes of followers determined reactions to leader's style. A recent study by Weed and others[45] updates the same effect. They found that followers who are high in dogmatism respond better to leaders who engage in high levels of structuring behavior. Low-dogmatism followers perform better with considerate leader behavior.

A number of other characteristics, including need for achievement,[46] work values,[47,48] and locus of control[49,50] have been shown to impact on leader behavior and follower attitudes. At this point, the literature on follower characteristics is not well integrated. However, the results occur frequently enough to suggest that leadership theorizing will benefit from attention to leader *and* follower characteristics and to the resultant relationship.

Cognitive Approaches

Perception and cognition have played a major role in leadership research. Many dependent measures such as leader-behavior ratings, satisfaction, and role ambiguity, are judgmental or memory processes. Social psychology has been strongly influenced by attribution theory[51-53] which is concerned with the cognitive processes which underlie interpersonal judgments. Recently, leadership theorists have begun to apply attribution-theory-based propositions to judgments involved in the process of leadership.

One of the key features of interpersonal judgments is the strong tendency for an observer to develop causal explanations for another person's behavior. Explanations of a person's behavior often center on the question of whether the behavior was determined by factors internal to the actor, such as ability or motivation, or factors external to the actor, such as situational forces, role demands, or luck. Reliable findings indicate that observers have a strong bias to attribute an actor's behavior to internal causes.[54] This tendency may result from the observer's desire for a sense of certainty and predictability about the actor's future behavior. Further, if the observer might be considered responsible for the actor's behavior, internal attributions to the actor remove that responsibility. For example, a teacher might be inclined to attribute a student's poor academic performance to a lack of ability, thereby relieving the teacher of responsibility for that performance.

Recent work by Green and Mitchell[55] has adapted some of the propositions of attribution theory to the processes which leaders use to make judgments about subordinate performance. They have shown that these processes are affected by factors which are not directly related to the subordinate's actual behavior. Studies[56,57] indicate that supervisors make more negative and more internal attributions when the negative outcomes of a subordinate's behavior are more severe. This happens even when the behavior in the two situations is identical. For example, nursing supervisors asked to judge a hypothetical subordinate's performance made more negative judgments of a nurse who left a railing down on a patient's bed if the patient fell out of bed than if the patient did not. These judgments have important implications for later actions the supervisor might take with respect to promotion, termination, or salary. The role-making processes which are discussed in the Vertical Dyad Linkage model might benefit from an analysis of the ways in which supervisory judgments affect leader-follower exchanges.

Calder's[58] attribution theory of leadership argues that leadership processes and effects exist primarily as perceptual processes in the minds of followers and observers. In fact, most of the measuring instruments used in leadership research ask the respondent for perceptions of the leadership process. These perceptions, judgments, and attributions are distorted by the biases which the perceiver brings to the situation. Each individual holds an implicit personal theory of leadership which serves as a cognitive filter to determine what the observer will notice, remember, and report about the leadership process.

A number of recent studies[59–61] indicate that such implicit theories are especially problematic in ratings of leader behavior. Raters who are led to believe that a group has performed well or poorly will modify their ratings of leader behavior to conform to the performance feedback. In other words, if I think that good leaders are very considerate of their followers, I am more likely to notice and report the consideration behavior of leaders whom I believe have performed well.

Ayman and Chemers[62] have found that the structure of leader-behavior ratings depends more on the culture of the raters than on the behavior of the leader. These researchers factor analyzed leader-behavior ratings made by Iranian subjects. They found that the structure of the behavior ratings was very different from the structure normally found in studies in the United States and Europe. In most leadership studies done in Western Europe and the United States, analyses of leader-behavior ratings yield two distinct and independent behavior clusters. These are the familiar structuring, task-directed behaviors and the considerate, relationship-directed behaviors. However, the

Ayman and Chemers analysis of ratings made by Iranian followers resulted in a single category of behavior which included both structuring and considerate items. This global factor depicting a directive but warm supervisor was labeled "benevolent paternalism." Furthermore, the factor was found to be strongly related to group performance as assessed by superiors and to satisfaction with supervision expressed by subordinates. Interestingly, this unique pattern of behavior ratings was found when the leaders being rated were Iranian or American. This led Ayman and Chemers to conclude that leader-behavior ratings are more a function of the implicit theories which guide the "eye of the beholder" than they are of what the leader actually does.

On the one hand, these distortions in the observation of leadership effects are very problematic. This is especially true for research with certain theories (for example, Path-Goal Theory, the Normative Decision Theory, and the Vertical Dyad Linkage Model) because in many tests of these theories subjects are asked to rate several aspects of the leadership situation, for example, their leader's behavior and their own satisfaction. The relationships observed among these measures may reflect the implicit theories held by the subjects rather than accurate reflections of the constructs studied. However, it is also true that perception, judgments, and expectations form the core of interpersonal relationships. The desire and expectations of a subordinate for some type of leader behavior (for example, consideration) may elicit or compel that behavior. This represents an interesting and necessary area for future research.

Cross-Cultural Approaches

Berry[63] has argued that American psychology is "culture bound" and "culture blind." The generalizability of our findings is bounded by the fact that most of our research is done with European or American samples. Furthermore, because we rarely compare cultures, we are blind to the potential effects of cultural differences. Chemers[64] points out that this problem becomes more salient when we attempt to export our theories and training programs to cultures which are different from those in which the theories were developed. Cross-cultural research can benefit leadership theory in two ways. Comparative studies can show us the generalizability of Euro-American theories, helping us to recognize the inherent limitations in their transfer to other cultures. More importantly, comparative research gives us a much broader range of variables which may highlight relationships previously ignored. For example, since most studies done in the developed countries are done on subjects who are relatively well educated and technologically sophisticated, educational level becomes a background variable to which we pay little attention. However, in a broader context, the socialization or educational background of workers may be an important determinant of work-related attitudes and responses.

Leadership researchers have not totally ignored culture, but the results of the research leave much to be desired. Reviews by Roberts,[65] Nath,[66] Barrett and Bass,[67] and Tannenbaum[68] all concluded that the cross-cultural research on leadership has been characterized by weak methodologies and by a paucity of theory, both of which make the interpretation of the scattered findings very difficult. However, a few cross-cultural models do exist. Neghandhi[69] presented a model of cultural effects on organizational structure in which cultural or national differences act indirectly on management practices by affecting the organizational environment. He argues that organizational structure and managerial policy are more important than cultural factors in determining behavior. This view contrasts with earlier views[70] which saw culture as directly determining managerial values, attitudes, and behavior.

The actual role of culture probably lies somewhere between these two views. Neither culture nor organizational structure are static forces. Rather, they interact in dynamic process influencing one another, and both contribute to managerial attitudes and behavior. For example, studies which have compared the attitudes or behaviors of managers have found national differences somewhat moderated by organizational policy.[71] Unfortunately, after we have dealt with the broad question of whether culture is important, we are still left with few theories which make any specific predictions about the role of culture in shaping leadership process.

A potentially useful theoretical framework relating values to managerial and organizational process has been offered by Hofstede.[72–74] Comparing responses to a value survey of managers from forty countries, Hofstede found that the pattern of results could be described by four factors. These were 1) power distance, that is, the relative importance of status; 2) tolerance for uncertainty; 3) individualism versus collectivism; and 4) masculinity. Hofstede[75] argues that a culture's standing on these four value dimensions determines the kind of organizational structure and managerial policies that will be most likely to develop. For example, he argues that cultures which have a low tolerance for uncertainty combined with a low emphasis on status are likely to develop highly bureaucratic organizational structures to reduce ambiguity. Cultures which are also low in tolerance for uncertainty but high in power distance will develop autocratic organizational structures, in which the high-status persons resolve ambiguity by fiat.

The validity of much of the cross-cultural research has been questioned by Ayman and Chemers.[76] In a study of the leadership behavior of Iranian managers, these researchers found that traditional measures of leadership behavior and subordinate satisfaction resulted in very different factor structures in their Iranian sample than did those measures when used with European or American samples. Ayman and Chemers[77] and Chemers[78] argue that the imposition of Euro-American theories, measures, and research designs on other cultures may lead to very inaccurate conclusions.

Summary and Conclusions

We can now look back on over seventy years of scientific research on leadership in small groups. For much of that time, the literature has been characterized by false starts, dead ends, and bitter controversies. Even today, the student of leadership is consistently confronted with acrimonious debates among theorists, giving the field an appearance of chaotic disarray. In fact, much of the controversy resembles a "tempest in a teapot." Various theories say much the same thing in slightly different ways, and advocates engage in quibbling over relatively minor differences. The current crop of theories has more which unites than separates them. The last twenty years of research has reinforced and clarified certain common threads, and the study of leadership stands poised for a thrust into a new era of growth. Let us examine these commonalities and the directions toward which they point.

At the broadest level, most contemporary theories adopt a contingency perspective. One would be hard put to find an empirical theory of leadership which holds that one style of leadership is appropriate for all situations. At a somewhat deeper level, the similarities continue. The most frequent dimensions on which leader behavior, style, or decision processes are differentiated are 1) the relative focus of the leader on goal-directed task functions versus morale-oriented interpersonal functions, and 2) the relative use of autocratic, directive styles versus democratic, participative styles. These related dichotomies have been part and parcel of the leadership equation since the first behavioral studies of the late 1940s and early 1950s.

Turning to the situational parameters embodied in most current theories, another area of commonality is revealed. Almost all of the contemporary approaches are concerned with the degree of predictability, certainty, and control which the environment affords to the leader. At an even more specific level most approaches integrate interpersonal and task features into the specification of the situation. Indeed, in retrospect, it is hard to imagine how it could be otherwise. Leadership involves a job to do and people to do it with. The likelihood of successful goal accomplishment must, then, depend upon the degree to which the support of the people and the control of the task are facilitative.

Finally, a careful examination of these leadership theories results in a common set of predictions as well. Autocratic decisions and directive styles in which the leader tells followers what to do are most likely to work when the leader knows exactly what to tell the subordinates (that is, a structured task) and when the subordinates are inclined to do what they are told (that is, good follower acceptance and loyalty). When the leader is not so sure what to do or not so sure that followers will go along, considerate and participative styles have the double benefit of encouraging follower acceptance and increasing follower input into the problem-solving process.

The presence of common themes in the research literature does not mean that we have answered all the questions and solved all the problems in leadership. The contingency approaches do provide us with a stable platform from which to step into the next set of issues. However, these issues are quite complex and will require a more integrated, multifaceted, and systemic view of leadership process.

A major gap in most current leadership theories is the lack of attention to the leaders and followers, as people. We focus on behavior or decision style with very little understanding of the values, needs, and motives which give rise to the observed behaviors. It is assumed that any leader can engage in any behavior, and that leaders and followers can easily identify the correct or ideal set of behaviors in a situation. When the possibility arises, as it has recently, that our observation of behavior may be flawed, we are left with nowhere to turn.

The differences in the factor structure of leader behavior across cultures highlight the role of personal values in the social process of leadership. In the research done in the Western industrialized nations, for example, leader behaviors which are directive and task oriented are usually differentiated from those that are more considerate and interpersonally oriented. The two sets of behaviors load on separate and distinct factors. However, Ayman and Chemers's[79] research in developing nations such as Iran and Mexico reveals a different pattern. The leaders who have the highest group performance and the most satisfied subordinates are those who combine directive task styles with interpersonal warmth and consideration. The factor structure of leader-behavior ratings in these cultures indicates that both structuring and considerate behavior correlate within a single global cluster.

In order to understand why leader-behavior factors differ across cultures, it is necessary to have some theory about the manner in which culture affects behavior. The culture, through the processes of socialization, helps to shape the needs, values, and personality of leaders and followers. The personality of the leader will affect the kinds of behaviors most often used. Further, cultural norms create expectations and judgments about the appropriate behavior of leaders and their group members. The cultural expectations of the society's members then influence the patterns of leadership exhibited.

Thus, one interpretation of the differences in leader-behavior patterns across cultures relates to the very strong emphasis on individualism in the Western democracies and on collective, group-oriented values in much of the rest of the world. When individual responsibility and individual autonomy are stressed, considerate supervisory behavior is that which reinforces the autonomy of subordinates; in other words, egalitarian, participative leadership. Thus considerate behavior is generally likely to be somewhat incompatible with high levels of directive and structuring behavior. However, in more collective and authoritarian cultures, in which group members subordinate individuals' goals to group needs, a leader can maintain control over subordinates *and* satisfy them, by being directive and structuring in a warm, supportive, "fatherly" manner. Cultural values are reinforced by social norms which prescribe elaborate codes of politeness and make the exercise of a "benevolent paternalism" the most acceptable mode of behavior.

The role of culture in leadership is much broader and more complex than the abbreviated explanation given here. But this analysis does turn our attention to the role of the leader's and the follower's personalities as an influence on behavior and the perception of behavior. The research on follower characteristics makes it very plain that the way in which one individual reacts to the behavior of another is dependent upon individual differences in styles and needs as well as variations in situational characteristics.

The transactional and exchange theories have shown that the relationship between leaders and followers is a dynamic one extending longitudinally in time. Roles are defined, negotiated, and redefined. People move toward or away from one another with effects on motivation, satisfaction, and individual and group performance. Observations and judgments are made which facilitate and enhance positive or negative relationships. Admittedly, such dynamic relationships are difficult to study. It is also true, however, that leadership theory will make major strides forward when we can begin to tie together the ways in which personal characteristics influence judgments which, in turn, influence role perception and performance which, subsequently, determine group behavior and effectiveness.

The simplistic trait approaches were superseded by the behavioral studies which were replaced by the contingency theories. The next major era of leadership research will begin with the recognition that group and organizational performance are dependent upon the interplay of social systems. A social-systems approach will recognize that the leadership process is a complex, multifaceted network of forces. Personal characteristics of leaders and followers interact in the perception of and reaction to task demands and to each other. The small group is further embedded in an organizational and societal context which influences personal characteristics, social roles, and situational contingencies. If general leadership theory can begin to span the gaps between the various levels of analysis (that is, individual, group, organization, society), the resultant theories will provide us with a much stronger base, not only for understanding leadership but also for improving its quality.

19

Transactional and
Transforming Leadership

James MacGregor Burns

James MacGregor Burns won a Pulitzer Prize and a National Book Award for his study of
Franklin D. Roosevelt. His book *Leadership* is considered to be a seminal work in leadership
studies. Burns has been Woodrow Wilson Professor of Government at Williams College, and he
has served as president of the American Political Science Association.

Some define leadership as leaders making followers do what *followers* would
not otherwise do, or as leaders making followers do what the *leaders* want
them to do; I define leadership as leaders inducing followers to act for certain
goals that represent the values and the motivations—the wants and needs,
the aspirations and expectations—*of both leaders and followers.* And the genius of leadership lies in the manner in which leaders see and act on their
own and their followers' values and motivations.

Leadership, unlike naked power-wielding, is thus inseparable from followers' needs and goals. The essence of the leader-follower relation is the interaction of persons with different levels of motivations and of power potential,
including skill, in pursuit of a common or at least joint purpose. That interaction, however, takes two fundamentally different forms. The first I will call

transactional leadership. . . . Such leadership occurs when one person takes the initiative in making contact with others for the purpose of an exchange of valued things. The exchange could be economic or political or psychological in nature: a swap of goods or of one good for money; a trading of votes between candidate and citizen or between legislators; hospitality to another person in exchange for willingness to listen to one's troubles. Each party to the bargain is conscious of the power resources and attitudes of the other. Each person recognizes the other as a *person*. Their purposes are related, at least to the extent that the purposes stand within the bargaining process and can be advanced by maintaining that process. But beyond this the relationship does not go. The bargainers have no enduring purpose that holds them together; hence they may go their separate ways. A leadership act took place, but it was not one that binds leader and follower together in a mutual and continuing pursuit of a higher purpose.

Contrast this with *transforming* leadership. Such leadership occurs when one or more persons *engage* with others in such a way that leaders and followers raise one another to higher levels of motivation and morality. . . . Their purposes, which might have started out as separate but related, as in the case of transactional leadership, become fused. Power bases are linked not as counterweights but as mutual support for common purpose. Various names are used for such leadership, some of them derisory: elevating, mobilizing, inspiring, exalting, uplifting, preaching, exhorting, evangelizing. The relationship can be moralistic, of course. But transforming leadership ultimately becomes *moral* in that it raises the level of human conduct and ethical aspiration of both leader and led, and thus it has a transforming effect on both. Perhaps the best modern example is Gandhi, who aroused and elevated the hopes and demands of millions of Indians and whose life and personality were enhanced in the process. Transcending leadership is dynamic leadership in the sense that the leaders throw themselves into a relationship with followers who will feel "elevated" by it and often become more active themselves, thereby creating new cadres of leaders. Transcending leadership is leadership *engagé*. Naked power-wielding can be neither transactional nor transforming; only leadership can be.

20

The Transformation
of Transforming Leadership

Richard A. Couto

Richard Couto currently serves as professor in the Jepson School of Leadership Studies at the University of Richmond. He has worked with community organizations and leaders in the Appalachian region and has published reports and articles related to that work. His recent, award-winning work, *Lifting the Veil*, examines the history of civil rights efforts in one county in Tennessee since Reconstruction.

Since its appearance in 1978, few books have commanded more attention of scholars in the field of leadership studies than *Leadership* by James MacGregor Burns.[1] Writers on the subject of leadership make their pilgrimage to this holy book from many different fields. They drink from the waters of wisdom they find there and take inspiration for what they need for their own work.

What they need is apparently different from what they find. The literature on leadership is replete with discussions of transformational leadership that have their obligatory reference to Burns's work but little relevance to it. This transition, from Burns's treatment of transforming leadership to others' treatment of transformational leadership indicates a bias within the field of leadership studies to interpret and apply scholarship to formal organizations. . . .

Excerpted from a paper delivered at the 1993 Annual Meeting of the American Political Science Association, Washington D.C., September 2–5, 1993. With permission of the author.

Transforming Leadership Revisited

Burns, like any dutiful and conscientious scholar, offers definitions of the concept he discusses. He informs his readers that transforming leadership "is a relationship of mutual stimulation and elevation that converts followers into leaders and may convert leaders into moral agents."[1] Not satisfied with having defined the term once, Burns offers another definition later in the book when he explains that transforming leadership "occurs when one or more persons *engage* with others in such a way that leaders and followers raise one another to higher levels of motivation and morality" . . .[1]

Transforming leadership, Burns asserts, changes some of those who follow into people whom others may follow in time. It also changes leaders into moral agents. Burns defines morality in terms of human development and of a hierarchy of human needs. He borrows from humanistic psychologists for these terms and concepts, Lawrence Kohlberg, Erik Erikson, and Abraham Maslow. Transforming leadership assists a group of people to move from one stage of development to a higher one and in doing so [to] address and fulfill better a higher human need.

> The leader's fundamental act is to induce people to be aware or conscious of what they feel—to feel their true needs so strongly, to define their values so meaningfully, that they can move to purposeful action.[1]

Transforming leadership has a nobility in Burns's descriptions that suggests very desirable and attractive characteristics of the person who incarnates it. The transforming leader shapes, alters, and elevates the motives and values and goals of followers.[1] The transforming leader achieves "significant change."[1] There is a special power entailed in transforming leadership. Leaders "armed with principles and rising above self-interest narrowly conceived" are invested with power that "may ultimately transform both leaders and followers into persons who jointly adhere to modal values and end-values."[1]

Burns is quick to distinguish this power from charisma and to distinguish transforming leadership from heroic leadership, a term he prefers to "charismatic leadership." Heroic leadership, according to Burns, is a relationship between followers and persons they believe in because of reputation aside from tested capacities, experience, or stands on issues. Followers place great confidence in heroic leaders and in their ability to overcome crises and obstacles.[1] Idolized heroes, such as Joan of Arc or Michael Jordan, lack essential characteristics of leaders, for Burns, because their relationship with followers is devoid of deeply held motives and goals, shared by leader and followers.[1]

Burns also adeptly distinguishes executive leadership from transforming leadership. Here Burns depends on Philip Selznick and Michael Crozier and their studies of formal organizations to identify a trinity of obstacles between executive leadership and transforming leadership: conditions of an organization; causal factors of problems within an organization; and the achievement of actual social change. Burns acknowledges the capacity of extraordinary executives to overcome limiting conditions and address causal factors of problems within an organization. Those accomplishments, Burns fears, would leave little energy for actual social change, which is the test of transforming leadership. . . .[1]

Given the clarity in Burns' work that transforming leadership is neither heroic nor executive leadership, it is surprising that most of the application of his work has been to these forms of leadership.

The Transformation of Transforming Leadership

Perhaps Bernard M. Bass has transformed the concept of transforming leader more than any other individual. Indeed, although explicitly related to Burns's work, Bass's development of the concept differs substantially. First, Bass uses the term "transformational leadership" rather than transforming leadership. The adjective form of a noun, transformation, modifies leadership and suggests a condition or a state. This contrasts with the adjective form of a verb, transform, that suggests leadership as a process. Since Bass, transformational leadership is more often used in leadership literature than transforming leadership with the implied change of state of being or character of a leader rather than of a process in which a leader participates. . . .

In Bass's terms, transformational leaders transform followers. The direction of influence is one-way, unlike Burns's treatment in which followers could transform leaders by the *interaction* of leaders and followers. For Bass, transformational leaders may expand a follower's portfolio of needs; may transform a followers' self-interest; and may elevate a follower's need to a higher Maslow level. In addition, leaders may increase the confidence of followers; elevate followers' expectations of success; and elevate the value of the leader's intended outcomes for the follower. These actions plus a change in organization culture create increased motivation in followers to attain the leader's designated outcome and eventually to perform beyond their own as well as the leader's initial expectations. The transformational leader has transformed followers into more highly motivated followers who provide extra effort to perform beyond expectations of leader and follower.[2]

The transformation that Bass conducts extends beyond the differences he has with Burns that he cites. Bass deals with the transformational style of executive leadership. He limits transformational leadership to the first two of the three tasks that Burns designated for transforming leadership of executives. Burns acknowledged the capacity of executive to change conditions and culture. The crucial, additional test for Burns, however, is social change, which is missing in Bass's analysis.

Bass's research on transformational leadership is conducted primarily in formal organizations, i.e. schools, industry and the military. Within these formal organizations, an array of studies of presidents of businesses, Methodist ministers, principals of private schools, and of "world-class industrial, military, and political leaders" demonstrate, according to Bass, that transformational leaders achieved more effective organizations with less effort on the part of subordinates.[3] Such findings fall short of the three part test of transforming leadership of Burns. . . .

Bass sees the payoff for this research on transformational leadership in "entrepreneurial champions", "organizational champions", and champions of "radical military innovations." . . .

In some ways, Bass has done for transforming leadership what David Lilienthal did for the concept "grassroots democracy" within the Tennessee Valley Authority (TVA). He has placed a radically transforming concept in the service of institutional practice. Bass, like Lilienthal, changed the test of the radical transformation from social change to the achievement of institutional goals, including preservation. Philip Selznick[4] criticized the grassroots policies of TVA and Lilienthal and introduced us to the concept of "cooptation." Selznick's work is part of the sociology of formal organizations from which Burns borrows and concludes the low probability of executive leadership reaching transforming leadership. Bass's work is part of the psychology of organizations and encourages a belief in the high probability of executive leadership reaching transformational leadership. . . .

Reclaiming a Lost Concept

The differences between Burns and Bass stem, in part, from the contexts in which they study leadership. Burns is dealing with leadership within social movements and politics; revolutionary leadership where politics and social movements overlap. In such a context, significant social change is extraordinary in scope: national independence, political revolution, the end of legal segregation. In this context, executive leaders become transforming leaders when they "mobilize political resources in groups, parties, public opinion, and legislatures."[1] However, Burns offers us more historical examples of transforming leaders—Lenin, Mao, Gandhi, and Luther—who become executive leaders in this manner than of executive leaders who become transforming leaders. Bass is dealing with leadership within formal organizations; organizational leadership where authority, management, and leadership blend. It may be gratifying for school principals, CEO's, and military officers to consider themselves exemplars of Gandhi and other transforming leaders but it [is] also a stretch. The contexts differ and this creates two distinct scales for the changes of followers and leaders, the moral issues, and the significant change entailed in transforming and transformational leadership.

Clearly, in some ways Bass's transformational leadership is an analogy of Burns's transforming leadership. The test of transforming leadership, for Burns, comes from social movements. "Significant change" entails the abolition of some caste-like restriction that impaired the recognition of the human worth of a group of people and the public expression of their values and needs. Such change is likely to come from outside of formal organizations and institutions, to entail involuntary changes of an organization, and to depend on causal factors and conditions that transforming leaders do not create or control. Followers are in a synergistic, reflexive relationship with transforming leaders and both are on a path of change towards uncertain but noble outcomes.

The test of transformational leadership, for Bass, comes from management goals. "Performance beyond expectations" entails the creation of an environment that enables followers to recognize and realize an organization goal that exceeds past accomplishments. This change is likely to come from inside formal organizations and institutions, to entail voluntary changes of an organization, and to depend on causal factors and conditions that transformational leaders create and control. Followers remain subordinates of the transformational leader whatever else might be transformed. . . .

To relate these concepts, we must come to terms with the differences in contexts for leadership, obviously. Burns's examples of epoch change risk idealizing and idolizing transforming leadership and removing it from the grasp of ordinary humans. Granted that a few transforming leaders exemplify dramatic social change, can other men and women involved in politics and social movements exemplify transforming leadership? Bass's examples of institutional change risk trivializing transformational leadership and placing it within the grasp of anyone in authority with the cost of a book or workshop on the topic. Granted that some managers manage better than others, can transformational be so common without manifesting itself in significant so-cial change? While Burns's transforming leadership is attractive, it may be unattainable and distract us from the important task of being as effective as one can be to transform this set of conditions and causal factors in the here and now with little hope of epoch change. While Bass's transformational leadership risks narcissism, it offers attainable goals and establishes for peo-ple with authority the conditions to lead and manage people more effective-ly and competently. Somehow we need to preserve an understanding of leadership in everyday life and not merely extraordinary human beings like Martin Luther, Lenin, Susan B. Anthony, Gandhi, Franklin Delano Roo-sevelt, Septima Clark, and Martin Luther King Jr. For example, Burns exem-plifies great leadership in Mao but uses terms that describe the principles of great teaching, as well.

> The classic role of the great leader . . . is to comprehend not only the existing needs of followers but to mobilize within them newer motivations and aspira-tions that would in the future furnish a popular foundation for the kind of leadership Mao hoped to supply.[1]

In adopting this role of great leader to teaching, for example, we very appro-priately extend the transforming power of the great leader. . . .

Conclusion

Burns turned away from the terms "charisma" and "charismatic" leadership because they had been hopelessly mangled. To a far less extent, perhaps his own term "transforming leader" has been modified almost to the point where it is no longer recognizable. The change has a great deal to do with the appli-cation of the concept to formal organizations, a context that dominates the field of leadership studies. . . . Examining the changes in "transforming lead-ership" enables us to identify elements of that analysis. . . . This . . . , it is hoped, permits us to understand better transforming leadership, in particular, and leadership, in general.

21

Beyond the Charismatic Leader: Leadership and Organizational Change

David A. Nadler and Michael L. Tushman

David A. Nadler is president of Delta Consulting Group and former professor at the Graduate School of Business, Columbia University. Michael L. Tushman is professor of management at Columbia University. He has lectured throughout Europe, Japan, and Brazil and has published several books and articles.

The Charismatic Leader

While the subject of leadership has received much attention over the years, the more specific issue of leadership during periods of change has only recently attracted serious attention.[1] What emerges from various discussions of leadership and organizational change is a picture of the special kind of leadership that appears to be critical during times of strategic organizational change. While various words have been used to portray this type of leadership, we prefer the label "charismatic" leader. It refers to a special quality that enables the leader to mobilize and sustain activity within an organization through specific personal actions combined with perceived personal characteristics.

Extracted from David A. Nadler and Michael L. Tushman, "Beyond the Charismatic Leader: Leadership and Organizational Change," *California Management Review* 32 (Winter, 1990): 77–97. Reprinted by permission.

The concept of the charismatic leader is not the popular version of the great speech maker or television personality. Rather, a model has emerged from recent work aimed at identifying the nature and determinants of a particular type of leadership that successfully brings about changes in an individual's values, goals, needs, or aspirations. Research on charismatic leadership has identified this type of leadership as observable, definable, and having clear behavioral characteristics.[2] We have attempted to develop a first cut description of the leader in terms of patterns of behavior that he/she seems to exhibit. The resulting approach is outlined in Figure 1, which lists three major types of behavior that characterize these leaders and some illustrative kinds of actions.

The first component of charismatic leadership is *envisioning*. This involves the creation of a picture of the future, or of a desired future state with which people can identify and which can generate excitement. By creating vision, the leader provides a vehicle for people to develop commitment, a common goal around which people can rally, and a way for people to feel successful. Envisioning is accomplished through a range of different actions. Clearly, the simplest form is through articulation of a compelling vision in clear and dramatic terms. The vision needs to be challenging, meaningful, and worthy of pursuit, but it also needs to be credible. People must believe that it is possible to succeed in the pursuit of the vision. Vision is also communicated in other ways, such as through expectations that the leader expresses and through the leader personally demonstrating behaviors and activities that symbolize and further that vision.

The second component is *energizing*. Here the role of the leader is the di-

FIGURE 1
The Charismatic Leader

Envisioning
- articulating a compelling vision
- setting high expectations
- modeling consistent behaviors

Energizing	*Enabling*
• demonstrating personal excitement	• expressing personal support
• expressing personal confidence	• empathizing
• seeking, finding, & using success	• expressing confidence in people

rect generation of energy—motivation to act—among members of the organization. How is this done? Different leaders engage in energizing in different ways, but some of the most common include demonstration of their own personal excitement and energy, combined with leveraging that excitement through direct personal contact with large numbers of people in the organization. They express confidence in their own ability to succeed. They find, and use, successes to celebrate progress towards the vision.

The third component is *enabling*. The leader psychologically helps people act or perform in the face of challenging goals. Assuming that individuals are directed through a vision and motivated by the creation of energy, they then may need emotional assistance in accomplishing their tasks. This enabling is achieved in several ways. Charismatic leaders demonstrate empathy—the ability to listen, understand, and share the feelings of those in the organization. They express support for individuals. Perhaps most importantly, the charismatic leader tends to express his/her confidence in people's ability to perform effectively and to meet challenges. . . .

Assuming that leaders act in these ways, what functions are they performing that help bring about change? First, they provide a psychological focal point for the energies, hopes, and aspirations of people in the organization. Second, they serve as powerful role models whose behaviors, actions and personal energy demonstrate the desired behaviors expected throughout the firm. The behaviors of charismatic leaders provide a standard to which others can aspire. Through their personal effectiveness and attractiveness they build a very personal and intimate bond between themselves and the organization. Thus, they can become a source of sustained energy; a figure whose high standards others can identify with and emulate.

Limitations of the Charismatic Leader

Even if one were able to do all of the things involved in being a charismatic leader, it might still not be enough. In fact, our observations suggest that there are a number of inherent limitations to the effectiveness of charismatic leaders, many stemming from risks associated with leadership which revolves around a single individual. Some of the key potential problems are:

- *Unrealistic Expectations*—In creating a vision and getting people energized, the leader may create expectations that are unrealistic or unattainable. These can backfire if the leader cannot live up to the expectations that are created.

- *Dependency and Counterdependency*—A strong, visible, and energetic leader may spur different psychological response. Some individuals may become overly dependent upon the leader, and in some cases whole organizations become dependent. Everyone else stops initiating actions and waits for the leader to provide direction; individuals may become passive or reactive. On the other extreme, others may be uncomfortable with strong personal presence and spend time and energy demonstrating how the leader is wrong—how the emperor has no clothes.
- *Reluctance to Disagree with the Leader*—The charismatic leader's approval or disapproval becomes an important commodity. In the presence of a strong leader, people may become hesitant to disagree or come into conflict with the leader. This may, in turn, lead to stifling conformity.
- *Need for Continuing Magic*—The charismatic leader may become trapped by the expectation that the magic often associated with charisma will continue unabated. This may cause the leader to act in ways that are not functional, or (if the magic is not produced) it may cause a crisis of leadership credibility.
- *Potential Feelings of Betrayal*—When and if things do not work out as the leader has envisioned, the potential exists for individuals to feel betrayed by their leader. They may become frustrated and angry, with some of that anger directed at the individual who created the expectations that have been betrayed.
- *Disenfranchisement of Next Levels of Management*—A consequence of the strong charismatic leader is that the next levels of management can easily become disenfranchised. They lose their ability to lead because no direction, vision, exhortation, reward, or punishment is meaningful unless it comes directly from the leader. The charismatic leader thus may end up underleveraging his or her management and/or creating passive/dependent direct reports.
- *Limitations of Range of the Individual Leader*—When the leadership process is built around an individual, management's ability to deal with various issues is limited by the time, energy, expertise, and interest of that individual. This is particularly problematic during periods of change when different types of issues demand different types of competencies (e.g., markets, technologies, products, finance) which a single individual may not possess. Different types of strategic changes make different managerial demands and call for different personal characteristics. There may be limits to the number of strategic changes that one individual can lead over the life of an organization.

In light of these risks, it appears that the charismatic leader is a necessary component—but not a sufficient component—of the organizational leadership required for effective organizational re-organization. There is a need to move beyond the charismatic leader.

Instrumental Leadership

Effective leaders of change need to be more than just charismatic. Effective re-orientations seem to be characterized by the presence of another type of leadership behavior which focuses not on the excitement of individuals and changing their goals, needs or aspirations, but on making sure that individuals in the senior team and throughout the organization behave in ways needed for change to occur. An important leadership role is to build competent teams, clarify required behaviors, build in measurement, and administer rewards and punishments so that individuals perceive that behavior consistent with the change is central for them in achieving their own goals.[3] We will call this type of leadership *instrumental leadership*, since it focuses on the management of teams, structures, and managerial processes to create individual instrumentalities. The basis of this approach is in expectancy theories of motivation, which propose that individuals will perform those behaviors that they perceive as instrumental for acquiring valued outcomes.[4] Leadership, in this context, involves managing environments to create conditions that motivate desired behavior.[5]

In practice, instrumental leadership of change involves three elements of behavior (see Figure 2). The first is *structuring*. The leader invests time in building teams that have the required competence to execute and implement the re-orientation[6] and in creating structures that make it clear what types of behavior are required throughout the organization. This may involve setting goals, establishing standards, and defining roles and responsibilities. Re-orientations seem to require detailed planning about what people will need to do and how they will be required to act during different phases of the change. The second element of instrumental leadership is *controlling*. This involves the creation of systems and processes to measure, monitor, and assess both behavior and results and to administer corrective action.[7] The third element is *rewarding*, which includes the administration of both rewards and punishments contingent upon the degree to which behavior is consistent with the requirements of the change.

Instrumental leadership focuses on the challenge of shaping consistent behaviors in support of the re-orientation. The charismatic leader excites indi-

FIGURE 2

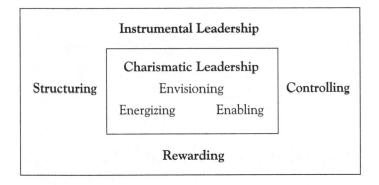

viduals, shapes their aspirations, and directs their energy. In practice, however, this is not enough to sustain patterns of desired behavior. Subordinates and colleagues may be committed to the vision, but over time other forces may influence their behavior, particularly when they are not in direct personal contact with the leader. This is particularly relevant during periods of change when the formal organization and the informal social system may lag behind the leader and communicate outdated messages or reward traditional behavior. Instrumental leadership is needed to ensure compliance over time consistent with the commitment generated by charismatic leadership. . . .

The Complementarity of Leadership Approaches

It appears that effective organizational re-orientation requires both charismatic and instrumental leadership. Charismatic leadership is needed to generate energy, create commitment, and direct individuals towards new objectives, values or aspirations. Instrumental leadership is required to ensure that people really do act in a manner consistent with their new goals. Either one alone is insufficient for the achievement of change.

22

What Leaders Really Do

John P. Kotter

John P. Kotter has published ten books, including *The Leadership Factor* and *A Force for Change: How Leadership Differs from Management*. He is professor of organizational behavior at the Harvard Business School.

Leadership is different from management, but not for the reasons most people think. Leadership isn't mystical and mysterious. It has nothing to do with having "charisma" or other exotic personality traits. It is not the province of a chosen few. Nor is leadership necessarily better than management or a replacement for it.

Rather, leadership and management are two distinctive and complementary systems of action. Each has its own function and characteristic activities. Both are necessary for success in an increasingly complex and volatile business environment.

Most U.S. corporations today are overmanaged and underled. They need to develop their capacity to exercise leadership. Successful corporations don't wait for leaders to come along. They actively seek out people with leadership potential and expose them to career experiences designed to develop that potential. Indeed, with careful selection, nurturing, and encouragement, dozens of people can play important leadership roles in a business organization.

But while improving their ability to lead, companies should remember that strong leadership with weak management is no better, and is sometimes actually worse, than the reverse. The real challenge is to combine strong leadership and strong management and use each to balance the other.

Of course, not everyone can be good at both leading and managing. Some people have the capacity to become excellent managers but not strong leaders. Others have great leadership potential but, for a variety of reasons, have great difficulty becoming strong managers. Smart companies value both kinds of people and work hard to make them a part of the team.

But when it comes to preparing people for executive jobs, such companies rightly ignore the recent literature that says people cannot manage *and* lead. They try to develop leader-managers. Once companies understand the fundamental difference between leadership and management, they can begin to groom their top people to provide both.

The Difference Between Management and Leadership

Management is about coping with complexity. Its practices and procedures are largely a response to one of the most significant developments of the twentieth century: the emergence of large organizations. Without good management, complex enterprises tend to become chaotic in ways that threaten their very existence. Good management brings a degree of order and consistency to key dimensions like the quality and profitability of products.

Leadership, by contrast, is about coping with change. Part of the reason it has become so important in recent years is that the business world has become more competitive and more volatile. Faster technological change, greater international competition, the deregulation of markets, overcapacity in capital-intensive industries, an unstable oil cartel, raiders with junk bonds, and the changing demographics of the work force are among the many factors that have contributed to this shift. The net result is that doing what was done yesterday, or doing it 5% better, is no longer a formula for success. Major changes are more and more necessary to survive and compete effectively in this new environment. More change always demands more leadership.

Consider a simple military analogy: a peacetime army can usually survive with good administration and management up and down the hierarchy, coupled with good leadership concentrated at the very top. A wartime army, however, needs competent leadership at all levels. No one yet has figured out how to manage people effectively into battle; they must be *led*.

These different functions—coping with complexity and coping with change—shape the characteristic activities of management and leadership. Each system of action involves deciding what needs to be done, creating networks of people and relationships that can accomplish an agenda, and then trying to ensure that those people actually do the job. But each accomplishes these three tasks in different ways.

Companies manage complexity first by *planning and budgeting*—setting targets or goals for the future (typically for the next month or year), establishing detailed steps for achieving those targets, and then allocating resources to accomplish those plans. By contrast, leading an organization to constructive change begins by *setting a direction*—developing a vision of the future (often the distant future) along with strategies for producing the changes needed to achieve that vision.

Management develops the capacity to achieve its plan by *organizing and staffing*—creating an organizational structure and set of jobs for accomplishing plan requirements, staffing the jobs with qualified individuals, communicating the plan to those people, delegating responsibility for carrying out the plan, and devising systems to monitor implementation. The equivalent leadership activity, however, is *aligning people*. This means communicating the new direction to those who can create coalitions that understand the vision and are committed to its achievement.

Finally, management ensures plan accomplishment by *controlling and problem solving*—monitoring results versus the plan in some detail, both formally and informally, by means of reports, meetings, and other tools; identifying deviations; and then planning and organizing to solve the problems. But for leadership, achieving a vision requires *motivating and inspiring*—keeping people moving in the right direction, despite major obstacles to change, by appealing to basic but often untapped human needs, values, and emotions.

A closer examination of each of these activities will help clarify the skills leaders need.

Setting a Direction vs. Planning and Budgeting

Since the function of leadership is to produce change, setting the direction of that change is fundamental to leadership.

Setting direction is never the same as planning or even long-term planning, although people often confuse the two. Planning is a management process, deductive in nature and designed to produce orderly results, not change. Setting a direction is more inductive. Leaders gather a broad range of data and look for patterns, relationships, and linkages that help explain things. What's more, the direction-setting aspect of leadership does not produce plans; it creates vision and strategies. These describe a business, technology, or corporate culture in terms of what it should become over the long term and articulate a feasible way of achieving this goal.

Most discussions of vision have a tendency to degenerate into the mystical. The implication is that a vision is something mysterious that mere mortals, even talented ones, could never hope to have. But developing good business direction isn't magic. It is a tough, sometimes exhausting process of gathering and analyzing information. People who articulate such visions aren't magicians but broad-based strategic thinkers who are willing to take risks.

Nor do visions and strategies have to be brilliantly innovative; in fact, some of the best are not. Effective business visions regularly have an almost mundane quality, usually consisting of ideas that are already well known. The particular combination or patterning of the ideas may be new, but sometimes even that is not the case.

For example, when CEO Jan Carlzon articulated his vision to make Scandinavian Airline Systems (SAS) the best airline in the world for the frequent business traveler, he was not saying anything that everyone in the airline industry didn't already know. Business travelers fly more consistently than other market segments and are generally willing to pay higher fares. Thus focusing on business customers offers an airline the possibility of high margins, steady business, and considerable growth. But in an industry known more for bureaucracy than vision, no company had ever put these simple ideas together and dedicated itself to implementing them. SAS did, and it worked.

What's crucial about a vision is not its originality but how well it serves the interests of important constituencies—customers, stockholders, employees—and how easily it can be translated into a realistic competitive strategy. Bad visions tend to ignore the legitimate needs and rights of important constituencies—favoring, say, employees over customers or stockholders. Or they are strategically unsound. When a company that has never been better than a weak competitor in an industry suddenly starts talking about becoming number one, that is a pipe dream, not a vision.

One of the most frequent mistakes that over-managed and underled corporations make is to embrace "long-term planning" as a panacea for their lack of direction and inability to adapt to an increasingly competitive and dynamic business environment. But such an approach misinterprets the nature of direction setting and can never work.

Long-term planning is always time consuming. Whenever something unexpected happens, plans have to be redone. In a dynamic business environment, the unexpected often becomes the norm, and long-term planning can become an extraordinarily burdensome activity. This is why most successful corporations limit the time frame of their planning activities. Indeed, some even consider "long-term planning" a contradiction in terms.

In a company without direction, even short-term planning can become a black hole capable of absorbing an infinite amount of time and energy. With no vision and strategy to provide constraints around the planning process or to guide it, every eventuality deserves a plan. Under these circumstances, contingency planning can go on forever, draining time and attention from far more essential activities, yet without ever providing the clear sense of direction that a company desperately needs. After awhile, managers inevitably become cynical about all this, and the planning process can degenerate into a highly politicized game.

Planning works best not as a substitute for direction setting but as a complement to it. A competent planning process serves as a useful reality check on direction-setting activities. Likewise, a competent direction-setting process provides a focus in which planning can then be realistically carried out. It helps clarify what kind of planning is essential and what kind is irrelevant.

Aligning People vs. Organizing and Staffing

A central feature of modern organizations is interdependence, where no one has complete autonomy, where most employees are tied to many others by their work, technology, management systems, and hierarchy. These linkages present a special challenge when organizations attempt to change. Unless many individuals line up and move together in the same direction, people will tend to fall all over one another. To executives who are overeducated in management and undereducated in leadership, the idea of getting people moving in the same direction appears to be an organizational problem. What executives need to do, however, is not organize people but align them.

Managers "organize" to create human systems that can implement plans as precisely and efficiently as possible. Typically, this requires a number of potentially complex decisions. A company must choose a structure of jobs and reporting relationships, staff it with individuals suited to the jobs, provide training for those who need it, communicate plans to the work force, and decide how much authority to delegate and to whom. Economic incentives also need to be constructed to accomplish the plan, as well as systems to monitor its implementation. These organizational judgments are much like architectural decisions. It's a question of fit within a particular context.

Aligning is different. It is more of a communications challenge than a design problem. First, aligning invariably involves talking to many more individuals than organizing does. The target population can involve not only a manager's subordinates but also bosses, peers, staff in other parts of the organization, as well as suppliers, governmental officials, or even customers. Anyone who can help implement the vision and strategies or who can block implementation is relevant.

Trying to get people to comprehend a vision of an alternative future is also a communications challenge of a completely different magnitude from organizing them to fulfill a short-term plan. It's much like the difference between a football quarterback attempting to describe to his team the next two or three plays versus his trying to explain to them a totally new approach to the game to be used in the second half of the season.

Whether delivered with many words or a few carefully chosen symbols, such messages are not necessarily accepted just because they are understood. Another big challenge in leadership efforts is credibility—getting people to believe the message. Many things contribute to credibility: the track record of the person delivering the message, the content of the message itself, the communicator's reputation for integrity and trustworthiness, and the consistency between words and deeds.

Finally, aligning leads to empowerment in a way that organizing rarely does. One of the reasons some organizations have difficulty adjusting to rapid changes in markets or technology is that so many people in those companies feel relatively powerless. They have learned from experience that even if they correctly perceive important external changes and then initiate appropriate actions, they are vulnerable to someone higher up who does not like what they have done. Reprimands can take many different forms: "That's against policy" or "We can't afford it" or "Shut up and do as you're told."

Alignment helps overcome this problem by empowering people in at least two ways. First, when a clear sense of direction has been communicated throughout an organization, lower level employees can initiate actions without the same degree of vulnerability. As long as their behavior is consistent with the vision, superiors will have more difficulty reprimanding them. Second, because everyone is aiming at the same target, the probability is less that one person's initiative will be stalled when it comes into conflict with someone else's.

Motivating People vs. Controlling and Problem Solving

Since change is the function of leadership, being able to generate highly energized behavior is important for coping with the inevitable barriers to change. Just as direction setting identifies an appropriate path for movement and just as effective alignment gets people moving down that path, successful motivation ensures that they will have the energy to overcome obstacles.

According to the logic of management, control mechanisms compare system behavior with the plan and take action when a deviation is detected. In a well-managed factory, for example, this means the planning process establishes sensible quality targets, the organizing process builds an organization that can achieve those targets, and a control process makes sure that quality lapses are spotted immediately, not in 30 or 60 days, and corrected.

For some of the same reasons that control is so central to management, highly motivated or inspired behavior is almost irrelevant. Managerial processes must be as close as possible to fail-safe and risk-free. That means they cannot be dependent on the unusual or hard to obtain. The whole purpose of systems and structures is to help normal people who behave in normal ways to complete routine jobs successfully, day after day. It's not exciting or glamorous. But that's management.

Leadership is different. Achieving grand visions always requires an occasional burst of energy. Motivation and inspiration energize people, not by pushing them in the right direction as control mechanisms do but by satisfying basic human needs for achievement, a sense of belonging, recognition, self-esteem, a feeling of control over one's life, and the ability to live up to one's ideals. Such feelings touch us deeply and elicit a powerful response.

Good leaders motivate people in a variety of ways. First, they always articulate the organization's vision in a manner that stresses the values of the audience they are addressing. This makes the work important to those individuals. Leaders also regularly involve people in deciding how to achieve the organization's vision (or the part most relevant to a particular individual). This gives people a sense of control. Another important motivational technique is to support employee efforts to realize the vision by providing coaching, feedback, and role modeling, thereby helping people grow professionally and enhancing their self-esteem. Finally, good leaders recognize and reward success, which not only gives people a sense of accomplishment but also makes them feel like they belong to an organization that cares about them. When all this is done, the work itself becomes intrinsically motivating.

The more that change characterizes the business environment, the more that leaders must motivate people to provide leadership as well. When this works, it tends to reproduce leadership across the entire organization, with people occupying multiple leadership roles throughout the hierarchy. This is highly valuable, because coping with change in any complex business demands initiatives from a multitude of people. Nothing less will work.

Of course, leadership from many sources does not necessarily converge. To the contrary, it can easily conflict. For multiple leadership roles to work together, people's actions must be carefully coordinated by mechanisms that differ from those coordinating traditional management roles.

Strong networks of informal relationships—the kind found in companies with healthy cultures—help coordinate leadership activities in much the same way that formal structure coordinates managerial activities. The key difference is that informal networks can deal with the greater demands for coordination associated with nonroutine activities and change. The multitude of communication channels and the trust among the individuals connected by those channels allow for an ongoing process of accommodation and adaptation. When conflicts arise among roles, those same relationships help resolve the conflicts. Perhaps most important, this process of dialogue and accommodation can produce visions that are linked and compatible instead of remote and competitive. All this requires a great deal more communication than is needed to coordinate managerial roles, but unlike formal structure, strong informal networks can handle it.

Of course, informal relations of some sort exist in all corporations. But too often these networks are either very weak—some people are well connected but most are not—or they are highly fragmented—a strong network exists inside the marketing group and inside R&D but not across the two departments. Such networks do not support multiple leadership initiatives well. In fact, extensive informal networks are so important that if they do not exist, creating them has to be the focus of activity early in a major leadership initiative.

Creating a Culture of Leadership

Despite the increasing importance of leadership to business success, the on-the-job experiences of most people actually seem to undermine the development of attributes needed for leadership. Nevertheless, some companies have consistently demonstrated an ability to develop people into outstanding leader-managers. Recruiting people with leadership potential is only the first step. Equally important is managing their career patterns. Individuals who are effective in large leadership roles often share a number of career experiences.

Perhaps the most typical and most important is significant challenge early in a career. Leaders almost always have had opportunities during their twenties and thirties to actually try to lead, to take a risk, and to learn from both triumphs and failures. Such learning seems essential in developing a wide range of leadership skills and perspectives. It also teaches people something about both the difficulty of leadership and its potential for producing change.

Later in their careers, something equally important happens that has to do with broadening. People who provide effective leadership in important jobs always have a chance, before they get into those jobs, to grow beyond the narrow base that characterizes most managerial careers. This is usually the result of lateral career moves or of early promotions to unusually broad job assignments. Sometimes other vehicles help, like special task-force assignments or a lengthy general management course. Whatever the case, the breadth of knowledge developed in this way seems to be helpful in all aspects of leadership. So does the network of relationships that is often acquired both inside and outside the company. When enough people get opportunities like this, the relationships that are built also help create the strong informal networks needed to support multiple leadership initiatives.

Corporations that do a better-than-average job of developing leaders put an emphasis on creating challenging opportunities for relatively young employees. In many businesses, decentralization is the key. By definition, it pushes responsibility lower in an organization and in the process creates more challenging jobs at lower levels. Johnson & Johnson, 3M, Hewlett-Packard, General Electric, and many other well-known companies have used that approach quite successfully. Some of those same companies also create as many small units as possible so there are a lot of challenging lower level general management jobs available.

Sometimes these businesses develop additional challenging opportunities by stressing growth through new products or services. Over the years, 3M has had a policy that at least 25% of its revenue should come from products introduced within the last five years. That encourages small new ventures, which in turn offer hundreds of opportunities to test and stretch young people with leadership potential.

Such practices can, almost by themselves, prepare people for small- and medium-sized leadership jobs. But developing people for important leadership positions requires more work on the part of senior executives, often over a long period of time. That work begins with efforts to spot people with great leadership potential early in their careers and to identify what will be needed to stretch and develop them.

Again, there is nothing magic about this process. The methods successful companies use are surprisingly straightforward. They go out of their way to make young employees and people at lower levels in their organizations visible to senior management. Senior managers then judge for themselves who has potential and what the development needs of those people are. Executives also discuss their tentative conclusions among themselves to draw more accurate judgments.

Armed with a clear sense of who has considerable leadership potential and what skills they need to develop, executives in these companies then spend time planning for that development. Sometimes that is done as part of a formal succession planning or high-potential development process; often it is more informal. In either case, the key ingredient appears to be an intelligent assessment of what feasible development opportunities fit each candidate's needs.

To encourage managers to participate in these activities, well-led businesses tend to recognize and reward people who successfully develop leaders. This is rarely done as part of a formal compensation or bonus formula, simply because it is so difficult to measure such achievements with precision. But it does become a factor in decisions about promotion, especially to the most senior levels, and that seems to make a big difference. When told that future promotions will depend to some degree on their ability to nurture leaders, even people who say that leadership cannot be developed somehow find ways to do it.

Such strategies help create a corporate culture where people value strong leadership and strive to create it. Just as we need more people to provide leadership in the complex organizations that dominate our world today, we also need more people to develop the cultures that will create that leadership. Institutionalizing a leadership-centered culture is the ultimate act of leadership.

PART V

THE LEADER

Leadership is a complex phenomenon, involving the constant interaction of three essential elements: the leader, the followers, and the surrounding situation or context. An effective leader must know something about each, and how they interact.

Perhaps the most obvious component of any leadership scenario is the leader himself or herself. Philosophers, scholars, politicians, and executives have all wondered what separates leaders from other people. One of the most enduring explanations has been the listing of what "traits" are associated with effective leaders. Until the middle 1940s many argued that leaders have special traits which distinguish them from others. Ralph Stogdill (selection 23) challenged any simplistic application of such notions, arguing that the traits of an effective leader can only be assessed in conjunction with other factors, such as the nature of the followers and the characteristics of the situation. In the aftermath of Stogdill's article, "trait theory" went into decline. However, there has been a recent resurgence of the idea that successful leaders have particular traits. Shelley A. Kirkpatrick and Edwin A. Locke revisit the issue and come up with their own list. Others who reflect on leadership credit a leader's success less to traits and more to his or her behavior. Paul Hersey and Kenneth Blanchard provide a clear and concise summary of some of the early studies of "relationship-centered" versus "task-oriented" leader behavior.

An inescapable question which presents itself when one thinks about leaders is whether one's gender affects his or her approach to leadership. This issue has generated a considerable amount of controversy; two selections presented here frame the debate. In a controversial Harvard Business Review *article, Judy Rosener suggests that "women do lead differently." In the accompanying piece, Virginia Schein poses precisely the same question, but comes to a different conclusion. These two readings are joined by a third, in which Ann Morrison and Mary Ann Von Glinow review the current thinking with respect to the "glass ceiling" which limits the advancement of both women and minorities into leadership positions.*

23

Personal Factors Associated with Leadership

Ralph M. Stogdill

Ralph M. Stogdill was professor emeritus of management science at Ohio State University, where he had served as associate director of the Ohio State Leadership Studies. He authored many books and articles, the most important of which was *Stogdill's Handbook of Leadership*.

Smith and Krueger[1] have surveyed the literature on leadership to 1933. Recent developments in leadership methodology, as related especially to military situations, were reviewed in 1947 by Jenkins.[2] The present survey is concerned only with those studies in which some attempt has been made to determine the traits and characteristics of leaders. In many of the studies surveyed, leadership was not defined. In others the methods used in the investigation appeared to have little relationship to the problem as stated. An attempt has been made to include all studies bearing on the problem of traits and personal factors associated with leadership. In all except four cases, the original book or article has been read and abstracted in detail. The data from one American and three German publications have been derived from competent abstracts.

From *The Journal of Psychology* 25 (1948): 35–71. Reprinted with permission of the Helen Dwight Reid Educational Foundation. Published by Heldref Publications, 1319 Eighteenth St., N.W., Washington, D.C., 20036-1802. Copyright 1948.

The present survey lists only those factors which were studied by three or more investigators. Evidence reported by fewer investigators has not been regarded as providing a satisfactory basis for evaluation. It is realized that the number of investigations in which a factor was studied is not necessarily indicative of the importance of the factor. However, the frequency with which a factor was found to be significant appears to be the most satisfactory single criterion for evaluating the data accumulated in this survey, but other criteria, such as the competency of the experimental methods employed and the adequacy of the statistical treatment of data, have also been regarded in evaluating the results of a particular study.

In analyzing data obtained from various groups and by various methods, the question arises as to the extent to which results may be influenced by differences in social composition of the groups, differences in methodology, and differences in leadership criteria. There is no assurance, for example, that the investigator who analyzes the biographies of great men is studying the same kind of leadership behavior that is revealed through observation of children's leadership activities in group situations. It is of interest, however, that some of the studies employing the two different methods yield remarkably similar results. On the other hand, there are some factors that appear only in certain age and social groups or only when certain methods are employed. . . .

Summary

1. The following conclusions are supported by uniformly positive evidence from 15 or more of the studies surveyed:
   a. The average person who occupies a position of leadership exceeds the average member of his group in the following respects: (1) intelligence, (2) scholarship, (3) dependability in exercising responsibilities, (4) activity and social participation, and (5) socio-economic status.
   b. The qualities, characteristics, and skills required in a leader are determined to a large extent by the demands of the situation in which he is to function as a leader.
2. The following conclusions are supported by uniformly positive evidence from 10 or more of the studies surveyed:
   a. The average person who occupies a position of leadership exceeds the average member of his group to some degree in the following respects: (1) sociability, (2) initiative, (3) persistence, (4) knowing

how to get things done, (5) self-confidence, (6) alertness to, and insight into, situations, (7) coöperativeness, (8) popularity, (9) adaptability, and (10) verbal facility.

3. In addition to the above, a number of factors have been found which are specific to well-defined groups. For example, athletic ability and physical prowess have been found to be characteristics of leaders in boys' gangs and play groups. Intellectual fortitude and integrity are traits found to be associated with eminent leadership in maturity.

4. The items with the highest overall correlation with leadership are originality, popularity, sociability, judgment, aggressiveness, desire to excel, humor, coöperativeness, liveliness, and athletic ability, in approximate order of magnitude of average correlation coefficient.

5. In spite of considerable negative evidence, the general trend of results suggests a low positive correlation between leadership and such variables as chronological age, height, weight, physique, energy, appearance, dominance, and mood control. The evidence is about evenly divided concerning the relation to leadership of such traits as introversion-extroversion, self sufficiency, and emotional control.

6. The evidence available suggests that leadership exhibited in various school situations may persist into college and into later vocational and community life. However, knowledge of the facts relating to the transferability of leadership is very meager and obscure.

7. The most fruitful studies, from the point of view of understanding leadership, have been those in which leadership behavior was described and analyzed on the basis of direct observation or analysis of biographical and case history data.

Discussion

The factors which have been found to be associated with leadership could probably all be classified under the general headings of *capacity, achievement, responsibility, participation*, and *status*:

1. *Capacity* (intelligence, alertness, verbal facility, originality, judgment).
2. *Achievement* (scholarship, knowledge, athletic accomplishments).
3. *Responsibility* (dependability, initiative, persistence, aggressiveness, self-confidence, desire to excel).
4. *Participation* (activity, sociability, coöperation, adaptability, humor).
5. *Status* (socio-economic position, popularity).

These findings are not surprising. It is primarily by virtue of participating in group activities and demonstrating his capacity for expediting the work of the group that a person becomes endowed with leadership status. A number of investigators have been careful to distinguish between the leader and the figure-head, and to point out that leadership is always associated with the attainment of group objectives. Leadership implies activity, movement, getting work done. The leader is a person who occupies a position of responsibility in coördinating the activities of the members of the group in their task of attaining a common goal. This leads to consideration of another significant factor.

6. *Situation* (mental level, status, skills, needs and interests of followers, objectives to be achieved, etc.).

A person does not become a leader by virtue of the possession of some combination of traits, but the pattern of personal characteristics of the leader must bear some relevant relationship to the characteristics, activities, and goals of the followers. Thus, leadership must be conceived in terms of the interaction of variables which are in constant flux and change. The factor of change is especially characteristic of the situation, which may be radically altered by the addition or loss of members, changes in interpersonal relationships, changes in goals, competition of extra-group influences, and the like. The personal characteristics of leader and of the followers are, in comparison, highly stable. The persistence of individual patterns of human behavior in the face of constant situational change appears to be a primary obstacle encountered not only in the practice of leadership, but in the selection and placement of leaders. It is not especially difficult to find persons who are leaders. It is quite another matter to place these persons in different situations where they will be able to function as leaders. It becomes clear that an adequate analysis of leadership involves not only a study of leaders, but also of situations.

The evidence suggests that leadership is a relation that exists between persons in a social situation and that persons who are leaders in one situation may not necessarily be leaders in other situations. Must it then be assumed that leadership is entirely incidental, haphazard, and unpredictable? Not at all. The very studies which provide the strongest arguments for the situational nature of leadership also supply the strongest evidence indicating that leadership patterns as well as nonleadership patterns of behavior are persistent and relatively stable. Jennings[3] observes that "the individual's choice behavior, in contrast to his social expansiveness, appears as an expression of needs which are, so to speak, so 'central' to his personality that he must strive to fulfill them whether or not the possibility of fulfilling them is at hand." A somewhat similar observation is made by Newstetter, Feldstein, and Newcomb,[4] who report that:

> Being accepted or rejected is not determined by the cordiality or antagonism of the individual's treatment of his fellows, nor evidently is the individual's treatment of his fellows much affected by the degree to which he is already being accepted or rejected by them. Their treatment of him is related to their acceptance or rejection of him. Their treatment of him is, of course, a reaction to some or all of his behaviors, but we have been completely unsuccessful in attempting to measure what these behaviors are.

The authors conclude that these findings provide "devastating evidence" against the concept of the operation of measurable traits in determining social interactions. The findings of Newstetter and his associates do not appear to provide direct evidence either for or against a theory of traits, but they do indicate that the complex of factors that determines an individual's status in a group is most difficult to isolate and evaluate.

The findings of Jennings and Newstetter suggest that the problem of selecting leaders should be much less difficult than that of training nonleaders to become leaders. The clinician or group worker who has observed the fruitless efforts of socially isolated individuals to gain group acceptance or leadership status is aware of the real nature of the phenomena described by Jennings and Newstetter. Some individuals are isolates in almost any group in which they find themselves, while others are readily accepted in most of their social contacts.

A most pertinent observation on this point is made by Ackerson,[5] who reports that "the correlation for 'leaders' and 'follower' are not of opposite sign and similar magnitude as would be expected of traits supposed to be antithetical." These may not be the opposite poles of a single underlying trait. "It may be that the true antithesis of 'leader' is not 'follower,' but 'indifference,' i.e., the incapacity or unwillingness either to lead or to follow. Thus it may be that some individuals who under one situation are leaders may under other conditions take the role of follower, while the true 'opposite' is represented by the child who neither leads nor follows."

The findings suggest that leadership is not a matter of passive status, or of the mere possession of some combination of traits. It appears rather to be a working relationship among members of a group, in which the leader acquires status through active participation and demonstration of his capacity for carrying coöperative tasks through to completion. Significant aspects of this capacity for organizing and expediting coöperative effort appear to be intelligence, alertness to the needs and motives of others, and insight into situations, further reinforced by such habits as responsibility, initiative, persistence, and self-confidence. The studies surveyed offer little information as to the basic nature of these personal qualifications. Cattell's[6] studies suggest that they may be founded to some degree on basic intelligence, but Cattell and others also suggest that they are socially conditioned to a high degree. Problems which appear to be in need of thorough investigation are those relating to factors which condition social participation, insight into situations, mood control, responsibility, and transferability of leadership from one situation to another. Answers to these questions seem basic not only to any adequate understanding of the personal qualifications of leaders, but also to any effective training for leadership.

24

Leadership: Do Traits Matter?

Shelley A. Kirkpatrick and Edwin A. Locke

Shelley A. Kirkpatrick received her Ph.D. in organizational behavior from the University of Maryland and has taught at Carnegie Mellon University and American University. She co-authored (with Edwin A. Locke, among others) the book *The Essence of Leadership.* Currently she is associated with Pelavin Research Institute. Edwin Locke is chairman of the Department of Management and Organizations at the University of Maryland's College of Business and Management. He has written over 140 books, chapters, and articles including (with Gary P. Latham) *A Theory of Goal Setting and Task Performance.*

Few issues have a more controversial history than leadership traits and characteristics. In the 19th and early 20th centuries, "great man" leadership theories were highly popular. These theories asserted that leadership qualities were inherited, especially by people from the upper class. Great men were born not made (in those days, virtually all business leaders were men). Today, great man theories are a popular foil for so-called superior models. To make the new models plausible, the "great men" are endowed with negative as well as positive traits. In a recent issue of the *Harvard Business Review*, for example, Slater and Bennis write,

Edited and reprinted from *Academy of Management Executive* 5 (1991): 48–60. By permission.

The passing years have . . . given the coup de grace to another force that has re-tarded democratization—the 'great man' who with brilliance and farsightedness could preside with dictatorial powers as the head of a growing organization.

Such great men, argue Slater and Bennis, become "outmoded" and dead hands on "the flexibility and growth of the organization." Under the new dem-ocratic model, they argue, "the individual *is* of relatively little significance."[1]

Early in the 20th century, the great man theories evolved into trait theo-ries. ("Trait" is used broadly here to refer to people's general characteristics, including capacities, motives, or patterns of behavior.) Trait theories did not make assumptions about whether leadership traits were inherited or ac-quired. They simply asserted that leaders' characteristics are different from non-leaders. Traits such as height, weight, and physique are heavily depen-dent on heredity, whereas others such as knowledge of the industry are de-pendent on experience and learning.

The trait view was brought into question during the mid-century when a prominent theorist, Ralph Stogdill, after a thorough review of the literature concluded that "A person does not become a leader by virtue of the posses-sion of some combination of traits."[2] Stogdill believed this because the re-search showed that no traits were universally associated with effective leadership and that situational factors were also influential. For example, mil-itary leaders do not have traits identical to those of business leaders.

Since Stogdill's early review, trait theory has made a comeback, though in altered form. Recent research, using a variety of methods, has made it clear that successful leaders are not like other people. The evidence indicates that there are certain core traits which significantly contribute to business leaders' success.

Traits alone, however, are not sufficient for successful business leader-ship—they are only a precondition. Leaders who possess the requisite traits must take certain actions to be successful (e.g. formulating a vision, role modeling, setting goals). Possessing the appropriate traits only makes it more likely that such actions will be taken and be successful. After summarizing the core leadership traits, we will discuss these important actions and the managerial implications.

The Evidence: Traits Do Matter

The evidence shows that traits do matter. Six traits on which leaders differ from non-leaders include: drive, the desire to lead, honesty/integrity, self-confidence, cognitive ability, and knowledge of the business.[3] These traits are shown in Figure 1.

Drive

The first trait is labeled "drive" which is not to be confused with physical need deprivation. We use the term to refer to a constellation of traits and motives reflecting a high effort level. Five aspects of drive include achievement motivation, ambition, energy, tenacity, and initiative.

Achievement. Leaders have a relatively high desire for achievement. The need for achievement is an important motive among effective leaders and even more important among successful entrepreneurs. High achievers obtain satisfaction from successfully completing challenging tasks, attaining standards of excellence, and developing better ways of doing things. To work their way up to the top of the organization, leaders must have a desire to complete challenging assignments and projects. This also allows the leader to gain technical expertise, both through education and work experience, and to initiate and follow through with organizational changes. . . .

Ambition. Leaders are very ambitious about their work and careers and have a desire to get ahead. To advance, leaders actively take steps to demonstrate their drive and determination. Ambition impels leaders to set hard, challenging goals for themselves and their organizations. Walt Disney, founder of Walt Disney Productions, had a "dogged determination to succeed" and C.E. Woolman of Delta Air Lines had "inexhaustible ambition."

Effective leaders are more ambitious than nonleaders. In their 20-year study, psychologists Ann Howard and Douglas Bray found that among a sample of managers at AT&T, ambition, specifically the desire for advancement, was the strongest predictor of success twenty years later. . . .

FIGURE 1
Leadership Traits

> Drive: Achievement, ambition, energy, tenacity, initiative
> Leadership Motivation (personalized vs. socialized)
> Honesty and Integrity
> Self-confidence (including emotional stability)
> Cognitive Ability
> Knowledge of the Business
> Other Traits (weaker support): charisma, creativity/originality, flexibility

Energy. To sustain a high achievement drive and get ahead, leaders must have a lot of energy. Working long, intense work weeks (and many weekends) for many years, requires an individual to have physical, mental, and emotional vitality. Leaders are more likely than nonleaders to have a high level of energy and stamina and to be generally active, lively, and often restless. Leaders have been characterized as "electric, vigorous, active, full of life" as well as possessing the "physical vitality to maintain a steadily productive work pace." . . .[4] The need for energy is even greater today than in the past, because more companies are expecting all employees, including executives, to spend more time on the road visiting the organization's other locations, customers, and suppliers.

Tenacity. Leaders are better at overcoming obstacles than nonleaders. They have the "capacity to work with distant objects in view" and have a "degree of strength of will or perseverance."[5] Leaders must be tirelessly persistent in their activities and follow through with their programs. Most organizational change programs take several months to establish and can take many years before the benefits are seen. Leaders must have the drive to stick with these programs, and persistence is needed to ensure that changes are institutionalized. . . . It is not just the direction of action that counts, but sticking to the direction chosen. Effective leaders must keep pushing themselves and others toward the goal. . . .

Persistence, of course, must be used intelligently. Dogged pursuit of an inappropriate strategy can ruin an organization. It is important to persist in the right things. But what are the right things? In today's business climate, they may include the following: satisfying the customer, growth, cost control, innovation, fast response time, and quality. Or, in Tom Peters' terms, a constant striving to improve just about everything.

Initiative. Effective leaders are proactive. They make choices and take action that leads to change instead of just reacting to events or waiting for things to happen; that is, they show a high level of initiative. . . .

Instead of sitting "idly by or [waiting] for fate to smile upon them," leaders need to "challenge the process."

Leaders are achievement-oriented, ambitious, energetic, tenacious, and proactive. These same qualities, however, may result in a manager who tries to accomplish everything alone, thereby failing to develop subordinate commitment and responsibility. Effective leaders must not only be full of drive and ambition, they must *want to lead others*.

Leadership Motivation

Studies show that leaders have a strong desire to lead. Leadership motivation involves the desire to influence and lead others and is often equated with the need for power. People with high leadership motivation think a lot about influencing other people, winning an argument, or being the greater authority. They prefer to be in a leadership rather than subordinate role. The willingness to assume responsibility, which seems to coincide with leadership motivation, is frequently found in leaders.

Sears psychologist Jon Bentz describes successful Sears executives as those who have a "powerful competitive drive for a position of . . . authority . . . [and] the need to be recognized as men of influence." . . .[6]

Psychologist Warren Bennis and colleague Burt Nanus state that power is a leader's currency, or the primary means through which the leader gets things done in the organization. A leader must want to gain the power to exercise influence over others. Also, power is an "expandable pie," not a fixed sum; effective leaders give power to others as a means of increasing their own power. Effective leaders do not see power as something that is competed for but rather as something that can be created and distributed to followers without detracting from their own power. . . .

Successful leaders must be willing to exercise power over subordinates, tell them what to do and make appropriate use of positive and negative sanctions. Previous studies have shown inconsistent results regarding dominance as a leadership trait. According to Harvard psychologist David McClelland, this may be because there are two different types of dominance: a personalized power motive or power lust, and a socialized power motive, or the desire to lead.[7]

Personalized Power Motive. Although a need for power is desirable, the leader's effectiveness depends on what is behind it. A leader with a personalized power motive seeks power as an end in itself. These individuals have little self-control, are often impulsive, and focus on collecting symbols of personal prestige. Acquiring power solely for the sake of dominating others may be based on profound self-doubt. The personalized power motive is concerned with domination of others and leads to dependent, submissive followers.

Socialized Power Motive. In contrast, a leader with a socialized power motive uses power as a means to achieve desired goals, or a vision. Its use is expressed as the ability to develop networks and coalitions, gain cooperation from others, resolve conflicts in a constructive manner, and use role modeling to influence others.

Individuals with a socialized power motive are more emotionally mature than those with a personalized power motive. They exercise power more for the benefit of the whole organization and are less likely to use it for manipulation. These leaders are also less defensive, more willing to take advice from experts, and have a longer-range view. They use their power to build up their organization and make it successful. The socialized power motive takes account of followers' needs and results in empowered, independent followers.

Honesty and Integrity

Honesty and integrity are virtues in all individuals, but have special significance for leaders. Without these qualities, leadership is undermined. Integrity is the correspondence between word and deed and honesty refers to being truthful or non-deceitful. The two form the foundation of a trusting relationship between leader and followers.

In his comprehensive review of leadership, psychologist Bernard Bass found that student leaders were rated as more trustworthy and reliable in carrying out responsibilities than followers. Similarly, British organizational psychologists Charles Cox and Cary Cooper's "high flying" (successful) managers preferred to have an open style of management, where they truthfully informed workers about happenings in the company. Morgan McCall and Michael Lombardo of the Center for Creative Leadership found that managers who reached the top were more likely to follow the following formula: "I will do exactly what I say I will do when I say I will do it. If I change my mind, I will tell you well in advance so you will not be harmed by my actions."[8]

Successful leaders are open with their followers, but also discreet and do not violate confidences or carelessly divulge potentially harmful information. One subordinate in a study by Harvard's John Gabarro made the following remark about his new president: "He was so consistent in what he said and did, it was easy to trust him." Another subordinate remarked about an unsuccessful leader, "How can I rely on him if I can't count on him consistently?"[9]

Professors James Kouzes, Barry Posner, and W.H. Schmidt asked 1500 managers "What values do you look for and admire in your superiors?" Integrity (being truthful and trustworthy, and having character and conviction) was the most frequently mentioned characteristic. Kouzes and Posner conclude:

"Honesty is absolutely essential to leadership. After all, if we are willing to follow someone whether it be into battle or into the boardroom, we first want to assure ourselves that the person is worthy of our trust. We want to know that he or she is being truthful, ethical, and principled. We want to be fully confident in the integrity of our leaders."

Effective leaders are credible, with excellent reputations, and high levels of integrity. The following description (from Gabarro's study) by one subordinate of his boss exemplifies the concept of integrity: "By integrity, I don't mean whether he'll rob a bank, or steal from the till. You don't work with people like that. It's whether you sense a person has some basic principles and is willing to stand by them."

Bennis and Nanus warn that today credibility is at a premium, especially since people are better informed, more cautious, and wary of authority and power. Leaders can gain trust by being predictable, consistent, and persistent and by making competent decisions. An honest leader may even be able to overcome lack of expertise, as a subordinate in Gabarro's study illustrates in the following description of his superior: "I don't like a lot of the things he does, but he's basically honest. He's a genuine article and you'll forgive a lot of things because of that. That goes a long way in how much I trust him."

Self-Confidence

There are many reasons why a leader needs self-confidence. Being a leader is a very difficult job. A great deal of information must be gathered and processed. A constant series of problems must be solved and decisions made. Followers have to be convinced to pursue specific courses of action. Setbacks have to be overcome. Competing interests have to be satisfied. Risks have to be taken in the face of uncertainty. A person riddled with self-doubt would never be able to take the necessary actions nor command the respect of others.

Self-confidence plays an important role in decision-making and in gaining others' trust. Obviously, if the leader is not sure of what decision to make, or expresses a high degree of doubt, then the followers are less likely to trust the leader and be committed to the vision.

Not only is the leader's self-confidence important, but so is others' perception of him. Often, leaders engage in impression management to bolster their image of competence; by projecting self-confidence they arouse followers' self-confidence. Self-confident leaders are also more likely to be assertive and decisive, which gains others' confidence in the decision. This is crucial for effective implementation of the decision. Even when the decision turns out to be a poor one, the self-confident leader admits the mistake and uses it as a learning opportunity, often building trust in the process. . . .

Emotional Stability. Self confidence helps effective leaders remain even-tempered. They do get excited, such as when delivering an emotionally-charged pep talk, but generally do not become angry or enraged. . . .

Emotional stability is especially important when resolving interpersonal conflicts and when representing the organization. A top executive who impulsively flies off the handle will not foster as much trust and teamwork as an executive who retains emotional control. . . .

Researchers at the Center for Creative Leadership found that leaders are more likely to "derail" if they lack emotional stability and composure. Leaders who derail are less able to handle pressure and more prone to moodiness, angry outbursts, and inconsistent behavior, which undermines their interpersonal relationships with subordinates, peers, and superiors. In contrast, they found the successful leaders to be calm, confident, and predictable during crisis.

Psychologically hardy, self-confident individuals consider stressful events interesting, as opportunities for development, and believe that they can influence the outcome. K. Labich in *Fortune* magazine argued that "By demonstrating grace under pressure, the best leaders inspire those around them to stay calm and act intelligently."

Cognitive Ability

Leaders must gather, integrate, and interpret enormous amounts of information. These demands are greater than ever today because of rapid technological change. Thus, it is not surprising that leaders need to be intelligent enough to formulate suitable strategies, solve problems, and make correct decisions.

Leaders have often been characterized as being intelligent, but not necessarily brilliant and as being conceptually skilled. Kotter states that a "keen mind" (i.e., strong analytical ability, good judgement, and the capacity to think strategically and multidimensionally) is necessary for effective leadership, and that leadership effectiveness requires "above average intelligence," rather than genius.

An individual's intelligence and the perception of his or her intelligence are two highly related factors. Professors Lord, DeVader, and Alliger concluded that intelligence is a key characteristic in predicting leadership perceptions."[10] Howard and Bray found that cognitive ability predicted managerial success twenty years later in their AT&T study. Effective managers have been shown to display greater ability to reason both inductively and deductively than ineffective managers.

Intelligence may be a trait that followers look for in a leader. If someone is going to lead, followers want that person to be more capable in *some* respects than they are. Therefore, the follower's perception of cognitive ability in a leader is a source of authority in the leadership relationship.

Knowledge of the Business

Effective leaders have a high degree of knowledge about the company, industry, and technical matters. For example, Jack Welch, president of GE, has a PhD in engineering; Geroge Hatsopolous of Thermo Electron Corporation, in the years preceding the OPEC boycott, had both the business knowledge of the impending need for energy-efficient appliances and the technical knowledge of thermodynamics to create more efficient gas furnaces. Technical expertise enables the leader to understand the concerns of subordinates regarding technical issues. Harvard Professor John Kotter argues that expertise is more important than formal education.

Effective leaders gather extensive information about the company and the industry. Most of the successful general managers studied by Harvard's Kotter spent their careers in the same industry, while less successful managers lacked industry-specific experiences. Although cognitive ability is needed to gain a through understanding of the business, formal education is not a requirement. Only forty percent of the business leaders studied by Bennis and Nanus had business degrees. In-depth knowledge of the organization and industry allows effective leaders to make well-informed decisions and to understand the implications of those decisions.

Other Traits

Charisma, creativity/originality, and flexibility are three traits with less clear-cut evidence of their importance to leadership.[11] Effective leaders may have charisma; however, this trait may only be important for political leaders. Effective leaders also may be more creative than nonleaders, but there is no consistent research demonstrating this. Flexibility or adaptiveness may be important traits for a leader in today's turbulent environment. Leaders must be able to make decisions and solve problems quickly and initiate and foster change.

There may be other important traits needed for effective leadership; however, we believe that the first six that we discussed are the core traits.

The Rest of the Story

A complete theory of leadership involves more than specifying leader traits. Traits only endow people with the potential for leadership. . . .

It is clear that leadership is a very demanding activity and that leaders who have the requisite traits—drive, desire to lead, self-confidence, honesty (and integrity), cognitive ability, and industry knowledge—have a considerable advantage over those who lack these traits. Without drive, for example, it is unlikely that an individual would be able to gain the expertise required to lead an organization effectively, let alone implement and work toward long-term goals. Without the desire to lead, individuals are not motivated to persuade others to work toward a common goal; such an individual would avoid or be indifferent to leadership tasks. Self-confidence is needed to withstand setbacks, persevere through hard times, and lead others in new directions. Confidence gives effective leaders the ability to make hard decisions and to stand by them. A leader's honesty and integrity form the foundation on which the leader gains followers' trust and confidence; without honesty and integrity, the leader would not be able to attract and retain followers. At least a moderate degree of cognitive ability is needed to gain and understand technical issues as well as the nature of the industry. Cognitive ability permits leaders to accurately analyze situations and make effective decisions. Finally, knowledge of the business is needed to develop suitable strategic visions and business plans.

Management Implications

Individuals can be *selected* either from outside the organization or from within non- or lower-managerial ranks based on their possession of traits that are less changeable or trainable. Cognitive ability (not to be confused with knowledge) is probably the least trainable of the six traits. Drive is fairly constant over time although it can change; it is observable in employees assuming they are given enough autonomy and responsibility to show what they can do. The desire to lead is more difficult to judge in new hires who may have had little opportunity for leadership early in life. It can be observed at lower levels of management and by observing people in assessment center exercises.

Two other traits can be developed through experience and *training*. Knowledge of the industry and technical knowledge come from formal training, job experience and a mentally active approach toward new opportunities for learning. Planned job rotation can facilitate such growth. Self-confidence is both general and task specific. People differ in their general confidence in mastering life's challenges but task-specific self-confidence comes from mastering the various skills that leadership requires as well as the technical and strategic challenges of the industry. Such confidence parallels the individual's growth in knowledge.

Honesty does not require skill building; it is a virtue one achieves or rejects by choice. Organizations should look with extreme skepticism at any employee who behaves dishonestly or lacks integrity, and should certainly not reward dishonesty in any form, especially not with a promotion. The key role models for honest behavior are those at the top. On this issue, organizations get what they model, not what they preach.

Conclusions

Regardless of whether leaders are born or made or some combination of both, it is unequivocally clear that *leaders are not like other people*. Leaders do not have to be great men or women by being intellectual geniuses or omniscient prophets to succeed but they do need to have the "right stuff" and this stuff is not equally present in all people. Leadership is a demanding, unrelenting job with enormous pressures and grave responsibilities. It would be a profound disservice to leaders to suggest that they are ordinary people who happened to be in the right place at the right time. Maybe the place matters, but it takes a special kind of person to master the challenges of opportunity. Let us not only give credit, but also use the knowledge we have to select and train our future leaders effectively. We believe that in the realm of leadership (and in every other realm), the individual *does* matter.

25

Behavioral Theories of Leadership

Paul Hersey and Kenneth H. Blanchard

Paul Hersey and Kenneth Blanchard have been at the forefront of leadership studies for a number of years, developing and refining the theory of Situational Leadership. Paul Hersey now heads the Center for Leadership Studies. Kenneth Blanchard has co-authored the internationally known *The One Minute Manager* and related books. He currently teaches at the School of Hotel Administration at Cornell University.

The recognition of task and relationships as two important dimensions of leader behavior has pervaded the works of management theorists[1] over the years. These two dimensions have been variously labeled as "autocratic" and "democratic;" "authoritarian" and "equalitarian;" "employee-oriented" and "production-oriented;" "goal achievement" and "group maintenance;" "task-ability" and "likeability;" "instrumental and expressive;" "efficiency and effectiveness." The difference between these concepts and task and relationships seems to be more semantic than real.

For some time, it was believed that task and relationships were either/or styles of leader behavior and, therefore, should be depicted as a single dimension along a continuum, moving from very authoritarian (task) leader behav-

Excerpted from Paul Hersey and Kenneth H. Blanchard, "Life Cycle Theory of Leadership," in *Training and Development Journal* (June, 1979): 94–100. Reprinted by permission.

ior at one end to very democratic (relationships) leader behavior at the other.[2]

In more recent years, the feeling that task and relationships were either/or leadership styles has been dispelled. In particular, the leadership studies initiated in 1945 by the Bureau of Business Research at Ohio State University[3] questioned whether leader behavior could be depicted on a single continuum.

In attempting to describe *how* a leader carries out his activities, the Ohio State staff identified "Initiating Structure" (task) and "Consideration" (relationships) as the two most important dimensions of leadership. "Initiating Structure" refers to "the leader's behavior in delineating the relationship between himself and members of the work-group and in endeavoring to establish well-defined patterns of organization, channels of communication, and methods of procedure." On the other hand, "Consideration" refers to "behavior indicative of friendship, mutual trust, respect, and warmth in the relationship between the leader and the members of his staff."[4]

In the leadership studies that followed, the Ohio State staff found that leadership styles vary considerably from leader to leader. The behavior of some leaders is characterized by rigidly structuring activities of followers in terms of *task* accomplishments, while others concentrate on building and maintaining good personal *relationships* between themselves and their followers.

Other leaders have styles characterized by both task and relationships behavior. There are even some individuals in leadership positions whose behavior tends to provide little structure or development of interpersonal relationships. No dominant style appears. Instead, various combinations are evident. Thus, task and relationships are not either/or leadership styles as an authoritarian-democratic continuum suggests. Instead, these patterns of leader behavior are separate and distinct dimensions which can be plotted on two separate axes, rather than a single continuum.

Thus, the Ohio-State studies resulted in the development of four quadrants to illustrate leadership styles in terms of Initiating Structure (task) and Consideration (relationships) as shown in Figure 1.

Robert R. Blake and Jane S. Mouton[5] in their Managerial Grid (Figure 2) have popularized the task and relationships dimensions of leadership and have used them extensively in organization and management development programs.

In the Managerial Grid, five different types of leadership based on concern for production (task) and concern for people (relationships) are located in the four quadrants identified by the Ohio State studies.

FIGURE 1

The Ohio State Leadership Quadrants

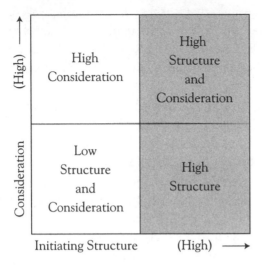

Concern for *production* is illustrated on the horizontal axis. Production becomes more important to the leader as his rating advances on the horizontal scale. A leader with a rating of 9 has a maximum concern for production.

Concern for people is illustrated on the vertical axis. People become more important to the leader as his rating progresses up the vertical axis. A leader with a rating of 9 on the vertical axis has a maximum concern for people.

The Managerial Grid, in essence, has given popular terminology to five points within the four quadrants identified by the Ohio State studies.

Suggesting a "Best" Style of Leadership

After identifying task and relationships as two central dimensions of any leadership situation, some management writers have suggested a "best" style of leadership. Most of these writers have supported either an integrated leader behavior style (high task and high relationships) or a permissive, democratic, human relations approach (high relationships).

Andrew W. Halpin,[6] of the original Ohio State staff, in a study of school superintendents, pointed out that according to his findings "effective or desirable leadership behavior is characterized by high ratings on both Initiating Structure and Consideration. Conversely, ineffective or undesirable leader-

FIGURE 2

The Managerial Grid Leadership Styles

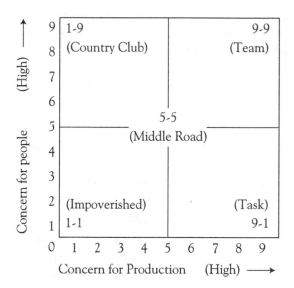

ship behavior is marked by low ratings on both dimensions." Thus, Halpin seemed to conclude that the high Consideration and high Initiating Structure style is theoretically the ideal or "best" leader behavior, while the style low on both dimensions is theoretically the "worst."

Blake and Mouton in their Managerial Grid also imply that the most desirable leadership style is "team management" (maximum concern for production and people) and the least desirable is "impoverished management" (minimum concern for production and people). In fact, they have developed training programs designed to change the behavior of managers toward this "team" style.[7]

Leadership Style Should Vary with the Situation

While the Ohio State and the Managerial Grid people seem to suggest there is a "best" style of leadership,[8] recent evidence from empirical studies clearly shows that there is no single all purpose leadership style which is universally successful.

Some of the most convincing evidence which dispels the idea of a single "best" style of leader behavior was gathered and published by A.K. Korman[9] in 1966. Korman attempted to review all the studies which examined the relationship between the Ohio State behavior dimensions of Initiating Structure (task) and Consideration (relationships) and various measures of effectiveness, including group productivity, salary, performance under stress, administrative reputation, work group grievances, absenteeism, and turnover. Korman reviewed over 25 studies and concluded that:

"Despite the fact that 'Consideration' and 'Initiating Structure' have become almost bywords in American industrial psychology, it seems apparent that very little is now known as to how these variables may predict work group performance and the conditions which affect such predictions. At the current time, we cannot even say whether they have any predictive significance at all."

Thus, Korman found the use of Consideration and Initiating Structure had no significant predictive value in terms of effectiveness as situations changed. *This suggests that since situations differ, so must leader style.*

Fred E. Fiedler,[10] in testing his contingency model of leadership in over 50 studies covering a span of 15 years (1951–1967), concluded that both directive, task-oriented leaders and non-directive, human relations-oriented leaders are successful under some conditions. Fiedler argues:

"While one can never say that something is impossible, and while someone may well discover the all-purpose leadership style or behavior at some future time, our own data and those which have come out of sound research by other investigators do not promise such miraculous cures."

A number of other investigators[11] besides Korman and Fiedler have also shown that different leadership situations require different leader styles.

In summary, empirical studies tend to show that there is no normative (best) style of leadership; that successful leaders are those who can adapt their leader behavior to meet the needs of their followers and the particular situation. Effectiveness is dependent upon the leader, the followers, and other situational elements. In managing for effectiveness a leader must be able to diagnose his own leader behavior in light of his environment. Some of the variables other than his followers which he should examine include the organization, superiors, associates, and job demands. This list is not all inclusive, but contains interacting components which tend to be important to a leader in many different organizational settings.

26

Ways Women Lead

Judy B. Rosener

Judy B. Rosener is a member of the faculty at the Graduate School of Management at the University of California, Irvine. She is co-author of *Workforce America*.

Women managers who have broken the glass ceiling in medium-sized, non-traditional organizations have proven that effective leaders don't come from one mold. They have demonstrated that using the command-and-control style of managing others, a style generally associated with men in large, traditional organizations, is not the only way to succeed.

The first female executives, because they were breaking new ground, adhered to many of the "rules of conduct" that spelled success for men. Now a second wave of women is making its way into top management, not by adopting the style and habits that have proved successful for men but by drawing on the skills and attitudes they developed from their shared experience as women. These second-generation managerial women are drawing on what is unique to their socialization as women and creating a different path to the top. They are seeking and finding opportunities in fast-changing and growing organizations to show that they can achieve results—in a different way. They are succeeding because of—not in spite of—certain characteristics generally considered to be "feminine" and inappropriate in leaders.

The women's success shows that a nontraditional leadership style is well suited to the conditions of some work environments and can increase an organization's chances of surviving in an uncertain world. It supports the belief that there is strength in a diversity of leadership styles.

In a recent survey sponsored by the International Women's Forum, I found a number of unexpected similarities between men and women leaders along with some important differences. (For more on the study and its findings, see "The IWF Survey of Men and Women Leaders" on page 152.) Among these similarities are characteristics related to money and children. I found that the men and women respondents earned the same amount of money (and the household income of the women is twice that of the men). This finding is contrary to most studies, which find a considerable wage gap between men and women, even at the executive level. I also found that just as many men as women experience work-family conflict (although when there are children at home, the women experience slightly more conflict than men).

But the similarities end when men and women describe their leadership performance and how they usually influence those with whom they work. The men are more likely than the women to describe themselves in ways that characterize what some management experts call "transactional" leadership.[1] That is, they view job performance as a series of transactions with subordinates—exchanging rewards for services rendered or punishment for inadequate performance. The men are also more likely to use power that comes from their organizational position and formal authority.

The women respondents, on the other hand, described themselves in ways that characterize "transformational" leadership—getting subordinates to transform their own self-interest into the interest of the group through concern for a broader goal. Moreover, they ascribe their power to personal characteristics like charisma, interpersonal skills, hard work, or personal contacts rather than to organizational stature.

Intrigued by these differences, I interviewed some of the women respondents who described themselves as transformational. These discussions gave me a better picture of how these women view themselves as leaders and a greater understanding of the important ways in which their leadership style differs from the traditional command-and-control style. I call their leadership style "interactive leadership" because these women actively work to make their interactions with subordinates positive for everyone involved. More specifically, the women encourage participation, share power and information, enhance other people's self-worth, and get others excited about their work. All these things reflect their belief that allowing employees to contribute and to feel powerful and important is a win-win situation—good for the employees and the organization.

Interactive Leadership

From my discussions with the women interviewees, several patterns emerged. The women leaders made frequent reference to their efforts to encourage participation and share power and information—two things that are often associated with participative management. But their self-description went beyond the usual definitions of participation. Much of what they described were attempts to enhance other people's sense of self-worth and to energize followers. In general, these leaders believe that people perform best when they feel good about themselves and their work, and they try to create situations that contribute to that feeling.

Encourage Participation

Inclusion is at the core of interactive leadership. In describing nearly every aspect of management, the women interviewees made reference to trying to make people feel part of the organization. They try to instill this group identity in a variety of ways, including encouraging others to have a say in almost every aspect of work, from setting performance goals to determining strategy. To facilitate inclusion, they create mechanisms that get people to participate and they use a conversational style that sends signals inviting people to get involved.

One example of the kinds of mechanisms that encourage participation is the "bridge club" that one interviewee, a group executive in charge of mergers and acquisitions at a large East Coast financial firm, created. The club is an informal gathering of people who have information she needs but over whom she has no direct control. The word *bridge* describes the effort to bring together these "members" from different functions. The word *club* captures the relaxed atmosphere.

Despite the fact that attendance at club meetings is voluntary and over and above the usual work demands, the interviewee said that those whose help she needs make the time to come. "They know their contributions are valued, and they appreciate the chance to exchange information across functional boundaries in an informal setting that's fun." She finds participation in the club more effective than memos.

The IWF Survey of Men and Women Leaders

The International Women's Forum was founded in 1982 to give prominent women leaders in diverse professions around the world a way to share their knowledge with each other and with their communities and countries. The organization now has some 37 forums in North America, Europe, Asia, Latin America, and the Middle East. To help other women advance and to educate the public about the contributions women can and are making in government, business, and other fields, the IWF created the Leadership Foundation. The foundation commissioned me to perform the study of men and women leaders on which this article is based. I conducted the study with the help of Daniel McAllister and Gregory Stephens (Ph.D. students at the Graduate School of Management at the University of California, Irvine) in the spring of 1989.

The survey consisted of an eight-page questionnaire sent to all the IWF members. Each respondent was asked to supply the name of a man in a similar organization with similar responsibilities. The men received the same questionnaire as the IWF members. The respondents were similar in age, occupation and educational level, which suggests that the matching effort was successful. The response rate was 31%.

The respondents were asked questions about their leadership styles, their organizations, work-family issues, and personal characteristics. The following are among the more intriguing findings, some of which contradict data reported in academic journals and the popular press:

☐ The women earn the same amount of money as their male counterparts. The average yearly income for men is $136,510; for women it is $140,573. (Most other studies have shown a wage gap between men and women.)

☐ The men's household income (their own and their spouse's) is much lower than that of the women—$166,454 versus $300,892. (Only 39% of the men have full-time employed spouses, as opposed to 71% of the women.)

☐ Both men and women leaders pay their female subordinates roughly $12,000 less than their male subordinates with similar positions and titles.

☐ Women are more likely than men to use transformational leadership–motivating others by transforming their self-interest into the goals of the organization.

☐ Women are much more likely than men to use power based on charisma, work record, and contacts (personal power) as opposed to power based on organizational position, title, and the ability to reward and punish (structural power).

☐ Most men and women describe themselves as having an equal mix of traits that are considered "feminine" (being excitable, gentle, emotional, submissive, sentimental, understanding, compassionate, sensitive, dependent), "masculine" (dominant, aggressive, tough, assertive, autocratic, analytical, competitive, independent), and "gender-neutral" (adaptive, tactful, sincere, conscientious, conventional, reliable, predictable systematic, efficient).

☐ Women who do describe themselves as predominately "feminine" or "gender-neutral" report a higher level of followership among their female subordinates than women who describe themselves as "masculine."

☐ Approximately 67% of the women respondents are married. (Other studies report that only 40% to 50% of women executives are married.)

☐ Both married men and women experience moderate levels of conflict between work and family domains. When there are children at home, women experience only slightly higher levels of conflict than men, even though they shoulder a much greater proportion of the child care–61% of the care versus 25% for the men.

Whether or not the women create special forums for people to interact, they try to make people feel included as a matter of course, often by trying to draw them into the conversation or soliciting their opinions. Frieda Caplan, founder and CEO of Frieda's Finest, a California-based marketer and distributor of unusual fruits and vegetables, described an approach she uses that is typical of the other women interviewed: "When I face a tough decision, I always ask my employees, 'What would you do if you were me?' This approach generates good ideas and introduces my employees to the complexity of management decisions."

Of course, saying that you include others doesn't mean others necessarily feel included. The women acknowledge the possibility that their efforts to draw people in may be seen as symbolic, so they try to avoid that perception by acting on the input they receive. They ask for suggestions before they reach their own conclusions, and they test—and sometimes change—particular decisions before they implement them. These women use participation to clarify their own views by thinking things through out loud and to ensure that they haven't overlooked an important consideration.

The fact that many of the interviewees described their participatory style as coming "naturally" suggests that these leaders do not consciously adopt it for its business value. Yet they realize that encouraging participation has benefits. For one thing, making it easy for people to express their ideas helps ensure that decisions reflect as much information as possible. To some of the women, this point is just common sense. Susan S. Elliott, president and founder of Systems Service Enterprises, a St. Louis computer consulting company, expressed this view: "I can't come up with a plan and then ask those who manage the accounts to give me their reactions. They're the ones who really know the accounts. They have information I don't have. Without their input I'd be operating in an ivory tower."

Participation also increases support for decisions ultimately reached and reduces the risk that ideas will be undermined by unexpected opposition. Claire Rothman, general manager of the Great Western Forum, a large sports and entertainment arena in Los Angeles, spoke about the value of open disagreement: "When I know ahead of time that someone disagrees with a decision, I can work especially closely with that person to try to get his or her support."

Getting people involved also reduces the risk associated with having only one person handle a client, project, or investment. For Patricia M. Cloherty, senior vice president and general partner of Alan Patricof Associates, a New York venture capital firm, including people in decision making and planning gives investments longevity. If something happens to one person, others will be familiar enough with the situation to "adopt" the investment. That way, there are no orphans in the portfolio, and a knowledgeable second opinion is always available.

Like most who are familiar with participatory management, these women are aware that being inclusive also has its disadvantages. Soliciting ideas and information from others takes time, often requires giving up some control, opens the door to criticism, and exposes personal and turf conflicts. In addition, asking for ideas and information can be interpreted as not having answers.

Further, it cannot be assumed that everyone wants to participate. Some people prefer being told what to do. When Mary Jane Rynd was a partner in a Big Eight accounting firm in Arizona (she recently left to start her own company—Rynd, Carneal & Associates), she encountered such a person: "We hired this person from an out-of-state CPA firm because he was experienced and smart—and because it's always fun to hire someone away from another firm. But he was just too cynical to participate. He was suspicious of everybody. I tried everything to get him involved—including him in discussions and giving him pep talks about how we all work together. Nothing worked. He just didn't want to participate."

Like all those who responded to the survey, these women are comfortable using a variety of leadership styles. So when participation doesn't work, they act unilaterally. "I prefer participation," said Elliott, "but there are situations where time is short and I have to take the bull by the horns."

Share Power and Information

Soliciting input from other people suggests a flow of information from employees to the "boss." But part of making people feel included is knowing that open communication flows in two directions. These women say they willingly share power and information rather than guard it and they make apparent their reasoning behind decisions. While many leaders see information as power and power as a limited commodity to be coveted, the interviewees seem to be comfortable letting power and information change hands. As Adrienne Hall, vice chairman of Eisaman, Johns & Laws, a large West Coast advertising firm, said: "I know territories shift, so I'm not preoccupied with turf."

One example of power and information sharing is the open strategy sessions held by Debi Coleman, vice president of information systems and technology at Apple Computer. Rather than closeting a small group of key executives in her office to develop a strategy based on her own agenda, she holds a series of meetings over several days and allows a larger group to develop and help choose alternatives.

The interviewees believe that sharing power and information accomplishes several things. It creates loyalty by signaling to coworkers and subordinates that they are trusted and their ideas respected. It also sets an example for other people and therefore can enhance the general communication flow. And it increases the odds that leaders will hear about problems before they explode. Sharing power and information also gives employees and coworkers the wherewithal to reach conclusions, solve problems, and see the justification for decisions.

On a more pragmatic level, many employees have come to expect their bosses to be open and frank. They no longer accept being dictated to but want to be treated as individuals with minds of their own. As Elliott said, "I work with lots of people who are bright and intelligent, so I have to deal with them at an intellectual level. They're very logical, and they want to know the reasons for things. They'll buy in only if it makes sense."

In some cases, sharing information means simply being candid about work-related issues. In early 1990, when Elliott hired as employees many of the people she had been using as independent contractors, she knew the transition would be difficult for everyone. The number of employees nearly doubled overnight, and the nature of working relationships changed. "I warned everyone that we were in for some rough times and reminded them that we would be experiencing them together. I admitted that it would also be hard for me, and I made it clear that I wanted them to feel free to talk to me. I was completely candid and encouraged them to be honest with me. I lost some employees who didn't like the new relationships, but I'm convinced that being open helped me understand my employees better, and it gave them a feeling of support."

Like encouraging participation, sharing power and information has its risks. It allows for the possibility that people will reject, criticize, or otherwise challenge what the leader has to say or, more broadly, her authority. Also, employees get frustrated when leaders listen to—but ultimately reject—their ideas. Because information is a source of power, leaders who share it can be seen as naive or needing to be liked. The interviewees have experienced some of these downsides but find the positives overwhelming.

Enhance the Self-Worth of Others

One of the by-products of sharing information and encouraging participation is that employees feel important. During the interviews, the women leaders discussed other ways they build a feeling of self-worth in co-workers and sub-ordinates. They talked about giving others credit and praise and sending small signals of recognition. Most important, they expressed how they refrain from asserting their own superiority, which asserts the inferiority of others. All those I interviewed expressed clear aversion to behavior that sets them apart from others in the company—reserved parking places, separate dining facilities, pulling rank.

Examples of sharing and giving credit to others abound. Caplan, who has been the subject of scores of media reports hailing her innovation of labeling vegetables so consumers know what they are and how to cook them, original-ly got the idea from a farmer. She said that whenever someone raises the sub-ject, she credits the farmer and downplays her role. Rothman is among the many note-writers: when someone does something out of the ordinary, she writes them a personal note to tell them she noticed. Like many of the women I interviewed, she said she also makes a point of acknowledging good work by talking about it in front of others.

Bolstering coworkers and subordinates is especially important in business-es and jobs that tend to be hard on a person's ego. Investment banking is one example because of the long hours, high pressures, intense competition, and inevitability that some deals will fail. One interviewee in investment banking hosts dinners for her division, gives out gag gifts as party favors, passes out M&Ms at meetings, and throws parties "to celebrate ourselves." These things, she said, balance the anxiety that permeates the environment.

Rynd compensates for the negativity inherent in preparing tax returns: "In my business we have something called a query sheet, where the person who reviews the tax return writes down everything that needs to be corrected. Criticism is built into the system. But at the end of every review, I always in-clude a positive comment—your work paper technique looked good, I appre-ciate the fact that you got this done on time, or something like that. It seems trivial, but it's one way to remind people that I recognize their good work and not just their shortcomings."

Energize Others

The women leaders spoke of their enthusiasm for work and how they spread their enthusiasm around to make work a challenge that is exhilarating and fun. The women leaders talked about it in those terms and claimed to use their enthusiasm to get others excited. As Rothman said, "There is rarely a person I can't motivate."

Enthusiasm was a dominant theme throughout the interviews. In computer consulting: "Because this business is on the forefront of technology, I'm sort of evangelistic about it, and I want other people to be as excited as I am." In venture capital: "You have to have a head of steam." In executive search: "Getting people excited is an important way to influence those you have no control over." Or in managing sports arenas: "My enthusiasm gets others excited. I infuse them with energy and make them see that even boring jobs contribute to the fun of working in a celebrity business."

Enthusiasm can sometimes be misunderstood. In conservative professions like investment banking, such an upbeat leadership style can be interpreted as cheerleading and can undermine credibility. In many cases, the women said they won and preserved their credibility by achieving results that could be measured easily. One of the women acknowledged that her colleagues don't understand or like her leadership style and have called it cheerleading. "But," she added, "in this business you get credibility from what you produce, and they love the profits I generate." While energy and enthusiasm can inspire some, it doesn't work for everyone. Even Rothman conceded, "Not everyone has a flame that can be lit."

Paths of Least Resistance

Many of the women I interviewed said the behaviors and beliefs that underlie their leadership style come naturally to them. I attribute this to two things: their socialization and the career paths they have chosen. Although socialization patterns and career paths are changing, the average age of the men and women who responded to the survey is 51—old enough to have had experiences that differed *because* of gender.

Until the 1960s, men and women received different signals about what was expected of them. To summarize a subject that many experts have explored in depth, women have been expected to be wives, mothers, community volunteers, teachers, and nurses. In all these roles, they are supposed to be cooperative, supportive, understanding, gentle, and to provide service to others. They are to derive satisfaction and a sense of self-esteem from helping others, including their spouses. While men have had to appear to be competitive, strong, tough, decisive, and in control, women have been allowed to be cooperative, emotional, supportive, and vulnerable. This may explain why women today are more likely than men to be interactive leaders.

Men and women have also had different career opportunities. Women were not expected to have careers, or at least not the same kinds of careers as men, so they either pursued different jobs or were simply denied opportunities men had. Women's career tracks have usually not included long series of organizational positions with formal authority and control of resources. Many women had their first work experiences outside the home as volunteers. While some of the challenges they faced as managers in volunteer organizations are the same as those in any business, in many ways, leading volunteers is different because of the absence of concrete rewards like pay and promotion.

As women entered the business world, they tended to find themselves in positions consistent with the roles they played at home: in staff positions rather than in line positions, supporting the work of others, and in functions like communications or human resources where they had relatively small budgets and few people reporting directly to them.

The fact that most women have lacked formal authority over others and control over resources means that by default they have had to find other ways to accomplish their work. As it turns out, the behaviors that were natural and/or socially acceptable for them have been highly successful in at least some managerial settings.

What came easily to women turned out to be a survival tactic. Although leaders often begin their careers doing what comes naturally and what fits within the constraints of the job, they also develop their skills and styles over time. The women's use of interactive leadership has its roots in socialization, and the women interviewees firmly believe that it benefits their organizations. Through the course of their careers, they have gained conviction that their style is effective. In fact, for some, it was their own success that caused them to formulate their philosophies about what motivates people, how to make good decisions, and what it takes to maximize business performance.

They now have formal authority and control over vast resources, but still they see sharing power and information as an asset rather than a liability. They believe that although pay and promotion are necessary tools of management, what people really want is to feel that they are contributing to a higher purpose and that they have the opportunity as individuals to learn and grow. The women believe that employees and peers perform better when they feel they are part of an organization and can share in its success. Allowing them to get involved and to work to their potential is a way of maximizing their contributions and using human resources most efficiently.

Another Kind of Diversity

The IWF survey shows that a nontraditional leadership style can be effective in organizations that accept it. This lesson comes especially hard to those who think of the corporate world as a game of survival of the fittest, where the fittest is always the strongest, toughest, most decisive, and powerful. Such a workplace seems to favor leaders who control people by controlling resources, and by controlling people, gain control of more resources. Asking for information and sharing decision-making power can be seen as serious disadvantages, but what is a disadvantage under one set of circumstances is an advantage under another. The "best" leadership style depends on the organizational context.

Only one of the women interviewees is in a traditional, large-scale company. More typically, the women's organizations are medium-sized and tend to have experienced fast growth and fast change. They demand performance and/or have a high proportion of professional workers. These organizations seem to create opportunities for women and are hospitable to those who use a nontraditional management style.

The degree of growth or change in an organization is an important factor in creating opportunities for women. When change is rampant, everything is up for grabs, and crises are frequent. Crises are generally not desirable, but they do create opportunities for people to prove themselves. Many of the women interviewees said they got their first break because their organizations were in turmoil.

Fast-changing environments also play havoc with tradition. Coming up through the ranks and being part of an established network is no longer important. What is important is how you perform. Also, managers in such environments are open to new solutions, new structures, and new ways of leading.

The fact that many of the women respondents are in organizations that have clear performance standards suggests that they have gained credibility and legitimacy by achieving results. In investment banking, venture capital, accounting, and executive placement, for instance, individual performance is easy to measure.

A high proportion of young professional workers—increasingly typical of organizations—is also a factor in some women's success. Young, educated professionals impose special requirements on their organizations. They demand to participate and contribute. In some cases, they have knowledge or talents their bosses don't have. If they are good performers, they have many employment options. It is easy to imagine that these professionals will respond to leaders who are inclusive and open, who enhance the self-worth of others, and who create a fun work environment. Interactive leaders are likely to win the cooperation needed to achieve their goals.

Interactive leadership has proved to be effective, perhaps even advantageous, in organizations in which the women I interviewed have succeeded. As the work force increasingly demands participation and the economic environment increasingly requires rapid change, interactive leadership may emerge as the management style of choice for many organizations. For interactive leadership to take root more broadly, however, organizations must be willing to question the notion that the traditional command-and-control leadership style that has brought success in earlier decades is the only way to get results. This may be hard in some organizations, especially those with long histories of male-oriented, command-and-control leadership. Changing these organizations will not be easy. The fact that women are more likely than men to be interactive leaders raises the risk that these companies will perceive interactive leadership as "feminine" and automatically resist it.

Linking interactive leadership directly to being female is a mistake. We know that women are capable of making their way through corporations by adhering to the traditional corporate model and that they can wield power in ways similar to men. Indeed, some women may prefer that style. We also know from the survey findings that some men use the transformational leadership style.

Large, established organizations should expand their definition of effective leadership. If they were to do that, several things might happen, including the disappearance of the glass ceiling and the creation of a wider path for all sorts of executives—men and women—to attain positions of leadership. Widening the path will free potential leaders to lead in ways that play to their individual strengths. Then the newly recognized interactive leadership style can be valued and rewarded as highly as the command-and-control style has been for decades. By valuing a diversity of leadership styles, organizations will find the strength and flexibility to survive in a highly competitive, increasingly diverse economic environment.

27

Would Women Lead Differently?

Virginia Schein

Virginia E. Schein is a former associate professor at the Wharton School and has held professional positions at Yale University and the City University of New York. She has held managerial positions at Metropolitan Life Insurance Company and the American Management Association. She is co-author of *Power and Organization Development*, and is currently professor of management at Gettysburg College.

The search for more effective leaders has led many to tout the virtues of the androgynous manager. Such a manager blends the characteristics of dominance, assertiveness, and competitiveness with those of concern for relationships, cooperativeness, and humanitarian values. As the argument goes, the former set of characteristics is too limited to meet the requirements of management and leadership in today's complex and changing environment. Effectiveness requires a broad range of characteristics, one that encompasses competence and compassion, toughness and tenderness.

The androgynous manager possesses both masculine characteristics, those seen as commonly held by men, and feminine characteristics, those viewed as more commonly held by women. The focus on feminine as well as masculine

---

Reprinted from William E. Rosenbach and Robert L. Taylor, eds., *Contemporary Issues in Leadership*, 2nd ed. (Boulder, Colo.: Westview Press, 1989). By permission of the author.

characteristics puts femininity into the leadership effectiveness equation. It highlights gender differences and suggests that, indeed, women would lead differently. Unlike the global warrior or John Wayne manager, a feminine leader would be oriented toward cooperation, teamwork, and concern for others.

That women would lead or govern differently is not a new idea. Women's leadership has been linked with enhancing world peace, reducing corruption, and improving opportunities for the downtrodden. If women, as keepers of the values of social justice, nurturance, and honesty, are put in charge, then the conflicts, corruption, and greed around us will go away—or so say proponents of this view. The maximalist perspective within the now fragmented feminist movement supports this idea. It argues for innate or highly socialized gender differences and views women as more likely to exhibit cooperative, compassionate, and humane types of behaviors than men.

At first glance, the new priority given to femininity and a feminine leadership style would seem to be a boon for women aspiring to leadership positions. The same sex role stereotyping that often excludes women from managerial positions can now be used to enhance their opportunities. Florence Nightingale meets John Wayne, and together they lead us into the sunset of greater leadership effectiveness.

In my opinion, however, this entire line of reasoning is both a foolhardy and dangerous one to pursue. It will not add to our understanding of leadership effectiveness, for it takes a narrow and simplistic approach to what is a broad and complex set of issues and activities. It will not promote equality of opportunity in the workplace because it perpetuates sex role stereotypical thinking that has no basis in reality. The androgynous orientation builds a managerial access bridge for women on a shaky foundation of sand.

The Leadership Labyrinth

Numerous researchers have shown that leadership effectiveness entails far more than a task versus people style or a trait approach. Yukl, for example, had identified more than 13 categories of relevant managerial behaviors, including representation, crisis management, problem solving, operations monitoring, etc. A large-scale study conducted by the American Management Association identified competency clusters such as entrepreneurial abilities, intellectual abilities, and socioemotional maturity, among others. Still other recent research stresses the importance of effective communication.

The view of the organization as a political coalition diverts us from a leader-follower concentration, where the style emphasis originated, and highlights the important role of external relationships. Effective managers need to deal with other groups and departments, form alliances and coalitions, and influence those over whom they have no direct authority in order to get things done. Effectiveness in an organization may be far more related to these behaviors than to leadership style.

Position is also a relevant variable. Dunnette and others have found that supervisory, middle-managerial, and executive positions differ as to the priority and importance of particular behaviors. The nature of the business and the environment in which it operates also determines the type of behaviors that are critical. Finally, as more and more organizations must undergo change in order to survive and compete successfully, transformational leadership has become valued and necessary.

Given the preceding factors, how much variance can specific characteristics, either masculine or feminine ones, account for in leadership effectiveness? Certainly, personality plays a part. But the Great Man (as it was called) trait theory of leadership went out with the buggy whip. Organizational cultures vary as much as the required behaviors within them. One constellation of behaviors may be appropriate within a bureaucratic, rigid structure but quite inappropriate in a loose, entrepreneurial type of organization. Creativity and flexibility may be important for the advertising executive, but stability and follow-through are probably more important for the effective insurance executive. The payoff in pursuing the trait theory is clearly limited.

Male and Female Managers—How Different Are They?

The focus on masculinity and femininity suggests significant innate or ingrained socialized differences between the sexes. Research does show some differences between males and females; however, there are far fewer differences than is commonly believed. Moreover, research indicates that the differences within each sex are greater than the differences between the sexes. That is, the differences among women (or men), considering variations in background, experience, and so on, are greater than the differences between women in general and men in general.

More to the point, the bulk of the evidence on managerial behaviors shows few differences between men and women. A major investigation by researchers at the Center for Creative Leadership, based on their own data as well as other research reports, concludes that "as individuals, executive women and men seem to be virtually identical psychologically, intellectually, and emotionally."[1]

Thus, even if the Great Man (or Great Person) trait theory had some validity, seeking those characteristics deemed relevant, such as intuitiveness or assertiveness, on the basis of the gender of the manager would not produce the desired results. Male and female managers appear to be cut from the same cloth, with some portions of it tattered and inappropriate and other parts of high quality. But gender will not predict the composition of the cloth. From a performance perspective, male and female leadership is more likely to be similar than different.

Within the corporate world, however, there is one glaring difference between the sexes. There are far fewer women in positions of power and influence than men. This is also true in the public sector. Although women have made significant inroads into lower and middle management ranks over the last 15 years, progress into senior ranks has been slow. There is a dearth of women in senior executive positions and among the ranks of the highest paid positions in major corporations. The barrier to the top, termed the "glass ceiling," has led to many female middle managers "bailing out." Some choose to seek power and influence through entrepreneurial channels; others choose to redirect the balance of the motherhood and managerhood juggling act in favor of the former, given the limited payoffs of the latter for women. Of the top 100 corporate women featured in a 1976 *Business Week* cover story, only 5 are working today in positions considered crucial for advancement to a senior executive post.

The Work and Family Interface—Meeting the Challenge

The glass ceiling barrier is both structural and attitudinal in nature. Although the male-female ratio in the work force in general, and in lower managerial ranks in particular, has changed dramatically, the recognition of the need for structural changes in the way work is accomplished as a result of this changed ratio has been much slower in coming. The gender-based division between work and family no longer exists, yet much of the work world is still structured as if there is a full-time spouse/parent at home attending to family responsibilities. Although some structural changes, such as child care benefits and flexible working hours, are being implemented, albeit on a limited basis, they will have little effect on the demands made in the "race for the top." Total attention, time, and energy must still be devoted to the endeavor.

It is the woman, by virtue of her biological role as childbearer, who gets squeezed out of the race. Called "super moms," many simply drop from exhaustion in what can only be a no-win contest with their male counterparts.

Asking women to choose between motherhood and career is the wrong question. Few have considered the implications if all of our bright, energetic women chose the latter. More importantly, such a question places a burden of choice on women that is not asked of their male counterparts. Although many men are asked to limit the amount of time they have available to devote to spouse and offspring, few are asked to give up the opportunity for spouse and offspring all together.

The right question is: "How can we restructure work in a society in which work and family no longer are separate, but interface?" This question should be addressed to, and serious responses expected of, our corporate and government leaders. It is when this question comes into play that the possibility emerges that *women would lead differently.* The biological responsibilities of women suggest that women as leaders might be more understanding of and willing to grapple with accommodating this work and family interface.

A case in point is the Norwegian government. Norway's prime minister is a woman and 7 of its 17 Cabinet members are female. Norway's Labor Party members of Parliament include more than 40 percent women as does the party's ruling National Board. Do women govern differently in Norway? Despite falling oil prices and huge spending cuts, the Norwegian government increased its emphasis on women and children. Child care subsidies are up, as are the number of weeks of paid parental leave. In addition, working parents have 10 days each (single parents have 20) to handle the "little crises" of child raising. At a recent Cabinet meeting, which was running overtime, the defense minister was neither uncomfortable nor frowned upon for excusing himself to pick up his son at nursery school.

If Norway is any example, women would indeed lead differently. They would focus on structural changes to facilitate the interface of work and family. This priority would encourage a work climate in which the work-family interface was recognized and accommodated, and its reality was not denied. As leaders, women would be more willing to grapple with the hard questions. These questions include: To what extent are some job expectations, such as last-minute travel demands, simply convenient in a corporate environment in which family responsibilities are handled by others? What work demands are essential and job related? What time frames, such as 7 years until partnership, are convenient only in the old order of a gender-based division of labor, and what career time frames are job related? In a society in which work and family must interface, "what is convenient to the corporation" and "what is job related" must be separated. This is a complex and challenging task.

Women as leaders have an investment in determining viable answers to these questions and restructuring the world of work accordingly. As such, they would foster an organizational climate receptive to and supportive of qualified and hard-working women and men. The race might not get any easier, but at least it would have the same type and number of bumps and hurdles for both sexes.

Attitudinal Barriers Revisited

Ironically, strongly held attitudinal barriers may well be blocking the very increases in the number of women in powerful positions necessary to bring about these vital changes. Although sex role stereotypes have little basis in reality, they can color our evaluations of people. In the early 1970s my research showed that both male and female managers viewed the characteristics required of a successful manager as more likely to be held by a man than a woman. This attitude limits women's opportunities for entry into and promotion within the managerial ranks.

A replication of this work in the mid-1980s reveals that this perception continues to hold true among male managers today. Males, predominant in senior managerial positions, are still more likely to see a man, rather than a woman, as next in line for an executive position. On the other hand, today's female managers no longer share the "think manager—think male" view. They see the characteristics necessary for success as just as likely to be held by a woman as by a man. To the extent women leaders, unlike their male counterparts, are more likely to be gender-blind in their promotional decision making, women leaders would foster more equal access to the race for the top as well as equalize the hurdles for male and female competitors.

The Leadership Difference

Evidence suggests few differences in the actual behaviors of men and women leaders. Effective leaders, male or female, seek to implement their visions, vary their behaviors contingent upon the situational requirements, and in general grapple successfully with the ever-changing and complex internal and external demands upon their organizations. Ineffective leaders, male or female, do not. Effective leadership is difficult. Both corporations and governments admit to a leadership shortage. The ever-increasing attention today on leadership evidences both its importance and the high priority placed on improving the quality of leadership in all of our institutions.

Women's attention to structural changes enhancing the work-family interface and a more gender-blind evaluation of qualifications can open the doors to allow more women entrants into the race for future leadership positions. If we want "the best and the brightest" to lead our major institutions, then the larger the supply of qualified candidates, the more selective we can be. The more rigorous the selection criteria, the better our chances for excellence in leadership in any one organization and in the number of organizations with such quality leadership.

This perspective need not be, and in many individual cases is not, "for women only." Although women leaders may be more instrumental in enhancing women's advancement opportunities, the real focus should be on erasing this difference between the sexes as well. Both men and women need to grapple seriously with the impact of a changing society on our organizations and to provide opportunities for the most qualified of either sex to apply their talents and energies to the leadership of our public and private institutions.

28

Women and Minorities in Management

Ann M. Morrison and Mary Ann Von Glinow

Ann M. Morrison has directed research on leadership diversity at the Center for Creative Leadership. She is lead author of *Breaking the Glass Ceiling: Can Women Reach the Top of America's Largest Corporations?* and *The New Leaders: Guidelines on Leadership Diversity in America*. Morrison is currently president of the New Leaders Institute. Mary Ann Von Glinow is professor of business management and international business at Florida International University. She has published six books and numerous articles, and currently serves as president of the Academy of Management and as a member of eleven editorial review boards.

Management and executive positions, along with professional and technical jobs, are among the fastest growing occupations between 1984 and 1995.[1] However, these occupations include jobs not traditionally held by women and minorities, who comprise the new work force. Therefore, one challenge for American organizations is to assimilate a more diverse labor force into high-status, high-skill management roles.

In this article we examine the current status of women and minorities in management, including some recent changes. We present theoretical models

Reprinted from Ann M. Morrison and Mary Ann Von Glinow, "Women and Minorities in Management," *American Psychologist* 45 No. 2 (Feb. 1990): 200–208. Copyright 1990 by American Psychological Association. Reprinted by permission.

from psychology and other social sciences, supported by recent data, to explain the progress and the barriers experienced by women and minorities. Finally, we explore potential remedies for the problems that endure, including programs and practices currently being applied in U.S. organizations as well as research directions that may increase our understanding of relevant issues.

We discuss White women and a wide range of minority groups, including Blacks, Hispanics, and Asians, but relevant research varies considerably in its coverage of various groups. The literature on White women is substantial, evidenced in part by the number of literature reviews done (nine reviews within the last 10 years were cited by Dipboye in 1987).[2] In contrast, the research base on other minorities in management is quite small and is dominated by studies of Black men. Even employment statistics are difficult to uncover for minority groups in management.[3-6] Reviews of research on White women are cited instead of individual studies whenever possible, and our focus is on U.S. studies published since 1980.

Current Data on the Status of Women and Minorities in Management

According to an Equal Employment Opportunity Commission (EEOC) report (cited by Bradsher),[7] the number of women, Blacks, and Hispanics in management has quadrupled since 1970, and the number of Asians has increased eightfold. However, the rate of upward movement of women and minority managers provides "clear evidence of nothing less than the abiding racism and sexism of the corporation."[7]

There is considerable evidence that White women and people of color encounter a "glass ceiling" in management. The glass ceiling is a concept popularized in the 1980s to describe a barrier so subtle that it is transparent, yet so strong that it prevents women and minorities from moving up in the management hierarchy. "Today, women fill nearly a third of all management positions (up from 19% in 1972), but most are stuck in jobs with little authority and relatively low pay."[8] A Korn/Ferry International survey[9] reported that only 2% of 1,362 senior executives were women. A study of the Fortune 500, the Fortune Service 500, and the 190 largest health care organizations in the United States[10] similarly found that only 3.6% of board directorships and 1.7% of corporate officerships in the Fortune 500 were held by women; the Fortune Service 500 and the health industry indicated that 4.4% of board members were women and that 3.8% and 8.5% of their corporate officers, respectively, were women.

Women do not fare any better in management in government or educational institutions. The U.S. government reported only 8.6% women in Senior Executive Service levels[11] with most female employees clustered in low-paying, nonprestigious GS 5–10 levels.[12] In education, Sandler's 1986 report shows that "on the average, colleges and universities nationwide employ 1.1 senior women (dean and above) per institution."[13]

With regard to the racial composition of management ranks, the statistics show less progress than for women. Only one Black heads a Fortune 1000 company.[5] In the senior ranks, studies by Korn/Ferry International (reported by Jones),[14] show little change. Of 1,708 senior executives surveyed in 1979, 3 were Black, 2 were Asian, and 2 were Hispanic; only 8 were women, all of them White. In 1985, the list showed 4 Blacks, 6 Asians, 3 Hispanics, and 29 women. In Jones's words, "I think it's fair to say that this is almost no progress at all."[14]

Some evidence also exists of a glass ceiling for Asians.[15] In 1988, only 2.2% of California's Career Executive Assignment positions were held by Asians despite larger representation at the journey and midmanagement levels "that could be considered as qualifying developmental experience for these assignments."[15]

With regard to management, one of the few surveys on minorities in business shows that in 1986 in 400 of the Fortune 1,000 companies, less than 9% of all managers were minorities, including Blacks, Hispanics, and Asians. A 1986 Equal Employment Opportunity Commission survey (cited by Leavitt)[16] shows that from 1974 to 1984, the percentage of Black women officials and managers grew at 0.7% of the total to 1.7%. Malveaux and Wallace,[17] Nkomo[18] and others claimed that minority women are doubly disadvantaged in terms of upward mobility. They also noted that research on certain minority women, particularly Asians and American Indians, has essentially slipped through the cracks.

Those women and minorities who have advanced into management often find reward differentials. There is evidence that at higher occupational levels, women are less satisfied with their pay than are men.[19] One study of 2,600 employees found substantial wage differences between men and women in managerial levels;[20] another reported that "women at the vice presidential levels and above earn 42% less than their male peers."[21] Earnings of Black men in management come closer to those of White men.[22]

The exodus of women and Blacks from corporate America is a disturbing trend sometimes attributed to differential treatment in management.[5,23–25] Women started their own businesses at six times the rate that men did between 1974 and 1984.[16] Of the 100 leading corporate women identified by a *Business Week* survey in 1976, nearly one third had left their corporate jobs for other pursuits 10 years later.[26]

A study by Morrison, White, Van Velsor, and the Center for Creative Leadership[27] concluded that obstacles related to the glass ceiling will impede women's progress toward top management for the next several decades. Others concur, citing little hope for women or minorities in the near future. Dipboye[2] claimed that even though female managers are progressing faster than their counterparts of decades ago, they still fail in terms of their rate of progress when compared with White males. *Business Week* recently concluded that "except for the true stars, the first generation of Black managers is destined to top out in middle levels."[28]

Theoretical Perspectives

A number of theories have been offered as to why sexual and racial differences exist within management. These theories tend to fall into three general groups. First are theories that assume that differences handicap women and minorities; these theories postulate that deficiencies in underrepresented groups are largely responsible for their differential treatment in management. Second are theories that cite discrimination by the majority population as the major cause of inequities. Here, bias and stereotyping on the part of White men in power are held to account for the slow progress of women and minorities. Third are theories that pinpoint structural, systemic discrimination as the root cause of differential treatment rather than actions or characteristics of individuals. These theories claim that widespread policies and practices in the social system perpetuate discriminatory treatment of women and people of color.

Theories Postulating Differences

Riger and Galligan[29] noted that psychological researchers have emphasized person-centered variables to explain women's low job status. Women's traits, behaviors, attitudes, and socialization are said to make them inappropriate or deficient as managers because of such factors as their alleged fear of success or their unwillingness to take risks. Riger and Galligan noted that investigations of sex differences have yielded mixed results overall but that current field studies have generally refuted this explanation.

Data disputing both sex and race deficiencies come from the AT&T Assessment Center reports,[30] which showed that female and male managers were more similar than different on personality and motivation factors as well as abilities. Race differences were greater than sex differences, but among the high-potential managers assessed, the relative weaknesses among Blacks in intellectual ability were compensated for by superior performance in interpersonal skills and stability of performance. There is considerable other evidence that women and men in management roles have similar aspirations, values, and other personality traits as well as job-related skills and behaviors.[2,27,29,31–37] Donnell and Hall's[38] unusually large field study of nearly 2,000 matched pairs of female and male managers led them to conclude that "the disproportionately low numbers of women in management can no longer be explained away by the contention that women practice a different brand of management from that practiced by men."

The human capital theory attempts to explain continued sex- and race-related differences in management by suggesting that individuals are rewarded in their current jobs for their past investment in education and job training.[39] Workers may choose to accept a wage or to invest in acquiring new skills and experiences to qualify for higher-paying jobs. Blau and Ferber contended that if this explanation is correct, then women should choose the occupational setting they prefer and invest accordingly in their own human capital. Any policy changes that may be called for to correct differential treatment should be directed to the educational process rather than the employment setting because no differences other than those in human capital are seen as operating.

The human capital explanation assumes that investment pays off equally for all groups, but recent studies suggest that investment yields higher returns for White men than for women and minorities. Education level has not fully accounted for discrepancies in level or pay in recent studies of sex and race differences in management.[4,40,41] Results of a survey of Asian Americans in professional and managerial positions indicate that education and work experience yield low returns in promotion or advancement.[42] Thus, person-centered theory cannot adequately explain differential treatment in management: other factors must also be considered.

Discrimination Explanations

The second group of theories targets bias on the part of the dominant group as the cause of differential treatment. The labor market discrimination explanation is an economic theory that assumes that relevant stakeholders—employers, customers, employees, and so forth—have discriminatory tastes even when women or minorities are perfect economic substitutes for White men in the workplace.[43] Blau and Ferber[33] pointed out that employers with discriminatory tastes hire women only at a wage discount large enough to compensate for the loss of utility or level of discomfort associated with employing them.

The rational bias explanation is a psychological theory that suggests that discrimination is influenced by contextual circumstances in which sexual or racial bias results in career rewards or punishments.[4,44,45] In this case, a manager's decision to discriminate is based on whether such discrimination will be viewed positively or negatively by relevant stakeholders and on the possibility of receiving rewards for discriminating. Rational bias illustrates why discrimination can continue to occur despite substantial regulations against it.[4,45]

Discrimination by the dominant group was also addressed by Wells and Jennings,[46] who argued that Black individuals are not rewarded on the basis of their performance. Organizations that espouse and even mandate racial equality are also characterized by a psychological mind-set of entitlement on the part of the dominant Whites. Blacks' access to resources is limited, Wells and Jennings claimed, and Blacks are systematically excluded from advancement except for a few who are allowed in "threshold" or acceptable positions.

Discrimination occurs in part because of the belief by White men that women and people of color are less suited for management than White men. Comparing actual performance in managerial jobs is difficult, but there is growing concern that differential treatment of women and Blacks is not related to performance alone. Some studies suggest that deficiencies are presumed even when no differences exist because stereotypes based on historical roles persist.[5,6,35,44,47–49] The "good manager" is still described as masculine, rather than androgynous, despite the growing number of female managers.[50] Ambiguity or lack of specific information about an individual contributes to bias against women and minorities because judgments are based on negative stereotypes of the group as a whole.[34,35,51,52] For example, pay differentials for women may be related more to the salary allocation process than to performance evaluation because salary decisions are made by people less familiar with female managers than are their immediate supervisors (who conduct their performance appraisals), and so bias is more likely.[20,53] The stereotypes are so strong that contrary data are sometimes ignored in managerial selection and other managerial decisions.[51,53,54] This research suggests that individuals, consciously or not, contribute to differential treatment of women and minorities in management.

Systemic Barriers

The third set of theories highlights structural discrimination. Intergroup theory[6,55] suggests that two types of groups exist in organizations—identity groups (based on race, ethnicity, family, gender, or age) and organization groups (based on common work tasks, work experiences, and position in the hierarchy). Tension results because organization group membership changes, whereas identity group membership does not. When the pattern of group relations within an organization mirrors the pattern in society as a whole, such as when Whites predominate in high-status positions and Blacks are concentrated in low-status jobs, then evaluations of Blacks (or members of other low-status groups) are likely to be distorted by prejudice or anxiety as racist assumptions go unquestioned in the organization.[6]

Intergroup theory has elements in common with the dual labor market concept in economics. Dual labor market theory was proposed as an alternative explanation to the human capital theory of the 1960s when education and training of inner-city minority workers did not reduce their unemployment rate as much as was anticipated by policymakers at the time.[56] The dual labor market consists of a set of better, or primary, jobs and a set of worse, or secondary, jobs, with little mobility between the two. Groups most frequently associated with the secondary labor market (including women and minorities) are largely confined there, and discrimination is often justified as economic efficiency.[57,58] Within management, the secondary jobs may be not only those at lower levels but also those in staff (vs. line) functions, wherein women and minorities are found in disproportionate numbers. Staff positions typically are out of the mainstream of the business and do not lead to top management posts.[14,50,57]

In the field of psychology, structural barriers are included as part of the situation-centered perspective[29] and the organization structure perspective,[59,60] which emphasize that women's lack of opportunity and power in organizations and the sex ratio of groups within organizations explain women's lack of managerial success. For example, Kanter's classic research pointed out that if a management cadre is at least 85% men, then the women in the group are "tokens" who very visibly represent women as a category whether they want to or not. These tokens' performances are hindered because of the pressure to which their visibility subjects them and because members of the dominant group exaggerate differences according to stereotypes they believe about women. Because people of color also become tokens in management ranks, the same dynamics may affect them.[54] Women, however, also face sexual harassment, which may be a result of skewed sex ratios favoring men.[61]

The dominance of White men in management poses another structural problem for underrepresented groups. Minorities struggle with fitting into two distinct cultural worlds, a concept called *biculturalism* that has been documented in studies of Black Americans.[6] Bell's[62] research on bicultural conflict among Black women shows that those from cultures other than that of the dominant work group must choose how to manage the stress of moving physically, cognitively, and emotionally between the two cultural systems. For women of all races, responsibility for home, family, and social activities still accompanies a demanding management job, adding other major sources of pressure.[2,27,35]

The impact of structural factors is shown by researchers such as Irons and Moore[63] in their study of the banking industry. They identified the three most significant problems faced by Blacks: (a) not knowing what is going on in the organization or not being in the network (rated as the most serious problem by 75% of survey respondents), (b) racism, and (c) inability to get a mentor. Irons and Moore pointed out that these results concur with those of Fernandez[64] in showing a strong perception that minorities are excluded from informal work groups. In a study of Asian Americans in professional and management jobs, similar barriers to upward mobility were most often cited: a corporate culture alien to some Asian Americans, management insensitivity, and a lack of networks, mentors, and role models.[42] Other research has shown that many female and Black managers feel excluded from informal relationships with their White male colleagues.[6,65,66]

Mentors and sponsors represent key relationships attributed to career success and, although research results are inconclusive as to whether women and minorities find fewer mentors than do White men, there is some indication that mentor relationships are harder to manage and provide a narrower range of benefits for women and minorities.[6,34,67–74] For example, crossrace relationships take longer to initiate, are more likely to end in an unfriendly fashion, and provide less psychosocial support than same-race relationships.[75,76] Cross-sex mentor relationships are subjected to sexual innuendo, and Black women face taboos across both sex and race.[74,76,77] Women and minorities may need more mentors or sponsors than do their White male counterparts—White male superiors in their own area and same-sex or same-race mentors in other areas of the organization who increase their comfort.[6]

Major career development theories do not consider race as a factor, yet evidence from recent studies of Black managers suggests that Black identity development may slow or alter the career development process and affect Blacks' willingness to accept White mentors.[6] Larwood and Gattiker[57] studied the career development of 215 employees in 17 firms and postulated a dual development model because career patterns differ between women and men as a result of widespread discrimination, competing demands outside work, and other structural barriers. Greenhaus, Parasuraman, and Wormley[78] studied the career success of 828 managers in three companies. They found differences by sex and race, with Black women having more negative experiences than any other group. To the extent that organizational structures and practices follow models based solely on how White men develop, women and minorities are disadvantaged.

It is possible that elements of all three theoretical approaches described are significantly related to the lack of upward mobility in management for women and minorities. According to some, the interaction of situational factors (in the organization and in society at large) with person-centered characteristics (related to sex and race) accounts for differential treatment.[29,54,59,79] For example, without opportunities to take challenging assignments, minority managers may fall behind their White cohorts in terms of knowledge and skill development, or they may internalize negative evaluations and stereotypes to the point where they limit themselves and turn down future opportunities for fear they will not succeed.[54] Tests of the interaction between gender and job factors lend some support to this combined approach[79–81] and suggest that remedies and continued research should be directed at all three sets of theories presented here.

Remedial Actions

In 1977, Kanter recommended that adjustments be made in the workplace to better accommodate women. She rejected the notion that women bear sole responsibility for equal opportunity in business. It is no longer uncommon to hear similar sentiment regarding both women and minorities,[4,44] although actual implementation of adjustments remains an unmet goal for many organizations.

Some organizations may be able to make adjustments more effectively than others depending on the current status of the diversity in their management. A team at Procter & Gamble recommended that firms go beyond two generations of affirmative action into true "multicultural management."[82] Most firms tend to be in what they describe as the first generation of affirmative action, characterized by a focus on numbers that stimulates superficial and crisis-oriented actions, racial or sexual hostility, lack of trust, and a widespread presumption that women and minorities are less capable. Compliance with government regulations is the main goal. Some organizations have evolved to a second generation, where they meet most numerical goals and attempt to provide the necessary critical mass for support and role models. Their concern over retaining high-performing women and minorities means implementing accountability for effectively managing these groups.

Merenivitch and Reigle[82] proposed that in multicultural organizations, the culture recognizes and appreciates diversity, resources and influence are distributed without regard to race or sex, and policies and practices are responsive to all employees' needs. In effect, the multicultural organization deliberately capitalizes on its diversity. As organizations evolve, different techniques for halting discrimination may be advocated depending on which phase the organization is in.

A variety of techniques are being used to reduce differential treatment and to bring diversity into organizations' cultures. Some techniques appear to be targeted toward the human capital issue, some toward discriminatory treatment, and some toward the structural and contextual barriers. Some techniques cover aspects of more than one theory. Education and training, for example, can be important steps for an organization. Some organizations, such as DuPont and GTE, provide additional classroom-training opportunities to women once they are hired, but the trend is to avoid segregating women or minorities so they are not seen as needing special help to become equally qualified. Many companies, such as IBM and Hewlett-Packard, provide no training at the corporate level for women per se, expecting that the training programs already being offered apply to all equally.[83]

A recent development in training is the variety of programs geared to help managers work together within a diverse workforce and reduce discrimination. The value of programs on managing diversity is that issues are brought out into the open, allowing people to discuss their beliefs. One problem this addresses is that women and minorities who have felt pressure to remain silent on issues of sexism and racism now can confront the system rather than have doubts raised about their loyalty or be seen as "too ambitious."[14,27,88-85] Eastman Kodak offers such a program to top division managers, and other firms run them for mixed groups, ensuring that at least one third to one half of the underrepresented groups participate in each program DuPont began running its "Men and Women Working Together" program specifically for managers of saleswomen, but it has since opened it to various employee groups. A spinoff is a program for women only.[83]

Despite these attempts to avoid treating women as different, demand for women-only programs is still strong. Because companies have made varying degrees of progress in attacking discrimination, and because some women and minorities rebel against attending segregated programs, the flexibility of organizations in providing different types of training is commendable. Limited research suggests that training may be most useful not in skill-building, but in areas such as career and self-awareness mentoring, and leadership development.[2,37,83,86]

Because women and minorities face special situations as tokens, they may need to perfect certain competencies such as conflict resolution. Researchers who have studied Black managers conclude that special skills and, therefore, specialized training may be needed by Blacks. If Blacks do not resolve conflicts that involve themselves or their area, they are likely to be blamed for the conflict.[67] Blacks need to be skilled at managing racism and at managing their own rage over the racism they encounter.[6,67,87,88] Thus, some skill-building programs, as well as awareness and assessment programs, may be appropriate to help women and minorities compete and cope in management.

Some research suggests that bias is most effectively decreased not only by education but also by exposure to and experience with members of the opposite sex and other races.[34,35] Working alongside a woman or a minority group member may be the key to quelling the discriminatory tastes of White men.

Incentives may also be needed to help overcome rational bias and other discrimination that legislation has failed to address and to reduce the effects of tokenism. Some organizations such as Corning Glass Works and Gannett are giving equal employment opportunity accountability to line managers, using bonuses as an incentive. Minority recruitment at Gannett, for example, is monitored by a committee of its publishers and factored into managers' bonus payouts.[89,90]

Other organizations use task forces to mandate and even implement changes. The Equitable Financial Company has been using the Women's Business Resource Group to identify and solve women's issues that emerge from the corporation's annual employee survey. According to Nelton and Berney,[21] this task force has been responsible for redesigning the job posting system as well as implementing flextime for working parents and toughening the company stand on sexual harassment. Task forces used in this way—to actually define the problem as well as create the cure—are more unusual than those aimed at problems already targeted, such as those on combining family and career. The task forces most highly praised seem to share several characteristics: direct access to the office of the president, influential members, and the resources required to try out new solutions.[21,83]

Career management is another key technique for eliminating the glass ceiling for women and people of color. Some research[27,91] has suggested that challenging, successfully completed assignments are important to executives' development. Yet some assignments cited most frequently by the male executives studied were rarely cited by female executives. The indicators are that these assignments are less available to women, including start-ups, troubleshooting, and international experience.[92] The same kind of restrictions on minority managers may also block their advancement. One unusual task force has taken on the challenge of increasing the mobility of women and minorities between "secondary" jobs and primary jobs. Mobil's Committee of Executives targets high-potential women and minorities and places them in key line jobs.[21]

Senior managers can help move women and minorities out of secondary or threshold management posts by giving them opportunities to take such challenging assignments in the mainstream of the organization and to reinforce their authority in those assignments. A recent study revealed that "only one woman in five found the professional impact of gender to be primarily negative abroad"[93] However, confronting superiors' resistance to get the assignment abroad was a major hurdle. Once a woman began the job, her senior male colleagues, particularly from the head office, became important in redirecting early client conversations away from her male colleagues and toward the woman herself to establish smooth, ongoing work relationships.[93]

Career development functions such as these are often attributed to mentors: yet, as we noted, women and minorities face special problems with mentoring relationships. Some companies such as Ortho Pharmaceutical Corporation[94] have tried formally assigning mentors to promising women and minorities, sometimes also including White male protégés in the program as well. However, there is little evidence that assigning mentors is effective.[77,95,96] One suggested alternative (or complement) to a formal mentor program is to provide training on how to be a mentor and how to be mentored.[67,77,97] Not only may this approach help build awareness of the barriers involved, but it may also allow the element of choice to continue in relationships initiated both by women and minorities seeking a mentor and by more senior managers who want to help.

Support groups may also help. Security Pacific National Bank created a program called Black Officers Support System (BOSS) to help recruit Blacks and reduce their turnover.[63] The Executive Leadership Council in Washington, DC, consists of about 50 Black line managers from major industries who recruit and hire minorities.[5] These groups, along with the many internal women's networks and community groups for women and minorities, may help by providing career guidance and psychological support in managing bi-culturalism and other tensions.

Despite the existence of these various remedies, the glass ceiling continues to frustrate ambitious women and minorities. Although employers' attitudes appear to be changing, the lack of results can be partly attributed to the lack of employers committed to equal opportunity. A 1983 survey of nearly 800 business opinion leaders, reported by Jones,[14] showed that of 25 possible human resource priorities, the issue of affirmative action for minorities and women ranked 23rd. Some efforts to attack discrimination in organizations have no doubt been piecemeal, and some may even have been harmful. When women believed they were hired only to meet EEOC guidelines, there was a negative effect on their self-image and development.[98]

Poor results may also be attributed to confusion over which remedies af-fect which symptoms or causes of differential treatment. As Dipboye[2] pointed out, few attempts have been made to evaluate training programs, as evi-denced by the sparsity of evaluation studies in the literature.

Research Needed

Evaluating potential remedies to sex- and race-based differential treatment in management is no small task. One difficulty is that the organizational con-text is so complicated that factors external to specific remedies may affect the outcome more than the remedies themselves. Interventions that can and should be made in critical organizational practices such as recruitment and selection, evaluation, career development, and promotion may be greatly in-fluenced by what Merlin Pope called "contextual prejudices," or exclusionary mechanisms that subtly keep women and minorities on the out-side.[13,27,34,35,83,99,100] A major challenge for researchers is to assess specific techniques, taking into account the effects of organizational culture and other contextual factors. Research across organizations to assess techniques would provide useful data that would allow executives to select those tech-niques shown to be more effective under circumstances matching those in their own organizations. Better links between specific techniques and theo-retical constructs such as those reviewed here are also needed.

Many more fundamental research issues are apparent by the questions that remain. These include unraveling the effects of race, sex, and age in studies by separating female subjects by age and race, separating Blacks by sex and age, and so on. Another needed step is separating one minority group from another rather than grouping them as "minorities": data on Hispanics and Asians are particularly needed. Assumptions are made about how White women experience the same or different treatment as men or women of color, but little research addresses this issue. Studies that separate the various groups would provide useful comparison data, particularly with regard to the impact of various remedial actions within organizations. Further theoretical refinement is also needed so that theories based on one group (such as White men) are not erroneously generalized to all others. Career development is one such area in which models developed on White males' career experiences may be inappropriately applied to women or minorities.[6]

The number of promising research areas is indicated by the number of questions this review has raised. We especially encourage research in organizations using actual managers and multiple methods so that the results reflect realistic situations. However, it is important that research be done on a variety of theoretical and applied issues. Research is needed to answer questions about whether actual or perceived differences are keeping women and minorities below a glass ceiling in management and the extent to which the structures and systems of organizations contribute to limited upward mobility. With the demographic changes already taking place in the U.S. labor force, restricting the pool of potential organizational leaders to White men only is foolhardy. Achieving diversity in management requires action. Continued research will help ensure that effective action is taken.

PART VI

THE FOLLOWERS

A*lthough an enormous amount of thinking and writing has addressed issues pertaining to the leader, much less attention has been paid to followers. This seems a rather puzzling oversight. It is difficult to imagine leadership without the participation of followers. Part VI addresses itself to the topic of followers in the leadership equation. John Gardner introduces us to the topic with a thoughtful essay on leaders and followers which poses the essential questions: what role should followers play? how should they interact with the leader? how should the leader behave toward followers? Joseph C. Rost amplifies this in the next selection, as he places followers firmly within his conception of the process of leadership, and forges a new, activist, definition of their role. The final reading on followers is by Robert Kelley, who expands upon Rost and creates an entirely new typology of followers which has become quite influential. Taken together, these readings on followers bring new emphasis and understanding to an important element of leadership.*

29

Leaders and Followers

John W. Gardner

John Gardner has served six presidents of the United States in various leadership capacities. He was Secretary of Health, Education, and Welfare, founding chairman of Common Cause, co-founder of the Independent Sector, chairman of the National Coalition, and president of the Carnegie Corporation and Foundation. He is currently the Miriam and Peter Haas Centennial Professor at Stanford Business School.

The interaction between leaders and constituents is one of the most central topics within the study of leadership. I would like to pass along some of my reflections from studying that topic over the past several months. Leaders are almost never as much in charge as they are pictured to be, and followers almost never are as submissive as one might imagine. That influence and pressure flow both ways is not a recent discovery. The earliest sociologists who wrote on the subject in the late nineteenth and early twentieth century made the same point. Max Weber, discussing charismatic leaders, asserted that such leaders generally appear in times of trouble and that their followers exhibit "a devotion born of distress." In other words, the state of mind of fol-

Excerpted from John W. Gardner, "Leaders and Followers," *Liberal Education* 73(2) (March–April, 1987): 4–6. By permission of the author.

lowers is a powerful ingredient in explaining the emergence of the charismatic leader.

Weber's great contemporary Georg Simmel was even more explicit, suggesting that followers have about as much influence on their leaders as leaders have on their followers. Leaders cannot maintain authority, he wrote, unless followers are prepared to believe in that authority. Weber and Simmel were writing in pre-World War I Germany. Their views were not the product of a populist environment!

There is a striking difference between the situation of political leaders and that of line executives in business or government. In the political process, people are free to follow any leader—and leaders must compete for approval. In corporate and governmental bureaucracies, employees appear to have less choice: They are supposed to accept their superiors in the hierarchy as their leaders. But, of course, quite often they do not. One reason corporate and governmental bureaucracies stagnate is the assumption by line executives that, given their rank and authority, they can lead without being leaders. They cannot. They can be given subordinates, but they cannot be given a following. A following must be earned. Surprisingly, many of them do not even know they are not leading. They mistake the exercise of authority for leadership, and as long as they persist in that mistake they will never learn the art of turning subordinates into followers.

Whatever one may say about the influence of constituents, leaders continue to play a crucial role in the interaction. How should they play that role? That is a question that explodes into a thousand questions. Does the group function most effectively when leaders make the decisions without consultation and impose their will—or when they invite varying degrees of participation in the decision? The tension between the two approaches is nicely illustrated in a quote attributed (probably inaccurately) to Woodrow Wilson when he was president of Princeton University. "How can I democratize this university," he demanded, "if the faculty won't do what I ask?"

Should there be a high degree of structure in the relationship—a sharp differentiation between the roles of leaders and followers, a clear hierarchy of authority with emphasis on detailed assignments and task specifications? Or should the relationship be more informal, less structured, with leaders making the goals clear and then letting constituents help determine the way of proceeding?

Should there be an atmosphere of discipline, constraints, controls—in Navy parlance, "a tight ship"—or should there be autonomy, individual responsibility, and freedom for growth, with the leader in the role of nurturer, supporter, listener, helper?

Should the leader focus on the job to be done—be "task-oriented" as the researchers put it—or should the leader be concerned primarily with the people performing the task, with their needs, their morale, their growth?

No Simple Answers

More than four decades of objective research have not produced clear answers to these questions. Simple answers have not emerged from the research because there are not any simple answers, only complicated answers hedged by conditions and exceptions. Followers do like being treated with consideration, do like having their say, do like being able to exercise their own initiative—and participation does increase acceptance of decisions. But there are times when followers welcome rather than reject authority, want prompt and clear decisions from the leader, want to close ranks around the leader.

In recent decades there has been increasing support for the view that the purposes of the group are best served by a relationship in which the leader helps followers to develop their own judgment and enables them to grow and to become better contributors. Industrial concerns are experimenting with measures that further such a relationship because of their hard-won awareness that some matters (for example, quality control, productivity, morale) simply cannot be dealt with unless highly motivated workers on site are committed to deal with them. Anyone who believes that people should be encouraged to the full development of their powers is bound to applaud the trend.

To the extent that leaders enable followers to develop their own initiative, they are creating something that can survive their own departure. If they have, in addition, the gift for institution-building, they may create a legacy that will last for a very long time. Some individuals who have dazzling powers of personal leadership not only fail to build institutions but create dependency in those below them. However spectacular their own performance, they leave behind a weakened organization staffed by weakened people.

The two-way conversation between leaders and followers is deeply influenced by the expectations of followers. Any social group, if it is more than a crowd of unrelated strangers, has certain shared needs, aspirations, values, hopes, and fears. The group creates norms that tend to control the behavior of its members, and these norms constitute the social order. It is in this context that leaders arise; and it is this context that determines what kinds of leaders will emerge and what will be expected of them. A loyal constituency is won when people consciously or unconsciously judge the leader to be capable of solving their problems and meeting their needs, when the leader is seen as symbolizing their norms, and when their image of the leader (whether or not it corresponds to reality) is congruent with their inner environment of myth and legend.

Effective leaders deal not only with the explicit decisions of the day—approving a budget, announcing a policy, disciplining a subordinate—but also with that partly conscious, partly buried world of needs and hopes, ideals and symbols. They serve as models; they symbolize the group's unity and identity; they retell the stories that carry shared meanings. William James says that the struggle between right and wrong is a matter of helping our best selves to act. Leaders can perform that function. Unfortunately, they can also help our worst selves to act. Their confidence—or, for that matter, their lack of confidence—communicates itself to followers. "For if the trumpet give an uncertain sound," says the Bible, "who shall prepare himself to the battle?"

To analyze complex problems, leaders must have a capacity for rational problem solving; but they must also have a penetrating intuitive grasp of the needs and moods of followers. Woodrow Wilson said, "The ear of the leader must ring with the voices of the people." The ablest leaders understand, rationally and intuitively, the embedded expectations of people with respect to their leadership. And they are adept at meeting those expectations not only with rational verbal pronouncements but with symbolic acts, ritual observances, and the like.

30

Leaders and Followers Are the People in this Relationship

Joseph C. Rost

Joseph C. Rost received his Ph.D. from the University of Wisconsin, and has served as a superintendent of schools. At the University of San Diego he inaugurated a doctoral program in leadership, as well as a leadership minor for undergraduates. He is currently professor of leadership and administration in the School of Education at the University of San Diego.

The second essential element flowing from the definition of leadership is that the people involved in this relationship are leaders and followers. This sounds rather innocuous, but there are several important points to be gained from examining this element, especially the meaning of the word *followers*.

Active Followers

I have no trouble with the word *followers*, but it does bother a number of other scholars and practitioners, who view the word as condescending. Gardner,[1,2] for instance, has rejected the word in favor of *constituents*. That word is problematic, however, because it has strong political connotations. People don't speak about constituents in small groups or clubs, business or religious

Joseph C. Rost, *Leadership for the Twenty-First Century*, pp. 107–109, reprinted with permission of Greenwood Publishing Group, Inc., Westport, CT. Copyright 1991 by Joseph C. Rost.

organizations, and the like. The word is mostly used in political organizations and as a result is unsatisfactory for a model of leadership that applies to all organizations and groups. Ford[3] used the word *participants*, which has much more generalizability to different organizations. Gardner and Ford are two of quite a number of leadership scholars who want to get rid of the word *followers* for mostly egalitarian reasons.

My view is that the problem is not with the word, but with the passive meaning given to the concept of followers by people who lived and worked and wrote in the industrial era. Followers, as a concept, connoted a group of people who were (1) part of the sweaty masses and therefore separated from the elites, (2) not able to act intelligently without the guidance and control of others, (3) willing to let other people (elites) take control of their lives, and (4) unproductive unless directed by others. In the leadership literature since the 1930s, therefore, followers were considered to be subordinates who were submissive and passive, and leaders were considered to be managers who were directive and active. Since leaders were managers, followers had to be the subordinate people in an organization. There is no other logical equation.

In a postindustrial frame, leaders are not equated with managers, so followers are not equated with subordinates. Since leaders can be anyone, followers can be anyone. That does not mean that leaders and followers are equal. No amount of egalitarian idealism will change the fact that there will be followers as long as human beings inhabit this planet. Only the meaning of the word *followers* will change, not the existence of human beings who are followers.

A distinction between leaders and followers remains crucial to the concept of leadership. Since leadership is a relationship, leaders must interact with other people. If all the people with whom leaders interacted were other leaders, leadership as a meaningful construct would not make much sense.

For one thing, leadership would be quite an elitist or exclusive group of people, since there are and will be many people who are not motivated to be leaders, who do not have the personal development needed to be leaders in a sophisticated and complex society, or who are not willing to use the power resources at their command to exercise significant influence through persuasion. I think we need to reject any elitist notion of leadership in spelling out who can participate in the relationship that is leadership.

One could argue that if all people were leaders, the notion of leadership would not be elitist. I agree. But everyone being leader is not consistent with what we know of human nature, even if we do not equate leadership with good management. Our human nature is not going to change all that much in the postindustrial era.

A second difficulty with the notion that we are all leaders is the complexity of our times and that of the postindustrial era. Active people may be involved in a dozen or more leadership relationships at any one time, and it is conceptually impossible to conceive of them being leaders in all of these influence relationships. Scholars tend to think of people being in only one leadership relationship, but that is not the way people live their lives. Even people who are less active may have several leadership relationships going on at any one time. The only possible way for people to cope with such multiple relationships is for them to be leaders in some relationships and followers in others. If one examines the many other relationships in which these active people are involved (love, friendship, professional, work, religious, etc.), the complexity of their lives becomes clear. Time restraints alone require that people be followers in some leadership relationships.

Realistically, we know from past experience that some people choose to be followers all the time and that many other people choose not to be involved in any leadership relationships. The complexity of life and our understanding of human nature based on centuries of experience would suggest that these two groups of people will continue to exist in the postindustrial era.

Thus, followers are part of the leadership relationship in a new paradigm of leadership. What is different about the emerging view of followers is the substantive meaning attached to the word and the clarity given to that understanding. The following five points give the concept of followers substance and clarity.

First, only people who are active in the leadership process are followers. Passive people are not in a relationship. They have chosen not to be involved. They cannot have influence. Passive people are not followers.

Second, active people can fall anywhere on a continuum of activity from highly active to minimally active, and their influence in the leadership process is, in large part, based on their activity, their willingness to get involved, their use of the power resources they have at their command to influence other people. Some followers are very active; others are not so active. Some followers are very active at certain times and not so active at other times.

Third, followers can become leaders and leaders can become followers in any one leadership relationship. People are not stuck in one or the other for the whole time the relationship exists. Followers may be leaders for a while, and leaders may be followers for a while. Followers do not have to be managers to be leaders. This ability to change places without changing organizational positions gives followers considerable influence and mobility.

Fourth, in one group or organization people can be leaders. In other groups and organizations they can be followers. Followers are not always followers in all leadership relationships.

Fifth, and most important, followers do not do followership, they do leadership. Both leaders and followers form one relationship that is leadership. There is no such thing as followership in the new school of leadership. Followership makes sense only in the industrial leadership paradigm, where leadership is good management. Since followers who are subordinates could not do management (since they were not managers), they had to do followership. No wonder followership connoted subordination, submissiveness, and passivity. *In the new paradigm, followers and leaders do leadership.* They are in the leadership relationship together. They are the ones who intend real changes that reflect their mutual purposes. Metaphorically, their activities are two sides of the same coin, the two it takes to tango, the composer and musicians making music, the female and male generating new life, the yin and the yang. Followers and leaders develop a relationship wherein they influence one another as well as the organization and society, and that is leadership. They do not do the same things in the relationship, just as the composers and musicians do not do the same thing in making music, but they are both essential to leadership.

31

In Praise of Followers

Robert E. Kelley

Robert E. Kelley is a professor at the Graduate School of Industrial Administration at Carnegie Mellon University and president of Consultants to Executives and Organizations, Ltd. His most recent book is *The Power of Followership*.

W e are convinced that corporations succeed or fail, compete or crumble, on the basis of how well they are led. So we study great leaders of the past and present and spend vast quantities of time and money looking for leaders to hire and trying to cultivate leadership in the employees we already have.

I have no argument with this enthusiasm. Leaders matter greatly. But in searching so zealously for better leaders we tend to lose sight of the people these leaders will lead. Without his armies, after all, Napoleon was just a man with grandiose ambitions. Organizations stand or fall partly on the basis of how well their leaders lead, but partly also on the basis of how well their followers follow.

In 1987, declining profitability and intensified competition for corporate clients forced a large commercial bank on the east coast to reorganize its operations and cut its work force. Its most seasoned managers had to spend most of their time in the field working with corporate customers. Time and energies were stretched so thin that one department head decided he had no choice but to delegate the responsibility for reorganization to his staff people, who had recently had training in self-management.

Despite grave doubts, the department head set them up as a unit without a leader, responsible to one another and to the bank as a whole for writing their own job descriptions, designing a training program determining criteria for performance evaluation, planning for operational needs, and helping to achieve overall organizational objectives.

They pulled it off. The bank's officers were delighted and frankly amazed that rank-and-file employees could assume so much responsibility so successfully. In fact, the department's capacity to control and direct itself virtually without leadership saved the organization months of turmoil, and as the bank struggled to remain a major player in its region, valuable management time was freed up to put out other fires.

What was it these singular employees did? Given a goal and parameters, they went where most departments could only have gone under the hands-on guidance of an effective leader. But these employees accepted the delegation of authority and went there alone. They thought for themselves, sharpened their skills, focused their efforts, put on a fine display of grit and spunk and self-control. They followed effectively.

To encourage this kind of effective following in other organizations, we need to understand the nature of the follower's role. To cultivate good followers, we need to understand the human qualities that allow effective followership to occur.

The Role of Follower

Bosses are not necessarily good leaders; subordinates are not necessarily effective followers. Many bosses couldn't lead a horse to water. Many subordinates couldn't follow a parade. Some people avoid either role. Others accept the role thrust upon them and perform it badly.

At different points in their careers, even at different times of the working day, most managers play both roles, though seldom equally well. After all, the leadership role has the glamour and attention. We take courses to learn it, and when we play it well we get applause and recognition. But the reality is that most of us are more often followers than leaders. Even when we have subordinates, we still have bosses. For every committee we chair, we sit as a member on several others.

So followership dominates our lives and organizations, but not our thinking, because our preoccupation with leadership keeps us from considering the nature and the importance of the follower.

What distinguishes an effective from an ineffective follower is enthusiastic, intelligent, and self-reliant participation—without star billing—in the pursuit of an organizational goal. Effective followers differ in their motivations for following and in their perceptions of the role. Some choose followership as their primary role at work and serve as team players who take satisfaction in helping to further a cause, an idea, a product, a service, or, more rarely, a person. Others are leaders in some situations but choose the follower role in a particular context. Both these groups view the role of follower as legitimate, inherently valuable, even virtuous.

Some potentially effective followers derive motivation from ambition. By proving themselves in the follower's role, they hope to win the confidence of peers and superiors and move up the corporate ladder. These people do not see followership as attractive in itself. All the same, they can become good followers if they accept the value of learning the role, studying leaders from a subordinate's perspective, and polishing the followership skills that will always stand them in good stead.

Understanding motivations and perceptions is not enough, however. Since followers with different motivations can perform equally well, I examined the behavior that leads to effective and less effective following among people committed to the organization and came up with two underlying behavioral dimensions that help to explain the difference.

One dimension measures to what degree followers exercise independent, critical thinking. The other ranks them on a passive/active scale. The resulting diagram identifies five followership patterns. [See Figure 1.]

Sheep are passive and uncritical, lacking in initiative and sense of responsibility. They perform the tasks given them and stop. Yes People are a livelier but equally unenterprising group. Dependent on a leader for inspiration, they can be aggressively deferential, even servile. Bosses weak in judgment and self-confidence tend to like them and to form alliances with them that can stultify the organization.

Alienated Followers are critical and independent in their thinking but passive in carrying out their role. Somehow, sometime, something turned them off. Often cynical, they tend to sink gradually into disgruntled acquiescence, seldom openly opposing a leader's efforts. In the very center of the diagram we have Survivors, who perpetually sample the wind and live by the slogan "better safe than sorry." They are adept at surviving change.

In the upper right-hand corner, finally, we have Effective Followers, who think for themselves and carry out their duties and assignments with energy and assertiveness. Because they are risk takers, self-starters, and independent problem solvers, they get consistently high ratings from peers and many superiors. Followership of this kind can be a positive and acceptable choice for parts or all of our lives—a source of pride and fulfillment.

Effective followers are well-balanced and responsible adults who can succeed without strong leadership. Many followers believe they offer as much value to the organization as leaders do, especially in project or task-force situations. In an organization of effective followers, a leader tends to be more an overseer of change and progress than a hero. As organizational structures flatten, the quality of those who follow will become more and more important. As Chester I. Barnard wrote 50 years ago in *The Functions of the Executive*, "The decision as to whether an order has authority or not lies with the person to whom it is addressed, and does not reside in 'persons of authority' or those who issue orders."

The Qualities of Followers

Effective followers share a number of essential qualities:

1. They manage themselves well.
2. They are committed to the organization and to a purpose, principle, or person outside themselves.
3. They build their competence and focus their efforts for maximum impact.
4. They are courageous, honest, and credible.

Self-Management

Paradoxically, the key to being an effective follower is the ability to think for oneself—to exercise control and independence and to work without close supervision. Good followers are people to whom a leader can safely delegate responsibility, people who anticipate needs at their own level of competence and authority.

Another aspect of this paradox is that effective followers see themselves—except in terms of line responsibility—as the equals of the leaders they follow. They are more apt to openly and unapologetically disagree with leadership and less likely to be intimidated by hierarchy and organizational structure. At

FIGURE 1

Five Followership Patterns

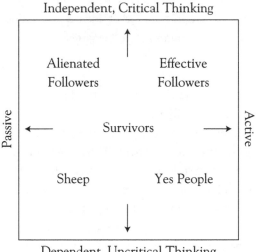

Independent, Critical Thinking

Alienated Followers   Effective Followers

Passive ←——   Survivors   ——→ Active

Sheep   Yes People

Dependent, Uncritical Thinking

the same time, they can see that the people they follow are, in turn, following the lead of others, and they try to appreciate the goals and needs of the team and the organization. Ineffective followers, on the other hand, buy into the hierarchy and, seeing themselves as subservient, vacillate between despair over their seeming powerlessness and attempts to manipulate leaders for their own purposes. Either their fear of powerlessness becomes a self-fulfilling prophecy—for themselves and often for their work units as well—or their resentment leads them to undermine the team's goals.

Self-managed followers give their organizations a significant cost advantage because they eliminate much of the need for elaborate supervisory control systems that, in any case, often lower morale. In 1985, a large midwestern bank redesigned its personnel selection system to attract self-managed workers. Those conducting interviews began to look for particular types of experience and capacities—initiative, teamwork, independent thinking of all kinds—and the bank revamped its orientation program to emphasize self-management. At the executive level, role playing was introduced into the interview process: how you disagree with your boss, how you prioritize your in-basket after a vacation. In the three years since, employee turnover has dropped dramatically, the need for supervisors has decreased, and administrative costs have gone down.

Of course not all leaders and managers like having self-managing subordinates. Some would rather have sheep or yes people. The best that good followers can do in this situation is to protect themselves with a little career self-management—that is, to stay attractive in the marketplace. The qualities that make a good follower are too much in demand to go begging for long.

Commitment

Effective followers are committed to something—a cause, a product, an organization, an idea—in addition to the care of their own lives and careers. Some leaders misinterpret this commitment. Seeing their authority acknowledged, they mistake loyalty to a goal for loyalty to themselves. But the fact is that many effective followers see leaders merely as coadventurers on a worthy crusade, and if they suspect their leader of flagging commitment or conflicting motives they may just withdraw their support, either by changing jobs or by contriving to change leaders.

The opportunities and the dangers posed by this kind of commitment are not hard to see. On the one hand, commitment is contagious. Most people like working with colleagues whose hearts are in their work. Morale stays high. Workers who begin to wander from their purpose are jostled back into line. Projects stay on track and on time. In addition, an appreciation of commitment and the way it works can give managers an extra tool with which to understand and channel the energies and loyalties of their subordinates.

On the other hand, followers who are strongly committed to goals not consistent with the goals of their companies can produce destructive results. Leaders having such followers can even lose control of their organizations.

A scientist at a computer company cared deeply about making computer technology available to the masses, and her work was outstanding. Since her goal was in line with the company's goals, she had few problems with top management. Yet she saw her department leaders essentially as facilitators of her dream, and when managers worked at cross-purposes to that vision, she exercised all of her considerable political skills to their detriment. Her immediate supervisors saw her as a thorn in the side, but she was quite effective in furthering her cause because she saw eye to eye with company leaders. But what if her vision and the company's vision had differed?

Effective followers temper their loyalties to satisfy organizational needs—or they find new organizations. Effective leaders know how to channel the energies of strong commitment in ways that will satisfy corporate goals as well as a follower's personal needs.

Competence and Focus

On the grounds that committed incompetence is still incompetence, effective followers master skills that will be useful to their organizations. They generally hold higher performance standards than the work environment requires, and continuing education is second nature to them, a staple in their professional development.

Less effective followers expect training and development to come to them. The only education they acquire is force-fed. If not sent to a seminar, they don't go. Their competence deteriorates unless some leader gives them parental care and attention.

Good followers take on extra work gladly, but first they do a superb job on their core responsibilities. They are good judges of their own strengths and weaknesses, and they contribute well to teams. Asked to perform in areas where they are poorly qualified, they speak up. Like athletes stretching their capacities, they don't mind chancing failure if they know they can succeed, but they are careful to spare the company wasted energy, lost time, and poor performance by accepting challenges that coworkers are better prepared to meet. Good followers see coworkers as colleagues rather than competitors.

At the same time, effective followers often search for overlooked problems. A woman on a new product development team discovered that no one was responsible for coordinating engineering, marketing, and manufacturing. She worked out an interdepartmental review schedule that identified the people who should be involved at each stage of development. Instead of burdening her boss with yet another problem, this woman took the initiative to present the issue along with a solution.

Another woman I interviewed described her efforts to fill a dangerous void in the company she cared about. Young managerial talent in this manufacturing corporation had traditionally made careers in production. Convinced that foreign competition would alter the shape of the industry, she realized that marketing was a neglected area. She took classes, attended seminars, and read widely. More important, she visited customers to get feedback about her company's and competitors' products, and she soon knew more about the product's customer appeal and market position than any of her peers. The extra competence did wonders for her own career, but it also helped her company weather a storm it had not seen coming.

Courage

Effective followers are credible, honest, and courageous. They establish themselves as independent, critical thinkers whose knowledge and judgment can be trusted. They give credit where credit is due, admitting mistakes and sharing successes. They form their own views and ethical standards and stand up for what they believe in.

Insightful, candid, and fearless, they can keep leaders and colleagues honest and informed. The other side of the coin of course is that they can also cause great trouble for a leader with questionable ethics.

Jerome LiCari, the former R&D director at Beech-Nut, suspected for several years that the apple concentrate Beech-Nut was buying from a new supplier at 20% below market price was adulterated. His department suggested switching suppliers, but top management at the financially strapped company put the burden of proof on R&D.

By 1981, LiCari had accumulated strong evidence of adulteration and issued a memo recommending a change of supplier. When he got no response, he went to see his boss, the head of operations. According to LiCari, he was threatened with dismissal for lack of team spirit. LiCari then went to the president of Beech-Nut, and when that, too, produced no results, he gave up his three-year good-soldier effort, followed his conscience, and resigned. His last performance evaluation praised his expertise and loyalty, but said his judgment was "colored by naiveté and impractical ideals."

In 1986, Beech-Nut and LiCari's two bosses were indicted on several hundred counts of conspiracy to commit fraud by distributing adulterated apple juice. In November 1987, the company pleaded guilty and agreed to a fine of $2 million. In February of this year, the two executives were found guilty on a majority of the charges. The episode cost Beech-Nut an estimated $25 million and a 20% loss of market share. Asked during the trial if he had been naive, LiCari said, "I guess I was. I thought apple juice should be made from apples."

Is LiCari a good follower? Well, no, not to his dishonest bosses. But yes, he is almost certainly the kind of employee most companies want to have: loyal, honest, candid with his superiors, and thoroughly credible. In an ethical company involved unintentionally in questionable practices, this kind of follower can head off embarrassment, expense, and litigation.

Cultivating Effective Followers

You may have noticed by now that the qualities that make effective followers are, confusingly enough, pretty much the same qualities found in some effective leaders. This is no mere coincidence, of course. But the confusion underscores an important point. If a person has initiative, self-control, commitment, talent, honesty, credibility, and courage, we say, "Here is a leader!" By definition, a follower cannot exhibit the qualities of leadership. It violates our stereotype.

But our stereotype is ungenerous and wrong. Followership is not a person but a role, and what distinguishes followers from leaders is not intelligence or character but the role they play. As I pointed out at the beginning of this article, effective followers and effective leaders are often the same people playing different parts at different hours of the day.

In many companies, the leadership track is the only road to career success. In almost all companies, leadership is taught and encouraged while followership is not. Yet effective followership is a prerequisite for organizational success. Your organization can take four steps to cultivate effective followers in your work force.

1. Redefining Followership and Leadership

Our stereotyped but unarticulated definitions of leadership and followership shape our expectations when we occupy either position. If a leader is defined as responsible for motivating followers, he or she will likely act toward followers as if they needed motivation. If we agree that a leader's job is to transform followers, then it must be a follower's job to provide the clay. If followers fail to need transformation, the leader looks ineffective. The way we define the roles clearly influences the outcome of the interaction.

Instead of seeing the leadership role as superior to and more active than the role of the follower, we can think of them as equal but different activities. The operative definitions are roughly these: people who are effective in the leader role have the vision to set corporate goals and strategies, the interpersonal skills to achieve consensus, the verbal capacity to communicate enthusiasm to large and diverse groups of individuals, the organizational talent to coordinate disparate efforts, and, above all, the desire to lead.

People who are effective in the follower role have the vision to see both the forest and the trees, the social capacity to work well with others, the strength of character to flourish without heroic status, the moral and psychological balance to pursue personal and corporate goals at no cost to either, and, above all, the desire to participate in a team effort for the accomplishment of some greater common purpose.

This view of leadership and followership can be conveyed to employees directly and indirectly—in training and by example. The qualities that make good followers and the value the company places on effective followership can be articulated in explicit follower training. Perhaps the best way to convey this message, however, is by example. Since each of us plays a follower's part at least from time to time, it is essential that we play it well, that we contribute our competence to the achievement of team goals, that we support the team leader with candor and self-control, that we do our best to appreciate and enjoy the role of quiet contribution to a larger, common cause.

2. Honing Followership Skills

Most organizations assume that leadership has to be taught but that everyone knows how to follow. This assumption is based on three faulty premises: (1) that leaders are more important than followers, (2) that following is simply doing what you are told to do, and (3) that followers inevitably draw their energy and aims, even their talent, from the leader. A program of follower training can correct this misapprehension by focusing on topics like:

Improving independent, critical thinking.

Self-management.
  Disagreeing agreeably.
  Building credibility.

Aligning personal and organizational goals and commitments.

Acting responsibly toward the organization, the leader, coworkers, and oneself.

Similarities and differences between leadership and followership roles.

Moving between the two roles with ease.

3. Performance Evaluation and Feedback

Most performance evaluations include a section on leadership skills. Followership evaluation would include items like the ones I have discussed. Instead of rating employees on leadership qualities such as self-management, independent thinking, originality, courage, competence, and credibility, we can rate them on these same qualities in both the leadership and followership roles and then evaluate each individual's ability to shift easily from the one role to the other. A variety of performance perspectives will help most people understand better how well they play their various organizational roles.

Moreover, evaluations can come from peers, subordinates, and self as well as from supervisors. The process is simple enough: peers and subordinates who come into regular or significant contact with another employee fill in brief, periodic questionnaires where they rate the individual on followership qualities. Findings are then summarized and given to the employee being rated.

4. Organizational Structures That Encourage Followership

Unless the value of good following is somehow built into the fabric of the organization, it is likely to remain a pleasant conceit to which everyone pays occasional lip service but no dues. Here are four good ways to incorporate the concept into your corporate culture:

In leaderless groups, all members assume equal responsibility for achieving goals. These are usually small task forces of people who can work together under their own supervision. However hard it is to imagine a group with more than one leader, groups with none at all can be highly productive if their members have the qualities of effective followers.

Groups with temporary and rotating leadership are another possibility. Again, such groups are probably best kept small and the rotation fairly frequent, although the notion might certainly be extended to include the administration of a small department for, say, six-month terms. Some of these temporary leaders will be less effective than others, of course, and some may be weak indeed, which is why critics maintain that this structure is inefficient. Why not let the best leader lead? Why suffer through the tenure of less effective leaders? There are two reasons. First, experience of the leadership role is essential to the education of effective followers. Second, followers learn that they must compensate for ineffective leadership by exercising their skill as good followers. Rotating leader or not, they are bound to be faced with ineffective leadership more than once in their careers.

Delegation to the lowest level is a third technique for cultivating good followers. Nordstrom's, the Seattle-based department store chain, gives each sales clerk responsibility for servicing and satisfying the customer, including the authority to make refunds without supervisory approval. This kind of delegation makes even people at the lowest levels responsible for their own decisions and for thinking independently about their work.

Finally, companies can use rewards to underline the importance of good followership. This is not as easy as it sounds. Managers dependent on yes people and sheep for ego gratification will not leap at the idea of extra rewards for the people who make them most uncomfortable. In my research, I have found that effective followers get mixed treatment. About half the time, their contributions lead to substantial rewards. The other half of the time they are punished by their superiors for exercising judgment, taking risks, and failing to conform. Many managers insist that they want independent subordinates who can think for themselves. In practice, followers who challenge their bosses run the risk of getting fired.

In today's flatter, leaner organization, companies will not succeed without the kind of people who take pride and satisfaction in the role of supporting player, doing the less glorious work without fanfare. Organizations that want the benefits of effective followers must find ways of rewarding them, ways of bringing them into full partnership in the enterprise. Think of the thousands of companies that achieve adequate performance and lackluster profits with employees they treat like second-class citizens. Then imagine for a moment the power of an organization blessed with fully engaged, fully energized, fully appreciated followers.

PART VII

LEADERS AND FOLLOWERS TOGETHER

After exploring leaders and their followers, it will come as no surprise that we now turn to the relationship between the two. One of the first and most influential attempts to track the interaction between leader and followers has been Paul Hersey and Kenneth Blanchard's model known as "Situational Leadership," described in selection 32. This is followed by one of the more innovative of the recent conceptions of leader–follower relations: the Charles C. Manz and Henry P. Sims, Jr. notion of "SuperLeadership," which argues that the most appropriate leader today is one who can lead others to lead themselves.

The discussion of the interactions between leaders and followers raises important questions about the impact of gender, race, ethnicity, and other forms of diversity upon the leadership relation. Our selections on this topic begin with an important conceptual piece from Jean Miller's important work, Toward a New Psychology of Women. *Miller's model for how unequal relationships form and persist is followed by the stark reality of Ann Morrison's field study of the "barriers to opportunity" faced by women and other minorities.*

32

Situational Leadership

Paul Hersey and Kenneth H. Blanchard

Paul Hersey and Kenneth Blanchard have been at the forefront of leadership studies for a number of years, developing and refining the theory of Situational Leadership. Paul Hersey now heads the Center for Leadership Studies. Kenneth Blanchard has co-authored the internationally known *The One Minute Manager* and related books. He is currently at the School of Hotel Administration at Cornell University.

Situational Leadership® is an attempt to demonstrate the appropriate relationship between the leader's behavior and a particular aspect of the situation—the readiness level exhibited by the followers. According to the model, the leader must remain sensitive to the follower's level of readiness. As personal problems arise, new tasks are assigned, or new goals are established, the level of readiness may change. The model prescribes that leaders should adjust their behavior accordingly. Thus, situational leadership assumes a dynamic interaction where the readiness level of the followers may change and where the leader's behavior must change appropriately in order to maintain the performance of the followers.

In Situational Leadership® readiness is defined as the ability and willing-

Adapted from course materials at the United States Military Academy. Situational Leadership® is a registered trademark of the Center for Leadership Studies, Inc. All rights reserved. Reprinted by permission.

ness of followers to perform a particular task. Ability is a function of the knowledge and/or skills which can be gained from education, training, and/or experience. Willingness is a combination of commitment, confidence and motivation. A confident follower is one who feels able to do a task well without much supervision, whereas motivation is defined as a person's interest and enthusiasm in doing the task.

Situational Leadership® identifies four readiness levels which combine the ability and willingness of the group as illustrated in Table 1.

According to Situational Leadership, as the readiness levels of individuals increase from R1 to R4, the followers' ability and willingness fluctuate. When first beginning a new task, where they have had little, if any, prior knowledge or experience, most individuals are tentative or insecure. Then, when they begin to get into the task, followers respond to the leader's assistance. This builds confidence which increases as skills are acquired (R2).

If they overcome this stage of development and learn to perform the task with help from the leader, most individuals then go through a self-doubt stage where they question whether they can perform the task well on their own. The leader would say that they are competent, but they are not sure of their competence. These alternating feelings of competence and self-doubt cause the variable commitment (sometimes excitement, other times self-doubt) associated with R3. Once the self-doubt is overcome, the followers move from (R3) to a peak performer (R4).

Depending on the development level of the followers, Situational Leadership prescribes the use of one of four different combinations of task and relationship leader behaviors as depicted in Table 2.

Task behavior is defined as the extent to which a leader engages in one-way communication; spells out the followers' role and tells the followers what to do, where to do it, and how to do it; and then the leader closely supervises

TABLE 1
Situational Leadership Readiness Levels

Follower's Level	Ability	Willingness
R1	Low	Low
R2	Moderate	High
R3	High	Variable
R4	High	High

performance. Relationship behavior is defined as the extent to which a leader engages in two-way communication, listens, provides encouragement, facilitates interaction, and involves the followers in decision-making.

High task and low relationship behavior (S1) is referred to as "Telling." The leader defines the roles of the followers and tells them what, how, when and where to do various tasks. Problem-solving and decision-making are initiated solely by the leader. Solutions and decisions are announced by the leader; communication is largely one-way, and implementation is closely supervised by the leader. Although this style may appear to be highly authoritarian, it is appropriate for a group with a low readiness level which lacks the necessary task competence (R1). Thus, a "Telling" style (S1) that provides clear, specific direction and close supervision has the highest probability of addressing their inability to do the task.

High task and high relationship behavior (S2) is referred to as "Selling." In this style, the leader still provides a great deal of direction and leads with his/her ideas, but the leader also attempts to hear the followers' feelings about decisions as well as their ideas and suggestions. While two-way communication and support are increased, control over decision-making remains with the leader. Followers who have some competence but are willing to learn (R2) and to take responsibility need both direction and support. A "selling" or coaching style (S2) that provides dual task behavior (because of their lack of competence) but also supportive behavior to build confidence and enthusiasm is most appropriate with individuals at this readiness level. This style encourages two-way communication in order to build the confidence and motivation of the person who is struggling to acquire new competence and skills. However, the leader must keep the responsibility for and control over decision-making until the group acquires the necessary task competence.

TABLE 2
Situational Leadership Task and Relationship Leader Behaviors

	Leader Behaviors	
	Task	Relationship
S1	High	Low
S2	High	High
S3	Low	High
S4	Low	Low

Low task and high relationship behavior (S3) is called "Participating." With this style, the control over day-to-day decision-making and problem-solving shifts from the leader to the followers. The leader's role is: to provide recognition; to actively listen; and to facilitate any problem-solving and decision-making that is done by the followers. This style is appropriate for a group with a moderate to high level of readiness (R3). People in this development level are competent but have variable commitment toward the assigned task.

Their variable motivation is often a function of a lack of confidence or insecurity in their newly acquired competence. However, if they are confident but uncommitted (remember that "commitment" includes both motivation and confidence), their reluctance to perform will be more of a motivation problem than a confidence problem. In either case, the leader needs to open up communication to support the follower's effort to use the skills they already have or those which they have recently acquired.

Low relationship and low task behavior (S4) is labeled "Delegating." With an S4 style, the leader discusses the problem with followers until a joint agreement is achieved on problem definition. Then the decision-making process is delegated totally to the followers. Now it is the followers who have the significant control for deciding how tasks are to be accomplished. Followers are allowed to "run their own show" and take responsibility for directing their own behavior. Thus, a "Delegating" style (S4) that provides little direction and support will be most appropriate for a group in the highest level of development (R4). This style does not mean that the leader is completely uninvolved. Rather, the leader can spend more time on goal-setting and problem identification because the group does not need the leader's constant attention.

In summary, Situational Leadership describes a way of adapting leadership behaviors to features of the situation and the followers. The key point is that the leader provides what is lacking in the situation, as depicted in Figure 1.

Even though Situational Leadership appears to be simple, you might think of a number of other situational variables that may influence the appropriateness of any leadership style. Hersey and Blanchard have based this approach to leadership on the factors they feel have the greatest impact on the choice of leadership style. The followers' effectiveness will ultimately depend on the manner in which the leader applies the appropriate combinations of directive and supportive behaviors. Effective leaders need to be able to adapt their chosen style to fit the requirements of the situation. Therefore, the leader must not only know when to use a particular style, but also know how to make each style fit into the situation in order to maximize the performance of subordinates.

FIGURE 1

Situational Leadership Leader Behavior

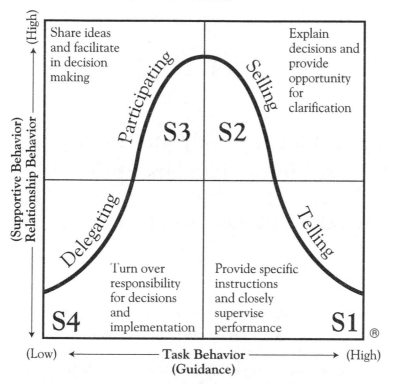

Adapted from Paul Hersey, *Situational Selling* (Escondido, Calif.: Center for Leadership Studies, 1985), p. 19.

33

SuperLeadership: Beyond the Myth of Heroic Leadership

Charles C. Manz and Henry P. Sims, Jr.

Charles C. Manz is co-author (with Henry Sims) of *SuperLeadership: Leading Others to Lead Themselves* and author of *Mastering Self-Leadership*. He is associate professor of management at Arizona State University. Henry P. Sims, Jr., has held management positions at Ford Motor Company, U.S. Steel Corporation, and Armco Corporation. He has published more than 75 articles, and is currently professor of management and organization at the University of Maryland.

When most of us think of leadership, we think of one person doing something to another person. This is "influence," and a leader is someone who has the capacity to influence another. Words like "charismatic" and "heroic" are sometimes used to describe a leader. The word "leader" itself conjures up visions of a striking figure on a rearing white horse who is crying "Follow me!" The leader is the one who has either the power or the authority to command others.

Many historical figures fit this mold: Alexander, Caesar, Napoleon, Washington, Churchill. Even today, the turnaround of Chrysler Corporation by Lee Iacocca might be thought of as an act of contemporary heroic leadership.

It's not difficult to think of Iacocca astride a white horse, and he is frequently thought of as "charismatic."

But is this heroic figure of the leader the most appropriate image of the organizational leader of today? Is there another model? We believe there is. In many modern situations, *the most appropriate leader is one who can lead others to lead themselves.* We call this powerful new kind of leadership "Super-Leadership".

Our viewpoint represents a departure from the dominant and, we think, incomplete view of leadership. Our position is that true leadership comes mainly from within a person, not from outside. At its best, external leadership provides a spark and supports the flame of the true inner leadership that dwells within each person. At its worst, it disrupts this internal process, causing damage to the person and the constituencies he or she serves.

Our focus is on a new form of leadership that is designed to facilitate the self-leadership energy within each person. This perspective suggests a new measure of a leader's strength—one's ability to maximize the contributions of others through recognition of their right to guide their own destiny, rather than the leader's ability to bend the will of others to his or her own. The challenge for organizations is to understand how to go about bringing out the wealth of talent that each employee possesses. Many still operate under a quasi-military model that encourages conformity and adherence rather than one that emphasizes how leaders can lead others to lead themselves.

Why Is SuperLeadership an Important Perspective?

This SuperLeadership perspective is especially important today because of several recent trends facing American businesses. First, the challenge to United States corporations from world competition has pressured companies to utilize more fully their human resources. Second, the workforce itself has changed a great deal in recent decades—for instance, "baby boomers" have carried into their organization roles elevated expectations and a need for greater meaning in their work lives.

As a consequence of these kinds of pressures, organizations have increasingly experimented with innovative work designs. Widespread introduction of modern management techniques, such as quality circles, self-managed work teams, Japanese business practices, and flatter organization structures, has led to the inherent dilemma of trying to provide strong leadership for workers who are being encouraged and allowed to become increasingly self-managed. The result is a major knowledge gap about appropriate new leadership approaches under conditions of increasing employee participation. The SuperLeadership approach is designed to meet these kinds of challenges.

Before presenting specific steps for becoming a SuperLeader, it is useful to contrast SuperLeadership with other views of leadership.

Viewpoints on what constitutes successful leadership in organizations have changed significantly over time. A simplified historical perspective on different approaches to leadership is presented in Table 1. As it suggests, four different types of leader can be distinguished: the "strong man," the "transactor," the "visionary hero," and the "SuperLeader."

The *strong-man view* of leadership is perhaps the earliest dominant form in our culture. The emphasis with this autocratic view is on the strength of the leader. We use the masculine noun purposely because when this leadership approach was most prevalent it was almost a completely male-dominated process.

The strong-man view of leadership still exists today in many organizations (and is still widely reserved for males), although it is not as highly regarded as it once was.

The strong-man view of leadership creates an image of a John Wayne type who is not afraid to "knock some heads" to get followers to do what he wants done. The expertise for knowing what should be done rests almost entirely in the leader. It is he who sizes up the situation and, based on some seemingly superior strength, skill, and courage, delivers firm commands to the workers. If the job is not performed as commanded, inevitably some significant form of punishment will be delivered by the leader to the guilty party. The focus is on the leader whose power stems primarily from his position in the organization. He is the primary source of wisdom and direction—strong direction. Subordinates simply comply. . . .

The second view of leadership is that of a *transactor*.

As time passed in our culture, the dominance of the strong-man view of leadership lessened somewhat. Women began to find themselves more frequently in leadership positions. With the development of knowledge of the power of rewards (such as that coming from research on behavior modification), a different view of influence began to emerge. With this view, the emphasis was increasingly placed on a rational exchange approach (exchange of rewards for work performed) in order to get workers to do their work. Even Taylor's views on scientific management, which still influence significantly many organizations in many industries, emphasized the importance of providing incentives to get workers to do work.

With the transactor type of leader, the focus is on goals and rewards; the

TABLE 1
Four Types of Leaders

	Strong Man	Transactor	Visionary Hero	SuperLeader
Focus	Commands	Rewards	Visions	Self-leadership
Type of power	Position authority	Rewards	Relational/ inspirational	Shared
Source of leader's wisdom and direction	Leader	Leader	Leader	Mostly followers (self-leaders) and then leaders
Followers' response	Fear-based compliance	Calculative compliance	Emotional commitment based on leader's vision	Commitment based on ownership
Typical leader behaviors	Direction command	Interactive goal setting	Communication of leader's vision	Becoming an effective self-leader
	Assigned goals	Contingent personal reward	Emphasis on leader's values	Modeling self-leadership
	Intimidation	Contingent material reward	Exhortation	Creating postitive thought patterns
	Reprimand	Contingent reprimand	Inspirational persuasion	Developing self-leadership through reward & constructive reprimand
				Promoting self-leading teams
				Facilitating a self-leadership culture

leader's power stems from the ability to provide rewards for followers doing what the leader thinks should be done. The source of wisdom and direction still rests with the leader. Subordinates will tend to take a calculative view of their work. "I will do what he (or she) asks as long as the rewards keep coming." . . .

The next type of leader, which probably represents the most popular view today, is that of the *visionary hero*. Here the focus is on the leader's ability to create highly motivating and absorbing visions. The leader represents a kind of heroic figure who is somehow able to create an almost larger-than-life vision for the workforce to follow. The promise is that if organizations can just find those leaders that are able to capture what's important in the world and wrap it up into some kind of purposeful vision, then the rest of the workforce will have the clarifying beacon that will light the way to the promised land.

With the visionary hero, the focus is on the leader's vision, and the leader's power is based on followers' desire to relate to the vision and to the leader himself or herself. Once again, the leader represents the source of wisdom and direction. Followers, at least in theory, are expected to commit to the vision and the leader.

The notion of the visionary hero seems to have received considerable attention lately, but the idea has not gone without criticism. Peter Drucker, for example, believes that charisma becomes the undoing of leaders. He believes they become inflexible, convinced of their own infallibility, and slow to really change. Instead, Drucker suggests that the most effective leaders are those not afraid of developing strength in their subordinates and associates. One wonders how Chrysler will fare when Iacocca is gone.

The final view of leadership included in our figure represents the focus of this article—the *SuperLeader*. We do not use the word "Super" to create an image of a larger-than-life figure who has all the answers and is able to bend others' wills to his or her own. On the contrary, with this type of leader, the focus is largely on the followers. Leaders become "super"—that is, can possess the strength and wisdom of many persons—by helping to unleash the abilities of the "followers" (self-leaders) that surround them.

The focus of this leadership view is on the followers who become self-leaders. Power is more evenly shared by leaders and followers. The leader's task becomes largely that of helping followers to develop the necessary skills for work, especially self-leadership, to be able to contribute more fully to the organization. Thus, leaders and subordinates (that are becoming strong self-leaders) together represent the source of wisdom and direction. Followers (self-leaders), in turn, experience commitment and ownership of their work. . . .

The Transition to Self-Leadership

Three basic assumptions underlie our ideas on self-leadership. First, everyone practices self-leadership to some degree, but not everyone is an effective self-leader. Second, self-leadership can be learned, and thus is not restricted to people who are "born" to be self-starters or self-motivated. And third, self-leadership is relevant to executives, managers, and all employees—that is, to everyone who works.

Few employees are capable of highly effective self-leadership the moment they enter a job situation. Especially at the beginning, the SuperLeader must provide orientation, guidance, and direction. The need for specific direction at the beginning stages of employment stems from two sources. First, the new employee is unfamiliar with the objectives, tasks, and procedures of his or her position. He or she will probably not yet have fully developed task capabilities. But more pertinent, the new employee may not yet have an adequate set of self-leadership skills. For the SuperLeader, the challenge lies in shifting employees to self-leadership. Thus the role of the SuperLeader becomes critical: He or she must lead others to lead themselves.

Throughout the entire process of leading others to lead themselves, aspects of SuperLeadership are involved that do not necessarily represent a distinct step but that are nevertheless quite important. For example, *encouragement* of followers to exercise initiative, take on responsibility, and to use self-leadership strategies in an effective way to lead themselves, is an important feature that runs through the entire process. Also, a feature we call *guided participation* is very important to SuperLeadership. This involves facilitating the gradual shifting of followers from dependence to independent self-leadership through a combination of initial instruction, questions that stimulate thinking about self-leadership (e.g., what are you shooting for? . . . what is your goal. How well do you think you're doing?), and increasing participation of followers.

Consider the goal setting process as an example of how the transition to self-leadership unfolds. Teaching an employee how to set goals can follow a simple procedure: First, an employee is provided with a model to emulate; second, he or she is allowed guided participation; and finally, he or she assumes the targeted self-leadership skill, which in this case is goal setting. Once again modeling is an especially key element in learning this skill. Because of their formal position of authority, SuperLeaders have a special responsibility to personally demonstrate goal setting behavior that can be emulated by other employees. Furthermore, goals need to be coordinated among the different levels of the hierarchy. Subordinate goals, even those that are self-set, need to be consistent with superior and organizational goals.

A SuperLeader takes into account the employee's time and experience on the job, as well as the degree of the employee's skill and capabilities. For a new employee, whose job-related and self-leadership skills may yet be undeveloped, an executive may wish to begin with assigned goals, while modeling self-set goals for himself or herself. Within a short period of time, the Super-Leader endeavors to move toward interactive goals. Usually the best way to accomplish this is by "guided participation," which includes asking the employee to propose his or her own goals. At this stage, the SuperLeader still retains significant influence over goal setting, actively proposing and perhaps imposing some of the goals. Usually, this is the give and take that is typical of the traditional MBO approach.

Finally, for true self-leadership to develop and flourish, the SuperLeader will deliberately move toward employee self-set goals. In this situation, the SuperLeader serves as a source of information and experience, as a sounding board, and as the transmitter of overall organizational goals. In the end, in a true self-leadership situation, the employee is given substantial latitude to establish his or her own goals.

We have found that sharing goal setting with subordinates is frequently one of the most difficult transitions for traditional leaders to understand and accept on their road to effective SuperLeadership. Often, an executive is reluctant to provide the full opportunity for a subordinate to lead himself or herself because it seems the executive is losing control. . . .

Good leaders intuitively understand the effects on performance of "knowing where they are going." During subordinate employees' critical transition from traditional external leadership to self-leadership, previous dependency on superior authority needs to be unlearned. In its place, employees must develop a strong sense of confidence in their own abilities to set realistic and challenging goals on their own.

Frequently this transition is not very smooth, leaving the employee wondering why "the boss" is not providing more help, and the executive biting his lip to avoid telling the employee to do the "right thing." Employees need to have some latitude in making mistakes during this critical period.

Reprimand takes on special importance during the critical transition phase, when the superior-subordinate relationship is very delicate. Careless use of reprimand can seriously set back the employee's transition to self-leadership. The issue becomes especially salient when employees make mistakes—sometimes serious mistakes. In our experience, during the transition to self-leadership, some mistakes are inevitable and should be expected as an employee reaches out. The way the SuperLeader responds to the mistakes can ensure or thwart a successful transition. . . .

Andrew Grove, CEO of chip maker Intel Corporation, discussed the issue of how to react when an employee seems to be making a mistake. Reacting too soon or too harshly can result in a serious setback in efforts to develop employee self-leadership. According to Grove, the manager needs to consider the degree to which the error can be tolerated or not. For example, if the task is an analysis for internal use, the experience the employee receives may be well worth some wasted work and delay. However, if the error involves a shipment to a customer, the customer should not bear the expense of boosting the employee further down the learning curve.

Sometimes the SuperLeader might *deliberately* hold back goals or decisions that, at other times, in other places, he or she would be more than willing to provide. Self-led employees must learn to stand on their own.

Once through this critical transition phase, the effects on the self-led employee's performance can be remarkable. Effectively leading themselves produces a motivation and psychological commitment that energizes employees to greater and greater achievements. SuperLeaders who have successfully unleashed the power of self-led employees understand the ultimate reward and satisfaction of managing these individuals. . . .

Ideally, the SuperLeader comes to be surrounded by strong people—self-leaders in their own right—who pursue exceptional achievement because they love to. The SuperLeader's strength is greatly enhanced since it is drawn from the strength of many people who have been encouraged to grow, flourish, and become important contributors. The SuperLeader becomes "Super" through the talents and capabilities of others. As self-leadership is nurtured, the power for progress is unleashed. . . .

SuperLeadership offers the most viable mechanism for establishing exceptional self-leading followers. True excellence can be achieved by facilitating the self-leadership system that operates within each person—by challenging each person to reach deep inside for the best each has to offer. Employee compliance is not enough. Leading others to lead themselves is the key to tapping the intelligence, the spirit, the creativity, the commitment, and most of all the tremendous unique potential of each individual.

To us, the message is clear: Excellence is achievable, but only if leaders are dedicated to tapping the vast potential within each individual. Most of all, this does *not* mean that more so-called charismatic or transformational leaders are needed to influence followers to comply with and carry out the vision of the leader. Rather, the vision itself needs to reflect and draw upon the vast resources contained within individual employees.

The currently popular notion that excellent leaders need to be visionary and charismatic may be a trap if taken too far. Wisdom on leadership for centuries has warned us about this potential trap. Remember what Abraham Lincoln said, "You cannot help men permanently by doing for them what they could and should do for themselves." Remember, also, the timeless words, "Give a man a fish and he will be fed for a day. Teach a man to fish and he will be fed for a lifetime."

It is time to transcend the notion of leaders as heroes and to focus instead on leaders as hero-makers. Is the spotlight on the leader, or on the achievements of the followers? To discover this new breed of leader, look *not* at the leader but at the followers. SuperLeaders have Super Followers that are dynamic self-leaders. The SuperLeader leads others to lead themselves. Perhaps this spirit was captured most succinctly by Lao-tzu, a sixth-century B.C. Chinese philosopher, when he wrote the following:

> A leader is best
> When people barely know he exists,
> Not so good when people obey and acclaim him.
> Worse when they despise him.
> But of a good leader, who talks little,
> When his work is done, his aim fulfilled,
> They will say:
> We did it ourselves.

Selected Bibliography

A more detailed description of the leadership approach addressed in this article is presented in the book *SuperLeadership: Leading Others to Lead Themselves* by Charles C. Manz and Henry P. Sims, Jr. (NY: Prentice-Hall, 1989, Berkley, 1990).

For an overview of self-leadership see Charles C. Manz's *Mastering Self-Leadership: Empowering Yourself for Personal Excellence*, Englewood Cliffs, NJ, Prentice-Hall, forthcoming in Summer 1991.

The book by Edward E. Lawler III, *High Involvement Management* (San Francisco: Jossey Bass, 1986) provides a good overview of various approaches for facilitating increasing involvement of employees in organizations. Also,

Richard Walton describes trends in "Control to Commitment in the Workplace," his article in *Harvard Business Review*, 63, 77–84.

For a good overview on the application of goal setting, see Gary Latham and Edwin Locke's "Goal Setting: A Motivational Technique That Works," *Organizational Dynamics*, Autumn 1979, pp. 68–80.

A recent study on the leadership of self-managing teams was presented in the article by Charles C. Manz and Henry P. Sims, Jr. entitled "Leading Workers to Lead Themselves: The External Leadership of Self-Managing Work Teams," *Administrative Science Quarterly*, 32, 1987, pp. 106–129.

Also, the practical challenge for managers transitioning into the role of leading self-managed employees is addressed in the article by Charles C. Manz, David E. Keating, and Anne Donnellon entitled "Preparing for an Organizational Change to Employee Self-Management: The Managerial Transition" in *Organizational Dynamics*, Autumn 1990, pp. 15–26.

34

Domination/Subordination

Jean B. Miller

Jean Baker Miller received her M.D. from Columbia University, and has been a practicing psychiatrist. She was the first director of the Stone Center for Developmental Studies at Wellesley College and subsequently scholar-in-residence there. She is clinical professor of psychiatry at the School of Medicine, Boston University.

What do people do to people who are different from them and why? On the individual level, the child grows only via engagement with people very different from her/himself. Thus, the most significant difference is between the adult and the child. At the level of humanity in general, we have seen massive problems around a great variety of differences. But the most basic difference is the one between women and men.

On both levels it is appropriate to pose two questions. When does the engagement of difference stimulate the development and the enhancement of both parties to the engagement? And, conversely, when does such a confrontation with difference have negative effects: when does it lead to great difficulty, deterioration, and distortion and to some of the worst forms of degradation, terror, and violence—both for individuals and for groups—that human beings can experience? It is clear that "mankind" in general, especially in our Western tradition but in some others as well, does not have a very glorious record in this regard.

It is not always clear that in most instances of difference there is also a factor of inequality—inequality of many kinds of resources, but fundamentally of status and power. One useful way to examine the often confusing results of these confrontations with difference is to ask: What happens in situations of inequality? What forces are set in motion? While we will be using the terms "dominant" and "subordinate" in the discussion, it is useful to remember that flesh and blood women and men are involved. Speaking in abstractions sometimes permits us to accept what we might not admit to on a personal level.

Temporary Inequality

Two types of inequality are pertinent for present purposes. The first might be called temporary inequality. Here, the lesser party is *socially* defined as unequal. Major examples are the relationships between parents and children, teachers and students, and, possibly, therapists and clients. There are certain assumptions in these relationships which are often not made explicit, nor, in fact, are they carried through. But they are the social structuring of the relationship.

The "superior" party presumably has more of some ability or valuable quality, which she/he is supposed to impart to the "lesser" person. While these abilities vary with the particular relationship, they include emotional maturity, experience in the world, physical skills, a body of knowledge, or the techniques for acquiring certain kinds of knowledge. The superior person is supposed to engage with the lesser in such a way as to bring the lesser member up to full parity; that is, the child is to be helped to become the adult. Such is the overall task of this relationship. The lesser, the child, is to be given to, by the person who presumably has more to give. Although the lesser party often also gives much to the superior, these relationships are *based in service* to the lesser party. That is their *raison d'être*.

It is clear, then, that the paramount goal is to end the relationship; that is, to end the relationship of inequality. The period of disparity is meant to be temporary. People may continue their association as friends, colleagues, or even competitors, but not as "superior" and "lesser." At least this is the goal.

The reality is that we have trouble enough with this sort of relationship.

Parents or professional institutions often tip toward serving the needs of the donor instead of those of the lesser party (for example, schools can come to serve teachers or administrators, rather than students). Or the lesser person learns how to be a good "lesser" rather than how to make the journey from lesser to full stature. Overall, we have not found very good ways to carry out the central task: to foster the movement from unequal to equal. In childrearing and education we do not have an adequate theory and practice. Nor do we have concepts that work well in such other unequal so-called "helping" relationships as healing, penology, and rehabilitation. Officially, we say we want to do these things, but we often fail.

We have a great deal of trouble deciding on how many rights "to allow" to the lesser party. We agonize about how much power the lesser party shall have. How much can the lesser person express or act on her or his perceptions when these definitely differ from those of the superior? Above all, there is great difficulty in maintaining the conception of the lesser person *as a person of as much intrinsic worth as the superior.*

A crucial point is that power is a major factor in all of these relationships. But power alone will not suffice. Power exists and it has to be taken into account, not denied. The superiors hold all the real power, but power will not accomplish *the task.* It will not bring the unequal party up to equality.

Our troubles with these relationships may stem from the fact that they exist within the context of a second type of inequality that tends to overwhelm the ways we learn to operate in the first kind. The second type molds the very ways we perceive and conceptualize what we are doing in the first, most basic kind of relationships.

The second type of inequality teaches us how to enforce inequality, but not how to make the journey from unequal to equal. Most importantly, its consequences are kept amazingly obscure—in fact they are usually denied. . . . We will concentrate on this second kind of inequality. However, the underlying notion is that this second type has determined, and still determines, the only ways we can think and feel in the first type.

Permanent Inequality

In these relationships, some people or groups of people are defined as unequal by means of what sociologists call ascription; that is, your birth defines you. Criteria may be race, sex, class, nationality, religion, or other characteristics ascribed at birth.[1] Here, the terms of the relationship are very different from those of temporary inequality. There is, for example, no notion that superiors are present primarily to help inferiors, to impart to them their advantages and "desirable" characteristics. There is no assumption that the goal of the unequal relationship is to end the inequality; in fact, quite the reverse. A series of other governing tendencies are in force, and occur with a great regularity. I shall suggest some of these tendencies first on a superficial level; we will then come back to them, to show how they operate at a much more intense, subtle, and profound personal level. While some of these elements may appear obvious, in fact there is a great deal of disagreement and confusion about psychological characteristics brought about by conditions as obvious as these.

Dominants

Once a group is defined as inferior, the superiors tend to label it as defective or substandard in various ways. These labels accrete rapidly. Thus, blacks are described as less intelligent than whites, women are supposed to be ruled by emotion, and so on. In addition, the actions and words of the dominant group tend to be destructive of the subordinates. All historical evidence confirms this tendency. And, although they are much less obvious, there are destructive effects on the dominants as well. The latter are of a different order and are much more difficult to recognize. . . .

Dominant groups usually define one or more acceptable roles for the subordinate. Acceptable roles typically involve providing services that no dominant group wants to perform for itself (for example, cleaning up the dominant's waste products). Functions that a dominant group prefers to perform, on the other hand, are carefully guarded and closed to subordinates. Out of the total range of human possibilities, the activities most highly valued in any particular culture will tend to be enclosed within the domain of the dominant group; less valued functions are relegated to the subordinates.

Subordinates are usually said to be unable to perform the preferred roles. Their incapacities are ascribed to innate defects or deficiencies of mind or body, therefore immutable and impossible of change or development. It becomes difficult for dominants even to imagine that subordinates are capable of performing the preferred activities. More importantly, subordinates themselves can come to find it difficult to believe in their own ability. The myth of their inability to fulfill wider or more valued roles is challenged only when a drastic event disrupts the usual arrangements. Such disruptions usually arise from outside the relationship itself. For instance, in the emergency situation of World War II, "incompetent" women suddenly "manned" the factories with great skill.

It follows that subordinates are described in terms of, and encouraged to develop, personal psychological characteristics that are pleasing to the dominant group. These characteristics form a certain familiar cluster: submissiveness, passivity, docility, dependency, lack of initiative, inability to act, to decide, to think, and the like. In general, this cluster includes qualities more characteristic of children than adults—immaturity, weakness, and helplessness. If subordinates adopt these characteristics they are considered well-adjusted.

However, when subordinates show the potential for, or even more dangerously have developed other characteristics—let us say intelligence, initiative, assertiveness—there is usually no room available within the dominant framework for acknowledgment of these characteristics. Such people will be defined as at least unusual, if not definitely abnormal. There will be no opportunities for the direct application of their abilities within the social arrangements. (How many women have pretended to be dumb!)

Dominant groups usually impede the development of subordinates and block their freedom of expression and action. They also tend to militate against stirrings of greater rationality or greater humanity in their own members. It was not too long ago that "nigger lover" was a common appellation, and even now men who "allow their women" more than the usual scope are subject to ridicule in many circles.

A dominant group, inevitably, has the greatest influence in determining a culture's overall outlook—its philosophy, morality, social theory, and even its science. The dominant group, thus, legitimizes the unequal relationship and incorporates it into society's guiding concepts. The social outlook, then, obscures the true nature of this relationship—that is, the very existence of inequality. The culture explains the events that take place in terms of other premises, premises that are inevitably false, such as racial or sexual inferiority. While in recent years we have learned about many such falsities on the larger social level, a full analysis of the psychological implications still remains to be developed. In the case of women, for example, despite overwhelming evidence to the contrary, the notion persists that women are meant to be passive, submissive, docile, secondary. From this premise, the outcome of therapy and encounters with psychology and other "sciences" are often determined.

Inevitably, the dominant group is the model for "normal human relationships." It then becomes "normal" to treat others destructively and to derogate them, to obscure the truth of what you are doing, by creating false explanations, and to oppose actions toward equality. In short, if one's identification is with the dominant group, it is "normal" to continue in this pattern. Even though most of us do not like to think of ourselves as either believing in, or engaging in, such domination, it is, in fact, difficult for a member of a dominant group to do otherwise. But to keep on doing these things, one need only behave "normally."

It follows from this that dominant groups generally do not like to be told about or even quietly reminded of the existence of inequality. "Normally" they can avoid awareness because their explanation of the relationship becomes so well integrated *in other terms*; they can even believe that both they and the subordinate group share the same interests and, to some extent, a common experience. If pressed a bit, the familiar rationalizations are offered: the home is "women's natural place," and we know "what's best for them anyhow."

Dominants prefer to avoid conflict—open conflict that might call into question the whole situation. This is particularly and tragically so, when many members of the dominant group are not having an easy time of it themselves. Members of a dominant group, or at least some segments of it, such as white working-class men (who are themselves also subordinates), often feel unsure of their own narrow toehold on the material and psychological bounties they believe they desperately need. What dominant groups usually cannot act on, or even see, is that the situation of inequality in fact deprives them, particularly on the psychological level.

Clearly, inequality has created a state of conflict. Yet dominant groups will tend to suppress conflict. They will see any questioning of the "normal" situation as threatening; activities by subordinates in this direction will be perceived with alarm. Dominants are usually convinced that the way things are is right and good, not only for them but especially for the subordinates. All morality confirms this view, and all social structure sustains it.

It is perhaps unnecessary to add that the dominant group usually holds all of the open power and authority and determines the ways in which power may be acceptably used.

Subordinates

What of the subordinates' part in this? Since dominants determine what is normal for a culture, it is much more difficult to understand subordinates. Initial expressions of dissatisfaction and early actions by subordinates always come as a surprise; they are usually rejected as atypical. After all, dominants *knew* that all women needed and wanted was a man around whom to organize their lives. Members of the dominant group do not understand why "they"—the first to speak out—are so upset and angry.

The characteristics that typify the subordinates are even more complex. A subordinate group has to concentrate on basic survival. Accordingly, direct, honest reaction to destructive treatment is avoided. Open, self-initiated action in its own self-interest must also be avoided. Such actions can, and still do, literally result in death for some subordinate groups. In our own society, a woman's direct action can result in a combination of economic hardship, social ostracism, and psychological isolation—and even the diagnosis of a personality disorder. Any one of these consequences is bad enough. . . .

It is not surprising then that a subordinate group resorts to disguised and indirect ways of acting and reacting. While these actions are designed to accommodate and please the dominant group, they often, in fact, contain hidden defiance and "put ons." Folk tales, black jokes, and women stories are often based on how the wily peasant or sharecropper outwitted the rich landowner, boss, or husband. The essence of the story rests on the fact that the overlord does not even know that he has been made a fool of.

One important result of this indirect mode of operation is that members of the dominant group are denied an essential part of life—the opportunity to acquire self-understanding through knowing their impact on others. They are thus deprived of "consensual validation," feedback, and a chance to correct their actions and expressions. Put simply, subordinates won't tell. For the same reasons, the dominant group is deprived also of valid knowledge about the subordinates. (It is particularly ironic that the societal "experts" in knowledge about subordinates are usually members of the dominant group.)

Subordinates, then, know much more about the dominants than vice versa. They have to. They become highly attuned to the dominants, able to predict their reactions of pleasure and displeasure. Here, I think, is where the long story of "feminine intuition" and "feminine wiles" begins. It seems clear that these "mysterious" gifts are in fact skills, developed through long practice, in reading many small signals, both verbal and non-verbal.

Another important result is that subordinates often know more about the dominants than they know about themselves. If a large part of your fate depends on accommodating to and pleasing the dominants, you concentrate on them. Indeed, there is little purpose in knowing yourself. Why should you when your knowledge of the dominants determines your life? This tendency is reinforced by many other restrictions. One can know oneself only through action and interaction. To the extent that their range of action or interaction is limited, subordinates will lack a realistic evaluation of their capacities and problems. Unfortunately, this difficulty in gaining self-knowledge is even further compounded.

Tragic confusion arises because subordinates absorb a large part of the untruths created by the dominants; there are a great many blacks who feel inferior to whites, and women who still believe they are less important than men. This internalization of dominant beliefs is more likely to occur if there are few alternative concepts at hand. On the other hand, it is also true that members of the subordinate group have certain experiences and perceptions that accurately reflect the truth about themselves and the injustice of their position. Their own more truthful concepts are bound to come into opposition with the mythology they have absorbed from the dominant group. An inner tension between the two sets of concepts and their derivatives is almost inevitable.

From a historical perspective, despite the obstacles, subordinate groups have tended to move toward greater freedom of expression and action, although this progress varies greatly from one circumstance to another. There were always some slaves who revolted; there were some women who sought greater development or self-determination. Most records of these actions are not preserved by the dominant culture, making it difficult for the subordinate group to find a supporting tradition and history.

Within each subordinate group, there are tendencies for some members to imitate the dominants. This imitation can take various forms. Some may try to treat their fellow subordinates as destructively as the dominants treat them. A few may develop enough of the qualities valued by the dominants to be partially accepted into their fellowship. Usually they are not wholly accepted, and even then only if they are willing to forsake their own identification with fellow subordinates. "Uncle Toms" and certain professional women have often been in this position. (There are always a few women who have won the praise presumably embodied in the phrase "she thinks like a man.")

To the extent that subordinates move toward freer expression and action, they will expose the inequality and throw into question the basis for its existence. And they will make the inherent conflict an open conflict. They will then have to bear the burden and take the risks that go with being defined as "troublemakers." Since this role flies in the face of their conditioning, subordinates, especially women, do not come to it with ease.

What is immediately apparent from studying the characteristics of the two groups is that mutually enhancing interaction is not probable between unequals. Indeed, conflict is inevitable. The important questions, then, become: Who defines the conflict? Who sets the terms? When is conflict overt or covert? On what issues is the conflict fought? Can anyone win? Is conflict "bad," by definition? If not, what makes for productive or destructive conflict?

35

Challenging the Barriers to Opportunity

Ann M. Morrison

Ann M. Morrison has directed research on leadership diversity at the Center for Creative Leadership. She is lead author of *Breaking the Glass Ceiling: Can Women Reach the Top of America's Largest Corporations?* and *The New Leaders: Guidelines on Leadership Diversity in America.* Morrison is currently president of the New Leaders Institute.

There are tremendous benefits to be had by fostering diversity in an organization, but they must be earned by successfully countering a host of stumbling blocks. The challenge of developing diversity should not be underestimated. Some of the problems have been with us for decades, while others are relatively new and unfamiliar. To find the best solutions to these problems, we need to understand.

There has been a significant reduction of some forms of racism, sexism, and other discrimination in this country. The Civil Rights Act of 1964, among other key pieces of legislation, helped reduce some of the most blatant forms of discrimination that put men of color and women in general at a disadvantage. There is evidence, however, that the force of these changes has

Excerpted from Ann M. Morrison, *The New Leaders: Guidelines on Leadership Diversity in America* (San Francisco: Jossey-Bass, 1992). Reprinted by permission.

essentially been checked in recent years, particularly with regard to the upward mobility of nontraditional managers.

In 1986,[1] Korn/Ferry found that of 1,362 senior executives only 29 were women and 13 were people of color, a total of 3 percent at a time when women and people of color made up 51.4 percent of the workforce. According to one survey reported by Braham,[2] in 1979, blacks occupied 0.2 percent of the senior executive positions and that figure had increased to only 0.3 percent by 1985. Another survey reported by Braham[2] showed a decrease in blacks at senior levels during the same period: from 0.4 percent to 0.2 percent. In addition, blacks have lost momentum in management overall. Blacks made up only 4.9 percent of the management ranks in 1987 compared with 4 percent in 1980.[3]

Hispanics, too, apparently lost advancement momentum in the 1980s. In California, for example, despite an increase in the Hispanic population from 19 percent of the total state population in 1980 to 30 percent in 1989, Hispanics still made up only 7 percent of the state's executives. Dan Cook[4] notes that the list of only seven Hispanic presidents or chairmen of large corporations nationwide is "rivetingly short."

Fortune magazine's 1990 survey[5] of 799 companies turned up only 19 women among the 4,012 directors and highest paid executives. Not much had changed since 1978, when the same survey located 10 women among 6,400 executives.

These statistics indicate that moving into middle management is still a problem for some traditionally underrepresented groups. Moving beyond middle management is an even greater problem for most nontraditional managers who confront a "glass ceiling" that limits their advancement. Although the U.S. government reports that 30 percent of corporate middle management is made up of women, blacks, and Hispanics, these groups make up less than 1 percent of chief executives and those who report directly to them.[6] Even if it takes fifteen or twenty years to develop a general manager, as some executive development specialists have concluded, if time were the only factor, we should have seen more advancement than this in the twenty-eight years since the passage of the 1964 Civil Rights Act, and we should have seen continued improvement throughout the period. Clearly, a lack of enough time is not the only force preventing upward mobility for nontraditional managers.

We can learn some lessons from what has been accomplished since the 1960s in reducing barriers for women and people of color. We can also learn something from the subsequent loss of some of this momentum as we confront the current situation. The problems of diversity that challenge us today are not entirely the same as the problems that confronted us as recently as the late 1980s. Our understanding of differential treatment and its consequences must continue to grow if we are to solve the problems facing us today.

A Historical Overview

In the past, a number of publicly accepted practices excluded people of color and white women from many institutions and positions of influence. Jobs were advertised separately by male or female, white or "colored," allowing organizations to exclude people they viewed as undesirable. People of color and white women were confined largely to low-paying jobs. As recently as 1983, white men, who made up about half of the labor force, held 96 percent of all the positions in this country that paid more than $18,000 a year.[7] In addition to job discrimination, prestigious schools denied admission to many women and people of color. Universities such as Yale and Princeton, among the schools typically considered feeder institutions for management jobs, explicitly refused to admit women as undergraduates until as recently as 1969.

In the past, racial and sexual discrimination also existed at levels of blatancy that may be hard for those who did not experience them to appreciate fully. It was socially and legally acceptable to treat blacks, Latinos, Asian-Americans, Native Americans, and other people of color as being inferior to whites and to give white men more career opportunities and preferential treatment than others. As antidiscrimination laws were passed, the resulting access to educational institutions and occupations helped people of color and white women compete more effectively. However, the university degrees and professional credentials that served as criteria for many jobs were still held largely by white men. "Lack of education" became a widely accepted explanation for the slow movement of nontraditional employees into and through management; this argument is still used today despite educational achievements that sometimes favor women over men and people of color over whites. . . .

When affirmative action legislation started to take hold, it did little to address the underlying assumptions and stereotypes that plagued nontraditional managers and created the barriers to advancement that persist today. Many white male managers viewed people of color and white women as inferior in intellect, training, and motivation. When the law forced them to hire and promote nontraditional employees, some responded with what one manager we interviewed termed "malicious compliance"—deliberately appointing nontraditional candidates who were weak or ill-suited to the jobs available so that they would have little chance of succeeding. Some managers delayed taking action until the last minute, and then they had to find people to hire or promote as a "quick fix" to meet the required quotas. When these hurriedly chosen people couldn't handle the job or couldn't get the resources they needed to carry out their new responsibilities, some managers' stereotype-based prejudice became even stronger. They pointed to these specific and inevitable failures as evidence that nontraditional managers in general couldn't do the work. Many employers have since become very cautious about hiring or promoting any nontraditional managers because of such early, ill-fated attempts. The lack of enforcement of affirmative action guidelines under the Reagan administration reinforced these employers' reluctance to keep trying, and the movement toward diversity slowed considerably.

Today the legal incentives operate in a different context. There is much more diversity in the workplace and in society overall. Managers are searching intensively for competitive advantage and often turn to their human resource practices to gain an edge. Employers now have compelling business reasons to follow and even exceed the legal requirements to comply with affirmative action guidelines. Many people have become aware of cultural differences, the value and the inevitability of diversity. But prejudice continues to permeate organizations in subtle, nearly invisible forms because stereotypic assumptions have been built into their organizational norms and everyday practices. For example, in our study we found that the recruitment process may continue to screen out people of color who do not have the same background as the whites who were recruited in the past. We learned that managers routinely pass over women for special assignments because they don't want to strain the family. And we discovered that nontraditional managers don't take outside classes because they don't know about them or don't believe they will ever pay off. These systemic barriers often predetermine the choice against nontraditional managers, and even well-meaning people perpetuate unfair treatment simply by using the organization's conventional processes. This not only restrains diversity, but it also powerfully restrains individuals from contributing in meaningful ways to the organization's goals.

The Most Critical Barriers to Advancement

The most significant barriers today are the policies and practices that systematically restrict the opportunities and rewards available to women and people of color. This is a fundamental finding of our study. We discovered twenty-one distinct barriers, which we categorized into thirteen types.

There is a remarkable consensus among the 196 managers in our study on the most critical barriers to advancement. Across industries, sectors, level and function, sex, and ethnic backgrounds, managers agree that the following six barriers are the most important.

1. Prejudice: treating differences as weaknesses
2. Poor career planning
3. A lonely, hostile, unsupportive working environment for nontraditional managers
4. Lack of organizational savvy on the part of nontraditional managers
5. Greater comfort in dealing with one's own kind
6. Difficulty in balancing career and family

These six barriers account for more than half of all the barriers mentioned by the managers in our study. They are also repeatedly revealed in various forms and combinations in other studies that focus on career development and advancement. These include a study commissioned by the Executive Leadership Council on driving and restraining forces for black senior executives[8]; a study conducted by Catalyst[9] on career barriers for women in management; and research by the U.S. Department of Labor[10] for the "glass ceiling initiative."

Prejudice: Still the Number One Barrier

The single most frequently mentioned barrier is prejudice. More than 12 percent of all managers' responses described how the perception of differences as weaknesses limited advancement opportunities for white women and people of color. Prejudice is defined here as the tendency to view people who are different from some reference group in terms of sex, ethnic background, or racial characteristics such as skin color as being deficient. In other words, prejudice is the assumption (without evidence) that nontraditional managers are less competent or less suitable than white male managers; it is the refusal to accept nontraditional managers as equals. Ethnic and sex differences are sometimes used, consciously or not, to define "inferior groups" in a kind of case system.

A survey by the University of Chicago's National Opinion Research Center,[11] along with other research findings, shows that stereotypes are still prevalent. This survey revealed that whites believe that people of other ethnic backgrounds are less intelligent, less hard working, less likely to be self-supporting, more violence prone, and less patriotic than whites. The Executive Leadership Council's study[8] found racism to be the most serious career hurdle for black executives, and Catalyst's[9] findings showed stereotypic preconceptions, or prejudice, to be the biggest advancement barrier women face today. Stereotypes about people of color and women in general are common among managers, and the managers we interviewed described a variety of them.

Some stereotypes apply to certain groups in particular. In our study, for example, we learned that Asian-Americans are said to be so research oriented and technically focused that they are not able to supervise people or communicate well in general. Hispanics are said to be unassertive; they "sit back" in meetings while others hurl and debate ideas. Some managers consider Asian-Americans and Hispanics "too polite" (and consequently, as lacking conviction), perhaps because of their concern for showing respect or maintaining cooperative teamwork. One white executive noted that there is also a trust barrier for Asian-Americans and Latinos, who are sometimes perceived as dishonest and corrupt. The prevailing stereotypes of blacks, we discovered, are that they are lazy, uneducated, and incompetent. Women are often assumed to be indecisive and unable to be analytical. . . .

Stereotypes make it acceptable among some traditional managers to ignore, disparage, or discount the qualities and contributions of nontraditional managers. As we learned in our study, people of color and white women are systematically screened out as candidates for more senior management posts when prejudice, as defined here, operates, that is, when a point of difference is highlighted as a flaw. Under such conditions, a nontraditional candidate's accent or hair style may be viewed as a flaw, and that may be enough for rejection. As one Hispanic manager who told us he faced "real animosities" at a previous workplace said, "The fact that I graduated first in my engineering class didn't make as much difference as the fact that I looked different."

Clearly, however, all differences are not based on stereotypes. Nontraditional managers, like everyone else, often have very real limitations that must be considered in hiring or promotion decisions. Nevertheless, the limitations of a nontraditional manager may be a greater liability than the limitations of a white male manager. A black manager in the employee relations field gave an example of how managers tend to isolate and emphasize the limitations of a person of color without giving appropriate attention to his or her strengths. This manager was invited to sit in on a meeting to select a manager for a department in turmoil. The black candidate had proved his skill in handling a troubled environment but not his administrative ability. A white candidate had demonstrated administrative skills. Others already in the department also had good administrative skills and could handle many of the administrative responsibilities. Yet the selection panel focused on the administrative aspects of the job and chose the white manager. In effect, the black manager was compared to the white manager on the basis of his area of relative weakness, even though that may have been less relevant to the job than was his area of strength.

Prejudice prevents many managers from seeing others without the filters that turn differences into liabilities. When prejudice operates this way, flaws are imagined, weaknesses are exaggerated, and failures are attributed to the nontraditional manager's sex or ethnicity rather than to individual differences. Managers we interviewed told us that expecting less from women and people of color is a notion so pervasive that it sometimes affects nontraditional managers' perceptions of themselves. . . .

Prejudice, a barrier in itself, can increase and create other barriers to advancement, such as contributing to the waning confidence and motivation that some nontraditional managers experience. In fact, prejudice is probably a contributing factor in most of the barriers we identified. By permeating policies and practices in very subtle ways, prejudice continues to deprive nontraditional managers of advocates, resources, and power. That is why, we believe, prejudice is the most often mentioned and most powerful barrier.

Poor Career Planning

The next most often mentioned barrier in our study was poor career planning and development. This is largely associated with the lack of opportunities for white women and people of color to get a series of varied work experiences that will qualify them for senior management posts. . . .

We also learned from our interviews that white male decision makers are often reluctant to assign nontraditional managers to the challenging, high-profile jobs that have rich learning potential and add credibility to a manager's track record. One manager described the problem in his organization this way: "The problem here is the syndrome of not wanting people to fail. The attitude of senior management is that we don't make bad people decisions and that we live with our decisions forever. The company wants to look good, and it won't move nontraditional managers into nontraditional positions, including higher-level jobs."

Some executives, as we have seen, have fallen into the trap of making prejudiced assessments of nontraditional managers' capability. Some executives have become reluctant to promote another nontraditional manager once an earlier nontraditional manager's promotion has been a failure. Some executives, when handing out key assignments, simply think first of the other white men with whom they have become better acquainted. In all these cases, the assignments such executives choose for nontraditional managers from the start are likely to be less visible and less central to the core business operations than the assignments given to white men. One manager in our study concluded that as these limiting assignments accumulate, the odds grow that the nontraditional managers will be limited in terms of future promotion because they do not have the required depth and range of job experience to be considered for senior-level jobs. . . .

Taking account of all these strands of evidence, we conclude that poor career development is cumulative because as a career progresses, it becomes increasingly difficult to overcome low-profile or ill-conceived assignments. Without the kinds of assignments that are considered prerequisites for senior management posts, nontraditional managers are likely to be overlooked. Thus it appears that early and continuing problems in career development are partly responsible for the discouraging situation today, a situation in which executives grumble that they can't find enough qualified nontraditional candidates for senior-level jobs.

Poor Working Environment

The working environment for many nontraditional managers is lonely, unfriendly, and pressure-packed. At the higher levels they are still dramatically outnumbered by white men, many of whom, deliberately or not, regularly treat them differently from the way they treat their white male colleagues. Our interviews revealed that nontraditional managers are excluded from luncheons, social events, and even the friendly camaraderie that occurs in most offices. They are often a curiosity to their colleagues, who watch them closely and sometimes scrutinize their work and behavior for possible mistakes. Some people of color and women have even commented that other people withhold information from them and sabotage their work in order to undermine them. Because they are still the exception in many groups and because prejudice shapes others' perceptions of them, many nontraditional managers find the working environment a frustrating, draining advancement barrier. . . .

Another factor we learned about that contributes to a poor working environment for nontraditional managers is that there are few if any other nontraditional managers to be role models and mentors for those rising beyond middle management. Many managers in our study pointed out that they were dependent on white men to advise and promote them, which was often ineffective. . . .

According to managers we interviewed, white men are not usually eager to support someone with a different perspective or different values, and many find it difficult even to communicate with such an individual. . . .

We also learned that nontraditional managers often have no one to talk to about their fears, their mistakes, and the rage they feel over being treated differently from others. There is often no one to help them objectively assess their abilities and their behavior or to help them cope with the uncertainty they may feel about their role in the organization and the expectations others have of them. There is often no one to help them feel comfortable. . . .

Lack of Organizational Savvy

The managers we interviewed told us that people of color and white women often fail to advance because they don't know "how to play the game" of getting along and getting ahead in business. They appear to lack the preparation and knowledge that would allow them to put their experiences and their expectations in the context of their organization's culture. Nontraditional managers don't seem to pay adequate attention to organizational politics and the agenda of their colleagues and bosses, and they don't seem to be strategic about their own career development. In some ways, all nontraditional managers share the problem of being newcomers who have been placed in management roles without any real expectation that they will advance to senior levels. Therefore, little if any effort has been made to prepare them for such advancement. In other ways, the problems seem to be distinctively different for Hispanics, for Asian-Americans, for blacks, for white women, and for other groups because of particular aspects of each group's organizational experience.

One of the problem areas mentioned for Hispanics, Asian-Americans, Native Americans, and sometimes women in general is an inability to assert themselves and their views. Some members of these groups feel that their upbringing makes it more difficult for them to behave competitively in many business settings. A Native American manager told us about how cultural traditions get in the way of effective corporate communication. For example, we learned that when Asian-Americans, Hispanics, and Native Americans show respect by not initiating conversation with older people or when they foster teamwork by not continuing to argue with a senior manager who doesn't accept their idea, they are seen as subservient yes-people not willing to take a stand. Women with these ethnic backgrounds have an especially hard time communicating this way because they have been reared to support men and seek their approval. More than one Asian-American employee group has asked for courses in assertiveness to help them combat this problem.

The opposite problem seems to plague many black managers, who are frequently seen as too aggressive. . . .

One disadvantage that seems to be common to all nontraditional groups is an inability to create and manage networks. Because their networks are not as strong as those of many white men, they don't get as much information about industry trends and where the company is headed. Without strong networks and mentors, it is difficult to gain expertise in corporate politics; yet naïveté in this domain can easily derail a career. . . .

Greater Comfort in Dealing with One's Own Kind

Consciously and unconsciously, managers, like people in general, tend to feel more comfortable around people who are like themselves. As a result, they often choose to associate with those who are like them rather than with those who are different. In the case of white male managers, this natural tendency would appear to be amplified by some of the institutionalized forms of prejudice discussed earlier. The president of a West Coast company, a white man, described the problem this way: "Cultural differences are tough for white males to deal with. We hire those who are like us; we perpetuate ourselves in the belief that it's easier to relate to someone with the same values, the same looks, the same perceptions. If anyone thinks about it, that's what they think."

Even without prejudice, then, many white male managers may be reluctant to embrace diversity. They may not intend to hire and promote candidates who are like them, but they may often favor white men because, through familiarity and comfort, white men seem to be the best people for the job.

On the other hand, discomfort with nontraditional managers, which can and often does come from prejudice, may also arise out of a simple lack of familiarity. Ethnic groups still do not mingle socially with others in many communities, so white male executives have little interaction with people of color outside the office. This social distance can create discomfort at work, perhaps because of a class issue. . . .

Difficulty in Balancing Career and Family

According to the managers we interviewed, the struggle to reconcile home and work is still largely a woman's problem, and the decisions that women must make often postpone and even preclude their advancement into senior management. Bearing and rearing children conflict with full-time dedication to a career. We learned that maternity leave is undefined or unavailable in many organizations, so women often put their jobs in jeopardy when they become pregnant. It is impossible for many women to continue to work evenings and weekends or to travel frequently once they have children, and many women don't want to. Many women wait until their thirties to have children, a time when they are expected to be proving themselves on the corporate fast track or on the tenure track in academia. Once this period is over, it is very difficult to be reconsidered as a high-potential executive candidate.

Organizations have historically provided little support for women who confront the dilemma of meeting both their career and their family needs, and we were told that there is still some reluctance to address this issue. . . .

Overall, a variety of barriers keep nontraditional managers from advancing in organizations. The majority of these barriers fall into two categories. The first is historical exclusion, the fact that white men have dominated the executive ranks of most organizations for many years. Because of their socialization, their reluctance to share their power and privilege with others, and their natural proclivity to associate with people like themselves, white men keep people of color and white women from moving into their circle. The second category involves deficits in various kinds of qualifications; this makes it difficult to find and accept nontraditional candidates for executive posts. Finding women and people of color with traditionally accepted credentials (such as an M.B.A. or an engineering degree) or experiences (such as military duty or line jobs) remains elusive to many managers; yet many managers are also reluctant to accept a different set of qualifications or to provide alternatives for those who cannot follow a traditional career path. These two themes amplify each other and create imposing barriers to the advancement of nontraditional managers.

The barriers to advancement have changed to some extent over time, and each level of progress has brought a new set of issues to be resolved. Until nontraditional managers began to be advanced into upper management, for example, the white male executives already in place did not feel so threatened by them. Until blatant discrimination became illegal and "politically incorrect," the subtly disguised versions of racism and sexism did not have to be confronted. Until diversity began to cover a greater variety of ethnic groups, the fewer nontraditional groups in a given organization received more attention and had greater solidarity. Therefore, within any organization, the specific problems that now exist may reflect the level of progress that has already been achieved. Discovering which concerns and barriers are the most critical to employees now is an essential part of moving ahead, and it is the first step in any effective diversity effort.

Although the specific barriers to advancement differ from one organization to another, their effect is the same. Barriers to nontraditional managers prevent any organization from preparing a full cadre of potential leaders to take over in the future. That cadre must be more diverse than it has ever been, and the techniques used to develop leadership talent must also be more diverse and creative than ever before.

PART VIII

THE LEADERSHIP ENVIRONMENT

Leaders and followers do not act in a vacuum. They are propelled, constrained, and buffeted by their environment. The effective leader must understand the nature of the leadership context, and how it affects the leadership process. Only then can he or she operate effectively in seeking to achieve the group's objectives.

Since anything and everything could legitimately be included within the notion of context, this topic is potentially so vast as to defy description. We are helped out of this bind by J. Thomas Wren and Marc J. Swatez in selection 36, who identify forces that shape the leadership environment. First—beginning at the most macro level—are the long-term forces of history (social, economic, political, and intellectual); the second sphere of the leadership context is colored by the values and beliefs of the contemporary culture; and finally, at the most micro level, leadership is shaped by such "immediate" aspects of the context as the nature of the organization, its mission, and the nature of the task.

Returning to the cultural influences on leadership, the next article in this segment presents an eye-opening account by Geert Hofstede of the limitations of traditional American conceptions of leadership. Taking us on a tour of differing cultures throughout the world, Hofstede provides us with key insights into assumptions about the nature of leadership in different cultures.

In selection 38, Edgar Schein introduces us to the impact of culture at a different level—that is, at the level of the organization itself. Just as national cultures have certain values which are "shared or held in common," so too organizations and groups have a "a pattern of shared basic assumptions." If one recognizes these assumptions and how they came to be, one can be a more effective leader. As Schein puts it, "cultural understanding is desirable for all of us, but it is essential to leaders if they are to lead." Schein's work is paired with a selection from Terrence Deal and Allan Kennedy's Corporate Cultures, which provides a striking example of how the careful shaping of corporate culture can yield positive effects.

The final readings in Part VIII explore how the demands of leadership change in differing settings—formal organizations, political systems, and social movements. John Gardner provides insight into the problems and possibilities facing leadership in large, bureaucratic organizations. Thomas Cronin and Cheryl Mabey explore the leadership demands of America's current political system, while Clayborne Carson analyzes Martin Luther King, Jr.'s, leadership of a mass social movement.

36

The Historical and Contemporary Contexts of Leadership: A Conceptual Model

J. Thomas Wren and Marc J. Swatez

J. Thomas Wren has a J.D. from the University of Virginia and a Ph.D. in history from the College of William and Mary. He is an associate editor of the *Journal of Leadership Studies*, and is currently associate professor of leadership studies at the Jepson School of Leadership Studies at the University of Richmond. Marc J. Swatez received his Ph.D. in sociology from Northwestern University and is currently assistant professor of leadership studies at the Jepson School.

Stating that leadership is a complex phenomenon repeats a truism that is painfully obvious to all who have ever participated in, observed, or analyzed the process as leaders, followers, students or scholars. Despite its inherent complexity, those who seek an understanding of the nature of leadership and leadership processes are well rewarded by the insights generated thereby. This essay provides an expanded conception of one of the key elements of the leadership process—the context of leadership.

It is now well accepted that an understanding of leadership requires careful attention to the contextual aspects of the process. In recent decades, for example, "contingency" theories and models of leadership have paid increasing attention to the impact of the surrounding situation upon the leadership process.[1] As laudable as these efforts have been, they remain inadequate due

---

to their myopic focus. This essay proposes a model designed to expand the notion of leadership context to embrace the impact of long-term historical forces and the influence of cultural values upon leadership. The study further suggests a procedure whereby these new insights into leadership can be infused into a rational approach to the problems of leadership.

The study of leadership in the twentieth century has been characterized by increasing levels of sophistication. Beginning with the simplistic study of leader traits and progressing to the study of leader behaviors, the focus was initially upon the characteristics and actions of the leader. As thinking about the leadership process has become more sophisticated, the key role played by followers came to be acknowledged and studied. Transactional approaches to leadership such as Hollander's notion of "idiosyncrasy credits" (which are built up by effective leaders in their interactions with their followers), and the exploration of "leader-member exchanges" represent the sorts of insights the study of followers can yield. Indeed, the study of followers and "follower-ship" appears to be something of a growth industry in the leadership studies field.[2]

While such theories have yielded important insights, the most all-encompassing conception of leadership can be found in the models and theories generally grouped together under the rubric "situational-contingency" approaches to leadership. These approaches seek to meld aspects of the leader, followers, and situation into models which help explain the dynamics of the process. Thus, for example, Fiedler's contingency theory includes consideration of such factors as leader-member relations, task structure, and leader position power in determining the appropriate syle of leader behavior, while path-goal theory considers task and environmental characteristics as well as the needs and expectations of the followers.[3]

Acknowledging the many contributions of this train of research (and the above summary is intended only to be illustrative rather than comprehensive), there remain serious omissions. These theories fail to adequately account for larger, more "macro" contextual factors. To be sure, the importance of such variables has not gone completely unrecognized,[4] but the focus has been concentrated upon variables at the organizational level. Little has been done to identify and integrate the larger influences of historical and cultural forces into the broader leadership equation.[5] This lack has not gone unremarked. At the conclusion of her summary of the developments in leadership theory from 1975–1995, Jean Phillips noted that "past leadership research has . . . tended to neglect the importance of the historical context in which leadership operates."[6] In an earlier survey of the trends of leadership research, Martin Chemers voiced a similar cry to acknowledge the role of the larger culture:

> The next major era of leadership research will begin with the recognition that group and organizational performance are dependent upon the interplay of social systems. A social-systems approach will recognize that the leadership process is a complex, multifaceted network of forces. . . . The small group is further imbedded in an organizational and societal context. . . . If general leadership theory can begin to span the gaps between the various levels of analysis (that is, individual, group, organization, society), the resultant theories will provide us with a much stronger base, not only for understanding leadership but also for improving its quality.[7]

In order to bridge these gaps, the impact of larger macro forces must be acknowledged. Leadership studies needs a model that identifies and affirms the various levels of historical and cultural forces that act upon the leadership process. This essay suggests such a typology.

The model presented here is admittedly simple, yet designed to provide the participant in the leadership process with a conceptual tool to help organize and make relevant the vast array of contextual variables which surround and influence any leadership scenario. The model itself is illustrated in Figure 1. Essentially, it portrays leadership as the interaction of leaders and followers within a sequence of overlapping contextual categories, represented by a series of concentric circles. Each category (the historical context of leadership; the contemporary context of leadership; and the immediate context of leadership) has its own unique attributes that impact the leadership process in distinct ways. By compartmentalizing the situation in this manner, the leader can begin to identify, prioritize, and adapt to the specific demands of his/her particular leadership scenario.

A summary of the impact of these three leadership contexts begins with a discussion of outermost circle, the historical context of leadership. It hardly needs remarking that any contemporary situation is at least partially a product of what has gone before. In leadership terms, however, one must move beyond this truism and begin to identify with some precision the long-term trends and influences which most impact any given leadership scenario, and shape the resulting leadership options. These trends may be long-term social, economic, political, or intellectual developments which operate as limitations on potential leadership solutions.

FIGURE 1

A Model of Leadership Contexts

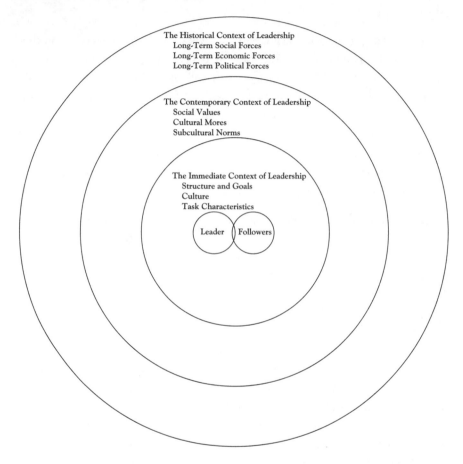

The Historical Context of Leadership
  Long-Term Social Forces
  Long-Term Economic Forces
  Long-Term Political Forces

The Contemporary Context of Leadership
  Social Values
  Cultural Mores
  Subcultural Norms

The Immediate Context of Leadership
  Structure and Goals
  Culture
  Task Characteristics

Leader   Followers

It is important to note that each leadership scenario has its own unique set of operative historical forces, each of which may have a distinct impact. To draw upon an historical example, the leadership options available to the leaders of Boston society on the eve of the American Revolution were severely constrained by long-term historical developments. Economically, a century of population pressure on the surrounding hinterland had filled Boston with a "rabble" of extremely poor, unemployed, and restive inhabitants. Bostonian society was highly stratified, and becoming more so. This recipe for unrest was flavored by decades of intellectual ferment which seemed to justify rebellion. It is small wonder, perhaps, that the conservative, rational responses to British aggravation counseled by leading citizen Thomas Hutchinson were swept away in the emotional fury encouraged by agitator Samuel Adams. Adams, a ne'er-do-well, ended up as governor, while Hutchinson, a member of the colony's elite with a history of service, ended up in exile.[8] In sum, Samuel Adams and his approach to leadership best fitted the demands of the times—demands which were largely a function of long-term developments.

A more recent example is provided by David J. Rothman in his 1993 article entitled "A Century of Failure: Health Care Reform in America."[9] Rothman argues that "to understand fully the persistent failure of the United States to enact national health insurance requires an appreciation not only of government and the dynamics of politics but of underlying social realities."[10] In support of his point Rothman cites longstanding American beliefs about the proper role of government, and an ethos of volunteerism. The history of the health care issue provides more specific insights. Beginning in the 1930s, the dominant political interest group in America—the middle class—has been co-opted on the health care issue by such health care providers as physicians and Blue Cross. The middle class, in other words, has never perceived it to be in its best interests to back national health care. Leaders who wish to enact such legislation can ignore this historical backdrop only at their own peril.

The second context category, the "contemporary" context of leadership, is closely related to the first. The term "contemporary context" of leadership represents the norms, values, and customs of the surrounding society—in short, the impact of cultural mores. Examples of the impact of societal values upon leadership can readily be seen in the political realm. In the American political debate of the 1990s, the polar star of all those aspiring to succeed is the value structure of the middle class. Although ill-defined, the middle class is the dominant political interest of contemporary politics. One of the most important political developments of the 1990s has been a perceived shift in middle class perceptions of self. Barbara Ehrenreich was one of the first to herald this change in her 1989 book *Fear of Falling*, in which she argued that the current middle class is insecure and deeply anxious about maintaining its status.[11] An analysis of the American political scene by Joe Klein in 1993 echoes this theme, suggesting that the essential challenge of American politics of the 1990s is facing up to what he called "The Big Fear"—the concern of the middle class for its future.[12] Rothman, in his study of the health care issue, agrees, and notes the policy implications:

> [There is a] persistence of a narrowed vision of middle-class politics. With no largesse of spirit, with no sense of mutual responsibility, the middle classes—

and their representatives—may advocate only minimal changes designed to provide protection only for them, not those in more desperate straits.[13]

Dispute regarding some of the specific conclusions of these authors undoubtedly exists, but their insights into the connection between societal values and the viable options open to political leaders are an example of the role of the contemporary context of leadership.

Nor are such influences restricted to the political realm. The leadership of all groups and entities is affected by societal values. Another obvious example is the multinational corporation. Geert Hofstede has demonstrated this with great clarity in his study of leadership in various cultures. Hofstede has studied the cultural contexts and histories of numerous nations, and concluded that the sorts of leadership values favored in the United States, *i.e.*, a stress on the individual, the confidence in market processes, and the focus on managers, are not well-received in many parts of the world. With the increasingly multinational character of most business operations, leaders who wish to succeed must attend to these cultural nuances.[14]

To add to the complexity of the analysis, it is significant to note that the contemporary sphere is not limited to the societal level. Societies are made up of countless subcultures that impact upon the leadership of each particular group. The values of these subcultures can generate quite specific expectations of leaders. For example, leadership in traditional Japanese-American subcultures is the province of the older generations,[15] just as ministers have been the expected leaders of the American civil rights movement.[16] In the domain of non-profit organizations and philanthropies, the leaders who are commonly identified and developed are those who demonstrate certain attributes—wealth, work, and wisdom—which reflect the needs and values of those sorts of organizations. Any careful consideration of a leadership environment must take into account the potential influence of subcultures.

The final context of leadership is the one undoubtedly most familiar, the "immediate context" of leadership, which embraces all those more "micro" situational factors which have such an impact upon leadership. These include, but are not limited to, the structure and goals of the group or organization, the culture of the organization itself, and the nature of the task at hand. These factors, when combined with the idiosyncrasies of the leader and followers, are the stuff of the contingency theories of leadership mentioned earlier. They need not detain us here.

In summary, the conceptual model outlined above is designed to bring prominence to several contextual factors which are often overlooked in efforts to analyze and diagnose the possibilities and constraints of any leadership scenario. Although it adds to the complexity of the analysis, ignoring such contextual influences risks failure in achieving leadership goals.

A conceptual model of the sort outlined above helps sort out the broad categories of contextual influences upon leadership. Such a model becomes more beneficial when supplemented by a structured procedure which helps the leader to identify and isolate the specific relevant historical and cultural influences that impact his or her unique leadership situation. The purpose of this final section is to suggest a protocol of questions that any leader can utilize to diagnose the historical and cultural factors which must be confronted and handled.

The questions set out below are quite simple and obvious; unfortunately, few leaders appear to pose them, and as a result, often overlook key environmental factors of their leadership situation. The questions:

1. Who are the important players in this leadership situation?
2. What are their interests/aspirations?
3. What aspects of the historical background threaten or challenge these interests/aspirations?
4. What aspects of the historical background support these interests/aspirations?
5. How do societal beliefs and values impinge, favorably or unfavorably, upon these interests/aspirations?
6. What cultural or subcultural precedents have been established that might influence these interests/aspirations?
7. How can my followers and I use this knowledge to maximize the potential for achieving our mutual goals?

It should be noted that this "environmental scan" purposely includes *all* interested parties, even (perhaps especially) those who might be opposed to one's interests. This approach is similar to the premise underlying Fisher, Ury, and Patton's conception of proper conflict resolution strategies. In their model of "principled negotiation", a knowledge of the true interests and demands upon all parties is the key to a successful resolution of any conflict.[17] So too here; the leader who can use this protocol to uncover the historical and cultural constraints which imbue any leadership situation will be best able to act constructively within those constraints.

The foregoing has been a brief overview of a perceived weakness in existing conceptions of the leadership process, together with a simple model intended as an initial remedy. The model has been operationalized so that leaders and followers facing the inevitable challenges to the achievement of group goals can diagnose the nature of the problems facing them. The ultimate objective of this article is to lead to a better and more rational leadership process in which mutual goals are more easily achieved.

37

Cultural Constraints in Management Theories

Geert Hofstede

Geert Hofstede is professor of organizational anthropology and international management at the University of Limburg at Maastricht, the Netherlands. He was founder and first director of the Institute for Research on Intercultural Cooperation. He has published over 100 articles, and the pathbreaking book *Culture's Consequences*.

Lewis Carroll's *Alice in Wonderland* contains the famous story of Alice's croquet game with the Queen of Hearts.

> Alice thought she had never seen such a curious croquet-ground in all her life; it was all ridges and furrows; the balls were live hedgehogs, the mallets live flamingoes, and the soldiers had to double themselves up and to stand on their hands and feet, to make the arches.

You probably know how the story goes: Alice's flamingo mallet turns its head whenever she wants to strike with it; her hedgehog ball runs away; and the doubled-up soldier arches walk around all the time. The only rule seems to be that the Queen of Hearts always wins. Alice's croquet playing problems are good analogies to attempts to build culture-free theories of management.

Geert Hofstede, "Cultural Constraints in Management Theories," *Academy of Management Executive* 7 (Feb. 1993): 81–94. Reprinted by permission.

Concepts available for this purpose are themselves alive with culture, having been developed within a particular cultural context. They have a tendency to guide our thinking toward our desired conclusion.

As the same reasoning may also be applied to the arguments in this article, I better tell you my conclusion before I continue—so that the rules of my game are understood. In this article we take a trip around the world to demonstrate that there are no such things as universal management theories.

Diversity in management practices as we go around the world has been recognized in U.S. management literature for more than thirty years. The term "comparative management" has been used since the 1960s. However, it has taken much longer for the U.S. academic community to accept that not only practices but also the validity of theories may stop at national borders, and I wonder whether even today everybody would agree with this statement.

An article I published in *Organizational Dynamics* in 1980 entitled "Do American Theories Apply Abroad?" created more controversy than I expected. The article argued, with empirical support, that generally accepted U.S. theories like those of Maslow, Herzberg, McClelland, Vroom, MacGregor, Likert, Blake and Mouton may not or only very partly apply outside the borders of their country of origin—assuming they do apply within those borders. Among the requests for reprints, a larger number were from Canada than from the United States.

Management Theorists are Human

Employees and managers are human. Employees as humans was discovered in the 1930s, with the Human Relations school. Managers as humans was introduced in the late 40's by Herbert Simon's "bounded rationality" and elaborated in Richard Cyert and James March's *Behavioral Theory of the Firm* (1963, and recently re-published in a second edition). My argument is that management scientists, theorists, and writers are human too: they grew up in a particular society in a particular period, and their ideas cannot help but reflect the constraints of their environment.

The idea that the validity of a theory is constrained by national borders is more obvious in Europe, with all its borders, than in a huge borderless country like the U.S. Already in the sixteenth century Michel de Montaigne, a Frenchman, wrote a statement which was made famous by Blaise Pascal about a century later: "Verité en-deca des Pyrénées, erreur au-dela"—There are truths on this side of the Pyrenees which are falsehoods on the other.

From Don Armado's Love to Taylor's Science

According to the comprehensive ten-volume *Oxford English Dictionary* (1971), the words "manage," "management," and "manager" appeared in the English language in the 16th century. The oldest recorded use of the word "manager" is in Shakespeare's "Love's Labour's Lost," dating from 1588, in which Don Adriano de Armado, "a fantastical Spaniard," exclaims (Act I, scene ii, 188): "Adieu, valour! rust, rapier! be still, drum! for your manager is in love; yea, he loveth".

The linguistic origin of the word is from Latin manus, hand, via the Italian maneggiare, which is the training of horses in the manege; subsequently its meaning was extended to skillful handling in general, like of arms and musical instruments, as Don Armado illustrates. However, the word also became associated with the French ménage, household, as an equivalent of "husbandry" in its sense of the art of running a household. The theatre of present-day management contains elements of both manege and menage and different managers and cultures may use different accents. The founder of the science of economics, the Scot Adam Smith, in his 1776 book *The Wealth of Nations*, used "manage," "management" (even "bad management") and "manager" when dealing with the process and the persons involved in operating joint stock companies (Smith, V.i.c.). British economist John Stuart Mill (1806–1873) followed Smith in this use and clearly expressed his distrust of such hired people who were not driven by ownership. Since the 1880s the word "management" appeared occasionally in writings by American engineers, until it was canonized as a modern science by Frederick W. Taylor in *Shop Management* in 1903 and in *The Principles of Scientific Management* in 1911.

While Smith and Mill used "management" to describe a process and "managers" for the persons involved, "management" in the American sense—which has since been taken back by the British—refers not only to the process but also to the managers as a class of people. This class (1) does not own a business but sells its skills to act on behalf of the owners and (2) does not produce personally but is indispensable for making others produce, through motivation. Members of this class carry a high status and many American boys and girls aspire to the role. In the U.S., the manager is a cultural hero.

Let us now turn to other parts of the world. We will look at management in its context in other successful modern economies: Germany, Japan, France, Holland, and among the Overseas Chinese. Then we will examine management in the much larger part of the world that is still poor, especially South-East Asia and Africa, and in the new political configurations of Eastern Europe, and Russia in particular. We will then return to the U.S. via mainland China.

Germany

The manager is not a cultural hero in Germany. If anybody, it is the engineer who fills the hero role. Frederick Taylor's Scientific Management was conceived in a society of immigrants—where large number of workers with diverse backgrounds and skills had to work together. In Germany this heterogeneity never existed.

Elements of the mediaeval guild system have survived in historical continuity in Germany until the present day. In particular, a very effective apprenticeship system exists both on the shop floor and in the office, which alternates practical work and classroom courses. At the end of the apprenticeship the worker receives a certificate, the Facharbeiterbrief, which is recognized throughout the country. About two thirds of the German worker population holds such a certificate and a corresponding occupational pride. In fact, quite a few German company presidents have worked their way up from the ranks through an apprenticeship. In comparison, two thirds of the worker population in Britain have no occupational qualification at all.

The highly skilled and responsible German workers do not necessarily need a manager, American-style, to "motivate" them. They expect their boss or Meister to assign their tasks and to be the expert in resolving technical problems. Comparisons of similar German, British, and French organizations show the Germans as having the highest rate of personnel in productive roles and the lowest both in leadership and staff roles.

Business schools are virtually unknown in Germany. Native German management theories concentrate on formal systems. The inapplicability of American concepts of management was quite apparent in 1973 when the U.S. consulting firm of Booz, Allen and Hamilton, commissioned by the German Ministry of Economic Affairs, wrote a study of German management from an American viewpoint. The report is highly critical and writes among other things that "Germans simply do not have a very strong concept of management." Since 1973, from my personal experience, the situation has not changed much. However, during this period the German economy has performed in a superior fashion to the U.S. in virtually all respects, so a strong concept of management might have been a liability rather than an asset.

Japan

The American type of manager is also missing in Japan. In the United States, the core of the enterprise is the managerial class. The core of the Japanese enterprise is the permanent worker group: workers who for all practical purposes are tenured and who aspire at life-long employment. They are distinct from the non-permanent employees—most women and subcontracted teams led by gang bosses, to be laid off in slack periods. University graduates in Japan first join the permanent worker group and subsequently fill various positions, moving from line to staff as the need occurs while paid according to seniority rather than position. They take part in Japanese-style group consultation sessions for important decisions, which extend the decision-making period but guarantee fast implementation afterwards. Japanese are to a large extent controlled by their peer group rather than by their manager.

Three researchers from the East-West Center of the University of Hawaii, Joseph Tobin, David Wu, and Dana Danielson, did an observation study of typical preschools in three countries: China, Japan, and the United States. Their results have been published both as a book and as a video. In the Japanese preschool, one teacher handled twenty-eight four-year olds. The video shows one particularly obnoxious boy, Hiroki, who fights with other children and throws teaching materials down from the balcony. When a little girl tries to alarm the teacher, the latter answers, "what are you calling me for? Do something about it!" In the U.S. preschool, there is one adult for every nine children. This class has its problem child too, Glen, who refuses to clear away his toys. One of the teachers has a long talk with him and isolates him in a corner, until he changes his mind. It doesn't take much imagination to realize that managing Hiroki thirty years later will be a different process from managing Glen.

American theories of leadership are ill-suited for the Japanese group-controlled situation. During the past two decades, the Japanese have developed their own "PM" theory of leadership, in which P stands for performance and M for maintenance. The latter is less a concern for individual employees than for maintaining social stability. In view of the amazing success of the Japanese economy in the past thirty years, many Americans have sought the secrets of Japanese management hoping to copy them.

There are no secrets of Japanese management, however; it is even doubtful whether there is such a thing as management, in the American sense, in Japan at all. The secret is in Japanese society; and if any group in society should be singled out as carriers of the secret, it is the workers, not the managers.

France

The manager, U.S. style, does not exist in France either. In a very enlightening book, unfortunately not yet translated into English, the French researcher Philippe d'Iribarne (1989) describes the results of in-depth observation and interview studies of management methods in three subsidiary plants of the same French multinational: in France, the United States, and Holland. He relates what he finds to information about the three societies in general. Where necessary, he goes back in history to trace the roots of the strikingly different behaviors in the completion of the same tasks. He identifies three kinds of basic principles (logiques) of management. In the USA, the principle is the fair contract between employer and employee, which gives the manager considerable prerogatives, but within its limits. This is really a labor market in which the worker sells his or her labor for a price. In France, the principle is the honor of each class in a society which has always been and remains extremely stratified, in which superiors behave as superior beings and subordinates accept and expect this, conscious of their own lower level in the national hierarchy but also of the honor of their own class. The French do not think in terms of managers versus nonmanagers but in terms of cadres versus non-cadres; one becomes cadre by attending the proper schools and one remains it forever; regardless of their actual task, cadres have the privileges of a higher social class, and it is very rare for a non-cadre to cross the ranks.

The conflict between French and American theories of management became apparent in the beginning of the twentieth century, in a criticism by the great French management pioneer Henri Fayol (1841–1925) on his U.S. colleague and contemporary Frederick W. Taylor (1856–1915). The difference in career paths of the two men is striking. Fayol was a French engineer whose career as a cadre superieur culminated in the position of President-Directeur-General of a mining company. After his retirement he formulated his experiences in a pathbreaking text on organization: Administration industrielle et générale, in which he focussed on the sources of authority. Taylor was an American engineer who started his career in industry as a worker and attained his academic qualifications through evening studies. From chief engineer in a steel company he became one of the first management consultants. Taylor was not really concerned with the issue of authority at all; his focus was on efficiency. He proposed to split the task of the first-line boss into eight specialties, each exercised by a different person, an idea which eventually led to the idea of a matrix organization.

Taylor's work appeared in a French translation in 1913, and Fayol read it and showed himself generally impressed but shocked by Taylor's "denial of the principle of the Unity of Command" in the case of the eight-boss-system.

Seventy years later André Laurent, another of Fayol's compatriots, found that French managers in a survey reacted very strongly against a suggestion that one employee could report to two different bosses, while U.S. managers in the same survey showed fewer misgivings. Matrix organization has never become popular in France as it has in the United States.

Holland

In my own country, Holland or as it is officially called, the Netherlands, the study by Philippe d'Iribarne found the management principle to be a need for consensus among all parties, neither predetermined by a contractual relationship nor by class distinctions, but based on an open-ended exchange of views and a balancing of interests. In terms of the different origins of the word "manager," the organization in Holland is more ménage (household) while in the United States it is more manege (horse drill).

At my university, the University of Limburg at Maastricht, every semester we receive a class of American business students who take a program in European Studies. We asked both the Americans and a matched group of Dutch students to describe their ideal job after graduation, using a list of twenty-two job characteristics. The Americans attached significantly more importance than the Dutch to earnings, advancement, benefits, a good working relationship with their boss, and security of employment. The Dutch attached more importance to freedom to adopt their own approach to the job, being consulted by their boss in his or her decisions, training opportunities, contributing to the success of their organization, fully using their skills and abilities, and helping others. This list confirms d'Iribarne's findings of a contractual employment relationship in the United States, based on earnings and career opportunities, against a consensual relationship in Holland. The latter has centuries-old roots; the Netherlands was the first republic in Western Europe (1609–1810), and a model for the American republic. The country has been and still is governed by a careful balancing of interests in a multi-party system.

In terms of management theories, both motivation and leadership in Holland are different from what they are in the United States. Leadership in Holland presupposes modesty, as opposed to assertiveness in the United States. No U.S. leadership theory has room for that. Working in Holland is not a constant feast, however. There is a built-in premium on mediocrity and jealousy, as well as time-consuming ritual consultations to maintain the appearance of consensus and the pretense of modesty. There is unfortunately another side to every coin.

The Overseas Chinese

Among the champions of economic development in the past thirty years we find three countries mainly populated by Chinese living outside the Chinese mainland: Taiwan, Hong Kong and Singapore. Moreover, overseas Chinese play a very important role in the economies of Indonesia, Malaysia, the Philippines and Thailand, where they form an ethnic minority. If anything, the little dragons—Taiwan, Hong Kong and Singapore—have been more economically successful than Japan, moving from rags to riches and now counted among the world's wealthy industrial countries. Yet very little attention has been paid to the way in which their enterprises have been managed. *The Spirit of Chinese Capitalism* by Gordon Redding (1990), the British dean of the Hong Kong Business School, is an excellent book about Chinese business. He bases his insights on personal acquaintance and in-depth discussions with a large number of overseas Chinese businesspeople.

Overseas Chinese American enterprises lack almost all characteristics of modern management. They tend to be small, cooperating for essential functions with other small organizations through networks based on personal relations. They are family-owned, without the separation between ownership and management typical in the West, or even in Japan and Korea. They normally focus on one product or market, with growth by opportunistic diversification; in this, they are extremely flexible. Decision making is centralized in the hands of one dominant family member, but other family members may be given new ventures to try their skills on. They are low-profile and extremely cost-conscious, applying Confucian virtues of thrift and persistence. Their size is kept small by the assumed lack of loyalty of non-family employees, who, if they are any good, will just wait and save until they can start their own family business.

Overseas Chinese prefer economic activities in which great gains can be made with little manpower, like commodity trading and real estate. They employ few professional managers, except their sons and sometimes daughters who have been sent to prestigious business schools abroad, but who upon return continue to run the family business the Chinese way. The origin of this system, or—in the Western view this lack of system—is found in the history of Chinese society, in which there were no formal laws, only formal networks of powerful people guided by general principles of Confucian virtue. The favors of the authorities could change daily, so nobody could be trusted except one's kinfolk—of whom, fortunately, there used to be many, in an extended family structure. The overseas Chinese way of doing business is also very well adapted to their position in the countries in which they form ethnic minorities, often envied and threatened by ethnic violence.

Overseas Chinese businesses following this unprofessional approach command a collective gross national product of some 200 to 300 billion US dollars, exceeding the GNP of Australia. There is no denying that it works.

Management Transfer to Poor Countries

Four-fifths of the world population live in countries that are not rich but poor. After World War II and decolonization, the stated purpose of the United Nations and the World Bank has been to promote the development of all the world's countries in a war on poverty. After forty years it looks very much like we are losing this war. If one thing has become clear, it is that the export of Western—mostly American—management practices and theories to poor countries has contributed little to nothing to their development. There has been no lack of effort and money spent for this purpose: students from poor countries have been trained in this country, and teachers and Peace Corps workers have been sent to the poor countries. If nothing else, the general lack of success in economic development of other countries should be sufficient argument to doubt the validity of Western management theories in non-Western environments.

If we examine different parts of the world, the development picture is not equally bleak, and history is often a better predictor than economic factors for what happens today. There is a broad regional pecking order with East Asia leading. The little dragons have passed into the camp of the wealthy; then follow South-East Asia (with its overseas Chinese minorities), Latin America (in spite of the debt crisis), South Asia, and Africa always trails behind. Several African countries have only become poorer since decolonization.

Regions of the world with a history of large-scale political integration and civilization generally have done better than regions in which no large-scale political and cultural infrastructure existed, even if the old civilizations had decayed or been suppressed by colonizers. It has become painfully clear that development cannot be pressure-cooked; it presumes a cultural infrastructure that takes time to grow. Local management is part of this infrastructure;

it cannot be imported in package form. Assuming that with so-called modern management techniques and theories outsiders can develop a country has proven a deplorable arrogance. At best, one can hope for a dialogue between equals with the locals, in which the Western partner acts as the expert in Western technology and the local partner as the expert in local culture, habits, and feelings.

Russia and China

The crumbling of the former Eastern bloc has left us with a scattering of states and would-be states of which the political and economic future is extremely uncertain. The best predictions are those based on a knowledge of history, because historical trends have taken revenge on the arrogance of the Soviet rulers who believed they could turn them around by brute power. One obvious fact is that the former bloc is extremely heterogeneous, including countries traditionally closely linked with the West by trade and travel, like Czechia, Hungary, Slovenia, and the Baltic states, as well as others with a Byzantine or Turkish past; some having been prosperous, others always extremely poor.

The industrialized Western world and the World Bank seem committed to helping the ex-Eastern bloc countries develop, but with the same technocratic neglect for local cultural factors that proved so unsuccessful in the development assistance to other poor countries. Free market capitalism, introduced by Western-style management, is supposed to be the answer from Albania to Russia.

Let me limit myself to the Russian republic, a huge territory with some 140 million inhabitants, mainly Russians. We know quite a bit about the Russians as their country was a world power for several hundreds of years before communism, and in the nineteenth century it produced some of the greatest writers in world literature. If I want to understand the Russians—including how they could so long support the Soviet regime—I tend to reread Lev Nikolayevich Tolstoy. In his most famous novel *Anna Karenina* (1876) one of the main characters is a landowner, Levin, whom Tolstoy uses to express his own views and convictions about his people. Russian peasants used to be serfs; serfdom had been abolished in 1861, but the peasants, now tenants, remained as passive as before. Levin wanted to break this passivity by dividing the land among his peasants in exchange for a share of the crops; but the peasants only let the land deteriorate further. Here follows a quote:

"(Levin) read political economy and socialistic works . . . but, as he had expected, found nothing in them related to his undertaking. In the political economy books—in (John Stuart) Mill, for instance, whom he studied first and with great ardour, hoping every minute to find an answer to the questions that were engrossing him he found only certain laws deduced from the state of agriculture in Europe; but he could not for the life of him see why these laws, which did not apply to Russia, should be considered universal. . . . Political economy told him that the laws by which Europe had developed and was developing her wealth were universal and absolute. Socialist teaching told him that development along those lines leads to ruin. And neither of them offered the smallest enlightenment as to what he, Levin, and all the Russian peasants and landowners were to do with their millions of hands and millions of acres, to make them as productive as possible for the common good."

In the summer of 1991, the Russian lands yielded a record harvest, but a large share of it rotted in the fields because no people were to be found for harvesting. The passivity is still there, and not only among the peasants. And the heirs of John Stuart Mill (whom we met before as one of the early analysts of "management") again present their universal recipes which simply do not apply.

Citing Tolstoy, I implicitly suggest that management theorists cannot neglect the great literature of the countries they want their ideas to apply to. The greatest novel in the Chinese literature is considered Cao Xueqin's *The Story of the Stone*, also known as *The Dream of the Red Chamber*, which appeared around 1760. It describes the rise and fall of two branches of an aristocratic family in Beijing, who live in adjacent plots in the capital. Their plots are joined by a magnificent garden with several pavilions in it, and the young, mostly female members of both families are allowed to live in them. One day the management of the garden is taken over by a young woman, Tan-Chun, who states:

"I think we ought to pick out a few experienced trust-worthy old women from among the ones who work in the Garden—women who know something about gardening—already and put the upkeep of the Garden into their hands. We needn't ask them to pay us rent; all we need ask them for is an annual share of the produce. There would be four advantages in this arrangement. In the first place, if we have people whose sole occupation is to look after trees and flowers and so on, the condition of the Garden will improve gradually year after year and there will be no more of those long periods of neglect followed by bursts of feverish activity when things have been allowed to get out of hand. Secondly there won't be the spoiling and wastage we get at present. Thirdly the women themselves will gain a little extra to add to their incomes which will compensate them for the hard work they put in throughout the year. And fourthly, there's no reason why we shouldn't use the money we should otherwise have spent on nurserymen, rockery specialists, horticultural cleaners and so on for other purposes."

As the story goes on, the capitalist privatization—because that is what it is—of the Garden is carried through, and it works. When in the 1980s Deng Xiaoping allowed privatization in the Chinese villages, it also worked. It worked so well that its effects started to be felt in politics and threatened the existing political order; hence the knockdown at Tienanmen Square of June 1989. But it seems that the forces of privatization are getting the upper hand again in China. If we remember what Chinese entrepreneurs are able to do once they have become Overseas Chinese, we shouldn't be too surprised. But what works in China—and worked two centuries ago—does not have to work in Russia, not in Tolstoy's days and not today. I am not offering a solution; I only protest against a naive universalism that knows only one recipe for development, the one supposed to have worked in the United States.

A Theory of Culture in Management

Our trip around the world is over and we are back in the United States. What have we learned? There is something in all countries called "management, but its meaning differs to a larger or smaller extent from one country to the other, and it takes considerable historical and cultural insight into local conditions to understand its processes, philosophies, and problems. If already the word may mean so many different things, how can we expect one country's theories of management to apply abroad? One should be extremely careful in making this assumption, and test it before considering it proven. Management is not a phenomenon that can be isolated from other processes taking place in a society. During our trip around the world we saw that it interacts with what happens in the family, at school, in politics, and government. It is obviously also related to religion and to beliefs about science. Theories of management always had to be interdisciplinary, but if we cross national borders they should become more interdisciplinary than ever.

Cultural differences between nations can be, to some extent, described using first four, and now five, bipolar dimensions. The position of a country on these dimensions allows us to make some predictions on the way their society operates, including their management processes and the kind of theories applicable to their management.

As the word culture plays such an important role in my theory, let me give you my definition, which differs from some other very respectable definitions. Culture to me is the collective programming of the mind which distinguishes one group or category of people from another. In the part of my work I am referring to now, the category of people is the nation.

Culture is a construct; that means it is "not directly accessible to observation but inferable from verbal statements and other behaviors and useful in predicting still other observable and measurable verbal and nonverbal behavior." It should not be reified; it is an auxiliary concept that should be used as long it proves useful but bypassed where we can predict behaviors without it.

The same applies to the dimensions I introduced. They are constructs too that should not be reified. They do not "exist"; they are tools for analysis which may or may not clarify a situation. In my statistical analysis of empirical data the first four dimensions together explain forty-nine percent of the variance in the data. The other fifty-one percent remain specific to individual countries.

The first four dimensions were initially detected through a comparison of the values of similar people (employees and managers) in sixty-four national subsidiaries of the IBM Corporation. People working for the same multinational, but in different countries, represent very well-matched samples from the populations of their countries, similar in all respects except nationality.

The first dimension is labelled Power Distance, and it can be defined as the degree of inequality among people which the population of a country considers as normal: from relatively equal (that is, small power distance) to extremely unequal (large power distance). All societies are unequal, but some are more unequal than others.

The second dimension is labelled Individualism, and it is the degree to which people in a country prefer to act as individuals rather than as members of groups. The opposite of individualism can be called Collectivism, so collectivism is low individualism. The way I use the word it has no political connotations. In collectivist societies a child learns to respect the group to which it belongs, usually the family, and to differentiate between in-group members and out-group members (that is, all other people). When children grow up they remain members of their group, and they expect the group to protect them when they are in trouble. In return, they have to remain loyal to their group throughout life. In individualist societies, a child learns very early to think of itself as "I" instead of as part of "we". It expects one day to have to stand on its own feet and not to get protection from its group any more; and therefore it also does not feel a need for strong loyalty.

The third dimension is called Masculinity and its opposite pole Femininity. It is the degree to which tough values like assertiveness, performance, success and competition, which in nearly all societies are associated with the role of men, prevail over tender values like the quality of life, maintaining warm personal relationships, service, care for the weak, and solidarity, which in nearly all societies are more associated with women's roles. Women's roles differ from men's roles in all countries; but in tough societies, the differences are larger than in tender ones.

The fourth dimension is labelled Uncertainty Avoidance, and it can be defined as the degree to which people in a country prefer structured over unstructured situations. Structured situations are those in which there are clear rules as to how one should behave. These rules can be written down, but they can also be unwritten and imposed by tradition. In countries which score high on uncertainty avoidance, people tend to show more nervous energy, while in countries which score low, people are more easy-going. A (national) society with strong uncertainty avoidance can be called rigid; one with weak uncertainty avoidance, flexible. In countries where uncertainty avoidance is strong a feeling prevails of "what is different, is dangerous." In weak uncertainty avoidance societies, the feeling would rather be "what is different, is curious."

The fifth dimension was added on the basis of a study of the values of students in twenty-three countries carried out by Michael Harris Bond, a Canadian working in Hong Kong. He and I had cooperated in another study of students' values which had yielded the same four dimensions as the IBM data. However, we wondered to what extent our common findings in two studies could be the effect of a Western bias introduced by the common Western background of the researchers: remember Alice's croquet game.

Michael Bond resolved this dilemma by deliberately introducing an Eastern bias. He used a questionnaire prepared at his request by his Chinese colleagues, the Chinese Value Survey (CVS), which was translated from Chinese into different languages and answered by fifty male and fifty female students in each of twenty-three countries in all five continents. Analysis of the CVS data produced three dimensions significantly correlated with the three IBM dimensions of power distance, individualism, and masculinity. There was also a fourth dimension, but it did not resemble uncertainty avoidance. It was composed, both on the positive and on the negative side, from items that had not been included in the IBM studies but were present in the Chinese Value Survey because they were rooted in the teachings of Confucius. I labelled this dimension: Long-term versus Short-term Orientation. On the long-term side one finds values oriented towards the future, like thrift (saving) and persistence. On the short-term side one finds values rather oriented towards the past and present, like respect for tradition and fulfilling social obligations.

Table 1 [omitted] lists the scores on all five dimensions for the United States and for the other countries we just discussed. The table shows that each country has its own configuration on the four dimensions. Some of the values in the table have been estimated based on imperfect replications or personal impressions. The different dimension scores do not "explain" all the differences in management I described earlier. To understand management in a country, one should have both knowledge of and empathy with the entire local scene. However, the scores should make us aware that people in other countries may think, feel, and act very differently from us when confronted with basic problems of society.

Idiosyncrasies of American Management Theories

In comparison to other countries, the U.S. culture profile presents itself as below average on power distance and uncertainty avoidance, highly individualistic, fairly masculine, and short-term oriented. The Germans show a stronger uncertainty avoidance and less extreme individualism; the Japanese are different on all dimensions, least on power distance; the French show larger power distance and uncertainty avoidance, but are less individualistic and somewhat feminine; the Dutch resemble the Americans on the first three dimensions, but score extremely feminine and relatively long-term oriented; Hong Kong Chinese combine large power distance with weak uncertainty avoidance, collectivism, and are very long-term oriented; and so on.

The American culture profile is reflected in American management theories. I will just mention three elements not necessarily present in other countries: the stress on market processes, the stress on the individual, and the focus on managers rather than on workers.

The Stress on Market Processes

During the 1970s and 80s it has become fashionable in the United States to look at organizations from a "transaction costs" viewpoint. Economist Oliver Williamson has opposed "hierarchies" to "markets." The reasoning is that human social life consists of economic transactions between individuals. We found the same in d'Iribarne's description of the U.S. principle of the contract between employer and employee, the labor market in which the worker sells his or her labor for a price. These individuals will form hierarchical organizations when the cost of the economic transactions (such as getting information, finding out whom to trust etc.) is lower in a hierarchy than when all transactions would take place on a free market.

From a cultural perspective the important point is that the "market" is the point of departure or base model, and the organization is explained from market failure. A culture that produces such a theory is likely to prefer organizations that internally resemble markets to organizations that internally resemble more structured models, like those in Germany or France. The ideal principle of control in organizations in the market philosophy is competition between individuals. This philosophy fits a society that combines a not-too-large power distance with a not-too-strong uncertainty avoidance and individualism; besides the USA, it will fit all other Anglo countries.

The Stress on the Individual

I find this constantly in the design of research projects and hypotheses; also in the fact that in the U.S. psychology is clearly a more respectable discipline in management circles than sociology. Culture however is a collective phenomenon. Although we may get our information about culture from individuals, we have to interpret it at the level of collectivities. There are snags here known as the "ecological fallacy" and the "reverse ecological fallacy." None of the U.S. college textbooks on methodology I know deals sufficiently with the problem of multilevel analysis.

Culture can be compared to a forest, while individuals are tree. A forest is not just a bunch of trees: it is a symbiosis of different trees, bushes, plants, insects, animals and micro-organisms, and we miss the essence of the forest if we only describe its most typical trees. In the same way, a culture cannot be satisfactorily described in terms of the characteristics of a typical individual. There is a tendency in the U.S. management literature to overlook the forest for the trees and to ascribe cultural differences to interactions among individuals.

A striking example is found in the otherwise excellent book *Organizational Culture and Leadership* by Edgar H. Schein (1985). On the basis of his consulting experience he compares two large companies, nicknamed "Action" and "Multi." He explains the differences in culture between these companies by the group dynamics in their respective boardrooms. Nowhere in the book are any conclusions drawn from the fact that the first company is an

American-based computer firm, and the second a Swiss-based pharmaceutics firm. This information is not even mentioned. A stress on interactions among individuals obviously fits a culture identified as the most individualistic in the world, but it will not be so well understood by the four-fifths of the world population for whom the group prevails over the individual.

One of the conclusions of my own multilevel research has been that culture at the national level and culture at the organizational level—corporate culture—are two very different phenomena and that the use of a common term for both is confusing. If we do use the common term, we should also pay attention to the occupational and the gender level of culture. National cultures differ primarily in the fundamental, invisible values held by a majority of their members, acquired in early childhood, whereas organizational cultures are a much more superficial phenomenon residing mainly in the visible practices of the organization, acquired by socialization of the new members who join as young adults. National cultures change only very slowly if at all; organizational cultures may be consciously changed, although this isn't necessarily easy. This difference between the two types of culture is the secret of the existence of multinational corporations that employ, as I showed in the IBM case, employees with extremely different national cultural values. What keeps them together is a corporate culture based on common practices.

The Stress on Managers Rather than Workers

The core element of a work organization around the world is the people who do the work. All the rest is superstructure, and I hope to have demonstrated to you that it may take many different shapes. In the U.S. literature on work organization, however, the core element, if not explicitly then implicitly, is considered the manager. This may well be the result of the combination of extreme individualism with fairly strong masculinity, which has turned the manager into a culture hero of almost mythical proportions. For example, he is supposed to make decisions all the time. Those of you who are or have been managers must know that this is a fable. Very few management decisions are just "made" as the myth suggests it. Managers are much more involved in maintaining networks; if anything, it is the rank-and-file worker who can really make decisions on his or her own, albeit on a relatively simple level.

An amusing effect of the U.S. focus on managers is that in at least ten American books and articles on management I have been misquoted as having studied IBM managers in my research, whereas the book clearly describes that the answers were from IBM employees. My observation may be biased, but I get the impression that compared to twenty or thirty years ago less research in this country is done among employees and more on managers. But managers derive their raison d'etre from the people managed: culturally, they are the followers of the people they lead, and their effectiveness depends on the latter. In other parts of the world, this exclusive focus on the manager is less strong, with Japan as the supreme example.

Conclusion

This article started with Alice in Wonderland. In fact, the management theorist who ventures outside his or her own country into other parts of the world is like Alice in Wonderland. He or she will meet strange beings, customs, ways of organizing or disorganizing and theories that are clearly stupid, old-fashioned or even immoral yet they may work, or at least they may not fail more frequently than corresponding theories do at home. Then, after the first culture shock, the traveller to Wonderland will feel enlightened, and may be able to take his or her experiences home and use them advantageously. All great ideas in science, politics and management have travelled from one country to another, and been enriched by foreign influences. The roots of American management theories are mainly in Europe: with Adam Smith, John Stuart Mill, Lev Tolstoy, Max Weber, Henri Fayol, Sigmund Freud, Kurt Lewin and many others. These theories were re-planted here and they developed and bore fruit. The same may happen again. The last thing we need is a Monroe doctrine for management ideas.

38

Defining Organizational Culture

Edgar H. Schein

Edgar H. Schein is considered one of the founders of the field of organizational psychology. He was chair of the Organization Studies Group of the Sloan School of Management at the Massachusetts Institute of Technology, and is currently professor of management there. His book *Organizational Culture and Leadership* has become a classic in the field.

Culture as a concept has had a long and checkered history. It has been used by the lay person as a word to indicate sophistication, as when we say that someone is very "cultured." It has been used by anthropologists to refer to the customs and rituals that societies develop over the course of their history. In the last decade or so it has been used by some organizational researchers and managers to indicate the climate and practices that organizations develop around their handling of people or to refer to the espoused values and credo of an organization.

In this context managers speak of developing the "right kind of culture" or a "culture of quality," suggesting that culture is concerned with certain values that managers are trying to inculcate in their organizations. Also implied in this usage is the assumption that there are better or worse cultures, stronger

Reprinted from Edgar H. Schein, *Organizational Culture and Leadership* 2d ed. (San Francisco: Jossey-Bass, 1992), pp. 3–15. Reprinted by permission.

or weaker cultures, and that the "right" kind of culture will influence how effective organizations are.

If a new and abstract concept is to be useful to our thinking, it should refer to a set of events that are otherwise mysterious or not well understood. From this point of view, I will argue that we must avoid the superficial models of culture and build on the deeper, more complex anthropological models. Culture will be most useful as a concept if it helps us better understand the hidden and complex aspects of organizational life. This understanding cannot be obtained if we use superficial definitions.

Most of us in our roles as students, employees, managers, researchers, or consultants work in and deal with organizations of all kinds. Yet we continue to find it amazingly difficult to understand and justify much of what we observe and experience in our organizational life. Too much seems to be bureaucratic, or political, or just plain irrational. People in positions of authority, especially our immediate bosses, often frustrate us or act incomprehensibly, and those we consider the leaders of our organizations often disappoint us.

If we are managers who are trying to change the behavior of subordinates, we often encounter resistance to change at a level that seems beyond reason. We observe departments in our organization that seem to be more interested in fighting with each other than getting the job done. We see communication problems and misunderstandings between group members that should not be occurring between "reasonable" people.

If we are leaders who are trying to get our organizations to become more effective in the face of severe environmental pressures, we are sometimes amazed at the degree to which individuals and groups in the organization will continue to behave in obviously ineffective ways, often threatening the very survival of the organization. As we try to get things done that involve other groups, we often discover that they do not communicate with each other and that the level of conflict between groups in organizations and in the community is often astonishingly high.

If we are teachers, we encounter the sometimes mysterious phenomenon that different classes behave completely differently from each other even though our material and teaching style remain the same. If we are employees considering a new job, we realize that companies differ greatly in their approach, even in the same industry and geographical area. We feel these differences even as we walk in the door of different organizations such as restaurants, banks, and stores.

The concept of culture helps explain all of these phenomena and to "normalize" them. If we understand the dynamics of culture, we will be less likely to be puzzled, irritated, and anxious when we encounter the unfamiliar and seemingly irrational behavior of people in organizations, and we will have a deeper understanding not only of why various groups of people or organizations can be so different but also why it is so hard to change them.

A deeper understanding of cultural issues in groups and organizations is necessary to decipher what goes on in them but, even more important, to identify what may be the priority issues for leaders and leadership. Organizational cultures are created in part by leaders, and one of the most decisive functions of leadership is the creation, the management, and sometimes even the destruction of culture.

Neither culture nor leadership, when one examines each closely, can really be understood by itself. In fact, one could argue that the only thing of real importance that leaders do is to create and manage culture and that the unique talent of leaders is their ability to understand and work with culture. If one wishes to distinguish leadership from management or administration, one can argue that leaders create and change cultures, while managers and administrators live within them.

By defining leadership in this manner, I am not implying that culture is easy to create or change or that leaders are the only determiners of culture. On the contrary, as we will see, culture refers to those elements of a group or organization that are most stable and least malleable. Culture is the result of a complex group learning process that is only partially influenced by leader behavior. But if the group's survival is threatened because elements of its culture have become maladapted, it is ultimately the function of leadership to recognize and do something about the situation. It is in this sense that leadership and culture are conceptually intertwined.

Two Brief Examples

To illustrate how "culture" helps illuminate organizational situations, I will describe two situations I encountered in my experience as a consultant. In the first case (the Action Company), I was called in to help a management group improve its communication, interpersonal relationships, and decision making. After sitting in on a number of meetings, I observed among other things (1) high levels of interrupting, confrontation, and debate; (2) excessive emotionalism about proposed courses of action; (3) great frustration over the difficulty of getting a point of view across; and (4) a sense that every member of the group wanted to win all the time.

Over a period of several months, I made many suggestions about better listening, less interrupting, more orderly processing of the agenda, the potential negative effects of high emotionalism and conflict, and the need to reduce the frustration level. The group members said that the suggestions were helpful, and they modified certain aspects of their procedure, such as lengthening some of their meetings. However, the basic pattern did not change. No matter what kind of intervention I attempted, the group's basic style remained the same.

In the second case (the Multi Company), I was asked, as part of a broader consultation project, to help create a climate for innovation in an organization that felt a need to become more flexible in order to respond to its increasingly dynamic business environment. The organization consisted of many different business units, geographical units, and functional groups. As I got to know more about these units and their problems, I observed that some very innovative things were occurring in many places in the company. I wrote several memos describing these innovations, added other ideas from my own experience, and gave the memos to my contact person in the company with the request that he distribute them to the various business unit and geographical managers who needed to be made aware of these ideas.

After some months, I discovered that the managers to whom I had personally given a memo thought it was helpful and on target, but rarely if ever did they pass it on. Moreover, none of the memos were ever distributed by my contact person. I also suggested meetings of managers from different units to stimulate lateral communication but found no support at all for such meetings. No matter what I did, I could not seem to get information flowing, especially laterally across divisional, functional, or geographical boundaries. Yet everyone agreed in principle that innovation would be stimulated by more lateral communication and encouraged me to keep on "helping."

I did not really understand what happened in either of these cases until I began to examine *my own assumptions* about how things should work in these organizations and began to test whether my assumptions fitted those operating in my client systems. This step of examining the shared assumptions in the organization or group one is dealing with takes one into "cultural" analysis and will be the focus from here on.

It turned out that in the Action Company senior managers and most of the other members of the organization shared the assumption that one cannot determine whether or not something is true unless one subjects that idea or proposal to intensive debate. Only ideas that survive such debate are worth acting on, and only ideas that survive such scrutiny will be implemented. The group assumed that what they were doing was discovering truth, and in this context being polite to each other was relatively less important.

In the case of the Multi Company I eventually discovered that there was a strong shared assumption that each manager's job was his or her private turf, not to be infringed on. Articulated was the strong image that one's job is like one's home, and if someone gives one unsolicited information, it is like walking into one's home uninvited. Sending memos to people implies that they do not already know what is in the memo and that is potentially insulting. In this organization managers prided themselves on knowing whatever they needed to know to do their job.

In both of these cases I did not understand what was going on because my basic assumptions about truth and turf differed from the shared assumptions of the group members. Cultural analysis, then, is the encountering and deciphering of such shared basic assumptions.

Toward a Formal Definition of Culture

The word *culture* has many meanings and connotations. When we apply it to groups and organizations, we are almost certain to have conceptual and semantic confusion because groups and organizations are also difficult to define unambiguously. Most people have a connotative sense of what culture is but have difficulty defining it abstractly. In talking about organizational culture with colleagues and members of organizations, I often find that we agree "it" exists and that "it" is important in its effects but that we have completely different ideas of what "it" is. I have also had colleagues tell me pointedly that they do not use the concept of culture in their work, but when I ask them what it is they do not use, they cannot define "it" clearly.

To make matters worse, the concept of culture has been the subject of considerable academic debate in the last five years, and there are various approaches to defining and studying culture.[1-4] This debate is a healthy sign in that it testifies to the importance of culture as a concept. At the same time, however, it creates difficulties for both the scholar and the practitioner if definitions are fuzzy and uses are inconsistent. . . . I will give only a brief overview of this range of uses and then try to give a precise and formal definition that makes the most sense from my point of view. Also, please note that from this point on I will use the term *group* to refer to social units of all sizes, including organizations and subunits of organizations except where it is necessary to distinguish type of social unit because of subgroups that exist within larger groups.

Commonly used words relating to culture emphasize one of its critical aspects—the idea that certain things in groups are *shared or held in common*. The major categories of such overt phenomena that are associated with culture in this sense are the following:

1. *Observed behavioral regularities when people interact*: the *language* they use, the *customs and traditions* that evolve, and the *rituals* they employ in a wide variety of situations.[5–10]

2. *Group norms*: the implicit standards and values that evolve in working groups, such as the particular norm of "a fair day's work for a fair day's pay" that evolved among workers in the Bank Wiring Room in the Hawthorne studies.[11,12]

3. *Espoused values*: the articulated, publicly announced principles and values that the group claims to be trying to achieve, such as "product quality" or "price leadership."[13]

4. *Formal philosophy*: the broad policies and ideological principles that guide a group's actions toward stockholders, employees, customers, and other stakeholders, such as the highly publicized "HP Way" of Hewlett-Packard.[14,15]

5. *Rules of the game*: the implicit rules for getting along in the organization, "the ropes" that a newcomer must learn to become an accepted member, "the way we do things around here."[10,16–19]

6. *Climate*: the feeling that is conveyed in a group by the physical layout and the way in which members of the organization interact with each other, with customers, or with other outsiders.[20,21]

7. *Embedded skills*: the special competencies group members display in accomplishing certain tasks, the ability to make certain things that gets passed on from generation to generation without necessarily being articulated in writing.[22–25]

8. *Habits of thinking, mental models, and/or linguistic paradigms*: the shared cognitive frames that guide the perceptions, thought, and language used by the members of a group and are taught to new members in the early socialization process.[10,26,27]

9. *Shared meanings*: the emergent understandings that are created by group members as they interact with each other.[28–30]

10. *"Root metaphors" or integrating symbols*: the ideas, feelings, and images groups develop to characterize themselves, that may or may not be appreciated consciously but that become embodied in buildings, office layout, and other material artifacts of the group. This level of the cul-

ture reflects group members' emotional and aesthetic responses as con-
trasted with their cognitive or evaluative response.[31-34]

All of these concepts relate to culture and/or reflect culture in that they
deal with things that group members share or hold in common, but none of
them are "the culture" of an organization or group. If one asks oneself why
one needs the word *culture* at all when we have so many other words such
as *norms, values, behavior patterns, rituals, traditions,* and so on, one recognizes that the word *culture* adds two other critical elements to the concept
of sharing.

One of these elements is that culture implies some level of *structural stability* in the group. When we say that something is "cultural," we imply that it is
not only shared but deep and stable. By deep I mean less conscious and
therefore less tangible and less visible. The other element that lends stability
is *patterning or integration* of the elements into a larger paradigm or gestalt
that ties together the various elements and that lies at a deeper level. Culture
somehow implies that rituals, climate, values, and behaviors bind together
into a coherent whole. This patterning or integration is the *essence* of what
we mean by "culture." How then do we think about this essence and formally
define it?

The most useful way to think about culture is to view it as the accumulated shared learning of a given group, covering behavioral, emotional, and cognitive elements of the group members' total psychological functioning. For
shared learning to occur, there must be a history of shared experience, which
in turn implies some stability of membership in the group. Given such stability and a shared history, the human need for parsimony, consistency, and
meaning will cause the various shared elements to form into patterns that
eventually can be called a culture.

I am not arguing, however, that all groups develop integrated cultures in
this sense. We all know of groups, organizations, and societies where cultural
elements work at cross purposes with other elements, leading to situations
full of conflict and ambiguity.[2,35] This may result from insufficient stability of
membership, insufficient shared history of experience, or the presence of
many subgroups with different kinds of shared experiences. Ambiguity and
conflict also result from the fact that each of us belongs to many groups so
that what we bring to any given group is influenced by the assumptions that
are appropriate to our other groups.

If the concept of culture is to have any utility, however, it should draw our
attention to those things that are the product of our human need for stability,

consistency, and meaning. Culture formation, therefore, is always, by definition, a *striving toward patterning and integration*, even though the actual history of experiences of many groups prevents them from ever achieving a clear-cut paradigm.

If a group's culture is that group's accumulated learning, how do we describe and catalogue the content of that learning? All group and organizational theories distinguish two major sets of problems that all groups, no matter what their size, must deal with: (1) survival, growth, and adaptation in their environment and (2) internal integration that permits daily functioning and the ability to adapt.

In conceptualizing group learning, we have to note that because of the human capacity to abstract and to be self-conscious, learning occurs not only at the behavioral level but also at an abstract level internally. Once people have a common system of communication and a language, learning can take place at a conceptual level and shared concepts become possible. Therefore, the deeper levels of learning that get us to the essence of culture must be thought of as concepts or, as I will define them, shared basic assumptions.

. . . The learning process for the group starts with one or more members taking a leadership role in proposing courses of action and as these continue to be successful in solving the group's internal and external problems, they come to be taken for granted and the assumptions underlying them cease to be questioned or debated. A group has a culture when it has had enough of a shared history to have formed such a set of *shared* assumptions.

Shared assumptions derive their power from the fact that they begin to operate outside of awareness. Furthermore, once formed and taken for granted, they become a defining property of the group that permits the group to differentiate itself from other groups, and in that process, value is attached to such assumptions. They are not only "our" assumptions, but by virtue of our history of success, they must be right and good. In fact, as we will see, one of the main problems in resolving intercultural issues is that we take culture so much for granted and put so much value on our own assumptions that we find it awkward and inappropriate even to discuss our assumptions or to ask others about their assumptions. We tend not to examine assumptions once we have made them but to take them for granted, and we tend not to discuss them, which makes them seemingly unconscious. If we are forced to discuss them, we tend not to examine them but to defend them because we have emotionally invested in them.[36]

Culture Formally Defined

The *culture* of a group can now be defined as: A pattern of shared basic assumptions that the group learned as it solved its problems of external adaptation and internal integration, that has worked well enough to be considered valid and, therefore, to be taught to new members as the correct way to perceive, think, and feel in relation to those problems.

Note that this definjition introduces three elements not previously discussed.

1. *The problem of socialization.* It is my view that what we think of as culture is primarily what is passed on to new generations of group members.[17,37–39] Studying what new members of groups are taught is, in fact, a good way to discover some of the elements of a culture, but one only learns about surface aspects of the culture by this means. This is especially so because much of what is at the heart of a culture will not be revealed in the rules of behavior taught to newcomers. It will only be revealed to members as they gain permanent status and are allowed to enter the inner circles of the group, where group secrets are shared.

On the other hand, *how* one learns and the socialization *processes* to which one is subjected may indeed reveal deeper assumptions. To get at those deeper levels one must try to understand the perceptions and feelings that arise in critical situations, and one must observe and interview regular members or old-timers to get an accurate sense of which deeper-level assumptions are shared.

Can culture be learned through anticipatory socialization or self-socialization? Can new members discover for themselves what the basic assumptions are? Yes and no. We certainly know that one of the major activities of any new member when she enters a new group is to decipher the norms and assumptions that are operating. But this deciphering can only be successful through the rewards and punishments that long-time members mete out to new members as they experiment with different kinds of behavior. In this sense, a teaching process is always going on, even though it may be quite implicit and unsystematic.

If the group does not have shared assumptions, as is sometimes the case, the new members' interaction with old members will be a more creative process of building a culture. Once shared assumptions exist, however, the culture survives through teaching them to newcomers. In this regard culture is a mechanism of social control and can be the basis of explicitly manipulating members into perceiving, thinking, and feeling in certain ways.[40,41]

Whether or not we approve of this as a mechanism of social control is a separate question that will be addressed later.

2. *The problem of "behavior."* Note that the definition of culture that I have given does *not* include overt behavior patterns, though some such behavior, especially formal rituals, would reflect cultural assumptions. Instead, the definition emphasizes that the critical assumptions deal with how we perceive, think about, and feel about things. Overt behavior is always determined both by the cultural predisposition (the perceptions, thoughts, and feelings that are patterned) and by the situational contingencies that arise from the immediate external environment.

Behavioral regularities could thus be as much a reflection of separate but similar individual experiences and/or common situational stimuli arising from the environment. For example, suppose we observe that all members of a group cower in the presence of a large and loud leader. Such cowering could be based on biological reflex reactions to sound and size, or individual learning, or shared learning. Such a behavioral regularity should not, therefore, be the basis for defining culture, though we might later discover that in a given group's experience, cowering is indeed a result of shared learning and therefore a manifestation of deeper shared assumptions. To put it another way, when we observe behavior regularities, we do not know whether we are dealing with a cultural manifestation. Only after we have discovered the deeper layers that I am defining as the essence of culture can we specify what is and what is not an "artifact" that reflects the culture.

3. *Can a large organization have one culture?* The definition provided does not specify the size of social unit to which it can legitimately be applied. Our experience with large organizations tells us that at a certain size, the variations among the subgroups are substantial, suggesting that it is not appropriate to talk of "the culture" of an IBM or a General Motors or a Shell Oil. My view is that this question should be handled empirically. If we find that certain assumptions are shared across all the units of an organization, then we can legitimately speak of an organizational culture, even though at the same time we may find a number of discrete subcultures that have their own integrity. In fact, as we will see, with time any social unit will produce subunits that will produce subcultures as a normal process of evolution. Some of these subcultures will typically be in conflict with each other, as is often the case with higher management and unionized labor groups. Yet in spite of such conflict one will find that organizations have common assumptions that come into play when a crisis occurs or when a common enemy is found.

Summary and Conclusions

The concept of culture is most useful if it helps to explain some of the more seemingly incomprehensible and irrational aspects of groups and organizations. Analysts of culture have a wide variety of ways of looking at the concept. My formal definition brings many of these various concepts together, putting the emphasis on shared, taken-for-granted basic assumptions held by the members of the group or organization. In this sense, any group with a stable membership and a history of shared learning will have developed some level of culture, but a group having either a great deal of turnover of members and leaders or a history without any kind of challenging events may well lack any shared assumptions. Not every collection of people develops a culture; in fact, we tend to use the term *group* rather than *crowd* or *collection of people* only when there has been enough of a shared history so that some degree of culture formation has taken place.

Culture and leadership are two sides of the same coin in that leaders first create cultures when they create groups and organizations. Once cultures exist, they determine the criteria for leadership and thus determine who will or will not be a leader. But if cultures become dysfunctional, it is the unique function of leadership to perceive the functional and dysfunctional elements of the existing culture and to manage cultural evolution and change in such a way that the group can survive in a changing environment.

The bottom line for leaders is that if they do not become conscious of the cultures in which they are embedded, those cultures will manage them. Cultural understanding is desirable for all of us, but it is essential to leaders if they are to lead.

39

Strong Cultures: A New "Old Rule" for Business Success

Terrence E. Deal and Allan A. Kennedy

Terrence E. Deal is the author of several books, including *Corporate Cultures* (with Allan Kennedy) and *Reframing Organizations* with Lee G. Bolman. He is professor of education at Peabody College of Vanderbilt University, and co-director of the National Center for Educational Leadership. Allan A. Kennedy served as a consultant with McKinsey and Company, then as president of Selkirk Associates.

S. C. Allyn, a retired chairman of the board, likes to tell a story about his company—the National Cash Register Corporation. It was August 1945, and Allyn was among the first allied civilians to enter Germany at the end of the war. He had gone to find out what had happened to an NCR factory built just before the war but promptly confiscated by the German military command and put to work on the war effort. He arrived via military plane and traveled through burned-out buildings, rubble, and utter desolation until he reached what was left of the factory. Picking his way through bricks, cement, and old timbers, Allyn came upon two NCR employees whom he hadn't seen for six years. Their clothes were torn and their faces grimy and blackened by smoke, but they were busy clearing out the rubble. As he came closer, one of the men

Terrence E. Deal and Allan A. Kennedy, *Corporate Cultures* (pp. 3–19), © 1982 by Addison-Wesley Publishing Company, Inc. Reprinted by permission of the publisher.

looked up and said, "We knew you'd come!" Allyn joined them in their work and together the three men began cleaning out the debris and rebuilding the factory from the devastation of war. The company had even survived the ravages of a world war.

A few days later, as the clearing continued, Allyn and his co-workers were startled as an American tank rumbled up to the site. A grinning GI was at its helm. "Hi," he said, "I'm NCR, Omaha. Did you guys make your quota this month?" Allyn and the GI embraced each other. The war may have devastated everything around them, but NCR's hard driving, sales-oriented culture was still intact.

This story may sound unbelievable, but there are hundreds like it at NCR and every other company. Together they make up the myths and legends of American business. What do they mean? To us these stories mean that businesses are human institutions, not plush buildings, bottom lines, strategic analysis, or five-year plans. NCR was never just a factory to the three men who dug it out of the rubble. Nor was it to others like them. Rather it was a living organization. The company's real existence lay in the hearts and minds of its employees. NCR was, and still is, a corporate culture, a cohesion of values, myths, heroes, and symbols that has come to mean a great deal to the people who work there.

Culture, as *Webster's New Collegiate Dictionary* defines it, is "the integrated pattern of human behavior that includes thought, speech, action, and artifacts and depends on man's capacity for learning and transmitting knowledge to succeeding generations." Marvin Bower, for years managing director of McKinsey & Company and author of *The Will to Manage*, offered a more informal definition—he described the informal cultural elements of a business as "the way we do things around here."

Every business—in fact every organization—has a culture. Sometimes it is fragmented and difficult to read from the outside—some people are loyal to their bosses, others are loyal to the union, still others care only about their colleagues who work in the sales territories of the Northeast. If you ask employees why they work, they will answer "because we need the money." On the other hand, sometimes the culture of an organization is very strong and cohesive; everyone knows the goals of the corporation, and they are working for them. Whether weak or strong, culture has a powerful influence throughout an organization; it affects practically everything—from who gets promoted and what decisions are made, to how employees dress and what sports they play. Because of this impact, we think that culture also has a major effect on the success of the business.

Today, everyone seems to complain about the decline in American productivity. The examples of industries in trouble are numerous and depressing. Books proclaim that Japanese management practices are the solution to America's industrial malaise. But we disagree. We don't think the answer is to mimic the Japanese. Nor do we think the solution lies with the tools of "scientific" management: MBAs' analyses, portfolio theories, cost curves, or econometric models. Instead we think the answer is as American as apple pie. American business needs to return to the original concepts and ideas that made institutions like NCR, General Electric, International Business Machines (IBM), Procter & Gamble, 3M, and others great. We need to remember that people make businesses work. And we need to relearn old lessons about how culture ties people together and gives meaning and purpose to their day-to-day lives.

The early leaders of American business such as Thomas Watson of IBM, Harley Procter of Procter & Gamble, and General Johnson of Johnson & Johnson believed that strong culture brought success. They believed that the lives and productivity of their employees were shaped by where they worked. These builders saw their role as creating an environment—in effect, a culture—in their companies in which employees could be secure and thereby do the work necessary to make the business a success. They had no magic formulas. In fact, they discovered how to shape their company's culture by trial and error. But all along the way, they paid almost fanatical attention to the culture of their companies. The lessons of these early leaders have been passed down in their own companies from generation to generation of managers; the cultures they were so careful to build and nourish have sustained their organizations through both fat and lean times. Today these corporations still have strong cultures and still are leaders in the marketplace.

We think that anyone in business can learn a lot from these examples. A major reason the Japanese have been so successful, we think, is their continuing ability to maintain a very strong and cohesive culture throughout the entire country. Not only do individual businesses have strong cultures, but the links among business, the banking industry, and the government are also cultural and also very powerful. Japan, Inc., is actually an expansion of the corporate culture idea on a national scale. Although this homogenization of values would not fit American culture on a national scale, we do think that it has been very effective for individual companies. In fact, a strong culture has almost always been the driving force behind continuing success in American business.

We came to this conclusion through our work and study—Kennedy at McKinsey & Company and Deal at Harvard's Graduate School of Education. The idea had several origins. One was at a meeting at Stanford. A group of sociologists was puzzling over the absence of relationships among variables that organizational theory said should be related. If the structure of an organization doesn't control work activities, what does it do? These questions led to new theories and views: structure and strategy may be more symbolic than substantive. The other was a McKinsey meeting. We were talking about the problems of organizations, and someone asked, "What makes for consistently outstanding company performance?" Another person offered the hypothesis that the companies that did best over the long haul were those that believed in something. The example was, "IBM means service." Others chimed in, and soon the table was full of examples:

- GE: "Progress is our most important product."
- DuPont: "Better things for better living through chemistry."
- Chubb Insurance: "Excellence in underwriting."

While the focus at that point was on slogan-like evidence of a paramount belief—which we later called a "superordinate goal"—we were struck by the fact that each of the companies named had an impressive track record in the marketplace.

Intrigued by this initial evidence of support for our somewhat unconventional hypothesis, we conducted an informal survey over the next several months by interviewing McKinsey consultants about companies or organizations[1] they knew on a firsthand basis. The questions we asked were:

- Does Company X have one or more visible beliefs?
- If so, what are they?
- Do people in the organization know these beliefs? If so, who? And how many?
- How do these beliefs affect day-to-day business?
- How are the beliefs communicated to the organization?
- Are the beliefs reinforced—by formal personnel processes, recognition, rewards?
- How would you characterize the performance of the company?

In total, over a period of about six months, we developed profiles of nearly eighty companies. Here's what we found out:

- Of all the companies surveyed, only about one third (twenty-five to be precise) had clearly articulated beliefs.
- Of this third, a surprising two-thirds had qualitative beliefs, or values, such as "IBM means service." The other third had financially oriented goals that were widely understood.
- Of the eighteen companies with qualitative beliefs, all were uniformly outstanding performers; we could find no correlations of any relevance among the other companies—some did okay, some poorly, most had their ups and downs. We characterized the consistently high performers as strong culture companies.[2]

These strong culture companies, we thought, were on to something. And so were we. Although this was far from a scientific survey, we did have evidence that the impact of values and beliefs on company performance was indeed real. We decided to follow up this "finding" by trying to figure out how these values got there and how they were transmitted throughout the corporation. We wanted to see what had made America's great companies not merely organizations, but successful, human institutions.

Here we stumbled onto a goldmine of evidence. Biographies, speeches, and documents from such giants of business as Thomas Watson of IBM, John Patterson (the founder of NCR), Will Durant of General Motors, William Kellogg of Kellogg's, and a host of others show a remarkable intuitive understanding of the importance of a strong culture in the affairs of their companies.

We read about Edwin Land, who built Polaroid into a successful $1 billion company (before losing control and having the company fall on hard times) and who developed a whole theory for Polaroid's culture; he called it "Semi-Topia" after the theories of Utopia. We also learned about Alfred Sloan, the manager who built General Motors into a monolith, who spent three full days every quarter reviewing person-by-person the career progression of his top 1,000 managers. And about Charles Steinmetz, the crippled Austrian dwarf who brought alternating current into electrical systems of the world while at GE, but who also adopted his lab assistant and the man's entire family. These, and many more stories, led us to one unmistakable conclusion: the people who built the companies for which America is famous all worked obsessively to create strong cultures within their organizations.

In our own research and consulting, we also found that many of the exciting, new, high-tech businesses springing up around Route 128 in Boston and Silicon Valley in California seem obsessed with culture. Consider the case of Tandem.

The Business of Culture

The Tandem Corporation, one of Silicon Valley's most highly publicized companies, is a company whose president deliberately manages the "informal," human side of the business. Founded by four former Hewlett-Packard employees, Tandem has built a highly successful company by solving a simple problem: the tendency of computers to break down. By yoking two computers together in one mainframe, Tandem offers customers the assurance that they will always have computer power available. If one of the processors breaks down, the other will carry on.

"Tandem is saying something about the product and people working together. Everything here works together. People with people; product with product; even processor with processor, within the product. Everything works together to keep us where we are." The quotation is not from Jim Treybig, Tandem's chief executive officer. It came from one of Tandem's managers, and the same sentiment is echoed through the ranks of the employees:

"I feel like putting a lot of time in. There is a real kind of loyalty here. We are all working in this together—working a process together. I'm not a workaholic—it's just the place. I love the place."

"I don't want anything in the world that would hurt Tandem. I feel totally divorced from my old company, but not Tandem."

These employees seem to be describing an ideal corporation, one most managers would give their eyeteeth to create. And by most standards, Tandem is enormously successful. It is growing at the rate of 25 percent per quarter, with annual revenues over $100 million. The turnover rate is nearly three times below the national average for the computer industry. Tandem's loyal employees like their jobs and the company's product. They are led by a talented group of experienced managers, a group which so far has been able to handle the phenomenal growth of the company.

Only time will tell whether Tandem can maintain its pattern of high performance. While it is easy to attribute the success of the company to fast growth and lack of competition, other things at work internally at Tandem suggest an interesting rival explanation—that the strong culture of Tandem produces its success. Here is how.

A Widely Shared Philosophy

Tandem is founded on a well-ordered set of management beliefs and practices. The philosophy of the company emphasizes the importance of people: "that's Tandem's greatest resource—its people, creative action, and fun."

This ethic is widely shared and exemplified by slogans that everyone knows and believes in:

"It's so nice, it's so nice, we do it twice."

"It takes two to Tandem."

"Get the job done no matter what it takes."

"Tandemize it—means make it work."

The slogans are broadcast by T-shirts, bulletin boards, and word of mouth.

Top management spends about half of its time in training and in communicating the management philosophy and the essence of the company. Work is underway on a book that will codify the philosophy for future generations of workers at Tandem. "The philosophy is our future," one senior manager notes:

"It mostly tells the 'whats' and 'hows' for selecting people and growing managers. Even though everything else around here changes, I don't want what we believe in and what we want to change."

At Tandem the management philosophy is not an afterthought, it's a principal preoccupation.

The Importance of People

Tandem has no formal organizational chart and few formal rules. Its meetings and memos are almost non-existent. Jobs are flexible in terms of duties and hours. The absence of name tags and reserved parking spaces suggests a less well-defined hierarchy than is typical in the corporate world. Despite this, the organization works and people get their jobs done.

What keeps employees off each other's toes and working in the same direction? One possibility is the unwritten rules and shared understandings. As one person put it: "There are a lot of unwritten rules. But there is also a lot of freedom to make a jerk out of yourself. Most of the rules are philosophical rules." Another is dispersed authority:

"The open door policy gives me access to anyone—even the president."

"Everyone here, managers, vice-presidents, and even janitors, communicate on the same level. No one feels better than anyone else."

Tandem seems to maintain a balance between autonomy and control without relying heavily on centralized or formalized procedures, or rigid status hierarchies.

Heroes: The President and the Product

Jim Treybig is a hero at Tandem, and his employees confirm it:

> "Jimmy is really a symbol here. He's a sign that every person here is a human being. He tries to make you feel part of the organization from the first day you are here. That's something people talk about."

> "The one thing you have to understand about the company—Treybig's bigger than life."

Treybig shares the hero's limelight with the Tandem Continuous 10 Computer—the backbone product of the company. The computer design is the company's logo and provides the metaphor for the "working together" philosophy.

> "The product is phenomenal, everyone is proud to be part of it."

> "When a big order was shipped, everyone in the plant was taking pictures. There were 'oh's' and 'ah's'. People were applauding. Can you believe it? For a computer."

Treybig and the computer share the main spotlight. But there are countless other heroes at Tandem—people whose achievements are regularly recognized on bulletin boards as "Our Latest Greatests."

Ritual and Ceremony

Tandem is renowned for its Friday afternoon "beer-busts" which everyone attends. But the ritual does more than help people wind down after a busy work week. It serves as an important vehicle for informal communication and mingling across groups.

Tandem's emphasis on ritual, ceremony, and play is not confined to beer-busts, however. There is a golf course, exercise room, and swimming pool. Company-wide celebrations are staged on important holidays. These provide opportunities for employees to develop a spirit of "oneness" and symbolize that Tandem cares about employees.

Tandem's attention to ritual and ceremony begins in its personnel selection interviews. During the hiring process, potential employees are called back two or three times for interviews and must accept the position before salary negotiations take place. The interviews have been likened to an "inquisition." The message conveyed to prospective employees is "we take longer, and take care of people we hire—because we really care." The impact of this process is significant.

"They had me here for four interviews. That's about four hours, for a position of stock clerk. It was clear that they were choosy about the people they hired. That said something about what they thought I was. They thought I was good."

Treybig personally appears at each orientation to welcome new employees and to explain the company's motivation and commitment philosophy. His appearance reinforces the honor of being accepted to work at Tandem. It's no surprise that people at Tandem feel special—after all, they were made to feel that way before they were hired. Moreover, they feel special because the company and its product are special. And their feelings are expressed in an unusual display of loyalty and commitment to the company.

"My goals follow the company's. It's the company and I. I think that's pretty true of everyone. We all want to see it work. You have to have it all or don't have any of it."

Employees see their work as linked to Tandem's success:

"My job is important, and if I don't do it, Tandem doesn't make a buck."

Tandem is a unique company. And much of its success appears as intimately tied to its culture as to its product and marketplace position. The company has explicit values and beliefs which its employees share. It has heroes. It has storytellers and stories. It has rituals and ceremonies on key occasions. Tandem appears to have a strong culture which creates a bond between the company and employees, and inspires levels of productivity unlike most other corporations. Established heroes, values, and rituals are crucial to a culture's continued strength, and Tandem has kept them. The trick is in sustaining the culture so that it in turn drives the company.

Will Tandem's culture last? Although Tandem is neither big enough nor old enough to judge whether or not it will ultimately take a place in the annals of great American business, we think it is off to a good start. Indeed, other companies like IBM and P&G have already succeeded in sustaining and evolving culture over generations. These strong culture companies truly are the giants of American industry. Yet, their cultures began taking shape in a way that was very similar to Tandem.

The Elements of Culture

What is it about Tandem's organization that exerts such a grip on its employees? Why do other strong culture companies seem to inspire such loyalty?

As we continued our research, we delved into the organizational literature to understand better the elements that make up a strong culture. What is it that determines the kind of culture a company will have in the first place? And how will that culture work in the day-to-day life of a company? . . . Let's summarize the elements now.

Business Environment

Each company faces a different reality in the marketplace depending on its products, competitors, customers, technologies, government influences, and so on. To succeed in its marketplace, each company must carry out certain kinds of activities very well. In some markets that means selling; in others, invention; in still others, management of costs. In short, the environment in which a company operates determines what it must do to be a success. This business environment is the single greatest influence in shaping a corporate culture. Thus, companies that depend for success on their ability to sell an undifferentiated product tend to develop one type of culture—what we call a work hard/play hard culture—that keeps its sales force selling. Companies that spend a great deal of research and development money before they even know if the final product will be successful or not tend to develop a different culture—one that we call a bet-your-company culture—designed to make sure decisions are thought through before actions are taken.

Values

These are the basic concepts and beliefs of an organization; as such they form the heart of the corporate culture. Values define "success" in concrete terms of employees—"if you do this, you too will be a success"—and establish standards of achievement within the organization. The strong culture companies that we investigated all had a rich and complex system of values that were shared by the employees. Managers in these companies talked about these beliefs openly and without embarrassment, and they didn't tolerate deviance from the company standards.

Heroes

These people personify the culture's values and as such provide tangible role models for employees to follow. Some heroes are born—the visionary institution builders of American business—and some are "made" by memorable moments that occur in day-to-day corporate life. Smart companies take a direct hand in choosing people to play these heroic roles, knowing full well that others will try to emulate their behavior. Strong culture companies have many heroes. At General Electric, for instance, the heroes include Thomas Edison, the inventor; Charles Steinmetz, the compleat engineer; Gerald Swope and now Jack Welch, the CEO entrepreneurs; and a legion of lesser-known but equally important internal figures: the inventor of the high-torque motor that powered the electric toothbrush; the chief engineer of the turbine works; the export salesman who survived two overseas revolutions; the international manager who had ghosts exorcised from a factory in Singapore; and many others. These achievers are known to virtually every employee with more than a few months' tenure in the company. And they show every employee "here's what you have to do to succeed around here."

The Rites and Rituals

These are the systematic and programmed routines of day-to-day life in the company. In their mundane manifestations—which we call rituals—they show employees the kind of behavior that is expected of them. In their extravaganzas—which we call ceremonies—they provide visible and potent examples of what the company stands for. Strong culture companies go to the trouble of spelling out, often in copious detail, the routine behavioral rituals they expect their employees to follow.

The Cultural Network

As the primary (but informal) means of communication within an organization, the cultural network is the "carrier" of the corporate values and heroic mythology. Storytellers, spies, priests, cabals, and whisperers form a hidden hierarchy of power within the company. Working the network effectively is the only way to get things done or to understand what's really going on.

The Importance of Understanding Culture

Companies that have cultivated their individual identities by shaping values, making heroes, spelling out rites and rituals, and acknowledging the cultural network have an edge. These corporations have values and beliefs to pass along—not just products. They have stories to tell—not just profits to make. They have heroes whom managers and workers can emulate—not just faceless bureaucrats. In short, they are human institutions that provide practical meaning for people, both on and off the job.

We think that people are a company's greatest resource, and the way to manage them is not directly by computer reports, but by the subtle cues of a culture. A strong culture is a powerful lever for guiding behavior; it helps employees do their jobs a little better, especially in two ways:

A strong culture is a system of informal rules that spells out how people are to behave most of the time. By knowing what exactly is expected of them, employees will waste little time in deciding how to act in a given situation. In a weak culture, on the other hand, employees waste a good deal of time just trying to figure out what they should do and how they should do it. The impact of a strong culture on productivity is amazing. In the extreme, we estimate that a company can gain as much as one or two hours of productive work per employee per day.

A strong culture enables people to feel better about what they do, so they are more likely to work harder. When a sales representative can say "I'm with IBM," rather than "I peddle typewriters for a living," he will probably hear in response, "Oh, IBM is a great company, isn't it?" He quickly figures out that he belongs to an outstanding company with a strong identity. For most people, that means a great deal. The next time they have the choice of working an extra half hour or sloughing off, they'll probably work. Overall, this has an impact on productivity too.

Unlike workers ten or twenty years ago, employees today are confused. According to psychologist Frederick Herzberg, they feel cheated by their jobs; they allow special interests to take up their time; their life values are uncertain; they are blameful and cynical; they confuse morality with ethics. Uncertainty is at the core of it all. Yet strong culture companies remove a great degree of that uncertainty because they provide structure and standards and a value system in which to operate. In fact, corporations may be among the last institutions in America that can effectively take on the role of shaping values. We think that workers, managers, and chief executive officers should recognize this and act on it.

People at all stages of their careers need to understand culture and how it works because it will likely have a powerful effect on their work lives. People just starting their careers may think a job is just a job. But when they choose a company, they often choose a way of life. The culture shapes their responses in a strong, but subtle way. Culture can make them fast or slow workers, tough or friendly managers, team players or individuals. By the time they've worked for several years, they may be so well conditioned by the culture they may not even recognize it. But when they change jobs, they may be in for a big surprise.

Take an up-and-coming executive at General Electric who is being wooed by Xerox—more money, a bigger office, greater responsibility. If his first reaction is to grab it, he's probably going to be disappointed. Xerox has a totally different culture than GE. Success (and even survival) at Xerox is closely tied to an ability to maintain a near frenetic pace, the ability to work and play hard, Xerox-style.

By contrast, GE has a more thoughtful and slow-moving culture. The GE culture treats each business activity seriously—almost as though each activity will have an enormous impact on the company. Success at GE is a function of being able to take work seriously, a strong sense of peer group respect, considerable deference for authority, and a sense of deliberateness. A person of proven success at GE will bring these values to Xerox because past experience in GE's culture has reinforced them. But these same values may not be held in high esteem elsewhere.

Bright young comers at GE could, for example, quickly fizzle out at Xerox—and not even understand why. They'll be doing exactly what they did to succeed at GE—maybe even working harder at it—but their deliberate approach to issues large and small will be seen by insiders at Xerox as a sign that they "lack smarts." Their loss of confidence, self-esteem, and ability will be confusing to them and could significantly derail their careers. For Xerox, the loss of productivity could be appreciable.

This is no imaginary scenario. It happens again and again at Xerox, General Electric, and many other companies when managers ignore the influence of culture on individual approaches to work. Culture shock may be one of the major reasons why people supposedly "fail" when they leave one organization for another. Where they fail, however, is not necessarily in doing the job, but in not reading the culture correctly.

People who want to get ahead within their own companies also need to understand—at least intuitively—what makes their culture tick. If product quality is the guiding value of your company, then you'd better be thinking about getting into manufacturing where you can contribute to the work on quality control teams. If you're a marketing whiz in a company where all of the heroes are number crunchers, then you may have a problem. You can start taking accounting courses, or you can start trying to find a more compatible environment. Unless the culture itself is in a state of change—shifting, say, from a financial emphasis to a marketing orientation—then the chances are very slim for any single person who is out of step with the culture to make it to the very top.

Aside from considerations of personal success, managers must understand very clearly how the culture works if they want to accomplish what they set out to do. If you're trying to institute a competitive, tough approach to marketing in a company that is full of hail-fellow-well-met salesmen, then you have your work cut out for you. Even if everyone agrees with what you want to do, you must know how to manage the culture—for instance; create new role model heroes—in order to teach your legion of easy-going salesmen the new rules of the game.

Finally, senior executives and especially chief executive officers may be missing out on one of the key ingredients for their companies' eventual success by ignoring either the influence of culture on corporate success or their own central role in shaping it. Their culture may be rich with lore or starved for shared values and stories. It may be coherent and cohesive, or fragmented and poorly understood. It may create meaning or contribute to blind confusion. It may be rich, fiery, focused, and strong; or weak, cold, and diffuse. Understanding the culture can help senior executives pinpoint why their company is succeeding or failing. Understanding how to build and manage the culture can help the same executives make a mark on their company that lasts for decades.

Can every company have a strong culture? We think it can. But to do that, top management first has to recognize what kind of culture the company already has, even if it is weak. The ultimate success of a chief executive officer depends to a large degree on an accurate reading of the corporate culture and the ability to hone it and shape it to fit the shifting needs of the marketplace.

In reading this book, we can imagine that many managers will ask themselves, is culture too "soft"? Can serious managers actually take the time to deal with it? Indeed, we believe that managers must. Management scientists sometimes argue that corporations are so complex and vulnerable to diverse external and internal forces that managers' freedom to act and lead is limited. Their argument is plausible, but our experience does not support it. By and large, the most successful managers we know are precisely those who strive to make a mark through creating a guiding vision, shaping shared values, and otherwise providing leadership for the people with whom they work.

It all comes down to understanding the importance of working with people in any organization. The institution builders of old knew the value of a strong culture and they worked hard at it. They saw themselves as symbolic players-actors in their corporations. They knew how to orchestrate, even dramatize events to drive their lessons home. They understood how corporations shape personal lives and were not shy about suggesting the standards that people should live by. If we are to have such great institutions tomorrow, the managers of today will have to take up this challenge again.

Our goal in this book is to provide business leaders with a primer on cultural management. In showing how several excellent companies[3] manage their cultures, this book is meant to be suggestive only, not hard and fast or prescriptive. Our aim is to heighten the awareness of our readers, to jog them into thinking about the workplace in its role as a mediator of behavior, and to show the positive effects of culture-building. Along the way, we hope to instill in our readers a new law of business life: In Culture There is Strength.

40

Leadership in Large-Scale Organized Systems

John W. Gardner

John Gardner has served six presidents of the United States in various leadership capacities. He was Secretary of Health, Education and Welfare, founding chairman of Common Cause, co-founder of the Independent Sector, chairman of the National Coalition, and president of the Carnegie Corporation and Foundation. He is currently the Miriam and Peter Haas Centennial Professor at Stanford Business School.

So far in our discussion, despite an occasional acknowledgment of historical and cultural context, we have given little attention to the fact that today's world is characterized by vast and interdependent organized systems. . . .

If one calls to mind ancient images of leadership—Moses leading the Is-raelites out of Egypt, Leonidas leading the Spartans in the defense of Ther-mopylae—and then reflects on the kind of leadership required to get anything done today, one might wonder whether the same word should be used for such spectacularly different activities. I am for keeping the word, even though the changes have been extraordinary.

The first thing that strikes one as characteristic of contemporary leadership is the necessity for the leader to work with and through extremely complex organizations and institutions—corporations, government agencies at all levels, the courts, the media of communication, and so on. Leaders must understand not only the intricate organizational patterns of their own segment but also the workings of neighboring segments. Business leaders must understand how our political system works. Political leaders must understand our economic system.

The leaders who succeed in making large and complex systems work may not achieve fame. Although their success is noted by those in the particular field in which they function, generally they do not achieve the "figure against the sky" visibility that they might have gained as individual performers. Some hire public relations people to pump them up and occasionally it works, but it is not a natural outcome.

Steven Muller, president of Johns Hopkins University and one of the wisest, most effective leaders in higher education today, points out how difficult it is to play a highly visible role nationally and still do justice to leadership of a great contemporary university with its size, complexity, huge investments in research, and so on. "We . . . are builders. Our task is to help to remodel our institutions for tomorrow."[1] If we want our complicated world to work, we had better revise our conception of leaders to make room for the Steven Mullers.

Large-Scale Organization

Many years ago, Max Weber, the great German sociologist, provided the first authoritative description of the bureaucratic form of organization that has dominated both governmental and corporate life throughout the twentieth century.[2] He pointed out that it was more efficient than the preindustrial modes it displaced, but warned that ultimately society might not like the "iron cage" it was constructing for itself. Not many people heard the warning. The division of labor, the specialization, and the rational allocation of functions characteristic of bureaucracy lent themselves to modern purposes, and the industrial societies proceeded hell-bent down that road.

One factor that blinded us to the difficulties that lay ahead was our belief that the word *bureaucracy* applied only to government agencies; we did not see that the problems were present in all large organizations, corporate as well as governmental.

A New Trend in Industry

There were some who looked at large-scale organization with a more perceiving and prophetic eye.[3] Alfred P. Sloan of General Motors recognized early that as systems increase in size and complexity, thought must be given to dispersing leadership and management functions throughout the system.

But most corporate leaders were not listening. They were against bureaucratic centralization by government, but embraced it unthinkingly in their own companies.

In the 1970s American industry was shaken to its foundations by the emergence of Japan as an immensely effective competitor, and we set out to examine the organizational practices behind Japan's phenomenal performance. The reexamination soon broadened to include every aspect of our own organizational functioning. And other segments of the society beyond industry began to reexamine their own practices. It is quite likely that historians will see the last half of the twentieth century as a time when we undertook a revolutionary reevaluation of large-scale organization and the sources of organizational vitality.

Problems of Large Organizations

We have come to recognize that the sheer size of an organization can create grave problems for the leader interested in vitality, creativity and renewal. We cannot escape the necessity for large-scale systems of organized human endeavor. A complex society—to say nothing of a complex world—requires such systems; but we now know that we can design them so that they do not suffer the worst ailments of size. There are ways of making them flexible and adaptive. There are ways of breaking them up into smaller subsystems.

All large-scale systems develop certain characteristic failings, some of which are destructive of organizational vitality. Largeness leads top executives to create huge headquarters staffs to monitor and analyze. Substructures proliferate, an elaborate organization chart emerges, and obsessive attempts to coordinate follow. Creative leaders work to reduce complexity, slim down central staff, eliminate excessive layering, and create units of manageable size.

In large organizations the chain of command becomes excessively long. Decisions are slowed and adventurous moves blocked by too many screening points and multiple sign-offs. As one production executive put it, "If I can get an idea past my boss and his boss and the financial vice-president and the general counsel, it's probably too feeble an idea to change anything."

The industrial community has in recent years expended great effort to accomplish the deeper involvement of workers in their jobs—through job redesign, autonomous working groups, schemes for feedback on performance, and various ways of providing recognition for work well done. Since sheer size creates problems in the organizational environment, some corporations have worked to counter the trend toward larger units. The chief executive officer of Hewlett-Packard Company, John Young, was recently rated as the most admired leader in the high-tech industries. He says, "Having small divisions is not the only way to organize a company, but having organizations that people can run like a small business is highly motivational. . . . Keeping that spirit of entrepreneurship is very important to us."[4]

Recognizing that the impersonality (some say dehumanization) of large-scale organization leaves many people feeling anonymous, powerless, and without a sense of their relationship to the whole, effective leaders create a climate that encourages two-way communication, participation, and a sense of belonging. They pay attention to people. They eliminate conditions that suppress individuality.

The goal is to give the individual employee and the lower levels of supervisors and district managers the conviction that their voices are heard, their participation welcomed. Everyone recognizes that autocratic practices work against this. Not everyone recognizes that depersonalization of the society may be a greater enemy than autocracy. My boss may be autocratic, but if he gets sore when I make a suggestion, at least I know he heard me. When a sense of impersonality pervades an organization, the conviction spreads that any suggestion I make will surely be lost in the complex processes of the organization.

The Turf Syndrome

Everyone who has worked in a large organization has memories of one or another zealous bureaucratic infighter. In the late 1940s, when I was serving as consultant to a large government agency, I had my first opportunity to observe over a considerable period a prime example of the species. Too timid to lead, too vain to follow, his game was turf defense. He was a master of the hidden move and the small betrayal. He understood with a surgeon's precision the vulnerabilities of his colleagues, and he masked calculated unresponsiveness in a thousand innocent guises. As a young observer eager to understand bureaucracy, I found him an open textbook.

Predictable characteristics of large-scale organization include a complex division of labor, specialization, fixed roles, and careful definitions of rank and status. Equally predictable are the proliferation of defined subsystems, increasingly rigid boundaries between subsystems and emergence of the turf syndrome. Rivalry and conflict develop, and effective internal communication is diminished. Referring to conflicts among his chief lieutenants, Henry Ford II once told me, "I try to remind them that the enemy is not the guy across the hall. It's the guys out there selling Chevys or Hondas."

All of this hampers adaptability, creativity and renewal. The organization most likely to renew itself enjoys good internal communication among its diverse elements. Effective leaders tear down rigid internal walls and bureaucratic enclaves, counter segmental loyalties through the creation of working groups that cut across boundaries, and foster informal exchange throughout the organization.

The Informal Organization

As everyone knows, the formal channels of communication and influence as defined by the organization chart do not constitute a complete description of what goes on. There are complex patterns of communication and influence that are generally spoken of as the *informal organization*. Because it is not one coherent system, it might be more accurate to speak of *informal groups* and *informal networks*.

Call them what you will, they are essential to the functioning of the system. They carry the bulk of communication relating to the organization's internal politics. They are the haunts of gossips and grumblers, sycophants and saboteurs, but they are also favored instruments of the natural leaders and power brokers scattered throughout every organization. Flexible and disrespectful of boundaries, the informal networks can serve the purposes of leaders shrewd enough to use them. . . .

The Leader's Advantage

Just about everything in large-scale organization seems to militate against leadership. All the intricate processes slow the leader down. Innumerable system manipulators push their particular agendas and block the leader's initiatives in untraceable ways. Cyert and March point out that an organization is generally a coalition of individuals and groups with diverse goals, engaged in continuous bargaining for power.[5] Elective officials have multiple constituencies that further complicate leadership.

But no matter how numerous the frustrations, leaders have advantages. They have a centrality that heightens their capacity to make strategic moves.

Unless they have foolishly isolated themselves, they are privy to more kinds of information than anyone else in the organization. They have many ways of granting or withholding favors and almost invariably have veto power over many decisions within the organization.

The leader generally has the power to set the agenda. I have known a number of mayors who essentially had no more power than any other member of the city council, but had the right to set the council's agenda. That, plus shrewd use of access to the media, enabled them to lead very effectively.

Leaders have the capacity to mobilize lower-level leaders within the system and to reach out to potential allies at all levels. With respect to most of the initiatives the leader wishes to take, there will be numbers of individuals down through the organization who are wholehearted allies, and the leader can often activate them regardless of intervening resistance in the chain of command. Leaders can turn on green lights throughout the organization with a minimum expenditure of energy.

Bennis and Nanus say that a major task of leadership is the management of attention.[6] The symbolic role of leaders, coupled with their privileges as the prime source of official information, gives them voice and visibility.

41

Leadership and Democracy

Thomas E. Cronin

Thomas Cronin is a former White House Fellow and White House aide. In 1986, he won the American Political Science Association's Charles E. Merriam Award for significant contributions to the art of government. He is widely published, and currently serves as President of Whitman College.

America's dream of a government by the people is about the most exacting venture a nation can undertake. Exhilarating, difficult, and demanding, the burden falls not just upon a select few, but on a large number of us if we would make democracy work.

For those of us who believe that the common human enterprise can best progress within a democracy—under a government of, by, and for the people—there is much to be studied and much to be done. For those of us who would make democracy work, these times cry out for better ways to keep the peace, eradicate discrimination, and revitalize our economy and exporting capabilities so that all might share its opportunities and the blessings of liberty.

At the very least, we must find:

Reprinted from Thomas E. Cronin, "Leadership and Democracy," *Liberal Education* 73(2) (March–April, 1987): 35–38. By permission of the author.

- Better ways for the individual to participate in government and politics and see that participation counts;
- Better ways to make government open, responsive, and accountable;
- Better ways to make government serve the common interests of us all rather than the narrow interests of the few.

Liberal arts colleges have an important role to play in all of this. The premise and promise of liberal arts colleges is their capacity to innovate, experiment, motivate, and educate the independent thinkers, writers, scientists, and citizen-leaders of our time. While their primary goal is the nurturing of the educated person, I would urge too that educating people about *both* good and evil leadership, effective and ineffective leadership, and about the preconditions and requisites of socially responsible democratic leadership be given a priority.

It is important to recall that most of our framers were skeptical of strong, centralized, national leadership institutions and equally skeptical and even hostile to notions of popular democracy. They had fought their war of independence in large part to get away from monarchy, royal governors, and unresponsive hierarchical leadership. Yet democracy was regarded as a dangerous and unworkable doctrine. The very term *democracy* appears neither in the Declaration of Independence nor in the U.S. Constitution.

A system of democracy implies a government in which ultimate political authority is vested in the people. The aspirations of a democracy are lofty; they celebrate the individual, personal liberty, equal political rights, and they are based on the noble premise that the people can be the masters of their own destiny, that the people can make moral judgments and practical decisions in their communities and in res publica as well as in their daily lives. It implies, as well, a searching for fairness and virtue in humanity's pursuit of improved ways of building social institutions and ordering human relations.

Warring Concepts

In many respects, leadership—the process whereby an individual or a few select individuals are in a position to provide the vision and make things happen—is at odds with much of what is implicit, if not explicit, in notions of democracy. These have been warring concepts, just as freedom and authority have long been fierce antagonists. The challenge, for those who care about our nation and the dreams of constitutional democracy, is to seek ways to reconcile these concepts—leadership and democracy. Whether we like it or not, our democracy will stand or fall on the quality of leaders as well as on the quality of citizens we produce and nurture here.

Governments throughout all history have been governments not of and by the masses, but of and by elites. At least in large-scale societies the question is not whether elites will exist and be important, but whether elites will govern on behalf of the many or on behalf of the few, most especially themselves.

Intellectuals and even average citizens have long been skeptical, if not cynical, toward the leaders of the nation-state. This is because leaders have done vast harm as well as served with noble motivations and in the cause of liberating ends. Leaders, in a sense, have to be mistrusted. None of them is ever infallible, and unquestioning subservience to those who wield public power corrupts the human spirit.

Americans admire power, yet fear it. We may love to unload our civic responsibilities on our leaders, yet we dislike—intensely dislike—being bossed around. We may admire Washington, Jackson, and Lincoln, yet we detested George the Third, and millions of Americans came here fleeing from nations ruled by tyrants and oppressors. We fear the abuse of power. We are fond of the saying that "power tends to corrupt" even if we know that the absence of power can also corrupt.

Our attitudes toward power and leadership are often as if they were poison: "A friend in power is a friend lost." "Power will intoxicate the best hearts, as wine the strongest heads." "There is something in politics that degrades." "Power turns good persons into bad and bad persons into worse." "Only the already corrupted seek power." "Power is ever stealing from the many for the few."

Plainly, a gap exists between what we think of the typical politician and the ideal statesperson. This gap exists in part because of unrealistic expectations. We want elected officials to be perfect and they are not. We want them to have all the answers and they do not. Politicians, like all individuals, live in the real world where perfection may be a goal, but compromises, approximations, negotiated settlements, and personal ambition are necessary. Our "ideal" leaders are usually dead.

Much of the criticism and skepticism about political and societal leaders is healthy. Evil leaders are all too real—past and present. Some Americans hate all kinds of leadership and are distrustful of any form of authority and power precisely because the evidence of the past is so compelling that leaders have it in their power to destroy civilization, corrupt societies, and abuse and repress the rights and freedoms of their people.

An Engagement Among Equals

I believe there can be an alternative form of leadership: I cling to the view that leadership can be of an enabling, facilitative kind. Leadership, reconceptualized as an engagement among equals, as a collegial collaboration, can empower and liberate people—and enlarge people's options, choices, and freedom.

Democratic leadership at its best recognizes the fundamental—unexpressed as well as felt—wants and needs of potential followers, encourages followers to a fuller consciousness of their higher needs, and helps convert the resulting hopes and aspirations into practical demands on other leaders. A democratic leader consults and listens and so engages with followers as to bring them to heightened political awareness and activity, and in the process enables many of these participating followers to become leaders in their own right. The desired leader in a democracy moves away from hierarchical commands and traditional leader-follower relations and instead helps inspire and mobilize others—citizens, contributors, participants—to undertake common problem-solving tasks.

The challenge of reconciling leadership and democracy is part definitional, part attitudinal, and part behavioral. We have too long held a view of leaders that is hierarchical, male, and upon which followers, like subjects or slaves, are dependent. That conception is antithetical to our democratic aspirations. The very word "followers" is a negative and demeaning word and ought, if possible, to be discarded or at least greatly modified. For a nation of subservient followers can never be a democratic one. A democratic nation requires educated, skeptical, caring, engaged, and contentious citizen-leaders—citizens who are willing to lead as well as follow, who are willing to point the way as often as they are persuaded in one way or another, and prize the spirit of liberty and free speech that animates our Bill of Rights.

The democratic citizen-leader I have in mind appreciates that power wielded justly today may be wielded corruptly tomorrow. The democratic citizen-leader is moved to protest when he or she knows a policy is wrong or when some of our sisters and brothers are finding their rights and liberties diminished. The citizen-leader appreciates that criticism of official error is not criticism of our country. The citizen-leader recognizes that democracy rests solidly upon a mixed view of human nature.

More than any other form of government, democracy requires a peculiar blend of faith in the people and skepticism of them. It requires a faith concerning the common human enterprise; a belief that if the people are informed and caring, they can be trusted with their own self-government; and an optimism that when things begin to go wrong, the people can be relied on to set them right. Plainly, however, a robust, healthy skepticism is needed as well. Democracy requires us to question our leaders and never to trust any group with too much power. Although we prize majority rule, we have to be skeptical enough to ask whether a majority is always right.

Democracy Demands Competing Leaders

Conceived this way, democratic politics is a forum or arena for excellence and responsibility where, by acting together, citizens become free. Politics in this sense is not a necessary evil but a realistic good, transcending the domains of narrow interests and power in the conventional sense, and providing citizens with opportunities to achieve a sustained educational process in which to seek agreement about the common good and the proper ordering of liberties.

Democracy is never self-activating. It needs competing leaders who have both a sense of the past and who are willing to share their competing conceptions of the public interest. Political leaders—both elected and unelected—are those who are bold enough to step forward in the midst of endless controversies. This requires ambition and assertiveness, leadership traits we sometimes undervalue. (There is a view that politics ought not to revolve around personal ambition. We ought to take another look at the important role of ambition, however, for it sparks just about anyone's efforts to excel. It motivates the great problem solvers just as it motivates the great cyclists, the great scientists, the great composers.) If elected politicians often seem bewildered in dealing with controversial issues, so are the rest of us. If elected officials sometimes make mistakes, so do the rest of us. If they sometimes postpone things rather than directly confront them, so do we.

The American people will never be completely satisfied with their politicians, nor should they be. The ideal politician is a fiction, because the ideal politician would be able to please absolutely everyone and make conflicts disappear. Such a person could exist within a small community of like-minded people, but American liberties invite diversity, and therefore conflict. Hence, politicians as well as the people they represent must have different, contending ideas about what is best for the nation.

Effective political leadership involves motivating people to create change when desirable, to uphold the status quo when necessary and to serve moral ends. All kinds of leadership—intellectual, educational, entrepreneurial, cultural, as well as political leadership—are necessary to make a diverse system live up to the ideals of the democratic creed.

The most lasting and pervasive leadership of all is often intangible and noninstitutional. It is leadership fostered or embodied in social, political, or artistic movements; in books, in documents, in speeches, and in the memory of great lives greatly lived. Intellectual leadership at its best is provided by those—often not in high political or corporate offices—who can clarify values and the implications of such values for policy. We have long ago, with Thomas Jefferson's assist, repudiated the tired idea that "leaders are born and not made." Today we realize leadership is forged out of competition and challenge of competence.

This, then, is the role of the liberal arts in higher education. Some things can be taught, other things have to be learned. Leadership must be learned. Learning about democratic leadership requires teaching and encouraging students to improve their capacities for observation, reflection, imagination, invention, and judgment. It requires refining one's ability to think, write, and communicate effectively; it requires an ability to gather and interpret evidence, marshal facts, and employ the most rigorous methods in the pursuit of knowledge. We should encourage the ability to ask the right questions and the ability to distinguish the significant from the trivial, and we should encourage an unyielding commitment to the truth combined with a full appreciation of what remains to be learned.

We have an obligation as well to encourage citizen-leaders who will not only organize and head interest groups but will learn how to unite a disparate people for responsible action, who will learn to appreciate the need for integrative thinking and understand the larger interrelationships. An indispensable quality of future citizen-leaders is breadth—the quality of mind and the capacity to relate disparate "facts" to a coherent theory, to fashion tactics that are part of a strategy, to act today in ways that are consistent with an informed theory of the future. This kind of societal leadership, writes Robert Bellah and his associates, will "discover enough common interest across the discontinuities of region, class, religion, race, and sex to order and regulate the affairs of a great industrial society." In short, we shall need leaders who will enlighten and exalt the mind and enlarge, empower, and unlock the forces for good that are with us in such abundance. A liberal arts education should nurture the premise, by a variety of means, that the liberally educated person should assume responsibility for more than his or her own private concerns and that civic and societal leadership is an obligation.

Freedom and obligation—they go together. Liberty *and* duty; that's the deal. The answer lies not in producing a few larger-than-life leaders. The answer lies in educating a nation of citizen-leaders who, regardless of their professional and private concerns, will at the very least make the concerns of the Republic and humankind their avocation.

We shall know we are making progress not when we discover or produce a handful of charismatic Mount Rushmore leaders, but when we can boast we are a nation no longer in need of those larger-than-life great leaders because we have become a nation of citizens who believe that one person can make a difference and every person should regularly try.

42

The Making of a Citizen Leader

Cheryl Mabey

Cheryl Mabey is a practicing attorney as well as executive director of the Women's Leadership Program and associate professor of political science at Mount St. Mary's College, Los Angeles, California. She is active in the field of leadership development, having founded the Leadership Center, and one of the pilot "Summer of Service" programs for AmeriCorps.

A current snapshot of contemporary American politics reveals largely cyni- cal, spectator-citizens waiting for the right type of leader(s) to resolve for them the critical problems in their neighborhoods, communities, states, and country. But the distance between citizens and leaders is greater than ever. Leaders appear detached or stripped of communal identity; citizens forfeit personal participation choosing instead to pass on unrealistic expectations to public leaders.

The picture is disquieting—but far from hopeless. The heterogeneity of Americans provides a powerful resource to revitalize political life and to fos- ter a public language involving freedom and responsibility, individualism and community, present needs and future plans. The potential for change is real.

Reprinted from Cheryl Mabey, "The Making of the Citizen Leader," in *Public Leadership Education: The Role of the Citizen Leader* (Dayton: Charles F. Kettering Foundation, 1992), pp. 10–16. By permission of the au- thor.

What must be done is to challenge commonly held assumptions about the dichotomy between leadership and citizenship. We need a much more inclusive definition of leadership in order to tap the potential to influence public life inherent in each of us. The crucial change needed on the political landscape in an America approaching the twenty-first century is the development of citizen leaders.

Traditional Leadership Models

At a time when sound bites are the prevalent mode of political discourse, images of leadership and citizenship may conform to an increasingly narrow definition. Research findings bear this out. Such diverse groups as politically active college women participating in the NEW Leadership Program at Rutgers University, and high school student leaders in Los Angeles, California, were asked to draw pictures describing what the word "leadership" meant to them. Two common elements emerged. First, the picture of the leader was always larger, more prominent than any other image on the page. Second, the leader was at a podium or on a stage, separate from a group passively listening to this larger, more important figure. Some drawings went so far as to include a line designating a space for the leader separate from that of the many followers.

This graphic illustration of the relationship between leaders and followers complements many prevailing theories about leadership. The leader is the one responsible for solving problems and for effectively communicating the answer(s) to the populace or group. The focal point in most leadership theories is on the leader.

The "trait theory" of leadership ascribes certain personality traits or attributes exclusively to leaders. Although research has failed to validate that leaders and followers possess different personality traits or that leaders share certain traits in common, a popular conception of leadership equates leadership with the personality of the leader. Journalists assessing potential presidential candidates daily demonstrate the durability of the trait theory. Not only does this approach create unrealistic expectations of potential leaders as superhumans nearing perfection, but it distorts the richly complex relationship between leading and following into a misleadingly simplistic focus on an individual. Leadership involves considerably more than a leader.

The "organizational theory" of leadership also narrows leadership to the position which any leader occupies within an organization. This fusion of leadership with office ignores the distinction between authority and leadership. The theory further assumes that a few are leaders and most are followers, failing to recognize the multiplicity of informal as well as formal leadership roles even within the most complex organizational structures. Perhaps it is the overlapping nature of these theories which results in the notion of leader *separate from* the group.

According to the "vision theory," a currently popular view of leadership, it is the job of the leader to imagine the future direction in which a company or country needs to go, and to communicate that vision effectively to others. Ideas, solutions to problems, personal meaning, and goals are the purview of leaders. The act of leading becomes the act of persuading others to adopt the leader's ideas through effective communication or marketing. All too often, expectations are raised that societal ills could be alleviated if only better individuals emerged in leadership positions.

Another prevalent leadership theory deriving from social sciences and management—the "situational theory"—acknowledges that leadership necessitates varying degrees of interaction between the group and a leader. In fact, this theory urges leaders to focus first upon the situation, the readiness of the group, to perform and work together. This transactive view of leadership suggests that effective leaders adapt their leadership style to provide what the group needs and in return the group "follows" the leader. Certainly, the situational leadership approach involves more complex interaction than the other three theories of leadership, but it measures leaders in terms of their ability to influence a group rather than to act in concert with it.

A fifth theory of leadership, labeled as the "power theory" and commonly associated with Machiavelli, can be considered as old as human nature. Leaders are the movers and shakers who get things done. Power in its different guises is a resource to be used prudently by the leader. A contemporary twist of the "power theory" is that the leader empowers others to use power. On the surface, Machiavelli and empowerment may appear paradoxical, but if the dominant paradigm is primarily leader-focused, "empowerment of others" can be viewed as simply another way of increasing the leader's power base.

These limited views of leadership are dangerous for two reasons: the group becomes overly dependent upon the leader to solve its problems, resulting in complacency or passivity among followers; and, the expectations that the leader can solve problems or create meaning are too high, resulting in the ultimate failure of society's leaders.

Today's leadership crisis may not lie in the caliber of our current leaders, but rather in our failure to mobilize group resources to solve the group's problems. In an analogy to the physician-patient relationship, Ronald Heifetz of

Harvard University identifies three situations that illustrate the shortcomings of a problem-solving model reliant on the leader alone.

In a Type I situation, the patient has an infection which the physician can treat with an antibiotic. The problem is relatively simple and the physician (leader) has the resources to treat the disease.

In a Type II situation, the patient has a chronic disease, such as high blood pressure. The physician may treat it partially through medication, but the patient shares in his or her own care by monitoring diet, exercise, stress, or other life-style factors. Both the physician and patient share in the responsibility for solving this problem.

In a Type III situation, the patient has a medically untreatable disease, such as an advanced stage of cancer. The options for treatment are negligible and the physician recognizes that the patient assumes the responsibility for facing the future. The physician may be a support, but the locus of power in handling such a crisis is the patient's alone.

The conventional paradigm of equating leadership with the leader's ability to solve problems overlooks the continuum of crises confronting society. Expecting the leader to initiate and carry out solutions in a straight-forward Type I problem may be realistic. In the majority of instances, however, the issues facing leaders are more complex, necessitating collective problem-solving strategies of the group and its leaders. The challenge is to develop a broader concept of leadership which emphasizes this dynamic relationship.

Redefining American Citizenship

Divergent meanings of citizenship have evolved throughout American history. The *republican* tradition, derived in part from Greek and Roman political thought, posited that civic participation was the foundation of a free society. Virtue, communal values, and a sense of mutual obligation formed the cornerstone which both Thomas Jefferson and James Madison viewed as necessary to secure liberty or happiness.

The *liberal* tradition inherited from the Enlightenment detached the concept of "citizen" from any communal ties or responsibilities. In the dominant liberal view, the citizen is seen mainly as a bearer of rights, such as the freedom to speak, to vote, or to worship. As Harry Boyte traces these approaches to citizenship in his book, *CommonWealth: A Return to Citizen Politics*, he points out that: "such an individualist conception of politics neglects the moral wellsprings of public life, the values like responsibility, fairness, and concern for others that were widespread at the nation's founding."

Even the *Progressive* movement of the twentieth century did not recapture the concept of an engaged citizenry. For most progressives, citizens acted by proxy and through the state with no broad popular involvement. The concept of "public" became specialized—the preserve of representatives, guided by the advice of experts, bureaucrats, and professionals.

The "managerial" era of the late twentieth century witnessed a transferal of the power to make key decisions about the public good, to experts, technical specialists, and professionals. Citizenship was defined in weak and attenuated ways, and citizens increasingly became spectators rather than participants in the political process.

Today, the operative paradigms for leadership and citizenship have stressed that the few exercise power over the many, and have reinforced passive rather than active behavior from average citizens. Individual or special interests supersede consideration for the general welfare or common good.

Broad-based and effective citizen leaders in our times are possible if—and only if—citizens develop the abilities to gain access to information of all kinds and the skills to put such information to effective use. At the same time, citizens committed to public life, community, and leadership will need to recognize and understand certain restraining forces in the world as it is.

American culture is predicated on an egocentric view of society: that is, a society made up of individuals freely able to contract to meet their individual needs. The unit of American society is the individual. Other cultures' basic units are groups or clans. Where a nation such as Kenya may aspire to "getting there together" or honor the "harambee" spirit, the American tradition is embedded in individual achievement that leaves a trail for others to follow. One obstacle for expanding leadership skills and opportunities to all citizens is our cultural bias in favor of individual action. In this view, groups are often suspect. Groups are voluntary associations, which individuals choose to affiliate with when their own interests are served.

Another obstacle to active citizenry is the exaltation of "the expert" in our culture. Even citizens knowledgeable about and committed to public life face an age of information of dizzying proportions. For the average student unacquainted with the institutions and processes of government or uninterested in contemporary issues, there is truth in the belief that others know more. If there is a societal problem, too often resources are expended in trying to find a technological fix even if the problem is political or social in nature. Many problems do not need experts to solve them. Neighborhoods or communities throughout the U.S. possess the resources to solve their own problems. Yet, the persistent belief that "professionals" or "experts" know more and should tell others what to do paralyze many community initiatives.

A further obstacle to developing a broader base of citizen leaders is the identification of leaders with certain positions. An office-holder is automatically defined as a leader whether or not he or she leads anyone. Nonoffice-holders are labeled outsiders or activists. Public space must be created for legitimizing informal citizen leaders and formal leaders to come together to discuss and offer alternative solutions to societal problems.

Somehow a language and a message must be forged outlining the positive expectations of citizenship. Millions of dollars have been spent on shaping negative campaigns, telling citizens why a particular candidate should not be elected. Youth are bombarded by negative messages: "Say No to Drugs," "Don't get pregnant!" "Don't drop out of school!" "Stay away from gangs!" Nowhere is there a positive creed for what society expects from its adult citizens or its youth. The skills and capabilities so necessary for citizen leaders begin with a positive invitation to become one.

"Couch citizens" must become active citizen leaders. The assumption is that each person is responsible for contributing to the common good in different areas. Participation at any level is an exercise of leadership, joining others to use power for constructive ends. Unlike the prevalent notion of solitary leaders finding answers and announcing solutions through mass media, the challenge for the twenty-first century is to prepare citizens to act together in a more interactive, dynamic process. The narrow command-and-control leadership style no longer works.

Making Citizen Leaders

Citizen leadership requires distinctive skills and capabilities that require development. Socialization in homes and schools must include the recognition that every citizen will lead. Civic participation is not an elective but a given. Each person matters. The axiom of Mount St. Mary's College Women's Leadership Program is that every student has the opportunity to enroll and participate in this program because the question is not *if* one will lead but rather *how effective* a leader one becomes. Such a message is important to this population of women, the majority of whom are women of color and first-generation college students.

Public life cannot be made synonymous with American government structures or processes. Public life—and political conversations—begin in the kitchens, neighborhoods, streets, cities, and organizations where we live and work. Caring passionately for something is the key to political participation. "Private" life impinges on "public" life. Likewise, public policy can limit or expand personal choices. Developing a citizen leader begins with encouraging opportunities for "doing something" with others and for giving "voice" to one's impressions and reactions. One of the objectives of Project Public Life based at the University of Minnesota's Humphrey Institute of Public Affairs is to teach a new kind of politics—citizen politics—in which citizens are powerful actors in public problem solving. In the workbook, *Making the Rules: A Guidebook for Young People Who Intend to Make a Difference*, readers are urged to develop "a big picture of politics, one that includes public life—an active, diverse, challenging arena in which we act on what matters to us."

Citizen leaders must obtain knowledge. Not only do citizen leaders need to become competent or knowledgeable about what they advocate, but they need to understand how the system operates. Too often, citizenship training is limited to formal knowledge about the institutions of government without ever addressing practical issues of access to civic knowledge. Community leadership programs, like the Industrial Areas Foundation (IAF) network, provide a model curriculum in public life. Policy issues are joined to theories of action that include concepts such as power, mediating institutions, public life, judgment, imagination, and self-interest. Such concepts are tied, in turn, to discussion of democratic and religious values, and the traditions that inform and frame them—justice, concern for the poor, the dignity of the person, diversity, participation, and cultural heritage. Strategies for change and community organizing techniques arise from the explicit assumption that neighborhood trainees have an important measure of responsibility for the public good of their community.

Action marks the citizen leader. Knowing is insufficient without action. Community service opportunities—even a school's community service requirement—expose others to a real world beyond their private lives. The Constitutional Rights Foundation, through its Youth in Community Service (YCS) program in southern California high schools, provides students with opportunities to learn and become involved with community problems. Linking action with reflection is a powerful learning model. "Skills for action" need to be recognized and nurtured by parents and educators alike. Time spent working with groups in student activities or volunteering may outdistance many more solitary, cognitive tasks in developing future citizen leaders.

While most learning involves working independently, educators are recognizing the importance of cooperative learning. Study groups, group projects, or small group discussions utilize a more collective view of work. Often ignored, though, is the necessity for teaching the social skills required for cooperativeness. If the dominant mode of playing, studying, and working is that of the independent competitor, different folkways of team-building and win-win problem solving need to be introduced and practiced. Outdoor leadership education such as programs sponsored by Outward Bound or the Wilderness Institute provide experiential laboratories in trust, team-building, and collective problem solving.

While others have addressed the importance of developing judgment, problem-solving and critical-thinking skills, a frequently overlooked skill for citizen leaders is learning to ask effective questions and to listen well. Given the scarcity of resources, concentrating on the "right set of questions" may be more critical than analyzing the "right answers" to questions of lesser importance. We will need to develop educational and civic programs or opportunities which develop the capacity for brainstorming and recognizing possibilities, rather than for limiting choices or critiquing ideas.

As recent events in Eastern Europe or southern California have demonstrated, citizen leaders do not possess the magical panacea for public life. They are bound by their definitions of leadership, history, and culture. The making of citizen leaders occurs too frequently in the cauldron of conflict and crisis rather than by design or invitation. Still, politics, as former Czech President Vaclav Havel has reminded the world, is not only the art of the possible: "It can also be the art of the impossible, that is, the art of making both ourselves and the world better."

43

Martin Luther King, Jr.: Charismatic Leadership in a Mass Struggle

Clayborne Carson

Clayborne Carson has been senior editor and director of the Martin Luther King, Jr., Papers Project at the Center for Nonviolent Social Change at Stanford University. He is a member of the history faculty of Stanford University.

The legislation to establish Martin Luther King, Jr.'s birthday as a federal holiday provided official recognition of King's greatness, but it remains the responsibility of those of us who study and carry on King's work to define his historical significance. Rather than engaging in officially approved nostalgia, our remembrance of King should reflect the reality of his complex and multifaceted life. Biographers, theologians, political scientists, sociologists, social psychologists, and historians have given us a sizable literature of King's place in the Afro-American protest tradition, his role in the modern black freedom struggle, and his eclectic ideas regarding nonviolent activism. Although King scholars may benefit from and may stimulate the popular interest in King generated by the national holiday, many will find themselves uneasy participants in annual observances to honor an innocuous, carefully cultivated image of King as a black heroic figure.

From Clayborne Carson, "Martin Luther King, Jr.: Charismatic Leadership in a Mass Struggle," *Journal of American History* 74 (Sept. 1987): 448–454. Reprinted by permission.

The King depicted in serious scholarly works is far too interesting to be encased in such a didactic legend. King was a controversial leader who challenged authority and who once applauded what he called "creative maladjusted nonconformity."[1] He should not be transformed into a simplistic image designed to offend no one—a black counterpart to the static, heroic myths that have embalmed George Washington as the Father of His Country and Abraham Lincoln as the Great Emancipator.

One aspect of the emerging King myth has been the depiction of him in the mass media, not only as the preeminent leader of the civil rights movement, but also as the initiator and sole indispensable element in the southern black struggles of the 1950s and 1960s. As in other historical myths, a Great Man is seen as the decisive factor in the process of social change, and the unique qualities of a leader are used to explain major historical events. The King myth departs from historical reality because it attributes too much to King's exceptional qualities as a leader and too little to the impersonal, large-scale social factors that made it possible for King to display his singular abilities on a national stage. Because the myth emphasizes the individual at the expense of the black movement, it not only exaggerates King's historical importance but also distorts his actual, considerable contribution to the movement.

A major example of this distortion has been the tendency to see King as a charismatic figure who single-handedly directed the course of the civil rights movement through the force of his oratory. The charismatic label, however, does not adequately define King's role in the southern black struggle. The term *charisma* has traditionally been used to describe the godlike, magical qualities possessed by certain leaders. Connotations of the term have changed, of course, over the years. In our more secular age, it has lost many of its religious connotations and now refers to a wide range of leadership styles that involve the capacity to inspire—usually through oratory—emotional bonds between leaders and followers. Arguing that King was not a charismatic leader, in the broadest sense of the term, becomes somewhat akin to arguing that he was not a Christian, but emphasis on King's charisma obscures other important aspects of his role in the black movement. To be sure, King's oratory was exceptional and many people saw King as a divinely inspired leader, but King did not receive and did not want the kind of unquestioning support that is often associated with charismatic leaders. Movement activists instead saw him as the most prominent among many outstanding movement strategists, tacticians, ideologues, and institutional leaders.

King undoubtedly recognized that charisma was one of many leadership

qualities at his disposal, but he also recognized that charisma was not a sufficient basis for leadership in a modern political movement enlisting numerous
self-reliant leaders. Moreover, he rejected aspects of the charismatic model
that conflicted with his sense of his own limitations. Rather than exhibiting
unwavering confidence in his power and wisdom. King was a leader full of
self-doubts, keenly aware of his own limitations and human weaknesses. He
was at times reluctant to take on the responsibilities suddenly and unexpectedly thrust upon him. During the Montgomery bus boycott, for example,
when he worried about threats to his life and to the lives of his wife and child,
he was overcome with fear rather than confident and secure in his leadership
role. He was able to carry on only after acquiring an enduring understanding
of his dependence on a personal God who promised never to leave him
alone.[2]

Moreover, emphasis on King's charisma conveys the misleading notion of
a movement held together by spellbinding speeches and blind faith rather
than by a complex blend of rational and emotional bonds. King's charisma
did not place him above criticism. Indeed, he was never able to gain mass
support for his notion of nonviolent struggle as a way of life, rather than simply a tactic. Instead of viewing himself as the embodiment of widely held
Afro-American racial values, he willingly risked his popularity among blacks
through his steadfast advocacy of nonviolent strategies to achieve radical social change.

He was a profound and provocative public speaker as well as an emotionally powerful one. Only those unfamiliar with the Afro-American clergy
would assume that his oratorical skills were unique, but King set himself
apart from other black preachers through his use of traditional black Christian idiom to advocate unconventional political ideas. Early in his life King
became disillusioned with the unbridled emotionalism associated with his father's religious fundamentalism, and, as a thirteen year old, he questioned
the bodily resurrection of Jesus in his Sunday school class.[3] His subsequent
search for an intellectually satisfying religious faith conflicted with the emphasis on emotional expressiveness that pervades evangelical religion. His
preaching manner was rooted in the traditions of the black church, while his
subject matter, which often reflected his wide-ranging philosophical interests,
distinguished him from other preachers who relied on rhetorical devices that
manipulated the emotions of listeners. King used charisma as a tool for mobilizing black communities, but he always used it in the context of other forms
of intellectual and political leadership suited to a movement containing
many strong leaders.

Recently, scholars have begun to examine the black struggle as a locally based mass movement, rather than simply a reform movement led by national civil rights leaders.[4] The new orientation in scholarship indicates that King's role was different from that suggested in King-centered biographies and journalistic accounts.[5] King was certainly not the only significant leader of the civil rights movement, for sustained protest movements arose in many southern communities in which King had little or no direct involvement.

In Montgomery, for example, local black leaders such as E. D. Nixon, Rosa Parks, and Jo Ann Robinson started the bus boycott before King became the leader of the Montgomery Improvement Association. Thus, although King inspired blacks in Montgomery and black residents recognized that they were fortunate to have such a spokesperson, talented local leaders other than King played decisive roles in initiating and sustaining the boycott movement.

Similarly, the black students who initiated the 1960 lunch counter sit-ins admired King, but they did not wait for him to act before launching their own movement. The sit-in leaders who founded the Student Nonviolent Coordinating Committee (SNCC) became increasingly critical of King's leadership style, linking it to the feelings of dependency that often characterize the followers of charismatic leaders.[6] The essence of SNCC's approach to community organizing was to instill in local residents the confidence that they could lead their own struggles. A SNCC organizer failed if local residents became dependent on his or her presence; as the organizers put it, their job was to work themselves out of a job. Though King influenced the struggles that took place in the Black Belt regions of Mississippi, Alabama, and Georgia, those movements were also guided by self-reliant local leaders who occasionally called on King's oratorical skills to galvanize black protestors at mass meetings while refusing to depend on his presence.

If King had never lived, the black struggle would have followed a course of development similar to the one it did. The Montgomery bus boycott would have occurred, because King did not initiate it. Black students probably would have rebelled—even without King as a role model—for they had sources of tactical and ideological inspiration besides King. Mass activism in southern cities and voting rights efforts in the deep South were outgrowths of large-scale social and political forces, rather than simply consequences of the actions of a single leader. Though perhaps not as quickly and certainly not as peacefully nor with as universal a significance, the black movement would probably have achieved its major legislative victories without King's leadership, for the southern Jim Crow system was a regional anachronism, and the forces that undermined it were inexorable.

To what extent, then, did King's presence affect the movement? Answering that question requires us to look beyond the usual portrayal of the black struggle. Rather than seeing an amorphous mass of discontented blacks acting out strategies determined by a small group of leaders, we would recognize King as a major example of the local black leadership that emerged as black communities mobilized for sustained struggles. If not as dominant a figure as sometimes portrayed, the historical King was nevertheless a remarkable leader who acquired the respect and support of self-confident, grass-roots leaders, some of whom possessed charismatic qualities of their own. Directing attention to the other leaders who initiated and emerged from those struggles should not detract from our conception of King's historical significance; such movement-oriented research reveals King as a leader who stood out in a forest of tall trees.

King's major public speeches—particularly the "I Have a Dream" speech—have received much attention, but his exemplary qualities were also displayed in countless strategy sessions with other activists and in meetings with government officials. King's success as a leader was based on his intellectual and moral cogency and his skill as a conciliator among movement activists who refused to be simply King's "followers" or "lieutenants."

The success of the black movement required the mobilization of black communities as well as the transformation of attitudes in the surrounding society, and King's wide range of skills and attributes prepared him to meet the internal as well as the external demands of the movement. King understood the black world from a privileged position, having grown up in a stable family within a major black urban community; yet he also learned how to speak persuasively to the surrounding white world. Alone among the major civil rights leaders of his time, King could not only articulate black concerns to white audiences, but could also mobilize blacks through his day-to-day involvement in black community institutions and through his access to the regional institutional network of the black church. His advocacy of nonviolent activism gave the black movement invaluable positive press coverage, but his effectiveness as a protest leader derived mainly from his ability to mobilize black community resources.

Analyses of the southern movement that emphasize its nonrational aspects and expressive functions over its political character explain the black struggle as an emotional outburst by discontented blacks, rather than recognizing that the movement's strength and durability came from its mobilization of black community institutions, financial resources, and grass-roots leaders.[7] The values of southern blacks were profoundly and permanently transformed not only by King, but also by involvement in sustained protest activity and community-organizing efforts, through thousands of mass meetings, workshops, citizenship classes, freedom schools, and informal discussions. Rather than merely accepting guidance from above, southern blacks were resocialized as a result of their movement experiences.

Although the literature of the black struggle has traditionally paid little attention to the intellectual content of black politics, movement activists of the 1960s made a profound, though often ignored, contribution to political thinking. King may have been born with rare potential, but his most significant leadership attributes were related to his immersion in, and contribution to, the intellectual ferment that has always been an essential part of Afro-American freedom struggles. Those who have written about King have too often assumed that his most important ideas were derived from outside the black struggle—from his academic training, his philosophical readings, or his acquaintance with Gandhian ideas. Scholars are only beginning to recognize the extent to which his attitudes and those of many other activists, white and black, were transformed through their involvement in a movement in which ideas disseminated from the bottom up as well as from the top down.

Although my assessment of King's role in the black struggles of his time reduces him to human scale, it also increases the possibility that others may recognize his qualities in themselves. Idolizing King lessens one's ability to exhibit some of his best attributes or, worse, encourages one to become a debunker, emphasizing King's flaws in order to lessen the inclination to exhibit his virtues. King himself undoubtedly feared that some who admired him would place too much faith in his ability to offer guidance and to overcome resistance, for he often publicly acknowledged his own limitations and mortality. Near the end of his life, King expressed his certainty that black people would reach the Promised Land whether or not he was with them. His faith was based on an awareness of the qualities that he knew he shared with all people. When he suggested his own epitaph, he asked not to be remembered for his exceptional achievements—his Nobel Prize and other awards, his academic accomplishments; instead, he wanted to be remembered for giving his life to serve others, for trying to be right on the war question, for trying to feed the hungry and clothe the naked, for trying to love and serve humanity. "I want you to say that I tried to love and serve humanity."[8] Those aspects of King's life did not require charisma or other superhuman abilities.

If King were alive today, he would doubtless encourage those who celebrate his life to recognize their responsibility to struggle as he did for a more just and peaceful world. He would prefer that the black movement be remembered not only as the scene of his own achievements, but also as a setting that brought out extraordinary qualities in many people. If he were to return, his oratory would be unsettling and intellectually challenging rather than remembered diction and cadences. He would probably be the unpopular social critic he was on the eve of the Poor People's Campaign rather than the object of national homage he became after his death. His basic message would be the same as it was when he was alive, for he did not bend with the changing political winds. He would talk of ending poverty and war and of building a just social order that would avoid the pitfalls of competitive capitalism and repressive communism. He would give scant comfort to those who condition their activism upon the appearance of another King, for he recognized the extent to which he was a product of the movement that called him to leadership.

The notion that appearances by Great Men (or Great Women) are necessary preconditions for the emergence of major movements for social changes reflects not only a poor understanding of history, but also a pessimistic view of the possibilities for future social change. Waiting for the Messiah is a human weakness that is unlikely to be rewarded more than once in a millennium. Studies of King's life offer support for an alternative optimistic belief that ordinary people can collectively improve their lives. Such studies demonstrate the capacity of social movements to transform participants for the better and to create leaders worthy of their followers.

PART IX

LEADING INDIVIDUALS

Leadership is, in essence, a process: *a series of actions and interactions among leaders and followers which lead to the attainment of group goals. A leader who aspires to be an effective leader must be proficient in this process. The next three parts of this volume (Leading Individuals, Leading Groups, The Skills of a Leader) are dedicated to exploring the means by which leaders and followers can succeed in positively affecting the outcome of group efforts.*

Although leadership is, almost by definition, a group phenomenon, at base it is a matter of individual leaders interacting with individual followers. Thus, before we turn to the group dynamics of the process, it is important to understand how this individual aspect of the leadership process operates. One of the most important challenges facing any leader is how to meld individual followers into a smoothly working whole, dedicated to the accomplishment of group objectives. The following readings address this problem. Both selections are drawn from the same source: Richard L. Hughes, Robert C. Ginnett, and Gordon J. Curphy's excellent leadership text, Leadership: Enhancing the Lessons of Experience. *In the first reading, Hughes et al. summarize the most important thinking on the motivation of followers. The following selection explores the related topic of the dynamics of power and influence among leaders and followers.*

44

Understanding and Influencing Follower Motivation

Richard L. Hughes, Robert C. Ginnett,
and Gordon J. Curphy

Richard L. Hughes has a Ph.D. in clinical psychology and heads the Department of Behavioral Sciences and Leadership at the United States Air Force Academy. Robert C. Ginnett has a Ph.D. in organizational behavior from Yale University and is currently deputy department head for leadership programs and counseling at the United States Air Force Academy. Gordon Curphy's graduate work was in industrial/organizational psychology. He was an associate professor at the Air Force Academy, and is now a senior consultant at Personnel Decisions, Inc.

Many people believe the most important quality of a good leader is the ability to motivate others to accomplish group tasks. The importance of motivation as a component of output is suggested in findings from diverse work groups that most people believe they could give as much as 15 percent or 20 percent more effort at work than they now do with no one, including their own bosses, recognizing any difference. Perhaps even more startling, these workers also believed they could give 15 percent or 20 percent *less* effort with no one noticing any difference. Moreover, variation in the output of jobs varies significantly across leaders and followers. Hunter, Schmidt, and Judiesch[1] estimated the top 15 percent of the workers for a particular job pro-

---

duced from 20 to 50 percent more output than the average worker, depending on the complexity of the job. What can leaders and followers do to enhance the motivation to perform? . . .

According to Kanfer,[2] **motivation** is anything that provides *direction, intensity*, and *persistence* to behavior. Another definition considers the term *motivation* a sort of shorthand to describe choosing an activity or task to engage in, establishing the level of effort to put forth on it, and determining the degree of persistence in it over time.[3] Like preferences and personality traits, motivation is not directly observable; it must be inferred from behavior. For example, if one person regularly assembles twice as many computers as any other person in his work group—assuming all have the same abilities, skills, and resources—then we likely would say this first person is more motivated than the others. We use the concept of motivation to explain differences we see among people in the energy and direction of their behavior. . . .

Few topics of human behavior have been the subject of so many books and articles as that of motivation. So much has been written about motivation that a comprehensive review of the subject is beyond the scope . . . [here]. This section will, however, overview several major approaches to understanding work motivation, as well as address their implications for followers' satisfaction and performance. (See[3,4] for more comprehensive reviews.) It is important for leadership practitioners to become familiar with these major approaches, which offer a variety of perspectives and ideas for influencing followers' decisions to choose, exert effort, or resist an activity. Additionally, through such understanding, leadership practitioners may recognize that some motivation theories are more applicable in certain situations, or for producing certain outcomes, than others. . . .

Need Theories

The two major need theories include Maslow's[4] hierarchy of needs and Alderfer's[5] existence-relatedness-growth (ERG) theory. These two theories assume all people share a common set of basic needs. **Needs** refer to internal states of tension or arousal, or uncomfortable states of deficiency people are motivated to change.[2]

Maslow's Hierarchy of Needs

According to Maslow,[4] people are motivated to satisfy five basic sorts of needs. These include the need to survive physiologically, the need for security, the need for affiliation with other people, the need to feel self-esteem, and

FIGURE 1
Maslow's Hierarchy of Needs

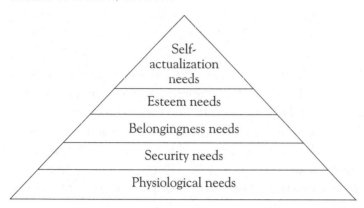

the need for self-actualization. Maslow's conceptualization of needs is usually represented by a triangle with the five levels of needs arranged in a hierarchy (see Figure 1) called, not surprisingly, the **hierarchy of needs**. According to Maslow, any person's behavior can be understood primarily as directed effort to satisfy one particular level of need in the hierarchy. Which level happens to be motivating one's behavior at any time depends on whether "lower" needs have been satisfied. According to Maslow, lower level needs must be satisfied before the next higher level would become salient in motivating behavior.

As an example, if Eric's salary were sufficient to meet his physiological needs, and his job security and retirement plan were sufficient to meet his security needs, neither of these two needs would serve to energize and direct his behavior. However, if he were in a secluded position on an assembly line and could not talk with others or be part of a close work group, he may still feel unfulfilled in his needs for affiliation and belongingness. This may cause him to put a lot of effort into forming friendships and socializing at work.

Maslow[4] said higher-level needs like those for self-esteem or self-actualization would not become salient (even when unfulfilled) until lower needs were satisfied. Thus, a practical implication of his theory is that leaders may only be successful in motivating follower behavior by taking account of the follower's position on the need hierarchy. For example, it might be relatively inefficient to try to motivate our lonely assembly-line worker by appealing to how much pride he would take in a job well done (i.e., to his self-esteem); Maslow said only *after* one feels part of a social group will such motives become energizing. At all levels of the hierarchy, the leader should watch for mismatches between his motivational efforts and the followers' lowest unsatisfied needs.

ERG Theory

Alderfer's[5] **existence-relatedness-growth (ERG) theory** has several similarities to Maslow's hierarchy of needs. In the terms of ERG theory, existence needs basically correspond to Maslow's physiological and security needs; relatedness needs are like Maslow's social and esteem needs; and growth needs are similar to the need for self-actualization. Beyond those similarities, however, are two important differences.

First, Alderfer reported that people sometimes try to satisfy more than one need at the same time. For example, even though a follower's existence needs may not be entirely satisfied, she may still be motivated to grow as a person. Second, he claimed frustration of a higher-level need can lead to efforts to satisfy a lower-level need. In other words, a follower who is continually frustrated in achieving some need might "regress" and exert effort to "satisfy" a lower need that already has been satisfied. For example, if the nature of work on an assembly line repeatedly frustrates Eric's need for relatedness with others, he may eventually stop trying to satisfy these needs at work and regress to demanding more pay—an existence need—and might, then, try to satisfy the relatedness need outside of work. Alderfer called this the **frustration-regression hypothesis**.

Concluding Thoughts on Need Theories

Although both Maslow's and Alderfer's need theories have played an important historical role in our understanding of motivation, they do have certain limitations. For one thing, neither theory makes specific predictions about what an individual will do to satisfy a particular need.[2,6] In the example above, Eric may exert considerable effort to establish new friendships at work, try to make friends outside of work, or even spend a lot of money on a new car or stereo equipment (the frustration-regression hypothesis). The theories' lack of specificity and predictive power severely limits their practical applicability in organizational, school, or team settings. On the other hand, awareness of the general nature of the various sorts of basic human needs described in these two theories seems fundamentally useful to leaders. . . .

FIGURE 2
Equity Theory Ratios

$$\frac{\text{Personal outcomes}}{\text{Personal inputs}} = \frac{\text{Reference group outcomes}}{\text{Reference group inputs}}$$

Cognitive Theories

The . . . cognitive theories we will describe here are concerned primarily with clarifying the conscious thought processes people use when deciding how hard or long to work toward some task or goal.

Equity Theory

As the name implies, **equity theory** emphasizes the motivational importance to followers of fair treatment by their leaders. It assumes that people value fairness in leader-follower exchange relationships.[3] Followers are said to be most satisfied when they believe that what they put into an activity or job and what they get out of it are roughly equivalent to what others put into and get out of it.[7,8] Equity theory proposes a very rational model for how followers assess these issues. Followers presumably reach decisions about equitable relationships by assigning values to the four elements in Figure 2 and then comparing the two ratios.[7] In looking at the specific elements in each ratio, personal outcomes refer to what one is receiving for one's efforts, such as pay, job satisfaction, opportunity for advancement, and personal growth. Personal inputs refer to all those things one contributes to a job such as time, effort, knowledge, and skills.

A key aspect of equity theory is that Figure 2 contains *two* ratios. Judgments of equity are always based on comparison to some reference group. It is the *relationship* between *the two ratios* that is important in equity theory, not the absolute value of either one's own outcomes or inputs, or those of others, considered by themselves. What matters most is the comparison between one's own ratio and that of a reference group such as one's co-workers or workers holding similar jobs in other organizations. For example, there may be many people who make more money than a particular follower; they may also, however, work longer hours, have more skills, or have to live in undesirable geographic locations to do so. In other words, although their outcomes are greater, so are their inputs, and thus the ratios may still be equal; there is equity.

In essence, equity theory does not try to evaluate "equality of inputs" or "equality of outcomes." It is concerned with "fairness" of inputs relative to outcomes. The perception of inequity creates a state of tension and an inherent pressure for change. As long as there is general equality between the two ratios, there is no motivation (at least based on inequity) to change anything, and people are reasonably satisfied. If, however, the ratios are significantly different, a follower will be motivated to take action likely to restore the balance. Exactly what the follower will be motivated to do depends on the direction of the inequality. Adams[9] suggested six ways people might restore balance: (a) changing their inputs; (b) changing their outcomes; (c) altering their self-perceptions; (d) altering their perceptions of their reference group; (e) changing their reference group; or, if all else fails, (f) leaving the situation. Thus, if a follower believed her ratio was lower than her co-worker's, she may reduce her level of effort or seek higher pay elsewhere. Research has shown that perceptions of underpayment generally resulted in actions in support of the model, but perceptions of overpayment did not. Instead of working harder in an over-payment condition (to make their own ratio more equitable), subjects often rationalized that they really deserved the higher pay.[4]

Expectancy Theory

First described by Tolman,[10] **expectancy theory** has been modified for use in work settings.[11–13] It involves two fundamental assumptions: (a) Motivated performance is the result of conscious choice and (b) people will do what they believe will provide them the highest (or surest) rewards. Thus, expectancy theory, like equity theory, is a highly rational approach to understanding motivation. It assumes that people act in ways that maximize their expectations of attaining valued outcomes and that reliable predictions of behavior are possible if the factors that influence those expectations can be quantified. In this model, there are three such factors to be quantified. The first two are probability estimates (expectancies), and the third is a vector sum of predicted positive and negative outcomes.

The first probability estimate is the **effort-to-performance expectancy**. Like all probabilities, it ranges from no chance of the event occurring to an absolute certainty of it occurring; or, in decimal form, from 0.0 to 1.0. Here, the follower estimates the likelihood of performing the desired behavior adequately, assuming she puts forth the required effort. The second probability estimate is the **performance-to-outcome expectancy**. In this case, our follower estimates the likelihood of receiving a reward, given that she achieves the desired level of performance. This is a necessary step in the sequence since it is not uncommon for people actually to do good work yet not be rewarded for it (e.g., someone else may be the teacher's pet). Finally, the follower must determine the likely outcomes, assuming that the previous conditions have been met, and determine whether their weighted algebraic sum (**valence**) is sufficiently positive to be worth the time and effort. To put it more simply, expectancy theory says that people will be motivated to do a task if three conditions are met; (1) They *can* do the task, (2) they will be rewarded if they do it, and (3) they value the reward. . . .

Situational Approaches

These approaches place considerably more emphasis on how the situation affects motivation. In other words, these approaches emphasize the leader's role in changing various aspects of the situation in order to increase followers' motivational levels. The three theories that emphasize situational influences in motivation are Herzberg's two-factor theory, the job characteristics model, and the operant approach.

Herzberg's Two-Factor Theory

Herzberg[14,15] developed the **two-factor theory** from a series of interviews he conducted with accountants and engineers. More specifically, he asked what satisfied them about their work and found that their answers usually could be sorted into five consistent categories. Furthermore, rather than assuming what dissatisfied people was always just the opposite of what satisfied them, he also specifically asked what dissatisfied people about their jobs. Surprisingly, the list of satisfiers and dissatisfiers represented entirely different aspects of work.

Herzberg labeled the factors that led to *satisfaction* at work **motivators**, and he labeled the factors that led to *dissatisfaction* at work **hygiene factors**. The most common motivators and hygiene factors can be found in Table 1. According to the two-factor theory, efforts directed toward improving hygiene factors will not increase followers' motivation. No matter how much leaders improve working conditions, pay, or sick-leave policies, for example, followers *will not* exert any additional effort or persist any longer at a task. For example, followers will probably be no more motivated to do a dull and boring job merely by being given pleasant office furniture. On the other hand,

TABLE 1
Motivators and Hygiene Factors of the Two-Factor Theory

Motivators	*Hygiene Factors*
Achievement	Supervision
Recognition	Working conditions
The work itself	Co-workers
Responsibility	Pay
Advancement and growth	Policies/procedures
	Job security

Source: Adapted from Herzberg, *Work and the Nature of Man* (Cleveland, Ohio: World Publishing, 1966).

followers may be asked to work in conditions so poor as to create dissatisfaction, which can distract them from constructive work.

Given limited resources on the leader's part, the key to increasing followers' effort levels according to two-factor theory is to just adequately satisfy the hygiene factors while maximizing the motivators for a particular job. It is important for working conditions to be adequate, but it is even more important (for enhancing motivation) to provide plenty of recognition, responsibility, and possibilities for advancement. In the words of Fred Herzberg, "if you don't want people to have Mickey Mouse attitudes, then don't give them Mickey Mouse work" (unpublished comments). . . .

The Job Characteristics Model

According to the **job characteristics model**, jobs or tasks having certain kinds of characteristics provide inherently greater motivation and job satisfaction than others. Hackman and Oldham[16,17] said that followers will work harder and be more satisfied if their tasks are meaningful, provide ample feedback, allow considerable latitude in deciding how to accomplish them, and require use of a variety of skills. The Hackman and Oldham model is based on five critical job characteristics: task identity, task significance, feedback, autonomy, and skill variety.

Note that while a job high in all these characteristics might seem intrinsically motivating, this model is not just another way of looking at intrinsic motivation. *Individuals* differ in their intrinsic motivation, whereas the job characteristics model says some *jobs* are, by their nature, more motivating and satisfying than others.

Actually, individual differences also play an important role in the job characteristics model. In this case the critical individual difference is called **growth-need strength**, which refers to the degree to which an individual is motivated by the need to fulfill herself (in Maslow's[4] terms, to increase one's self-esteem or self-actualization). Hackman and Oldham[16,17] said that individuals with high growth-need strength especially desire jobs high on the five characteristics in the model; they are even more motivated and satisfied than others with such jobs, and even less motivated and satisfied than others with jobs very low on those characteristics. Thus, if leaders were to follow the tenets of the job characteristics model to increase followers' satisfaction and motivation, then they would hire followers with high growth-need strength, and they would restructure followers' jobs to have more favorable task characteristics.

The Operant Approach

The **operant approach** focuses on modifying rewards and punishments in order to change the direction, intensity, or persistence of *observable behavior*. It will help at the outset of this discussion to define several terms. A **reward** is any consequence that *increases* the likelihood that a particular behavior will be repeated. For example, if a student receives an A on a science project, then she will be more likely to work hard on the next science project. **Punishment** is the administration of an aversive stimulus or the withdrawal of something desirable, each of which *decreases* the likelihood a particular behavior will be repeated.[18] Thus, if a child loses his allowance for talking back to his parents, then he will be less likely to do so again in the future. Both rewards and punishments can be administered in a contingent or noncontingent manner. **Contingent** rewards or punishments are administered as consequences of a particular behavior. Examples might include giving a runner a medal immediately after she won a race or grounding a teenage son after he comes home late. **Noncontingent** rewards and punishments are not associated with a particular behavior and might include receiving the same monthly paycheck even after working considerably less hard than the month before or getting a better parking slot because of seniority rather than performance. Rewards and punishments can also be administered using different schedules, such as those found in Table 2. Finally, behaviors that are not rewarded will eventually be eliminated through the process of **extinction**.

Research evidence has consistently shown that the operant approach is a

TABLE 11–2
Schedules of Reinforcement

Continuous: When rewards are given every time a person manifests a specific response. An example would be giving a golfer praise every time he broke par.

Fixed ratio: When rewards are given after a certain number of responses occur. For example, a coach may give her players a reward every time they shoot 100 free throws before practice.

Fixed interval: When rewards are given after a fixed period of time has elapsed, such as a weekly or monthly paycheck.

Variable ratio: When rewards are administered on a variable basis, but on average after a certain number of responses have occurred. An example would be a worker who gets rewarded after successfully assembling as few as 10 or as many as 20 computers, but on average the worker receives reinforcement after an average of 15 computers have been assembled.

Variable interval: Similar to the variable ratio schedule, except in this case rewards are administered after an average amount of time has elapsed. A worker might get a reward after 3, 8, or 1 days of good work, but on average receives a reward once a week.

---

very effective way of modifying followers' motivation and performance levels.[19–21] Other evidence has shown that rewards were more strongly related to satisfaction and performance than was punishment,[20,22,23] and that contingent rewards and punishments were more strongly related to satisfaction and performance than noncontingent rewards and punishments.[21,24,25]

Although these findings paint an encouraging picture of the practical utility of the operant approach, implementing it correctly in a work setting can be difficult.[26] Using operant principles properly to improve followers' motivation and hence performance requires following several steps. First, leaders need to *clearly specify* what behaviors are important. Second, leaders need to determine if those behaviors are currently being punished, rewarded, or ignored. Believe it or not, sometimes followers are actually rewarded for behavior that leaders are trying to extinguish and are punished for behaviors that leaders want to increase. For example, followers may get considerable positive attention from peers by talking back to the leader or by violating dress codes. Similarly certain overly competitive employees may be promoted ahead of their peers (by walking over their backs, we might say), even when management's rhetoric extols the need for cooperation and teamwork. It also may be the case that leaders sometimes just ignore the very behaviors they would like to see strengthened. An example here would be if a leader consistently failed to provide reward when followers produced high-quality products despite the leader's rhetoric always emphasizing the importance of quality.

Third, leaders need to find out what followers actually find rewarding and punishing. Leaders should *not* make the mistake of assuming that followers will find the same things rewarding and punishing as they do, nor should they assume that all followers will find the same things to be rewarding and punishing. What may be one follower's punishment may be another follower's reward. For example, some followers may dislike public attention and actually exert *less* effort after being publicly recognized; other followers may find public attention to be extremely rewarding. Fourth, leaders need to be wary of creating perceptions of inequality and decreasing intrinsic motivation when administering individually tailored rewards. Fifth, leaders should not limit themselves to administering organizationally sanctioned rewards and punishments. Using a bit of ingenuity, leaders can often come up with an array of potential rewards and punishments that are effective, inexpensive, and do not violate company policies. Finally, because the administration of noncontingent consequences has relatively little impact, leaders should administer rewards and punishments in a contingent manner whenever possible.

Concluding Thoughts on Situational Approaches to Motivation

The two-factor theory, the job characteristics model, and the operant approach all make one important point that is often overlooked in other theories of motivation: By changing the situation, leaders can enhance followers' motivation, performance, and satisfaction. Unfortunately, the same approaches tend to pay too little attention to the importance of needs, individual difference variables, and cognitive processes in the direction, intensity, and persistence of followers' behaviors (with the exception of growth-need strength in the job characteristics model). Perhaps the best strategy for leaders is to recognize that some motivational theories are more applicable to some situations than others, and to be flexible in the types of motivational interventions they use. However, leaders will only be able to adopt a flexible motivation intervention strategy if they become familiar with the strengths and weaknesses of the different theories and approaches. Just as a carpenter can more effectively build a house by using a variety of tools, a leader can be more effective by using a variety of motivational interventions to resolve work problems.

45

Power, Influence, and Influence Tactics

Richard L. Hughes, Robert C. Ginnett,
and Gordon J. Curphy

Richard L. Hughes has a Ph.D. in clinical psychology and heads the Department of Behavioral Sciences and Leadership at the United States Air Force Academy. Robert C. Ginnett has a Ph.D. in organizational behavior from Yale University and is currently deputy department head for leadership programs and counseling at the United States Air Force Academy. Gordon Curphy's graduate work was in industrial/organizational psychology. He was an associate professor at the Air Force Academy, and is now a senior consultant at Personnel Decisions, Inc.

One cannot understand leadership without understanding the concepts of power, influence, and influence tactics. Many people use these concepts synonymously[1] but it may be useful to distinguish among power, influence, and influence tactics. **Power** has been defined as the capacity to produce effects on others[2] or the potential to influence.[1] **Influence** can be defined as the change in a target agent's attitudes, values, beliefs, or behaviors as the result of influence tactics. **Influence tactics** refer to one person's actual behaviors designed to change another person's attitudes, beliefs, values, or behaviors. Although power, influence, and influence tactics are typically examined from the leader's perspective, it is important to remember that followers can also wield a considerable amount of power and influence, and that followers also use a variety of influence tactics to change the attitudes, values, beliefs, and behaviors of their leaders. Leadership practitioners can improve their effectiveness by reflecting on the types of power they and their followers have and the types of influence tactics that they may use or that may be used on them. . . .

A Taxonomy of Social Power

French and Raven[3] identified five sources, or bases, of power by which an individual can potentially influence others. These five sources include one that is primarily a function of the leader; one that is a function of the relationship between leaders and followers; one primarily a function of the leader and the situation; one primarily a function of the situation; and finally, one that involves aspects of all three elements. The five bases of power are organized from the leader's perspective, yet it is important to note that followers also have varying amounts of power they can use to resist a leader's influence attempts. Because both leaders and followers can use all five bases of power to influence each other, this section describes the bases of power from both the leader's and followers' perspectives. Understanding these bases of power from both perspectives can help leadership practitioners be more effective, because these bases can be used (a) to help determine why subordinates and superiors may successfully resist different influence attempts and (b) to improve the potential amount of influence leadership practitioners can have with subordinates and superiors. The following is a more detailed discussion of French and Raven's five bases of social power.

Expert Power. Expert power is the power of knowledge. Some people are able to influence others through their relative expertise in particular areas. A surgeon may wield considerable influence in a hospital because others are dependent on her knowledge, skill, and judgment, even though she may not have any formal authority over them. A mechanic may be influential among his peers because he is widely recognized as the best in the city. A longtime employee may be influential because his "corporate memory" provides a useful historical perspective to newer personnel. Legislators who are expert in the intricacies of parliamentary procedure, athletes who have played in championship games before, and soldiers who have been in combat before are valued for the "lessons learned" and wisdom they can share with others.

Because expert power is a function of the amount of knowledge one possesses relative to the rest of the members of the group, it is possible for followers to have considerably more expert power than leaders in certain situations. For example, new leaders often possess less knowledge of the jobs and tasks performed in a particular work unit than the followers do, and in this case the followers can potentially wield considerable influence when decisions are made regarding work procedures, new equipment, or the hiring of additional workers. Probably the best advice for leaders in this situation is to ask a lot of questions and perhaps seek additional training to help fill this knowledge gap. So long as different followers have considerably greater amounts of expert power, it will be difficult for a leader to influence the work unit on the basis of expert power alone.

Referent Power. One way to counteract the problems stemming from a lack of expertise is to build strong interpersonal ties with subordinates. Referent power refers to the potential influence one has due to the strength of the relationship between the leader and the followers. When people admire a leader and see her as a role model, we say she has referent power. For example, students may respond positively to advice or requests from teachers who are well liked and respected, while the same students might be unresponsive to less popular teachers. This relative degree of responsiveness is primarily a function of the strength of the relationship between the students and the different teachers. We knew one young lieutenant who had enormous referent power with the military security guards working for him due to his selfless concern for them, evident in such habits as bringing them hot chocolate and homemade cookies on their late-night shifts. The guards, sometimes taken for granted by other superiors, understood and valued the extra effort and sacrifice this young supervisor put forth for them. When Buddy Ryan was fired as head coach of the Philadelphia Eagles football team, many of the players expressed fierce loyalty to him. One said, "We'd do things for Buddy that we wouldn't do for another coach. I'd sell my body for Buddy" (Associated Press, January 9, 1991). That is referent power.

It is important to note that the relationships between leaders and followers take time to develop and often limit the actions leaders may take in a particular leadership situation. For example, a leader who has developed a strong relationship with a follower may be reluctant to discipline the follower for poor work or chronic tardiness, as these actions could disrupt the nature of the relationship between the leader and the follower. Thus, referent power is a two-way street; the stronger the relationship, the more influence leaders and followers exert over each other. Moreover, just as it is possible for leaders to

develop strong relationships with followers and, in turn, acquire more referent power, it is also possible for followers to develop strong relationships with
other followers and acquire more referent power. Followers with relatively
more referent power than their peers are often the spokespersons for their
work units and generally have more latitude to deviate from work-unit
norms. Followers with little referent power have little opportunity to deviate
from group norms. For example, in an episode of the television show "The
Simpsons," Homer Simpson was fired for wearing a pink shirt to work (everybody else at the Springfield nuclear power plant had always worn white
shirts). Homer was fired partly because he "was not popular enough to be different."

Legitimate Power. Legitimate power depends on a person's organizational role.
It can be thought of as one's formal or official authority. Some people make
things happen because they have the power or authority to do so. The boss
can assign projects; the coach can decide who plays; the colonel can order
compliance with uniform standards; the teacher assigns the homework and
awards the grades. Individuals with legitimate power exert influence through
requests or demands deemed appropriate by virtue of their role and position.
In other words, legitimate power means a leader has authority because he or
she has been assigned a particular role in an organization (and the leader has
this authority only as long as he or she occupies that position and operates
within the proper bounds of that role).

It is important to note that legitimate authority and leadership are not the
same thing. Holding a position and being a leader are not synonymous, despite the relatively common practice of calling position holders in bureaucracies the leaders. The head of an organization may be a true leader, but he also
may not be. Effective leaders often intuitively realize they need more than legitimate power to be successful. Before he became president, Dwight Eisenhower commanded all Allied troops in Europe during World War II. In a
meeting with his staff before the Normandy invasion, Eisenhower pulled a
string across a table to make a point about leadership. He was demonstrating
that just as you can pull a string, not push it, officers must lead soldiers and
not "push" them from the rear.

It is also possible for followers to use their legitimate power to influence
leaders. In these cases, followers can actively resist a leader's influence attempt by only doing work specifically prescribed in job descriptions, bureaucratic rules, or union policies. For example, many organizations have job
descriptions that limit both the time spent at work and the types of tasks and

activities performed. Similarly, bureaucratic rules and union policies can be invoked by followers to resist a leader's influence attempts. Often the leader will need to change the nature of his or her request or find another way to resolve the problem if these rules and policies are invoked by followers. If this is the case, then the followers will have successfully used legitimate power to influence their leader.

Reward Power. Reward power involves the potential to influence others due to one's control over desired resources. This can include the power to give raises, bonuses, and promotions; to grant tenure; to select people for special assignments or desirable activities; to distribute desired resources like computers, offices, parking places, or travel money; to intercede positively on another's behalf; to recognize with awards and praise; and so on. Many corporations use rewards extensively to motivate employees. At McDonald's, for example, there is great status accorded the "All-American Hamburger Maker," the cook who makes the fastest, highest-quality hamburgers in the country. At individual fast-food restaurants, managers may reward salespersons who handle the most customers during rush periods. Tupperware holds rallies for its salespeople. Almost everyone wins something, ranging from pins and badges to lucrative prizes for top performers.[4] Schools pick "teachers of the year" and professional athletes are rewarded by selection to all-star teams for their superior performance.

The potential to influence others through the ability to administer rewards is a joint function of the leader, the followers, and the situation. Leaders vary considerably in the types and frequency in which they mete out rewards, but the position they fill also helps to determine the frequency and types of rewards administered. For example, employees of the month at Kentucky Fried Chicken are not given new cars; the managers of these franchises do not have the resources to offer such awards. Similarly, leaders in other organizations are limited to some extent in the types and frequency in which they can administer awards. Nevertheless, leadership practitioners can enhance their reward power by spending some time reflecting on the followers and the situation. Often a number of alternative or innovative rewards can be created, and these rewards, along with ample doses of praise, can help a leader overcome the constraints his or her position puts on reward power.

Although using the power to administer rewards can be an effective way to change the attitudes and behaviors of others, there are several situations where a leader's use of reward power can be problematic. For example, the perception that a company's monetary bonus policy is handled equitably may be as important in motivating good work (or avoiding morale problems) as the amount of the bonus itself. Moreover, a superior may mistakenly assume that a particular reward is valued when it is not. This would be the case if a particular subordinate were publicly recognized for her good work when she actually dislikes public recognition. Leadership practitioners can avoid the latter problem by developing good relationships with subordinates and administering rewards that they, not the leader, value.

Another potential problem with reward power is that it may produce compliance but not other desirable outcomes like commitment.[5] In other words, subordinates may perform only at the level necessary to receive a reward and may not be willing to put forth the extra effort needed to make the organization better. An overemphasis on rewards as "payoff" for performance may also lead to resentment and feelings by workers of being manipulated, especially if it occurs in the context of relatively cold and distant superior-subordinate relationships. Extrinsic rewards like praise, compensation, promotion, privileges, and time off may not have the same effects on behavior as intrinsic rewards such as feelings of accomplishment, personal growth, and development. There is evidence under some conditions extrinsic rewards can even decrease intrinsic motivation toward a task and make the desired behavior less likely to persist when extrinsic rewards are not available.[6,7] Overemphasis on extrinsic rewards may instill an essentially contractual or economic relationship between superiors and subordinates, diluting important aspects of the relationship like mutual loyalty or shared commitment to higher ideals.[8]

All these cautions about reward power should not cloud its usefulness and effectiveness, which is very real. As noted previously, top organizations make extensive use of both tangible and symbolic rewards in motivating their workers. Furthermore, some of the most important rewards are readily available to all leaders—sincere praise and thanks to others for their loyalty and work. The bottom line is that leadership practitioners can enhance their ability to influence others based on reward power if they (*a*) determine what rewards are available, (*b*) determine what rewards are valued by their subordinates, and (*c*) establish clear policies for the equitable and consistent administration of rewards for good performance.

Finally, because reward power is partly determined by one's position in the organization, some people may believe followers have little, if any, reward power. This may not be the case. If followers have control over scarce resources, then they may use the administration of these resources as a way of getting leaders to act in the manner they want. Moreover, followers may reward their leader by putting out a high level of effort when they feel their leader is doing a good job, and they may put forth less effort when they feel their leader is doing a poor job. By modifying their level of effort, followers may in turn modify a leader's attitudes and behaviors. And when followers compliment their leader (e.g., for running a constructive meeting), it is no less an example of reward power than when a leader compliments a follower. Thus, leadership practitioners should be aware that followers can also use reward power to influence leaders.

Coercive Power. Coercive power, the opposite of reward power, is the potential to influence others through the administration of negative sanctions or the removal of positive events. In other words, it is the ability to control others through the fear of punishment or the loss of valued outcomes. Like reward power, coercive power is partly a function of the leader, but the situation often limits the coercive actions a leader can take. Examples of coercive power include policemen giving tickets for speeding, the army court-martialing AWOL soliders, a teacher detaining disruptive students after school, employers firing lazy workers, and parents spanking children.[9] Even presidents resort to their coercive powers. Historian Arthur Schlesinger, Jr., for example, described Lyndon Johnson as having a "devastating instinct for the weaknesses of others." Lyndon Johnson was familiar and comfortable with the use of coercion; he once told a White House staff member, "Just you remember this. There's only two kinds at the White House. There's elephants and there's ants. And I'm the only elephant."[10]

Coercive power, like reward power, can be used appropriately or inappropriately. It is carried to its extreme in harsh and repressive totalitarian societies. One of the most tragic instances of coercive power was in the cult led by Jim Jones, which tragically and unbelievably self-exterminated in an incident known as the Jonestown massacre.[11] Virtually all of the 912 who died there drank, at Jones's direction, from large vats of a flavored drink containing cyanide. The submissiveness and suicidal obedience of Jones's followers during the massacre was due largely to the long history of rule by fear Jones had practiced. For example, teenagers caught holding hands were beaten, and adults judged slacking in their work were forced to box for hours in marathon public matches against as many as three or four bigger and stronger opponents. Jim Jones ruled by fear, and his followers became self-destructively compliant.

Perhaps the preceding example is so extreme that we can dismiss its relevance to our own lives and leadership activities. On the other hand, it does provide dramatic reminder that reliance on coercive power has inherent limitations and drawbacks. This is not to say the willingness to use disciplinary sanctions is never necessary. Sometimes it is.

Informal coercion, as opposed to the threat of formal punishment, can also be used to change the attitudes and behaviors of others. Informal coercion is usually expressed implicitly, and often nonverbally, rather than explicitly. It may be the pressure employees feel to donate to the boss's favorite charity, or it may be his glare when they bring up an unpopular idea. One of the most common forms of coercion is simply a superior's temperamental outbursts. The intimidation of a leader's poorly controlled anger is usually, in its long-term effects, a dysfunctional style of behavior for leaders.

It is also possible for followers to use coercive power to influence their leader's behavior. For example, a leader may be hesitant to take disciplinary action against a large, emotionally unstable follower. Followers can threaten leaders with physical assaults, industrial sabotage, or work slowdowns and strikes, and these threats can serve to modify a leader's behavior. In all likelihood, followers will be more likely to use coercive power to change their leader's behavior if they have a relatively high amount of referent power with their fellow co-workers. This may be particularly true if threats of work slowdowns or strikes are used to influence a leader's behavior.

Concluding Thoughts About French and Raven's Power Taxonomy. There has been considerable research addressing French and Raven's[3] taxonomy of power, and generally the findings indicate that leaders who relied primarily on referent and expert power had subordinates who were more motivated and satisfied, were absent less, and performed better.[12] However, Yukl[12] and Podsakoff and Schriesheim[13] have criticized these findings, and much of their criticism centers on the instrument used to assess a leader's bases of power. Recently, Hinkin and Schriesheim[14] have developed an instrument that overcomes many of the criticisms, and future research should more clearly delineate the relationship between the five bases of power and various leadership effectiveness criteria.

Even though much research to date about the five bases of power may be flawed, three generalizations about power and influence still seem warranted. First, effective leaders typically take advantage of all their sources of power. They understand the relative advantages and disadvantages of the different power sources, and they selectively emphasize one or another depending on their particular objectives in a given situation. Second, whereas leaders in well-functioning organizations have strong influence over their subordinates, they are also open to being influenced by them. High degrees of reciprocal influence between leaders and followers characterize the most effective organizations.[5] Third, leaders vary in the extent to which they share power with subordinates. Some leaders seem to view their power as a fixed resource that, when shared with others (like cutting a pie into pieces), reduces their own portion. They see power in zero-sum terms. Other leaders see power as an expandable pie. They see the possibility of increasing a subordinate's power without reducing their own. Needless to say, which view a leader subscribes to can have a major impact on the leader's support for power-sharing activities like delegation and participative management. Support for them is also affected by the practice of holding leaders responsible for subordinates' decisions and actions as well as their own. It is, after all, the coach or manager who often gets fired when the team loses. . . .[15,16]

Leader Motives

People vary in their motivation to influence or control others. McClelland[17] called this the **need for power**, and individuals with a high need for power derive psychological satisfaction from influencing others. They seek positions where they can influence others, and they are often involved concurrently in influencing people in many different organizations or decision-making bodies. In such activities they readily offer ideas, suggestions, and opinions, and also seek information they can use in influencing others. They are often astute at building trusting relationships and assessing power networks, though they can also be quite outspoken and forceful. They value the tangible signs of their authority and status as well as the more intangible indications of others' deference to them. Two different ways of expressing the need for power have been identified: **personalized power** and **socialized power**. Individuals who have a high need for personalized power are relatively selfish, impulsive, and uninhibited, and lacking in self-control. These individuals exercise power for their own self-centered needs, not for the good of the group or the organization. Socialized power, on the other hand, implies a more emotionally mature expression of the motive. Socialized power is exercised in the service of higher goals to others or organizations and often involves self-sacrifice toward those ends. It often involves an empowering rather than autocratic style of management and leadership. . . .

Findings concerning both the need for power and the motivation to manage have several implications for leadership practitioners. First, not all individuals like being leaders. One reason may be that some have a relatively low need for power or motivation to manage. Because these scores are relatively stable and fairly difficult to change, leaders who do not enjoy their role may want to seek positions where they have few supervisory responsibilities.

Second, a high need for power or motivation to manage does not guarantee leadership success. The situation can play a crucial role in determining whether the need for power or the motivation to manage is related to leadership success. For example, McClelland and Boyatzis[18] found the need for power to be related to leadership success for nontechnical managers only, and Miner[19] found motivation to manage was related to leadership success only in hierarchical or bureaucratic organizations.

Third, in order to be successful in the long term, leaders may have to have both a high need for socialized power and a high level of activity inhibition. Leaders who impulsively exercise power merely to satisfy their own selfish needs will probably be ineffective in the long term.

Finally, it is important to remember that followers as well as leaders differ in the need for power, activity inhibition, and motivation to manage. Certain followers may have stronger needs or motives in this area. Leaders may need to behave differently toward these followers than they might toward followers having a low need for power or motivation to manage. . . .

Influence Tactics

Whereas power is the capacity or potential to influence others, influence tactics are the actual behaviors used by an agent to change the attitudes, opinions, or behaviors of a target person. Kipnis and his associates accomplished much of the early work on the types of influence tactics one person uses to influence another, and developed the Profile of Organizational Influence Strategies (POIS) to assess these behaviors.[20] Several methodological problems, however, limit the usefulness of this instrument.[21] For example, influence tactics are evaluated only from the perspective of the influencing agent; the target's perceptions are ignored. Others, fortunately, have developed an alternative measure of influence tactics: the Influence Behavior Questionnaire, or IBQ.[22] The IBQ is completed by both agents and targets, and appears to be a more valid instrument than the POIS. The following is a more detailed discussion of the tactics assessed by the IBQ.

Types of Influence Tactics

The IBQ is designed to assess nine types of influence tactics. **Rational persuasion** occurs when an agent uses logical arguments or factual evidence to influence others. Agents make **inspirational appeals** when they make a request or proposal designed to arouse enthusiasm or emotions in targets. **Consultation** occurs when agents ask targets to participate in planning an activity, and **ingratiation** occurs when the agent attempts to get you in a good mood before making a request. Agents use **personal appeals** when they ask another to do a favor out of friendship, whereas influencing a target through the exchange of favors is labeled **exchange.** **Coalition tactics** are different from consultation in that they are used when agents seek the aid or support of others to influence the target. Threats or persistent reminders used to influence targets are known as **pressure tactics**, and **legitimizing tactics** occur when agents make requests based on their position or authority.

Influence Tactics and Power

As alluded to throughout this . . . [selection], a strong relationship exists between the powers possessed by agents and targets, and the type of influence tactic used by the agent to modify the attitudes, values, or behavior of a target. Because leaders with relatively high amounts of referent power have built up close relationships with followers, they may be more able to use a wide variety of influence tactics to modify the attitudes and behaviors of their followers. For example, leaders with a lot of referent power could use inspirational appeals, consultations, ingratiation, personal appeals, exchanges, and even coalition tactics to increase the amount of time a particular follower spends doing work-related activities. Note, however, that leaders with high referent power generally do not use legitimizing or pressure tactics to influence followers since by threatening followers leaders risk some loss of referent power. Leaders who have only coercive or legitimate power may be able to use only coalition, legitimizing, or pressure tactics to influence followers. In this case, coalition tactics are just pressure tactics one step removed, as these leaders can threaten other followers with disciplinary action if they do not persuade a fellow follower to change his attitudes or behavior.

Other factors also can affect the choice of influence tactics.[23] People typically use hard tactics (i.e., the legitimizing or pressure tactics of the IBQ) when an influencer has the upper hand, when she anticipates resistance, or when the other person's behavior violates important norms. People typically use soft tactics (e.g., ingratiation) when they are at a disadvantage, when they expect resistance, or when they will personally benefit if the attempt is successful. People typically use rational tactics (i.e., the exchange and rational appeals tactics of the IBQ) when parties are relatively equal in power, when resistance is not anticipated, and when the benefits are organizational as well as personal. . . .

Concluding Thoughts about Influence Tactics

In the above discussion, an implicit lesson for leaders is the value of being conscious of what influence tactics one uses and what effects are typically associated with each tactic. Knowledge of such effects can help a leader make better decisions about her manner of influencing others. It might also be helpful for leaders to think more carefully about why they believe a particular influence tactic might be effective. Research indicates that some reasons for selecting among various possible influence tactics lead to successful outcomes more frequently than others. More specifically, thinking an act would improve an employee's self-esteem or morale was frequently associated with successful influence attempts. On the other hand, choosing an influence tactic because it followed company policy and choosing one because it was a way to put a subordinate in his place were frequently mentioned as reasons for unsuccessful influence attempts.[24] In a nutshell, these results suggest that leaders should pay attention not only to the actual influence tactics they use—to *how* they are influencing others—but also to *why* they believe such methods are called for. It is consistent with these results to conclude that influence efforts intended to build others up more frequently lead to positive outcomes than influence efforts intended to put others down.

Summary

This . . . . [selection] has defined power as the capacity or potential to exert influence; influence tactics as the behaviors used by one person to modify the attitudes and behaviors of another; and influence as the degree of change in a person's attitudes, values, or behaviors as the result of another's influence tactic. Because power, influence, and influence tactics play such an important role in the leadership process, this . . . . [selection] provides ideas to help leadership practitioners improve their effectiveness. Leadership practitioners can help themselves become more effective by reflecting on their leadership situation and considering the relative amounts of the five bases of social power both they and their followers possess. By reflecting on their bases of power, leadership practitioners can better understand how they can affect followers and how they can expand the amount of power they possess. In addition, the five bases of power also provide clues as to why subordinates are able to influence leaders and successfully resist leaders' influence attempts.

Leaders also may gain insight about why they may not enjoy their job by considering their own need for power or motivation to manage, or may better understand why some leaders exercise power selfishly by considering McClelland's concepts of personalized power and activity inhibition. . . .

Although power is an extremely important concept, having power is relatively meaningless unless a leader is willing to exercise it. The exercise of power occurs primarily through the influence tactics leaders and followers use to modify the attitudes and behaviors of each other. The types of influence tactics used seem to depend on the amount of different types of power possessed, the degree of resistance expected, and the rationale behind the different influence tactics. Because influence tactics designed to build up others are generally more successful than those that tear down others, leadership practitioners should always consider why they are using a particular influence attempt before they actually use it. By carefully considering the rationale behind the tactic, leaders may be able to avoid using pressure and legitimizing tactics and to find ways to influence followers that build them up rather than tear them down. Being able to use influence tactics that modify followers' attitudes and behaviors in the desired direction at the same time they build up followers' self-esteem and self-confidence should be a skill all leaders strive to master.

PART X

LEADING GROUPS

Although an appreciation of the art of leading individuals is a necessary first step toward an understanding of the process of leadership, leadership itself occurs in group situations. Moreover, it is important to recognize that groups are more than simply an aggregation of individuals. Groups have special characteristics, and their own dynamics, which must be understood if one is to lead successfully.

The selections below represent two classic contributions to the literature on group process. The first is Bruce Tuckman's description of the stages of group process. Tuckman's "forming, storming, norming, and performing" typology of group development serves as the basis for our modern understanding of groups. In identifying the typical problems groups encounter at each stage, Tuckman provides a digest of the obstacles effective leaders must identify and overcome. In the second reading, Irving Janis describes the evils of "groupthink," and outlines potential remedies.

Taken together, these selections provide leaders with important insights into the essence of leadership: group process.

353

46

Developmental Sequence in Small Groups

Bruce W. Tuckman

Bruce W. Tuckman received his Ph.D. in psychology from Princeton. He has published extensively in the fields of motivation, group dynamics, and personality measurement. His books include *Conducting Educational Research* and *Educational Psychology: From Theory to Application*. Tuckman is currently professor of educational research at Florida State University.

The purpose of this article is to review the literature dealing with the developmental sequence in small groups, to evaluate this literature as a body, to extrapolate general concepts about group development, and to suggest fruitful areas for further research. . . .

Classification Model

Realm: Interpersonal versus Task

Within the studies reviewed, an attempt will be made to distinguish between *interpersonal* stages of group development and *task* behaviors exhibited in the group. The contention is that any group, regardless of setting, must address

Excerpted from Bruce W. Tuckman, "Developmental Sequence in Small Groups," *Psychological Bulletin* 63 No. 6 (1965): 384–389. Copyright 1965 by the American Psychological Association. Adapted by permission of the author and publisher.

itself to the successful completion of a task. At the same time, and often through the same behaviors, group members will be relating to one another interpersonally. The pattern of *interpersonal relationships* is referred to as *group structure* and is interpreted as the interpersonal configuration and interpersonal behaviors of the group at a point in time, that is, the way the members act and relate to one another as persons. The content of interaction as related to the task at hand is referred to as *task activity*. The proposed distinction between the group as a social entity and the group as a task entity is similar to the distinction between the task-oriented functions of groups and the social-emotional-integrative functions of groups, both of which occur as simultaneous aspects of group functioning. . . .

Proposed Developmental Sequence

The following model is offered as a conceptualization of changes in group behavior, in both social and task realms, across all group settings, over time. It represents a set of hypotheses reflecting the author's biases (rather than those of the researchers) and the perception of trends in the studies reviewed which become considerably more apparent when these studies are viewed in the light of the model. The model of development stages presented below is not suggested for primary use as an organizational vehicle, although it serves that function here. Rather, it is a conceptual statement suggested by the data presented and subject to further test.

In the realm of group structure the first hypothesized stage of the model is labeled as *testing and dependence*. The term "testing" refers to an attempt by group members to discover what interpersonal behaviors are acceptable in the group, based on the reactions of the therapist or trainer (where one is present) and on the reactions of the other group members. Coincident to discovering the boundaries of the situation by testing, one relates to the therapist, trainer, some powerful group member, or existing norms and structures in a dependent way. One looks to this person, persons, or standards for guidance and support in this new and unstructured situation.

The first stage of task-activity development is labeled as *orientation to the task*, in which group members attempt to identify the task in terms of its relevant parameters and the manner in which the group experience will be used to accomplish the task. The group must decide upon the type of information they will need in dealing with the task and how this information is to be obtained. In orienting to the task, one is essentially defining it by discovering its "ground rules." Thus, orientation, in general, characterizes behavior in both interpersonal and task realms during this stage. It is to be emphasized that orientation is a general class of behavior which cuts across settings; the specifics of orientation, that is, what one must orient to and how, will be setting-specific.

The second phase in the development of group structure is labeled as *intragroup conflict*. Group members become hostile toward one another and toward a therapist or trainer as a means of expressing their individuality and resisting the formation of group structure. Interaction is uneven and "infighting" is common. The lack of unity is an outstanding feature of this phase. There are characteristic key issues that polarize the group and boil down to the conflict over progression into the "unknown" of interpersonal relations or regression to the security of earlier dependence.

Emotional response to task demands is identified as the second stage of task-activity development. Group members react emotionally to the task as a form of resistance to the demands of the task on the individual, that is the discrepancy between the individual's personal orientation and that demanded by the task. This task stage will be most evident when the task has as its goal self-understanding and self-change, namely, the therapy- and training-group tasks, and will be considerably less visible in groups working on impersonal intellectual tasks. In both task and interpersonal realms, emotionality in response to a discrepancy characterizes this stage. However, the source of the discrepancy is different in the different realms.

The third group structure phase is labeled as the *development of group cohesion*. Group members accept the group and accept the idiosyncrasies of fellow members. The group becomes an entity by virtue of its acceptance by the members, their desire to maintain and perpetuate it, and the establishment of new group-generated norms to insure the group's existence. Harmony is of maximum importance, and task conflicts are avoided to insure harmony.

The third stage of task activity development is labeled as the *open exchange of relevent interpretations*. In the therapy- and training-group context, this takes the form of *discussing oneself and other group members*, since self and other personal characteristics are the basic task inputs. In the laboratory-task context, exchanged interpretations take the form of opinions. In all cases one sees information being acted on so that alternative interpretations of the information can be arrived at. The openness to other group members is characteristic in both realms during this stage.

The fourth and final developmental phase of group structure is labeled as *functional role-relatedness*. The group, which was established as an entity during the preceding phase, can now become a problem-solving instrument. It does this by directing itself to members as objects, since the subjective relationship between members has already been established. Members can now adopt and play roles that will enhance the task activities of the group, since they have learned to relate to one another as social entities in the preceding stage. Role structure is not an issue but an instrument which can now be directed at the task. The group becomes a "sounding board" off which the task is "played."

In task-activity development, the fourth and final stage is identified as the *emergence of solutions*. It is here that we observe constructive attempts at successful task completion. In the therapy- and training-group context, these solutions are more specifically *insight* into personal and interpersonal processes and instructive self-change, while in the laboratory-group context the solutions are more intellectual and impersonal. Here, as in the three preceding stages, there is an essential correspondence between group structural and task realms over time. In both realms the emphasis is on constructive action, and the realms come together so that energy previously invested in the structural realm can be devoted to the task. . . .

Discussion . . .

In order to isolate those concepts common to the various studies reviewed (across settings), a developmental model was proposed. This model was aimed at serving a conceptual function as well as an integrative and organizational one. The model will be summarized here.

Groups initially concern themselves with orientation accomplished primarily through testing. Such testing serves to identify the boundaries of both interpersonal and task behaviors. Coincident with testing in the interpersonal realm is the establishment of dependency relationships with leaders, other group members, or preexisting standards. It may be said that orientation, testing, and dependence constitute the group process of *forming*.

The second point in the sequence is characterized by conflict and polarization around interpersonal issues, with concomitant emotional responding in the task sphere. These behaviors serve as resistance to group influence and task requirements and may be labeled as *storming*.

Resistance is overcome in the third stage in which ingroup feeling and cohesiveness develop, new standards evolve, and new roles are adopted. In the task realm, intimate, personal opinions are expressed. Thus, we have the stage of *norming*.

Finally, the group attains the fourth and final stage in which interpersonal structure becomes the tool of task activities. Roles become flexible and functional, and group energy is channeled into the task. Structural issues have been resolved, and structure can now become supportive of task performance. This stage can be labeled as *performing*.

47

Groupthink

Irving Janis

Irving Janis has written extensively on psychological stress, attitude change, and decision making. He is best known, however, for his classic book *Groupthink*. Janis has been a member of the department of psychology at Yale University since 1947.

"How could we have been so stupid?" President John F. Kennedy asked after he and a close group of advisers had blundered into the Bay of Pigs invasion. For the last two years I have been studying that question, as it applies not only to the Bay of Pigs decision makers but also to those who led the United States into such other major fiascos as the failure to be prepared for the attack on Pearl Harbor, the Korean War stalemate, and the escalation of the Vietnam War.

Stupidity certainly is not the explanation. The men who participated in making the Bay of Pigs decision, for instance, comprised one of the greatest arrays of intellectual talent in the history of American government—Dean Rusk, Robert McNamara, Douglas Dillon, Robert Kennedy, McGeorge Bundy, Arthur Schlesinger, Jr., Allen Dulles and others.

It also seemed to me that explanations were incomplete if they concentrated only on disturbances in the behavior of each individual within a decision-making body: temporary emotional states of elation, fear, or anger that reduce a man's mental efficiency, for example, or chronic blind spots arising from a man's social prejudices or idiosyncratic biases.

I preferred to broaden the picture by looking at the fiascos from the standpoint of group dynamics as it has been explored over the past three decades, first by the great social psychologist Kurt Lewin and later in many experimental situations by myself and other behavioral scientists. My conclusion after poring over hundreds of relevant documents—historical reports about formal group meetings and informal conversations among the members—is that the groups that committed the fiascos were victims of what I call "groupthink."

"Groupy"

In each case study, I was surprised to discover the extent to which each group displayed the typical phenomena of social conformity that are regularly encountered in studies of group dynamics among ordinary citizens. For example, some of the phenomena appear to be completely in line with findings from social-psychological experiments showing that powerful social pressures are brought to bear by the members of a cohesive group whenever a dissident begins to voice his objections to a group consensus. Other phenomena are reminiscent of the shared illusions observed in encounter groups and friendship cliques when the members simultaneously reach a peak of "groupy" feelings.

Above all, there are numerous indications pointing to the development of group norms that bolster morale at the expense of critical thinking. One of the most common norms appears to be that of remaining loyal to the group by sticking with the policies to which the group has already committed itself, even when those policies are obviously working out badly and have unintended consequences that disturb the conscience of each member. This is one of the key characteristics of groupthink.

1984

I use the term groupthink as a quick and easy way to refer to the mode of thinking that persons engage in when *concurrence-seeking* becomes so dominant in a cohesive ingroup that it tends to override realistic appraisal of alternative courses of action. Groupthink is a term of the same order as the words in the newspeak vocabulary George Orwell used in his dismaying world of *1984*. In that context, groupthink takes on an invidious connotation. Exactly such a connotation is intended, since the term refers to a deterioration in mental efficiency, reality testing, and moral judgments as a result of group pressures.

The symptoms of groupthink arise when the members of decision-making groups become motivated to avoid being too harsh in their judgments of their leaders' or their colleagues' ideas. They adopt a soft line of criticism, even in their own thinking. At their meetings, all the members are amiable and seek complete concurrence on every important issue, with no bickering or conflict to spoil the cozy, "we-feeling" atmosphere.

Kill

Paradoxically, soft-headed groups are often hard-hearted when it comes to dealing with outgroups or enemies. They find it relatively easy to resort to dehumanizing solutions—they will readily authorize bombing attacks that kill large numbers of civilians in the name of the noble cause of persuading an unfriendly government to negotiate at the peace table. They are unlikely to pursue the more difficult and controversial issues that arise when alternatives to a harsh military solution come up for discussion. Nor are they inclined to raise ethical issues that carry the implication that *this fine group of ours, with its humanitarianism and its high-minded principles, might be capable of adopting a course of action that is inhumane and immoral.*

Norms

There is evidence from a number of social-psychological studies that as the members of a group feel more accepted by the others, which is a central feature of increased group cohesiveness, they display less overt conformity to group norms. Thus we would expect that the more cohesive a group becomes, the less the members will feel constrained to censor what they say out of fear of being socially punished for antagonizing the leader or any of their fellow members.

In contrast, the groupthink type of conformity tends to increase as group cohesiveness increases. Groupthink involves nondeliberate suppression of critical thoughts as a result of internalization of the group's norms, which is quite different from deliberate suppression on the basis of external threats of social punishment. The more cohesive the group, the greater the inner compulsion on the part of each member to avoid creating disunity, which inclines him to believe in the soundness of whatever proposals are promoted by the leader or by a majority of the group's members.

In a cohesive group, the danger is not so much that each individual will fail to reveal his objections to what the others propose but that he will think the proposal is a good one, without attempting to carry out a careful, critical scrutiny of the pros and cons of the alternatives. When groupthink becomes dominant, there also is considerable suppression of deviant thoughts, but it takes the form of each person's deciding that his misgivings are not relevant and should be set aside, that the benefit of the doubt regarding any lingering uncertainties should be given to the group consensus.

Stress

I do not mean to imply that all cohesive groups necessarily suffer from group-think. All ingroups may have a mild tendency toward groupthink, displaying one or another of the symptoms from time to time, but it need not be so dom-inant as to influence the quality of the group's final decision. Neither do I mean to imply that there is anything necessarily inefficient or harmful about group decisions in general. On the contrary, a group whose members have properly defined roles, with traditions concerning the procedures to follow in pursuing a critical inquiry, probably is capable of making better decisions than any individual group member working alone.

The problem is that the advantages of having decisions made by groups are often lost because of powerful psychological pressures that arise when the members work closely together, share the same set of values and, above all, face a crisis situation that puts everyone under intense stress.

The main principle of groupthink, which I offer in the spirit of Parkinson's Law, is:

> The more amiability and esprit de corps there is among the members of a poli-cy-making ingroup, the greater the danger that independent critical thinking will be replaced by groupthink, which is likely to result in irrational and dehu-manizing actions directed against outgroups.

Symptoms

In my studies of high-level governmental decision makers, both civilian and military, I have found eight main symptoms of groupthink.

1. Invulnerability

Most or all of the members of the ingroup share an *illusion* of invulnerability that provides for them some degree of reassurance about obvious dangers and leads them to become overoptimistic and willing to take extraordinary risks. It also causes them to fail to respond to clear warnings of danger.

The Kennedy ingroup, which uncritically accepted the Central Intelligence Agency's disastrous Bay of Pigs plan, operated on the false assumption that they could keep secret the fact that the United States was responsible for the invasion of Cuba. Even after news of the plan began to leak out, their belief remained unshaken. They failed even to consider the danger that awaited them: a worldwide revulsion against the U.S.

A similar attitude appeared among the members of President Lyndon B. Johnson's ingroup, the "Tuesday Cabinet," which kept escalating the Vietnam War despite repeated setbacks and failures. "There was a belief," Bill Moyers commented after he resigned, "that if we indicated a willingness to use our power, they [the North Vietnamese] would get the message and back away from an all-out confrontation.

"There was a confidence—it was never bragged about, it was just there— that when the chips were really down, the other people would fold."

A most poignant example of an illusion of invulnerability involves the ingroup around Admiral H. E. Kimmel, which failed to prepare for the possibility of a Japanese attack on Pearl Harbor despite repeated warnings. Informed by his intelligence chief that radio contact with Japanese aircraft carriers had been lost, Kimmel joked about it: "What, you don't know where the carriers are? Do you mean to say that they could be rounding Diamond Head (at Honolulu) and you wouldn't know it?" The carriers were in fact moving full-steam toward Kimmel's command post at the time. Laughing together about a danger signal, which labels it as a purely laughing matter, is a characteristic manifestation of groupthink.

2. Rationale

As we see, victims of groupthink ignore warnings; they also collectively construct rationalizations in order to discount warnings and other forms of negative feedback that, taken seriously, might lead the group members to reconsider their assumptions each time they recommit themselves to past decisions. Why did the Johnson ingroup avoid reconsidering its escalation policy when time and again the expectations on which they based their decisions turned out to be wrong? James C. Thompson, Jr., a Harvard historian who spent five years as an observing participant in both the State Department and the White House, tells us that the policymakers avoided critical discussion of their prior decisions and continually invented new rationalizations so that they could sincerely recommit themselves to defeating the North Vietnamese.

In the fall of 1964, before the bombing of North Vietnam began, some of the policymakers predicted that six weeks of air strikes would induce the North Vietnamese to seek peace talks. When someone asked, "What if they don't?" the answer was that another four weeks certainly would do the trick.

Later, after each setback, the ingroup agreed that by investing just a bit more effort (by stepping up the bomb tonnage a bit, for instance), their course of action would prove to be right. *The Pentagon Papers* bear out these observations.

In *The Limits of Intervention*, Townsend Hoopes, who was acting Secretary of the Air Force under Johnson, says that Walt A. Rostow in particular showed a remarkable capacity for what has been called "instant rationalization." According to Hoopes, Rostow buttressed the group's optimism about being on the road to victory by culling selected scraps of evidence from news reports or, if necessary, by inventing "plausible" forecasts that had no basis in evidence at all.

Admiral Kimmel's group rationalized away their warnings, too. Right up to December 7, 1941, they convinced themselves that the Japanese would never dare attempt a full-scale surprise assault against Hawaii because Japan's leaders would realize that it would precipitate an all-out war which the United States would surely win. They made no attempt to look at the situation through the eyes of the Japanese leaders—another manifestation of groupthink.

3. Morality

Victims of groupthink believe unquestioningly in the inherent morality of their ingroup; this belief inclines the members to ignore the ethical or moral consequences of their decisions.

Evidence that this symptom is at work usually is of a negative kind—the things that are left unsaid in group meetings. At least two influential persons had doubts about the morality of the Bay of Pigs adventure. One of them, Arthur Schlesinger, Jr., presented his strong objections in a memorandum to President Kennedy and Secretary of State Rusk but suppressed them when he attended meetings of the Kennedy team. The other, Senator J. William Fulbright, was not a member of the group, but the President invited him to express his misgivings in a speech to the policymakers. However, when Fulbright finished speaking the President moved on to other agenda items without asking for reactions of the group.

David Kraslow and Stuart H. Loory, in *The Secret Search for Peace in Vietnam*, report that during 1966 President Johnson's ingroup was concerned primarily with selecting bomb targets in North Vietnam. They based their selection on four factors—the military advantage, the risk to American aircraft and pilots, the danger of forcing other countries into the fighting, and the danger of heavy civilian casualties. At their regular Tuesday luncheons, they weighed these factors the way school teachers grade examination papers, averaging them out. Though evidence on this point is scant, I suspect that the group's ritualistic adherence to a standardized procedure induced the members to feel morally justified in their destructive way of dealing with the Vietnamese people—after all, the danger of heavy civilian casualties from U.S. air strikes was taken into account on their checklists.

4. Stereotypes

Victims of groupthink hold stereotyped views of the leaders of enemy groups: they are so evil that genuine attempts at negotiating differences with them are unwarranted, or they are too weak or too stupid to deal effectively with whatever attempts the ingroup makes to defeat their purposes, no matter how risky the attempts are.

Kennedy's groupthinkers believed that Premier Fidel Castro's air force was so ineffectual that obsolete B-26s could knock it out completely in a surprise attack before the invasion began. They also believed that Castro's army was so weak that a small Cuban-exile brigade could establish a well-protected beachhead at the Bay of Pigs. In addition, they believed that Castro was not smart enough to put down any possible internal uprisings in support of the exiles. They were wrong on all three assumptions. Though much of the blame was attributable to faulty intelligence, the point is that none of Kennedy's advisers even questioned the CIA planners about these assumptions.

The Johnson advisers' sloganistic thinking about "the Communist apparatus" that was "working all around the world" (as Dean Rusk put it) led them to overlook the powerful nationalistic strivings of the North Vietnamese government and its efforts to ward off Chinese domination. The crudest of all stereotypes used by Johnson's inner circle to justify their policies was the domino theory ("If we don't stop the Reds in South Vietnam, tomorrow they will be in Hawaii and next week they will be in San Francisco," Johnson once said). The group so firmly accepted this stereotype that it became almost impossible for any adviser to introduce a more sophisticated viewpoint.

In the documents on Pearl Harbor, it is clear to see that the Navy commanders stationed in Hawaii had a naive image of Japan as a midget that would not dare to strike a blow against a powerful giant.

5. Pressure

Victims of groupthink apply direct pressure to any individual who momentarily expresses doubts about any of the group's shared illusions or who questions the validity of the arguments supporting a policy alternative favored by the majority. This gambit reinforces the concurrence-seeking norm that loyal members are expected to maintain.

President Kennedy probably was more active than anyone else in raising skeptical questions during the Bay of Pigs meetings, and yet he seems to have encouraged the group's docile, uncritical acceptance of defective arguments in favor of the CIA's plan. At every meeting, he allowed the CIA representatives to dominate the discussion. He permitted them to give their immediate refutations in response to each tentative doubt that one of the others expressed, instead of asking whether anyone shared the doubt or wanted to pursue the implications of the new worrisome issue that had just been raised. And at the most crucial meeting, when he was calling on each member to give his vote for or against the plan, he did not call on Arthur Schlesinger, the one man there who was known by the President to have serious misgivings.

Historian Thomson informs us that whenever a member of Johnson's in-group began to express doubts, the group used subtle social pressures to "domesticate" him. To start with, the dissenter was made to feel at home, provided that he lived up to two restrictions: (1) that he did not voice his doubts to outsiders, which would play into the hands of the opposition; and (2) that he kept his criticisms within the bounds of acceptable deviation, which meant not challenging any of the fundamental assumptions that went into the group's prior commitments. One such "domesticated dissenter" was Bill Moyers. When Moyers arrived at a meeting, Thomson tells us, the President greeted him with, "Well, here comes Mr. Stop-the-Bombing."

6. Self-Censorship

Victims of groupthink avoid deviating from what appears to be group consensus; they keep silent about their misgivings and even minimize to themselves the importance of their doubts.

As we have seen, Schlesinger was not at all hesitant about presenting his strong objections to the Bay of Pigs plan in a memorandum to the President and the Secretary of State. But he became keenly aware of his tendency to suppress objections at the White House meetings. "In the months after the Bay of Pigs I bitterly reproached myself for having kept so silent during those crucial discussions in the cabinet room," Schlesinger writes in *A Thousand Days*. "I can only explain my failure to do more than raise a few timid questions by reporting that one's impulse to blow the whistle on this nonsense was simply undone by the circumstances of the discussion."

7. Unanimity

Victims of groupthink share an *illusion* of unanimity within the group concerning almost all judgments expressed by members who speak in favor of the majority view. This symptom results partly from the preceding one, whose effects are augmented by the false assumption that any individual who remains silent during any part of the discussion is in full accord with what the others are saying.

When a group of persons who respect each other's opinions arrives at a unanimous view, each member is likely to feel that the belief must be true. This reliance on consensual validation within the group tends to replace individual critical thinking and reality testing, unless there are clear-cut disagreements among the members. In contemplating a course of action such as the invasion of Cuba, it is painful for the members to confront disagreements within their group, particularly if it becomes apparent that there are widely divergent views about whether the preferred course of action is too risky to undertake at all. Such disagreements are likely to arouse anxieties about making a serious error. Once the sense of unanimity is shattered, the members no longer can feel complacently confident about the decision they are inclined to make. Each man must then face the annoying realization that there are troublesome uncertainties and he must diligently seek out the best information he can get in order to decide for himself exactly how serious the risks might be. This is one of the unpleasant consequences of being in a group of hardheaded, critical thinkers.

To avoid such an unpleasant state, the members often become inclined, without quite realizing it, to prevent latent disagreements from surfacing when they are about to initiate a risky course of action. The group leader and the members support each other in playing up the areas of convergence in their thinking, at the expense of fully exploring divergencies that might reveal unsettled issues.

"Our meetings took place in a curious atmosphere of assumed consensus," Schlesinger writes. His additional comments clearly show that, curiously, the consensus was an illusion—an illusion that could be maintained only because the major participants did not reveal their own reasoning or discuss their idiosyncratic assumptions and vague reservations. Evidence from several sources makes it clear that even the three principals—President Kennedy, Rusk, and McNamara—had widely differing assumptions about the invasion plan.

8. Mindguards

Victims of groupthink sometimes appoint themselves as mindguards to protect the leader and fellow members from adverse information that might break the complacency they shared about the effectiveness and morality of past decisions. At a large birthday party for his wife, Attorney General Robert F. Kennedy, who had been constantly informed about the Cuban invasion plan, took Schlesinger aside and asked him why he was opposed. Kennedy listened coldly and said, "You may be right or you may be wrong, but the President has made his mind up. Don't push it any further. Now is the time for everyone to help him all they can."

Rusk also functioned as a highly effective mindguard by failing to transmit to the group the strong objections of three "outsiders" who had learned of the invasion plan—Undersecretary of State Chester Bowles, USIA Director Edward R. Murrow, and Rusk's intelligence chief, Roger Hilsman. Had Rusk done so, their warnings might have reinforced Schlesinger's memorandum and jolted some of Kennedy's ingroup, if not the President himself, into reconsidering the decision.

Products

When a group of executives frequently displays most or all of these interrelated symptoms, a detailed study of their deliberations is likely to reveal a number of immediate consequences. These consequences are, in effect, products of poor decision-making practices because they lead to inadequate solutions to the problems being dealt with.

First, the group limits its discussions to a few alternative courses of action (often only two) without an initial survey of all the alternatives that might be worthy of consideration.

Second, the group fails to reexamine the course of action initially preferred by the majority after they learn of risks and drawbacks they had not considered originally.

Third, the members spend little or no time discussing whether there are nonobvious gains they may have overlooked or ways of reducing the seemingly prohibitive costs that made rejected alternatives appear undesirable to them.

Fourth, members make little or no attempt to obtain information from experts within their own organizations who might be able to supply more precise estimates of potential losses and gains.

Fifth, members show positive interest in facts and opinions that support their preferred policy; they tend to ignore facts and opinions that do not.

Sixth, members spend little time deliberating about how the chosen policy might be hindered by bureaucratic inertia, sabotaged by political opponents, or temporarily derailed by common accidents. Consequently, they fail to work out contingency plans to cope with foreseeable setbacks that could endanger the overall success of their chosen course.

Support

The search for an explanation of why groupthink occurs has led me through a quagmire of complicated theoretical issues in the murky area of human motivation. My belief, based on recent social psychological research, is that we can best understand the various symptoms of groupthink as a mutual effort among the group members to maintain self-esteem and emotional equanimity by providing social support to each other, especially at times when they share responsibility for making vital decisions.

Even when no important decision is pending, the typical administrator will begin to doubt the wisdom and morality of his past decisions each time he receives information about setbacks, particularly if the information is accompanied by negative feedback from prominent men who originally had been his supporters. It should not be surprising, therefore, to find that individual members strive to develop unanimity and esprit de corps that will help bolster each other's morale, to create an optimistic outlook about the success of pending decisions, and to reaffirm the positive value of past policies to which all of them are committed.

Pride

Shared illusions of invulnerability, for example, can reduce anxiety about taking risks. Rationalizations help members believe that the risks are really not so bad after all. The assumption of inherent morality helps the members to avoid feelings of shame or guilt. Negative stereotypes function as stress-reducing devices to enhance a sense of moral righteousness as well as pride in a lofty mission.

The mutual enhancement of self-esteem and morale may have functional value in enabling the members to maintain their capacity to take action, but it has maladaptive consequences insofar as concurrence-seeking tendencies interfere with critical, rational capacities and lead to serious errors of judgment.

While I have limited my study to decision-making bodies in Government, groupthink symptoms appear in business, industry, and any other field where small, cohesive groups make the decisions. It is vital, then, for all sorts of people—and especially group leaders—to know what steps they can take to prevent groupthink.

Remedies

To counterpoint my case studies of the major fiascos, I have also investigated two highly successful group enterprises, the formulation of the Marshall Plan in the Truman Administration and the handling of the Cuban missile crisis by President Kennedy and his advisers. I have found it instructive to examine the steps Kennedy took to change his group's decision-making processes. These changes ensured that the mistakes made by his Bay of Pigs ingroup were not repeated by the missile-crisis ingroup, even though the membership of both groups was essentially the same.

The following recommendations for preventing groupthink incorporate many of the good practices I discovered to be characteristic of the Marshall Plan and missile-crisis groups:

1. The leader of a policy-forming group should assign the role of critical evaluator to each member, encouraging the group to give high priority to open airing of objections and doubts. This practice needs to be reinforced by the leader's acceptance of criticism of his own judgments in order to discourage members from soft-pedaling their disagreements and from allowing their striving for concurrence to inhibit criticism.
2. When the key members of a hierarchy assign a policy-planning mission to any group within their organization, they should adopt an impartial stance instead of stating preferences and expectations at the beginning. This will encourage open inquiry and impartial probing of a wide range of policy alternatives.

3. The organization routinely should set up several outside policy-planning and evaluation groups to work on the same policy question, each deliberating under a different leader. This can prevent the insulation of an ingroup.

4. At intervals before the group reaches a final consensus, the leader should require each member to discuss the group's deliberations with associates in his own unit of the organization—assuming that those associates can be trusted to adhere to the same security regulations that govern the policy makers—and then to report back their reactions to the group.

5. The group should invite one or more outside experts to each meeting on a staggered basis and encourage the experts to challenge the views of the core members.

6. At every general meeting of the group, whenever the agenda calls for an evaluation of policy alternatives, at least one member should play devil's advocate, functioning as a good lawyer in challenging the testimony of those who advocate the majority position.

7. Whenever the policy issue involves relations with a rival nation or organization, the group should devote a sizable block of time, perhaps an entire session, to a survey of all warning signals from the rivals and should write alternative scenarios on the rivals' intentions.

8. When the group is surveying policy alternatives for feasibility and effectiveness, it should from time to time divide into two or more subgroups to meet separately, under different chairmen, and then come back together to hammer out differences.

9. After reaching a preliminary consensus about what seems to be the best policy, the group should hold a "second-chance" meeting at which every member expresses as vividly as he can all his residual doubts, and rethinks the entire issue before making a definitive choice.

How

These recommendations have their disadvantages. To encourage the open airing of objections, for instance, might lead to prolonged and costly debates when a rapidly growing crisis requires immediate solution. It also could cause rejection, depression, and anger. A leader's failure to set a norm might create cleavage between leader and members that could develop into a disruptive power struggle if the leader looks on the emerging consensus as anathema. Setting up outside evaluation groups might increase the risk of security leakage. Still, inventive executives who know their way around the organizational maze probably can figure out how to apply one or another of the prescriptions successfully, without harmful side effects.

They also could benefit from the advice of outside experts in the administrative and behavioral sciences. Though these experts have much to offer, they have had few chances to work on policy-making machinery within large organizations. As matters now stand, executives innovate only when they need new procedures to avoid repeating serious errors that have deflated their self-images.

In this era of atomic warheads, urban disorganization and ecocatastrophes, it seems to me that policy makers should collaborate with behavioral scientists and give top priority to preventing groupthink and its attendant fiascos.

PART XI

THE SKILLS OF A LEADER

No matter how well one knows the leadership definitions, theories, and processes, if one aspires to actually lead, that individual must also possess the ability to lead. While the definition of "the ability to lead" is open to interpretation, it would seem that there are some competencies which are indispensable to leadership (and, indeed, followership as well). This part brings together a collection of insights on the most important leadership skills.

Our survey begins with a short selection by Warren Bennis, who has devised a list of leadership competencies necessary for effective leadership through the intensive study of actual leaders in many fields. Bennis's conclusion—that effective leadership "knows what it wants, communicates those intentions accurately, empowers others and knows how to stay on course and when to change"—provides an appropriate framework for the ensuing selections.

Any overview of leadership competencies must begin with one that all leaders must possess: the ability to think critically. Without this capability, leadership is—at best—misguided; it may even become dangerous. In selection 49, Stephen Brookfield investigates what it means to think critically. In the ensuing selection, Lee Bolman and Terrence Deal provide an example of one of the essential elements of critical thinking: the ability to view a problem from multiple perspectives.

If leadership is the ability to cope with change, as John Kotter suggests in selection 22, the effective leader must be able to identify the forces of change, develop and articulate a vision which adapts to (or initiates) change, and then implement the chosen change strategy. Richard Beckhard and Wendy Pritchard offer their recommendations for the approach leaders must take in the face of change. Marshall Sashkin elaborates, with his view of how a leader should implement his or her vision.

Leadership also requires certain competencies in facilitating the group's activities. A central part of most leadership situations is making decisions and subsequently implementing them. E. Frank Harrison provides an overview of "the managerial decision-making process," while Victor Vroom describes how to decide which decision style is appropriate for any given leadership scenario.

Michael Z. Hackman and Craig E. Johnson turn to the key leadership issue of communication. All the envisioning and rational decision-making in the world is of little utility if the leader cannot communicate his or her vision or policy determination to his or her followers. Likewise, the group process itself depends for its success upon effective communications among all group members. Hackman and Johnson explore leadership communication skills and roles.

One of the inevitable concomitants of group interaction is conflict: either between leader and follower, or among followers, or between groups. The effective leader needs to have the capability to live with conflict, and to manage it in such a way as it does not become dysfunctional to the group. Jeanne Brett, Stephen Goldberg, and William Ury discuss the principles of dispute settlement, and suggest how an effective leader can design systems of resolving disputes in organizations.

The leadership skills surveyed above only tap the surface of the sorts of competencies required to operate effectively in a leadership position. Nevertheless, any individual who strives to become proficient at the skills discussed in this segment will be well on his or her way to becoming an effective leader.

48

The Artform of Leadership

Warren Bennis

Warren Bennis is one of the best-known and most well-respected names in leadership studies. He has published hundreds of articles and twenty books, including *On Becoming a Leader* and *Why Leaders Can't Lead*, and he co-authored *Leaders: Strategies for Taking Charge*. He has served as consultant, faculty member, and university president. He is currently Distinguished Professor of Business Administration at the University of Southern California.

Without any question, "leadership" is the most studied and least understood topic of any I can think of. To start with, there are more than 350 definitions with more coined by the dozens each month. Leadership training contains as many variants as there are definitions, which is appropriate since the state of that art can most appropriately be called formless.

In order to get closer to understand the artform of leadership, it helps to address the following question: *How do organizations translate intention into reality and sustain it?* Leadership is the major component, though it must be held within a context of organizational factors.

The question of "translating-intention-into-reality" contains complexity and depth, as well as chronic elusiveness. This undoubtedly explains why it tends to be avoided, though it is the essence of what is ordinarily meant to be organizational leadership. Even when it is indirectly touched on, the orchestral richness inherent in the question is bypassed in favor of the doctrinal, predictable and prosaic cliches. Between the blur produced by saying too much at once and the banality which comes from dismissing mysteries, there remains the possibility of articulating just what it is that causes some organizations to translate an intention into reality and sustain it.

The Leader

Important clues about the nature of effective leadership have come out of a study I recently completed of 90 CEOs. These studies provide a basis for generalizing about those "chiefs" who successfully achieved mastery over the noisy, incessant environments, rather than throwing up their hands and living in a perpetual state of "present shock."

What all these effective CEOs shared and embodied was directly related to how they construed their roles. To use a popular distinction, they viewed themselves as leaders, not managers; they were concerned with their organization's basic purposes, why it exists and its general direction. They did not spend time on the "how to," but with purpose and paradigms of action. In short, they were concerned not with "doing things right" (the overriding concern of managers) but with "doing the right thing." They were capable of transforming doubts into the psychological grounds of common purpose.

I found that all the CEOs, in varying degrees, possessed the following competencies:

- *Vision*: the capacity to create and communicate a compelling vision of a desired state of affairs, a vision (or paradigm, context, frame) that induces the commitment and clarity to the vision;
- *Communication and alignment*: the capacity to communicate a vision in order to gain the support of multiple constituencies;
- *Persistence, consistency, focus*: the capacity to maintain the organization's direction, especially when the going gets rough;
- *Empowerment*: the capacity to create environments—the appropriate social architecture—that can tap and harness the energies and abilities necessary to bring about the desired results.

In short, nothing serves an organization better—especially during these times of agonizing doubts and paralyzing ambiguities—than leadership that knows what it wants, communicates those intentions accurately, empowers others and knows how to stay on course and when to change.

49

What It Means to Think Critically

Stephen D. Brookfield

Stephen D. Brookfield is among the foremost commentators and scholars in the field of adult learning. He has been chair of the Adult Education Research Conference and a consultant and workshop leader. Brookfield has written several books, including the award-winning *Understanding and Facilitating Adult Learning*. He has taught in several institutions of higher education in the United States, Great Britain, and Canada, and been associated with the Center for Adult Education at Teacher's College, Columbia University.

The need to develop critical thinkers is currently something of a cause célèbre. The *New York Times* reports that "the public schools have discovered the importance of critical thinking, and many of them are trying to teach children how to do it."[1] Educational journals regularly advertise conferences on critical thinking, and three recent major reports on American education, *Involvement in Learning*,[2] *A Nation at Risk*,[3] and *Higher Education and the American Resurgence*,[4] all call for the development of critical thinkers as a national priority for both civic and economic reasons. Civically, a critically informed populace is seen as more likely to participate in forms of democratic political activity. Economically, a critically active and creative work force is

Stephen D. Brookfield, *Developing Critical Thinkers: Challenging Adults to Explore Alternative Ways to Thinking and Acting* (San Francisco: Jossey-Bass, 1987), pp. 3–14. Reprinted by permission.

seen as the key to American economic resurgence in the face of crippling foreign trade competition. Johnston[5] observes that "it is generally agreed that nothing is more important to the nation's ability to meet the competitive challenge of the future than what Samuel Ehrenhalt[6] of the Department of Labor has termed a 'flexible, adaptable labor force.'" That the message contained in these reports is having some practical effect is evident from case studies of education for critical thinking,[7-9] from special issues being devoted to this topic in such journals as *Phi Delta Kappan* and *National Forum* in 1985, from a flow of grant monies for projects to research applications of critical thinking, and from a recent upsurge in conferences on critical thinking. There have been attempts to propose a new concept described as *critical literacy*[10] and to outline the foundations of a critical pedagogy[11,12] that would foster this capacity. As Sternberg[13] observes, "It would be difficult to read anything at all in the contemporary literature of education without becoming aware of this new interest in teaching critical thinking."

But critical thinking is an activity that can be observed in settings and domains very far removed from the school or college classroom. Indeed, there is no clear evidence that any of the skills of critical thinking learned in schools and colleges have much transferability to the contexts of adult life. Sternberg[13] points out the lack of correspondence between what is required for critical thinking in adulthood and what is taught in school programs intended to develop critical thinking. He writes that "the problems of thinking in the real world do not correspond well with the problems of the large majority of programs that teach critical thinking. We are preparing students to deal with problems that are in many respects unlike those that they will face as adults" (p. 194). In adulthood, we are thinking critically whenever we question why we, or our partners, behave in certain ways within relationships. Critical thinking is evident whenever employees question the appropriateness of a certain technique, mode of production, or organizational form. Managers who are ready to jettison outmoded organizational norms or unwieldy organizational hierarchies, and who are prepared to open up organizational lines of communication in order to democratize the workplace and introduce participatory forms of management, are critical thinkers. Citizens who ask "awkward" questions regarding the activities of local, regional, and national government offices, who call for political leaders to account for their actions, and who are ready to challenge the legitimacy of existing policies and political structures are critical thinkers. Television viewers who are skeptical of the accuracy of media depictions of what are portrayed as "typical" families, or of the neutrality and objectivity of television's reporting of political events, are critical thinkers.

Recognizing Critical Thinking

What characteristics do we look for in critical thinkers? How can we recognize when critical thinking is happening? What are the chief capacities we are trying to encourage when we help people to become critical thinkers? What activities and processes are taking place when people are thinking critically? These questions, and others, are addressed in the nine critical thinking "themes." . . .

1. Critical thinking is a productive and positive activity.

Critical thinkers are actively engaged with life. They see themselves as creating and re-creating aspects of their personal, workplace, and political lives. They appreciate creativity, they are innovators, and they exude a sense that life is full of possibilities. Critical thinkers see the future as open and malleable, not as closed and fixed. They are self-confident about their potential for changing aspects of their worlds, both as individuals and through collective action. Critical thinkers are sometimes portrayed as cynical people who often condemn the efforts of others without contributing anything themselves. Those who hold this view see being critical as somehow antisocial; it is seen as a belittling activity engaged in only by those with false assumptions of superiority. In fact, the opposite is true. When we think critically we become aware of the diversity of values, behaviors, social structures, and artistic forms in the world. Through realizing this diversity, our commitments to our own values, actions, and social structures are informed by a sense of humility; we gain an awareness that others in the world have the same sense of certainty we do—but about ideas, values, and actions that are completely contrary to our own.

2. Critical thinking is a process, not an outcome.

Being critical thinkers entails a continual questioning of assumptions. People can never be in a state of complete critical development. If we ever felt that we had reached a state of fully developed or realized critical awareness, we would be contradicting one of the central tenets of critical thinking— namely, that we are skeptical of any claims to universal truth or total certainty. By its nature, critical thinking can never be finished in some final, static manner.

3. Manifestations of critical thinking vary according to the contexts in which it occurs.

The indicators that reveal whether or not people are thinking critically vary enormously. For some people, the process appears to be almost wholly internal; very few external features of their lives appear to change. With these individuals, we can look for evidence of the critical process in their writing or talking. With others, critical thinking will manifest itself directly and vividly in their external actions. People who renegotiate aspects of their intimate relationships, managers who deliberately depart from their habitual ways of coming to decisions or solving problems, workers who reshape their workplace according to nonhierarchical organizational norms after establishing a worker cooperative, or citizens campaigning for a nuclear freeze after observing the effects of a radiation leak in their community are all examples of how critical thinking can prompt dramatic action.

4. Critical thinking is triggered by positive as well as negative events.

A theme common to many discussions of critical thinking is that this activity usually results from people having experienced traumas or tragedies in their lives. These events, so the argument goes, cause people to question their previously trusted assumptions about how the world works; and this questioning prompts a careful scrutiny of what were previously unquestioned ways of thinking and living. This often happens. It is also true, however, that critical thinking is triggered by a joyful, pleasing, or fulfilling event—a "peak" experience such as falling in love, being unexpectedly successful in some new workplace role, or finding that others place great store by abilities or accomplishments that we exhibit almost without being aware of them. In such circumstances we begin to reinterpret our past actions and ideas from a new vantage point. We begin to wonder if our old assumptions about our roles, personalities, and abilities were completely accurate. We begin to be aware of and to explore new possibilities with our intimates, at our workplace, and in our political involvements.

5. Critical thinking is emotive as well as rational.

Critical thinking is sometimes regarded as a kind of pure, ascetic cognitive activity above and beyond the realm of feeling and emotions. In fact, emotions are central to the critical thinking process. As we try to think critically and help others to do so, we cannot help but become aware of the importance of emotions to this activity. Asking critical questions about our previously accepted values, ideas, and behaviors is anxiety-producing. We may well feel fearful of the consequences that might arise from contemplating alternatives to our current ways of thinking and living; resistance, resentment, and confusion are evident at various stages in the critical thinking process. But we also feel joy, release, relief, and exhilaration as we break through to new ways of looking at our personal, work, and political worlds. As we abandon assumptions that had been inhibiting our development, we experience a sense of liberation. As we realize that we have the power to change aspects of our lives, we are charged with excitement. As we realize these changes, we feel a pleasing sense of self-confidence. Critical thinkers and helpers ignore these emotions at their peril.

Components of Critical Thinking

1. Identifying and challenging assumptions is central to critical thinking.

Trying to identify the assumptions that underlie the ideas, beliefs, values, and actions that we (and others) take for granted is central to critical thinking. Once these assumptions are identified, critical thinkers examine their accuracy and validity. They ask awkward questions concerning whether the taken-for-granted, common-sense ideas about how we are supposed to organize our workplaces, act in our intimate relationships, become politically involved, and view television fit the realities of our lives. They are open to jettisoning old assumptions when these are clearly inappropriate (for example, "Workers are there to work, not to think"; "Decisions made by executive directors, parents, and presidents are infallible and inviolable"; "Women should be kept barefoot and pregnant") and to search for new assumptions that fit more closely their experiences of the world.

2. Challenging the importance of context is crucial to critical thinking.

When we are aware of how hidden and uncritically assimilated assumptions are important to shaping our habitual perceptions, understandings, and interpretations of the world, and to influencing the behaviors that result from these interpretations, we become aware of how context influences thoughts and actions. Critical thinkers are aware that practices, structures, and actions are never context-free. What we regard as appropriate ways of organizing the workplace, of behaving toward our intimates, of acting politically, and of viewing television reflect the culture and time in which we live. In realizing this, critical thinkers are contextually aware.

3. Critical thinkers try to imagine and explore alternatives.

Central to critical thinking is the capacity to imagine and explore alternatives to existing ways of thinking and living. Realizing that so many ideas and actions spring from assumptions that might be inappropriate for their lives, critical thinkers are continually exploring new ways of thinking about aspects of their lives. Being aware of how context shapes what they consider normal and natural ways of thinking and living, critical thinkers realize that in other contexts entirely different norms of organizing the workplace, behaving politically, interpreting media, and living in relationships are considered ordinary. These contexts are scrutinized for assumptions that might be adopted and integrated into their own lives.

4. Imagining and exploring alternatives leads to reflective skepticism.

When we realize that alternatives to supposedly fixed belief systems, habitual behaviors, and entrenched social structures always exist, we become skeptical of claims to universal truth or to ultimate explanations. In short, we exhibit what might be called *reflective skepticism*. People who are reflectively skeptical do not take things as read. Simply because a practice or structure has existed for a long time does not mean that it is the most appropriate for *all* time, or even for this moment. Just because an idea is accepted by everyone else does not mean that we have to believe in its innate truth without first checking its correspondence with reality as we experience it. Just because a chief executive officer, executive director, prime minister, president, religious leader, or parent says something is right or good does not make it so. Critical thinkers become immediately suspicious of those who say they have the answers to all of life's problems. They are wary of the management consultant who argues that "if only you will buy my training package and follow these steps to executive development, your executives will double the company's output in the next fiscal quarter." They distrust the educator who purports to have a curriculum or model of teaching appropriate for all learners or subjects. They scrutinize carefully the therapist or counselor who argues that he or she has discovered the key to resolving difficulties within intimate relationships.

How Others Contribute to Critical Thinking

On a very personal level, practically all adults function in some way as critical thinkers. At some time or another, most people decide that some aspect of their lives is unsatisfactory, and decide of their own volition to change this. Such self-initiated changes are often (though not always) connected to externally imposed crises. Being fired or suffering crippling mental or physical disability is not something we choose to happen. When an intimate relationship dissolves, or a loved one dies, several reactions are possible. We may be thrown into an apathetic resignation to these changed circumstances, or we may deny this disappearance of a previously stable element in our life. We may well fluctuate between periods of acceptance of, and flight from, these changes. Energy alternates with apathy as we first scramble to deny or forget the changes forced upon us, and then become aware of their overwhelming reality. The rollercoaster turbulence of these changes is tiring and debilitating, and we describe ourselves as exhausted, burned out, or finished.

As people try to make sense of these externally imposed changes, they are frequently at teachable moments as far as the process of becoming critical thinkers is concerned. As people begin to look critically at their past values, common-sense ideas, and habitual behaviors, they begin the precarious business of contemplating new self-images, perspectives, and actions. Skilled helpers can support these first tentative stages in critical thought by listening empathetically to people's "travelers' tales" of their journeys into unexplored personal and political territories. Helpers act as sounding boards, providing reactions to people's experiences, pleasures, and anxieties. They help to make connections between apparently disparate occurrences and assist people in reflecting on the reasons for their actions and reactions. They encourage people to identify the assumptions underlying their behaviors, choices, and decisions. They help clients, learners, friends, and colleagues to recognize aspects of their situations that are of their own making and hence open to being changed by an act of will. They encourage skepticism of anyone claiming to have "the answer." They help people to realize that while actions are shaped by context, context can be altered to be more congruent with people's desires.

When helpers and educators work in these ways, they are encouraging critical thinking. Critical thinking is complex and frequently perplexing, since it requires the suspension of belief and the jettisoning of assumptions previously accepted without question. As people strive for clarity in self-understanding, and as they try to change aspects of their lives, the opportunity to discuss these activities is enormously helpful. By providing an opportunity for reflection and analysis, educators and other helpers, such as counselors, therapists, trainers, and friends, are crucial. They are sympathizers, empathizers, reactors, devil's advocates, initiators, and prompters. They help people to articulate and understand the assumptions underlying their actions. In short, they assist people to become critical thinkers.

Concepts of Critical Thinking

Phrases such as *critical thinking, critical analysis, critical awareness, critical consciousness,* and *critical reflection* are exhortatory, heady, and often conveniently vague. We can justify almost any action with a learner, client, friend, or colleague by claiming that it assists the process of critical thinking. Haranguing a friend who feels satisfied with life, forcing a learner to view things the way we do, and requiring that lovers re-evaluate their relationship or that colleagues change their work patterns may all be claimed (inaccurately) as examples of facilitating critical thinking. Central to developing critical thinkers must be some minimal level of consent on the part of those involved. Trying to force people to analyze critically the assumptions under which they have been thinking and living is likely to serve no function other than intimidating them to the point where resistance builds up against this process. We can, however, try to awaken, prompt, nurture, and encourage this process without making people feel threatened or patronized. These are the skills of critical helpers.

As a concept, critical thinking has been interpreted in a variety of ways. It has been equated with the development of logical reasoning abilities,[14,15] with the application of reflective judgment,[16] with assumption hunting,[17] and with the creation, use, and testing of meaning.[18] Ennis[19] lists twelve aspects of critical thinking, which include analytical and argumentative capacities such as recognizing ambiguity in reasoning, identifying contradictions in arguments, and ascertaining the empirical soundness of generalized conclusions. D'Angelo[20] specifies ten attitudes that are necessary conditions for being critical, including curiosity, flexibility, skepticism, and honesty. As the central component of critical thinking, O'Neill[21] proposes the ability to distinguish bias from reason and fact from opinion. To Halpern,[22] critical thought is a rational and purposeful attempt to use thought in moving toward a future goal.

Critical thinking is generally conceptualized as an intellectual ability suitable for development by those involved in higher education.[7,9,23,24] Empirical studies of the development of critical thinking capacities focus on young adults[16,25] or college students.[26,27] While this setting for critical thinking is undoubtedly crucial, it is but one of the many settings in which critical thinking is practiced, particularly in adult life. This book takes the concepts of critical thinking, analysis, and reflection out of the classroom and places them firmly in the contexts of adults' lives—in their relationships, at their workplaces, in their political involvements, and in their reactions to mass media of communication. Critical thinking is not seen as a wholly rational, mechanical activity. Emotive aspects—feelings, emotional responses, intuitions, sensing—are central to critical thinking in adult life. In particular, the ability to imagine alternatives to one's current ways of thinking and living is one that often entails a deliberate break with rational modes of thought in order to prompt forward leaps in creativity.

One alternative interpretation of the concept of critical thinking is that of *emancipatory learning*. The idea of emancipatory learning is derived from the work of Habermas,[28] who distinguished this as one of the three domains of learning (technical and communicative learning being the other two). As interpreted by adult educators,[29-31] emancipatory learning is evident in learners becoming aware of the forces that have brought them to their current situations and taking action to change some aspect of these situations. To Apps, "emancipatory learning is that which frees people from personal, institutional, or environmental forces that prevent them from seeing new directions, from gaining control of their lives, their society and their world."[31]

A second concept closely related to that of critical thinking is *dialectical thinking*. Dialectical thinking is viewed as a particular form of critical thinking that focuses on the understanding and resolution of contradictions. Morgan[32] writes that "dialectical analysis (thus) shows us that the management of organization, of society, and of personal life ultimately involves the management of contradiction." As proposed by Riegel[33] and Basseches,[34] dialectical thinking is thinking in which elements of relativistic thought (for example, "Morality can be understood only in the context of the culture concerned") are fused with elements of universalistic thought (for example, "Moral conduct is recognizable in any society by certain innate features"). Dialectical thinkers engage in a continual process of making judgments about aspects of their lives, identifying the general rules implicit in these judgments, modifying the original judgments in light of the appropriateness of these general rules, and so on. To Deshler,[35] "dialectical thinking is thinking which looks for, recognizes, and welcomes contradictions as a stimulus to development." Change is regarded as the fundamental reality, forms and structures are perceived as temporary, relationships are held to involve developmental transformations, and openness is welcomed. Hence, we are involved in a constant process of trying to create order in the world—to discover what elements are missing from our existing ordering and to create new orderings that include these. Daloz[36] echoes this idea in his belief that dialectical thinking "presumes change rather than a static notion of 'reality.' As each assertion is de-rived from the one before, truth is always emergent, never fixed; relative, not absolute."

Being a critical thinker involves more than cognitive activities such as log-ical reasoning or scrutinizing arguments for assertions unsupported by empiri-cal evidence. Thinking critically involves our recognizing the assumptions underlying our beliefs and behaviors. It means we can give justifications for our ideas and actions. Most important, perhaps, it means we try to judge the rationality of these justifications. We can do this by comparing them to a range of varying interpretations and perspectives. We can think through, pro-ject, and anticipate the consequences of those actions that are based on these justifications. And we can test the accuracy and rationality of these justifica-tions against some kind of objective analysis of the "real" world as we under-stand it.

Critical thinking, then, involves a reflective dimension. The idea of *reflec-tive learning* is a third concept closely related to that of critical thinking. Boyd and Fales[37] define reflective learning as "the *process* of internally examining and exploring an issue of concern, triggered by an experience, which creates and clarifies meaning in terms of self, and which results in a changed concep-tual perspective." Boud, Keogh, and Walker[38] view reflection as "a generic term for those intellectual and affective activities in which individuals engage to explore their experiences in order to lead to new understandings and ap-preciation." To Schlossberg,[39] the outcome of these activities is "a change in assumptions about oneself and the world" requiring "a corresponding change in one's behavior and relationships."

Conclusion

Critical thinking is a lived activity, not an abstract academic pastime. It is something we all do, though its frequency, and the credibility we grant it, vary from person to person. Our lives are sufficiently complex and perplexing that it would be difficult to escape entirely from feeling that at times the world is not working the way we thought it was supposed to, or that there must be other ways of living. . . . The capacity for critical thinking [is] at the heart of what it means to be a developed person living in a democratic society. I argue that the ability to think critically is crucial to understanding our personal rela-tionships, envisioning alternative and more productive ways of organizing the workplace, and becoming politically literate.

50

Common Views of Organizations

Lee G. Bolman and Terrence E. Deal

Lee G. Bolman has served as lecturer on education at the Harvard Graduate School of Education. His primary research interests have been in leadership and organizational behavior. Terrence E. Deal is professor of education at Peabody College of Vanderbilt University. Bolman and Deal serve as co-directors of the National Center for Educational Leadership. They have co-authored *Modern Approaches to Understanding and Managing Organizations* and *Reframing Organizations*.

The difficulties of managing organizations have been well documented and widely recognized. Organizations do not change when we want them to, yet they change rapidly when we wish they would not. They control and stifle with red tape, rigid rules, and bureaucratic lethargy but seem unable to control waste, inefficiency, and misdirected effort. Organizations have huge appetites and can swallow almost unlimited resources but often produce disappointing results. A substantial slice of organizational resources goes to employees in the form of salary, benefits, and perquisites, yet employees are frequently more discontented and apathetic than committed and satisfied.

Solving such organizational problems—and many others—is the appoint-

Lee G. Bolman and Terrence E. Deal, *Modern Approaches to Understanding and Managing Organizations* (San Francisco: Jossey-Bass, 1984), pp. 1–7. Reprinted by permission.

ed task of a special group called managers. To assist them in this awesome task, aspiring managers are armed with decision trees, PERT charts, consultants, management information systems, "management by objectives" programs, and a panoply of theories and rational techniques. Managers go forth with this arsenal to tame the wild and savage social creations that we mundanely call "organizations." Yet in the end it is often the beast who wins. Defeated and battle-scarred managers retreat to management seminars and universities for tools that may give them a better chance in the next encounter. Often, they are mystified by what went wrong and seek some way to avoid the same mistakes or, at least, to face the same old problems with more confidence and less trauma.

Theories of Organization

The dominance of economic and governmental activity by large organizations is a relatively recent development. It is only in the last twenty-five years that social scientists have devoted significant time and attention to studying organizations and developing ideas about how they work (or why they often fail to work). Within the social sciences, major schools of thought have evolved, each with its own view of organizations, its own well-defended concepts and assumptions, and its own ideas about how managers can best bring social collectives under control.

Rational systems theorists emphasize organizational goals, roles, and technology. They look for ways to develop organizational structures that best fit organizational purpose and the demands of the environment.

Human resource theorists emphasize the interdependence between people and organizations. They focus on ways to develop a better fit between people's needs, skills, and values and the formal roles and relationships required to accomplish collective goals and purposes.

Political theorists see power, conflict, and the distribution of scarce resources as the central issues in organizations. They suggest that organizations are very like jungles and that managers need to understand and manage power, coalitions, bargaining, and conflict.

Symbolic theorists focus on problems of meaning in organizations. They are more likely to find serendipitous virtue in organizational misbehavior and to focus on the limits of managers' abilities to create organizational cohesion through power or rational design. In this view, managers must rely on images, luck, and sometimes the supernatural to bring some semblance of order to organizations.

We summarize these schools at this point only to contrast their basic differences. Each body of theory purports to be based on a scientific foundation—but each is also a theology that offers scripture and preaches its own version of the gospel to modern managers. Each gospel tells them what organizations are like, and each has a vision of how they should be. Each provides a range of ideas and techniques to make organizations better. A modern manager wanting to do better and understand more is consistently confronted with a cacophony of different voices and visions.

Examples of this division and diversity are numerous. A manager of a large corporation recently called several university-based consultants for help in dealing with turnover among middle managers. "It's obvious," said one. "You are probably neglecting your managers' needs for autonomy and opportunities to participate in important decisions. You need an attitude survey to pinpoint the problems."

Another consultant offered different advice. "When did you last reorganize? As your firm has grown, managers' responsibilities have probably become blurred and overlapping. When reporting relationships are confused, you get stress and conflict. You need to restructure."

Still another consultant called attention to the company's recent collective bargaining experience. "What do you expect? You've given up basic management prerogatives. If you want managers to stay, you'll have to get back to the table and fight to restore their power. Why the hell did you give away the store to the unions?"

A final call yielded one more opinion: "Your company has never developed a strong value system, and growth has made the situation worse. Your managers don't find any meaning in their work. You need to revitalize your company culture."

We call this state of organizational consulting—and of organization theory—"conceptual pluralism." . . . We will not join the battle over which school of thought is better or more valuable for managers. We do not believe that managers have to choose the strongest voice or to visit a succession of organizational gurus in order to obtain a more comprehensive view. Instead, we advocate the use of diverse outlooks to obtain a more comprehensive understanding of organizations and a broader range of options for managerial action.

Theories as Frames

We have consolidated the major schools of organizational thought into four relatively coherent perspectives. We have chosen the label "frames" to characterize these different vantage points. Frames are windows on the world. Frames filter out some things while allowing others to pass through easily. Frames help us to order the world and decide what action to take. Every manager uses a personal frame, or image, of organizations to gather information, make judgments, and get things done.

Understanding organizations is nearly impossible when the manager is unconsciously wed to a single, narrow perspective. Modern organizations are complicated. Think of the complexities and perils in introducing computers into a small elementary school. Consider the difficulties faced by a large, multi-divisional company like Johnson & Johnson as it attempts to integrate more than fifty different, semiautonomous businesses under one corporate roof. Think of the enormous pressures facing managers in "Ma Bell"—the telephone giant that was forced to divest all its local operating companies. Ask yourself how you might try to reduce red tape in government agencies or reform the United States Congress.

Managers in all organizations—large or small, public or private—can increase their effectiveness and their freedom through the use of multiple vantage points. To be locked into a single path is likely to produce error and self-imprisonment. We believe that managers who understand their own frame—and who can adeptly rely on more than one limited perspective—are better equipped to understand and manage the complex everyday world of organizations. Sometimes they can make a significant difference in how that world responds.

The four frames . . . are based on the major schools of organizational research and theory. For each frame, we have provided a label and consolidated the central assumptions and propositions.

The *structural frame* emphasizes the importance of formal roles and relationships. Structures—commonly depicted in organization charts—are created to fit an organization's environment and technology. Organizations allocate responsibilities to participants ("division of labor") and create rules, policies, and management hierarchies to coordinate diverse activities. Problems arise when the structure does not fit the situation. At that point, some form of reorganization is needed to remedy the mismatch.

The *human resource frame* establishes its territory because organizations are inhabited by people. Individuals have needs, feelings, and prejudices. They have both skills and limitations. They have great capacity to learn and a sometimes greater capacity to defend old attitudes and beliefs. From a human resource perspective, the key to effectiveness is to tailor organizations to people—to find an organizational form that will enable people to get the job done while feeling good about what they are doing. Problems arise when human needs are throttled.

The *political frame* views organizations as arenas of scarce resources where power and influence are constantly affecting the allocation of resources among individuals or groups. Conflict is expected because of differences in needs, perspectives, and life-styles among different individuals and groups. Bargaining, coercion, and compromise are all part of everyday organizational life. Coalitions form around specific interests and may change as issues come and go. Problems may arise because power is unevenly distributed or is so broadly dispersed that it is difficult to get anything done. Solutions are developed through political skill and acumen—much as Machiavelli suggested centuries ago.

The *symbolic frame* abandons the assumptions of rationality that appear in each of the other frames and treats the organization as theater or carnival. Organizations are viewed as held together more by shared values and culture than by goals and policies. They are propelled more by rituals, ceremonies, stories, heroes, and myths than by rules, policies, and managerial authority. Organization is drama; the drama engages actors inside, and outside audiences form impressions based on what they see occurring on-stage. Problems arise when actors play their parts badly, when symbols lose their meaning, when ceremonies and rituals lose their potency. Improvements come through symbol, myth, and magic.

Each frame has its own vision of reality. Only when managers can look at organizations through the four are they likely to appreciate the depth and complexity of organizational life. Successful managers rely intuitively on the different frames, blending them into a coherent, pragmatic, personal theory of organizations. We believe that an explicit introduction to and grounding in all four frames can enrich any manager's native intuition. Success becomes possible even for the great majority of us who were not born with the ability to understand and act effectively in such a complicated and ambiguous world.

Learning the Frames

For the past five years, we have taught the four frames to managers in a variety of situations. Our primary setting has been a required introductory course for doctoral students at Harvard's Graduate School of Education. But we have also taught public-sector managers at the Kennedy School of Government and in summer institutes and private-sector managers in university programs and in corporate seminars.

Our experience across these diverse settings has taught us several things about people who manage organizations (at least, those with whom we have had the opportunity to work).

1. Most managers have relatively limited views of organizations. Generally, they are likely to diagnose most organizational problems as caused by the defects of particular individuals or groups. Although the causes of problems are often seen as personal, the solutions are often rational: restructuring, rational discourse, the use of facts and logic as a basis for influence.

2. A majority of the people we work with have had very powerful negative experiences in organizations. For many, the frustrations of organizational life have outweighed the satisfactions. Attempts to improve organizations have often ended in failure and disillusionment. Feelings of cynicism and impotence are widespread.

3. When we introduce the four frames, people often respond with initial confusion. The frames seem to contradict one another; there is no right answer. Exploration of this issue often produces tension and conflict.

4. As people become more comfortable with the frames and have an opportunity to apply them—particularly in important, real-world situations—they report a liberating feeling of choice and power. They are much better able to understand what is happening around them. Sometimes they are able to develop effective ideas of how things might be changed. They are less often surprised and more often able to predict what will happen.

Our experience encourages us to believe that the frames have a wider audience than the participants in our courses and seminars. The frames can be helpful to any manager—senior executives in large corporations, hospital administrators, agency heads, and junior high assistant principals. They can even help in many of the informal settings of daily life—bridge clubs, sororities and fraternities, marriages, country fairs, or therapy groups. The nature of the setting and an individual's place in the setting will influence the specific application of the ideas.

51

Choosing a Fundamental Change Strategy

Richard Beckhard and Wendy Pritchard

Richard Beckhard is considered one of the founders of the field of organizational development. He spent much of his career at the Sloan School at the Massachusetts Institute of Technology. He has authored numerous books and articles; his contributions to the field were recognized in 1984 when a paper prize was established in his name. Wendy Pritchard is an occupational psychologist who has worked for Rank Xerox (UK), Shell International Petroleum Company and served as board director for Wolff Olins. She currently runs her own consulting practice in London.

Forces Requiring Fundamental Change

The world in which we live and will live, and the environment in which organizations will operate, are without precedent. Although the elements are the same, the pace and complexity of changes to new forms, ways of living, and values are of an order of magnitude never before experienced. Changes in the political landscape and new relationships between the First World and the Third World are redefining the marketplace, the means of production, and the location of human, financial, and technical resources.

Richard Beckhard and Wendy Pritchard, *Changing the Essence: The Art of Creating and Leading Fundamental Change in Organizations* (San Francisco: Jossey-Bass Publishers, 1992), pp. 1–8. Reprinted by permission.

The explosion of technology in communications and information has indeed created one world in which transactions take a microsecond, and news travels as fast as it can be reported. Worldwide changes in social values, such as concern for the environment, the role of women in society, and the role of wealth-producing organizations, all define the environment in which organizations function.

This environment is making unprecedented demands on organizational leaders, who have the task and responsibility of determining both the functioning and the future of their organizations. This "white water" turbulence is forcing most leaders to examine the very essence of their organizations— their basic purposes, their identities, and their relationships with customers, competitors, and suppliers.

The assumptions that guided organizations in the past were (1) that they could control their own destinies and (2) that they operated in a relatively stable and predictable environment. These assumptions are challenged in today's world by, for example, the vulnerability of even the largest organizations to takeovers and recession, the changing nature of industries, and the increased concern with social issues such as protecting the physical environment.

To respond effectively to these demands, chief executives must rethink their own priorities and behavior. Competitive supremacy will be a function not only of increased profits and performance, but of the organization's capacity to innovate, learn, respond quickly, and design the appropriate infrastructure to meet demands and to have maximum control over its own destiny.

For this to occur, top leaders will need to reduce their personal "hands-on" involvement in current operations and replace it with management systems and structures. Leaders must focus on taking the organization into the future. This means developing a vision of the desired future state of the enterprise, creating management structures and systems to achieve this state, and providing personal leadership in directing the process of managing the dynamics of both the organization and its interfaces with its environment.

The management journalist Christopher Lorenz wrote in a recent *London Financial Times* article: "Under relentless pressure from competitors and costs, and egged on by management gurus such as Tom Peters who preach that 'the only constant thing today is change,' virtually every self-respecting large European and American company these days is running at least one 'organization-wide change programme.' . . . Many of these ambitious, but varied, efforts will either fail entirely, or have a short-term impact and then die.

For the management of change is a much more challenging and multi-faceted process than most companies realize."[1]

It is our conviction that for a change effort to move an organization into the future, the process (see Figure 1) must involve an understanding of the outside forces that require business decisions for change, such as going global, becoming customer driven rather than technology driven, or becoming service oriented rather than product focused. All these kinds of business decisions have such profound consequences for the organization that the essence of the organization must change. The topic of this . . . [selection] is the creation and leadership of changes to the essence of organizations, a process that we have called *fundamental change*.

Choosing a Fundamental Change Strategy

In considering the forces for change, the business decisions to be made, and their organizational consequences, leaders need to choose between treating the change in an incremental and linear way or in a fundamental, systems-based, and diagnostic way.

If an incremental change strategy is chosen, it is likely to deal with "first things first" and to make the necessary changes in sequential order. If a fundamental change strategy is chosen, the implications for the organization are that the organization itself, its parts, and their relationships will simultaneously change. The subparts of the organization must be committed to change and have action plans in place that fit the constellation of changes needed and that are aligned with the leaders' vision of an end state.

FIGURE 1
Fundamental Change Model.

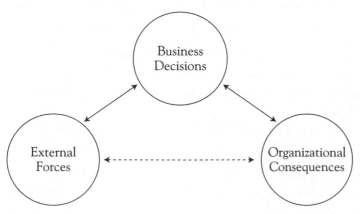

Characteristics of a Fundamental Change Strategy

The leaders of the organization must have a clear vision of the desired end state of the entire system, including such dimensions as its business, its organization, and its ways of working. This vision must be used as a common context both for diagnosing the need for changes and for managing the process of change, so that it acts as an integrating force for the multitude of apparently disparate changes to be made. The plan for making the changes must be an integrated one.

An integral part of a fundamental change strategy must be a conscious decision to move to a learning mode, where both learning and doing are equally valued. This is an essential precondition for managing fundamental change effectively and is also a fundamental change in its own right. A further essential ingredient is a clear commitment by top leaders to making a significant personal investment in developing and building commitment to an inspirational vision, and to examining and using their own time and behavior in ways that are congruent with this vision.

Many leaders have responded to outside forces by developing an immediate action plan to effect changes. It is not "natural" for dynamic leaders to respond to pressures by saying, "Let's stop and look at where we want to be, let's see how that is different from where we are now, and let's make a plan to get there."

A Shift from an Incremental to a Fundamental Change Strategy

A chief executive officer (CEO) of a multibillion-dollar financial organization doing business worldwide was discussing with one of us some deep concerns about business strategy. His "products" were almost identical to those of key competitors. He was concerned that his company was losing market share in several markets as a result of a number of factors, including:

- Aggressive marketing strategies and practices of competitors
- Customer resistance to changing buying habits
- Lack of organizational capacity to respond quickly to changes in the business environment
- Inconsistency in management philosophy and practices among top managers around the world

The organization had been developed through a series of mergers with other companies and therefore it had a patchwork culture. The organizational design, a country-based central management, was organized around the creation of financial products and the development and installation of the systems needed to support their delivery. The products were issued by financial institutions.

The chief executive had concluded that to penetrate other markets effectively, the design of the organization would have to change from one centrally directed organization to strong, highly autonomous regional organizations. The central management would resemble a holding company and would be required to develop partnerships with regional management.

From his analysis of the change needed, the CEO had posed the following urgent questions:

- How should authority be distributed between regional managements and the center?
- How should policies such as pricing and marketing strategy be determined?
- How should authority be divided between central staff functions that created products and the decision to use them?
- What impact would structural change have on information management, financial management, and human resource policies?

To respond to these questions, he and his colleagues had developed a strategy. The first step was to appoint and brief the regional executives, then to establish local headquarters and divide roles and responsibilities. Management would determine policies affecting the adoption and use of products by the regions, while at the same time producing a new information management system to ensure that information requirements were successfully met.

To implement this strategy, the management group had developed a timetable that would put regional executives in place within three months, with the rest following as soon as possible.

After describing the change strategy and plan, the CEO paused and reflected that he still had an uneasy feeling that something was not quite right about management's thinking and plans. How quickly could he expect this change to have positive effects on the business? How would be measure success?

The consultant with whom he was working raised a series of questions:

- Did the CEO have a clear vision of what the company would look like in five years' time? What businesses would it be in? Where would it be and how would it be positioned?

- If he had such a vision, was it known, understood, and supported by key staff?
- Had he done an analysis of what would have to be changed to move the organization from its present state to its envisaged state?
- Had he explored the interrelationships between the questions he himself had raised?
- What were the benefits of a region acting autonomously and owning its own resources compared to those of a centrally managed information resource?
- What was the relationship between the staff function of creating products and the regional authority to determine appropriate products?
- Should the basic relationship between regions and the center be that of financial borrower and lender or that of an independent business joined in a network with a central executive?

After considerable thought and discussion, the CEO declared that he felt it was necessary to rethink the situation. He would have to go "back to the drawing board" with his senior colleagues and produce a vision statement that clearly defined what the business and organization should look like in three years. Using this vision, the management group would be able to look at what in the organization needed changing and what interrelationships, policies, and systems would have to be developed.

He also decided that he and his senior colleagues would have to develop a dedicated structure to manage these changes. He accepted that this structure would not be the same as the structure for managing the day-to-day operations.

In [the above] example, the CEO's main insight was that an incremental change strategy based on action and reaction would not produce the results he wanted over time. What he needed was a more diagnostic approach to the constellation of issues that was involved and an integrated plan to move the organization where he wanted it to be.

He had recognized that there was a relationship between outside pressures (poor competitive position and market share) and his business response (a more aggressive business strategy), as well as a need for some organizational changes (regionalizing to carry out the business strategy), but had approached these elements in a linear, incremental way rather than looking at them as an integrated whole. What he had not realized was the importance of considering the organizational consequences of his business decision as much more complex clusters of changes.

His *revised* plan was, first, to recognize his personal responsibility to look at a "whole-picture" view of the relationships and connections between the outside demand for change and what the business needed to become. This would be the context for his business decisions and organizational change strategy. He also realized that he needed to establish an integrated way to manage the process of making the changes effectively.

Diagnosing Changes

The first step in the process of mounting fundamental change is an adequate diagnosis. This involves an analysis of the present reality, including the demands of the environment and the organization's capacity to respond to these demands, and the development of a clear vision of the changed state after the change effort has taken place.

We believe that this diagnostic approach is better than an action approach in managing fundamental change; that is, the vision is used as a guide to determining what should change, rather than today's presenting symptoms being triggers for action.

Designing an Integrated Management Strategy

A change of this magnitude cannot be described as a single change: in reality it is a constellation of changes that are both discrete and interdependent and that must be managed simultaneously. Success in managing fundamental change includes moving the organization to a mode in which learning and improving the quality of performance are equally valued.

52

Visionary Leadership

Marshall Sashkin

Marshall Sashkin holds a doctorate in organizational psychology from the University of Michigan and teaches as adjunct professor at George Washington University. For several years his primary assignment has been in the U.S. Department of Education's Office of Educational Research and Improvement, where he developed and guided applied research aimed at improving leadership and organization in schools. His most recent book (with Kenneth Kizer) is *Putting Total Quality Management to Work*.

To some, history is the story of great leaders. Throughout the first half of this century, most managers and scholars probably accepted the basic premises of the "great person" theory of leadership. But, by the late 1940s, studies at Harvard, in human relations and group dynamics, had shown that only a small proportion of leaders actually fit this theory. Subsequent theories of leadership centered on behavior; perhaps if one were to act like a great leader, the act would become real. As we began to understand how leaders behaved, perhaps it was reasonable to train people to act that way.

But the next 30 years of research failed to yield substantial evidence that

Reprinted from Marshall Sashkin, "Visionary Leadership" The Perspective from Education," in *Contemporary Issues in Leadership*, 2d. Ed., William E. Rosenbach and Robert L. Taylor, eds., 1989, by permission of Westview Press, Boulder, Colorado.

leaders who behaved in a task-directed manner, while simultaneously be-having in a relationship-directed manner, were especially successful or "great." Thus, researchers turned to situational factors in the hope of finding that different behavioral approaches would be effective for different situations. Although these situational or "continuing" approaches were somewhat more successful in helping to guide managers, they did little to improve our understanding of top-level, creative leadership. Researchers were still at a loss to explain outstanding leadership at the top—leadership characterized by vision.

My theory of effective executive leadership, or visionary leadership, considers not only the leader's personal characteristics, not only the leader's behavior, and not only the situation; it considers all three. Only by looking at each of these factors as they relate to one another can we truly understand visionary leadership. Visionary leaders share certain characteristics that are different from the personality traits on which early leadership research was focused. In addition, they have a deep, basic awareness of key situational factors that dictate what leadership approach and actions are required. Furthermore, these leaders not only know what behaviors are required, they can also carry out those behaviors.

Visionary Leadership in Action

There are three major aspects to visionary leadership. The first consists of constructing a vision, creating an ideal image of the organization and its culture. The second involves defining an organizational philosophy that succinctly states the vision and developing programs and policies that put the philosophy into practice within the organization's unique context and culture. The third aspect centers on the leaders' own practices, the specific actions in which leaders engage on a one-to-one basis in order to create and support their visions.

Visioning: Creating a Cultural Ideal

The process of conceiving a vision calls for certain cognitive skills. Central to the ability to conceive a vision is the ability to think in terms of a period of time, that is, not just in terms of daily or weekly goals but in terms of actions carried out over a period of years. Elliott Jaques[1] has shown that there are reliable differences among individuals in terms of the span of time over which they think and work. Effective executive leaders must, according to Jaques, be able to think clearly, to "vision," over periods of at least 5 years and, more often, 10 years or longer. In more recent work, Jaques[2] has constructed a theory of cognitive development, based on Piagetian concepts, specifying in detail the series of hierarchical cognitive tasks required to construct visions over increasingly long spans of time. But whether one is involved in creating a 10-year or 10-week vision, the ability to do so involves four distinct actions, each requiring certain thinking skills.

The first such cognitive skill is in *expressing* the vision—behaving in a way that advances the goal of the vision. Consider the case of a manufacturer's chief executive who wishes to create a plant-level operation to involve all employees in managing the firm. To make this vision real, the CEO must be able to perform these steps:

- write a proposed set of policy actions that would create a plant-level worker involvement program;
- meet with relevant parties—plant-level managers as well as workers—to develop a document detailing the new policy and program;
- meet with, and arrange meetings of, all plant-level managers and all employees to review and revise the program and to plan for its implementation;
- work with relevant managers to identify ways to track the program's effects and effectiveness; and
- oversee the monitoring of the program and work with relevant parties on any further modifications needed.

Leaders must understand and express by their behavior the sequence of actions to be taken to make a vision real.

The second important thinking skill is *explaining* the vision to others—making the nature of the vision clear in terms of its required action steps and its aims. Let us return to the example of the CEO who envisions worker involvement at the plant level. The CEO who can express this vision still may not succeed in implementing it unless he or she can clearly explain to others the steps involved in carrying it out. Unless the CEO can clearly explain the vision to the program manager, uncertainty will arise as to the steps and handling of problems and issues. And unless the CEO can explain the program to plant managers, their support for the vision will fade as the CEO loses touch with the day-to-day program details (as is inevitable for any chief executive). Explaining involves more than mere restatement of the vision's nature or aim. The visionary leader must be able to describe how the actions required for the vision link together until, step by step, the goal is reached.

The third required thinking skill is *extending* the vision—applying the sequence of activities to a variety of situations so that the vision can be implemented in several ways and places. To continue with the above example, the CEO will probably, at some point, wish to extend the vision to other parts of the organization. This might mean working with the program manager to revise the worker involvement plan and apply it to the headquarters staff departments as well as to the plant. Doing so will call for changes in how the program is implemented and may even require alterations in the worker involvement program itself. The expressed vision is an important frame of reference, but the visionary leader must be able to adapt it to varied circumstances, as required. Again, he or she must be able to explain these changes to others and to demonstrate the steps necessary to carry them out.

The fourth thinking skill involves *expanding* the vision—applying it not just in one limited way, and not even in a variety of similar ways, but in many different ways and in a broad range of circumstances. The CEO who has a vision of worker involvement at the operating level, and who goes about implementing this vision in the manner outlined above, still may not be a visionary leader. The true visionary leader will also have the conceptual skill needed to look at the overall plan and effects of worker involvement in the organization. This means more than extending the program to another unit. The visionary leader will think through the effects of the worker involvement vision throughout the organization, consider different ways the program might be spread (for example, unit by unit, or by divisions), and speculate about how to "revise" the entire organization in consistence with the new employee involvement system.

Just about anyone can carry out the four skills of visioning—expressing, explaining, extending, and expanding—with respect to short-range visions—those implemented in a day, a week, or a month. Many individuals can do this over time spans as long as a year. Few people, however, can do so over periods of 1 to 3 years, and fewer still can vision over periods of 5 to 10 years. The person who can think through a vision over a time span of 10 to 20 years is the rare, visionary leader.

In addition to these thinking skills, visionary leaders must also possess the personal conviction that what they do can make a difference. Without this belief these actions would be no more than "going through the motions." Nor will their efforts suffice or their visions endure unless those visionary leaders desire and can use power and influence in positive ways, so that followers are "empowered" to carry out the leaders' visions.[3,4]

Implementing the Vision Organizationally

Elsewhere I have detailed the process by which visionary leaders turn their cultural ideals into organizational realities.[5,6] The most important part of this process is creating an explicit organizational philosophy and then enacting that philosophy by means of specific policies and programs. The specific statement of the philosophy is best developed by the leader and his or her key subordinates. In this manner, the visionary leader begins the process of implementing the vision with a strong base of support from the key actors in the system. The statement of philosophy must then be put into practice by means of actual, operational policies and programs. That is, the philosophy must be articulated through action, not just words. Deal[7] offered some insight as to how this process of articulating the vision takes place. He spoke of identifying heroes, of creating rituals and ceremonies, and of telling stories that support and strengthen the philosophy—and the values behind it—and that make more visible the policies and programs derived from the philosophy. Deal also noted that this process is best accomplished if the visionary leader can identify an "informal network of cultural players"—informal advisers (or even just gossips) and secretaries, for example—who, in effect, preside over the organization's culture, serve as key links to the community, and are keepers of the organization's history. These are the keys to organizational implementation of the leader's vision.

Implementing the Vision Through Personal Practices

Finally, effective visionary leaders put their visions into practice by means of their own specific interpersonal behaviors on a one-to-one basis. Warren Bennis[8,9] studied 90 exceptionally effective CEOs and identified several sets of characteristics common to many of these visionary leaders. Based on this work I defined five specific behavior categories.[6,10–12] These behaviors have since proven to be strongly associated with organizational performance.[13]

The first category of behavior consists of focusing others' attention on key issues—helping people grasp, understand, and become committed to the leader's vision. A second group of behaviors is centered on effective communication: listening for understanding, rephrasing to clarify, giving constructive feedback (e.g., being descriptive and not evaluative, being specific and not general), and summarizing when appropriate. These behaviors are easy to describe, but they take tremendous skill to perform.

The third behavior category concerns consistency and trustworthiness. Bennis found that outstanding CEOs exhibited consistent behavior. They did not ever flip-flop on their positions; it was always clear where they stood on issues. People might not agree with the leader, but they could trust that what the leader said was, in fact, what was really meant. Visionary leaders do not shift their positions with every shift in the political winds.

Displaying respect for self and others is the fourth type of visionary leadership behavior and is similar in essence to what Carl Rogers called "unconditional positive regard." Leaders must start with self-respect because they cannot really care about others without caring first about themselves. Visionary executive leaders are self-assured, certain of their abilities. This trait is not manifested in an arrogant or superior attitude, but in a simple display of self-confidence. This sense of self-respect, of confidence in themselves and their abilities, comes across not only in leaders' attitudes but also in how they treat others. One of the characteristics of visionary leaders is that we feel good around them because they boost our sense of self-worth by paying attention to us, by trusting us, by sharing ideas with us, by making it clear how important we are as persons. They tell us we are important—"I really value your ability to do that, John; we need you"—and they demonstrate what they say through their behavior.

The final category of behavior involves taking calculated risks and making a commitment to risks once they are decided on. Visionary leaders have no energy to spare for recouping their losses; all their efforts go toward achieving their goals. Moreover, these leaders build into their risks opportunities for others to buy in, to take the risks with the leaders and share in the effort and the rewards. These leaders motivate by "pulling" us along with them, as Bennis put it, rather than by trying to push us in the direction they want to go. Franklin D. Roosevelt displayed this sort of behavior often; he took risks and made commitments and inspired others to join him.

Behaviors of a kind other than these five types surely contribute to the sense of inspiration and commitment we feel when responding to visionary leadership. Most important, however, is what visionary leaders are trying to accomplish through their behavior. They attempt to create cultures that will guide their organizations into the future. . . .

53

The Decision-Making Process

E. Frank Harrison

E. Frank Harrison has served as management educator, consultant, university president and chancellor. His books include *The Managerial Decision-Making Process* and *Management and Organizations*. He is currently professor of management at San Francisco State University.

Decision making in formal organizations should take place as an interrelated and dynamic process. Since the making of decisions in the real world is often unstructured,[1] a process-oriented approach may seem different from traditional ways of arriving at a choice. Nonetheless, the benefits of this approach are considerable, and its use seems certain to improve managerial decision making in organizations of all types. Moreover, business executives, government administrators, military officers, and managers in any type of formal organization all perform the several functions that make up the decision-making process. In effect, then, the process approach provides a comprehensive framework for students intent on learning about management, as well as a means for practicing managers to evaluate and improve their own performance as decision makers.

The definition of decision making as a process consisting of several functions is advantageous for several reasons: (1) it indicates the dynamic nature of decision making; (2) it depicts decision-making activities as occurring over varying spans of time; (3) it implies that the decision-making process is continuous and, thus, that it is an ever-present reality of organizational life; and (4) it suggests that, at least to some extent, managerial decision making can direct and control the nature, degree, and pace of change within the organization.

Nature of the Process

There are various views on the process of decision making. Simon assigns three major elements to the process: (1) finding occasions for making a decision, (2) finding possible courses of action, and (3) choosing among courses of action.[2] Witte advances the notion of decision making as a total process involving discernible and separate activities: (1) information gathering, (2) development of alternatives, (3) evaluation of alternatives, and (4) choices.[3] The process espoused by Schrenk focuses on three elements: (1) problem recognition, (2) problem diagnosis, and (3) action selection.[4] Janis envisions a decision-making process with five stages: (1) recognition of a challenge, (2) acceptance of the challenge, (3) meeting the challenge through a choice, (4) committing oneself to the choice, and (5) adherence to the choice.[5] Eilon advances a comprehensive process composed of eight stages, which begins with information input and culminates in a choice.[6] Mintzberg and his associates offer an incredibly complex formal structure derived from twenty-five "unstructured" decision-making processes that are then organized into a general model of interrelated strategic decision processes.[7] Fredrikson proposes a method for organizing noneconomic criteria in a decision-making process that includes four stages: (1) developing a criteria set, (2) posing criteria questions, (3) scaling the responses, and (4) choosing among alternatives.[8] And, finally, Holsapple and Moskowitz set forth several principal constraints that limit the use of whatever decision-making process is being used.[9]

There is no doubt that the process-oriented approach to managerial decision making is on the rise.[10] . . . We will consider the decision-making process from a three-dimensional perspective. We base this perspective on the premise that decision making is synonymous with management, and, therefore, the process of decision making should have as its central focus the management of formal organizations. The first dimension of decision making is the individual functions of the process, each with certain inherent properties. The second dimension is the total process, characterized by a host of interrelationships among its functions and by certain properties of its own. The third dimension is the dynamism of the total process, which is a product of the properties and relationships of the individual functions and the total process.

The Functions of Decision Making

The components of the decision-making process are the functions of decision making. This definition is in keeping with the standard definition of a *function* as "one of a group of related actions contributing to a larger action."[11] In a social science context, the concept of function

> involves the notion of a structure consisting of a set of relations among unit entities, the continuity of the structure being maintained by a life-process made up of the activities of the constituent units. . . . "function" is the contribution which a partial activity makes to the total activity of which it is a part.[12]

The functions of decision making are:

1. *Setting managerial objectives*. The decision-making process starts with the setting of objectives, and a given cycle within the process culminates upon reaching the objectives that gave rise to it. The next complete cycle begins with the setting of new objectives.
2. *Searching for alternatives*. In the decision-making process, search involves scanning the internal and external environments of the organization for information. Relevant information is formulated into alternatives that seem likely to fulfill the objectives.
3. *Comparing and evaluating alternatives*. Alternatives represent various courses of action that singly or in combination may help attain the objectives. By formal and informal means alternatives are compared based on the certainty or uncertainty of cause-and-effect relationships and the preferences of the decision maker for various probabilistic outcomes.
4. *The act of choice*. Choice is a moment in the ongoing process of decision making when the decision maker chooses a given course of action from among a set of alternatives.

5. *Implementing the decision.* Implementation causes the chosen course of action to be carried out within the organization. It is that moment in the total decision-making process when the choice is transformed from an abstraction into an operational reality.

6. *Follow-up and control.* This function is intended to ensure that the implemented decision results in an outcome that is in keeping with the objectives that gave rise to the total cycle of functions within the decision-making process.

Decision Making: An Interrelated Process

The functions of decision making are highly interrelated within the decision-making process. Bass notes the interrelatedness of the process as follows:

> Decision making is an orderly process beginning with the discovery by the decision maker of a discrepancy between the perceived state of affairs and the desired state. This desired state is usually between an ideal and a realistically attainable state. Alternative actions . . . are selected or invented. One of these alternatives emerges as the action of choice followed by justification for it. Then comes its authorization and implementation. The process cycle is completed with feedback about whether the action resulted in movement toward the desired state of affairs. If the perceived and desired state of affairs have not narrowed sufficiently, a new cycle is likely to commence.[13]

Figure 1 illustrates the interrelationships among the functions of decision making set forth. . . . The process begins with the setting of objectives the attainment of which requires a search for information. The analysis of the information derived from the search compares the alternatives discovered in light of (1) attaining the objectives, (2) the opportunity costs of alternatives not selected, and (3) likely internal effects on the organization following a choice. The comparison considers the trade-off values among these features and a choice is made based on the trade-off values.*

The chosen alternative is normally implemented through established organizational structures and processes. At this point the decision is implemented. For follow-up and control of the implemented decision, established information systems quickly reveal to management the actual outcome of the

---

Trade-off value means that some amount of one kind of performance may be substituted for another kind of performance—for example, an increase in the probability of attaining objectives may be worth an adverse internal effect on the organization.

FIGURE 1

The Decision-Making Process

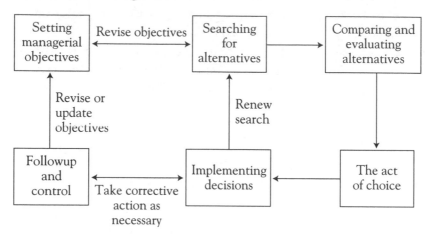

decision. Thus, management can determine how implementation affects the intended outcome inherent in the managerial objectives.

The success of the decision-making process is highly dependent on the functions that are the components of the process. *Success* in this context means the attainment of the objectives that started the process. The process is normally sequential, rather than hit-or-miss. For example, if managerial objectives are absent, there is no basis for a search. Without the information obtained through a search, there are no alternatives to compare. Without a comparison of alternatives, the choice of a particular course of action is unlikely to yield desired results. Without effective implementation of a choice, the actual outcome of the decision is unlikely to be the attainment of the managerial objectives. And, finally, in the absence of follow-up and control, the successful implementation of a decision is difficult. Thus the functions constituting the decision-making process must be organized if the process is to accomplish its purposes effectively. We can easily demonstrate the interrelatedness of the process by starting with any one of the functions of decision making and working forward or backward through the process. There is a definite need for a framework that organizes the functions of decision making, if only to improve the making of managerial decisions in formal organizations. The framework illustrated in Figure 1 shows both the interrelatedness of the functions and their sequential organization. . . .

Setting Managerial Objectives

The foundation of the decision-making process lies in the objectives that give it purpose, direction, and continuity.[14] The setting of managerial objectives is the first function of decision making, and attainment of the objectives represents the culmination of a given cycle within the decision-making process.

Objectives, which underlie the effective management of any type of formal organization, are not abstractions. They are the commitments to action through which the mission of the organization is carried out, and they are the standards against which the performance of management is measured. "If objectives are only good intentions they are worthless. They must degenerate into work. And work is always specific, always has—or should have—unambiguous, measurable results, a deadline and a specific assignment of responsibility."[15] The importance of objectives as a foundation for the managerial decision-making process is expressed in the following statement of the principle of the objective: "Before initiating any course of action, the objectives in view must be clearly determined, understood, and stated."[16] *Thus an objective may be defined as the end point toward which management directs its decision making.*

It is particularly useful to differentiate between the terms *objective* and *goal*. "An objective is a specific category of purpose that includes the attainment by an organization of certain states or conditions; a goal may be viewed as a subset of an objective, expressed in terms of one or more specific dimensions."[17]

Advantages of Managerial Objectives

Objectives are required for all activities that contribute to the basic purposes of the organization. Objectives enable management to plan and organize such activities. With objectives, management explains the whole range of organizational phenomena in a small number of general statements that can be tested in practice. Objectives enable managers to appraise the soundness of their decisions while they are being made; and objectives offer a framework for predicting and analyzing managerial performance in pursuing successful outcomes of decisions.[18]

Objectives serve as yardsticks for measuring, comparing, and evaluating the success of decisions in accomplishing organizational purposes. Indeed objectives serve as the basis for rational decision making by managers in formal organizations. Objectives can also be good motivators because they make it easier for individuals to relate reaching personal goals to the work of the organization. They know what is expected of them and are thus more certain of how to carry out their duties and responsibilities. In turn, they are able to serve themselves and the organization more efficiently. Managerial objectives, then, provide a means to fuse the fulfillment of human need and the accomplishment of the organizational mission.

The Hierarchy of Managerial Objectives

Managerial objectives tend to create a kind of hierarchy that can be related to the formal structure of managerial responsibilities and authority.

> In complex organizations objectives are structured in a hierarchy in which the objectives of each unit contribute to the objectives of the next higher unit. And a broad objective . . . states the purpose of the entire organization. This is true of all organizations—military, educational, government, and business.[19]

In effect, there are "objectives within objectives within objectives."[20] A useful technique for analyzing the hierarchy of objectives in a formal organization is to view it as a means-end chain.[21] As Simon says, "The fact that [objectives] may be dependent for their force on other more distant ends leads to the arrangement of these [objectives] in a hierarchy—each level to be considered as an end relative to the levels below it and a means relative to the levels above it."[22]

Managerial objectives, then, serve not only as a primary function of decision making that initiates and completes a given cycle within the decision-making process. They also link together the total organization by fostering common purpose and unified action. The sum of all the objectives below the level of top management serves as a means to attain the objectives of the total organization. This in turn permits the organization to accomplish its basic purposes. In one sense, therefore, all objectives are means, although, at various times and depending on its level in the hierarchy, a given objective will also serve as an end.

Characteristics of Managerial Objectives

One approach to ensuring that managerial objectives possess the characteristics essential for successful decision making is to make them satisfy relevant criteria. Such criteria may be applied by asking a series of questions:

1. *Relevance.* Are the objectives related to and supportive of the basic purposes of the organization?

2. *Practicality*. Do the objectives recognize obvious constraints?
3. *Challenge*. Do the objectives provide a challenge for managers at all levels in the organization?
4. *Measurability*. Can the objectives be quantified, if only in an order-of-importance ranking?
5. *Schedulability*. Can the objectives be scheduled and monitored at interim points to ensure progress toward their attainment?
6. *Balance*. Do the objectives provide for a proportional emphasis on all activities and keep the strengths and weaknesses of the organization in proper balance?
7. *Flexibility*. Are the objectives sufficiently flexible or is the organization likely to find itself locked into a particular course of action?
8. *Timeliness*. Given the environment within which the organization operates, is this the proper time to adopt these objectives?
9. *State of the art*. Do the objectives fall within the boundaries of current technological development?
10. *Growth*. Do the objectives point toward the growth of the organization, rather than toward mere survival?
11. *Cost effectiveness*. Are the objectives cost effective in that the anticipated benefits clearly exceed the expected costs?
12. *Accountability*. Are the assignments for the attainment of the objectives made in a way that permits the assessment of performance on the part of individual managers throughout the organization?

If a given set of managerial objectives meets most of these criteria, it possesses the characteristics essential to effective decision making at all levels of management. . . .

Searching for Alternatives

Once the managerial objectives are set, the next function in the decision-making process is the search for information from which to fashion alternatives. For purposes of explanation, this function of decision making will be simply designated as *search* or *search activity*. . . .

Comparing and Evaluating Alternatives

Once the search yields a sufficient amount of information to fashion a set of alternatives, the next function in the decision-making process is to compare and evaluate these alternatives. This function epitomizes the interrelatedness of the decision-making process. For example, in using the available information to compare and evaluate alternatives, the decision maker must focus on anticipated outcomes that will probably meet the objectives only through follow-up and control after a choice is made and implemented.

The overriding purpose in the decision-making process is to attain the objectives that serve as a foundation for the process. There will be, for any objective, many ways of seeking attainment. Each alternative will produce a different degree of attainment of a given objective and hence a different value of the measure of effectiveness. "The number of alternatives depends on how much effort the decision maker puts into a search for them. Thus, there are possible alternatives which the decision maker is completely unaware of, just as there are alternatives which the decision maker will disregard without consideration."[23] The alternatives are not given but must be sought out by an expenditure of resources. From the known set of alternatives deemed worthy of additional consideration, the decision maker must determine which one is most likely to meet the objective at hand. Thus the decision maker is confronted with the need to make an estimate of effectiveness for each alternative. To accomplish these estimates, the decision maker must have some idea of the relationships between alternatives and outcomes in relation to the objectives.[24] . . .

The Act of Choice

The act of choice is, in one sense, the high point of the decision-making process. "The *decision* itself is the culmination of the process. Regardless of the problem, the alternatives, the decision aids, or the consequences to follow, once a decision is made, things begin to happen. Decisions trigger action, movement, and change."[25] However, the act of choice is still only a part of the process, not, as is so often assumed, the entire process in itself. In this regard, Simon noted:

> All of these images have a significant point in common. In them, the decision maker is a man at the moment of choice, ready to plant his foot on one or another of the routes that lead from the crossroads. All of the images falsify decision by focusing on its final moment. All of them ignore the whole lengthy, complex process of alerting, exploring, and analyzing that precede that final moment.[26]

Simon's point is well taken. To focus solely on the act of choice is to disregard or minimize all the actions necessary to create the conditions of choice, not to mention the succession of postdecision actions essential to transform the choice into acceptable results. To be sure, if the act of choice "is given exclusive attention, many antecedent and associated phenomena are excluded from analysis."[27]

By now we are familiar with the antecedent phenomena referred to: (1) setting managerial objectives, (2) searching for alternatives, and (3) comparing and evaluating alternatives. And we know that the decision-making process does not stop with the act of choice. It continues on through implementation and follow-up and control, with new alternatives being identified and existing objectives reset or updated to reflect changing conditions and emerging knowledge. Indeed, decision making directed toward the attainment of managerial objectives is a dynamic, interrelated process and not a simple series of discrete actions.

54

Decision Making and the Leadership Process

Victor H. Vroom

Victor H. Vroom is John G. Searle Professor of Organization and Management at Yale University. He has received awards from such varied sources as the American Psychological Association, the McKinsey Foundation, and the Ford Foundation. He has published several works which have become classics: *Work and Motivation, Motivation in Management* (with Edward Deci), and *Leadership and Decision Making*, written with Phillip Yetton. His most recent work is *The New Leadership: Managing Participation in Organizations*.

This article deals with the intersection of two areas of scientific inquiry and with the results of an extensive program of research to explore that intersection. The first area is the process of decision making. Recent developments in the theory of decision making suggest the usefulness of focussing on the processes by which decisions are made by individuals, groups and organizations.[1] Instead of treating the social system as a "black box," research underscores the necessity of identifying the processes which intervene between problem and solution—those which ultimately control the decisions that are made.

The second area of inquiry is the study of leadership. From its early beginnings in the search for universal leadership traits and from more recent ef-

Reprinted courtesy of the *Journal of Contemporary Business*, 3 (Autumn 1974), published by the School of Business Administration, University of Washington, Seattle, WA.

forts to uncover patterns of leader behavior which are consistently related to group effectiveness has come widespread support for situational or contingency conceptions of the leadership process. Such questions as, "Who would be the best leader?" or "How should a leader behave so as to stimulate the greatest productivity?" cannot be answered without a detailed knowledge of the situation.[2]

To put these two developments together, one can conceive of the leader's role, at least in part, as controlling the processes by which decisions are made in that part of the organization for which he or she is responsible. The processes vary in a number of respects, but the one of most immediate interest and relevance to the study of leadership is the extent to which the leader encourages the participation of his or her subordinates in the decision-making process.

To illustrate this connection between leadership and decision making, assume that you are a manager who has five subordinates reporting to you. Each subordinate has a clearly defined and distinct set of responsibilities. When one of them resigns to take a position with another organization due to a recent cost-cutting program which makes it impossible to hire new employees, you cannot replace this subordinate with someone else. Now it will be necessary to find some way to reallocate the departing subordinate's responsibilities among the remaining four in order to maintain the present workload and effectiveness of the unit.

This situation represents many circumstances faced by persons in leadership positions. There is some need for action—a problem exists and a solution, or decision, must be found. You, as leader, have some area of freedom or discretion (there are a number of possible ways in which the work can be reallocated), but there are also some constraints on your actions. For example, you cannot solve the problem by hiring someone from outside the organization. Furthermore, the solution is going to have effects on people other than yourself; your subordinates must carry out whatever decision is reached.

In this situation, one can envision a number of possible decision-making processes that could be employed. You could make the decision by yourself and announce it to your subordinates; you could obtain additional information from your subordinates and then make the decision; you could consult your subordinates, individually or collectively before making the decision; or you could convene them as a group, share the problem and attempt to reach an agreement on the solution. These alternatives vary in terms of not cognitive but social processes—specifically, the amount and type of opportunity afforded subordinates to participate in the decision. . . .

Toward a Normative Model

What would be a rational way of deciding on the form and amount of partici-pation in decision-making to be used in different situations? One can agree with the basic tenet of contingency theories that "leadership must depend upon the situation" but despair over the vacuous nature of this statement when faced with the task of specifying the kinds of situations which call for different approaches.

Clearly, one wants to select a decision process in a given situation that has the greatest likelihood of resulting in effective decisions, but the concept of effectiveness is far too general to be of much use for analytical purposes. There are at least three classes of outcomes that bear on the ultimate effec-tiveness of decisions:

- The quality or rationality of the decision
- The acceptance or commitment on the part of subordinates to execute the decision effectively
- The amount of time required to make the decision.

Research dealing with the effects of the degree of subordinate participa-tion in decision making on each of these outcomes concluded:

> The results suggest that allocating problem-solving and decision-making tasks to entire groups requires a greater investment of manhours but produces high-er acceptance of decisions and a higher probability that the decision will be executed efficiently. Differences between these two methods in quality of de-cisions and in elapsed time are inconclusive and probably highly variable . . . It would be naive to think that group decision-making is always more "effective" than autocratic decision-making, or vice versa; the relative effectiveness of these two extreme methods depends both on the weights attached to quality, acceptance and time variables and on differences in amounts of these out-comes resulting from these methods, neither of which is invariant from one situation to another. The critics and proponents of participative management would do well to direct their efforts toward identifying the properties of situa-tions in which different decision-making approaches are effective rather than wholesale condemnation or deification of one approach.[3]

Vroom and Yetton described a taxonomy of decision processes that is used throughout this article. The taxonomy is shown in Table 1. Each process is represented by a symbol, e.g., AI, CI, GII; the first letter signifies the basic properties of the process (A stands for autocratic, C for consultative and G

TABLE 1

Types of Management Decision Styles

AI   You solve the problem or make the decision yourself, using information available to you at that time.

AII   You obtain the necessary information from your subordinate(s), then decide on the solution to the problem yourself. You may or may not tell your subordinates what the problem is in getting the information from them. The role played by your subordinates in making the decision is clearly one of providing the necessary information to you, rather than generating or evaluating alternative solutions.

CI   You share the problem with relevant subordinates individually, getting their ideas and suggestions without bringing them together as a group. Then *you* make the decision that may or make not reflect your subordinates' influence.

CII   You share the problem with your subordinates as a group, collectively obtaining their ideas and suggestions. Then *you* make the decision that may or may not reflect your subordinates' influence.

GII* You share a problem with your subordinates as a group. Together you generate and evaluate alternatives and attempt to reach agreement (consensus) on a solution. Your role is much like that of chairman. You do not try to influence the group to adopt "your" solution and you are willing to accept and implement any solution that has the support of the entire group.

---

*GI is omitted because it applies only to more comprehensive models outside the scope of this article.

for group) and the Roman numerals constitute variants on that process. Thus, AI represents the first variant on an autocratic process and AII represents the second variant, etc.

The next step is to identify, in a manner consistent with available research evidence, properties of the situation that can be used in a model. In the model to be described, the situational attributes are characteristics of the problem to be solved or decision to be made rather than more general properties of the role of the leader. Table 2 shows the problem attributes in the present form of the model. For each attribute a question is provided that can be used by leaders in diagnosing problems. The terms used in Table 2 and the empirical basis for their inclusion in the model are described more completely in a more recent book by Vroom and Yetton.[4]

It has been found that trained managers can diagnose a particular problem quickly and quite reliably by answering this set of seven relevant questions. But how can such responses generate a prediction concerning the most effective decision process to be employed by the leader? What kind of normative model of leadership style can be constructed using this set of problem attributes? (See Table 2.)

Figure 1 shows one such model expressed in the form of a decision tree, the seventh version of such a model that we have developed over the last 3 years. The problem attributes, expressed in question form, are arranged along the top of the figure. To use the model for a particular decision-making situation, one starts at the left-hand side and works toward the right asking oneself the question immediately above any box encountered. When a terminal node is reached, a number will be found designating the problem type and one of the decision-making processes appearing in Table 1.

AI is prescribed for four problem types (1, 2, 4 and 5); AII is prescribed for two problem types (9 and 10); CI is prescribed for only one problem type (8); CII is prescribed for four problem types (7, 11, 13 and 14); and GII is prescribed for three problem types (3, 6 and 12). The relative frequency with which each of the five decision processes would be prescribed for any manager would, of course, depend on the distribution of problem types encountered in his decision-making.

Rationale Underlying the Model

The decision processes specified for each problem type are not arbitrary. The model's behavior is governed by a set of principles intended to be consistent with evidence concerning the consequences of participation in decision-making on organizational effectiveness.

Two mechanisms underlie the behavior of the model. The first is a set of seven rules that protect the quality and acceptance of the decision by eliminating alternatives that risk one or the other of these decision outcomes. The second mechanism is a principle for choosing among alternatives in the feasible set where more than one exists.

The rules are examined first because they do much of the work of the model. As previously indicated, they intend to protect both the quality and acceptance of the decision.

Rules protecting decision quality. In the form of the model shown, three rules protect decision quality.

TABLE 2
Problem Attributes Used in the Model

Problem Attributes	*Diagnostic Questions*
A. The importance of the quality of the decision.	Is there a quality requirement such that one solution is likely to be more rational than another?
B. The extent to which the leader possesses sufficient information/ expertise to make a high-quality decision by himself or herself.	Do I have sufficient information to make a high-quality decision?
C. The extent to which the problem is structured.	Is the problem structured?
D. The extent to which acceptance or commitment on the part of subordinates is critical to the effective implementation of the decision.	Is acceptance of the decision by subordinates critical to effective implemenation?
E. The prior probability that the leader's autocratic decision will receive acceptance by subordinates.	If I were to make the decision by myself, is it reasonably certain that it would be accepted by my subordinates?
F. The extent to which subordinates are motivated to attain the organizational goals as represented in the objectives explicit in the statement of the problem.	Do subordinates share the organizational goals to be obtained in solving the problem?
G. The extent to which subordinates are likely to be in conflict over preferred solutions	Is conflict among subordinates likely in preferred solutions?

FIGURE 1
Decision Model

A. Is there a quality requirement such that one solution is likely to be more rational than another?

B. Do I have sufficient information to make a high-quality decision?

C. Is the problem structured?

D. Is acceptance of the decision by subordinates critical to effective implementation?

E. If I were to make the decision by myself, is it reasonably certain that it would be accepted by my subordinates?

F. Do subordinates share the organizational goals to be obtained in solving the problem?

G. Is conflict among subordinates likely in preferred solutions?

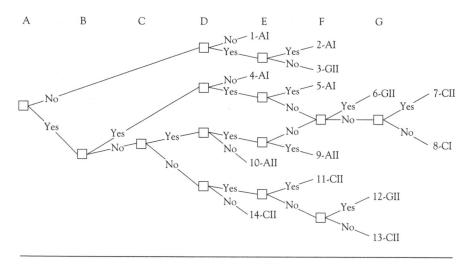

- *The Information Rule.* If the quality of the decision is important and if the leader does not possess enough information or expertise to solve the problem by himself or herself, AI is eliminated from the feasible set. (Its use risks a low-quality decision.)
- *The Goal-Congruence Rule.* If the quality of the decision is important and if the subordinates do not share the organizational goals to be obtained in solving the problem, GII is eliminated from the feasible set. (Alternatives

that eliminate the leader's final control over the decision reached may jeopardize the quality of the decision.)

- *The Unstructured-Problem Rule.* In decisions in which the quality of the decision is important, if the leader lacks the necessary information or expertise to solve the problem alone, and if the problem is unstructured, i.e., he or she does not know exactly what information is needed and where it is located, the method used must provide not only for collection of information but also for collection in an efficient and effective manner. Methods that involve interaction among all subordinates with full knowledge of the problem are likely to be both more efficient and to generate a high-quality solution. Under these conditions, AI, AII and CI are eliminated from the feasible set. (AI does not allow the leader to collect the necessary information, and AII and CI represent more cumbersome, less effective and less efficient means of bringing the necessary information to bear on the solution of the problem than methods that permit persons with the necessary information to interact.)

Rules protecting acceptance. In addition to the decision quality rules, there are four rules to protect acceptance.

- *The Acceptance Rule.* If the acceptance of the decision by subordinates is critical to effective implementation, and if it is not certain that an autocratic decision made by the leader would receive that acceptance, AI and AII are eliminated from the feasible set. (Neither provides an opportunity for subordinates to participate in the decision and both risk the necessary acceptance.)
- *The Conflict Rule.* If the acceptance of the decision is critical; if an autocratic decision is not certain to be accepted; and if subordinates are likely to be in conflict or disagreement over the appropriate solution, AI, AII and CI are eliminated from the feasible set. (The method used in solving the problem should enable those disagreeing to resolve their differences with full knowledge of the problem. Accordingly, under these conditions, AI, AII and CI, which involve no interaction or only "one-on-one" relationships and, therefore, provide no opportunity for those in conflict to resolve their differences, are eliminated from the feasible set. Their use runs the risk of leaving some subordinates with less than the necessary commitment to the final decision.)
- *The Fairness Rule.* If the quality of decision is unimportant and if acceptance is critical and not certain to result from an autocratic decision, AI, AII, CI and CII are eliminated from the feasible set. (The method used

should maximize the probability of acceptance as this is the only relevant consideration in determining the effectiveness of the decision. Under these circumstances, AI, AII, CI and CII, which create less acceptance or commitment than GII, are eliminated from the feasible set. To use them is to run the risk of getting less than the needed acceptance of the decision.)

• *The Acceptance Priority Rule.* If acceptance is critical and is not assured by an autocratic decision, and if subordinates can be trusted, AI, AII, CI and CII are eliminated from the feasible set. (Methods that provide greater partnership in the decision-making process can provide greater acceptance without risking decision quality. Use of any method other than GII results in an unnecessary risk that the decision will not be fully accepted or receive the necessary commitment on the part of subordinates.)

After these seven rules have been applied to a given problem, a feasible set of decision processes is generated (see Table 3). Clearly, there are some problem types for which only one method remains in the feasible set and others for which five methods remain feasible.

Choosing among alternatives. When more than one method remains in the feasible set, there are a number of ways to choose among them. In Figure 1, the mechanism underlying choices utilizes the number of man-hours used in solving the problem. Given a set of methods with equal likelihood of meeting both quality and acceptance requirements for the decision, it chooses that method that requires the least investment in manhours. On the basis of the empirical evidence summarized earlier, this is the method furthest to the left within the feasible set. For example, because AI, AII, CI, CII and GII are all feasible as in Problem Types 1 and 2, AI would be the method chosen.

The model just described seeks to protect the quality of the decision and to expend the least number of manhours in the process. Because it focuses on conditions surrounding making and implementing a particular decision rather than on any long-term considerations, it can be termed a short-term model.

However, it seems likely that leadership methods that may be optimal for short-term results may be different from those that would be optimal over a longer period of time. The manager who uses more participative methods could, in time, develop his or her subordinates, increasing not only the knowledge and talent that they could bring to bear on decisions but also their identification with the organization goals. A promising approach to development of a long-term model is one that places less weight on manhours as the basis for choice of method within the feasible set. Given a long-term orienta-

TABLE 3
Problem Types and the Feasible Set of Decision Processes

Problem Type	Acceptable Methods
1	AI, AII, CI, CII, GII
2	AI, AII, CI, CII, GII
3	GII
4	AI, AII, CI CII, GII*
5	AI, AII, CI CII, GII*
6	GII
7	CII
8	CI, CII
9	AII, CI, CII, GII*
10	AII, CI, CII, GII*
11	CII, GII*
12	GII
13	CII
14	CII, GII*

*Within the feasible set only when the answer to question F is yes.

tion, one would be interested in the possibility of a tradeoff between man-hours in problem solving and team development, both of which increase with participation. Viewed in these terms, the time-minimizing model places maximum relative weight on manhours and no weight on development, hence, it chooses the style furthest to the left within the feasible set. If these assumptions are correct, a model that places less weight on manhours and more weight on development would choose a style further to the right within the feasible set.

The model just described is the latest of a set of such models which have been devised over the last few years. Undoubtedly, it is not perfect and will be amended or altered as additional research evidence becomes available.

55

Leadership Communication Skills

Michael Z. Hackman and Craig E. Johnson

Michael Z. Hackman is on the faculty at the University of Colorado–Colorado Springs. Craig E. Johnson is associated with George Fox College.

We believe that leadership is best understood from a communication stand-point. . . .

We offer the following communication-based definition of leadership:

> Leadership is human (symbolic) communication which modifies the attitudes and behaviors of others in order to meet group goals and needs.

Viewing leadership from a communication perspective recognizes that leadership effectiveness depends on developing effective communication skills. Frank Dance and Carl Larson identify three functions of human communication.[1] First, *symbolic communication links humans to other humans and to the physical environment.* Conversations, parties, weather reports, meetings and so on tie us to one another and to the world. Second, *higher mental processes develop as a result of symbol usage.* Language makes reasoning and conceptualizing possible. Third, *human communication allows for the regulation*

From Michael Z. Hackman and Craig E. Johnson, *Leadership: A Communication Perspective* (Prospect Heights, Ill.: Waveland Press, 1991). Reprinted by permission.

of our own behavior as well as the behavior of others. We can suggest, plead, command or convince—to name a few of the possible means to regulate behavior.

Each of the functions of human communication identified by Dance and Larson plays a critical role in effective leadership. Successful leaders are experts in processing cues from the environment. They attend to current events, to the activities of other groups and organizations, to their own group norms and cultures, as well as to the physical environment. Most importantly, they solicit feedback from others. Listening which accurately interprets verbal and nonverbal messages is a primary linking skill. Effective leadership also involves the establishment and maintenance of satisfying group relationships. Creating a trusting, cooperative work atmosphere and building an effective team are key linking abilities.

Thinking and reasoning skills are essential to leaders since leaders direct groups toward goals. The term "envisioning" best describes the type of conceptual activity needed for leadership. Leaders must be able to take the inputs they receive from linking with others and the environment and convert them into an agenda or vision for the future. In many cases, these visions are creative in nature; that is, they combine previously existing needs, wants and demands into new images or realities.

We noted earlier that influence is an important element in the definition of leadership. Skills that involve regulating the behavior of others are part of the leader's repertoire. To influence others successfully, leaders must be able to:

1. Develop perceptions of credibility
2. Develop and use power bases effectively
3. Make effective use of verbal and nonverbal influence cues
4. Develop positive expectations for others
5. Manage change
6. Gain compliance
7. Negotiate productive solutions. . . .

Playing to a Packed House: Leaders as Impression Managers

From a communication standpoint, leaders are made, not born. We increase our leadership competence as we increase our communication skills. We can compare the leadership role to a part played on stage to illustrate how effective communication skills translate into effective leadership.

Sociologist Erving Goffman adapts Shakespeare's adage that life is a stage and we are all actors on it to argue that most communication interactions can be viewed as performances complete with actors, stages, dialogues, and dressing rooms.[2] Let's look at a typical date, for example. The date is a performance which may take place on any number of stages: the dance floor, the living room, the movie theater, the football game. The actors (the couple) prepare in their dressing rooms at home before the performance and may return to the same locations for a critique session after the date ends. Particularly on the first date, the interactants may work very hard to create desired impressions—they engage in "impression management." Each dating partner tries to manage the perceptions of the other person by using appropriate behaviors, which might include dressing in the latest fashions, acting in a courteous manner, engaging in polite conversation, and paying for meals and other activities.

Leaders also engage in impression management. When leaders perform, they play to packed houses. People in organizations, for example, carefully watch the behavior of the CEO for information about the executive officer's character and for clues as to organizational priorities, values, and future direction. They seek answers to such questions as: "Can I trust him/her?" "What kind of behavior gets rewarded around here?" "Is he or she really interested in my welfare?" "Is dishonesty tolerated?" "Are we going to survive the next five years?"

Successful leaders use communication as a tool to reach their ends; they match their behaviors with their goals. If they want to emphasize customer service, they spend more time with customers and reward good service providers. If they want to foster cooperation, they downplay power and status cues and emphasize listening. These leaders promote communication on a first-name basis and refuse such luxuries as executive washrooms and reserved parking places. Effective leaders know what they want to accomplish, what communication skills are needed to reach their goals, and how to put those behaviors into action.[3]

To see how impression management works, change one aspect of your usual communication and watch how others respond. If friends have told you that you seem unfriendly because you are quiet when meeting new people, try being more assertive the next time you meet strangers at a party. If you make a conscious effort to greet others, introduce yourself and learn more about them, you may shake your cool, unfriendly image.

Many people are uncomfortable with the idea of impression management. They equate playing a role with being insincere since true feelings and beliefs might be hidden. While this is a very real danger, followers continually watch for inconsistencies and often "see through" performances of insincere leaders. Frequently, we have no choice but to play many roles. We are forced into performances as job applicants, students, dating partners and leaders each day. The real problem is that we often mismanage the impressions we make. Our behaviors may make us appear dull or untrustworthy when we really are interesting and honest.

Some fear that leaders can manipulate impressions to mislead the group. This is a legitimate concern. . . . Because impression management can be used to further group goals or to subvert them, it should be judged by its end product. Ethical impression management meets group wants and needs and, in the ideal, spurs the group to reach higher goals. Unethical impression management subverts group needs and lowers purpose and aspiration.[4] . . .

Three clusters of communication skills are essential for leaders: 1) linking, 2) envisioning, and 3) regulating. Linking skills include monitoring the environment, creating a trusting climate and team building. Envisioning involves creating new agendas or visions out of previously existing elements. Regulating means influencing others by developing credibility and power, using effective verbal and nonverbal communication, creating positive expectations, managing change, gaining compliance, and negotiation. Successful leaders match their communication behaviors to their goals through a process called impression management. They monitor their actions to create desired impressions in the minds of others. Ethical leaders use impression management to reach group goals rather than to satisfy selfish, personal goals.

56

Designing Systems for Resolving
Disputes in Organizations

Jeanne M. Brett, Stephen B. Goldberg, and William L. Ury

Jeanne M. Brett is DeWitt W. Buchanan, Jr. Distinguished Professor of Dispute Resolution and Organizations at the Kellogg Graduate School of Management at Northwestern University and serves as director of Northwestern's Dispute Resolution Center. She is the author of over thirty articles and three books. Stephen B. Goldberg is professor of law at Northwestern University Law School. He has mediated and arbitrated many disputes, including serving as a salary arbiter for major league baseball from 1981–1992. Professor Goldberg is president of Mediation Research and Education Project, Inc. William Ury, co-author of the seminal book *Getting to Yes*, is associate director of the Harvard Negotiation Project, and a noted consultant and lecturer on negotiation. Brett, Goldberg, and Ury have collaborated to write *Getting Disputes Resolved: Designing Systems to Cut the Cost of Conflict*, which received the 1988 Center for Public Resources Award for excellence and innovation in alternative dispute resolution.

Two oil companies, about to engage in a joint venture, agree in advance to try to resolve all disputes in a partnership committee. If direct negotiations fail, senior executives from each company who are otherwise uninvolved in the joint venture will try to resolve the dispute by using a mix of mediation and negotiation procedures.[1] If they cannot, the dispute will be sent to arbitration.[2]

At the Catholic Archdiocese of Chicago, school administrators, looking for a better way to resolve disputes about teacher dismissals and student suspensions, designed a multistep dispute resolution system that requires negotiation between disputing parties, provides advice from a school conflict-management board, and offers the services of a trained mediator.[3]

IBM and Fujitsu, after disputing for years over hundreds of charges that Fujitsu had wrongfully used IBM software, negotiated a system that allowed Fujitsu to examine and use IBM software in exchange for adequate compensation. Future disputes about use will be resolved by a neutral technical expert; future disputes about compensation will be resolved by arbitration.[4]

In these situations managers and the consultants who worked with them designed multiprocedure systems for resolving disputes without resort to litigation. Their dispute systems designs were intuitive, based on their recognition that an ongoing series of disputes was inevitable and that currently available procedures were costly.

In 1980 we found ourselves in a similar situation. We had been asked to consult at Caney Creek (a pseudonym), a coal mine in eastern Kentucky, where conflict had reached monumental proportions. In the prior two years there had been 27 wildcat strikes, management had regularly taken the union to court for breach of the no-strike clause in the contract, and 115 miners had been jailed overnight. There had been bomb threats, sabotage, and theft. Productivity was so low that management was considering closing the mine.

The union contract provided for a four-step procedure for the resolution of grievances: (a) negotiation between miner and supervisor; (b) negotiation between local mine management and a committee that represented the miners; (c) negotiation between a representative of the company and a district-level representative of the union; and (d) binding arbitration. At Caney Creek, as at other high strike mines,[5] little serious negotiation occurred at the local level, and miners had little confidence that arbitration would resolve disputes satisfactorily. Working with union and management officials, we designed a program of changes intended to encourage miners and managers to resolve their disputes by negotiating the interests underlying their positions rather than focusing on intractable positional differences and then helped them put the program into practice. Afterward, bomb threats ceased, sabotage and theft decreased, and productivity improved.[6] There were no wildcat strikes until the national contract expired, nearly a year later.

At the same time we were working at Caney Creek, we began an experiment in mediating grievances in the coal industry. On the basis of our prior research and Stephen B. Goldberg's own experience as an arbitrator in the industry, Goldberg thought that mediation inserted between the negotiation (third) and arbitration (fourth) steps of the coal industry grievance procedure would be able to uncover and resolve the problems underlying a grievance, problems that seldom surfaced at arbitration where grievances were typically dealt with exclusively on contractual terms. One of Goldberg's arbitration cases illustrates this point. A miner filed a series of grievances claiming that his foreman was doing work that should have been done by union members. Goldberg denied the miner's grievances and only learned later that the miner believed that his frequent assignments to shovel muck from the mine's sump hole were unfair, but because he had no grounds to file a grievance on the job assignment, he sought other contractual grounds on which to file a grievance against his foreman. Arbitration neither resolved the real problem, the miner's job assignments, nor did anything to improve the relationship between the miner and his foreman.

The mediation of grievances experiment, too, was successful[5] and led us to reflect on just what it was from the perspective of the theory of dispute resolution that we and others were trying to do. We were not mediators—that is, we were not helping to settle specific disputes. Rather we were dispute systems designers—helping disputants change the way they handled disputes. Our interventions were not limited to suggesting new procedures but extended to organizing procedures into a sequence and working with the parties to help them acquire the motivation, negotiation skills, and resources to use their new system successfully. Our reflections led to *Getting Disputes Resolved: Designing Systems to Cut the Costs of Conflict.*[7]

This article reviews our principles of dispute systems design as they apply to intra- and interorganizational conflict. It draws on our own experiences, those of other dispute systems designers, and current research on negotiations and dispute resolution in organizational settings. The article begins with a look at the costs and benefits of conflict in organizations—the criteria by which any dispute systems design project must ultimately be evaluated. We then introduce our fundamental proposition that resolving disputes on the basis of interests rather than rights or power results in lower costs and greater benefits. Then we discuss six principles for designing systems to cut the costs of conflict. We conclude with some advice about working with the parties to make the dispute systems design viable and an appeal to psychologists to help move dispute systems design out of its infancy by testing its assumptions and prescriptions in their own research and practice.

Costs and Benefits of Conflict

At York Computer (a pseudonym), a high-technology company in which the corporate culture stresses the appearance of harmony, avoidance of confrontation, and deference to authority, conflicts between managers over budget and project authority are avoided until they reach major proportions, at which point the company president steps in and decides what should be done.[8] The results have been disastrous.

Driven to early success by the creativity and charisma of its founder, York Computer has been unable to make the transition to professional management. At the same time it has failed to keep pace with the changes in its market and technological environments. Why? From our perspective much of the problem is due to management's failure to understand two fundamental facts about conflict: First, conflict is inevitable within organizations. Although certainly affected by the personalities and ideologies of the parties, conflict within and between organizations is primarily due to the roles, rules, incentives, and constraints of the organizational structure within which parties interact.[9] Second, if successfully managed, conflict can produce high quality, creative solutions that lead to innovation and progress.[9]

It is usually the crippling costs of poorly managed conflict that stimulate organizations to reevaluate the way conflict is being managed. Although there are many organizational costs and benefits of disputing, we focus on four criteria in evaluating a conflict management system: transaction costs, satisfaction with outcomes, effect on the relationship, and recurrence of disputes.

Costs

Transaction costs. Transaction costs refer to the time, money, and emotional energy expended in disputing; the resources consumed and destroyed; and the opportunities lost. The IBM-Fujitsu disputes over the use of software threatened to consume millions of dollars in litigation costs. The wildcat strikes at Caney Creek had made the mine so unprofitable that management was ready to close the mine, with the resulting loss of 300 jobs. Managers at York Computer, by failing to recognize that their conflict reflected among other things differing views of their customers' changing needs, missed the rapid shift in word processing technology from stand alone processors to personal computers. Because they did not have the equipment to replace their customers' office systems with personal computers, York Computer lost many of its customers to competitors.

Satisfaction with outcomes. Satisfaction with outcomes depends primarily on the degree to which the outcomes of the dispute meet the parties' interests—their needs, desires, concerns—and secondarily on whether the parties believe the dispute resolution process is fair. At Caney Creek the outcome of a wildcat strike was usually the continuation of the status quo. Mine management, angry with the costs of the strike, typically refused to make concessions in the face of a strike. Thus, the miners seldom got more from a strike than an opportunity to vent their frustration.

Procedures that allow disputing parties to vent their emotions, voice their concerns, and participate in determining the final decision are perceived as providing fairer outcomes than procedures that involve the disputants less.[10,11] Wildcat strikes, for instance, provided miners with both emotional venting and voice. The new dispute system for Caney Creek was designed to provide opportunities for both but in the context of negotiations, not a strike.

Effect on the relationship. The outcomes of disputes and the procedures that generate those outcomes may not only affect the parties' ability to resolve future disputes but also their ability to work together day to day. The long-term effect of the procedures and outcomes on the parties' relationship is a third criterion for evaluating a dispute resolution system. This may have been the primary concern of school administrators at the Catholic Archdiocese of Chicago in designing their new dispute resolution system. They were concerned that teachers who believed themselves to be unfairly disciplined would find it difficult to fulfill their classroom responsibilities and follow directives from school administrators.

Recurrence of disputes. The final criterion is recurrence—whether disputes once resolved stay resolved or recur. Recurrence can take three forms: same dispute, same parties; different dispute, same parties; different dispute, same parties; same dispute, different parties. All three types of recurrence could result from the same situation. For example, a teacher in need of additional income begins to work for the park district after school. When she receives a disciplinary warning for moonlighting, she quits her park district job and begins to do private tutoring and is again reprimanded (same dispute, same parties). At the same time five other teachers who are tutoring receive reprimands (same dispute, different parties).

The Benefits of Conflict

There are benefits associated with managing conflict that go well beyond minimizing its costs. Conflict within and between organizations often stems from differing perceptions of the present and the future. The resolution of disputes is a major factor driving incremental change in an organization or in a relationship. York Computer with its centralized decision-making system and its culture of conflict avoidance lacked mechanisms for incremental change. Whether this company can catch up with its competitors and then remain competitive depend on whether overdue change in corporate strategy can be implemented successfully, especially if the change in strategy is not accompanied by internal changes in decision-making, reward, and dispute resolution systems.

Interests, Rights, and Power

To resolve a dispute, opposed positions—the claim of one party and its rejection by the other—have to be turned into one outcome. Our principles for dispute systems design rest on an assumption, a proposition, and an observation about dispute resolution.

An Assumption

Resolving a dispute will not alter the underlying conflict of interests that generated the dispute. As long as the relationship endures, future disputes will arise. For example, determining what Fujitsu should pay IBM for the use of some IBM systems software will not alter Fujitsu's strategy to produce IBM compatible mainframes and IBM's desire for proprietary control over its software. Fujitsu will need continued access to IBM systems software. Even after IBM agrees to provide that access, future disputes about what Fujitsu should pay IBM for access to the software are likely.

A Proposition

From the long-term perspective of the organization or interorganizational relationship, reconciling conflicting interests is generally a less costly way to resolve disputes than determining who is right or more powerful.

Interests. Reconciling interests often involves identifying underlying concerns, prioritizing them, and devising tradeoffs in which parties concede on low-priority interests in order to receive satisfaction of high-priority interests.[12] Tradeoffs are a particularly effective means of resolving disputes when parties' interests dovetail, that is, when interests of high priority to one party are low priority to the other, and vice versa.[13]

Another technique for reconciling interests, called *bridging*, involves devising creative solutions that serve the disputants' primary interests.[13] Bridging is like trading-off in that both parties are likely to have to make concessions on low-priority interests. It goes beyond trading-off, however, in that the resolution turns on a new element, the bridge, that is added to the negotiation.[14] In this, Pruitt gave Follett's[15] example to illustrate bridging. Two companies were in conflict because each wanted to use a loading platform at the same time. Taking turns was for some reason unacceptable. The bridge solution was to enlarge the platform.

Three other techniques for reconciling interests rely on creative use of resources.[16] In *cost cutting* some disputants get what they want in return for acting to reduce or eliminate costs likely to be incurred by others. In *nonspecific compensation* some disputants get what they want, and the others receive some type of substitute compensation. Finally, when a dispute is about resources and new resources sufficient to satisfy all disputants can be made available, the dispute can be resolved at least until resources again become scarce. Pruitt and Rubin[16] called this *expanding the pie.*

Reconciling interests does not mean that disputants ignore the distributive aspects of the negotiation. Unless new resources can be added, reconciling interests means that one or more of the disputants will have to take less than they would like. The question of how much each takes is as salient in negotiations that focus on interests as those that do not. The difference is that interests-based negotiations take a more creative look at the distribution problem.

Rights. Another approach to resolving disputes is to determine who is right according to some independent standard of perceived legitimacy or fairness. Laws, contracts, and social norms, such as reciprocity and precedent, are all potential rights standards. The difficulty is in choosing a standard and then determining what it implies with respect to the dispute. For instance, when IBM and Fujitsu first began disputing over systems software, both sides focused on rights: IBM lawyers argued that according to legal standards, systems software was proprietary; Fujitsu lawyers argued that it was not, invoking different legal standards.

Power. Determining who is more powerful is yet another way to resolve disputes. Without a decisive power contest—a fight, strike, or war—in which power is exercised and costs are imposed, it is often difficult to determine which party is more powerful. This is because power stems from interdependency,[17] and each party's perceptions of the quality of its own and the other party's alternatives to resolving the dispute may not coincide. It is therefore difficult to predict at what point each will prefer its alternatives to continuing to deal with the other.

Interests versus rights. Reconciling interests tends to produce higher satisfaction with outcomes, better working relationships, and less recurrence of conflicts, and it may incur lower transaction costs than determining who is right. This conclusion follows from research that has compared mediation (an interests-based dispute resolution procedure) with arbitration (a rights-based procedure). In the context of labor grievances,[5] small claims,[18] and child-custody disputes,[19] as well as in simulated management decision making,[20] disputants prefer mediation to arbitration or court. Why? Agreements that reconcile interests often provide all parties with much of what they wanted. The information shared in the process of searching for a resolution may increase mutual understanding and benefit the relationship. An additional benefit of mediation is that recurrence is low.[19]

The transaction costs associated with reconciling interests are sometimes higher than those associated with rights or power procedures. For instance, it is likely to take a supervisor longer to help subordinates find an interests-based resolution to their dispute than to decide it herself or himself. But low recurrence of disputes resolved by reconciling interests should compensate for the time taken by the interests-based procedure.

Social psychologists and organizational development specialists have known at least since Lewin's famous experiments[21] that it is more effective to involve people in a decision to change than for a third party to exhort them to change. Our prescription about the costs and benefits of interests-based procedures is consistent both with this and subsequent research on change.

Rights versus power. Determining who is right or more powerful often becomes a contest distinguished primarily by transaction costs. Violence quite simply costs more than litigation. Power contests often create new injuries and disputes and leave a residue of anger, distrust, and a desire for revenge.

An Observation

Dispute resolution procedures differentially focus parties on reconciling interests versus determining who is right or more powerful. Negotiation, of course, can focus on all three, depending on what is being communicated. Parties may focus on interests and approach the dispute as a problem to be solved together. Alternatively, they may discuss rights and search for an organizational rule or precedent. When threatening each other, parties are engaged in power negotiations. In the course of a single negotiation, the focus may shift from rights to interests to power and back.

Other procedures tend to have a dominant focus. Mediation, in which a third party assists the disputants in reaching an agreement, typically focuses on interests. Adjudicative procedures, like court or arbitration, in which the disputants or their representatives present evidence and arguments to a neutral third party who has the power to make a binding decision, focus on rights. Power procedures, like proxy fights, elections, strikes, and wars, focus on who is more powerful.

Cutting the Costs and Reaping the Benefits of Conflict: Principles of Dispute Systems Design

Before introducing our prescriptions about how conflict within and between organizations ought to be handled in order to minimize costs and maximize benefits, it may be useful to consider briefly how organizations tend to handle disputes.

Disputes within organizations are typically handled by hierarchy and other forms of organizational structure like task forces, liaisons, integrating departments, and so on.[22,23] Organizational structure serves to funnel disputes to third-party decision makers with the authority to resolve them but is neutral with respect to whether disputes should be resolved primarily on the basis of interests, rights, or power. Thus, managers acting as conflict handlers and dispute resolvers have an option as to which approach they take. Our dispute systems design prescriptions indicate what approach managers might take to resolve disputes and should reduce the frequency with which mangers must become involved as third parties to disputes.

Disputes between organizations, or between organizations and their customers or suppliers, although initially negotiated, often end up in court. Corporations, sensitive to the high costs of resolving disputes in court, are beginning to explore alternative dispute resolution procedures. Agreements among joint-venture partners to arbitrate disputes are becoming more common.[24] In the service sector car dealers and stock brokers provide for arbitration that is binding on them but not on their complaining customer.[24]

Our seven principles of dispute system design are guidelines for cutting the costs of conflict and realizing its benefits and are applicable to disputes within and between organizations.

Principle 1: Consultation Before Disputing, Feedback After

Our assumptions that conflict is inevitable in organizations and is often an early warning of need for change imply that organizations should make a significant effort to discuss issues that may cause disputes and to learn from those disputes that do occur. Consultation before disputes erupt can minimize the occurrence of unnecessary disputes. Feedback after a dispute has occurred helps managers take action to prevent recurrence. Two examples illustrate these points.

Consultation. When Pacific Bell went through the transition of deregulation, the company and the union formed Common Interest Forums to discuss ways to work together and prevent unnecessary disputes. These forums provided opportunities for management to consult with the union before initiating action. Management was not committed to negotiate over such intended actions but could do so if the union raised unexpected opposition.[25]

Feedback. Managers and lawyers at some consumer-product companies regularly analyze consumer complaints to determine what changes in product design might reduce the likelihood of similar disputes in the future. In some states consumer mediation agencies keep records of complaints against each merchant. The agency alerts the proper state authorities when repeated complaints are lodged against the same merchant.[26] In this way state action to prevent the merchant from continued unlawful practices can be instituted.

Principle 2: Put the Focus on Interests

Negotiation is almost always available to disputants. The challenge lies in using negotiation to reconcile interests. Framing negotiations as a cooperative rather than competitive exercise facilitates interests-based resolutions,[14] as does an exchange of information about interests, either directly by sharing information or indirectly through the exchange of proposals.[27] Providing negotiation skills training that focuses on techniques for reconciling interests[13,28] may not only increase skills but may also establish norms about how disputes are to be handled within an organization. Additionally, successful resolution of disputes in simulated negotiations training may generate expectations that interests-based negotiations can be successful and may thus motivate disputants to use interests-based procedures.

Interests-based negotiations, of course, are not always successful. Often disputants are so emotionally involved with the dispute that they need to vent their emotions before they can negotiate successfully. In these situations mediation, in which a third party tries to help the disputants reach an agreement but does not have the power to impose a settlement on them, may be effective in reconciling interests. A mediator may provide a controlled environment in which one or both parties may express emotions and feelings and acknowledge those of the other. A mediator may also help the parties understand their interests as well as the other parties' interests, induce them to evaluate their alternatives if no resolution is reached, and encourage each to think about agreements that both can accept.

A major question is the circumstances under which managers will mediate. When their role gives them authority over the disputants, managers acting as third parties in disputes seldom act like mediators.[29,30] Nevertheless, a mediation approach to dispute resolution may have long-term benefits for managers.[5,31] For example, Karambayya and Brett[20] found that when management students simulated an organizational dispute in which a third-party manager became involved, the disputants judged the procedures and outcomes to be more fair when the third party used mediation techniques rather than authoritarian approaches.

Principle 3: Build in "Loop-Backs" to Negotiations

Sometimes negotiations fail because the parties' perceptions of who is right or who is more powerful are so different that they cannot establish a range in which to negotiate. Information about how rights standards have been applied in other disputes can serve to narrow the gap between the parties' expectations of the outcome of a rights contest and thus make agreement possible.

For interorganizational disputes advisory arbitration (in which a third party provides a nonbinding decision concerning how a case would be resolved in court) may be the simplest procedure for acquiring rights information.[24] Disputants within organizations may use information about corporate norms to help them establish a bargaining range. An example illustrates this point.

Two strategic business units of an organization were negotiating over what one would pay the other in return for the transfer of some magnet technology. When negotiations broke down, the directors of the two units could have turned the dispute over to the corporation's president, but this was risky in the absence of information about what the president might do. Instead, they went to the director of another unit, whom they asked about previous transfers of technology between units, in particular, how profits had been shared. Precedent provided a norm to help them to define the bargaining range and negotiate a resolution.

There are also loop-back procedures that help avoid power contests. Rarely does a negotiated agreement look so attractive as when the parties are on the verge of a costly power contest. For this reason a cooling-off period, a specified time during which the disputants refrain from a power contest, can be effective. Such periods are mandated by the Taft-Hartley Act and the Railway Labor Act before strikes that threaten to cause a national emergency, but they are just as applicable to small-scale conflict. For example, "sleeping on" a decision or talking it over with an uninvolved third party before taking action are practical rules of thumb that let emotions cool and rationality reassert itself.

Separation of disputing parties by a third party may help avoid power contests. Kolb[29] described a manager, "Restructure-it Roger," who assumes that conflict within his division is due to personality differences. His primary dispute resolution technique is to reorganize or restructure his division so that disputing managers no longer have to interact directly.

The problem with this approach is that, at least in Restructure-it Roger's case, the assumption is wrong. Within organizations conflict is often due to roles that people play, not merely to personalities. New people in the same roles are likely to have the same disputes. Furthermore, restructuring reporting relationships in the division and adding hierarchy exacerbates communications problems and makes reconciliation of interests less likely.

Principle 4: Provide Low-Cost Rights and Power Procedures

In some disputes interests are so opposed that agreement is not possible. Thus, effective dispute resolution systems have low-cost procedures for providing final resolution of disputes on the basis of rights or power. Joint-venture agreements like the one entered into by the oil companies in our example often provide for arbitration. Management hierarchy provides the same mechanism for final resolution of disputes within organizations. Voting resolves proxy battles like the one between Texaco and Carl Icahn, the corporate raider.

Principle 5: Arrange Procedures in a Low-to-High Cost Sequence

Our design principles—consultation before disputing, feedback after—put the focus on interests, provide procedures that loop back to negotiations, and provide low-cost rights and power procedures; the principles suggest creating dispute resolution systems in which procedures are arranged in a low-to-high cost sequence. These principles are the building blocks of a dispute resolution system. Table 1 shows a menu of procedures to draw on in designing such a sequence.

Depending on the characteristics of the organization or interorganizational relationship in which the new dispute resolution system is to be embedded, the designer may wish to select more than one procedure from a category. For example, in our grievance-mediation experiment in the coal industry, we added interests-based mediation to a system that already provided for negotiation. Our decision about where to place mediation in the coal industry's se-

TABLE 1
Menu of Procedures Least Costly to Most Costly

Procedure	Example
Prevention procedures	Consultation
	Feedback
Interests-based procedures	Negotiation
	Mediation
"Loop-back" procedures	Rights
	Information procedures
	Advisory arbitration
	Power
	Cooling-off periods
	Third-party intervention
Low-cost rights and power procedures	Rights—arbitration
	Power—voting

Note. Adapted from *Getting Disputes Resolved: Designing a Dispute Resolution System to Cut the Costs of Conflict* (pp. 62–63) by W. L. Ury, J.M. Brett, and S.B. Goldberg, 1988, San Francisco: Jossey-Bass. Copyright 1988 by Jossey-Bass. Adapted by permission.

quence of procedures for resolving grievances was based both on considerations of cost and the effect of the new procedure on old ones. Mediation at the mine site would not only be prohibitively expensive but also would likely encourage disputants to treat negotiation as pro forma and become dependent on the mediator instead of themselves for resolving disputes. Thus, a sequence of procedures, each only slightly more costly than the previous one, may have the paradoxical effect of encouraging use of higher cost procedures. The best means to guard against this is to space procedures sufficiently far apart that increased transaction costs are noticeable.

Principle 6: Provide Disputants With the Necessary Negotiation Skills, Resources, and Motivation

Designing procedures according to these principles is not sufficient to reduce the costs of dispute resolution and to realize its benefits. Disputants must have the negotiation skills, the resources, and the motivation to use the system.

Issues in training negotiation skills. A dispute resolution system that meets our costs criteria is one in which a relatively high proportion of disputes are resolved through interests-based procedures. The Achilles heel of our system may be negotiation skills. Negotiators seem to be better at maximizing their own gains (distributive bargaining) than they are at maximizing joint gains (integrative bargaining). It is intuitive to many that when negotiating over a single issue, say the purchase price of a company, the buyer makes a low initial offer, the seller makes a high initial demand, and the two make concessions in a reciprocal fashion until they reach agreement or impasse. Negotiators also seem to know intuitively how to compromise by splitting the difference between their positions. What they do not do very well is to find agreements that integrate interests, agreements by which they receive more than they would had they simply compromised on each issue.[32]

In an exercise derived from the magnet technology transfer situation discussed earlier, management students and executives negotiating the terms of the transfer frequently fail to find the integrative agreement. The situation involves two issues (which should be a tip-off that a solution involving trade-offs may be possible). The first is what the buyer should pay for the technology. The second is how long the buyer should refrain from selling the magnet to the seller's competitors. Parties who find the integrative trade-off that maximizes joint gains in this case are ones who discuss the two issues together and consider alternative arrangements of transfer price and protection from competitors.

Several cognitive biases prevent people from finding integrative solutions. One important one is what Bazerman and Neale[33] called the *bias of the fixed pie.* Parties approach a negotiation with the perspective that the task is solely one of distribution.[34] Then, they tend to deal with multi-issue situations issue by issue.[14] It is cognitively simpler to resolve each issue separately, yet doing so usually precludes making trade-offs between them.[14] Finally, satisficing may occur. Once negotiators have found an agreement that is satisfactory to them, they tend to resolve the dispute or close the deal and move on, not realizing that one or both of them could have done better.[12]

Numerous experiments to teach negotiators to overcome their cognitive biases have been unsuccessful.[34,35] Recently, however, Neale, Northcraft, and Earley[36] found that experimental subjects' performance on an integrative negotiation task improved dramatically when they were given specific goals about how many points to try for and a lecture on problem-solving negotiation. In contrast, the subjects whose goals were "do your best" did not profit from the same lecture and increase their scores. Their performance remained stable over time.

Experienced managers with no prior training in interests-based or problem-solving negotiation find the integrative solution in the magnet technology transfer exercise about 40% of the time. Management students negotiating this exercise after having been exposed through lecture, readings, and prior exercises to interests-based negotiations do better; they find the integrative solution about 60% to 80% of the time. Furthermore when told there is a settlement as good or better than the one they negotiated, most students continue negotiating and find it.

Searching for a postsettlement settlement[12] helps avoid the bias of satisficing when a distributive rights or power-based focus has dominated negotiations. Information is shared more easily in postsettlement negotiations because the initial settlement determines the distribution. Postsettlement negotiations can therefore focus on integrating the parties' interests.

Overcoming cognitive biases that limit effectiveness of interests-based negotiations may take rather sophisticated negotiations training. Does this mean that dispute systems design is limited to situations in which such training is possible or to people whose attitudes or abilities indicate that they would benefit from training? We do not think so. In many seriously distressed dispute resolution situations, like Caney Creek mine, schools, or even penitentiaries, disputes are normally resolved by power contests, such as strikes and fights. Dispute systems design coupled with training that does little more than expose disputants to interests-based negotiations has been successful in getting disputants to talk their disputes through to resolution instead of fighting them out. Although these resolutions may show signs of cognitive biases, transaction and other costs of disputing have been reduced.

At Bryant High School in New York, for example, a program to mediate disputes that ranged across student-student, student-teacher, and student-parent problems was instituted in 1980. More than 3,000 students received some training through classroom seminars on nonviolent problem solving. As a result almost any time a dispute arose, several students were present who knew about taking a problem-solving approach to resolving it. Either they stepped in to help resolve it or they encouraged the disputants to go to the mediation committee (that consisted of parents, teachers, and students).

Consider, too, the story of the inmate, "Heavy":

The first prison that we worked in New York was a big maximum security place, a couple thousand men locked up. And one of the men on the design committee who later became a committee member was a guy named Heavy. I don't remember what his first name was but they called him Heavy because he just sat there. I don't know how smart Heavy was, he was just a moose of a guy who apparently had a very quick temper, which we saw a little bit of, and who also in his earlier days had been very quick with his fists. When we got this thing going, Heavy got the training. Sometime after it started, a grievance clerk said, "I can't believe it. Yesterday Heavy got into an argument and I thought he was going to drop the sucker right in his tracks. Heavy just kept talking to him!" I don't know how much of this you can attribute to the training, but the guy who was talking to us was attributing all of it to the fact that Heavy had learned that he didn't have to drop people in their tracks, he could talk to them and get something out of that.[37]

Resources for dispute systems design. Experts, information, and institutions are the resources needed to support some dispute systems designs. The IBM-Fujitsu agreement required all three. The parties agreed to set up a facility where Fujitsu could examine IBM software and IBM could examine Fujitsu software. If either party wants to use any element of the other's software, negotiations are to take place over the proper compensation for the developer. These negotiations can be assisted by the technical director of the facility, who is neutral and is paid jointly by IBM and Fujitsu. Unresolved disputes about compensation are resolved by arbitration.[4]

Informational resources are particularly important for supporting loop-back procedures (Principle 3) that focus on rights. For example, some courts have set up data bases for information about the characteristics and results of asbestos claims that have been resolved by trial or by settlement. When a new claim is filed, similar claims are identified in the data base. Information about how these similar claims have been resolved helps lawyers for both sides determine the range within which their claim is likely to be resolved. This information reduces uncertainty about the likely outcome of the case and provides an independent standard for settlement negotiations.[38]

Motivating disputants to use new low-cost procedures. One of the most difficult issues in dispute system design is motivating the parties to use interests-based procedures, procedures that loop back to negotiations, and low-cost rights or power procedures. Parties often engage in procedures that generate high costs and fail to use procedures that would seem to be less costly and potentially more beneficial. Why? Sometimes interests-based procedures are not available, parties lack negotiation skills to use them successfully, or they do not have the necessary resources. Often, however, the problem is one of motivation.

At Caney Creek mine we were faced with frequent wildcat strikes despite the availability of a contractual grievance procedure that provided for three stages of negotiation and binding arbitration. We found some miners were reluctant to raise grievances with their foremen because of fear of retaliation. Others felt that the grievance procedure deprived them of voice. Union and company representatives would argue about contractual technicalities far removed from the actual problem as the miner perceived it. Miners were passive observers at arbitration and often would have to wait months for the arbitrator's decision. Any miner, in contrast, could instigate a wildcat strike and receive immediate attention. Even if the strike failed to get the miners what they wanted, their voice would be heard, and they would receive the emotional satisfaction of revenge. In many instances the motivation to strike outweighed the motivation to use the contractual grievance procedure.

We are doubtful that a Caney Creek miner with a grievance weighed the pros and cons of alternative courses of action before striking. However, for a dispute systems designer who is trying to understand why parties are using what seem to be high cost procedures, it is useful to analyze the incentives associated with the use of alternative procedures. Some incentives have to do with expected outcomes, others with characteristics of the procedures themselves.

Incentives associated with outcomes. Disputants prefer procedures that generate outcomes that meet their interests[11] and avoid those in which they believe outcomes are risky.[39] As a result, powerful parties who believe they have been winning with old procedures may be extremely reluctant to cooperate with dispute systems design. It may be that the weaker party will have to champion the dispute systems design and the focus on interests. In the long run, however, the stronger party should also prefer a system that preserves its strength but reduces transaction costs and increases satisfaction with outcomes. The costs of imposing one's will can be high. Threats must be backed up by actions from time to time. The weaker party may fail to comply fully with a settlement imposed by power and thereby force the more powerful party to engage in expensive policing. Thus, even for a party who has been winning, a focus on interests, within the bounds set by power, may be more desirable than would appear at first glance.

Incentives associated with process. Empirical research has identified several procedural characteristics that affect parties' procedural preferences. Two of these are outcome control and voice. Evidence from a wide variety of contexts indicates that disputants prefer procedures in which they retain out-come control or final authority over the resolution of the dispute.[5,18,19,40] Fur-thermore, despite laboratory evidence to the contrary,[41] mediation, an interest-based procedure in which disputants retain outcome control, appears to be quite effective in resolving disputes when parties have an ongoing rela-tionship[5,19] and even when they do not.[18] Other research suggests that proce-dures in which disputants simply have a veto, for example, advisory arbitration in which the third party makes a recommendation after hearing evidence presented in an adjudicative format, are not particularly successful in resolving disputes,[42,43] possibly because the parties do not participate in formulating the resolution and, therefore, feel little ownership of it.

Parties also prefer procedures that give them voice, the opportunity to pre-sent their side of the dispute or to frame the dispute from their own perspec-tive.[11,41] However, it is not entirely clear whether it is voice qua voice that is important or whether having voice results in perceptions of greater influence over the ultimate decision.[5,11]

Another aspect of voice that has not received empirical attention is the opportunity to express emotions. It may be that in emotionally charged dis-putes parties prefer procedures that provide for the controlled expression of emotion and the acknowledgment by the blamed party of the validity of such emotions. An apology, for instance, can often defuse emotion and make problem-solving negotiation possible.[42]

Working with the Parties to Make the Dispute Systems Design Viable

At York Computers dispute systems design is unlikely to be successful without major changes in the corporate culture, centralized decision-making struc-ture, and system of rewarding managers for avoiding conflict. Dispute systems design in other organizations or interorganizational relationships may not re-quire such a total intervention. Working with the parties, the designer needs to assess how much change is needed and how much is possible.

Without the active support of parties on all sides of the conflict, it will be exceedingly difficult to make any substantial changes in the way disputes are resolved. The process of design is as much a political task as it is a technical one. (Those who practice organizational development know this all too well.) We have found that in working with the parties, dispute systems designers play the roles of coach, evaluator, and evangelist, in addition to those of ex-pert, mediator, and negotiator. They act as experts when analyzing the current system and considering potential changes. Acting as mediators, they seek to bring the parties to agreement on changes to the system. In doing so they are at the same time negotiating with the parties to adopt changes the designers think are worthwhile. In helping the parties begin to use the new system, the designers become coaches, working to develop the parties' skills and sustaining their enthusiasm when interests cannot be reconciled. They may also evaluate the system, helping the parties determine how well it is working and what adjustments should be made. If they take on the task of diffusion, they play yet another role, that of evangelist.

The Role of the Psychologist in Dispute Systems Design

Dispute systems design is in its infancy as an area of research and practice for psychologists. The gaps in empirical knowledge are numerous: What motivates the use of different procedures? How do different procedures vary with respect to different effectiveness criteria? How can a balance be achieved between a system that encourages parties to make claims and one that is overwhelmed by claims? How can sequences of procedures be designed to discourage pro forma behavior in early steps? What is the most effective means of training people in skills for reconciling interests? Are there differences between the standard practice of organizational development and dispute systems design?

We have extrapolated from prior research, practice, and our own experience in making prescriptions in all these areas. We are prepared to be wrong in some, but we have taken the prescriptive leap to encourage others to begin studying and practicing dispute systems design. In an increasingly interdependent world, we need to find better ways of resolving disputes than fighting over them or going to court. Dispute systems design is intended to meet this challenge.

PART XII

LEADERSHIP IN PRACTICE

Many insights into leadership can be gleaned from academicians and observers of the phenomenon, but leadership remains a practical art. Those who have been intimately engaged in the actual "doing" of leadership have a perspective which is unmatched. The readings in this segment represent observations on the art of leadership from successful leaders.

In the first selection, Max De Pree, CEO of Herman Miller, Inc., likens leadership to a jazz band, and reflects upon the skills required of a leader. The second selection is drawn from 21st Century Leadership: Dialogues with 100 Top Leaders, compiled by Lynne Joy McFarland, Larry E. Senn, and John R. Childress, and distills the insights of a large and distinguished group of leaders. The final two selections are addresses on leadership given by two leading executives, Roger B. Smith and Michele Darling. The conclusions these practitioners come to about the nature of leadership in the upcoming century cannot be ignored by anyone who hopes to be an effective player in tomorrow's world.

451

57

Leadership Jazz

Max De Pree

Max De Pree is chairman of the board of Herman Miller, Inc., a firm regularly on *Fortune*'s list of the most admired companies in the United States. He is the author of the bestsellers *Leadership Is an Art* and *Leadership Jazz*. De Pree was recently elected by *Fortune* magazine to the National Business Hall of Fame.

Leadership is, as you know, not a position but a job. It's hard and exciting and good work. It's also a serious meddling in other people's lives. One examines leadership beginning not with techniques but rather with premises, not with tools but with beliefs, and not with systems but with understandings. This I truly believe.

On a recent trip to England, I looked out of the window just before sunrise as the plane circled over central London on its way to Heathrow. The gauze of a light fog diffused the yellow lights of the city and created a brief but exciting feeling of a new Narnia. I was looking at something I had seen many times before through a new lens.

Leaders need an ability to look through a variety of lenses. We need to look through the lens of a follower. We need to look through the lens of a new reality. We need to look through the lens of hard experience and failure. We need to look through the lens of unfairness and mortality. We need to look hard at our future.

What will be needed by the next generations, our own children and grandchildren? When will we stop being boxed in by national boundaries and cultural stereotypes? What does it mean to modulate individual rights with the common good? Are we ready to make a commitment to civility and inclusiveness? Are we ready to think seriously about a fairer way to distribute economic results among all people? Where will we find new metaphors for these essential ideas?

I enjoy jazz, and one way to think about leadership is to consider a jazz band. Jazz-band leaders must choose the music, find the right musicians, and perform—in public. But the effect of the performance depends on so many things—the environment, the volunteers playing in the band, the need for everybody to perform as individuals and as a group, the absolute dependence of the leader on the members of the band, the need of the leader for the followers to play well. What a summary of an organization!

A jazz band is an expression of servant leadership. The leader of a jazz band has the beautiful opportunity to draw the best out of the other musicians. We have much to learn from jazz-band leaders, for jazz, like leadership, combines the unpredictability of the future with the gifts of individuals.

Leaders certainly need to know where they stand. But *how* do leaders stand? A sound philosophy isn't enough; we all need to connect voice and touch. So much discussion these days talks of ethics as a legal line in the sand, a prohibition against certain actions. But leadership is constructive, the right actions taken in the context of clear and well-considered thinking. The active pursuit of a common good gives us the right to ask leaders and managers of all kinds to be not only successful, but faithful. While measuring success in our society seems to be hardly mysterious enough, judging faithfulness is another matter. After all, a philosophy of leadership or management cannot be caught like a cold.

In an effort to be helpful, let me suggest five criteria as a way to start thinking about faithfulness.

Integrity in all things precedes all else. The open demonstration of integrity is essential; followers must be wholeheartedly convinced of their leaders' integrity. For leaders, who live a public life, perceptions become a fact of life. Leaders understand the profound difference between gestures and commitment. It's just impossible to be a closet leader.

The servanthood of leadership needs to be felt, understood, believed, and practiced if we're to be faithful. The best description of this kind of leadership is found in the book of Luke: "The greatest among you should be like the youngest, and the one who rules, like the one who serves." The finest instruction in how to practice it can be found in *Servant Leadership* by Robert Greenleaf, a lovely grace note to the melody in Luke.

Accountability for others, especially those on the edges of life and not yet experienced in the ways of the world, is one of the great directions leaders receive from the prophet Amos. Amos tells us that leaders should encourage and sustain those on the bottom rung first and then turn to those on the top. Should we call this the trickle-up theory?

There is a great misconception in organizations: that a manager must be either in control or not in control. The legitimate alternative is *the practice of equity*. This is surely a reasonable component in anyone's philosophy of management. While equity should certainly guide the apportioning of resources, it is far more important in our human relationships. . . .

The last criterion for faithfulness (in this list, that is; of course you will think of more) is that leaders have to be *vulnerable*, have to offer others the opportunity to do their best. Leaders become vulnerable by sharing with others the marvelous gift of being personally accountable. People in a capitalist system become vulnerable by creating a genuine opportunity for others to reach their potential at the same time that all work together toward corporate goals.

In finding one's voice and connecting it to one's touch, three questions come to mind: "What shall I promise?" "Can the so-called bottom line truly be the bottom line?" and "Who speaks for whom?" . . .

You've recently been promoted. You're now a vice president or a provost or a department supervisor. Now the work begins. You haven't arrived, you've only begun to travel. In the same way, having children means only that the work of becoming a parent has begun. The biological event is very different from the love and commitment, the skinned knees and dirty diapers, the faithfulness to homework and Little League, the sacrifices for tuition and music lessons, the laughter and the tears—these kinds of things add up to earning the title "Mom" or "Dad."

One becomes a leader, I believe, through doing the work of a leader. It's often difficult and painful and sometimes even unrewarding, and it's work. There are also times of joy in the work of leadership, and doing the work of a leader is necessary in our society.

58

Redefining Leadership for the Next Century

Lynn Joy McFarland, Larry E. Senn, and John R. Childress

Lynn Joy McFarland is founder, chairman and CEO of LINC (Leadership into the Next Century), a not-for-profit leadership education organization. She has held executive positions at Xerox, Honeywell, Bank of America, and McDonnell Douglas. Larry Senn has taught at UCLA and the University of Southern California, and co-founded—with John Childress—America's first leadership consulting group. John Childress graduated from Harvard and has extensive experience in training and personal development. McFarland, Senn, and Childress collaborated to write *Twenty-First Century Leadership: Dialogues with 100 Top Leaders*.

"I think the ideal leader for the 21st Century will be one who creates an environment that encourages everyone in the organization to stretch their capabilities and achieve a shared vision, who gives people the confidence to run farther and faster than they ever have before, and who establishes the conditions for people to be more productive, more innovative, more creative and feel more in charge of their own lives than they ever dreamed possible," says Robert Crandall, Chairman and President of American Airlines.

As leadership is the currency for the 21st Century, what is being called for at this time? While many leaders acknowledge that some qualities of leader-

From Lynne Joy McFarland, Larry E. Senn, and John R. Childress, *Twenty-First Century Leadership: Dialogues with 100 Top Leaders* (Long Beach, CA: The Leadership Press, Inc., 1993). Reprinted by permission.

ship are timeless, they also indicate that we are in a whole new era, one that challenges our old frameworks, assumptions and beliefs. Leadership, in fact, needs to be redefined for the next century. Just as our organizations have required dramatic transformation, the face of leadership too must change.

In the preceding chapters, our dialogues with leaders established the importance of using a new set of leadership technologies, such as the greater use of empowerment, vision and winning shared values, building a healthy culture, and focusing on superior quality and service. With these tools gaining new focus, what does that imply for a leader to personally be successful in the 21st Century?

As we conversed with leaders, the answer became very clear: new behaviors will be required and old habits will have to be broken. Many of the existing behaviors of leaders are based on their past successful experience and their beliefs about what it took to win. However, that model came from an earlier era, rooted in such hero figures as John Wayne and military models like General Patton.

Some of the old beliefs that have become self-limiting for leaders include:

- "If I'm the boss, I'm supposed to have all the answers."
- "If I'm the boss, I'm not supposed to make any mistakes."
- "I'm in charge, no one should question my authority."
- "If you want the job done right, you have to do it yourself."
- "If we create new things around here, they should be my ideas."

Unfortunately, most of these beliefs are inconsistent with the new era of empowering leadership. The behaviors that flow from these disempowering beliefs do not create the quality of organization that will succeed now or in the years ahead.

Many current leaders would be well served to take some time out and reevaluate their lifelong beliefs and behaviors by acknowledging "that may have worked for me then, but what is most appropriate for today and tomorrow?" We are in a time when using the old skills, even while working harder, will not move us toward success. What we need is a new set of beliefs and behaviors, new technologies, and a fundamental shift in the relationship between leaders and their organizations.

There is a useful metaphor that relates to the current leadership paradigm shift: In high jumping years ago, from high school track meets to the Olympics, the men and women who won always used the traditional scissors kick. Then Dick Fosbury showed up and invented a whole new way to jump over the bar, which came to be called the "Fosbury Flop." Very soon, if you couldn't convert your old belief in the scissors kick to a new belief in this more effective "Fosbury Flop," then you could no longer compete in the event.

In the complexity and intensity of the Changing Game, a parallel situation has arisen in business. As a result of holding onto past beliefs and behaviors, we have seen once dominant organizations lose to the competition. So the question now is will leaders convert to a new "Fosbury" leadership model in order to make it over the high bar of the 21st Century?

New Definitions for Leaders in the 21st Century

As we spoke with leaders about the most important changes they see in leadership, several themes emerged. The first is a shift in who we see as leaders. **Leadership is no longer the exclusive domain of the "boss at the top."** Ray Smith, Chairman and CEO of Bell Atlantic, sums it up well: "*Everyone in an organization has an obligation to lead.*"

A second theme follows from the first: **The new leader must facilitate excellence in others**. This is made clear by Patricia Aburdene: "*To be a leader for the next century, you have to be able to bring out the best in people.*" Understandably, this approach, like the "Fosbury Flop" replaces the insensitive "drill sergeant," who barked out the orders and pressured others to achieve short-term results.

The third theme is the distinction between leadership and management. Kate Rand Lloyd, Editor-At-Large of *Working Woman* magazine, says, "*It's only been in the last decade, really, that people have become aware that management and leadership are not the same thing at all. And we're beginning to see the return of true leadership.*" We will see why it's important to understand the difference.

A fourth theme explores the newly emerging, sensitive and humanistic dimension to leadership. As Howard Allen, Chairman of the Executive Committee of Southern California Edison, states, "*I don't think you can be a successful leader without interpersonal sensitivity.*"

A fifth theme is the growing need for leaders to take a holistic approach, embracing a wide variety of qualities, skills, and capabilities. Carolyn Burger, President and CEO of Diamond State Telephone, A Bell Atlantic Company, tells us, "*To be a well-rounded and successful leader of a corporation in the 21st Century, many broad qualities will be essential.*"

A final theme in the new leadership definition is mastery over change, which goes beyond merely reacting to change as it comes up, but rather

predicting and redirecting change before it comes up. *"The first aspect of leadership for the future is openness to, and maybe even eagerness for, change,"* says Blenda Wilson, President of California State University, Northridge.

It is our hope that as you read this chapter, you will open up to new ideas and possibilities to assist you personally in your own leadership effectiveness. Perhaps we can learn together with these leaders how to reinvent ourselves and our organizations for the 21st Century.

Section 1: Everyone As a Leader

"The biggest change in leadership is our perception of who can be a leader," observes Rieva Lesonsky, Editor-In-Chief of *Entrepreneur* magazine.

The response we heard over and over is "Everyone can be a leader." In this Changing Game, leadership and power—like information—needs to be shared throughout an enterprise. We saw in earlier dialogues that in order to build a successful, empowered, high-performance organization, the leaders at the top had to share their power and distribute leadership out to the far reaches of their organization.

We were also shown that leadership itself is shifting from an autocratic, militaristic model toward an empowering, participatory model. The new leadership definition recognizes the greatness and unique contributions of everyone. "Everybody does have a leader inside," says Robert Reich, Secretary of Labor and former Professor at John F. Kennedy School of Government, Harvard University.

So if every single person must be utilized in a leadership capacity, how does that reflect on the leaders at the top? The classic definition of a leader is a charismatic, often forceful, individual taking command over followers, whether that leader is a corporate CEO, an army general, or a high school principal. While we still need charismatic leaders, the command-and-control style has outlived its usefulness, because people no longer want to be dominated.

William T. Solomon, Chairman and CEO of Austin Industries, Inc., says, "There has been a massive change in corporate leadership in the last 15 to 20 years. Leadership and a sense of accountability for what really goes on in the organization have been pushed down and distributed throughout the organization."

Therefore, we will also need visionary leaders, facilitative leaders, inspiring leaders, collaborative leaders—in other words, leaders of all types arising at every level of an enterprise. Leadership is no longer exclusively top-down, but also bottom-up and "omni-directional."

Leaders at the top will need to make it popular to lead, invite everyone to take a leadership role and then educate and strengthen each person's capacity to lead.

Reuben Mark, Chairman, President, and CEO of Colgate-Palmolive Company, adds, "It is crucial for our future that we find ways to lead better. Because in the final analysis, it's not the general who wins, but the army. And the more that you can help people be self-sufficient, proud of themselves and truly skillful, the more the organization and society are going to accomplish." . . .

Section 2: Bringing Out the Best in Everyone

"The most important quality that a 21st Century leader needs is the ability to inspire other people, first to pull together in the direction of the vision, and second to do their very best in producing excellent results," poignantly states Kathy Keeton, President of Omni Publications International.

Leaders in our dialogue underscore that once the leadership responsibility has been distributed to everyone in the organization, the next imperative is to bring out the best in everyone. In some ways this is not new—successful leaders have historically raised the performance of people. Yet for the years ahead there are important distinctions.

In the past, leaders often have gotten results from their people, at least for the short term, by using non-empowering methods, including intimidation and force at the one extreme, or paternalistic, "care-taking" approaches at the other. By contrast the leaders in this dialogue point out more effective ways to bring out the best in people through trust, respect, listening, inspiration, setting the example, alignment of vision and values, nourishing, educating, coaching, mentoring, welcoming risk-taking and mistakes, recognizing creativity and genius, harnessing talent, awakening latent potential, and even having fun. . . .

Section 3: Leadership versus Management

"More and more people will be asked not just to manage; they will be asked to provide leadership," states John Kotter, Professor at Harvard Business School.

As we progress toward the 21st Century, while aspects of management will still be very necessary, there will be a tremendous premium on leadership.

This fact is dictated by the need for individual and organizational excellence in the midst of constant, complex change. In simpler times, when the market was far more predictable, customers were not as knowledgeable and demanding, and employees were more accepting of the traditional command-and-control model, effective management was often all that was required. The classic business school definition of management was "planning, organizing, directing, and controlling." The distinctions between "leadership" and "management" were blurred, and they were often used interchangeably. Not so today. . . .

Section 4: Sensitivity in Leadership

"Some of the best leaders have a spiritual side," says Larry Miller, author of Barbarians to Bureaucrats and President of the Miller Consulting Group.

As we spoke with leaders, we were impressed by the sensitivity many of them displayed in talking about the humanistic aspects of leadership. Words like courage, hope, caring, heart, love, compassion, listening, cooperation and service kept cropping up. This should not be surprising, given the shift towards empowerment and bringing out the best in people. . . .

Section 5: The Holistic Leader

"To be a well-rounded and successful leader in the 21st Century, many broad qualities will be essential," says Carolyn Burger, President and CEO of Diamond State Telephone, A Bell Atlantic Company.

We are living in an increasingly holistic era. For example, we see the earth more and more as an integrated holistic ecosystem. In health, the trend is toward a holistic approach with added emphasis on wellness, prevention, diet and fitness. In business, we are operating within an interconnected, mutually-dependent global market place.

These factors call out for holistic leadership. 21st Century leaders will be well-rounded and balanced in a myriad of ways. They will pay attention not only to the bottom-line of their organizations but also to the well-being of their employees. They will balance the objective elements of strategy with the subjective aspects of their organization's value system.

In order to effectively lead a balanced holistic organization, leaders will need to cultivate many different dimensions within themselves. This may call for being committed and hard-driving and simultaneously having a healthy peaceful mind and a fit body. At times it may require making difficult decisions which have a human price, while also demonstrating care and compassion. It may periodically require long hours while still sharing quality time with family.

During our dialogues with the leaders it becomes increasingly clear that they feel the definition of leadership is moving far beyond traditional boundaries, and that much more will be expected of future leaders—wherever they are in an organization. The successful leaders of the 21st Century will in fact have to approach their lives and their organizations from a much more holistic standpoint, embracing within themselves a broad range of qualities, skills, and behaviors.

The leaders in this section suggest these kinds of capabilities: more global perspectives in terms of understanding economies, markets, and people; the capabilities to learn and grow; broad multi-media communication skills; excellent fitness—physically, emotionally and intellectually; and tremendous courage, conviction and hope.

As a result, leaders are going to have to drop the "I've got it all together" image and become "life-long learners." This new leadership image will mean that leaders will be far more aggressive about personal growth and development opportunities.

They will be more reflective, constantly inviting feedback from peers and others in order to improve themselves and become more effective. The internal conversation will shift from "I have arrived" to "I'm learning more every day!" . . .

Section 6: Leaders As Change Masters

"What it takes to be a leader in the 1990s and beyond is really handling change," says Roberto Goizueta, Chairman and CEO of The Coca-Cola Company.

Given the reality of "The Changing Game," a very essential skill for 21st Century leaders is the mastery of change. We have moved from the evolutionary changes that past leaders had to face to more revolutionary changes today. This is one reason why courage has been mentioned often as an essential trait.

To prepare for the next century, many changes will include difficult adjustments in both the structure and size of organizations. Leaders will need to guide their organizations through these disruptions and yet retain a motivated, committed organization that can build for the future. . . .

Taking a Fresh Look at Ourselves as Leaders

While a great deal is being written in the media about "reinventing the organization," not enough has been written about the need to redefine ourselves as leaders. One will not happen without the other. We invite you to explore some of the ways it may be appropriate for you to revise elements of your style, your priorities, your beliefs, and your habits by asking yourself the following questions:

1. Am I paying enough attention to the subjective aspects of leadership, including the values, culture and tone in my organization?
2. Am I doing all I can to bring out the best in others by valuing and respecting their differences and by motivating and inspiring them?
3. Am I a developmental leader who is coaching others on an ongoing basis?
4. Is my attitude toward change a healthy one? Do I see change as an opportunity vs. a threat? Am I an effective change master?
5. Would others say that I am living in integrity by walking my talk and modeling the values I espouse?
6. What other leadership dimensions should I be adding? How am I balancing my focus on results vs. people? My commitment to career vs. my personal life? How can I improve my business skills, my physical fitness, my relationships, and my inner self?
7. Am I a leader in a big enough game? How can I make more of a difference in my family, organization, community, nation, and world?

59

Talent and Training for Leadership

Roger B. Smith

Roger B. Smith is former chairman and chief executive officer of General Motors Corporation. These remarks were presented at the University of Tennessee MBA Symposium in Knoxville, Tennessee, on November 2, 1990.

It is a pleasure to be here at this outstanding school of business and a real honor to have been selected to receive your MBA Distinguished Executive Award. Some of the best advice on public speaking that I've ever heard came from Franklin Delano Roosevelt; "Be sincere; be brief; and be seated." Well, I'm going to try to go three-for-three today, and I'll be looking forward to our Q&A session right afterward.

My subject today is leadership which, as someone once observed, is like the abominable snowman: you see the tracks, but never the thing itself. So then, what is leadership, really? What makes it work? And—most relevant to our MBA students in my audience—how can people about to enter the world business develop their own leadership skills?

Those are the questions I'd like to address in the next few minutes. But first, let me put leadership in its proper context.

Reprinted from *Executive Speeches* (Feb/March 1994): pp. 6–9. By permission.

All businesses have, of course, a competitive agenda: winning in the marketplace. They also have a social agenda. And really, the two intertwine. If a company can't be competitive—that is to say, profitable—then it won't have the resources to fulfill society's expectations; it won't be able to support education, charities, the arts, and so on—and it'll have fewer resources to develop the technology that makes its products environmentally acceptable. On the other hand, a company's reputation itself is a competitive asset; if it doesn't fulfill society's expectations, it'll jeopardize its good name—and the market's acceptance of its products—and it won't be profitable. All of which means that a company has to pursue its competitive goals *and* fulfill its social responsibilities—both at the same time, and each without compromising the other.

Now there's a third set of challenges, and they're even more fundamental . . . because, if companies don't pay attention to them, there's no way they can take on the other two. These are what I call the "people issues." To me, these will absolutely be the key issues for business in the 1990s and on into the 21st century. I believe it was Tip O'Neill who once said that "all politics is local politics." By the same token, all business issues are, at the bottom, people issues. Yes, it's critical to have leading-edge automation and R&D facilities. You also need first-rate information and communications technology. And you definitely need state-of-the-art accounting, reporting, planning, and decision-making systems. But let's face it: those are only tools . . . tools that are useless—*unless* they are put in the hands of trained and dedicated men and women who will give their best and most creative efforts.

What are the people issues? Well, as I see it, they cluster around four main themes. First, there's training. How can companies do the most effective job of preparing their work forces for the onrush of new technologies that are transforming the way they do their jobs? And to what degree should business be responsible for training people whom the educational system has not adequately prepared for their rapidly changing, high-tech environment?

The second people issue is retraining. How can companies best retrain those workers whose job skills are made obsolete by new technology or economic shifts in production?

Then there's management. How do you balance the need to share information with your people—and involve them more fully in the success of the business—with the need for managerial responsibility and accountability?

And the final people issue is the one I regard as "first among equals"—*leadership*. Under the intense pressure of global competition, cutbacks, retrenchments, and mergers, how can companies make the correct decisions about training, retraining, and management—*and also* evoke loyalty, stimulate risk-taking, and encourage commitment to the organization's goals?

Any business that's not bearing down—and bearing down hard—on these questions is not going to be a serious competitor, much less a winner, in the decade ahead. And since it's business schools like this one that train the people who will cope with the challenges I've described. I'd like to offer a few thoughts about business schools and business leaders.

What's the connection between the two? Is it your mission to train full-fledged leaders? Or to graduate very bright, well-prepared people, some of whom have natural talents that will, in the right situation, flower into true leadership?

To my mind, leadership is like any other human talent: some people are more inclined toward it than others, but there are some techniques that can be taught. The key that unlocks it all, though, is situation: leadership occurs when people with the talent and training find themselves in circumstances that enable them to put that talent and training into action.

Let me try to give you some idea of the role I think business schools should play by going into a little more detail on those three components of leadership: training, talent, and situation. The business leaders of the 21st century—and I trust I'm speaking to a roomful of them—will need certain basic survival skills, some of which can most readily be acquired in school.

A business leader must be able to live with powerful ambiguities and to make trade-offs in the pursuit of more than one goal at the same time. The familiar conflict between having to fulfill the expectations of stockholders and investors . . . and deliver short-term results on the one hand . . . and having to invest for the long-term health of the business on the other . . . is a familiar one to most of us. And it's certainly one that we had plenty of experience with at in the 1980s, we made massive investments in new plants, equipment and training—investments that took years to start paying off in lower costs, better quality, and attractive new products. Now the corporation faces another set of ambiguities on the environmental issues: people want cars and trucks that offer roominess, comfort, and performance—and that are as environmentally clean and fuel-efficient as possible. And again, the company's management team will have to employ that key leadership skill: reconciling conflict and moving in two partly incompatible directions at the same time.

There's another leadership skill—a set of them, really—that I think business school can give you a good foundation in. I'm talking about a global outlook and a multicultural orientation. This is one area where GM has been providing a lot of training right on the job. The company has been in Europe, for example, for over 60 years. It was there before Volkswagen, Jaguar, and Volvo were even founded. And there are GM people who spend much of their professional lives in one overseas assignment after another. But today, it has to bring its North American and overseas operations closer together, sharing components, products, people and overall strategy.

Consider how interdependent our world has become. Between 1980 and 1988, total two-way trade between major industrial powers rose 16%. In 1987 alone, there were 19 international mergers of $1 billion or more, part of nearly $100 billion worth of international mergers, acquisition and divestitures. While the U.S. will remain the world's largest economy as far out as I can see, it's never going to get back the unchallenged economic dominance that it enjoyed in the 1950s and 60s. So tomorrow's business leaders should come prepared to live in an interdependent world and to manage in an international environment. As Lester Thurow says, "To be trained as an *American* manager is to be trained for a world that is no longer there."

Tomorrow's business leaders must also have an in-depth understanding of technology. Whether it's lap-top computers for staff professionals, or assembly-line robots for production workers, you have to stay abreast of the latest innovations and aware of their potential for helping to run every aspect of the business more effectively. This is one place where I think business schools do an especially good job. But since technology is changing so rapidly, it's also an area where they need to make a special effort to keep up. Because it's not just a matter of new tools improving old processes. New technology makes new things possible. Today's information systems, for example, are literally transforming the nature of our organizations. They make information available to everyone. And that eliminates the jobs of people whose function has been to assemble and verify information . . . it flattens out the organizational chart and it creates a class of what Peter Drucker calls "knowledge workers." These are specialists who actually know more about their particular function than their bosses. And the boss' job is then to organize these knowledge workers and make sure they have the information they need.

Finally, to the extent that it's possible, tomorrow's business leader must be a specialist/generalist—an expert in one field, but also reasonably familiar with a number of others. Finance is a good place to start out; heck, I started out there. But to lead in the organization, you have to really know it, inside out, including staff operations, and right down to the factory floor. It's especially important to get a good grasp of advisory functions like legal, economics, communications, and government relations, because political and social forces are—and will continue to be—a powerful influence on how the business is run. And you have to be able to factor the effects of these forces into your business plan—remember what I said earlier about the intertwining of the social and competitive agendas. One more thing about being a specialist: given the enormous importance of international and people issues, it would be very helpful to have certain key non-technical abilities—excellent communication and interpersonal skills, a broad social and historical perspective, and an appreciation of quality and excellence—many of the skills you get from liberal-arts studies.

Well, so much for skills that can be taught in school. What about the second component of leadership—talent? Are some of us natural leaders? I think many people come at this question from the wrong direction. They look at the most famous political leaders and assume that leadership has something to do with whipping up passionate emotions, preferably through passionate oratory. Well, you do need the confidence of your convictions. As Confucius said long ago, "It is better to have a lion at the head of an army of sheep than a sheep at the head of an army of lions." But that's only one leadership style; it's not the only one.

The award that you're so kind to bestow on me is, according to the letter I received from Dean Jenkins, "given . . . for outstanding leadership in the world of business and government." So all of the recipients must have something in common. But what would that be? I'd bet that if you got all their biographies and laid them side by side, you'd find a wide variety of backgrounds, both personal and educational. The various individuals probably got to their high positions by many different routes. If you looked a little deeper, you'd also find different leadership styles—this person's autocratic, that one's charismatic, another is democratic. What defines them as leaders?

Well, if they have anything in common, I would guess that all of them have been able to get people to work together for a common goal—a "vision," if you will, that happened to be right for the times. All of them are people of integrity and consistency. All of them have earned trust, and thus have been able to mobilize the energies of others, and bring about their commitment to work together in pursuit of that vision. Yes, I'm aware that "vision" is one of those overused buzz words—but I insist that it does have a specific meaning. Speaking just from the business world that I know best, I would say that vision has an external side—satisfied customers, profitability, and industry leadership for the company, all of which mean material benefits and pride for its people. And vision has an equally important internal side—creating a work environment in which everyone can participate fully and achieve personal and professional growth, in the pursuit of that common goal.

Now that's all the generalizing I'm willing to do about the other recipients of your Distinguished Executive Award. Frankly, I don't think we could learn all that much about leadership by examining every detail of people's lives and careers. You'll remember that I compared leadership to the abominable snowman—it's really hard to see it at work. I also think that leadership is not always one person leading many, although that's the most prominent model. Anybody whose ideas are fresh and timely and who gets along well with people is a potential leader, even if that person has no one reporting to him. And there are things that anybody can do to develop whatever leadership talents he or she may have.

To begin with I'd advise you MBA students to forget about the so-called "corporate ladder." That implies a series of rungs, which you climb in an orderly and mechanical way, until you get to the top. Instead, I would urge you to think in terms of a "mountain"—because climbing requires you to use a variety of tools and techniques, including descending a little bit before you can go back upward. Also, the higher up you go, the farther you can see, and that helps orient you for the rest of the climb.

The second thing I've learned is that leadership is a lot of hard work. And so is learning to be a leader. I always did the best job I could in whatever assignment I was given. When you show you can act with the interests of the team at heart, that not only reflects well on you; it also builds credibility and trust.

Leaders are also willing—in fact, determined—to communicate—constantly. People need to be able to sense your consistency and integrity. They need to know where you stand and what your priorities are, so they can decide whether to give you their support. And as you rise in responsibility, you have to communicate your vision, as well as a credible plan to achieve it— again, that's essential in getting people behind you.

Leaders also need to be able to ask for—and listen to—bad news—not repress it, but listen—and then respond rationally. If your subordinates get the message that you only want good news, that's all you'll get. And that's the first step towards a very dangerous isolation from reality.

Finally, and most important, a leader needs a TEAM. Andrew Carnegie once said that he wanted, for his epitaph, the following words: "Here lies a man who was wise enough to bring into his service men who know more than he." The point is, you need to be able to surround yourself with bright, competent people, people who can really run this or that aspect of the business and give you their best advice on what's best for the whole organization. Without them, there's no way you can be successful, which is why I always give plenty of credit to the exceptional people I worked with on our GM team.

Well, I've talked about training for leadership and talent for leadership. I now come to the third component of leadership, the match that ignites the fire—situation. It doesn't have to be outright crisis, though that often is the case. Sometimes, though, an organization or an entire industry is in need of—or already in the throes of—a massive overhaul, in order to avert crisis. But crisis or not, I think there are certain kinds of organizations that are fertile grounds for the development of leadership skills; just by being there, you'll have a better chance of developing the abilities I've described.

What kind of organizations? Well, first, I'd advise you to give very serious consideration to companies whose business is manufacturing. Manufacturing is where the action is these days. It's at the forefront of our nation's struggle to stay competitive in world markets. It's where great things are happening in technology, design, automation, financial analysis, strategic planning, and management. In fact, manufacturing is where the 21st century organization—electronically integrated, technologically-advanced, customer-responsive, and people-oriented—is being born. And manufacturing firms need the very best business minds to make it all happen.

Second, if you're looking for a breeding ground for leaders, make sure you're in an organization that really rewards outstanding performance. Just about every company wants to do this, almost all say they do, and most believe they do. But spend a few months or a year there, and you'll find out how well they measure up to their ideal. Are there defined career paths, clear succession plans, regular performance reviews whose results are taken seriously and acted on? An organization that grooms its talent in these and similar ways . . . is an organization that builds leadership.

You also want to get yourself into a company with a long tradition of leadership in its industry. Organizations with a history of being in the vanguard have cultures that show the influence of this experience. They have high expectations of their people. They have an aggressive can-do attitude. And they expect—and accept—the penalties of leadership: criticism, skepticism, imperfect success that's long in coming, because they know the rewards; doing what's never been done, showing others the way, and creating the future.

I would humbly submit that General Motors is just such an organization—

a manufacturing company that rewards excellent performance and has a long tradition of industry leadership. But of course, I admit to a certain built-in bias. The real point is, in order for leadership to occur, individuals who seek to be leaders must find their way into industries and companies that build leaders.

Let me close with a fundamental question—so basic that you almost never hear it asked: Why would anyone even want to be a leader today? In times past, the reasons were pretty obvious: you wanted to be a leader because leadership meant power; it meant control over others; it meant being served. True, we still do have some of those old-style leaders around. But today, at least in the capitalist democracies that so many countries around the world are emulating these days, the power of leaders is diffuse. Leaders themselves have many constituencies to answer to, and the people they lead are better-informed, more questioning, and far less obedient. There have to be different motives for leadership—and indeed there are. Today's leaders—and this is true of the more enlightened leaders of history as well—want to help others realize their own power and dignity. They lead because they want to create an environment in which people are free to think, innovate, and unite into teams and groups, in order to solve problems that are too big for any one person to solve alone. And that, I think, is the final piece of the leadership puzzle—the desire to build and to serve. Schools can teach it, people can grow up with it, and organizations can foster it. And a society in which all of this happens need never fear the future; it is creating it, every day.

60

A New Vision of Leadership

Michele Darling

Michele Darling is executive vice president of human resources at Canadian Imperial Bank of Commerce. These remarks were presented to Rotary International in Niagara-on-the-Lake, Ontario on April 11, 1992.

If I wanted to cite a badly led corporation, I could think of no better example than Springfield Nuclear Power. Springfield Nuclear is best known for its most famous employee, the bumbling everyman Homer Simpson of television's hit animated show, *The Simpsons*. But the reedy, slit-eyed CEO, C. Montgomery Burns, is the perfect caricature of the bad, old corporate leader. Burns, as those of you who are Simpsons' fans already know, is autocratic, covetous of money and power, contemptuous and flint-hearted.

His employee Homer is capable of indulging in petty malfeasance or precipitating a meltdown. Whatever the feckless Simpson does, however, C. Montgomery Burns can be counted on to respond with the sensitivity of Attila the Hun and the deviousness of a Borgia. He knows who number one is and how to look out for him.

The cartoon Mr. Burns has no perfect parallel in real life. The caricature is

Reprinted from *Executive Speeches* (Feb/March 1994): pp. 77–80. By permission.

only interesting because it's a stereotype of the classic notion of what a big corporate boss is supposed to be like. And perhaps to a greater extent than we imagine, old stereotypes condition our thinking about leadership and what we think a leader ought to be.

It's easy to slip into. Modern corporations can face a daunting array of problems at any given time. Changing markets for products and services, competitive pressures, regulatory issues, labor problems, trade pacts—the list is endless. Wouldn't it be comforting to think that there was an all-seeing eye in the executive suite? A decisive, autocratic, knowledgeable and courageous leader? Someone who, as one former prime minister told us, realizes that a leader must be a leader?

I don't think so. The leadership profile I've just described is no longer effective. That's because our concept of what constitutes appropriate and effective corporate leadership is always changing. It is always being redefined. Let me give you a couple of examples.

Only a decade ago, we didn't automatically assume that CEOs would be aggressive corporate image builders or public spokespeople. Lee Iacocca of Chrysler showed us what CEOs could do in this regard. Others as diverse as George Cohon of McDonald's and Conrad Black of Hollinger have followed, refining the art of visible leadership.

In the early 80s, business leaders weren't routinely expected to be corporate visionaries. Leaders like Xerox Corporation CEO David Kearns, who set corporate direction with a clearly expressed vision, stood out among their peers. Today, most major corporations, including my own, have visions and statements of purpose that set their behavior.

Business realities are changing all the time. And as they do, corporate leadership—what the boss is doing, and ought to be seen to be doing—evolves and improves as well. What I want to talk about today are some of the directions in which it has been evolving.

I'm going to suggest that we are heading toward a kind of business leadership that, in certain respects, is quite unlike the traditional form we've known. It's different from what most of us are used to and will require changes in our attitudes and actions, whether we're CEOs, managers or line employees.

A new reality has grown up around us and we have to reckon with it.

By the time I'm finished we'll be contemplating corporate leaders who are radically different from the fictional C. Montgomery Burns. If the trends I'm going to be talking about prevail, the best person to run Springfield Nuclear will turn out to be caring rather than caustic, generous with information rather than secretive. This person will be a mentor who will encourage, guide and support rather than bark orders.

We are already moving in this direction. Internationally respected CEOs such as Yotaro Kobayashi of Japan's Fuji-Xerox or Paul O'Neil at Alcoa have been described as charismatic leaders, people with the ability to inspire in the traditional sense. But they are also renowned for their skills in motivating employees with coaching, training and moral support.

Corporate leaders reserve the right to make decisions, but they're also interested in democratizing their companies and getting increased employee involvement. Corporate structures are still more often than not hierarchical, but leaders are more aware than ever of the needs and feelings of their subordinates. There's a decided willingness to communicate and consult. There's systematic delegation of responsibility to lower levels of management.

These developments are expressed in many different ways. Management theorist Peter Drucker has likened the corporation to a symphony orchestra with the CEO/leader as conductor. In more practical terms, companies such as Heinz and Colgate-Palmolive do everything from reducing the middle layers of corporate management, thus freeing up communication between the CEO and line managers, to having different parts of the company treat each other as if they were independent suppliers. There is no one magic method, only a host of initiatives.

All these changes reflect the new realities that large corporations face. One person can no longer effectively control a large, multifaceted corporate enterprise. I don't care how many hours a leader works, how much management by walking around the leader may do, how intelligent or financially adept that person is. It is simply impossible to pull all the strands together on one desk.

Why is this so? To start with, we are in a period of increasingly rapid change in business. Take the financial services industry as an example. In the past year, we have had to deal with external issues including legislative changes that have further eroded the competitive barriers in the industry. We have faced public scrutiny over specific segments of our business such as credit cards.

And we've had to ponder the potential impact of Canada's participation in a North American Free Trade Agreement. Those are just a few of the items our corporate leaders have to contemplate in addition to day-to-day competitive pressures.

I don't think the financial services industry is unique in this. The degree and pace of change seems greater in all businesses. And as this happens, corporations are becoming more and more accountable—to customers, share-holders, suppliers, regulators, fiscally-strapped governments and, increasingly, the general public.

If you doubt what I'm saying, ask yourself any or all of the following questions. How many of you have experienced more intense competition in recent years? How many of you feel your competitive position has been eroded since the last recession? How many of you feel your employees are more demanding than they used to be and, as a corollary, how many of you find it harder than ever to find the right kind of employees with the right skills? How many of you have noticed that your customers are more demanding and prone to dictating the terms of your business relationship?

In this kind of challenging environment, unresponsive leadership runs the risk of failure. On the other hand, the right kind of leadership can make a huge difference; it can turn established thinking upside down. In this respect, I think of the great supermarket object lesson of the 1980s. The major producers of foods and household goods, the Procter and Gamble's and General Mills' of the world, used to dictate terms to the stores that stocked their products. You always knew that Tide and Wheaties would get good display and shelf space.

That is, until David Nichol of Loblaws came along. He proved with the development of the "President's Choice" product line that you could turn house brands into formidable national brands and completely upset a traditional supplier/customer relationship. It is not an isolated example.

The evolution of corporate leadership is also being influenced by changes in society. One way we see this happening is in the employee population. Society has become less rigid and more democratic. People question the status quo, sometimes to an extraordinary degree. We see this in family life, schools and universities, religious life and government. It is only logical that this trend should affect business.

Employees today are far less inclined to accept corporate bureaucracy and authoritarian management than their parents were. The word "career" used to suggest lifetime employment with one company. Now we understand it to mean that an individual seeks betterment, in challenging work and improved living standards, wherever possible.

Internally, we can see this in the ambition people show to move into different areas of the corporation. And if we can't accommodate them, we know there's a reasonable chance that they'll seek satisfaction somewhere else.

You hear a lot in this country about the skills shortage and how it's luring us as we attempt to compete in global markets. What we sometimes ignore is the fact that employees very often have great skills and are highly motivated to use them. They want to make a contribution; they want to be recognized and rewarded.

How many times have you heard business leaders say their greatest resource is their people? It sounds trite, but it's true. One of the most compelling tasks for the evolving corporate leadership I've been talking about is to harness the enormous resource represented by employees.

How well are we doing at this and the other tasks of leadership? In many respects I think we're doing very well. In the past few years business leaders have to an unprecedented extent been rethinking what their companies do and how they operate. Abroad, there are some well chronicled examples such as General Electric Corporation chairman Jack Welch or Drake Business School CEO May Ann Lawlor. Here in Canada we can point to people such as IPSCO CEO Roger Phillips. All of them have shown leadership by helping their companies—their employees—adjust to new realities.

My own company, CIBC, has spent a great deal of time and effort in recent years redefining what we do. We've tried to isolate the values that drive us and the things we want to achieve.

Our values—commitment to stewardship, respect for individuals, encouragement of initiative and creativity, the quest for excellence—are the clear and simple refined outpourings of arduous self-examination. So is our basic purpose—to be the leading performer in all our product areas.

Like all those authorities and books that we have been delighted with in recent times, I'm telling you that CIBC and other corporations are reinventing themselves to cope with new realities. And at the center of it all is the need for a vision, a sense of purpose and direction.

This affects the way we look at corporate leadership. I believe that the new realities we face, the pace of change and the uncertainty of life in general requires that leaders increasingly be visionaries who are capable of directing, encouraging and coaching others.

Peter Senge of the MIT Sloan School of Management put it very well in an article for the *Sloan Management Review* a little over a year ago. He described what he called "learning organizations," companies that grow and prosper over the long term by adapting and regenerating themselves in the face of change. In these kinds of companies, he said, the role of the leader is no longer that of the charismatic decision-maker.

"Leaders are designers, teachers and stewards," he wrote. "These roles require new skills: the ability to build shared vision, to bring to the surface and challenge prevailing mental models, and to foster more systematic patterns of thinking. In short, leaders in learning organizations are responsible for building organizations where people are continually expanding their capabilities to shape their future—that is, leaders are responsible for learning."

Senge provides evidence that this style works. His best example recalls how Johnson & Johnson responded when one of its key products, Tylenol, was tampered with in 1982. The company referred to the credo developed by its founder 40 years before, a firmly implanted vision that starts with the assertion that "service to the customers comes first," and withdrew all stocks of the product from the market. The move was costly, but effective, and eventually Tylenol reclaimed its dominant place as a headache remedy.

Leadership that seeks to take a simple vision and then teach, nurture and shape a company is a challenging, demanding and exciting concept that ultimately brings success. Companies like Johnson & Johnson have known this for a long time; now many more realize it. It shows just how far we've come along the evolutionary cycle.

Implicit in this style of leadership are a number of things. As I've said, information is not to be hoarded, but communicated freely. People at all levels of an organization are to be looked at not merely as employees with specific work-related functions, but as well rounded human beings who are the sum of their parts.

And as someone whose company is engaged in a major effort to improve service, I can tell you that this style of leadership changes our notions of who supports who. As our Service/Quality campaign has taught us, it isn't the bottom of the organization that supports the top, but rather the other way around. The customer doesn't deal with the chairman or an executive vice president, but with loan officers and tellers.

This brings us to another of those truths about leadership. Power doesn't accrue to those who hoard it. Real power is obtained only by those who give it away. Or, as Colgate-Palmolive CEO Reuben Mark once put it: "You consolidate and build power by empowering others."

When leaders ignore these truths, when they attempt to be aloof or dictatorial, it's noticed. Consider a management practices survey that was done about a year ago in the U.S. by *Industry Week* magazine. In essence, it showed that as you move down through the ranks of many business organizations, confidence in top managements' leadership ability deteriorates.

Decrying this tendency, *Industry Week* concluded: "Today, top executives are being called upon to behave as leaders—to set direction, establish goals and strategy, and help their workforces see clearly how they can contribute to improvements in quality and productivity."

This survey's findings seem consistent with what I see happening in business and society as a whole. People crave strong leadership; all you need to do to realize this is read the newspaper or listen to radio phone-in shows or talk to your friends. Nobody out there knows how to lead, we seem to be telling each other.

I think this attitude overstates the case. We live in an age where problems can sometimes be more imagined than real. This is the era of the scare headline and the superficial analysis and a lot of the information we get is foreboding.

I also think, however, that we have to try to deal with people's fears and clarify their uneasy perceptions. And I happen to believe that leadership that shares information and knowledge, real knowledge, and brings more people into the folds of events, is a very good way to do it.

We've come a long way with our evolving idea of leadership. I found a good indication of this in a recent book by the American journalist Sally Helgesen. Helgesen went back to the work of management scientist Henry Mintzberg in the late 1960s and re-examined the profile he had assembled of top business leaders.

The pattern won't surprise you. Mintzberg's executive leaders worked at an unrelenting pace through their days. They felt disrupted by the unexpected. They made little or no time for non-work activities. They were highly absorbed in the day-to-day matter of their jobs and had little time for reflection. They kept information to themselves.

By way of comparison, Helgesen looked at some of today's top executives and made some interesting discoveries. She found that they tend to work at a steady pace and schedule breaks in their day. They see interruptions as an important part of their job because they feel a need to be accessible and caring about the activities of people around them. They make time for non-work activities.

They focus on what Helgesen calls "the ecology of leadership," seeing management as a continuum with long range implications. They see dimensions of their lives beyond their jobs. They share information.

There were other differences, not to mention some interesting similarities Helgesen's executive leaders had with their historically distant counterparts, but the point is this. Generally speaking, the style of leadership has evolved considerably.

I have to put in an important qualifier here. The corporate leaders that Mintzberg studied were all men. The leaders Helgesen profiled were women. That's another measurement of how leadership has evolved. Roughly 20 years ago, the notion of a female CEO was a foreign one. But not any more, as we see more women assuming the top role.

You could conceivably make a case that women are intrinsically better suited to the style of corporate leadership that we practice today than men are. After all, women are supposed to be naturally more consultative, more caring, more liable to share power.

It will be a long while before we have any hard proof that women will make a difference in the realm of leadership. In my bank, women now constitute 14 percent of senior management. Five years ago, women held down perhaps three or four percent of those jobs so that's an impressive gain.

Indeed, there are more women generally in the management ranks at CIBC. And while it's too soon to be conclusive, there are indications that the most effective teams in our organization are those where there is a balance between men and women.

That's a positive sign, but we would like to have more senior women because it's simply good business—it widens the pool of talent available to us and it better reflects our customer base. Our chairman has set a goal of having women in one-third of all senior jobs.

In the end, though, such corrective actions aren't necessarily about leadership. Certainly, the qualities of leadership that I've been talking about have no reference to gender, race or creed.

Most of the references I've made have been to companies led by men. The development of less rigid hierarchies, the improved communication and consultation, increased delegation and the nurturing of employees' abilities and feelings—all have come in companies run by men. But they could have just as easily been companies led by women or minorities. Nobody, to my knowledge, has cornered the market on leadership ability.

PART XIII

PRACTICING MORAL LEADERSHIP

An understanding of the nature and processes of leadership must be coupled with a clear sense of the moral and ethical overtones of leadership; that is to say, the group goals which are the objective of leadership must be moral, and the process of achieving these goals must be ethical. If either the ends of leadership or the means to achieve it be improper, the ultimate goal of leadership—the betterment of society—is compromised.

Accordingly, important issues must be confronted. What is moral leadership? How can a leader affect the ethical choices and conduct of others (his or her followers)? To what extent are the followers' decisions the responsibility of the leader? What are the responsibilities of followers? The selections in this segment address some of the issues surrounding the exercise of moral leadership.

In the first selection, James MacGregor Burns defines "moral leadership" in terms of the fundamental needs of followers. The next reading by Howard T. Prince II reviews the major theories of moral development to determine whether it is possible for a leader to shape the moral and ethical behavior of followers. Joanne Ciulla draws from examples in the real world to demonstrate how to structure a work environment "where employees want to act responsibly and find it easy to do so." The concluding selection returns to the larger issues which should shape all leadership. Rushworth M. Kidder suggests that there are, after all, certain universal human values that peoples of all cultures acknowledge and admire. These values—truthfulness, fairness, responsibility, and the like—seem very much akin to the notion of moral leadership first described by Burns.

481

61

Moral Leadership

James MacGregor Burns

James MacGregor Burns won a Pulitzer Prize and a National Book Award for his study of Franklin D. Roosevelt. His book *Leadership* is considered to be a seminal work in leadership studies. Burns has been Woodrow Wilson Professor of Government at Williams College, and he has served as president of the American Political Science Association.

This last concept, *moral leadership*, concerns me the most. By this term I mean, first, that leaders and led have a relationship not only of power but of mutual needs, aspirations, and values; second, that in responding to leaders, followers have adequate knowledge of alternative leaders and programs and the capacity to choose among those alternatives; and, third, that leaders take responsibility for their commitments—if they promise certain kinds of economic, social, and political change, they assume leadership in the bringing about of that change. Moral leadership is not mere preaching, or the uttering of pieties, or the insistence on social conformity. Moral leadership emerges from, and always returns to, the fundamental wants and needs, aspirations, and values of the followers. I mean the kind of leadership that can produce social change that will satisfy followers' authentic needs. I mean less the Ten Commandments than the Golden Rule. But even the Golden Rule is inadequate, for it measures the wants and needs of others simply by our own.

62

Moral Development in Individuals

Howard T. Prince II

Howard T. Prince II received his Ph.D. in psychology from the University of Texas. He retired as a brigadier general after more than twenty-eight years of service in the U.S. Army. He developed one of the first undergraduate programs in leadership at the United States Military Academy and developed a graduate program in leader development there. He currently serves as the dean of the Jepson School of Leadership Studies at the University of Richmond.

Moral development is to a great extent determined by the cultural standards of the larger society from which organizational members come. . . . Individuals are prepared by their previous experiences to behave in accordance with societal standards of right and wrong. The resultant personal ethic consisting of the values, beliefs and attitudes about what is proper and acceptable behavior is one of the major sources of influence on individual moral behavior within an organizational setting. These individual moral standards influence and are in turn conditioned by group and organizational factors. The impact of individual moral development is particularly crucial if the individual in question is an organizational leader.

To what extent can the leader influence the moral development of others? If the answer is relatively little, then the leader who wishes or is required to

From *Leadership in Organization*, Howard T. Prince II, ed. et al., © 1988. Published by Avery Publishing Group, Inc. Garden City Park, N.Y. 11040. Reprinted by permission.

establish and maintain an ethical climate is faced primarily with a problem of selecting moral people. On the other hand, if moral development is not fixed at some particular stage in a sequence of development, then perhaps the leader can do more than merely select those who are most moral (assuming this could be assessed). How then do we develop into human beings capable of moral action and of deciding between right and wrong? What is the nature of the process of moral development and how, if at all, can the leader influence that process within an organization?

The Psychoanalytic Approach to Moral Development

There are several contemporary theories which attempt to explain how moral development occurs. One approach is that of the renowned psychoanalyst, Sigmund Freud.[1] We need to examine Freud's approach first because if he is correct, then there may be little that the leader can do beyond selecting and eliminating people based on moral standards.

Freud observed that many of his patients suffered severe feelings of guilt. These feelings served both to inhibit their behavior, usually sexual or aggressive in nature, and to punish themselves for engaging in, or merely for thinking about, improper behavior. In Freud's approach to understanding human behavior, several personality structures are proposed. To account for the observations just described, he developed the concept of a superego, which we may roughly compare to the conscience. Freud theorized that the superego developed fairly early in life, around age 5 or 6, when the child identified intensely with the parent of the same sex as a way of resolving the famous Oedipal complex (based on unconscious feelings of sexual attraction for the parent of the opposite sex). By making the values of the same-sex parent his or her own, a child acquires a sense of right and wrong as well as other values held by that parent along with a strengthened sense of sex-role identity. Young boys increase their sense of masculinity and young girls their sense of femininity, according to this theory. In Freud's view an individual's basic personality, including the superego, is for the most part determined by early childhood experiences.

What evidence is there for the Freudian approach to moral development? If Freud were right, then we would expect to see a dramatic change at some point around age 5 or 6 from little or no morality to an almost adult-like morality in the young child. Neither our experience nor scientific research provides evidence for such a change. As the child enters school there is an increased sense of morality and, as we shall discover in a moment, there is support for the concept of moral development over time among children (although not as dramatic as we would expect if Freud were correct). A more subtle check on Freud's theory can be made by comparing the processes of moral development and the establishment of sex-role identity. If Freud were right, we should expect these processes to develop in parallel fashion. Moral people should have clear sex-role identities and immoral people should have poorly defined sex-role identities. There is no evidence that this is the case. Thus, Freud may have provided a useful concept in the form of the superego to help us label and communicate about what we usually call the conscience, but it appears that Freud's theory is not well supported by independent evidence. The lack of research support for the implication that moral development occurs very early in life is important to the organizational leader. If moral development is instead a continuing process, then the leader may be able to foster moral development among organizational members.

The Cognitive Approach to Moral Development

We all know people whom we describe as very moral and others whom we consider less moral. We also know that people who engage in moral behavior, such as telling the truth, may give different reasons for doing so. For example, one person may explain that he or she told the truth "so that I wouldn't get in trouble." Another person might explain telling the truth by maintaining that "if I didn't tell the truth, I would lose the respect of others when they found out." Lawrence Kohlberg, of Harvard, has taken these two basic observations, namely that people appear to be at different stages of moral development and that the reasons people give for their behavior may differ, and has attempted to give us a cognitive-developmental theory of individual moral development.

According to Kohlberg, there are six different stages of moral development as shown in Table 1.[2] Each stage is characterized by a typical way of moral reasoning.

In stage 1 (preconventional) moral reasoning is very primitive and for the most part based on avoiding punishment. In the second stage (preconventional), morality is still very self-centered. The individual follows rules, for example, not just to avoid punishment but because it is in his or her interest to do so. In stages 3 and 4 (conventional) the person begins to consider relationships with others as important in moral reasoning. In stage 3 there is morality based on a desire for approval from others while in stage 4 there is more awareness of an obligation to live up to one's word, to do one's duty,

TABLE 1
Kohlberg's Stages of Moral Development

Level		Dominant Theme When Reasoning About a Moral Choice
Level 1 *Preconventional* (Children, a few adults)	• Stage 1 • Stage 2	• Fear of punishment • Opportunistic—"what's in it for me?"
Level 2 *Conventional* (Most adults)	• Stage 3 • Stage 4	• Good boy-nice girl—"will people think well of me?" • Law and order—"can't break the rules."
Level 3 *Post-conventional* (A few highly developed adults)	• Stage 5 • Stage 6	• Social contract—"the greatest good for the greatest number. Laws should generally be followed, but there are exceptions." • Universal ethical principles—there are a few basic moral principles which apply in all situations, e.g., life, liberty, human rights, respect for the dignity of man—irrespective of specific laws or rules.

and to help maintain the social system. In the fifth stage (post-conventional) a person becomes more aware that while it is well to live up to the rules of society, there are a variety of possible value systems. There is greater sensitivity to deciding what the rules should be in the first place. Finally, in stage 6 (post-conventional) the individual operates from a set of universal moral principles which guide moral judgments and which even may conflict with existing societal values.

According to Kohlberg, this sequence is fixed and develops over time from one stage to the next as our capacity for moral reasoning increases. We may also become fixated at any stage if development ceases. Typically, the majority of our moral reasoning is centered on one level at a time, although some of our moral judgments are also at the next lower and next higher levels as well. Intelligence as well as social influences help to determine the level of moral reasoning we attain. One important social influence is our capacity to understand another person's point of view. As this capacity increases, so does our potential for higher levels of moral reasoning.

Notice that Kohlberg's theory has as its most essential characteristic the quality of the moral reasoning process. This means that, according to Kohlberg, it is the thought process behind moral behavior which determines whether the person is moral rather than the behavior itself. For example, two students may each refrain from taking advantage of an opportunity to submit someone else's work as their own. One may choose not to do so because of fear of punishment. The other may choose not to do so on the grounds that truth-telling is a high ethical principle and that a written submission should therefore truly be one's own and not a misrepresentation of ideas taken from someone else. Both people behave in the same way and yet the reasons differ, reflecting different stages of moral development, according to Kohlberg.

Development from one stage to the next appears to depend upon both the maturation process and the quality of one's experiences. New experiences and challenges to one's moral reasoning framework have been shown to lead to the development of higher levels of reasoning ability in children.[3] There is also evidence to support Kohlberg's assumption of a progression of moral development with age through a fixed sequence of stages.[4]

What are the implications of Kohlberg's approach to moral development for the organizational leader? This approach would suggest that moral development is something which can be influenced, although Kohlberg is not especially clear about how this can be done. Kohlberg also has little to offer concerning the question of what specific moral actions people will choose, even for people at the same level of moral development. Further, he recognizes that situational factors will influence the actions which are taken as a result of moral reasoning. That is, a moral person may act differently in one set of circumstances than in another, even though there may be a highly developed thought process which precedes moral conduct in each case. In this regard, Kohlberg is similar not only to the next approach to moral development that we will consider, social learning theory, but also to the approach of some moral philosophers who apply abstract moral principles in specific situations.

The Social Learning Approach to Moral Development

Social learning theory is a general approach to understanding how we learn, retain and eventually choose to perform or not perform any given class of behavior—including moral behavior. In contrast to Freud and Kohlberg, social learning theorists such as the social psychologist, Albert Bandura,[5,6] have generated considerable evidence for the effects of variables which influence what we do and even whether we will do it in specific situations calling for ethical choices. Indeed, the fundamental approach of social learning theorists is based on the recognition that behavior is in large measure determined by situational factors outside the individual. However, the individual is not overlooked and is given a central role in processing the components of the situations in terms of perception, reasoning, memory and other internal psychological responses.

The key features of the social learning approach to learning moral behavior are conditioning and imitation. For example, a young child may be punished for some wrongdoing such as stealing money. The child is scolded, perhaps spanked, told to return the money and made to feel bad by the experience of anxiety and guilt brought on by the punishment received for the unacceptable action. The experience of negative feelings becomes associated through this conditioning experience with stealing, a behavior which then is subsequently inhibited. An even more powerful way of learning moral behavior is through the process of observing others. We learn not only appropriate or inappropriate actions but also what consequences are associated with those actions. As a result of watching others tell the truth, we may learn, for example, that telling the truth is valued and rewarded by powerful figures such as parents or teachers. We are then capable, through our own psychological processes, of imagining ourselves engaging in similar behavior under similar future circumstances and expecting similar consequences to accrue to our own behavior, without ever performing the behavior ourselves. This makes observational learning leading to imitation (or inhibition of observed behavior if the model is punished) unique and different from conditioning in which direct experience is our teacher.

What determines whether we learn by observing others? Bandura has described a four-stage process in which we attend to actions of others, retain the observed information, are motivated to perform or not, and behave.[7] Whether we are influenced by others depends upon whether or not we pay attention to them in the first place. Certain characteristics of models make us more or less likely to notice them and observe their actions. Status, power, control over rewards and punishments, and similarity between model and observer are all factors which make us likely to observe a model. Parents, teachers, peers and coaches are all examples of possible models from whom we might learn. How would an organizational leader influence our attention as a model in terms of the characteristics just described?

TABLE 2
Comparison of the Three Major Theories of Moral Development

	Psychoanalytic (Freud)	Cognitive–Developmental (Kohlberg)	Social Learning (Bandura)
Basic emphasis	Feeling (conscience, guilt, remorse)	Thought (quality of moral reasoning, stages)	Behavior (influence of models and the situation, rewards, punishments, expectations)
How morality is acquired	Formation of a superego by internalizing parental values	Through invariant stages of increased capacity for reason based on intelligence and experience	Learning through observation of others, rewards and punishments
Principal agents of socialization	Parents (especially same-sex parent)	People who are at a higher stage	Any significant model (parents, peers) or person who controls rewards and punishments
Research support	Slight	Moderate	Strong
Implications for organizational leader	Leadership exerts little influence except through selection	Leadership influences stage of development through increasing capacity for moral reasoning, e.g, education	Leadership influences moral behavior directly by example, communication of expectations and consequences, control of rewards and punishments

We retain information about two aspects of observed behavior. First, we remember what was done. Second, we remember what happened to the model. Assuming we are capable of performing an observed behavior which is rewarded, what determines whether we will engage in that behavior in some future situation? When the rewards which a model received are perceived as rewarding to ourselves and we expect that there is a good chance of receiving similar rewards, then we are likely to engage in behavior similar to that which we observed the model perform. Similarly, we tend to inhibit behaviors similar to those of a model when the model was punished in a way that we would consider punishing ourselves.

Evidence for this social learning point of view is found in several studies relevant to moral behavior. The behavior of models and the consequences of the models' actions have been shown to influence not only moral reasoning,[8,9] but also socially acceptable behavior.[10,11] The influence of model characteristics has been demonstrated by other researchers who showed that children imitate adult models who are powerful and rewarding but fail to imitate adults who are low on these attributes.[12]

It may be argued that instilling ethical standards and changing values is not the business of the organization—that this is the task of such institutions as the family, school and church. But surely it could also be argued that the organization would be better served if it could foster the further moral development of its members and reinforce the basic ethical standards which individuals bring to the organization. Of the three approaches to moral development which have been presented, social learning theory with its emphasis on learning by observing others appears to have considerable relevance for the organizational leader in this regard. Table 2 contains a summary of the key features of each approach. Of special interest is the section on implications for the leader in the organization. In essence, the leader can influence the moral conduct of others by demonstrating the desired behavior, rewarding ethical behavior and punishing unethical conduct.

63

Messages from the Environment: The Influence of Policies and Practices on Employee Responsibility

Joanne B. Ciulla

Joanne B. Ciulla received her Ph.D. in philosophy from Temple University. Her specialty is in business ethics, and she has held faculty positions at the Wharton School, the Harvard University Graduate School of Business Administration, and Oxford University. She currently holds the Coston Family Chair in Leadership and Ethics at the Jepson School of Leadership Studies at the University of Richmond.

One morning in 1955, a 43-year-old black woman named Rosa Parks took a seat in the front of the Cleveland Avenue bus in Montgomery, Alabama. When she refused to relinquish her seat to a white man, she was arrested. For an act that millions of Americans perform daily, Rosa Parks was taken to jail and fined $10. There was something obviously right about Mrs. Parks's act and obviously wrong with a society that arrests middle-aged ladies for sitting in the front of a bus. The case of Rosa Parks illustrates the fact that courage is a quality that can be found in ordinary people doing ordinary things under extraordinary circumstances.

Joanne Ciulla, "Messages from the Environment: The Influence of Policies and Practices on Employee Responsibility", in Chimezie A.B. Osigweh, Yg., ed., *Communicating Employee Responsibilities and Rights: A Modern Management Mandate* (New York: Quorum Books, 1987), pp. 133–140, reprinted with permission of Greenwood Publishing Group, Inc., Westport CT. Copyright © 1987 by Chimezie A. B. Osigueh, Yg.

Aristotle recognized the importance of morally good social organizations for the development of responsible members. According to Aristotle, governments and other social institutions should be set up so that it is both possible and sensible for people to be honest, loyal, compassionate, fair, etc. It is unwise to create and perpetuate work environments that make ethically responsible behavior into acts of moral courage. Yet, sometimes companies unwittingly implement policies or tolerate behavior that make it difficult for employees to act responsibly.

This chapter looks at how the interaction of certain policies and practices in an organization can inadvertently create an unhealthy moral environment—meaning one that does not encourage employees to act in a morally responsible way. Looking at an organization as a moral environment provides a way for managers to take stock of how corporate policies and practices encourage, or fail to encourage, responsible employee behavior.

Environmental Influence

A moral environment is a system of customs and habits found in daily life that take on a logic of their own. They influence the dispositions and sensibilities of people given the structure, tradition, beliefs, leadership, policies, and practices of an organization.[1] An unhealthy moral environment is one where it does not make sense for a person to be, for example, honest, fair, loyal or trustworthy. In an unhealthy moral environment, doing what is morally right is more difficult than usual and sometimes requires great courage.

The practice of segregation in America produced an unhealthy moral environment. One need only visit some of the older parts of southern towns and see the worn signs on rest rooms and water fountains that say "colored" and "white." What ideas and attitudes do separate and unequal facilities foster? What kind of people does this environment produce? Is it responsible for people to follow these social norms?

The fact that it took an act of heroism for a black woman to ride in the front of the bus highlighted the fact that there was something seriously wrong with our society. Similarly, there is something seriously wrong with an organization in which telling simple truths and doing what is morally right exposes employees to the danger of being fired or not promoted. Rosa Parks's rights as an American were undercut by the fact that she was black. Our rights as Americans are sometimes undercut by the fact that we are employees. However, perhaps more important, our moral values as persons are at times compromised or diminished by the necessity of doing what makes sense in the moral environment of the work place.

A healthy moral environment is one where it makes sense to be honest, fair, loyal, forthright, etc. Businesses and society should be places where these virtues thrive and even cowards can do the right thing. A responsible employee not only obeys rules and follows orders, but also attempts to do what is morally right. In a healthy moral environment, these two sets of responsible behavior overlap, i.e., by doing one's job and acting in the interest of the company, one also does the right thing. The point is that organizations need to be places where ordinary life is not a daily moral struggle.

The Heinz Case

A case concerning an incident at the H. J. Heinz company illustrates how a corporate incentive program, combined with other aspects of the Heinz organization, produced a fertile environment for dishonest attitudes and behavior.[2] The case is rich with issues concerning leadership, control, and corporate policy, but I will focus on the dynamics of its moral environment.

In April of 1979, Heinz's president and CEO, James Cunningham, discovered that certain divisions of the company had been making improper income transfers since 1972. Vendors were being prepaid for services and then repaid or had services exchanged in the succeeding year. Managers had recorded expenses and sales in different fiscal years so that they would be assured of reaching the goals of the Management Incentive Program (MIP). Further investigation by the Heinz audit committee uncovered other more serious irregularities such as questionable payments and unrecorded transactions. Basically, the Heinz managers broke every one of the articles in the company's code of ethics.

The Heinz policy of corporate ethics was adopted in May of 1976. It stated that no division should:

1. have any form of unrecorded assets or false entries on its books or records;
2. make or approve any payment with the intention or understanding that any part of such payment was to be used for any purpose other than that described by the documents supporting the payment;
3. make political contributions;
4. make payments or gifts to public officials or customers; or
5. accept gifts or payments of more than a nominal account.[2]

Every year either the president or managing director, along with the chief financial officer of each division, was required to sign a letter affirming their compliance with the code of ethics.

Heinz's MIP was established in 1972 as an aggressive means for attaining corporate financial goals. The MIP was based on a point system. By earning the maximum amount of points, managers could earn bonuses as high as 40 percent of their salary. MIP points were awarded on the basis of reaching certain goals that were determined in the following ways:

1. Personal goals were set by one's immediate supervisor.
2. Division goals were set by the chief executive officer, the chief operating officer, and the senior vice-presidents of finance and corporate development.
3. Corporate goals were set yearly by the development and compensation committee of the board of directors.
4. Corporate officers could also make adjustments or award arbitrary points without consulting division personnel.

There were two types of goals set. The first was called the "fair" goal. It was based on a fixed percentage more than the preceding year's net profit after taxes. The second, called the "outstanding goal," awarded the greatest amount of points and was higher than the fair goal. Division net profit after tax goals was not always in line with the division's budgeted profits. Yet, once the goals were determined, they were rarely changed. Hence, a division could get stuck with an impossible goal and not receive any points in a given year.

To understand what went wrong, we can begin by looking at the kinds of messages that might have been conveyed by this MIP in the context of the structure, policies, and practices of the Heinz organization. One manager said that it had become a "mortal sin" not to achieve these goals.[2] Therefore, the MIP was not only considered as an incentive, but was regarded as a norm of professional competence. Also, in this competitive environment, the focus on the goals of the program was raised to the level of a fetish. Inadequate reporting relationships, poor leadership, and weak accounting controls (among other things) did not reinforce the importance of using the appropriate means to reach profit goals. So, this became an environment where winning was more important than playing by the rules. And because the goals were sometimes unrealistic, it was difficult or impossible to win without cheating.

The managers who did juggle their books knew that it was wrong, particularly those who had to sign the code of ethics every year. However, they had probably substituted their own ethical rationale—i.e., it was okay because the practice did not hurt anyone. It was more like telling a "little white lie" than being overtly dishonest. Over the seven years that the improper income transfers were being made, the practice no longer needed ethical justification because it had become a well-established custom or convention. In the moral environment of Heinz, it might not have made sense not to juggle one's books. The practice had then become important for maintaining the status quo.

Upon discovering the accounting irregularities, Heinz ordered a complete audit by an outside accounting firm. The accounting firm presented their recommendations to the audit committee of the board of directors, commenting that if their recommendations were followed, the "likelihood of the reoccurrence of any of the practices would be materially reduced." Senior management was blamed for poor "control consciousness" and creating an atmosphere of unreasonable pressure to meet and exceed economic goals."[2] One of the more interesting audit committee suggestions was that Heinz should make it clear to all levels of managers "that a directive to achieve a particular financial result carries a corresponding obligation to ascertain whether that result can and will be obtained in the proper legal manner."[2] The question left unanswered by the audit committee was how this point would be communicated—in a memo, a meeting, personal conversations, a new code of ethics complete with spelled-out penalties, or perhaps a good rap on the knuckles.

In May of 1980, after considering the findings of the audit committee, the Heinz board of directors recommended that none of the employees involved in the improper income transferal practices be fired; however, some were "taken to the woodshed" through salary adjustments. An unidentified company source told the *Wall Street Journal* that one reason no one was fired was because some of the most talented managers were involved. The company source said: "This company doesn't believe in this sort of thing philosophically or morally. But nobody got hurt and nobody benefited, except some guys got a leg up (on their incentive goals) for the next year. The amount of money involved was peanuts."[2]

The Heinz Company reorganized their reporting relationships and tightened up their control system, but did they improve the moral environment? Here we have to ask ourselves: What did Heinz's action on this case communicate to employees? They removed the tempting situation, but did they remove the attitudes that went with it? Can talented managers "get away with murder" as long as they are not caught? And when they are caught, should they be excused because they are talented? Does cheating show ingenuity and leadership? What about the managers who did not cheat and made their goals honestly? At stake here is the question: What kind of moral behavior is being encouraged, or is employee responsibility encouraged in the Heinz Corporation?

Critics say that corporate codes of ethics are useless because they have no teeth. Some codes of ethics are regarded as laws and carry particular sanctions for violations. However, ethical norms or mores are usually reinforced and punished through informal social channels. Lying about one's abilities may not be against the law or incur harm. Yet, when caught in a lie, a person can be subject to embarrassment, ridicule, and/or ostracism. For example, getting caught in a lie may be more embarrassing in a monastery than in a used car lot. These social sanctions depend on what is valued, expected, and desired of people in a particular context.

The Heinz code of ethics came in four years after the account juggling had already been in practice. To many it may have been a joke or mere window dressing, since it was basically contrary to what had become "sensible" or customary practice. It is unclear whether Heinz was committed to its own principles. While juggling invoices is not on par with embezzlement or murder, the audit did uncover other irregularities including bribes. What then does one have to do to violate the code of ethics? Get caught with their hand in the till? Ethical codes may not need formal sanctions, but they do need managers who are willing to take a strong stand on their contents. In the Heinz case this would mean not only sanctions against the people involved, but a massive reassessment of their incentive system. The code of ethics and the MIP seemed to be giving off conflicting messages.

Another way of looking at this case is to focus on the moral character of the individuals involved. If the managers had been better persons, this might not have happened. Although we might say that cheating on the MIP had become a common part of the moral environment, this does not excuse managers from intentionally doing things that they knew to be wrong (particularly those who signed the code of ethics). So the question here is: Did the environment make it extraordinarily hard for most managers to do the right thing?

A similar question can be asked concerning the U.S. government's Abscam operation: Did the FBI uncover sleazy politicians? Or did it show that most politicians are not of heroic moral stature? Each of the Abscam defendants were men of different moral makeups with different reasons for being tempted. One Philadelphia congressman had six children, all approaching college age. His sole source of income was his salary as a congressman. He had a reputation for being a decent guy and was, by the norms of Philadelphia politics, fairly honest.

Another congressman had a reputation as a ruthless, self-interested schemer who was not wanting for money. No one who knew him was surprised when the videotapes showed him enthusiastically accepting the payoff (insiders commented this congressman had had a lot of practice at taking bribes).

These two congressmen were equally guilty of wrongdoing; however, the issue is whether the temptation was the same for both men. The FBI administered a very difficult test of moral character. A morally strong person would conquer the temptation. But, as Aristotle points out, people are morally weak, not just because they give in to temptation, but because they do so easily.[3] A person demonstrates his moral strength not just by triumphing over temptation, but by putting up a good fight. The history of western civilization is filled with stories of human resistance to temptation. What is most interesting in the study of ethics is how they have struggled, not whether they won or lost. In the Bible, God or the devil did the tempting; today, it's an MIP or the FBI.

Everybody's Doin' It

All of us have faced difficult tests of moral principles, but hopefully we do not do so every day. When doing the right thing is heroic, stupid, or socially unacceptable, then it becomes too hard for many people. Not everyone is cut out to be a hero or a martyr. Unethical practices that go unchallenged can become the norm of a society or business. Difficult circumstances can produce moral laxity—most people simply do not want to put up a daily struggle. Morality should not be made too easy or too hard in any culture or organization.

When practices that involve some form of lying and cheating become commonplace, they prescribe the way that a sensible person should act in that environment. We have all heard arguments like these: "Everyone cheats on their income tax, or inflates their expense account, so why shouldn't I?" Or "All the kids smoke pot, so why can't I?" This line of thought does not necessarily indicate that doing these things is right, but rather that they are acceptable, or not so very wrong. Responsible behavior requires adherence to principles and resistance to the tyranny of the perceived majority.

Conclusion

Chester Barnard once said that the best managers are "those who possess the art of sensing the whole."[4] Employee responsibilities must be compatible with the social and moral obligations of a culture. Rosa Parks, Heinz, and Abscam give us three things to consider when taking stock of a moral environment.

First, there is something wrong with an environment where a Rosa Parks has to stand on principle in order to sit in the front of a bus—where doing what is sensible or right takes a heroic gesture. This point is particularly important when one considers cases of whistleblowing. Basically, morality in the workplace should not be drastically different from morality in the culture outside of it.

Second, ethical responsibilities are, or should be, inseparable from business policies and practices. It must "make sense" to be honest, fair, loyal, etc. in carrying out the requirements of one's job and the goals of a business. This is all part of what it means to be responsible. Heinz was able to stop the spread of cancer, but it is unclear whether they cured the disease. From what the case tells us, Heinz never took a strong stand on the ethical wrongdoing. Excusing the talented managers was rather like pardoning Richard Nixon. No one admitted that he was wrong, no one was really punished, no one apologized, and no one promised he would not do anything like that again. Rather than taking measures to encourage more responsible behavior in the future, Heinz chose to enforce adherence to rules by implementing strict controls. They will probably have to be vigilant in the future.

Third, while it is true that employee behavior may be controlled by force, responsible behavior is not fostered by it. Abscam was rather like leaving the cash register open and then posting a security guard at the door to catch the thieves. Part of what is required to improve the health of a moral environment is to close the cash drawer. By limiting temptation, one limits the need for control and makes it easier for employees to act responsibly.

The work environment should be a place where employees want to act responsibly and find it easy to do so. This involves management policies and practices that are reasonable and worthy of respect. However, it also requires adequate control systems that keep the weak or the overly ambitious from temptation. A delicate balance must be struck here between the rights and autonomy of individuals and managerial control. Authoritarian management may, by stripping employees of their say in the work process, also free them from responsibility for their actions. On the other hand, overly lax management can lead to abuses and irresponsible behavior. Here again, we might take Aristotle's advice and search for a balance, or the "golden mean" between these two extremes.

64

Universal Human Values:
Finding an Ethical Common Ground

Rushworth M. Kidder

Rushworth M. Kidder formerly served as senior columnist for *The Christian Science Monitor*. He is currently president of the Institute for Global Ethics. His most recent book is *Shared Values for a Troubled World: Conversations with Men and Women of Conscience*.

In the remote New Zealand village of Panguru, tucked into the mountains at the end of a winding gravel road, a Maori woman nearly a century old pauses for a moment as she talks about the moral values of her people. "This is God's country!" says Dame Whina Cooper with great feeling, gesturing toward the flowers blooming among the bird songs outside her modest frame house. "Only, we the people running it must be doing something wrong."

Halfway around the world, in a United Nations office perched under the eaves of a fifteenth-century building in Florence, a leading journalist from Sri Lanka is asked what will happen if the world enters the twenty-first century with the ethics of the twentieth. "I feel it will be disastrous," Varindra Tarzie Vittachi replies simply.

Midway between, in his well-appointed residence in San Jose, Costa Rica, former president Oscar Arias explains that our global survival "will become

Reproduced with permission from the *The Futurist*, published by the World Future Society, 7910 Woodmont Avenue, Suite 450, Bethesda, Maryland 20814.

more complicated and precarious than ever before, and the ethics required of us must be correspondingly sophisticated."

Turn where you will in the world and the refrain is the same. The ethical barometer is falling, and the consequences appear to be grave. That, at least, is one of the impressions to be drawn from the two dozen individuals from 16 nations interviewed over the past few years by the Institute for Global Ethics.

These interviews did not seek to discover the ethical failings of various nations, but rather to find the moral glue that will bind us together in the twenty-first century. These voices speak powerfully of an underlying moral presence shared by all humanity—a set of precepts so fundamental that they dissolve borders, transcend races, and outlast cultural traditions.

There is a pressing need for shared values in our age of global interdependence without consensus. But there is one very real question unanswered: Is there in fact a single set of values that wise, ethical people around the world might agree on? Can there be a global code of ethics? If there is a common core of values "out there" in the world, it ought to be identifiable through examination of contemporary modes of thought in various cultures around the world. Can it be found?

On that topic, the two dozen "men and women of conscience" interviewed had a clear point of view. "Yes," they said, "there is such a code, and it can be clearly articulated." These interviewees were chosen not because they necessarily know more about ethics than their peers—although some do, having made it a lifelong study. Nor were they chosen because they are the single most exemplary person of their nation or community—though some could easily be nominated for that honor. They are, however, ethical thought-leaders within their different cultures, each viewed by his or her peers as a kind of ethical standard-bearer, a keeper of the conscience of the community, a center of moral gravity.

Each of the interviews began with a common question: If you could help create a global code of ethics, what would be on it? What moral values, in other words, would you bring to the table from your own culture and background?

In an ideal world, one would have assembled all the interviewees around a table, had each talk for an hour, had each listen intently to all the others, and finally had them arrive at a consensus. If they could have done so, here's the core of moral values upon which they probably would have agreed:

Love

Despite the concern of foundation executive James A. Joseph in Washington that "the L-word, Love," is falling sadly into disuse, it figured prominently in these interviews. "Love, yes," said children's author Astrid Lindgren in Stockholm. "This is the main word for what we need—love on all stages and with all people."

"The base of moral behavior is first of all solidarity, love, and mutual assistance," said former first lady Graça Machel of Mozambique. Buddhist monk Shojun Bando in Tokyo agreed, detailing three different kinds of love and insisting that "it shouldn't be that *others* should tell you to love others: It should just come of its own will, spontaneously." Or, as author Nien Cheng from China put it, "You cannot guide without love."

For tribal chief Reuben Snake of Nebraska, the central word is *compassion*. "We have to be compassionate with one another and help one another, to hold each other up, support one another down the road of life," he recalled his grandfather telling him. Thinking back on her dealings with a global spectrum of cultures at the United Nations, former ambassador Jeane Kirkpatrick in Washington noted that, no matter how severe the political differences, "there was a kind of assumption, on the part of almost everyone, that people would help one another at the personal level."

Truthfulness

Of the four theses that form Harvard University ex-president Derek Bok's code of ethics, two center on truth. "You should not obtain your ends through lying and deceitful practices," he said, and you have a "responsibility to keep [your] promises." Astrid Lindgren put it with equal clarity when she spoke of the need to "be honest, not lying, not afraid to say your opinion."

Looking through the lens of science, the late economist Kenneth Boulding of Colorado also put "a very high value on veracity—telling the truth. The thing that gets you run out of the scientific community is being caught out telling a lie." Fortunately, said Bangladeshi banker Muhammad Yunus, the spread of technology makes it increasingly difficult for the truth to be hidden. In the future, "people will be forced to reveal themselves," he said. "Nothing can be kept hidden or secret—not in computers, not in the halls of government, nothing. People will feel much more comfortable when they're dealing in truth. You converge around and in truth."

Here, however, as with many of these global values, there was also a residue of concern—a fear that trust, which is central to honesty and truthfulness, seems to be falling into abeyance. "The idea that you ought to be able to trust somebody is out of fashion," worried Katharine Whitehorn, columnist for *The Observer* of London. That's a point seconded by corporate executive James K. Baker of Indiana. "Little by little," he said, "if we let that trust go out of our personal dealings with one another, then I think the system really begins to have trouble."

Fairness

Elevating the concept of justice to the top of his list, philosopher and author John W. Gardner of Stanford University said, "I consider that probably the number-one candidate for your common ground." By *justice*, he meant "fair play, or some word for even-handedness."

"Here, one could get caught up in the very complicated theories of social justice," warned James A. Joseph. "Or one could simply look at the Golden Rule. I relate fairness to treating other people as I would want to be treated. I think that [rule] serves humanity well. It ought to be a part of any ethic for the future."

For many, the concern for fairness goes hand in hand with the concept of equality. "The pursuit of equality is basic," said columnist and editor Sergio Muñoz of Mexico City and Los Angeles. "The people who come from Mexico and El Salvador have the same values, in my point of view, as the person who comes from Minnesota or from Alabama or from California—those basic principles that are common to all civilizations."

For some, like Joseph, the concept of fairness and equality focuses strongly on racial issues. Others, like author Jill Ker Conway from Australia, see the need for "greater equity between the sexes." Still others, like UNESCO Director-General Federico Mayor of Spain, see the problem as one of international relations: Despite the groundswell of interest in democracy arising within the former East Bloc nations, Westerners "have not reacted as humans, but only as economic individuals. . . . Even equity—the most important value in all the world—has collapsed."

Freedom

Very early in human history, said John Gardner, "the concept of degrees of freedom of my action—as against excessive constraints on my action by a tyrant or by military conquerors—emerged." Even the earliest peoples "knew when they were subjugated"—and didn't like it. That desire for liberty, he said, persists to the present as one of the defining values of humanity.

But liberty requires a sense of individuality and the right of that individual to express ideas freely, many of the interviewees said. "Without the principle of individual conscience, every attempt to institutionalize ethics must necessarily collapse" said Oscar Arias. "The effect of one upright individual is incalculable. World leaders may see their effect in headlines, but the ultimate course of the globe will be determined by the efforts of innumerable individuals acting on their consciences."

Such action, for many of these thinkers, is synonymous with democracy. "I think democracy is a must for all over the world," said Salim El Hoss, former prime minister of Lebanon. He defined the ingredients of democracy as "freedom of expression plus accountability plus equal opportunity." While he worried that the latter two are lacking in many countries, he noted that the first condition, freedom of expression, is increasingly becoming available to "all peoples."

Unity

As a counterbalance to the needs of individual conscience, however, stands the value that embraces the individual's role in a larger collective. Of the multitude of similar terms used for that concept in these interviews (*fraternity, solidarity, cooperation, community, group allegiance, oneness*) *unity* seems the most encompassing and the least open to misconstruction. For some, it is a simple *cri de coeur* in a world that seems close to coming undone. "I want unity," said Dame Whina Cooper of New Zealand, adding that "God wants us to be one people." For Tarzie Vittachi of Sri Lanka, the idea of unity embraces a global vision capable of moving humanity from "unbridled competition" to cooperation. "That is what is demanded of us now: putting our community first, meaning the earth first, and all living things."

The problem arises when the common good is interpreted "by seeing the relation between the individual and the common in individualistic terms," said Father Bernard Przewozny of Rome. Carried to the extreme, individualism is "destructive of social life, destructive of communal sharing, destructive of participation," he said, adding that "the earth and its natural goods are the inheritance of all peoples."

Tolerance

"If you're serious about values," said John Gardner, "then you have to add tolerance very early—*very* early. Because you have to have constraints. The more you say, 'Values are important,' the more you have to say, 'There are limits to which you can impose your values on me.'"

"It is a question of respect for the dignity of each of us," said Graça Machel. "If you have a different idea from mine, it's not because you're worse than me. You have the right to think differently." Agreeing, Derek Bok defined tolerance as "a decent respect for the right of other people to have ideas, an obligation or at least a strong desirability of listening to different points of view and attempting to understand why they are held."

"You have your own job, you eat your own food," said Vietnamese writer and activist Le Ly Hayslip. "How you make that food is up to you, and how I live my life is up to me."

Reuben Snake traced the idea of tolerance back to a religious basis. "The spirit that makes you stand up and walk and talk and see and hear and think is the same spirit that exists in me—there's no difference," he said. "So when you look at me, you're looking at yourself—and I'm seeing me in you."

Abstracting from the idea of tolerance the core principle of respect for variety, Kenneth Boulding linked it to the environmentalist's urgency over the depletion of species. "If the blue whale is endangered, we feel worried about this, because we love the variety of the world," he explained. "In some sense I feel about the Catholic Church the way I feel about the blue whale: I don't think I'll be one, but I would feel diminished if it became extinct."

Responsibility

Oxford don A.H. Halsey placed the sense of responsibility high on his list of values because of its impact on our common future. "We are responsible for our grandchildren," he explained, "and we will make [the world] easier or more difficult for our grandchildren to be good people by what we do right here and now." This was a point made in a different way by Katharine Whitehorn, who noted that, while as a youth "it's fun to break away," it's very much harder to "grow up and have to put it together again."

For Nien Cheng, the spotlight falls not so much on the actions of the future as on the sense of self-respect in the present. "This is Confucius' teaching," she said. "You must take care of yourself. To rely on others is a great shame."

Responsibility also demands caring for others, Hayslip said. But, under the complex interactions of medicine, insurance, and law that exists in the West, "If you come into my house and see me lying here very sick, you don't dare move me, because you're not a doctor," she pointed out. "So where is your human obligation? Where is your human instinct to try to save me? You don't have it. You lost it, because there are too many rules."

Yet, paradoxically, "responsibility is not often mentioned in discussions of world politics or ethics," said Oscar Arias. "There, the talk is all of rights, demands, and desires." Human rights are "an unquestionable and critical priority for political societies and an indispensable lever for genuine development," he said. "But the important thing is not just to assert rights, but to ensure that they be protected. Achieving this protection rests wholly on the principle of responsibility."

Chicago attorney Newton Minow agreed. "I believe the basic reason we got off the track was that rights became more important than responsibilities, that individuals became more important than community interests. We've gotten to the point where everybody's got a right and nobody's got a responsibility."

At its ultimate, this sense of responsibility extends to the concept of the right use of force. "You shouldn't perpetrate violence," said Derek Bok simply, finding agreement with Jeane Kirkpatrick's insistence that "war is always undesirable" and that "any resort to force should be a very late option, never a first option."

Respect for Life

Growing out of this idea of the responsible use of force, but separate from and extending beyond it, is a value known most widely in the West from the Ten Commandments: Thou shalt not kill. For Shojun Bando, it is an inflexible principle: Even if ordered in wartime to defend his homeland by killing, he said, "I would refuse. I would say, 'I cannot do this.'"

Such an idea, expressed in today's peaceable Japan, may seem almost naive when examined through the lens of such war-riddled areas as the Middle East. Yet, Salim El Hoss took much the same view. "I was a prime minister [of Lebanon] for seven and a half years. I can't imagine myself signing a death penalty for anybody in the world. I think that is completely illegitimate, and I think that is the kind of thing a code of ethics should deal with."

Reuben Snake, noting that the North American Indians have a war-like reputation, said, "Probably the most serious shortcoming of tribal governments is their inability to effectively resolve conflict within the tribe and externally." He described earlier Indian traditions, however, in which great efforts were made by the tribal elders to prevent killing. That's a point with which Tarzie Vittachi—himself from the much-bloodied nation of Sri Lanka—felt perfectly at home. The first element of the Buddhist "daily prayer" under which he was raised, he recalled, is "I shall not kill." It is also central to the Ten Commandments of the Jewish decalogue under which Newton Minow was raised and which he said he still feels form the basis for the world's code of ethics.

Other Shared Values

There were, of course, other significant values that surfaced in these interviews. Nien Cheng, for instance, pointed to *courage*. "One should basically know what is right and what is wrong," she said, "and, when you know that, be courageous enough to stand for what is right."

Figuring strongly in Shojun Bando's pantheon was *wisdom*, which he defined as "attaining detachment, getting away from being too attached to things."

Whina Cooper put *hospitality* high on her list, recalling that her father said, "If you see any strangers going past, you call them—*Kia Ora*—that means to call them to come here." Astrid Lindgren put an emphasis on *obedience*—a quality that runs throughout the life of her most famous character, Pippi Longstocking, though usually in reverse.

Kenneth Boulding pointed to *peace*, which he defined simply as "well-managed conflict." Thinking of peace brought Salim El Hoss to the concept of *stability*. "Peace is equivalent to stability," he said, adding that "stability means a long-term perspective of no problems." These and other values, while they don't find broad support, had firm proponents among those we interviewed and deserve serious attention.

Other values mentioned included the burning public concerns for racial harmony, respect for women's place, and the protection of the environment. Many of the interviewees touched on them, and some elevated them to high priority. Speaking of the need for racial harmony, James Joseph put at the top of his list a sense of "respect for the cultures of other communities, respect for the need to begin to integrate into our collective memory appreciation of the contributions and traditions of those who are different." Jill Conway topped her list with a warning about the "increasing exploitation of women" around the world. And of the many human rights identified by Father Bernard Prze-wozny, the one to which he has dedicated his life is the "right to a healthy environment."

So what good is this code of values? It gives us a foundation for building goals, plans, and tactics, where things really happen and the world really changes. It unifies us, giving us a home territory of consensus and agreement. And it gives us a way—not *the* way, but *a* way—to reply when we're asked, "Whose values will you teach?" Answering this last question, as we tumble into the twenty-first century with the twentieth's sense of ethics, may be one of the most valuable mental activities of our time.

REFERENCES

PREFACE

1. James MacGregor Burns, *Leadership* (New York: Harper & Row, 1978).

SELECTION 7

1. Different definitions and conceptions of leadership have been reviewed briefly by Morris and Seeman,[5] Shartle,[6-8] L. F. Carter,[9] C. A. Gibb,[10-11] Bass,[12] Stogdill,[13] and Schriesheim and Kerr.[14]
2. Pfeffer, J. (1977). The ambiguity of leadership. *Academy of Management Review 2*, 104–112.
3. Bavelas, A. (1960). Leadership: Man and Function. *Administrative Science Quarterly 4*, 491–498.
4. Hollander, E. P., & Julian, J. W. (1969). Contemporary trends in the analysis of leadership processes. *Psychological Bulletin*, 71, 387–397.
5. Morris, R. T., & Seeman, M. (1950). The problem of leadership: An interdisciplinary approach. *American Journal of Sociology 56*, 149–155.
6. Shartle, C. L. (1951). Leader behavior in jobs. *Occupations*, 30, 164–166.
7. Shartle, C. L. (1951). Studies in naval leadership. In H. Guetzkow (Ed.), *Groups, leadership, and men*. Pittsburgh, PA: Carnegie Press.
8. Shartle, C. L. (1956). *Executive performance and leadership*. Englewood Cliffs, NJ: Prentice-Hall.
9. Carter, L. F. (1953). Leadership and Small Group Behavior. In M. Sherif & M. O. Wilson (Eds.) *Group relations at the crossroads*. New York: Harper.
10. Gibb, C. A. (1954). Leadership. In G. Lindzey (Ed.) *Handbook of social psychology*. Cambridge, MA: Addison-Wesley.

11. Gibb, C. A. (1969). Leadership. In G. Lindzey & E. Aronson (Eds.) *The handbook of social psychology*, 2nd ed., Vol. 4. Reading, MA: Addison-Wesley.

12. Schriesheim, C. A., & Kerr, S. (1977). Theories and measures of leadership: A critical appraisal of present and future directions. In J. G. Hunt & L. L. Larson (Eds.) *Leadership: The cutting edge*. Carbondale: Southern Illinois University Press.

13. Stogdill, R. M. (1975). The evolution of leadership theory. *Proceedings, Academy of Management*, New Orleans, LA, 4–6.

SELECTION 8

1. Read, P. P. *Alive*. New York: J. B. Lippincott, 1974.

2. Meindl, J. R., and S. B. Erlich. "The Romance of Leadership and the Evaluation of Organizational Performance." *Academy of Management Journal* 30 (1987), pp. 90–109.

3. Munson, C. E. "Style and Structure in Supervision." *Journal of Education Social Work* 17 (1981), pp. 65–72.

4. Bennis, W. G. "Leadership Theory and Administrative Behavior: The Problem of Authority." *Administrative Science Quarterly* 4(1959).

5. Hollander, E. P., and J. W. Julian. "Contemporary Trends in the Analysis of Leadership Processes." *Psychological Bulletin* 71 (1969), pp. 387–91.

6. Fiedler, F. E. *A Theory of Leadership Effectiveness*. New York: McGraw-Hill, 1967.

7. Merton, R. K. *Social Theory and Social Structure*. New York: Free Press, 1957.

8. Bass, B. M. *Leadership and Performance Beyond Expectations*. New York: The Free Press, 1985.

9. Tichy, N. M., and M. A. Devanna. *The Transformational Leader*. New York: Wiley, 1986.

10. Roach, C. F., and O. Behling. "Functionalism: Basis for an Alternate Approach to the Study of Leadership," in *Leaders and Managers: International Perspectives on Managerial Behavior and Leadership*, ed. J. G. Hunt, D. M. Hosking, C. A. Schriesheim, and R. Stewart. Elmsford, N.Y.: Pergamon, 1984.

11. Campbell, D. P. *Campbell Leadership Index Manual*. Minneapolis: National Computer Systems, 1991.

SELECTION 9

1. Paige, G. D. (1977). *The scientific study of political leadership*. New York: The Free Press.

2. Lichtheim, M. (1973). *Ancient Egyptian literature. Vol. I: The old and middle kingdoms*. Los Angeles: University of California Press.

3. Sarachek, B. (1968). Greek concepts of leadership. *Academy of Management Journal*, 11, 39–48.

4. Kellerman, B. (1987). *The politics of leadership in America: Implications for higher education in the late twentieth century.* Paper, Invitational Interdisciplinary Colloquium on Leadership in Higher Education, National Center for Postsecondary Governance and Finance, Teacher's College, Columbia University, New York.
5. Machiavelli, N. (1513/1962). *The prince.* New York: Mentor Press.
6. Christie, R., & Geis, F. L. (1970). *Studies in Machiavellianism.* New York: Academic Press.
7. Hegel, G. F. (1830/1971). Philosophy of mind. (Trans. W. Wallace) *Encyclopedia of the philosophical sciences.* Oxford: Clarendon Press.

SELECTION 11

1. In 1806 Napoleon issued a decree forbidding all trade with England and closing all European ports to her ships. He compelled his allies to accede to this policy, which was disadvantageous to many countries. It led to great injury to trade and to much smuggling: the system was often infringed, and even Napoleon himself could not dispense with English goods and at times admitted them to France. It was particularly irksome to Russia, and her evasion of it was treated by Napoleon as a violation of the treaty. In conjunction with other causes it led to his invasion of Russia in 1812. One result of the Continental System was the issue of the English Orders in Council in reply to it. These Orders occasioned much inconvenience to neutral nations and, together with the intrigues conducted by Napoleon, led to the war between England and the United States of America in 1812–14.—A.M.
2. The demand that Napoleon should withdraw beyond that river was Alexander's last effort to avoid war, and Napoleon's refusal led directly to the commencement of hostilities in 1812.—A.M.
3. In May, 1812, immediately before the war, Napoleon spent about a month in Dresden with his new allies: the Emperor of Austria, the King of Prussia, the King of Saxony, etc.—attending a series of magnificent banquets and fetes and receiving flattery and honors from all sides.—A.M.

SELECTION 16

1. Throughout this chapter the words *passive resistance* are generally used for Satyagraha.

SELECTION 18

1. Ralph M. Stogdill. "Personal Factors Associated with Leadership: A Survey of the Literature." *Journal of Psychology,* 25 (1948), pp. 35–71.

2. Kurt Lewin, Ronald Lippitt, and Ralph K. White, "Patterns of Aggressive Behavior in Experimentally Created Social Climates," *Journal of Social Psychology*, 10 (1939), pp. 271–99.

3. Ralph M. Stogdill, Carroll L. Shartle, Willis L. Scott, Alvin E. Coons, and William E. Jaynes, *A Predictive Study of Administrative Work Patterns* (Columbus: Ohio State University, Bureau of Business Research, 1956).

4. Robert L. Kahn and Daniel Katz, "Leadership Practices in Relation to Productivity and Morale," in Dorwin Cartwright and Alvin Zander, eds., *Group Dynamics* (New York: Harper & Row, 1953).

5. Robert F. Bales and Paul E. Slater, "Role Differentiation in Small Decision Making Groups," in Talcott Parsons and Robert F. Bales, eds., *Family, Localization, and Interaction Processes* (New York: Free Press, 1945).

6. Ralph M. Stogdill and Alvin E. Coons, eds., *Leader Behavior: Its Description and Measurement* (Columbus: Ohio State University, Bureau of Business Research, 1957).

7. Kahn and Katz, *Group Dynamics*.

8. Bales and Slater, *Family, Localization, and Interaction Processes*.

9. Abraham Korman, "Consideration, Initiating Structure, and Organizational Criteria—A Review," *Personnel Psychology*, 19 (1966), pp. 349–62.

10. Fred E. Fiedler, "A Contingency Model of Leadership Effectiveness," in Leonard Berkowitz, ed., *Advances in Experimental Social Psychology*, vol. 1 (New York: Academic Press, 1964).

11. ———, *A Theory of Leadership Effectiveness* (New York: McGraw-Hill, 1967).

12. ———, "The Contingency Model and the Dynamics of the Leadership Process," in Leonard Berkowitz, ed., *Advances in Experimental Social Psychology*.

13. Fred E. Fiedler and Martin M. Chemers, *Leadership and Effective Management* (New York: Scott, Foresman, 1974).

14. Robert W. Rice, "Construct Validity of the Least Preferred Co-worker Score," *Psychological Bulletin*, 85 (1978), pp. 1199–1237.

15. Ibid.

16. Fiedler, *A Theory of Leadership Effectiveness*.

17. Ahmed S. Ashour, "Further Discussion of Fiedler's Contingency Model of Leadership Effectiveness: An Evaluation," *Organizational Behavior and Human Performance*, 9 (1973), pp. 339–55.

18. George Graen, Kenneth M. Alveres, James B. Orris, and John A. Martella, "Contingency Model of Leadership Effectiveness: Antecedent and Evidential Results," *Psychological Bulletin*, 74 (1970), pp. 285–96.

19. Terrence R. Mitchell, Anthony Biglan, Gerald R. Oncken, and Fred E. Fiedler, "The Contingency Model: Criticism and Suggestions," *Academy of Management Journal*, 13 (1970), pp. 253–67.

20. Michael J. Strube and Joseph E. Garcia, "A Meta-analytical Investigation of

Fiedler's Contingency Model of Leadership Effectiveness," *Psychological Bulletin*, 90 (1981), pp. 307–21.

21. Robert J. House, "T-Group Education and Leadership Effectiveness: A Review of the Empirical Literature and a Critical Evaluation," *Personnel Psychology*, 20 (1967), pp. 1–32.

22. Martin M. Chemers, Robert W. Rice, Eric Sundstrom, and William M. Butler, "Leader LPC. Training and Effectiveness: An Experimental Examination," *Journal of Personality and Social Psychology*, 31 (1975), pp. 401–9.

23. Fred E. Fiedler, "The Effects of Leadership Training and Experience: A Contingency Model Interpretation," *Administrative Science Quarterly*, 17 (1972), pp. 453–70.

24. Victor H. Vroom and Paul W. Yetton, *Leadership and Decision-Making* (Pittsburgh: University of Pittsburgh Press, 1973).

25. Arthur G. Jago and Victor H. Vroom, "An Evaluation of Two Alternatives to the Vroom Yetton Normative Model," *Academy of Management Journal*, 23 (1980), pp. 347–55.

26. Victor H. Vroom and Arthur G. Jago, "On the Validity of the Vroom-Yetton Model," *Journal of Applied Psychology*, 63 (1978), pp. 151–62.

27. Martin M. Chemers, Barbara K. Goza, and Sheldon I. Plumer, "Leadership Style and Communication Process: An Experiment Using the Psychological Isotope Technique," *Resources in Education* (September 1979).

28. Martin M. Chemers and George J. Skrzypek, "An Experimental Test of the Contingency Model of Leadership Effectiveness," *Journal of Personality and Social Psychology*, 24 (1972), pp. 172–77.

29. Rice, "Construct Validity of the Least Preferred Co-worker Score."

30. Bernard M. Bass, Enzo R. Valenzi, Dana L. Farrow, and Robert J. Solomon, "Management Styles Associated With Organizational, Task, Personal, and Interpersonal Contingencies," *Journal of Applied Psychology*, 60 (1975), pp. 720–29.

31. Robert J. House, "A Path-Goal Theory of Leadership," *Administrative Science Quarterly*, 16 (1971), pp. 321–38.

32. Robert J. House and Gary Dessler, "The Path-Goal Theory of Leadership: Some Post Hoc and A Priori Tests," in James G. Junt and Lars L. Larsen, eds., *Contingency Approaches to Leadership* (Carbondale, Il: Southern Illinois University Press, 1974).

33. Ricky N. Griffin, "Relationships Among Individual, Task Design, and Leader Behavior Variables," *Academy of Management Journal*, 23, (1980), pp. 665–83.

34. Edwin P. Hollander, "Conformity, Status, and Idiosyncrasy Credit," *Psychological Review*, 65, pp. 117–27.

35. Edwin P. Hollander and James W. Julian, "Studies in Leader Legitimacy, Influence, and Innovation," in Leonard Berkowitz, ed., *Advances in Experimental Social Psychology*, vol. 5 (New York: Academic Press, 1970).

36. Fred Dansereau, Jr., George Graen, and William J. Haga, "Vertical Dyad Linkage Approach to Leadership Within Formal Organizations: A Longitudinal Investigation of the Role Making Process," *Organizational Behavior and Human Performance*, 13 (1975), pp. 46–78.

37. George Graen and James F. Cashman, "A Role-Making Model of Leadership in Formal Organizations: A Developmental Approach," in J. G. Hunt and L. L. Larsen, eds., *Leadership Frontiers* (Kent, Ohio: Kent State University Press, 1975).

38. George Graen, James F. Cashman, Steven Ginsburgh, and William Schiemann, "Effects of Linking-Pin Quality of Work Life of Lower Participants," *Administrative Science Quarterly*, 22 (1977), pp. 491–504.

39. George Graen and Steven Ginsburgh, "Job Resignation as a Function of Role Orientation and Leader Acceptance: A Longitudinal Investigation of Organizational Assimilation," *Organizational Behavior and Human Performance*, 19 (1977), pp. 1–17.

40. Alex Bavelas, Albert H. Hastorf, Alan E. Gross, and W. Richard Kite, "Experiments on the Alteration of Group Structure," *Journal of Experimental Social Psychology*, 1 (1965), pp. 55–70.

41. Lawrence Beckhouse, Judith Tanur, John Weiler, and Eugene Weinstein, "And Some Men Have Leadership Thrust Upon Them," *Journal of Personality and Social Psychology*, 31 (1975), pp. 557–66.

42. Leopold W. Gruenfeld, David E. Rance, and Peter Weissenbert, "The Behavior of Task Oriented (Low LPC) and Socially Oriented (High LPC) Leaders Under Several Conditions of Social Support," *Journal of Social Psychology*, 79 (1969), pp. 99–107.

43. William Haythorn, Arthur Couch, Don Haefner, Peter Langham, and Launor F. Carter, "The Effects of Varying Combinations of Authoritarian and Egalitarian Leader and Follower," *Journal of Abnormal and Social Psychology*, 53 (1956), pp. 210–19.

44. Frederick Sanford, "Research on Military Leadership," in John Flanagan, ed., *Psychology in the World Emergency* (Pittsburgh: University of Pittsburgh Press, 1952).

45. Stanley E. Weed, Terrence R. Mitchell, and William Moffitt, "Leadership Style, Subordinate Personality, and Task Type as Predictors of Performance and Satisfaction With Supervision," *Journal of Applied Psychology*, 61 (1976), pp. 58–66.

46. Richard M. Steers, "Task-goal Attributes, N Achievement, and Supervisory Performance," *Organizational Behavior and Human Performance*, 13 (1975), pp. 392–103.

47. Milton R. Blood, "Work Values and Job Satisfaction," *Journal of Applied Psychology*, 53 (1969), pp. 456–59.

48. Ramon J. Aldage and Arthur P. Brief, "Some Correlates of Work Values," *Journal of Applied Psychology*, 60 (1975), pp. 757–60.

49. Thomas L. Ruble, "Effects of One's Locus of Control and the Opportunity to Participate in Planning," *Organizational Behavior and Human Performance*, 16 (1976), pp. 63–73.

50. Douglas E. Durand and Walter R. Nord, "Perceived Leader Behavior as a Function of Personality Characteristics of Supervisors and Subordinates," *Academy of Management Journal*, 19 (1976), pp. 427–31.

51. Fritz Heider, *The Psychology of Interpersonal Relations* (New York: John Wiley, 1958).

52. Edward E. Jones and Keith E. Davis, "From Acts to Dispositions," in Leonard Berkowitz, ed., *Advances in Experimental Social Psychology*, vol 2. (New York: Academic Press, 1965).

53. Harold H. Kelley, "The Processes of Causal Attribution," *American Psychologists*, 28 (1973), pp. 107–28.

54. Jones and Davies, "From Acts to Dispositions."

55. Stephen G. Green and Terrence R. Mitchell, "Attributional Processes of Leaders in Leader-Member Interactions," *Organizational Behavior and Human Performance*, 23 (1979), pp. 429–58.

56. Terrence R. Mitchell and Laura S. Kalb, "Effects of Outcome Knowledge and Outcome Valence in Supervisors' Evaluations," *Journal of Applied Psychology*, 66 (1981), pp. 604–12.

57. Terrence R. Mitchell and Robert E. Wood, "Supervisors' Responses to Subordinate Poor Performance: A Test of an Attributional Model," *Organizational Behavior and Human Performance*, 25 (1980), pp. 123–38.

58. Billy J. Calder, "An Attribution Theory of Leadership," in Barry M. Staw and Gerald R. Slancik, eds., *New Directions in Organizational Behavior* (Chicago: St. Clair, 1977).

59. Dov Eden and Uri Leviatan, "Implicit Leadership Theory as a Determinant of the Factor Structure Underlying Supervisory Behavior Scales," *Journal of Applied Psychology*, 60 (1975), pp. 736–41.

60. Robert G. Lord, John F. Binning, Michael C. Rush, and Jay C. Thomas, "The Effect of Performance Cues and Leader Behavior in Questionnaire Rating of Leadership Behavior," *Organizational Behavior and Human Performance*, 21 (1978), pp. 27–39.

61. H. Kirk Downey, Thomas I. Chacko, and James C. McElroy, "Attribution of the 'Causes' of Performance: A Constructive, Quasi-Longitudinal Replication of the Staw (1975) Study," *Organizational Behavior and Human Performance*, 24 (1979), pp. 287–89.

62. Rova Avman and Martin M. Chemers, "The Relationship of Leader Behavior to Managerial Effectiveness and Satisfaction in Iran," *Journal of Applied Psychology*, 68 (1983), pp. 338–341.

63. John W. Berry, "On Cross-Cultural Comparability," *International Journal of Psychology*, 4 (1969), pp. 119–28.

64. Martin M. Chemers, "Leadership and Social Organization in Cross-Cultural Psychology," paper presented to the Meetings of the American Psychological Association, Los Angeles, 1981.

65. Karlene H. Roberts, "On Looking at an Elephant: An Evaluation of Cross-Cultural Research Related to Organizations," *Psychological Bulletin*, 74 (1970), pp. 327–50.

66. Robert A. Nath, "A Methodological Review of Cross-Cultural Management Research," in Jean Boddewyn, ed., *Comparative Management and Marketing* (Glenview, Il.: Scott, Foresman, 1969).

67. Gerald V. Barrett and Bernard M. Bass, "Cross-Cultural Issues in Industrial and Organizational Psychology," in M. D. Dunnette, ed., *Handbook of Industrial and Organizational Psychology* (Chicago: Rand McNally, 1975).

68. Arnold S. Tannenbaum, "Organizational Psychology," in Harry C. Triandis and Richard W. Brislin, eds., *Handbook of Cross-Cultural Psychology, Social Psychology*, vol. 5 (Boston: Allyn & Bacon, 1980).

69. Anant R. Negandhi, "Comparative Management and Organizational Theory: A Marriage Needed," *Academy of Management Journal*, 18 (1975), pp. 334–44.

70. Richard N. Farmer and Barry M. Richman, *Comparative Management and Economic Progress* (Homewood, Il.: Richard D. Irwin, 1965).

71. Tannenbaum, "Organizational Psychology."

72. Geert Hofstede, "Nationality and Espoused Values of Managers," *Journal of Applied Psychology*, 61 (1976), pp. 148–55.

73. ———, "Motivation, Leadership, and Organization: Do American Theories Apply Abroad?" *Organizational Dynamics* (Summer 1980).

74. ———, *Culture's Consequences: International Differences in Work-Related Values* (London: Sage, 1981).

75. Ibid.

76. Ayman and Chemers, "The Relationship of Leader Behavior to Managerial Effectiveness and Satisfaction in Iran."

77. Ibid.

78. Chemers, "Leadership and Social Organization in Cross-Cultural Psychology."

79. Ayman and Chemers, "The Relationship of Leader Behavior to Managerial Effectiveness and Satisfaction in Iran."

SELECTION 20

1. Burns, James MacGregor. 1878. *Leadership*. New York: Harper & Row, Publishers.

2. Bass, Bernard M. 1985. *Leadership and Performance Beyond Expectations*. New York: The Free Press.

3. Ibid.

4. Selznick, Philip. 1948. *TVA and the Grassroots: A Study in the Sociology of Formal Organizations.* New York: Harper & Row, Publishers.

SELECTION 21

1. J. M. Burns, *Leadership* (New York, NY: Harper & Row, 1978); W. Bennis and B. Nanus, *Leaders: The Strategies for Taking Charge* (New York, NY: Harper & Row, 1985); N. M. Tichy and D. Ulrich, "The Leadership Challenge: A Call for the Transformational Leader," *Sloan Management Review* (Fall 1984); N. M. Tichy and M. A. Devanna, *The Transformational Leader* (New York, NY: Wiley, 1986).
2. D. E. Berlew, "Leadership and Organizational Excitement," in D. A. Kolb, I. M. Rubin, and J. M. McIntyre, eds., *Organizational Psychology* (Englewood Cliffs, NJ: Prentice-Hall, 1974); R. J. House, "A 1976 Theory of Charismatic Leadership," in J. G. Hunt and L. L. Larson, eds., *Leadership: The Cutting Edge* (Carbondale, IL: Southern Illinois University Press, 1977); H. Levinson and S. Rosenthal, *CEO* (New York, NY: Basic Books, 1984); B. M. Bass, *Performance Beyond Expectations* (New York, NY: Free Press, 1985); R. House et al., "Personality and Charisma in the U.S. Presidency," Wharton Working Paper, 1989.
3. D. Hambrick, "The Top Management Team," *California Management Review* 30/1 (Fall 1987): 88–108; D. Ancona and D. Nadler, "Teamwork at the Top: Creating High Performing Executive Teams," *Sloan Management Review* (in press).
4. V. H. Vroom, *Work and Motivation* (New York, NY: John Wiley & Sons, 1964); J. P. Campbell, M. D. Dunnette, E. E. Lawler, and K. Weick, *Managerial Behavior, Performances, and Effectiveness* (New York, NY: McGraw-Hill, 1970).
5. R. J. House, "Path-Goal Theory of Leader Effectiveness," *Administrative Science Quarterly*, 16 (1971):321–338; G. R. Oldham, "The Motivational Strategies Used by Supervisors: Relationships to Effectiveness Indicators," *Organizational Behavior and Human Performance*, 15 (1976):66–86.
6. See Hambrick, op. cit.
7. E. E. Lawler and J. G. Rhode, *Information and Control in Organizations* (Pacific Palisades, CA: Goodyear, 1976).

SELECTION 23

1. Smith, H. L., & Krueger, L. M. A brief summary of literature on leadership. *Bull. Sch. Educ., Indiana Univ.*, 1993, **9**, No. 4.
2. Jenkins, W. O. A review of leadership studies with particular reference to military problems. *Psychol. Bull.*, 1947, **44**, 54–79.
3. Jennings, H. H. Leadership and Isolation. New York: Longmans Green, 1943.
4. Newstetter, W. I., Feldstein, M. J., & Newcomb, T. M. Group Adjustment: A Study in Experimental Sociology. Cleveland: Western Reserve Univ., 1938.

5. Ackerson, L. Children's Behavior Problems: Relative Importance and Intercorrelation among Traits. Chicago: Univ. Chicago Press, 1942.

6. Cattell, R. B. Description and Measurement of Personality. New York: World Book, 1946.

SELECTION 24

1. P. Slater and W. G. Bennis, "Democracy is Inevitable," *Harvard Business Review*, Sept-Oct, 1990, 170 and 171. For a summary of trait theories, see R. M. Stogdill's *Handbook of Leadership* (New York: Free Press, 1974). For reviews and studies of leadership traits, see R. E. Boyatzis, *The Competent Manager* (New York: Wiley & Sons, 1982); C. J. Cox and C. L. Cooper, *High Flyers: An Anatomy of Managerial Success* (Oxford: Basil Blackwell): G. A. Yukl, *Leadership in Organizations* (Englewood Cliffs, NJ: Prentice Hall, 1989), Chapter 9.

2. R. M. Stogdill, "Personal Factors Associated with Leadership: A Survey of the Literature," *Journal of Psychology*, 1948, 25, 64.

3. See the following sources for evidence and further information concerning each trait: 1) drive: B. M. Bass's *Handbook of Leadership* (New York: The Free Press, 1990); K. G. Smith and J. K. Harrison, "In Search of Excellent Leaders" (in W. D. Guth's *The Handbook of Strategy*, New York: Warren, Gorham, & Lamont, 1986). 2) desire to lead: V. J. Bentz, "The Sears Experience in the Investigation, Description, and Prediction of Executive Behavior," (In F. R. Wickert and D. E. McFarland's *Measuring Executive Effectiveness*, (New York: Appleton-Century-Crofts, 1967); J. B. Miner, "Twenty Years of Research on Role-Motivation Theory of Managerial Effectiveness," *Personnel Psychology*, 1978, 31, 739–760. 3) honesty/integrity: Bass, op cit.; W. G. Bennis and B. Nanus, *Leaders: The Strategies for Taking Charge* (New York: Harper & Row, 1985); J. M. Kouzes and B. Z. Posner, *The Leadership Challenge: How to Get Things Done in Organizations* (San Francisco: Jossey-Bass); T. Peters, *Thriving on Chaos* (New York: Harper & Row, 1987); A. Rand, *For the New Intellectual* (New York: Signet, 1961). 4) self-confidence: Bass, op cit. and A. Bandura, *Social Foundations of Thought and Action: A Social Cognitive Theory*, (Englewood Cliffs, NJ: business: Bennis and Nanus, op. cit.; J. P. Prentice-Hall). Psychological hardiness is discussed by S. R. Maddi and S. C. Kobasa, *The Hardy Executive: Health Under Stress* (Chicago: Dorsey Professional Books, 1984); M. W. McCall Jr. and M. M. Lombardo, *Off the Track: Why and How Successful Executives get Derailed* (Technical Report No. 21, Greensboro, NC: Center for Creative Leadership, 1983). 5) cognitive ability: R. G. Lord, C. L. DeVader, and G. M. Alliger, "A Meta-analysis of the Relation Between Personality Traits and Leadership Perceptions: An Application of Validity Generalization Procedures," *Journal of Applied Psychology*, 1986; 61, 402–410; A. Howard and D. W. Bray, *Managerial*

Lives in Transition: Advancing Age and Changing Times (New York: Guilford Press, 1988). 6) knowledge of the business: Bennis and Nanus, op. cit.; J. P. Kotter, *The General Managers* (New York: Macmillan); Smith and Harrison, op. cit.

4. From Kouzes and Posner, op. cit., pp. 122 and V. J. Bentz, op cit. The Sam Walton quote is from J. Huey, "Wal-Mart: Will it take over the world?," *Fortune*, January 30, 1989, 52–59.

5. From Bass, op. cit.

6. From Bentz, op. cit.

7. The distinction between a personalized and a socialized power motive is made by D. C. McClelland, "N-achievement and entrepreneurship: A longitudinal study," Journal of Personality and Social Psychology, 1965, *1*, 389–392. These two power motives are discussed further by Kouzes and Posner, op. cit.

8. From McCall and Lombardo, op cit.

9. From Gabarro, op. cit.

10. From Lord, DeVader, and Alliger, op cit.

11. For research on charisma, see Bass, op. cit. and R. J. House, W. D. Spangler, and J. Woycke, "Personality and charisma in the U.S. presidency: A psychological theory of leadership effectiveness (Wharton School, University of Pennsylvania, 1989, unpublished manuscript), on creativity/originality, see Howard and Bray, op. cit. and A. Zaleznik, *The Managerial Mystique* (New York: Harper and Row, 1989); on flexibility, see Smith and Harrison, op. cit.

CHAPTER 25

1. As examples see the following: Robert F. Bales, "Task Roles and Social Roles in Problem-Solving Groups," in *Readings in Social Psychology*, E. E. Maccoby, T. M. Newcomb and E. L. Hartley (eds.), Holt, Rinehart and Winston, 1958; Chester I. Barnard, *The Functions of the Executive*, Harvard University Press, 1938; Dorwin Cartwright and Alvin Zander (eds.), *Group Dynamics: Research and Theory*, second edition, Row, Peterson and Co., 1960; D. Katz, N. Maccoby, and Nancy C. Morse, *Productivity Supervision, and Morale in an Office Situation*, The Darel Press, Inc., 1950; Talcott Parsons, *The Social System*, The Free Press, 1951.

2. Robert Tannenbaum and Warren H. Schmidt, "How to Choose a Leadership Pattern," *Harvard Business Review*, Mar.-Apr. 1957, pp. 95–101.

3. Roger M. Stogdill and Alvin E. Coons (eds.), *Leader Behavior: Its Description and Measurement*, Research Monograph No. 88, Bureau of Business Research, The Ohio State University, 1957.

4. *Ibid*; See also Andrew W. Halpin, *The Leadership Behavior of School Superintendents*, Midwest Administration Center, The University of Chicago, 1959.

5. Robert R. Blake and Jane S. Mouton, *The Managerial Grid*, Gulf Publishing, 1964.
6. Halpin, *The Leadership Behavior of School Superintendents*.
7. Robert R. Blake *et al.*, "Breakthrough in Organization Development," *Harvard Business Review*, Nov.–Dec. 1964.
8. See also, Rensis Likert, *New Patterns of Management*, McGraw-Hill, 1961.
9. A. K. Korman, "'Consideration,' 'Initiating Structure,' and Organizational Criteria—A Review," *Personnel Psychology: A Journal of Applied Research*, Vol. 19, No. 4 (Winter, 1966), pp. 349–361.
10. Fred E. Fiedler, *A Theory of Leadership Effectiveness*, McGraw-Hill, 1967.
11. See C. A. Gibb, "Leadership"; A. P. Hare, *Handbook of Small Group Research*, Wiley, 1965; and D. C. Pelz, "Leadership Within a Hierarchial Organization," *Journal of Social Issues*, 1961, 7, pp. 49–55.

SELECTION 26

1. Transactional and transformational leadership were first conceptualized by James MacGregor Burns in *Leadership* (New York: Harper & Row, 1978) and later developed by Bernard Bass in *Leadership and Performance Beyond Expectations* (New York: Free Press, 1985).

SELECTION 27

1. Morrison, A., R. White, and E. Velsor. 1987. Executive women: substance plus style. *Psychology Today*, August, 18–21.

SELECTION 28

1. U.S. Department of Labor. (1987, May). *Work force 2000*. Washington, DC: Employment and Training Administration, U.S. Department of Labor.
2. Dipboye, R. L. (1987). Problems and progress of women in management. In K. S. Koziara, M. H. Moskow, & L. D. Tanner (Eds.), *Working women: Past, present, future* (pp. 118–153). Washington, DC: BNA Books.
3. Cox, T., Jr., & Nkomo, S. (1987). *Race as a variable in OB/HRM research. A review and analysis of the literature.* Paper presented at the Symposium on Black Career Research, Drexel University, Philadelphia, PA.
4. Larwood, L., Szwajkowski, E., & Rose, S. (1988). Sex and race discrimination resulting from manager-client relationships: Applying the rational bias theory of managerial discrimination. *Sex Roles, 18,* 9–29.
5. Leinster, C. (1988, January 18). Black executives: How they're doing. *Fortune*, pp. 109–120.

6. Thomas, D. A., & Alderfer, C. P. (1989). The influence of race on career dynamics: Theory and research on minority career experiences. In M. Arthur, D. Hall, & B. Lawrence (Eds.), *Handbook of career theory*: Cambridge, England: Cambridge University Press.

7. Bradsher, K. (1988, March 17). Women gain numbers, respect in board rooms. *The Los Angeles Times*, pp. 1, 6.

8. Hymowitz, C., & Schellhardt, T. D. (1986, March 24). The glass ceiling. *The Wall Street Journal*, pp. 1D, 4D–5D.

9. Korn/Ferry International. (1982). *Profile of women senior executives*. New York: Author.

10. Von Glinow, M. A., & Krzyczkowska-Mercer, A. (1988, Summer). Women in corporate America: A caste of thousands. *New management*, 6, pp. 36–42.

11. U.S. Office of Personnel Management (1989). *Report on minority group and sex by pay plan and appointing authority* (EPMD Report No. 40, March 31, 1989). Washington, DC: U.S. Office of Personnel Management.

12. U.S. Department of Labor. (1986). *Meeting the challenges of the 1980's.* Washington, DC: Women's Bureau, U.S. Department of Labor.

13. Sandler, B. R. (1986, October). *The campus climate revisited: Chilly for women faculty, administrators, and graduate students.* Washington, DC: The Project on the Status and Education of Women, Association of American Colleges.

14. Jones, E. W., Jr. (1986, May-June). Black managers: The dream deferred. *Harvard Business Review*, pp. 84–93.

15. Lan, D. (1988, September 7). *Information hearing on Asian, Filipino, Pacific Islander (AFPI) demographics and employment.* Memo presented to the California State Personnel Board.

16. Leavitt, J. A. (1988). *Women in administration and management: An information sourcebook.* New York: Oryx Press.

17. Malveaux, J., & Wallace, P. (1987). Minority women in the work-place. In K. S. Koziara, M. H. Moskow, & L. D. Tanner (Eds.), *Working women: Past, present, future* (pp. 265–298). Washington, DC: BNA Books.

18. Nkomo, S. M. (1988). Race and sex: The forgotten case of the black female manager. In S. Rose & L. Larwood (Eds.), *Women's careers: Pathways and pitfalls.* New York: Praeger.

19. Varca, P., Shaffer, G. S., & McCauley, C. D. (1983, June). Sex differences in job satisfaction revisited. *Academy of Management Journal*, 26, 348–353.

20. Drazin, R., & Auster, E. R. (1987, Summer). Wage differences between men and women: Performance appraisal ratings vs. salary allocation as the locus of bias. *Human Resource Management*, 26, 157–168.

21. Nelton, S., & Berney, K. (1987, May). Women: The second wave. *Nation's Business*, pp. 18–27.

22. Ploski, H. A., & Williams, J. (1983). *The Negro almanac: A reference work on the Afro-American.* New York: Wiley.

23. Ellis, J. (1988, March 14). The black middle class. *Business Week*, pp. 62–70.
24. James, F. E. (1988, June 7). More blacks quitting white-run firms: Many cite bias, desire to help minority firms. *The Wall Street Journal*, p. 37.
25. Taylor, A., III. (1986). Why women managers are bailing out. *Fortune*, pp. 16–23.
26. DeGeorge, G. (1987, June 22). Where are they now? Business Week's leading corporate women of 1976. *Business Week*, pp. 76–77.
27. Morrison, A. M., White, R. P., Van Velsor, E., & the Center for Creative Leadership (1987). *Breaking the glass ceiling: Can women reach the top of America's largest corporations?* Reading, MA: Addison Wesley.
28. Progress report on the Black executive: The top spots are still elusive. (1984). *Business Week*, pp. 104–105.
29. Riger, S., & Galligan, P. (1980). An exploration of competing paradigms. *American Psychologist, 35*, 902–910.
30. Howard, A., & Bray, D. W. (1988). *Managerial lives in transition*. New York: Guilford.
31. Dobbins, G. H., & Platz, S. J. (1986). Sex differences in leadership: How real are they? *Academy of Management Review, 11*, 118–127.
32. Harlan, A., & Weiss, C. (1981, September). *Moving up: Women in managerial careers* (Working Paper No. 86). Wellesley, MA: Wellesley College, Center for Research on Women.
33. Liden, R. C. (1985). Female perceptions of female and male managerial behavior. *Sex Roles, 12*, 421–433.
34. Noe, R. A. (1988). Women and mentoring: A review and research agenda. *Academy of Management Review, 13*, 65–78.
35. Powell, G. N. (1988). *Women and men in management*. Newbury Park, CA: Sage.
36. Ritchie, R. J., & Moses, J. L. (1983, May). Assessment center correlates of women's advancement into middle management: A 7-year longitudinal analysis. *Journal of Applied Psychology, 68*, 227–231.
37. White, M. C., Crino, M. D., & DeSanctis, G. L. (1981). A critical review of female performance, performance training and organizational initiatives designed to aid women in the work-role environment. *Personnel Psychology, 34*, 227–248.
38. Donnell, S. M. & Hall, J. (1980, Spring). Men and women as managers: A significant case of no significant difference. *Organizational Dynamics, 8*, 60–76.
39. Blau, F. D., & Ferber, M. A. (1987). Occupations and earnings of women workers. In K. S. Koziara, M. H. Moskow, & L. D. Tanner (Eds.), *Working women: Past, present, future* (pp. 37–68). Washington, DC: BNA Books.
40. Cabezas, A., Shinagawa, L. H., & Kawaguchi, G. (1989). Income and status differences between White and minority Americans: A persistent inequality. In S. Chan (Ed.), *Persistent inequality in the United States*. Lewiston, New York: Edwin Mellen Press.
41. Madden, J. F. (1985). The persistence of pay differentials: The economics of sex

discrimination. In L. Larwood, A. H. Stromberg, & B. A. Gutek (Eds.), *Women and work: An annual review*, (Vol. 1, pp. 76–114). Beverly Hills, CA: Sage.

42. Cabezas, A., Tam, T. M., Lowe, B. M., Wong, A., & Turner, K. (in press). Empirical study of barriers to upward mobility of Asian Americans in the San Francisco Bay area. In G. Nomura, R. Endo, R. Leong, & S. Sumida (Eds.), *Frontiers of Asian American studies*. Pullman: Washington State University Press.

43. Becker, G. (1957). *The economics of discrimination*. Chicago: University of Chicago Press.

44. Larwood, L., Gutek, B., & Gattiker, U. E. (1984). Perspectives on institutional discrimination and resistance to change. *Group and Organization Studies, 9,* 333–352.

45. Larwood, L., Szwajkowski, E., & Rose, S. (1988). When discrimination makes "sense"—The rational bias theory of discrimination. In B. A. Gutek, A. H. Stromberg, & L. Larwood (Eds.). *Women and work*. Beverly Hills, CA: Sage.

46. Wells, L., & Jennings, C. L. (1983). Black career advances and white reactions: Remnants of Herrenvolk democracy and the scandalous paradox. In D. Vails-Webber & W. N. Potts (Eds.), *Sunrise seminars* (pp. 41–47). Arlington, VA: NTL Institute.

47. Davis, G., & Watson, G. (1982). *Black life in corporate America*. Garden City, NY: Anchor Press/Doubleday.

48. Dubno, P. (1985). Attitudes toward women executives: A longitudinal approach. *Academy of Management Journal, 28,* 235–239.

49. Stevens, G. E. (1984, June). Attitudes toward blacks in management are changing. *Personnel Administrator*, pp. 163–171.

50. Powell, G. N., & Butterfield, D. A. (1989). The "good manager": Did androgyny fare better in the 1980's? *Group and Organization Studies, 14*(2), 216–233.

51. Heilman, M. E., & Martell, R. F. (1986). Exposure to successful women: Antidote to sex discrimination in applicant screening decisions? *Organizational Behavior and Human Decision Processes, 37,* 376–390.

52. Nieva, V. F., & Gutek, B. A. (1981). *Women and work: A psychological perspective*. New York: Praeger.

53. Freedman, S. M., & Phillips, J. S. (1988). The changing nature of research on women at work. *Journal of Management, 14,* 231–251.

54. Ilgen, D. R., & Youtz, M. A. (1986). Factors affecting the evaluation and development of minorities in organizations. *Personnel and Human Resources Management, 4,* 307–337.

55. Alderfer, C. P. (1986). An intergroup perspective on group dynamics. In J. Lorsch (Ed.). *Handbook of organizational behavior* (pp. 190–222). Englewood Cliffs. NJ: Prentice-Hall.

56. Thurow, L. (1969). *Poverty and discrimination*. Washington, DC: The Brookings Institute.

57. Larwood, L., & Gattiker, U. E. (1987). A comparison of the career paths used by successful women and men. In B. A. Gutek & L. Larwood (Eds.), *Women's career development* (pp. 129–156). Newbury Park, CA: Sage.

58. Osajima, K. (1988). Asian Americans as the model minority: An analysis of the popular press image in the 1960s and 1980s. In G. Y. Okihiro, S. Hune, A. A. Hansen, & J. M. Liu (Eds.), *Reflections on shattered windows: Promises and prospects for Asian American studies*. Pullman: Washington State University Press.

59. Fagenson, E. A. (1988). *At the heart of women in management research: Theoretical and methodological approaches and their biases*. Paper presented at the Women in Management (WIM) Conference. Halifax, Nova Scotia.

60. Kanter, R. (1977). *Men and women of the corporation*. New York: Basic Books.

61. Gutek, B. A. (1985). *Sex and the workplace*. San Francisco: Jossey-Bass.

62. Bell, E. L. (1988). *The bicultural life experience of career oriented black women*. Unpublished manuscript.

63. Irons, E. D., & Moore, G. W. (1985). *Black managers: The case of the banking industry*. New York: Praeger.

64. Fernandez, J. P. (1981). *Racism and sexism in corporate life*. Lexington, MA: Lexington Books.

65. Rogan, H. (1984, October 26). Young executive women advance farther, faster than predecessors. *The Wall Street Journal*, p. 31.

66. Rosen, B., Templeton, N. C., & Kichline, K. (1981, December). First few years on the job: Women in management. *Business Horizons, 24,* 26–29.

67. Dickens, F., Jr., & Dickens, J. B. (1982). *The black manager: Making it in the corporate world*. New York: Amacom.

68. Fagenson, E. A. (1988). The power of a mentor. *Group & Organization Studies, 13,* 182–194.

69. Fitt, L. W., & Newton, D. A. (1981, March-April). When the mentor is a man and the protege a woman. *Harvard Business Review,* pp. 56–60.

70. Ford, D., & Wells, L., Jr. (1985). Upward mobility factors among black public administrators. *Centerboard: Journal of the Center for Human Relations Studies, 3*(1), 38–48.

71. Gooden, W. (1980). *The adult development of black men*. Unpublished doctoral dissertation. Yale University.

72. Herbert, J. I. (1986). *The adult development of black male entrepreneurs*. Unpublished doctoral dissertation. Yale University.

73. Hunt, D. M., & Michael, C. (1983, July). Mentorship: A career training and development tool. *Academy of Management Review, 8,* 475–486.

74. Kram, K. E. (1985). *Mentoring at work*. Glenview, IL: Scott, Foresman.

75. Bearden, K. W. (1984). *Women proteges' perception of the mentoring process*. Unpublished doctoral dissertation. University of Louisville.

76. Thomas, D. A. (1986). *An intra-organizational analysis of black and white patterns of sponsorship and the dynamics of cross-racial mentoring*. Unpublished doctoral dissertation. Yale University.

77. Feinstein, S. (1987, November 10). Women and minority workers in business find a mentor can be a rare commodity. *The Wall Street Journal*, p. 39.

78. Greenhaus, J. H., Parasuraman, S., & Wormley, W. M. (1988, August). *Organizational experiences and career success of black and white managers.* Paper presented at the Annual Meeting of the Academy of Management, Anaheim, CA.

79. Fagenson, E. A., & Horowitz, S. V. (1985). On moving up: A rest of the person-centered, organization-centered and interactionist perspectives. *Academy of Management Proceedings,* 345–348.

80. Mainiero, L. A. (1986). Coping with powerlessness: The relationship of gender and job dependency to empowerment-strategy usage. *Administrative Science Quarterly, 31,* 633–653.

81. Yammarino, F. J., & Dubinsky, A. J. (1988). Employee responses: Gender- or job-related differences? *Journal of Vocational Behavior, 32,* 366–383.

82. Merenivitch, J., & Reigle, D. (1979, January). *Toward a multicultural organization.* (Available from The Procter & Gamble Company, Personnel Development Department, Cincinnati, OH.)

83. Lee, C. (1986, December). Training for women: Where do we go from here? *Training,* pp. 26–40.

84. Blacks in management: No progress. (1983, January). *Management World,* p. 24.

85. Rosener, J. B. (1986, December 7). Coping with sexual static. *The New York Times Magazine,* pp. 89, 120–121.

86. Staley, C. C. (1984, September). Managerial women in mixed groups: Implications of recent research. *Groups and Organization Studies, 9,* 316–332.

87. Cox, T., Jr., & Nkomo, S. (1986). Differential performance appraisal criteria: A field study of black and white managers. *Group and Organization Studies, 11,* 101–119.

88. Simpson, J. C. (1981, January). The woman boss. *Black Enterprise,* pp. 20–25.

89. Roberts, J. L. (1988, May 11). Gannett surpasses other newspaper firms in the hiring and promotion of minorities. *The Wall Street Journal,* p. 25.

90. Schmidt, P. (1988, October 16). Women and minorities: Is industry ready? *The New York Times,* pp. 25, 27.

91. McCall, M. W., Jr., Lombardo, M. M., & Morrison, A. M. (1988). *The lessons of experience.* Lexington, MA: Lexington Books.

92. Morrison, A. M. (1988, May). *Comparing the career paths of men and women.* Paper presented at The Conference Board's conference on *Women in the corporation: The value added,* New York, NY.

93. Jelinek, M., & Adler, N. J. (1988, February). Women: World-class managers for global competition. *Executive, II,* 11–19.

94. Zintz, A. C. (1988, May). *Succession planning, career tracks and mentoring.* Paper presented at The Conference Board, Inc.'s conference on "Women in the Corporation: The Value Added," New York, NY.

95. Noe, R. A. (1988). An investigation of the determinants of successful assigned mentoring relationships. *Personnel Psychology, 41,* 457–479.

96. Zey, M. (1985, February). Mentor programs: Making the right moves. *Personnel Journal*, pp. 53–57.
97. Willbur, J. (1987, November). Does mentoring breed success? *Training and Development Journal*, pp. 38–41.
98. Heilman, M. E., Simon, M. C., & Repper, D. P. (1987). Intentionally favored, unintentionally harmed? Impact of sex-based preferential selection on self-perceptions and self-evaluations. *Journal of Applied Psychology, 72*, 62–68.
99. Jaffe, B. (1985, September). A forced fit. *Training and Development Journal, 39*(9), 82–83.
100. Nelton, S. (1988, July). Meet your new work force. *Nation's Business*, pp. 14–21.

SELECTION 30

1. Gardner, J. W., *The Nature of Leadership*, Independent Sector, Washington, D.C., 1986
2. Gardner, J. W., *On Leadership*, The Free Press, New York, 1990.
3. Ford, J. F., *Education for Christian Leadership*, Doctoral dissertation, University of San Diego, 1990.

SELECTION 34

1. There have been many earlier presentations of similar ideas with somewhat different emphases. See Gunnar Myrdal, "A Parallel to the Negro Problem," Appendix 5 in *An American Dilemma* (New York: Harper, 1944), pp. 1073–78; and Helen Mayer Hacker, "Women as a Minority Group," *Social Forces 30* (October 1951), 60–69.

SELECTION 35

1. Korn/Ferry International. *Korn/Ferry's International Executive Profile: A Survey of Corporate Leaders in the 80s*. New York: Korn/Ferry International, 1986.
2. Braham, J. "Is the Door Really Open?" *Industry Week*, Nov. 16, 1987, pp. 64–70.
3. "Debate—Affirmative Action Is Doing the Right Thing." *USA Today*, June 29, 1990, p. 10A.
4. Cook, D. "The Silent Minority." *California Business*, Oct. 1989, pp. 23–27.
5. "The Fortune 500—The Largest U.S. Industrial Corporations." *Fortune*, Apr. 23, 1990, pp. 338–365.
6. "Bias in Promotions at the Very Top Targeted." *San Diego Union*, July 30, 1990, pp. A1–A2.
7. "Blacks in Management: No Progress." Editorial. *Management World*, Jan. 1983, p. 24.

8. Baskerville, D. M., and Tucker, S. H. "A Blueprint for Success." *Black Enterprise*, Nov. 1991, pp. 85–93.

9. Catalyst. *Women in Corporate Management: Results of a Catalyst Survey*. New York: Catalyst, 1990.

10. U.S. Department of Labor. *A Report on the Glass Ceiling Initiative*. Washington, D.C.: U.S. Department of Labor, 1991.

11. Smith, T. W. *Ethnic Images*. National Opinion Research Center, GSS Topical Report No. 19. Chicago: University of Chicago, Dec. 1990.

SELECTION 36

1. *See generally* Gary Yukl, *Leadership in Organizations* 3d ed. Englewood Cliffs, NJ: Prentice-Hall, 1994), pp. 285–312.

2. Martin M. Chemers, "The Social, Organizational, and Cultural Context of Effective Leadership", in Barbara Kellerman, ed., *Leadership: Multidisciplinary Perspectives* (Englewood Cliffs, NJ: Prentice-Hall, 1984), pp. 91–112; Ralph M. Stogdill, "Historical Trends in Leadership Theory and Research", *Journal of Contemporary Business* 3 (Autumn, 1974): 1–17; Jean M. Phillips, "Leadership Since 1975: Advancement or Inertia?" *Journal of Leadership Studies* 2 (Winter, 1995): 58–80. *See also* Robert E. Kelley, *The Power of Followership* (New York: Doubleday, 1992). *Note* that Joseph C. Rost argues that "followership" should not be distinguished from leadership. Rost, *Leadership for the Twenty-First Century* (New York: Praeger, 1991).

3. Yukl, *Leadership in Organizations*, pp. 285–312; Chemers, "The Social, Organizational, and Cultural Context", pp. 95–100; Stogdill, "Historical Trends", pp. 3–4, 7–10; Phillips, "Leadership Since 1975", pp. 62–64.

4. R. N. Osborne and J. G. Hunt, "An Adaptive-Reaction Theory of Leadership: The Role of Macro Variables in Leadership Research", in J. G. Hunt and L. L. Larson, eds., *Leadership Frontiers* (Carbondale, Ill.: Southern Illinois University Press, 1975); J. G. Hunt and R. N. Osborne, "Toward a Macro-Oriented Model of Leadership: An Odyssey", in J. G. Hunt, U. Sekaran, and C. Schriescheim, eds., *Leadership: Beyond Establishment Views* (Carbondale, Ill.: Southern Illinois University Press, 1982), pp. 196–221.

5. Very little indeed has been done with historical forces. Several comparative studies of leadership in varying cultures has at least identified the role culture plays in the leadership process. *See* Chemers, "The Social, Organizational, and Cultural Context", pp. 103–105.

6. Phillips, "Leadership Since 1975", p. 77.

7. Chemers, "The Social, Organizational, and Cultural Context", pp. 107–108.

8. *See generally* E. James Ferguson, *The American Revolution: A General History, 1763–1790* (Homewood, Ill.: Dorsey Press, 1974); John R. Galvin, *Three Men of Boston* (New York: Thomas Y. Crowell co., 1976); Bernard Bailyn, *The Ordeal of*

Thomas Hutchinson (Cambridge: Harvard University Press, 1974); William Bruce Wheeler and Susan D. Becker, *Discovering the American Past: A Look at the Evidence* 2d. ed. (Boston: Houghton Mifflin Company, 1990, pp. 48–66; Richard A. Luecke. *Scuttle Your Ships before Advancing* (New York: Oxford University Press, 1994), pp. 126–145.

9. David J. Rothman, "A Century of Failure: Health Care Reform in America", *Journal of Health Politics, Policy, and Law* 18 (Summer, 1993): 270–286.

10. Id at 271.

11. Barbara Ehrenreich, *Fear of Falling: The Inner Life of the Middle Class* (New York: Pantheon Books, 1989).

12. Joe Klein, "Facing Up to the Big Fear", *Newsweek* 27 September 1993, p. 38.

13. Rothman, "A Century of Failure", p. 285.

14. Geert Hofstede, "Cultural Constraints in Management Theories", *Academy of Management Executive* 7 (Feb. 1993): 81–94.

15. Ronald Tataki, *Strangers from a Different Shore* (Boston: Little, Brown & Co., 1989).

16. Alden Morriss, *The Origins of the Civil Rights Movement* (New York: The Free Press, 1984).

17. Roger Fisher, William Ury, and Bruce Patton, *Getting to Yes* 2d. ed. (Boston: Houghton Mifflin Company, 1991).

SELECTION 38

1. Barley, S. R., Meyer, G. W., and Gash, D. "Cultures of Culture: Academics, Practitioners, and the Pragmatics of Normative Control." *Administrative Science Quarterly*, 1988, *33*, 24–60.

2. Martin, J. "A Personal Journey: From Integration to Differentiation to Fragmentation to Feminism." In P. Frost and others (eds.). *Reframing Organizational Culture*. Newbury Park, Calif.: Sage, 1991.

3. Ott, J. S. *The Organizational Culture Perspective*. Belmont, Calif.: Dorsey Press, 1989.

4. Smircich, L., and Calas, M. B. "Organizational Culture: A Critical Assessment." In F. M. Jablin, L. L. Putnam, K. H. Roberts, and L. W. Porter (eds.), *Handbook of Organizational Communication*. Newbury Park, Calif.: Sage, 1987.

5. Goffman, E. *The Presentation of Self in Everyday Life*. New York: Doubleday, 1959.

6. Goffman, E. *Interaction Ritual*. Hawthorne, N.Y.: Aldine, 1967.

7. Jones, M. O., Moore, M. D., and Snyder, R. C. (eds.). *Inside Organizations*. Newbury Park, Calif.: Sage, 1988.

8. Trice, H. M., and Beyer, J. M. "Studying Organizational Cultures Through Rites and Ceremonials." *Academy of Management Review*, 1984, *9*, 653–669.

9. Trice, H. M., and Beyer, J. M. "Using Six Organizational Rites to Change Cul-

ture." In R. H. Kilmann, M. J. Saxton, R. Serpa, and Associates, *Gaining Control of the Corporate Culture*. San Francisco: Jossey-Bass, 1985, pp. 370–399.

10. Van Maanen, J. "The Self, the Situation, and the Rules of Interpersonal Relations." In W. Bennis and others, *Essays in Interpersonal Dynamics*. Belmont, Calif.: Dorsey Press, 1979.

11. Homans, G. *The Human Group*. Orlando, Fla.: Harcourt Brace Jovanovich, 1950.

12. Kilmann, R. H., and Saxton, M. J. *The Kilmann-Saxton Culture Gap Survey*. Pittsburgh: Organizational Design Consultants, 1983.

13. Deal, T. E., and Kennedy, A. A. *Corporate Cultures*. Reading, Mass.: Addison-Wesley, 1982.

14. Ouchi, W. G. *Theory Z*. Reading, Mass.: Addison-Wesley, 1981.

15. Pascale, R. T., and Athos, A. G. *The Art of Japanese Management*. New York: Simon & Schuster, 1981.

16. Schein, E. H. "Organizational Socialization and the Profession of Management." *Industrial Management Review*, 1968, 9, 1–15.

17. Schein, E. H. *Career Dynamics: Matching Individual and Organizational Needs*. Reading, Mass.: Addison-Wesley, 1978.

18. Van Maanen, J. "Breaking In: Socialization to Work." In R. Dubin (ed.), *Handbook of Work, Organization and Society*. Skokie, Ill.: Rand McNally, 1976.

19. Ritti, R. R., and Funkhouser, G. R. *The Ropes to Skip and the Ropes to Know*. Columbus, Ohio: Grid, 1982.

20. Schneider, B. (ed.). *Organizational Climate and Culture*. San Francisco: Jossey-Bass, 1990.

21. Tagiuri, R., and Litwin, G. H. (eds.). *Organizational Climate: Exploration of a Concept*. Boston: Division of Research, Harvard Graduate School of Business, 1968.

22. Argyris, C., and Schön, D. A. *Organizational Learning*. Reading, Mass.: Addison-Wesley, 1978.

23. Cook, S. D. N., and Yanow, D. "What Does It Mean for a Culture to Learn? Organizational Learning from a Culture Perspective." Paper presented at the third National Symposium of Public Administration Theory Network, Los Angeles, Calif., April 1990.

24. Henderson, R. M., and Clark, K. B. "Architectural Innovation: The Reconfiguration of Existing Product Technologies and the Failure of Established Firms." *Administrative Science Quarterly*, 1990, 35, 9–30.

25. Peters, T. J., and Waterman, R. H., Jr. *In Search of Excellence*. New York: Harper & Row, 1982.

26. Douglas, M. *How Institutions Think*. Syracuse, N.Y.: Syracuse University Press, 1986.

27. Hofstede, G. *Culture's Consequences*. Newbury Park, Calif.: Sage, 1980.

28. Geertz, C. *The Interpretation of Cultures*. New York: Basic Books, 1973.

29. Smircich, L. "Concepts of Culture and Organizational Analysis." *Administrative Science Quarterly*, 1983, 28, 339–358.

30. Van Maanen, J., and Barley, S. R. "Occupational Communities: Culture and Control in Organizations." In B. M. Staw and L. L. Cummings (eds.), *Research in Organizational Behavior*. Vol. 6. Greenwich, Conn.: JAI Press, 1984.

31. Gagliardi, P. (ed.). *Symbols and Artifacts: Views of the Corporate Landscape*. New York: de Gruyter, 1990.

32. Hatch, M. J. *The Dynamics of Organizational Culture*. Copenhagen Business School Paper in Organization, no. 4. Copenhagen, Denmark: Copenhagen Business School, 1991.

33. Pondy, L. R., Frost, P. J., Morgan, G., and Dandridge, T. (eds.). *Organizational Symbolism*. Greenwich, Conn.: JAI Press, 1983.

34. Schultz, M. *Transition Between Symbolic Domains in Organizations*. Copenhagen Business School Papers in Organization, no. 1. Copenhagen, Denmark. Copenhagen Business School, 1991.

35. Martin, J., and Meyerson, D. "Organizational Cultures and the Denial, Channeling and Acknowledgment of Ambiguity." In L. R. Pondy, R. J. Boland, Jr., and H. Thomas (eds.), *Managing Ambiguity and Change*. New York: Wiley, 1988.

36. Bohm, D. *On Dialogue*. Ojai, Calif.: David Bohm Seminars, 1990.

37. Louis, M. R. "Surprise and Sense Making." *Administrative Science Quarterly*, 1980, *25*, 226–251.

38. Louis, M. R. "Newcomers as Lay Ethnographers: Acculturation During Organizational Socialization." In B. Schneider (ed.), *Organizational Climate and Culture*. San Francisco: Jossey-Bass, 1990.

39. Van Maanen, J., and Schein, E. H. "Toward a Theory of Organizational Socialization." In B. M. Staw and L. L. Cummings (eds.), *Research in Organizational Behavior*. Vol. 1. Greenwich, Conn.: JAI Press, 1979.

40. Van Maanen, J., and Kunda, G. "'Real Feelings': Emotional Expression and Organizational Culture." In B. Staw (ed.), *Research in Organizational Behavior*. Vol. 11. Greenwich, Conn.: JAI Press, 1989.

41. Kunda, G. *Engineering Culture*. Philadelphia: Temple University Press, 1992.

SELECTION 39

1. Our survey covered both profit-making companies and a few non-profit organizations we found particularly intriguing. For simplicity we refer in the text to all of these as "companies."

2. These were: Caterpillar Tractor, General Electric, DuPont, Chubb Insurance, Price Waterhouse & Co., 3M, Jefferson-Smurfit, The Training Services Administration Agency of the British government, Digital Equipment Corporation, International Business Machines, Dana Corporation, Procter & Gamble, Hewlett-Packard, Leo Burnett Advertising Agency, Johnson & Johnson, Tandem Computer, Continental Bank, and the Rouse Corporation.

3. You may see several companies—such as General Electric—and several individuals—such as Thomas Watson—named again and again throughout the book. This is because we consider them the absolutely best examples we could find to illustrate our ideas. Managers could do worse than to emulate these examples.

SELECTION 40

1. Steven Muller, "The University Presidency Today," *Science* 237, 14 August 1987.
2. Max Weber, *The Theory of Social and Economic Organization*, trans. A. M. Henderson and Talcott Parsons (New York: Oxford University Press, 1947).
3. For example, Elton Mayo, an industrial psychologist at the Harvard Graduate School of Business, did pioneering work on the morale and motivation of workers. In 1938, Chester Barnard, in his book *The Functions of the Executive* (republished by Harvard University Press in 1984) contributed importantly to a new understanding. In the 1950s and 1960s writers such as Rensis Likert, *New Patterns of Management* (New York: McGraw-Hill, 1961) and Douglas McGregor, *The Professional Manager* (New York: McGraw-Hill, 1967) pursued the same questions.
4. Daniel Yankelovich, *Work and Human Values* (New York: Public Agenda Foundation, 1983).
5. Richard M. Cyert and James G. March, *A Behavioral Theory of the Firm* (Englewood Cliffs, N.J.: Prentice-Hall, 1963).
6. Warren Bennis and Burt Nanus, *Leaders* (New York: Harper and Row, 1965).

SELECTION 43

1. Martin Luther King, Jr., speech at the University of California, Berkeley, tape recording, May 17, 1967, Martin Luther King, Jr., Papers Project (Stanford University, Stanford, Calif.).
2. Martin Luther King, Jr., described this episode, which occurred on the evening of January 27, 1956, in a remarkable speech delivered in September 1966. It is available on a phonograph record; "Dr. King's Entrance into the Civil Rights Movement," *Martin Luther King, Jr.: In Search of Freedom* (Mercury SR 61170).
3. Martin Luther King, Jr., "An Autobiography of Religious Development," [c. 1950], Martin Luther King, Jr. Papers (Mugar Library, Boston University). In this paper, written for a college class, King commented: "I guess I accepted Biblical studies uncritically until I was about twelve years old. But this uncritical attitude could not last long, for it was contrary to the very nature of my being."
4. The new orientation is evident in William H. Chafe, *Civilities and Civil Rights: Greensboro, North Carolina and the Black Struggle for Equality* (New York, 1980); David R. Colburn, *Racial Change and Community Crisis St. Augustine, Florida,*

1877–1980 (New York, 1985); Robert J. Norrell, *Reaping the Whirlwind: The Civil Rights Movement in Tuskegee* (New York, 1985); and John R. Salter, *Jackson, Mississippi: An American Chronicle of Struggle and Schism* (Hicksville, N.Y. 1979).

5. The tendency to view the struggle from King's perspective is evident in the most thoroughly researched of the King biographies, despite the fact that the book concludes with Ella Baker's assessment: "The movement made Martin rather than Martin making the movement." See David J. Garrow, *Bearing the Cross: Martin Luther King Jr., and the Southern Christian Leadership Conference* (New York, 1986), esp. 625. See also David L. Lewis, *King A Biography* (Urbana, 1978); Stephen B. Oates, *Let the Trumpet Sound* (New York, 1982); and Adam Fairclough, *To Redeem the Soul of America: The Southern Christian Leadership Conference and Martin Luther King, Jr.* (Athens, 1987).

6. See Clayborne Carson. *In Struggle: SNCC and the Black Awakening of the 1960s* (Cambridge, Mass., 1981); and Howard Zinn, *SNCC: The New Abolitionists* (Boston, 1965).

7. For incisive critiques of traditional psychological and sociological analyses of the modern black struggle, see Doug McAdam, *Political Process and the Development of Black Insurgency, 1930–1970* (Chicago, 1982); and Aldon D. Morris, *Origins of the Civil Rights Movement: Black Communities Organizing for Change* (New York, 1984).

8. James M. Washington, ed., *A Testament of Hope: The Essential Writings of Martin Luther King, Jr.* (San Francisco, 1986), 267.

SELECTION 44

1. Hunter, J. E.; F. L. Schmidt; and M. K. Judiesch. "Individual Differences in Output Variability as a Function of Job Complexity." *Journal of Applied Psychology* 74 (1990), pp. 28–42.

2. Kanfer, R. "Motivation Theory in Industrial and Organizational Psychology." In *Handbook of Industrial and Organizational Psychology*, ed. M. D. Dunnette and L. M. Hough. Vol. 1. Palo Alto, Calif.: Consulting Psychologists Press, 1990, pp. 75–170.

3. Campbell, J. P., and R. D. Pritchard. "Motivation Theory in Industrial and Organizational Psychology." In *Handbook of Industrial and Organizational Psychology*, ed. M. D. Dunnette. Chicago: Rand McNally, 1976, pp. 60–130.

4. Maslow, A. H. *Motivation and Personality.* New York: Harper & Row, 1954.

5. Alderfer, C. P. "An Empirical Test of a New Theory of Human Needs." *Organizational Behavior and Human Performance* 4 (1969), pp. 142–75.

6. Betz, E. L. "Two Tests of Maslow's Theory of Need Fulfilment." *Journal of Vocational Behavior,* 24 (1984), pp. 204–20.

7. Adams, J. S. "Toward an Understanding of Inequity." *Journal of Abnormal and Social Psychology* 67 (1963), pp. 422–36.

8. Vecchio, R. P. "Predicting Worker Performance in Inequitable Settings." *Academy of Management Review* 7 (1982), pp. 103–10.

9. Adams, J. S. "Inequity in Social Exchange." In *Advances in Experimental Social Psychology.* ed. L. Berkowitz. Vol. 2. New York: Academic Press, 1965, pp. 267–96.

10. Tolman, E. C., *Purposeful Behavior in Animals and Men,* Appleton-Century Crofts: New York, 1932.

11. Vroom, V. H. *Work and Motivation.* New York: Wiley, 1964.

12. Porter, L. W., and E. E. Lawler, III. *Managerial Attitudes and Performance.* Homewood, Ill.: Dorsey, 1968.

13. Lawler, E.E. III. *Motivation in Work Organizations.* Pacific Grove, Calif.: Brooks/Cole, 1973.

14. Herzberg, F. "The Motivation-Hygiene Concept and Problems of Manpower." *Personnel Administrator* 27 (1964), pp. 3–7.

15. Herzberg, F. *Work and the Nature of Man.* Cleveland, Ohio: World Publishing, 1966.

16. Hackman, J. R., and G. R. Oldham. "Motivation through the Design of Work: Test of a Theory." *Organizational Behavior and Human Performance* 16 (1976), pp. 250–79.

17. ———. *Work Redesign.* Reading, Mass.: Addison-Wesley, 1980.

18. Arvey, R. D., and J. M. Ivancevich. "Punishment in Organizations: A Review, Propositions, and Research Suggestions." *Academy of Management Review* 5 (1980), pp. 123–32.

19. Komacki, J. L.; S. Zlotnick; and M. Jensen. "Development of an Operant-based Taxonomy and Observational Index on Supervisory Behavior." *Journal of Applied Psychology* 71 (1986), pp. 260–69.

20. Luthans, F., and R. Kreitner. *Organizational Behavior Modification and Beyond: An Operant and Social Learning Approach.* Glenview, Ill.: Scott, Foresman, 1985.

21. Pritchard, R. D.; J. Hollenback; P. J. DeLeo. "The Effects of Continuous and Partial Schedules of Reinforcement of Effort, Performance, and Satisfaction." *Organizational Behavior and Human Performance* 25 (1980), pp. 336–53.

22. Podsakoff, P. M.; W. D. Todor; and R. Skov. "Effects of Leader Contingent and Noncontingent Reward and Punishment Behaviors on Subordinate Performance and Satisfaction." *Academy of Management Journal.* 25 (1982), pp. 810–25.

23. Sims, H. P., and A. D. Szilagyi. "Leader Reward Behavior and Subordinate Satisfaction and Performance." *Organizational Behavior and Human Performance* 14 (1975), pp. 426–38.

24. Arvey, R. D.; G. A. Davis; and S. M. Nelson. "Use of Discipline in an Organization: A Field Study." *Journal of Applied Psychology* 69 (1984), pp. 448–60.

25. Podsakoff, P. M., and W. D. Todor. "Relationships between Leader Reward and Punishment Behavior and Group Process and Productivity." *Journal of Management* 11 (1985), pp. 55–73.

26. Saal, F. E., and P. A. Knight. *Industrial Organizational Psychology: Science and Practice.* Belmont, Calif.: Brooks/Cole, 1988.

SELECTION 45

1. Bass, B. M. *Bass and Stogdill's Handbook of Leadership.* 3rd ed. New York: Free Press, 1990.
2. House, R. J. "Power in Organizations: A Social Psychological Perspective." Unpublished manuscript, University of Toronto, Toronto, Canada, 1984.
3. French, J., and B. H. Raven. "The Bases of Social Power," In *Studies of Social Power,* ed. D. Cartwright. Ann Arbor, Mich.: Institute for Social Research, 1959. Friedland, W. H. "For a Sociological Concept of Charisma." *Social Forces* no. 1 (1964), pp. 18–26.
4. Peters, T. J., and R. H. Waterman, *In Search of Excellence* (New York: Harper & Row), 1982.
5. Yukl, G. A. *Leadership in Organizations.* 2nd ed. Englewood Cliffs, N.J.: Prentice Hall, 1989.
6. Deci, E. L. "Effects of Contingent and Noncontingent Rewards and Controls on Intrinsic Motivation." *Organizational Behavior and Human Performance* 22 (1972?), pp. 113–20.
7. Ryan, E. M.; V. Mims; and R. Koestner. "Relation of Reward Contingency and Interpersonal Context to Intrinsic Motivation: A Review and Test Using Cognitive Evaluation Theory." *Journal of Personality and Social Psychology* 45 (1983), pp. 736–50.
8. Wakin, M. M. "Ethics of Leadership." In *Military Leadership,* ed. J. H. Buck and L. J. Korb. Beverly Hills, Calif.: Sage, 1981.
9. Klein, S. B. *Learning.* 2nd ed. New York: McGraw-Hill, 1991.
10. Barnes, F. "Mistakes New Presidents Make." *Reader's Digest* (January 1989), p. 43.
11. Conway, F., and J. Siegelman. *Snapping.* New York: Delta, 1979.
12. Yukl, G. A. *Leadership in Organizations.* 1st ed. Englewood Cliffs, N.J.: Prentice Hall, 1981.
13. Podsakoff, P. M., and C. A. Schriesheim. Field Studies of French and Raven's Bases of Power: Critique, Reanalysis, and Suggestions for Future Research." *Psychological Bulletin* 97 (1985), pp. 387–411.
14. Hinkin, T. R., and C. A. Schriesheim. "Development and Application of New Scales to Measure the French and Raven (1959) Bases of Social Power." *Journal of Applied Psychology* 74 (1989), pp. 561–67.
15. Hollander, E. P., and L. R. Offermann. "Power and Leadership in Organizations." *American Psychologist* 45 (1990), pp. 179–89.
16. Pfeffer, J. "The Ambiguity of Leadership." In *Leadership: Where Else Can We Go?,* ed. M. W. McCall, Jr., and M. M. Lombardo. Durham, N.C.: Duke University Press, 1977.
17. McClelland, D. C. *Power: The Inner Experience.* New York: Irvington (distributed by Halstead Press), 1975.

18. McClelland, D. C., and R. E. Boyatzis. "Leadership Motive Pattern and Long-Term Success in Management." *Journal of Applied Psychology* 67 (1982), pp. 737–43.
19. Miner, J. B. "Twenty Years of Research on Role Motivation Theory of Managerial Effectiveness." *Personnel Psychology* 31 (1978), pp. 739–60.
20. Kipnis, D., and S. M. Schmidt. *Profiles of Organizational Strategies.* (Form M). San Diego, Calif.: University Associates, 1982.
21. Schriesheim, C. A., and T. R. Hinkin. "Influence Tactics Used by Subordinates: A Theoretical and Empirical Analysis and Refinement of the Kipnis, Schmidt, and Wilkinson Subscales." *Journal of Applied Psychology* 75 (1990), pp. 246–57.
22. Yukl, G. A.; R. Lepsinger; and T. Lucia. "Preliminary Report on the Development and Validation of the Influence Behavior Questionnaire." In *Impact of Leadership,* ed. K. E. Clark, M. B. Clark, and D. P. Campbell. Greensboro, N.C.: Center for Creative Leadership, 1992.
23. Kipnis, D., and S. M. Schmidt. "The Language of Persuasion." *Psychology Today* 19, no. 4 (1985), pp. 40–46.
24. Dosier, L.; T. Case; and B. Keys. "How Managers Influence Subordinates: An Empirical Study of Downward Influence Tactics." *Leadership and Organization Development Journal* 9, no. 5 (1988), pp. 22–31.

SELECTION 49

1. Hechinger, F. M. "Thinking Critically." *New York Times*, Feb. 24, 1987, p. 27.
2. National Institute of Education. *Involvement in Learning: Realizing the Potential of American Higher Education.* Washington, D.C.: U.S. Department of Education, 1984.
3. National Commission on Excellence in Education. *A Nation at Risk: The Imperative for Educational Reform.* Washington, D.C.: U.S. Department of Education, 1983.
4. Newman, F. *Higher Education and the American Resurgence.* Princeton, N.J.: Carnegie Foundation for the Advancement of Teaching, 1985.
5. Johnston, J. S., Jr., and Associates. *Educating Managers: Executive Effectiveness Through Liberal Learning.* San Francisco: Jossey-Bass, 1986.
6. Ehrenhalt, S. H. "No Golden Age for College Graduates." *Challenge,* 1983, 26, 42–50.
7. Young, R. E. (ed.). *Fostering Critical Thinking.* New Directions for Teaching and Learning, no. 3. San Francisco: Jossey-Bass, 1980.
8. Gamson, Z. F., and Associates. *Liberating Education.* San Francisco: Jossey-Bass, 1984.
9. Stice, J. (ed.). *Developing Critical Thinking and Problem-Solving Abilities.* New Directions for Teaching and Learning, no. 30. San Francisco: Jossey-Bass, 1987.

10. Kretovics, J. R. "Critical Literacy: Challenging the Assumptions of the Mainstream." *Journal of Education*, 1985, *167*(2), 50–62.

11. Greene, M. "In Search of a Critical Pedagogy." *Harvard Educational Review*, 1986, *56*(4), 427–441.

12. Livingstone, D. W. (ed.). *Critical Pedagogy and Cultural Power*. South Hadley, Mass.: Bergin & Garvey, 1987.

13. Sternberg, R. J. "Teaching Critical Thinking, Part 1: Are We Making Critical Mistakes?" *Phi Delta Kappan*, 1985, *67*(3), 194–198.

14. Hallet, G. L. *Logic for the Labyrinth: A Guide to Critical Thinking*. Washington, D.C.: University Press of America, 1984.

15. Ruggiero, V. R. *Beyond Feelings: A Guide to Critical Thinking*. Palo Alto, Calif.: Mayfield Publications, 1975.

16. Kitchener, K. S. "The Reflective Judgment Model: Characteristics, Evidence, and Measurement." In R. A. Mines and K. S. Kitchener (eds.), *Adult Cognitive Development: Methods and Models*. New York: Praeger, 1986.

17. Scriven, M. *Reasoning*. New York: McGraw-Hill, 1976.

18. Hullfish, H. G., and Smith, P. G. *Reflective Thinking. The Method of Education*. Westport, Conn.: Greenwood Press, 1964.

19. Ennis, R. H. "A Concept of Critical Thinking." *Harvard Educational Review*, 1962, *32*(1), 81–111.

20. D'Angelo, E. *The Teaching of Critical Thinking*. Amsterdam: B. R. Gruner, 1971.

21. O'Neill, T. *Censorship—Opposing Views*. St. Paul, Minn.: Greenhaven Press, 1985.

22. Halpern, D. F. *Thought and Knowledge: An Introduction to Critical Thinking*. Hillsdale, N.J.: Erlbaum, 1984.

23. Drake, J. *Teaching Critical Thinking*. Danville, Ill.: Interstate Publishers, 1976.

24. Meyers, C. *Teaching Students to Think Critically: A Guide for Faculty in All Disciplines*. San Francisco: Jossey-Bass, 1986.

25. King, P. M., Kitchener, K. S., and Wood, P. K. "The Development of Intellect and Character: A Longitudinal-Sequential Study of Intellectual and Moral Development in Young Adults." *Moral Education Forum*, 1985, *10*(1), 1–13.

26. Perry, W. G. *Forms of Intellectual and Ethical Development in the College Years: A Scheme*. New York: Holt, Rinehart & Winston, 1970.

27. Perry, W. G. "Growth in the Making of Meaning." In A. W. Chickering (ed.). *The Modern American College*. San Francisco: Jossey-Bass, 1981.

28. Habermas, J. *Communication and the Evolution of Society*. Boston: Beacon Press, 1979.

29. Collins, M. "Jurgen Habermas's Concept of Communicative Action and Its Implications for the Adult Learning Process." *Proceedings of the Adult Education Research Conference*, no. 26. Tempe: Arizona State University, 1985.

30. Hart, M. "Thematization of Power, the Search for Common Interests, and Self-Reflection: Towards a Comprehensive Concept of Emancipatory Education." *International Journal of Lifelong Education*, 1985, *4*(2), 119–134.

31. Apps, J. W. *Improving Practice in Continuing Education: Modern Approaches for Understanding the Field and Determining Priorities.* San Francisco: Jossey-Bass, 1985.

32. Morgan, G. *Images of Organizations.* Beverly Hills, Calif.: Sage, 1986.

33. Riegel, K. F. "Dialectic Operations: The Final Period of Cognitive Development." *Human Development,* 1973, 16, 346–370.

34. Basseches, M. *Dialectical Thinking and Adult Development.* Norwood, N. J.: Ablex Publishing Corporation, 1984.

35. Deshler, D. "Moral Faith and Cognitive Development: Aspects of Critical Awareness on the Part of Professors of Adult Education." Paper presented to the Commission of Professors of Adult Education Conference, Milwaukee, Nov. 5, 1985.

36. Daloz, L. *Effective Teaching and Mentoring: Realizing the Transformational Power of Adult Learning Experiences.* San Francisco: Jossey-Bass, 1986.

37. Boyd, E. M., and Fales, A. W. "Reflective Learning: Key to Learning from Experience." *Journal of Humanistic Psychology,* 1983, 23(2), 99–117.

38. Boud, D., Keogh, R., and Walker, D. *Reflection: Turning Experience into Learning.* London: Kogan Page, 1985.

39. Schlossberg, N. K. "A Model for Analyzing Human Adaptation to Transition." *The Counseling Psychologist,* 1981, 9(2), 2–18.

SELECTION 51

1. Lorenz, C. *London Financial Times,* Jan. 9, 1991.

SELECTION 52

1. Jaques, E. 1979. Taking time seriously in evaluating jobs. *Harvard Business Review.* 57(5), 124–132.

2. ———. 1986. The development of intellectual capability: A discussion of stratified systems theory. *Journal of Applied Behavioral Science,* 22, 361–383.

3. Burke, W. W. 1986. Leadership as empowering others. In S. Srivastra et al. (eds.), *Executive power.* San Francisco: Jossey-Bass.

4. McClelland, D. C., and D. H. Burnham. 1976. Power is the great motivator. *Harvard Business Review,* 54 (2), 100–110.

5. Sashkin, M. 1985, August. "Creating organizational excellence: Developing a top management mind set and implementing a strategy." Paper presented at the annual meeting of the Academy of Management, Organization Development Division, San Diego.

6. ———. 1988. The visionary leader: A new theory of organizational leadership. In J. A. Conger and R. N. Kanungo (eds.), *Charismatic leadership in management.* San Francisco: Jossey-Bass.

7. Deal, T. E. 1987. The culture of schools. In L. T. Sheive and M. B. Schoenbeit (eds.), *Leadership: Examining the elusive: 1987*. Yearbook of the Association for Supervision and Curriculum Development (pp. 3–15). Alexandria, VA: ASCD.

8. Bennis, W. 1984. The four competencies of leadership. *Training and Development Journal*, 38 (8), 15–19.

9. Bennis, W., and B. Nanus. 1985. *Leaders*. New York: Harper & Row.

10. Sashkin, M. 1984. *The leadership behavior questionnaire*. Bryn Mawr, PA: Organization Design and Development.

11. Sashkin, M., and R. M. Fulmer. 1985. "A new framework for leadership: vision, charisma, and culture creation." Paper presented at the Biennial Leadership Symposium, Texas Tech University, Lubbock, TX.

12. ———. 1987. Toward an organizational leadership theory. In J. G. Hunt et al. (eds.), *Emerging leadership vistas*. Boston: Lexington Press.

13. Major, K. D. 1988. Dogmatism, visionary leadership, and effectiveness of secondary principals. Unpublished doctoral dissertation, University of LaVerne, LaVerne, CA.

SELECTION 53

1. See, for example, James G. March and Johan P. Olsen, *Ambiguity and Choice in Organizations*, 2nd ed. (Norway: Universitetsforlaget, 1979).

2. Herbert A. Simon, *The New Science of Management Decision* (New York: Harper & Row, 1960), p. 1.

3. Eberhard Witte, "Field Research on Complex Decision-Making Processes—The Phase Theorem," *International Studies of Management and Organization* (Summer 1972), 156–182.

4. L. P. Schrenk, "Aiding the Decision Maker—A Decision Process Model," *Ergonomics*, 12 (July 1969), 543–557.

5. Irving L. Janis, "Stages in the Decision-Making Process," in *Theories of Cognitive Consistency: A Sourcebook*, ed. Robert P. Abelson et al. (Chicago: Rand McNally, 1968), pp. 577–588.

6. Samuel Eilon, *Management Control*, 2nd ed. (New York: Pergamon, 1979), pp. 135–162.

7. Henry Mintzberg, Duru Raisinghani, and Andre Theoret, "The Structure of 'Unstructured' Decision Processes," *Administrative Science Quarterly*, 21 (June 1976), 246–275.

8. E. Bruce Frederikson, "Noneconomic Criteria and the Decision Process," *Decision Sciences*, 2 (January 1971), 25–52.

9. Clyde W. Holsapple and Herbert Moskowitz, "A Conceptual Framework for Studying Complex Decision Processes," *Policy Sciences*, 13 (1980), 83–104.

10. See, for example, Margaret K. Park, "Decision-Making Processes for Information Managers," *Special Libraries* (October 1981), pp. 307–318.
11. *Webster's New Collegiate Dictionary* (Springfield, Mass.: G. & C. Merriam: 1977), p. 465.
12. A. R. Radcliffe-Brown, "Concept of Function in Social Science," *American Anthropologist*, 37 (July–September 1935), 19.
13. Bernard M. Bass, *Organizational Decision Making* (Homewood, Ill.: Richard D. Irwin, 1983), p. 4.
14. This section is adapted from E. Frank Harrison, *Management and Organizations* (Boston: Houghton Mifflin, 1978), p. 81–91.
15. Peter F. Drucker, *Management: Tasks—Responsibilities—Practices* (New York: Harper & Row, 1973), p. 101.
16. John F. Mee, "Objectives in a Management Philosophy," in *Management in Perspective*, ed. William E. Schlender, William G. Scott, and Alan C. Filley (Boston: Houghton Mifflin, 1965), p. 61.
17. Dalton E. McFarland, *Management: Principles and Practices*, 4th ed. (New York: Macmillan, 1974), p. 7.
18. Drucker, *Management*, p. 101.
19. Herbert G. Hicks, *The Management of Organizations: A Systems and Human Resources Approach*, 2nd ed. (New York: McGraw-Hill, 1972), p. 62.
20. Charles H. Granger, "The Hierarchy of Objectives," *Harvard Business Review* (May–June 1964), 63.
21. Hicks, *Management of Organizations*, p. 62.
22. Herbert A. Simon, *Administrative Behavior*, 2nd ed. (New York: Free Press, 1957), p. 63.
23. Howard E. Thompson, "Management Decisions in Perspective," in *Management in Perspective*, ed. William E. Schlender, William G. Scott, and Alan C. Filley (Boston: Houghton Mifflin, 1965), p. 137.
24. Ibid.
25. Percy H. Hill et al., *Making Decisions: A Multidisciplinary Introduction* (Reading, Mass.: Addison-Wesley, 1978), p. 24.
26. Simon, *New Science of Management Decision*, p. 1.
27. Fremont A. Shull, Jr., Andre L. Delbecq, and L. L. Cummings, *Organizational Decision Making* (New York: McGraw-Hill, 1970), p. 30.

SELECTION 54

The research on which this paper is based was sponsored by the Organizational Effectiveness Research Programs, Psychological Sciences Division Office of Naval Research. (Control No. N0014-67-A-0097-0027, Control Authority Identification No. NR-177-935.)

1. J. G. March and H. A. Simon, *Organizations* (New York: Wiley, 1958); R. M. Cyert and J. G. March, *A Behavioral Theory of the Firm* (Englewood Cliffs, N.J.: Prentice-Hall, 1963); A. Newell and H. A. Simon, *Human Problem Solving* (New York: Prentice Hall, 1972).
2. F. E. Fiedler, *A Theory of Leadership Effectiveness* (New York: McGraw Hill, 1967); V. H. Vroom, "Leadership," *Handbook of Industrial and Organizational Psychology*, M. Dunnette, ed. (Chicago: Rand McNally, 1974, in press).
3. V. H. Vroom, "Industrial Social Psychology," in G. Lindzey and E. Aronson, eds., *Handbook of Social Psychology*, Vol. 5 (Reading, Mass.: Addison-Wesley, 1970), pp. 239–240.
4. V. H. Vroom and P. W. Yetton, *Leadership and Decision-Making* (Pittsburgh: University of Pittsburgh Press, 1973).

SELECTION 55

1. Dance, F. E. X., & Larson, C. (1976). *The functions of human communication: A theoretical approach*. New York: Holt, Rinehart and Winston.
2. Goffman, E. (1959). *The presentation of self in everyday life*. Garden City, NY: Doubleday.
3. For more information on the prerequisites for effective goal directed (instrumental) communication see: Hart, R. P., & Burks, D. M. (1972). Rhetorical sensitivity and social interaction. *Speech Monographs*, 39, 75–91. Hart, R. P., Carlson, R. E., & Eadie, W. F. (1980). Attitudes toward communication and the assessment of rhetorical sensitivity. *Communication Monographs*, 47, 3–22.
4. The term "transformational" was coined by James McGregor Burns to describe the type of leadership that creates high moral purpose. We'll have more to say about transformational leadership in Chapter 3.

SELECTION 56

1. A dispute resolution procedure is a pattern of interactive behavior directed toward resolving a dispute. Mediation and arbitration are two such procedures that are discussed in more detail in this article.
2. The "Wise Man" Procedure. (1987). *Alternatives to the High Cost of Litigation*, 5(105), 110–111.
3. Friedman, E. (1988, January). *Dispute resolution in the Catholic Archdiocese of Chicago*. Paper presented at the Dispute Resolution Research Colloquium, Northwestern University, Evanston, IL.
4. International Business Machines Corporation v. Fujitsu Limited, American Arbitration Association, Commercial Arbitration Tribunal, Case No. 13-I-117-0636-85 (1987, September 15).

5. Brett, J. M., & Goldberg, S. B. (1983). Grievance mediation in the coal industry: A field experiment. *Industrial and Labor Relations Review, 37,* 49–69.
6. Ury, W. L. (1982). *Talk out or walk out: The role of control and conflict in a Kentucky coal mine.* Unpublished doctoral dissertation, Harvard University, Cambridge, MA.
7. Ury, W. L., Brett, J. M., & Goldberg, S. B. (1988). *Getting disputes resolved: Designing a dispute resolution system to cut the costs of conflict.* San Francisco: Jossey-Bass.
8. Kolb, D. M., personal communication, 1987.
9. Kilmann, R. H., & Thomas, K. W. (1978). Four perspectives on conflict management: An attributional framework for organizing descriptive and normative theory. *Academy of Management Review, 3,* 59–68.
10. Brett, J. M. (1986). Commentary on procedural justice papers. In R. Lewicki, M. Bazerman, & B. Sheppard (Eds.), *Research on negotiations in organizations* (Vol. 1, pp. 81–90). Greenwich, CT: JAI Press.
11. Lind, E. A., & Tyler, T. R. (1988). *The social psychology of procedural justice.* New York: Plenum Press.
12. Raiffa, H. (1982). *The art and science of negotiation.* Cambridge, MA. Harvard University Press.
13. Fisher, R., & Ury, W. (1981). *Getting to yes: Negotiating agreements without giving in.* Boston: Houghton-Mifflin.
14. Pruitt, D. G. (1981). *Negotiation behavior.* New York: Academic Press.
15. Follett, M. P. (1940). Constructive conflict. In H. C. Metcalf & L. Urwick (Eds.), *Dynamic administration: The collected papers of Mary Parker Follett.* New York: Harper.
16. Pruitt, D. G., & Rubin, J. Z. (1986). *Social conflict: Escalation, stalemate and settlement.* New York: Random House.
17. Emerson, R. M. (1962). Power dependency relations. *American Sociological Review, 27,* 31–41.
18. McEwen, C. A., & Maiman, R. J. (1981). Small claims mediation in Maine: An empirical assessment. *Maine Law Review, 37,* 237–268.
19. Pearson, J. (1982). An evaluation of alternatives to court adjudication *The Justice System Journal, 7,* 420–444.
20. Karambayya, R., & Brett, J. M. (1989). *Managers handling disputes Third party roles and perceptions of fairness. Academy of Management Journal, 32,* 687–704.
21. Lewin, K. (1951). *Field theory in social science.* New York. Harper & Row.
22. Brett, J. M. (1984). Managing organizational conflict. *Professional Psychology: Research and Practice, 15,* 664–678.
23. Szilagyi, A. D., Jr., & Wallace, M. J. (1980). *Organizational behavior and performance* (2nd. ed.). Glenview, IL: Scott, Foresman.
24. Goldberg, S. B., Green, E. D., & Sander, F. E. A. (1985). *Dispute resolution.* Boston: Little Brown.

25. Kanter, R. M., & Morgan, E. (1988). The new alliances: First report on the formation and significance of a labor-management "business partnership." *Harvard Business School Working Paper* (No. 87-042). Cambridge, MA: Harvard Business School.

26. McGillis, D. (1985). *Consumer dispute resolution: A survey of programs* Washington, DC: National Institute for Dispute Resolution.

27. Pruitt, D. G., & Carnevale, P. J. D. (1982). The development of integrative agreements. In V. J. Derlega & J. Grezlak (Eds.), *Cooperation and helping behavior* (pp. 151–181). New York: Academic Press.

28. Lax, D. A., & Sebenius, J. K. (1986). *The manager as negotiator*. New York: Free Press.

29. Kolb, D. M. (1986). Who are organizational third parties and what do they do? In R. J. Lewicki, B. H. Sheppard, & M. H. Bazerman (Eds.). *Research on negotiations in organizations* (pp. 207–227). Greenwich, CT: JAI Press.

30. Sheppard, B. H. (1983). Managers as inquisitors: Some lessons from the law. In M. H. Bazerman & R. J. Lewicki (Eds.), *Negotiating in organizations* (pp. 193–213). Beverly Hills, CA: Sage.

31. Kolb, D. M., & Glidden, P. (1986). Getting to know your conflict options *Personnel Administrator, 31*, 77–90.

32. Bazerman, M. H. (1983). Negotiator judgment. *American Behavioral Scientist, 27*, 211–228.

33. Bazerman, M. H., & Neale, M. A. (1983). Heuristics in negotiation: Limitations to dispute resolution effectiveness. In M. H. Bazerman & R. J. Lewicki (Eds.), *Negotiating in organizations* (pp. 51–67). Beverly Hills, CA: Sage.

34. Thompson, L. (1988). *Social perception in negotiation*. Unpublished doctoral dissertation, Northwestern University, Evanston, IL.

35. Bazerman, M. H., Magliozzi, T., & Neale, M. A. (1985). Integrative bargaining in a competitive market. *Organizational Behavior and Human Decision Processes, 35*, 294–313.

36. Neale, M. A., Northcraft, G. B., & Earley, P. C. (1988). *Joint effects of goal setting and expertise on negotiator behavior*. Unpublished manuscript, Northwestern University, Evanston, IL.

37. Lewis, M., personal communication, May 14, 1987.

38. McGovern, F. E. (1986). Toward a functional approach for managing complex litigation. *University of Chicago Law Review, 33*, 440–493.

39. Neale, M. A. (1984). The effects of negotiation and arbitration cost salience on bargainer behavior: The role of the arbitrator and constituency on negotiator judgment. *Organizational Behavior and Human Performance, 34*, 97–111.

40. McGillis, D., & Mullen, J. (1977). *Neighborhood justice centers. An evaluation of potential models*. Washington, DC: U.S. Law Enforcement Assistance Administration.

41. Thibaut, J., & Walker, L. (1975). *Procedural justice: A psychological analysis*. Hillsdale, NJ: Earlbaum.
42. Brett, J. M., & Shapiro, D. (1988). *Procedural justice: A test of competing models*. Unpublished manuscript, Northwestern University, Evanston, IL.
43. Kochan, T. A. (1980). *Collective bargaining and industrial relations*. Homewood, IL: Irwin.
44. Goldberg, S. B., & Sander, F. E. A. (1987). Saying you're sorry. *Negotiation Journal, 3*, 221–224.

SELECTION 62

1. Hall, C. S. & Lindsey, G., *Theories of Personality*, 2d Ed. (New York: John Wiley & Sons, 1970).
2. Adapted from Lawrence Kohlberg, "Moral Stages and Moralization," in *Moral Development and Behavior*, ed. Thomas Lickona. Copyright © 1976 by Holt, Rinehart and Winston, Inc. Reprinted by permission of CBS College Publishing.
3. Turiel, E., "Developmental Processes in the Child's Moral Thinking," in *Trends and Issues in Developmental Psychology*, eds. Mussen, P., Langer L., & Covington, M. (New York: Holt, Rinehart and Winston, 1969).
4. Kohlberg, L., *The Development of Children's Orientation Toward a Moral Order: 1. Sequence in the Development of Moral Thought* (Vita Humana, 1963), 6, pp. 11–33.
5. Bandura, A., *Social Learning Theory* (Englewood Cliffs, N.J.: Prentice-Hall, Inc., 1977).
6. Bandura, A. *Aggression: A Social Learning Analysis* (Englewood Cliffs, N.J.: Prentice-Hall, Inc., 1973).
7. Bandura, *op. cit.*, 1977.
8. Bandura, A. & McDonald, F. J., "The Influence of Social Reinforcement and the Behavior of Models in Shaping Children's Moral Judgments," *Journal of Abnormal and Social Psychology*, (1963), 67, pp. 274–281.
9. Prentice, N. M., "The influence of live and symbolic modeling on promoting moral judgment of adolescent delinquents," *Journal of Abnormal Psychology*, (1972), 80, pp. 157–161.
10. Bryan, J. H. & Test, M. A., "Models and Helping: Naturalistic Studies in Aiding Behavior," *Journal of Personality and Social Psychology*, (1967), 6, pp. 400–407.
11. Staub, E., *The Development of Prosocial Behavior in Children* (New York: General Learning Press, 1975).
12. Mischel, W., & Grusec, J., "Determinants of the Rehearsal and Transmission of Neutral and Aversive Behaviors," *Journal of Personality and Social Psychology*, (1966), 3, pp. 197–205.

SELECTION 63

1. Ciulla, Joanne B. "Note on the Corporation as a Moral Environment." Boston: Harvard Business School Case Services no. 0-385-324, 1985.
2. Post, Richard J. "The H. J. Heinz Company: The Administration of Policy," parts A, B, C, and D. Boston: Harvard Business School Case Services nos. 382-034, 035, 036, and 037.
3. Aristotle. *Nichomachean Ethics*, trans. Terence Irwin. Indianapolis: Hackett Publishing Company, 1985.
4. Barnard, Chester. *The Functions of the Executive*. Cambridge, Mass.: Harvard University Press, 1969, p. 238.

Name Index

SUBJECT INDEX